GREAT BRITAIN & II

GW00373098

TOURIST and MOTORING ATLAS / ATLAS ROUTIER et TOURISTIQUE /
TOERISTISCHE WEGENATLAS / ATLANTE STRADALE e TURISTICO / ATLAS [

Contents
Sommaire / Inhaltsübersicht / Inhoud / Sommario / Sumario

Inside front cover: key to map pages
Intérieur de couverture : tableau d'assemblage / Umschlaginnenseite: Übersicht / Binnenzijde van het omslag: overzichtskaart
-Copertina interna: quadro d'insieme / Portada interior: mapa índice

II - III

Channel Tunnel - Tunnel sous la Manche
Folkestone Terminal - Terminal de Calais (F)
Shipping Services
Liaisons maritimes / Schiffsverbindungen / Scheepvaartverbindingen / Collegamenti marittimi / Líneas marítimas

IV - XXI

Main road map
Grands axes routiers / Durchgangsstraßen / Grote verbindingswegen / Grandi arterie stradali / Carreteras principales
1 inch = 15.8 miles - 1:1 000 000 - 1 cm = 10 km

1 - 119

Key · 1
Légende / Zeichenerklärung / Verklaring van de tekens / Legenda / Signos convencionales

Great Britain & Ireland · 2 - 119
Grande-Bretagne & Irlande / Großbritannien & Irland / Groot-Brittannië & Ierland
Gran Bretagna & Irlanda / Gran Bretaña & Irlanda
1 inch = 4.75 miles - 1: 300 000 - 1 cm = 3 km

120 - 147

Index Great Britain · 120 - 138
Index Grande-Bretagne / Register Großbritannien / Register Groot-Brittannië / Indice Gran Bretagna / Índice Gran Bretaña

Index Ireland · 139 - 147
Index Irlande / Register Irland / Register Ierland / Indice Irlanda / Índice Irlanda

148 - 192

Key · 148
Légende / Zeichenerklärung / Verklaring van de tekens / Legenda / Signos convencionales

Town plans Great Britain · 149 - 185
Plans de ville Grande-Bretagne / Stadtpläne Großbritannien / Stadsplattegronden Groot-Brittannië
Piante di città Gran Bretagna / Planos de ciudades Gran Bretaña

Town plans Ireland · 186 - 191
Plans de ville Irlande / Stadtpläne Irland / Stadsplattegronden Ierland / Piante di città Irlanda / Planos de ciudades Irlanda

Eochair / Allwedd / Comnarthai ar phleanna bailte / Symbolau ar gynlluniau'r trefi · 192

Back of the guide: distances
En fin de volume : distances / Am Ende des Buches: Entfernungen / Achter in het boek: afstanden
Alla fine del volume: distanze / Al final del volumen: distancias

Channel Tunnel
Tunnel sous la Manche

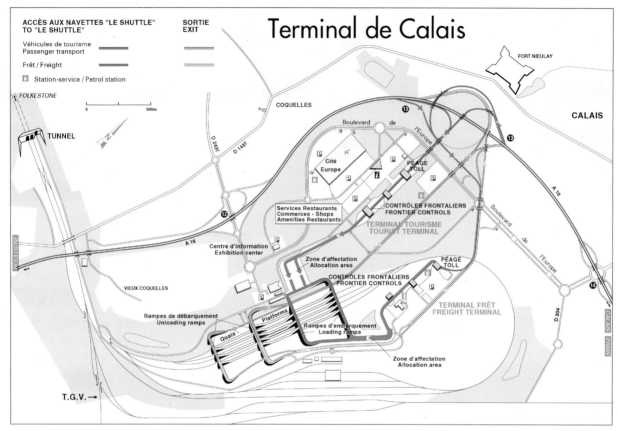

Terminal de Calais

ACCÈS AUX NAVETTES "LE SHUTTLE"
TO "LE SHUTTLE"

SORTIE
EXIT

Véhicules de tourisme
Passenger transport

Frêt / Freight

Station-service / Petrol station

FOLKESTONE

TUNNEL

COQUELLES

FORT NIEULAY

CALAIS

Boulevard   de   l'Europe

Cité Europe

PÉAGE TOLL

CONTRÔLES FRONTALIERS
FRONTIER CONTROLS

Services Restaurants
Commerces - Shops
Amenities Restaurants

TERMINAL TOURISME
TOURIST TERMINAL

Centre d'information
Exhibition center

Zone d'affectation
Allocation area

CONTRÔLES FRONTALIERS
FRONTIER CONTROLS

PÉAGE TOLL

Boulevard   de   l'Europe

VIEUX COQUELLES

Rampes de débarquement
Unloading ramps

Platforms

Quais -

Rampes d'embarquement
Loading ramps

TERMINAL FRÊT
FREIGHT TERMINAL

Zone d'affectation
Allocation area

T.G.V. →

CALAIS PARIS

A 16

D 243E

D 143E

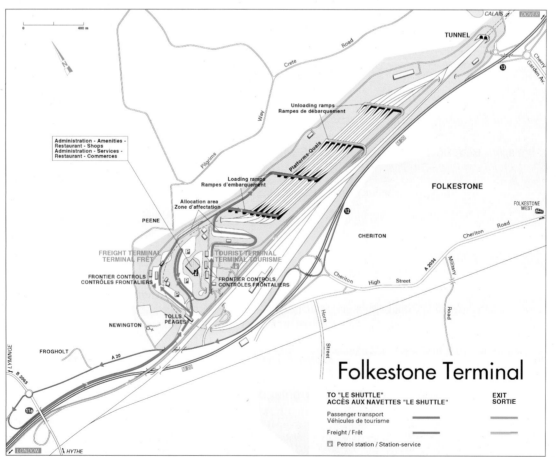

Folkestone Terminal

CALAIS   DOVER

TUNNEL

Crete   Road

Unloading ramps
Rampes de débarquement

Way

Pilgrims

Administration - Amenities -
Restaurant - Shops
Administration - Services -
Restaurant - Commerces

Platforms-Quais

Loading ramps
Rampes d'embarquement

Allocation area
Zone d'affectation

PEENE

FREIGHT TERMINAL
TERMINAL FRÊT

TOURIST TERMINAL
TERMINAL TOURISME

FRONTIER CONTROLS
CONTRÔLES FRONTALIERS

FRONTIER CONTROLS
CONTRÔLES FRONTALIERS

TOLLS
PÉAGES

NEWINGTON

FROGHOLT

LYMINGE

B 2068

A 20

M 20

LONDON   HYTHE

FOLKESTONE

FOLKESTONE WEST

CHERITON

Cheriton   Road

Cheriton   High   Street

A 20A

Military   Road

Horn   Street

TO "LE SHUTTLE"
ACCÈS AUX NAVETTES "LE SHUTTLE"

EXIT
SORTIE

Passenger transport
Véhicules de tourisme

Freight / Frêt

Petrol station / Station-service

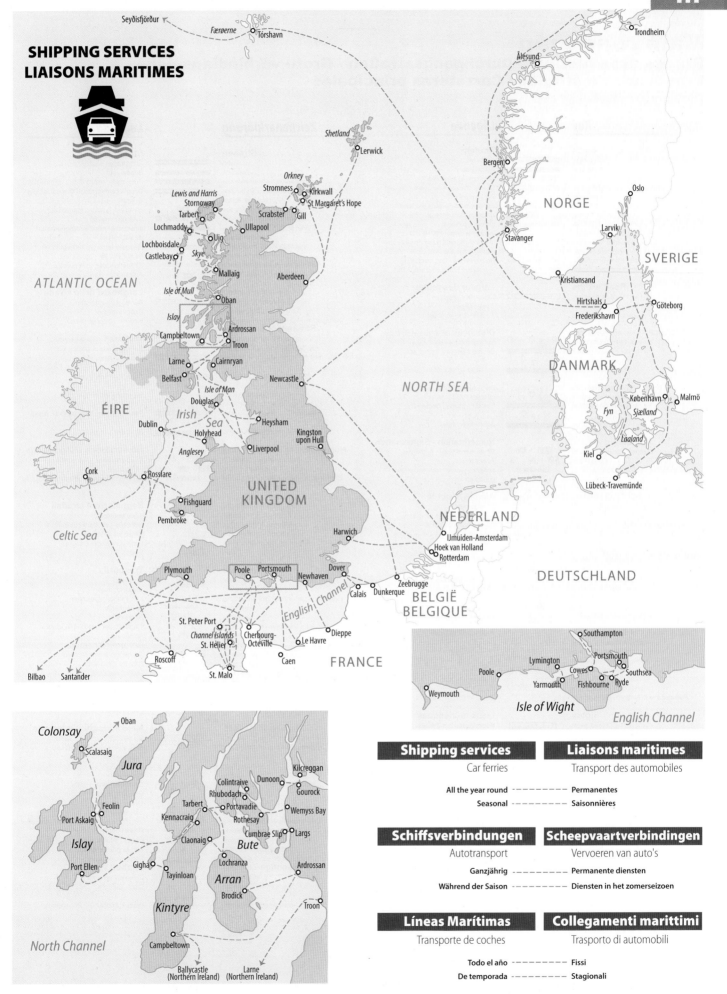

SHIPPING SERVICES
LIAISONS MARITIMES

ATLANTIC OCEAN

Seyðisfjörður
Færøerne
Tórshavn
Trondheim
Ålesund
Shetland
Lerwick
Bergen
Oslo
NORGE
Orkney
Stromness
Kirkwall
St Margaret's Hope
Scrabster
Gill
Lewis and Harris
Stornoway
Tarbert
Ullapool
Lochmaddy
Uig
Skye
Lochboisdale
Castlebay
Mallaig
Aberdeen
Stavanger
SVERIGE
Kristiansand
Isle of Mull
Oban
Hirtshals
Göteborg
Islay
Ardrossan
Frederikshavn
Campbeltown
Troon
Larne
Cairnryan
DANMARK
Belfast
Newcastle
NORTH SEA
ÉIRE
Isle of Man
København
Malmö
Douglas
Fyn
Sjælland
Irish Sea
Heysham
Dublin
Holyhead
Kingston upon Hull
Låaland
Liverpool
Anglesey
Kiel
Cork
Rosslare
UNITED KINGDOM
Lübeck-Travemünde
Fishguard
NEDERLAND
Pembroke
Celtic Sea
Harwich
IJmuiden-Amsterdam
Hoek van Holland
Rotterdam
Plymouth
Poole Portsmouth
DEUTSCHLAND
Newhaven
Dover
Zeebrugge
St. Peter Port
Calais
Dunkerque
BELGIË
Channel Islands
Cherbourg-Octeville
Dieppe
BELGIQUE
St. Hélier
Le Havre
English Channel
Roscoff
Caen
Bilbao
Santander
St. Malo
FRANCE

Isle of Wight inset
Southampton
Lymington
Portsmouth
Poole
Cowes
Southsea
Yarmouth
Fishbourne
Ryde
Weymouth
Isle of Wight
English Channel

Scotland inset
Colonsay
Oban
Scalasaig
Jura
Kilcreggan
Colintraive
Dunoon
Rhubodach
Gourock
Tarbert
Portavadie
Feolin
Kennacraig
Rothesay
Wemyss Bay
Port Askaig
Claonaig
Cumbrae Slip
Largs
Islay
Bute
Port Ellen
Gigha
Lochranza
Ardrossan
Tayinloan
Arran
Brodick
Kintyre
Troon
Campbeltown
North Channel
Ballycastle (Northern Ireland)
Larne (Northern Ireland)

Main road map
Grands axes routiers / Durchgangsstraßen / Grote verbindingswegen
Grandi arterie stradali / Carreteras principales

Key	Légende	Zeichenerklärung	Legenda
Roads	**Routes**	**Straßen**	**Strade**
Motorway	Autoroute	Autobahn	Autostrada
Motorway: single carriageway	Route-auto	Autostraße	Strada-auto
Motorway (unclassified)	Autoroute et assimilée	Autobahn oder Schnellstraße	Autostrada, strada di tipo autostradale
Dual carriageway with motorway characteristics	Double chaussée de type autoroutier	Schnellstraße mit getrennten Fahrbahnen	Doppia carreggiata di tipo autostradale
Interchanges:	Échangeurs :	Anschlussstellen:	Svincoli:
complete, limited, not specified	complet, partiels, sans précision	Voll- bzw. Teilanschluss, ohne Angabe	completo, parziale, imprecisato
Interchange numbers	Numéros d'échangeurs	Anschlussstellennummern	Svincoli numerati
Recommended MICHELIN main itinerary	Itinéraire principal recommandé par MICHELIN	Von MICHELIN empfohlene Hauptverkehrsstraße	Itinerario principale raccomandato da MICHELIN
Recommended MICHELIN regional itinerary	Itinéraire régional ou de dégagement recommandé par MICHELIN	Von MICHELIN empfohlene Regionalstraße	Itinerario regionale raccomandato da MICHELIN
Road surfaced - unsurfaced	Route revêtue - non revêtue	Straße mit Belag - ohne Belag	Strada rivestita - non rivestita
Motorway/Road under construction	Autoroute - Route en construction	Autobahn/Straße im Bau	Autostrada - Strada in costruzione
Road widths	**Largeur des routes**	**Straßenbreiten**	**Larghezza delle strade**
Dual carriageway	Chaussées séparées	Getrennte Fahrbahnen	Carreggiate separate
2 wide lanes	2 voies larges	2 breite Fahrspuren	2 corsie larghe
2 lanes - 2 narrow lanes	2 voies - 2 voies étroites	2 Fahrspuren - 2 schmale Fahrspuren	2 corsie - 2 corsie strette
Distances (total and intermediate)	**Distances** (totalisées et partielles)	**Straßenentfernungen** (Gesamt- und Teilentfernungen)	**Distanze** (totali e parziali)
On motorway in kilometers	Sur autoroute en kilomètres	Auf der Autobahn in Kilometern	Su autostrada in chilometri
Toll roads - Toll-free section	Section à péage - Section libre	Mautstrecke - Mautfreie Strecke	Tratto a pedaggio - Tratto esente da pedaggio
On road in kilometers	Sur route en kilomètres	Auf der Straße in Kilometern	Su strada in chilometri
On motorway (GB) in miles - in kilometers	Sur autoroute (GB) en miles - en kilomètres	Auf der Autobahn (GB) in Meilen - in Kilometern	Su autostrada (GB) in miglia - in chilometri
Toll roads - Toll-free section	Section à péage - Section libre	Mautstrecke - Mautfreie Strecke	Tratto a pedaggio - Tratto esente da pedaggio
On road in miles	Sur route en miles	Auf der Straße in Meilen	Su strada in miglia
Numbering - Signs	**Numérotation - Signalisation**	**Nummerierung - Wegweisung**	**Numerazione - Segnaletica**
European route - Motorway	Route européenne - Autoroute	Europastraße - Autobahn	Strada europea - Autostrada
Other roads	Autres routes	Sonstige Straßen	Altre strade
Destination on primary route network	Localités jalonnant les itinéraires principaux	Richtungshinweis auf der empfohlenen Fernverkehrsstraße	Località delimitante gli itinerari principali
Safety Warnings	**Alertes Sécurité**	**Sicherheitsalerts**	**Segnalazioni stradali**
Snowbound, impassable road during the period shown	Enneigement : période probable de fermeture	Eingeschneite Straße: voraussichtl. Wintersperre	Innevamento: probabile periodo di chiusura
Pass and its height above sea level	Col et sa cote d'altitude	Pass mit Höhenangabe	Passo ed altitudine
Steep hill - Toll barrier	Forte déclivité - Barrière de péage	Starke Steigung - Mautstelle	Forte pendenza - Casello
Ford	Gué	Furt	Guado
Transportation	**Transports**	**Verkehrsmittel**	**Trasporti**
Airport	Aéroport	Flughafen	Aeroporto
Transportation of vehicles: year-round - seasonal	Transport des autos : permanent - saisonnier	Autotransport: ganzjährig - saisonbedingte Verbindung	Trasporto auto: tutto l'anno - stagionale
by boat	par bateau	per Schiff	su traghetto
by ferry	par bac	per Fähre	su chiatta
Ferry (passengers and cycles only)	Bac pour piétons et cycles	Fähre für Personen und Fahrräder	Traghetto per pedoni e biciclette
Motorail	Auto/Train	Autoreisezug	Auto/treno
Administration	**Administration**	**Verwaltung**	**Amministrazione**
Administrative district seat	Capitale de division administrative	Verwaltungshauptstadt	Capoluogo amministrativo
Parador / Pousada	Parador / Pousada	Parador / Pousada	Parador / Pousada
Administrative boundaries	Limites administratives	Verwaltungsgrenzen	Confini amministrativi
National boundary	Frontière	Staatsgrenze	Frontiera
Principal customs post	Douane principale	Hauptzollamt	Dogana principale
Secondary customs post	Douane avec restriction	Zollstation mit Einschränkungen	Dogana con limitazioni
Restricted area for foreigners / Military property	Zone interdite aux étrangers / Zone militaire	Sperrgebiet für Ausländer / Militärgebiet	Zona vietata agli stranieri / Zona militare
Sights	**Lieux touristiques**	**Sehenswürdigkeiten**	**Mete e luoghi d'interesse**
2- and 3-star MICHELIN Green Guide sites	Sites classés 2 et 3 étoiles par le Guide Vert MICHELIN	Sehenswürdigkeiten mit 2 und 3 Sternen im Grünen Reiseführer MICHELIN	Siti segnalati con 2 e 3 stelle dalla Guida Verde MICHELIN
Religious building	Édifice religieux	Sakral-Bau	Edificio religioso
Historic house, castle	Château	Schloss, Burg	Castello
Monastery	Monastère	Kloster	Monastero
Stave church	Église en bois debout	Stabkirche	Chiesa in legno di testa
Wooden church	Église en bois	Holzkirche	Chiesa in legno
Open air museum	Musée de plein air	Freilichtmuseum	Museo all'aperto
Antiquities	Site antique	Antike Fundstätte	Sito antico
Rock carving - Prehistoric monument	Gravure rupestre - Monument mégalithique	Felsbilder - Vorgeschichtliches Steindenkmal	Incisione rupestre - Monumento megalitico
Rune stone - Ruins	Pierre runique - Ruines	Runenstein - Ruine	Pietra runica - Rovine
Cave - Windmill	Grotte - Moulin à vent	Höhle - Windmühle	Grotta - Mulino a vento
Other places of interest	Autres curiosités	Sonstige Sehenswürdigkeit	Altri luoghi d'interesse
Scenic route	Parcours pittoresque	Landschaftlich schöne Strecke	Percorso pittoresco
Other signs	**Signes divers**	**Sonstige Zeichen**	**Simboli vari**
Recreation ground	Parc de loisirs	Erholungspark	Parco divertimenti
Dam - Waterfall	Barrage - Cascade	Staudamm - Wasserfall	Diga - Cascata
National park / Nature park	Parc national / Parc naturel	Nationalpark / Naturpark	Parco nazionale / Parco naturale

Signos Convencionales

Carreteras
Autopista
Carretera
Autopista, Autovía
Autovía
Accesos:
completo, parcial, sin precisar
Números de los accesos
Itinerario principal recomendado por MICHELIN
Itinerario regional recomendado por MICHELIN
Carretera asfaltada - sin asfaltar
Autopista - Carretera en construcción

Ancho de las carreteras
Calzadas separadas
Dos carriles anchos
Dos carriles - Dos carriles estrechos

Distancias (totales y parciales)
En autopista en kilómetros
Tramo de peaje - Tramo libre

En carretera en kilómetros

En autopista (GB)
en millas - en kilómetros
Tramo de peaje - Tramo libre

En carretera en millas

Numeración - Señalización
Carretera europea - Autopista
Otras carreteras
Localidades situadas en los principales itinerarios

Alertas Seguridad
Nevada:
Período probable de cierre
Puerto y su altitud
Pendiente Pronunciada - Barrera de peaje
Vado

Transportes
Aeropuerto
Transporte de coches:
todo el año - de temporada
por barco
por barcaza
Barcaza para el paso de peatones y vehículos dos ruedas
Auto-tren

Administración
Capital de división administrativa
Parador / Pousada
Limites administrativos
Frontera
Aduana principal
Aduana con restricciones
Zona prohibida a los extranjeros / Propiedad militar

Curiosidades
Lugares clasificados con 2 y 3 estrellas por la Guía Verde MICHELIN
Edificio religioso
Castillo
Monasterio
Iglesia de madera
Iglesia de madera
Museo al aire libre
Zona de vestigios antiguos
Grabado rupestre - Monumento megalítico
Piedra rúnica - Ruinas
Cueva - Molino de viento
Otras curiosidades
Recorrido pintoresco

Signos diversos
Zona recreativa
Presa - Cascada

Parque nacional / Parque natural

Verklaring van de tekens

Wegen
Autosnelweg
Autoweg
Autosnelweg of gelijksoortige weg
Gescheiden rijbanen van het type autosnelweg
Aansluitingen: volledig, gedeeltelijk, zonder aanduiding
Afritnummers
Hoofdweg

Regionale weg

Verharde weg - onverharde weg
Autosnelweg - Weg in aanleg

Breedte van de wegen
Gescheiden rijbanen
2 brede rijstroken
2 rijstroken - 2 smalle rijstroken

Afstanden (totaal en gedeeltelijk)
Op autosnelwegen in kilometers
Gedeelte met tol - Tolvrij gedeelte

Op andere wegen in kilometers

Op autosnelwegen (GB)
in mijlen - in kilometers
Gedeelte met tol - Tolvrij gedeelte

Op andere wegen in mijlen

Wegnummers - Bewegwijzering
Europaweg - Autosnelweg
Andere wegen
Plaatsen langs een hoofdweg met bewegwijzering

Veiligheidswaarschuwingen
Sneeuw:
vermoedelijke sluitingsperiode
Bergpas en hoogte boven de zeespiegel
Steile helling - Tol
Wad

Vervoer
Luchthaven
Vervoer van auto's:
het hele jaar - tijdens het seizoen
per boot
per veerpont
Veerpont voor voetgangers en fietsers
Autotrein

Administratie
Hoofdplaats van administratief gebied
Parador / Pousada
Administratieve grenzen
Staatsgrens
Hoofddouanekantoor
Douanekantoor met beperkte bevoegdheden
Terrein verboden voor buitenlanders / Militair gebied

Bezienswaardigheden
Locaties met 2 en 3 sterren volgens de Groene Gids van MICHELIN
Kerkelijk gebouw
Kasteel
Klooster
Stavkirke (houten kerk)
Houten kerk
Openluchtmuseum
Overblijfsel uit de Oudheid
Rotstekening - Megaliet
Runensteen - Ruïne
Grot - Molen
Andere bezienswaardigheden
Schilderachtig traject

Diverse tekens
Recreatiepark
Stuwdam - Waterval

Nationaal park / Natuurpark

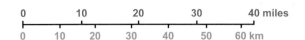

Republic of Ireland: All distances and speed limits are signed in kilometres.

République d'Irlande: Les distances et les limitations de vitesse sont exprimées en kilomètres.

Irland: Alle Entfernungsangaben und Geschwindigkeitsbegrenzungen in km.

Ierland: Alle afstanden en maximumsnelheden zijn uitsluitend in kilometers aangegeven.

Repubblica d'Irlanda: Distanze e limiti di velocità sono espressi soltanto in chilometri.

República de Irlanda: Distancias y límites de velocidad están expresados sólo en kilómetros.

Key to 1:1 000 000 map pages
Légende des cartes au 1/1 000 000
Zeichenerklärung der Karten 1:1 000 000
Verklaring van de tekens voor kaarten met schaal 1:1 000 000
Legenda carte scala 1:1 000 000
Signos convencionales de los mapas a escala 1:1 000 000

ENGLAND

UNITARY AUTHORITIES

1	Bath and North East Somerset		43	North East Lincolnshire
	Bedford		44	North Lincolnshire
	Blackburn with Darwen		45	North Somerset
	Blackpool		46	North Yorkshire
	Bracknell Forest		47	Northamptonshire
	Brighton and Hove		48	Northumberland
7	Buckinghamshire		49	Nottinghamshire
8	Cambridgeshire			Nottingham
9	Central Bedfordshire		51	Oxfordshire
10	Cheshire East			Peterborough
11	Cheshire West and Chester			Plymouth
	City of Bristol			Portsmouth
13	Cornwall			Reading
14	Cumbria		56	Redcar and Cleveland
	Derby		57	Rutland
16	Derbyshire		58	Shropshire
17	Devon		59	Somerset
18	Dorset		60	South Gloucestershire
19	Durham		61	South Yorkshire
20	East Riding of Yorkshire			Southend-on-Sea
21	East Sussex		63	Staffordshire
22	Essex			Stockton-on-Tees
23	Gloucestershire			Stoke-on-Trent
	Greater London		66	Suffolk
	Greater Manchester		67	Surrey
26	Halton			Swindon
27	Hampshire		69	Telford and Wrekin
	Hartlepool		70	Thurrock
29	Herefordshire			Torbay
30	Hertfordshire		72	Tyne and Wear
31	Kent			Warrington
	Kingston-upon-Hull		74	Warwickshire
33	Lancashire		75	West Berkshire
	Leicester		76	West Midlands
35	Leicestershire		77	West Sussex
36	Lincolnshire		78	West Yorkshire
	Luton		79	Wiltshire
38	Medway			Windsor and Maidenhead
39	Merseyside			Wokingham
	Middlesbrough		82	Worcestershire
41	Milton Keynes			York
42	Norfolk			

SCOTLAND

UNITARY AUTHORITIES

1	Aberdeen City		17	Inverclyde
2	Aberdeenshire		18	Midlothian
3	Angus		19	Moray
4	Argyll and Bute		20	North Ayrshire
5	Clackmannanshire		21	North Lanarkshire
6	City of Edinburgh		22	Orkney Islands
7	City of Glasgow		23	Perth and Kinross
8	Dumfries and Galloway		24	Renfrewshire
9	Dundee City		25	Scottish Borders
10	East Ayrshire		26	Shetland Islands
11	East Dunbartonshire		27	South Ayrshire
12	East Lothian		28	South Lanarkshire
13	East Renfrewshire		29	Stirling
14	Falkirk		30	West Dunbartonshire
15	Fife		31	West Lothian
16	Highland		32	Western Isles

NORTHERN IRELAND

DISTRICT COUNCILS

1	Antrim		14	Down
2	Ards		15	Dungannon
3	Armagh		16	Fermanagh
4	Ballymena		17	Larne
5	Ballymoney		18	Limavady
6	Banbridge		19	Lisburn
7	Belfast		20	Magherafelt
8	Carrickfergus		21	Moyle
9	Castlereagh		22	Newry and Mourne
10	Coleraine		23	Newtownabbey
11	Cookstown		24	North Down
12	Craigavon		25	Omagh
13	Derry		26	Strabane

WALES

UNITARY AUTHORITIES

1	Anglesey/Sir Fôn		12	Merthyr Tydfil/Merthyr Tudful
2	Blaenau Gwent		13	Monmouthshire/Sir Fynwy
3	Bridgend/Pen-y-bont ar Ogwr		14	Neath Port Talbot/Castell-nedd Phort Talbot
4	Caerphilly/Caerffili		15	Newport/Casnewydd
5	Cardiff/Caerdydd		16	Pembrokeshire/Sir Benfro
6	Carmarthenshire/Sir Gaerfyrddin		17	Powys
7	Ceredigion		18	Rhondda Cynon Taff/Rhondda Cynon Taf
8	Conwy		19	Swansea/Abertawe
9	Denbighshire/Sir Ddinbych		20	Torfaen/Tor-faen
10	Flintshire/Sir y Fflint		21	Vale of Glamorgan/Bro Morgannwg
11	Gwynedd		22	Wrexham/Wrecsam

 = UNITARY AUTHORITIES

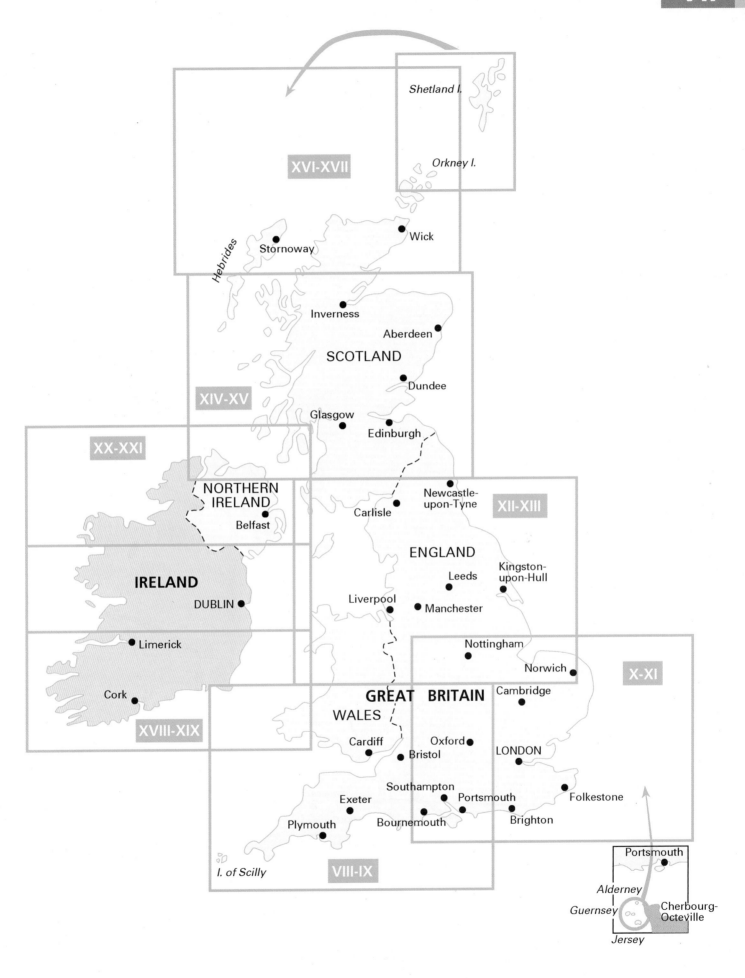

Shetland I.

Orkney I.

XVI-XVII

Hebrides

Stornoway

Wick

Inverness

Aberdeen

SCOTLAND

Dundee

Glasgow

Edinburgh

XIV-XV

XX-XXI

NORTHERN
IRELAND

Belfast

Carlisle

Newcastle-
upon-Tyne

XII-XIII

IRELAND

ENGLAND

Kingston-
upon-Hull

DUBLIN

Leeds

Liverpool

Manchester

Limerick

Nottingham

Norwich

X-XI

Cork

Cambridge

GREAT BRITAIN

WALES

Cardiff

Oxford

Bristol

LONDON

XVIII-XIX

Southampton

Exeter

Portsmouth

Folkestone

Plymouth

Bournemouth

Brighton

I. of Scilly

VIII-IX

Portsmouth

Alderney

Guernsey

Cherbourg-
Octeville

Jersey

ST. GEORGE'S CHANNEL

BRISTOL CHANNEL

e Harbour/
Ros Láir
Point

Saltee Islands

Strumble Head

Pembrokeshire Coast National Park

St. David's Head
St. David's
A 487
A 487 16
A 40
17
15
Haverfordwest/Hwlffordd
St. Bride's Bay
Milford Haven/
Aberdaugleddau
10
Neyland
Pembroke Dock
Pembroke
A 4139
St. Govan's Head

Newport
A 487
19
Fishguard/
Abergwaun
26
537
B 4329
A 478
Narberth
11
16
Whitland
23
Kidwelly
Pendine
132
52
Saundersfoot
Tenby/
Dinbych-y-pysgod
Carmarthen Bay
Rhossili
Worms Head
Port-
Eynon
The Mumbles

Cardigan
A 484
31
Newcastle
Emlyn
Crymmych
Llandysul
6
A 484
23
A 475
St. Clears
A 40
74
46 21
Carmarthen/
Caerfyrddin
16
85 53
16
30
48
Cross
Hands
Ammanford
A 474
Burry
Port
19
A 476
Pontarddulais
40
14
47
45
44
43
42
Llanelli
Neath/
Castell Nedd
SWANSEA/
ABERTAWE
6
40
Port Talbot
53
33
37
39
Porthcawl
Bridgend/
Pen-y-bont
21

New Quay
7
Aberaeron
A 487
58
93
Aberporth
16
Synod
Inn
A 482
A 486
A 475
Tregaron
Lampeter
A 485
7
CAM
14
11
A 482
19
Teifi
593
Elan Valley
Wye
Llanwrtyd
Wells
12
A 483
A 40
Llandovery
4
Llandeilo
Llangadog
A 4069
Black Mountain
23
25
802
Brecon
National
Sennybridge
68
42
Merthyr
Hirwaun
Aberdare/
Aberda
Mount
14
3
Maesteg
A 4061
Rh
C.
Po
21

Lundy

Ilfracombe
10
Combe
Martin
Lynton
Lynmouth
Porlock
A 39
A 399
Exmoor
30
519
Duns
National
Tarr
steps
Croyde
14
B 3231
B 3230
12
11
A 399
13
B 3358
B 3233
Simonsbath
493
Braunton
B 3233
Northam
Barnstaple
South
Molton
B 3227
B 3226
35
56
16
Hartland Point
Clovelly
Bideford
16
B 3232
Great
Torrington
B 3227
A 3137
Tiverton
17
Cliffs of
Morwenstow
32
A 39
A 388
13
A 386
B 3220
40
Exe
Kilkhampton
13
Holsworthy
B 3072
Hatherleigh
22
Winkleigh
Crediton
28
EXETER
Stratton
Bude
19
19
A 3072
A 3072
28
A 30
A 3212
Tamar
A 388
A 3079
Okehampton
15
A 30
621
High
Willhays
11
Moretonhampstead
A 382
18
Tintagel
B 3263
B 3254
Launceston
A 395
12
Lydford
Gorge
Dartmoor
26
A 382
Camelford
420
B 3362 13
National
Bovey
Tracey
Padstow
177
109
A 39
12
A 30
B 3254
Tavistock
Park
B 3357
Wadebridge
9
B 3274
13
113
182
Callington
A 390
20
B 3212
Ashburton
Princetown
Newton
Abbot
Bodmin
A 389
12
A 38
12
Liskeard
17
Buckland Abbey
Buckfastleigh
6
A 384
A 381
Newquay
A 3059
8
A 30
21
78
126
17
A 38
Plympton
41
66
Totnes
A 3122
B
P
Fraddon
12
A 3075
13
B 3269
Lostwithiel
13
A 387
West
Looe
Saltash
Torpoint
PLYMOUTH
Plymstock
Modbury
20
A 381
Dartmouth
Ki
14
A 3058
A 3082
Fowey
Polperro
Newton
Ferrers
A 379
Kingsbridge
St. Austell
A 30
Truro
14
6
Trewithen
Tregony
Mevagissey
St. Ives
6
Camborne
14
Trelissick Garden
B
Salcombe
Start Poi
B 3306
Redruth
St. Mawes
Hayle
B 3300
Penryn
B 3275
A 3078
St. Just
252
Penzance
9
B 3302
A 3297
Falmouth
A 394
10
Subtropical
Gardens
Land's End
A 30
Sennen
10
St. Michael's
Mount
Helston
14
Glendurgan
Garden
B 3293
Tresco
St. Martin's
Isles of Scilly
St. Mary's
Mount's Bay
11
A 3083
St. Keverne
Lizard
Lizard Point

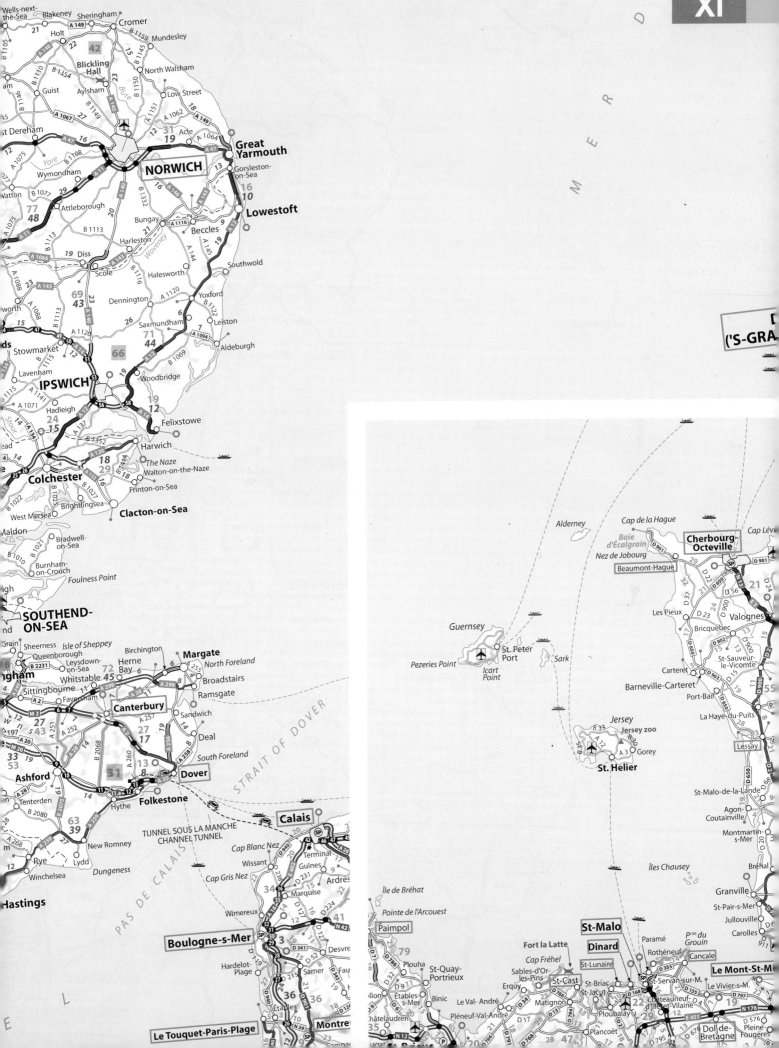

MER DU

D
('S-GRA

Wells-next-the-Sea
Blakeney
Sheringham
Cromer
Holt
Mundesley
21
22
B 149
B 1159
Blickling Hall
42
North Walsham
Aylsham
23
Guist
27
Low Street
Acle
31
Great Yarmouth
Gorsleston-on-Sea
NORWICH
13
st Dereham
16
12
19
A 1064
A 47
Wymondham
Lowestoft
16
10
29
Attleborough
Bungay
Beccles
77
48
Harleston
Halesworth
Southwold
Diss
19
Scole
69
43
Dennington
Yoxford
Leiston
Saxmundham
71
44
Aldeburgh
66
Stowmarket
Woodbridge
53
IPSWICH
19
12
Hadleigh
Felixstowe
24
15
Harwich
18
29
The Naze
Walton-on-the-Naze
Colchester
Frinton-on-Sea
Brightlingsea
Clacton-on-Sea
West Mersea
Maldon
Bradwell-on-Sea
Burnham-on-Crouch
Foulness Point
SOUTHEND-ON-SEA
Sheerness
Isle of Sheppey
Birchington
Margate
Queenborough
Herne Bay
North Foreland
Whitstable
72
Broadstairs
Sittingbourne
Faversham
Canterbury
Ramsgate
27
S 43
Sandwich
27
17
Deal
33
19
13
Ashford
8
Dover
Folkestone
63
39
New Romney
Hythe
South Foreland
Tenterden
STRAIT OF DOVER
Rye
Lydd
Winchelsea
Dungeness
Hastings
TUNNEL SOUS LA MANCHE
CHANNEL TUNNEL
Calais
PAS DE CALAIS
Cap Blanc Nez
Wissant
Terminal
Cap Gris Nez
Guines
Ardres
34
Marquise
Wimereux
Boulogne-s-Mer
41
Desvres
Hardelot-Plage
Samer
Le Touquet-Paris-Plage
36
36
Étaples
Montre

Alderney
Cap de la Hague
Cap Lév
Baie d'Écalgrain
Cherbourg-Octeville
Nez de Jobourg
Beaumont-Hague
Guernsey
Les Pieux
Valognes
St. Peter Port
Bricquebec
Pezeries Point
Sark
St-Sauveur-le-Vicomte
Icart Point
Carteret
Barneville-Carteret
Port-Bail
La Haye-du-Puits
Jersey
Jersey zoo
Lessay
St. Helier
Gorey
St-Malo-de-la-Lande
Agon-Coutainville
Montmartin-s-Mer
Îles Chausey
Bréhal
Granville
St-Pair-s-Mer
Jullouville
Carolles
Pointe de l'Arcouest
St-Malo
Paimpol
Dinard
Paramé
P^nte du Grouin
Rothéneuf
Cancale
Fort la Latte
Cap Fréhel
St-Lunaire
Le Mont-St-M
Sables-d'Or-les-Pins
St-Cast
St-Servan-sur-M.
St-Quay-Portrieux
St-Briac
Le Vivier-s-M.
Plouha
St-Jacut
Erquy
Châteauneuf-d'Ille-et-Vilaine
Binic
Le Val-André
Matignon
Dol-de-Bretagne
Étables-s-Mer
Ploubalay
Pleine-Fougères
Pléneuf-Val-André
Plancoët
âtelaudren

Jarrow, South Shields, SUNDERLAND, Gateshead, Stanley, Washington, Chester-le-Street, Seaham, Houghton-le-Spring, Horden, Durham, Crook, Spennymoor, Peterlee, Hartlepool, Redcar, Marske-by-the-Sea, Saltburn-by-the-Sea, Brotton, Loftus, Whitby, Auckland, Newton Aycliffe, Sedgefield, Billingham, Guisborough, Stockton-on-Tees, MIDDLESBROUGH, Darlington, Eaglescliffe, Richmond, Northallerton, Cleveland Hills, North York Moors National Park, Rievaulx Abbey, Scalby, Scarborough, Bedale, Helmsley, Pickering, Filey, Thirsk, Ripon, Easingwold, Malton, Norton, Bridlington, Pateley Bridge, Boroughbridge, Flamborough Head, Knaresborough, YORK, Driffield, Beeford, Harrogate, Wetherby, Wetwang, Hornsea, Tadcaster, Market Weighton, Leven, Otley, Bingley, Harewood, Beverley, KINGSTON UPON HULL, LEEDS, Selby, Barlby, Hedon, Withernsea, Garforth, Castleford, Howden, Goole, Patrington, Kilnsea, Halifax, Snaith, Barton-upon-Humber, Spurn Head, Dewsbury, Pontefract, Immingham Dock, Immingham, Wakefield, Thorne, Crowle, Scunthorpe, Grimsby, Cleethorpes, HUDDERSFIELD, Barnsley, Bentley, Doncaster, Brigg, Conisbrough, Bawtry, Caistor, Rotherham, Market Rasen, Louth, Mablethorpe, SHEFFIELD, Maltby, Gainsborough, Sutton-on-Sea, Stocksbridge, Chapel-en-le-Frith, Dronfield, Staveley, Worksop, Retford, Wragby, Alford, Dovedale, Castleton, Baslow, Chesterfield, Tuxford, Lincoln, Horncastle, Partney, Spilsby, Skegness, Bakewell, Haddon Hall, Clay Cross, Ollerton, Woodhall Spa, Matlock, Alfreton, Sutton-in-Ashfield, Mansfield, Southwell, Leadenham, Boston, Holkham Hall, Wells-next-the-Sea, Blakeney, Ashbourne, Belper, Heanor, Ripley, Hucknall, Newark-on-Trent, Sleaford, Hunstanton, Holt, Ilkeston, NOTTINGHAM, Bingham, Donington, Sutterton, The Wash, Sandringham House, Houghton Hall, Fakenham, Guist, DERBY, West Bridgford, Grantham, Holbeach, Long Sutton, King's Lynn, East Dereham, Long Eaton, Belvoir Castle, Bourne, Spalding, Wisbech, Swaffham, Burton-upon-Trent, Loughborough, Melton Mowbray, Stamford, Crowland, Outwell, Stradsett, Oxburgh Hall, Watton, Wymondham, Swadlincote, Shepshed, Oakham, Guyhirn, Downham Market, Ashby de la Zouch, Coalville, Oadby, Uppingham, Eye, Whittlesey, March, Brandon, Lichfield, Tamworth, Hinckley, LEICESTER, Corby, Weldon, Oundle, PETERBOROUGH, Chatteris, Ramsey, Littleport, Thetford, Diss, Sutton Coldfield, Nuneaton, Bedworth, Lutterworth, Market Harborough, Husbands Bosworth, Desborough, Boughton House, Kettering, Thrapston, Ely, Attleborough

Inverness
ABERDEEN
Peterhead
Fraserburgh
DUNDEE
Perth
Stirling
Falkirk
Alloa **Dunfermline**
Kirkcaldy
Glenrothes
St. Andrews
EDINBURGH
Livingston
Cumbernauld
East Kilbride
Kilmarnock
Berwick-upon-Tweed
Alnwick
Morpeth
Blyth

Alness, Invergordon, Cromarty, Black Isle, Fortrose, Nairn, Forres, Elgin, Lossiemouth, Buckie, Cullen, Banff, Macduff, Fochabers, Keith, Rothes, Craigellachie, Dufftown, Huntly, Turriff, New Deer, Mintlaw, Rattray Head, Buchan Ness, Cruden Bay, Newburgh, Ellon, Oldmeldrum, Inverurie, Kintore, Alford, Mossat, Rhynie, Tomintoul, Carrbridge, Dulnain Bridge, Grantown-on-Spey, Dava, Aviemore, Kingussie, Newtonmore, Carn Ban, Laggan, Dalwhinnie, Pass of Drumochter, Blair Castle, Blair Atholl, Kinloch Rannoch, Pitlochry, Aberfeldy, Dunkeld, Killin, Lochearnhead, Callander, Doune, Crieff, Auchterarder, Dunblane, Bridge of Allan, Alva, Dollar, Kinross, Lochgelly, Cowdenbeath, Kincardine, Culross, Rosyth, Inverkeithing, S. Queensferry, Grangemouth, Bo'Ness, Linlithgow, Bathgate, Armadale, Whitburn, Airdrie, Coatbridge, Motherwell, Wishaw, Carluke, Lanark, Biggar, Abington, Elvanfoot, Sanquhar, Thornhill, Moffat, Beattock, Lockerbie, Lochmaben, Langholm

Craigievar Castle, Crathes Castle, Balmoral Castle, Craigellachie, Glamis Castle, Hopetoun House, Rosslyn Chapel, Drumlanrig Castle, Bamburgh Castle

Stonehaven, Inverbervie, Laurencekirk, Marykirk, Brechin, Montrose, Kirriemuir, Forfar, Glamis, Arbroath, Carnoustie, Monifieth, Tayport, Newport-on-Tay, Buddon Ness, Leuchars, Cupar, Auchtermuchty, Newburgh, Falkland, Leven, Methil, Buckhaven, Crail, Anstruther, Pittenweem, Saint Monans, Elie, Kelty, Burntisland, North Berwick, Dunbar, Cockburnspath, Eyemouth, Coldstream, Duns, Greenlaw, Earlston, Mellerstain, Kelso, Abbey, Dryburgh, Melrose, Galashiels, Innerleithen, Peebles, West Linton, Carnwath, Penicuik, Loanhead, Dalkeith, Musselburgh, Prestonpans, Aberlady, East Linton, Haddington, Tranent, Leith, St. Abb's Head, Holy Island, Belford, Wooler, Rothbury, Warkworth, Amble, Felton, Otterburn, Ashington, Newbiggin-by-the-Sea

St Boswells, Newtown, Selkirk, Hawick, Jedburgh, Carter Bar, The Cheviot

Grampian Mountains, Cairngorms National Park, Glenmore Forest Park, Cairn Gorm, Ben Macdui, Devil's Elbow, Glas Maol, Beinn a' Ghlò, Schiehallion, Ben Lawers, Ben Chonzie, Ben Vorlich, Ochil Hills, Sidlaw Hills, Pentland Hills, Moorfoot Hills, Lammermuir Hills, Southern Uplands, The Cheviot Hills, Northumberland National Park, Kielder Res., Broad Law, Fife Ness, Firth of Forth, Loch of Strathbeg, Pitmedden Garden, The Pleasance, St Abb's Head National Nature Reserve

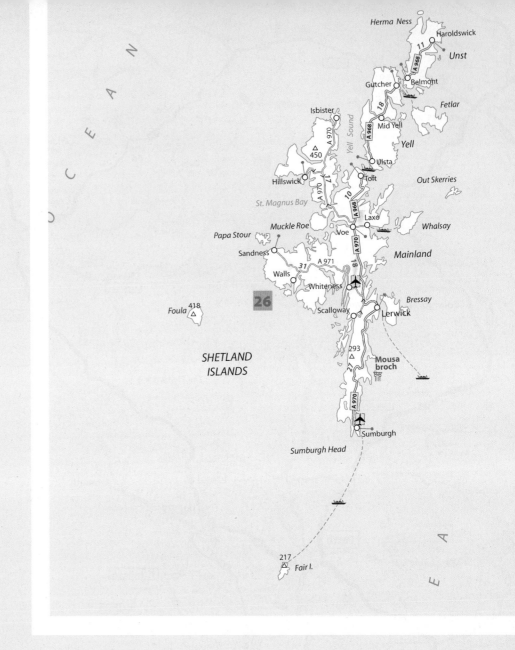

Herma Ness

Haroldswick

Unst

11

Gutcher

Belmont

A 968

Fetlar

18

Isbister

Mid Yell

Yell

A 970

Ulsta

450

Out Skerries

Toft

A 968

Hillswick

17

10

A 970

St. Magnus Bay

Laxo

Muckle Roe

Whalsay

Papa Stour

Voe

A 970

18

Mainland

Sandness

A 971

Walls

31

Whiteness

Bressay

26

Scalloway

Lerwick

Foula 418

SHETLAND
ISLANDS

293

27

Mousa
broch

A 970

Sumburgh

Sumburgh Head

217 Fair I.

E A

Butt of Lewis

Port of Ness

Kinle

A 857

16

THE MINCH

LEWIS

Barvas

Scourie

A 858

A 857

Flannan I.

Carloway

292

12

Portnaguran

Eddrachillis
Bay

Callanish
Standing
Stones

Stornoway

Broad
Bay

Tiumpan Head

Garynahine

34

A 858

A 866

Eye Peninsula

574

Rubha Còigeach

Lochir

36

Kebock Head

A 859

Hushinish

572

Coigach
743

B 887

Clisham
799

WESTERN

West Loch Tarbert

Tarbert

32

Gruinard
Bay

St. Kilda

Toe Head

A 859

24

Rubha Réidh

Laide

29

Harris

Dundonnel

26

Papa

Walls

Whiten

Scallo

Foula 418 △

SHETLAND
ISLANDS

Sumburgh He

217 △ Fair I.

22

North Ronaldsay

Westray

Pierowall

The North
Sound

Westray Firth

Kettletoft

Sanday

Rousay

Brough Head

Eday

Stronsay Firth

Stronsay

ORKNEY
ISLANDS

38

A 966

Shapinsay

Skara
Brae

A 967

A 996

A 965

Mainland

Stromness

Kirkwall

Skaill

Stenness

15

A 964

20

Scapa Flow

A 961

A 990

△
479

Rora Head

A 961

Lyness

St Margaret's Hope

Hoy

South Ronaldsay

Pentland Firth

Burwick

Dunnet Head

Duncansby Head

Cape Wrath

Strathy Point

Scrabster

Dunnet

A 836

Gills

John O' Groats

Durness

Whiten Head

Kyle of Tongue

Thurso

20

Castletown

Noss Head

hbervie

A 838

Coldbackie

Bettyhill

A 836

A 836

34

B 876

17

A 99

20

27

Melvich

16

21

Reiss

31

Tongue

Roadside

A 882

Wick

Foinaven
△ 908

927

Ben Hope

Syre

40

A 837

B 871

A 836

B 873

B 871

39

183
114

A 9

172
107
A 99

Laxford Bridge

A 838

Kylestrome

Altnaharra

L. Naver

Kinbrace

Morven
△ 706

Latheron

A 9

17

39

34

Ben Klibreck
961

△ 713

Ben Armine

A 897

20

Inchnadamph

A 838

A 836

△ 998

Ben More Assynt

A 837

Loch Shin

A 897

Helmsdale

A 9

Ledmore

Lairg

21

18

A 837

27

A 839

14

A 839

11

Golspie

Brora

Ullapool

A 837

Bonar Bridge

A 949

14

Dornoch

Dornoch Firth

12

Aran Island

Gweebarra B

Rossan Point   Glencolumbkille

R 263   17   Killybegs

Bunglass Cliffs

Donegal B

Bun
Bun D

Inishmurray

65
40
Rosses
Point

Erris Head

Broad
Haven

Ballycastle   Killala
Bay   Easky   Slygo Bay

Strandhill

Belmullet   Glénamoy   31   379 △   R 314   R 297

R 314   12   17   Inishcrone   N 59   Mountains △   33   543   Ballysadare

Inishkea   12   R 315   543

R 313   Bangor   Oweniny   N 59   20   Crossmolina   Ballina/   The   20   SLIGO   18

BlacksodBay   720   19   R 312   R 316   L.   Béal an Átha Ó.   47   29

670   Ballycroy   20   10   Cóng   R 294   Tubbercurry   R 294   Ballymo

Keel   698   Nephin   May   Charlestown   Gorteen

Achill Island   R 319   1   804   Foxford   N 26   25   21   L. Gara

Mulrany   11   R 317   R 310   Pontoon   39   Swinford   28

Corraun   521   Castlebar/   24   Kiltimagh   R 320   Ballaghaderreen

Clare Island   Newport   Caisléan an   R 321   N 5   Frenchpark

Clew   Bay   17   Bharraigh   R 324   R 322   20   ROSC

Westport/   18   N 5   Manulla   R 324   R 323   N 83

Louisburgh   Cathair na Mart   11   R 330   18   18   Ballyhaunis   Castlere

Croagh   763   14   R 331   Claremorris   10   N 60   6   Ballym

Patrick   66   19   Robe   22   R 360   Rosc

Mweelrea   41   Ballintubber   97   Clare   R 364   R

Mts   Murrisk   14   60   Dunmore   Glennamaddy

817   Partry Mountains   Ballinrobe   N 17   19   R 328

Killary Harbour   681   Lough   Kilmaine   R 332

Inishturk   Letterfrack   22   Mask   R 345   31   R 332   17

Inishbofin   9   R 336   Clonbur   R 334   Tuam/Tuaim   Mount

RinvylePt.   728   Leenane   19   Cong   Lough   12   R 341   23   Bellew   R 359   R 358

Inishshark   The   Maumturk Mts   5   Corrib   Headford   N 63

Twelve Pins   22   701   Connemara   N 59   17   Ballinas

Clifden   N 59   22   Maam   13   Oughterard   27   R 332   Béal

N 341   49   Cross   R 363   na Slua

Slyne Head   79   Gortmore   13   GALWAY   R 348   21

Roundstone   R 340   9   R 332   20   Athenry   63   M 6

Carna   12   Galway/   6   17   39   R 350   19

Lettermullan   R 374   24   Gaillimh   R 348

Gorumna   R 336   Spiddal   Barna   Oranmore

Island   104   Craughwell   R 353

Inishmore   Kilronan   BlackHead   65   R 347   Ardrahan   Loughrea   R 352

Dún   Inishmaan   25   Kinvarra   28

Aonghasa   Inisheer   R 477   Ballyvaughan   15

Aran   Islands   R 67   Lisdoonvarna   18   R 480   R 460   Gort

Cliffs of Mol   R 478   R 481   R 476   R 460

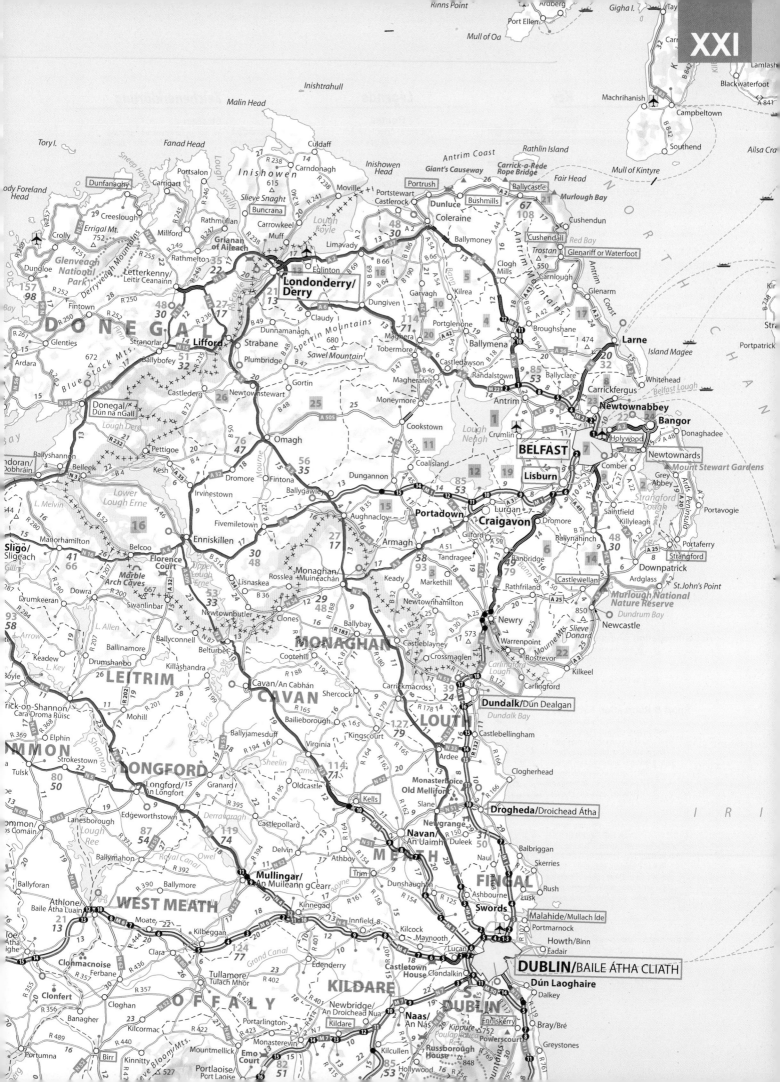

Key	**Légende**	**Zeichenerklärung**

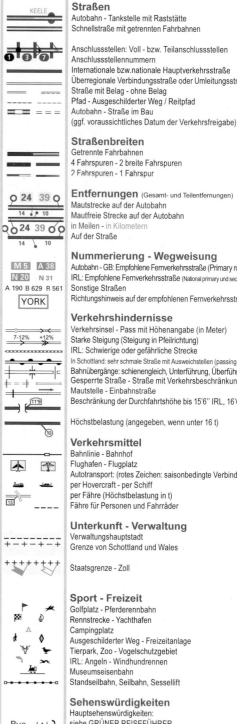

Roads / Routes / Straßen

Key	Légende	Zeichenerklärung
Motorway - Service areas	Autoroute - Aires de service	Autobahn - Tankstelle mit Raststätte
Dual carriageway with motorway characteristics	Double chaussée de type autoroutier	Schnellstraße mit getrennten Fahrbahnen
Interchanges: complete, limited	Échangeurs : complet, partiels	Anschlussstellen: Voll - bzw. Teilanschlussstellen
Interchange numbers	Numéros d'échangeurs	Anschlussstellennummern
International and national road network	Route de liaison internationale ou nationale	Internationale bzw.nationale Hauptverkehrsstraße
Interregional and less congested road	Route de liaison interrégionale ou de dégagement	Überregionale Verbindungsstraße oder Umleitungsstrecke
Road surfaced - unsurfaced	Route revêtue - non revêtue	Straße mit Belag - ohne Belag
Footpath - Waymarked footpath / Bridle path	Sentier - Sentier balisé/Allée cavalière	Pfad - Ausgeschilderter Weg / Reitpfad
Motorway / Road under construction	Autoroute - Route en construction	Autobahn - Straße im Bau
(when available: with scheduled opening date)	(le cas échéant : date de mise en service prévue)	(ggf. voraussichtliches Datum der Verkehrsfreigabe)

Road widths / Largeur des routes / Straßenbreiten

Key	Légende	Zeichenerklärung
Dual carriageway	Chaussées séparées	Getrennte Fahrbahnen
4 lanes - 2 wide lanes	4 voies - 2 voies larges	4 Fahrspuren - 2 breite Fahrspuren
2 lanes - 2 narrow lanes	2 voies - 2 voies étroites	2 Fahrspuren - 1 Fahrspur

Distances (total and intermediate) / Distances (totalisées et partielles) / Entfernungen (Gesamt- und Teilentfernungen)

Key	Légende	Zeichenerklärung
Toll roads on motorway	Section à péage sur autoroute	Mautstrecke auf der Autobahn
Toll-free section on motorway	Section libre sur autoroute	Mautfreie Strecke auf der Autobahn
in miles - en kilometers	en miles - en kilomètres	in Meilen - in Kilometern
on road	sur route	Auf der Straße

Numbering - Signs / Numérotation - Signalisation / Nummerierung - Wegweisung

Key	Légende	Zeichenerklärung
Motorway - GB: Primary route	Autoroute - GB : itinéraire principal (Primary route)	Autobahn - GB: Empfohlene Fernverkehrsstraße (Primary route)
IRL : National primary and secondary route	IRL : itinéraire principal (National primary et secondary route)	IRL: Empfohlene Fernverkehrsstraße (National primary und secondary route)
Other roads	Autres routes	Sonstige Straßen
Destination on primary route network	Localités jalonnant les itinéraires principaux	Richtungshinweis auf der empfohlenen Fernverkehrsstraße

M 5   A 38   N 20   N 31   A 190   B 629   R 561   YORK

Obstacles / Obstacles / Verkehrshindernisse

Key	Légende	Zeichenerklärung
Roundabout - Pass and its height above sea level (meters)	Rond-point - Col et sa cote d'altitude (en mètres)	Verkehrsinsel - Pass mit Höhenangabe (in Meter)
Steep hill (ascent in direction of the arrow)	Forte déclivité (flèches dans le sens de la montée)	Starke Steigung (Steigung in Pfeilrichtung)
IRL: Difficult or dangerous section of road	IRL : Parcours difficile ou dangereux	IRL: Schwierige oder gefährliche Strecke
In Scotland: narrow road with passing places	En Écosse : route très étroite avec emplacements pour croisement	In Schottland: sehr schmale Straße mit Ausweichstellen (passing places)
Level crossing: railway passing, under road, over road	Passages de la route : à niveau, supérieur, inférieur	Bahnübergänge: schienengleich, Unterführung, Überführung
Prohibited road - Road subject to restrictions	Route interdite - Route réglementée	Gesperrte Straße - Straße mit Verkehrsbeschränkungen
Toll barrier - One way road (on major and regional roads)	Barrière de péage - Route à sens unique	Mautstelle - Einbahnstraße
Height limit under 15'6'' IRL, 16'6'' GB	Hauteur limitée au dessous de 15'6'' IRL, 16'6''GB	Beschränkung der Durchfahrtshöhe bis 15'6' IRL, 16'6' GB
Load limit (under 16 t.)	Limites de charge (au-dessous de 16 t.)	Höchstbelastung (angegeben, wenn unter 16 t)

Transportation / Transports / Verkehrsmittel

Key	Légende	Zeichenerklärung
Railway - Passenger station	Voie ferrée - Gare	Bahnlinie - Bahnhof
Airport - Airfield	Aéroport - Aérodrome	Flughafen - Flugplatz
Transportation of vehicles: (seasonal services in red)	Transport des autos: (liaison saisonnière en rouge)	Autotransport: (rotes Zeichen: saisonbedingte Verbindung)
by hovercraft - by boat	par aéroglisseur - par bateau	per Hovercraft - per Schiff
by ferry (load limit in tons)	par bac (charge maximum en tonnes)	per Fähre (Höchstbelastung in t)
Ferry (passengers and cycles only)	Bac pour piétons et cycles	Fähre für Personen und Fahrräder

Accommodation - Administration / Hébergement - Administration / Unterkunft - Verwaltung

Key	Légende	Zeichenerklärung
Administrative boundaries	Limites administratives	Verwaltungshauptstadt
Scottish and Welsh borders	Limite de l'Écosse et du Pays de Galles	Grenze von Schottland und Wales
National boundary - Customs post	Frontière - Douane	Staatsgrenze - Zoll

Sport & Recreation Facilities / Sports - Loisirs / Sport - Freizeit

Key	Légende	Zeichenerklärung
Golf course - Horse racetrack	Golf - Hippodrome	Golfplatz - Pferderennbahn
Racing circuit - Pleasure boat harbour	Circuit automobile - Port de plaisance	Rennstrecke - Yachthafen
Caravan and camping sites	Camping, caravaning	Campingplatz
Waymarked footpath - Country park	Sentier balisé - Base ou parc de loisirs	Ausgeschilderter Weg - Freizeitanlage
Safari park, zoo - Bird sanctuary, refuge	Parc animalier, zoo - Réserve d'oiseaux	Tierpark, Zoo - Vogelschutzgebiet
IRL: Fishing - Greyhound track	IRL : Pêche - Cynodrome	IRL: Angeln - Windhundrennen
Tourist train	Train touristique	Museumseisenbahn
Funicular, cable car, chairlift	Funiculaire, téléphérique, télésiège	Standseilbahn, Seilbahn, Sessellift

Sights / Curiosités / Sehenswürdigkeiten

Key	Légende	Zeichenerklärung
Principal sights:	Principales curiosités :	Hauptsehenswürdigkeiten:
see THE GREEN GUIDE	voir LE GUIDE VERT	siehe GRÜNER REISEFÜHRER
Towns or places of interest, Places to stay	Localités ou sites intéressants, lieux de séjour	Sehenswerte Orte, Ferienorte
Religious building - Historic house, castle	Édifice religieux - Château	Sakral-Bau - Schloss, Burg
Ruins - Prehistoric monument - Cave	Ruines - Monument mégalithique - Grotte	Ruine - Vorgeschichtliches Steindenkmal - Höhle
Garden, park - Other places of interest	Jardin, parc - Autres curiosités	Garten, Park - Sonstige Sehenswürdigkeit
IRL: Fort - Celtic cross - Round Tower	IRL : Fort - Croix celte - Tour ronde	IRL: Fort, Festung - Keltisches Kreuz - Rundturm
Panoramic view - Viewpoint - Scenic route	Panorama - Point de vue - Parcours pittoresque	Rundblick - Aussichtspunkt - Landschaftlich schöne Strecke

Rye (▲)   Ergol

Other signs / Signes divers / Sonstige Zeichen

Key	Légende	Zeichenerklärung
Industrial cable way	Transporteur industriel aérien	Industrieschwebebahn
Telecommunications tower or mast - Lighthouse	Tour ou pylône de télécommunications - Phare	Funk-, Sendeturm - Leuchtturm
Power station - Quarry	Centrale électrique - Carrière	Kraftwerk - Steinbruch
Mine - Industrial activity	Mine - Industries	Bergwerk - Industrieanlagen
Refinery - Cliff	Raffinerie - Falaise	Raffinerie - Klippen
National forest park - National park	Parc forestier national - Parc national	Waldschutzgebiet - Nationalpark

Verklaring van de tekens	*Legenda*	*Signos convencionales*

Wegen / Strade / Carreteras

Nederlands	Italiano	Español
Autosnelweg - Serviceplaatsen	Autostrada - Aree di servizio	Autopista - Áreas de servicio
Gescheiden rijbanen van het type autosnelweg	Doppia carreggiata di tipo autostradale	Autovía
Aansluitingen: volledig, gedeeltelijk	Svincoli: completo, parziale	Enlaces: completo, parciales
Afritnummers	Svincoli numerati	Números de los accesos
Internationale of nationale verbindingsweg	Strada di collegamento internazionale o nazionale	Carretera de comunicación internacional o nacional
Interregionale verbindingsweg	Strada di collegamento interregionale o di disimpegno	Carretera de comunicación interregional o alternativo
Verharde weg - Onverharde weg	Strada rivestita - non rivestita	Carretera asfaltada - sin asfaltar
Pad - Bewegwijzerd wandelpad / Ruiterpad	Sentiero - Sentiero segnalato / Pista per cavalli	Sendero - Sendero señalizado / Camino de caballos
Autosnelweg in aanleg - weg in aanleg (indien bekend: datum openstelling)	Autostrada, strada in costruzione (data di apertura prevista)	Autopista, carretera en construcción (en su caso: fecha prevista de entrada en servicio)

Breedte van de wegen / Larghezza delle strade / Ancho de las carreteras

Gescheiden rijbanen	Carreggiate separate	Calzadas separadas
4 rijstroken - 2 brede rijstroken	4 corsie - 2 corsie larghe	Cuatro carriles - Dos carriles anchos
2 rijstroken - 2 smalle rijstroken	2 corsie - 2 corsie strette	Dos carriles - Dos carriles estrechos

Afstanden (totaal en gedeeltelijk) / Distanze (totali e parziali) / Distancias (totales y parciales)

Gedeelte met tol op autosnelwegen	Tratto a pedaggio su autostrada	Tramo de peaje en autopista
Tolvrij gedeelte op autosnelwegen	Tratto esente da pedaggio su autostrada	Tramo libre en autopista
in mijlen - in kilometers	in migla - in chilometri	en millas - en kilómetros
op andere wegen	su strada	en carretera

Wegnummers - Bewegwijzering / Numerazione - Segnaletica / Numeración - Señalización

Autosnelweg - GB: Hoofdweg (Primary route)	Autostrada - GB: itinerario principale (Strada «Primary»)	Autopista - GB: Vía principal (Primary route)
IRL: Hoofdweg (National primary en secondary route)	IRL: itinerario principale (Strada «National primary» e «Secondary»)	IRL: Vía principal (National primary et secondary route)
Andere wegen	Altre Strade	Otras carreteras
Plaatsen langs een autosnelweg of Primary route met bewegwijzering	Località delimitante gli itinerari principali	Localidad en itinerario principal

Hindernissen / Ostacoli / Obstáculos

Rotonde - Bergpas en hoogte boven de zeespiegel (in meters)	Rotonda - Passo ed altitudine (in metri)	Rotonda - Puerto y su altitud (en métros)
Steile helling (pijlen in de richting van de helling)	Forte pendenza (salita nel senso della freccia)	Pendiente Pronunciada (las flechas indican el sentido del ascenso)
IRL: Moeilijk of gevaarlijk traject	IRL: Percorso difficile o pericoloso	IRL: Recorrido difícil o peligroso
In Schotland: smalle weg met uitwijkplaatsen	In Scozia: Strada molto stretta con incrocio	En escocia: carretera muy estrecha con ensanchamientos para poder cruzarse
Wegovergangen: gelijkvloers, overheen, onderdoor	Passaggi della strada: a livello, cavalcavia, sottopassaggio	Pasos de la carretera: a nivel, superior, inferior
Verboden weg - Beperkt opengestelde weg	Strada vietata - Strada a circolazione regolamentata	Tramo prohibido - Carretera restringida
Tol - Weg met eenrichtingsverkeer	Casello - Strada a senso unico (su collegamenti principali e regionali)	Barrera de peaje - Carretera de sentido único
Vrije hoogte indien lager dan 15' 6'' IRL, 16'6'' GB	Limite di altezza inferiore a 15'6'' IRL, 16'6''GB	Altura limitada (15'6'' IRL, 16'6''GB)
Maximum draagvermogen (indien minder dan 16 t)	Limite di portata (inferiore a 16 t.)	Limite de carga (inferior a 16 t)

Vervoer / Trasporti / Transportes

Spoorweg - Reizigersstation	Ferrovia - Stazione viaggiatori	Línea férrea - Estación de viajeros
Luchthaven - Vliegveld	Aeroporto - Aerodromo	Aeropuerto - Aeródromo
Vervoer van auto's: (tijdens het seizoen: rood teken)	Trasporto auto: (stagionale in rosso)	Transporte de coches: (Enlace de temporada: signo rojo)
per hovercraft - per boot	su idrovolante - su traghetto	por overcraft - por barco
per veerpont (maximum draagvermogen in t.)	su chiatta (carico massimo in t.)	por barcaza (carga máxima en toneladas)
Veerpont voor voetgangers en fietsers	Traghetto per pedoni e biciclette	Barcaza para el paso de peatones y vehículos dos ruedas

Verblijf - Administratie / Risorse alberghiere - Amministrazione / Alojamiento - Administración

Administratieve grenzen	Confini amministrativi	Limites administrativos
Grens van Schotland en Wales	Confine di Scozia e Galles	Limites de Escocia y del País de Gales
Staatsgrens - Douanekantoor	Frontiera - Dogana	Frontera - Puesto de aduanas

Sport - Recreatie / Sport - Divertimento / Deportes - Ocio

Golfterrein - Renbaan	Golf - Ippodromo	Golf - Hipódromo
Autocircuit - Jachthaven	Circuito Automobilistico - Porto turistico	Circuito de velocidad - Puerto deportivo
Kampeerterrein (tent, caravan)	Campeggi, caravaning	Camping, caravaning
Sentiero segnalato - Recreatiepark	Sentiero segnalato - Area o parco per attività ricreative	Sendero señalizado - Parque de ocio
Safaripark, dierentuin - Vogelreservaat	Parco con animali, zoo - Riserva ornitologica	Reserva de animales, zoo - Reserva de pájaros
IRL: Vissen - Hondenrenbaan	IRL: Pesca - Cinodromo	IRL: Pêche - Cynodrome
Toeristentreintje	Trenino turistico	Tren turístico
Kabelspoor, kabelbaan, stoeltjeslift	Funicolare, funivia, seggiovia	Funicular, Teleférico, telesilla

Bezienswaardigheden / Mete e luoghi d'interesse / Curiosidades

Belangrijkste bezienswaardigheden: zie DE GROENE GIDS	Principali luoghi d'interesse, vedere LA GUIDA VERDE	Principales curiosidades: ver LA GUÍA VERDE
Interessante steden of plaatsen, vakantieoorden	Località o siti interessanti, luoghi di soggiorno	Localidad o lugar interesante, lugar para quedarse
Kerkelijk gebouw - Kasteel	Edificio religioso - Castello	Edificio religioso - Castillo
Ruïne - Megaliet - Grot	Rovine - Monumento megalitico - Grotta	Ruinas - Monumento megalítico - Cueva
Tuin, park - Andere bezienswaardigheden	Giardino, parco - Altri luoghi d'interesse	Jardín, parque - Curiosidades diversas
IRL: Fort - Keltisch kruis - Ronde toren	IRL: Forte - Croce celtica - Torre rotonda	IRL: Fortaleza - Cruz celta - Torre redonda
Panorama - Uitzichtpunt - Schilderachtig traject	Panorama - Vista - Percorso pittoresco	Vista panorámica - Vista parcial - Recorrido pintoresco

Rye (▲)
Ergol

Diverse tekens / Simboli vari / Signos diversos

Kabelvrachtvervoer	Teleferica industriale	Transportador industrial aéreo
Telecommunicatietoren of -mast - Vuurtoren	Torre o pilone per telecomunicazioni - Faro	Emisor de Radiodifusión - Faro
Elektriciteitscentrale - Steengroeve	Centrale elettrica - Cava	Central eléctrica - Cantera
Mijn - Industrie	Miniera - Industrie	Mina - Industrias
Raffinaderij - Klif	Raffineria - Falesia	Refinería - Acantilado
Staatsbos - Nationaal park	Parco forestale nazionale - Parco nazionale	Parque forestal nacional - Parque nacional

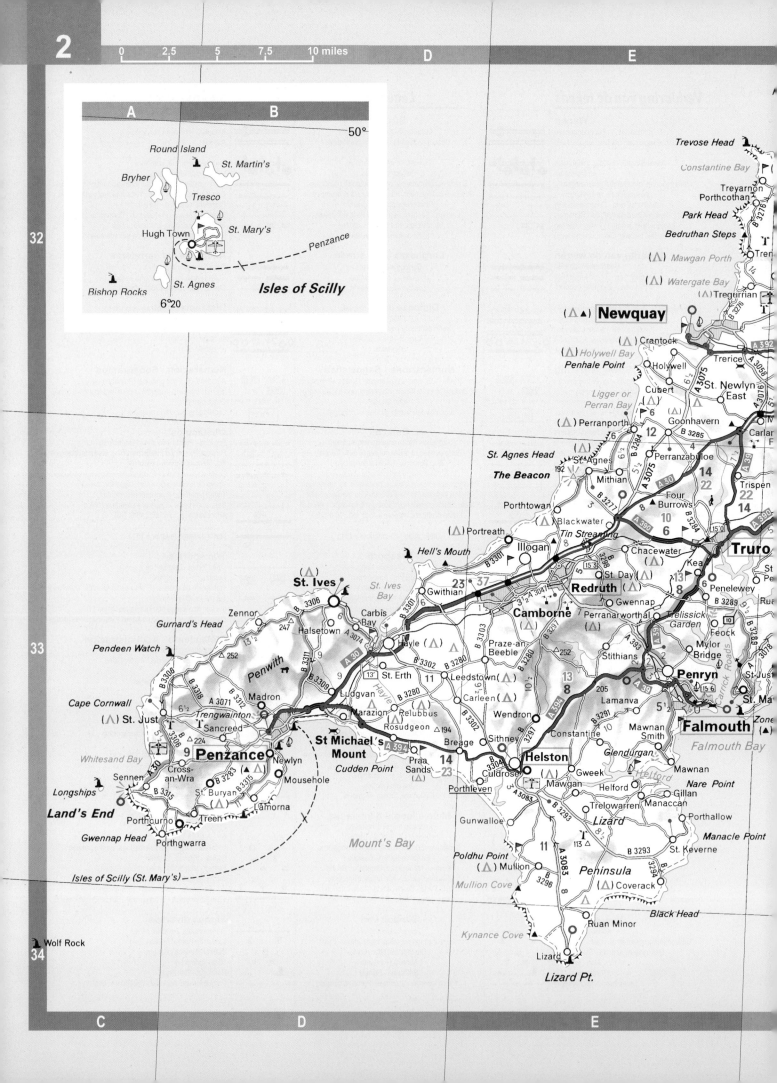

0   2.5   5   7.5   10 miles

D

E

50°

A

B

Round Island

St. Martin's

Bryher

Tresco

Hugh Town

St. Mary's

Penzance

Bishop Rocks

St. Agnes

Isles of Scilly

6°20

32

33

34

Trevose Head
Constantine Bay
Treyarnon
Porthcothan
Park Head
Bedruthan Steps
Tren
(∆) Mawgan Porth
(∆) Watergate Bay
(∆) Treguirrian
(∆▲) **Newquay**
(∆) Crantock
(∆) Holywell Bay
Penhale Point
Holywell
Trerice
St. Newlyn East
Cubert
Ligger or Perran Bay
Goonhavern
(∆) Perranporth
12
B 3285
Carlar
St. Agnes Head
The Beacon
St. Agnes
Perranzabuloe
14
22
Trispen
Mithian
Four Burrows
Porthtowan
Blackwater
10
6
(∆) Portreath
Tin Streaming
Chacewater
Truro
Hell's Mouth
Illogan
St. Day (∆)
13
Kea
(∆)
23 • 37
Penelewey
St. Ives Bay
Gwithian
Redruth
8
Carbis Bay
Camborne
Perranarworthal
Trelissick Garden
Feock
Zennor
252
Halsetown
Praze-an-Beeble
Stithians
Mylor Bridge
St. Ives
Penryn
Gurnard's Head
Hayle (∆)
St. Erth
Penzance
Leedstown (∆)
13
Lamanva
St. Ma
Pendeen Watch
Penwith
Ludgvan
11
Carleen (∆)
8
205
Madron
Wendron
Mawnan Smith
Falmouth
Cape Cornwall
Trengwainton
Marazion
Rosudgeon
Sithney
Constantine
Falmouth Bay
(∆) St. Just
Sancreed
Relubbus
Breage
Helston
Glendurgan
St Michael's Mount
14
Gweek
Mawnan
Cross-an-Wra
Newlyn
Cudden Point
23
Culdrose
Mawgan
Helford
Nare Point
9 **Penzance**
Mousehole
Praa Sands
Porthleven
Gillan
St. Buryan
Gunwalloe
Trelowarren
Manaccan
Longships
Lamorna
11
113
Porthallow
Land's End
Treen
Mount's Bay
Poldhu Point
Peninsula
Manacle Point
Gwennap Head
Porthcurno
(∆) Mullion
St. Keverne
Porthgwarra
Mullion Cove
(∆) Coverack
Lizard
Black Head
Isles of Scilly (St. Mary's)
Ruan Minor
Kynance Cove
Wolf Rock
Lizard
Lizard Pt.

C

D

E

Tintagel 308 △ B 3266 17 Davidstow 26 Egloskerry Yeolmbridge Carey

B 3263 B 3314 42 La Castle N. Bre Brent

F Delabole 6 Camelford 6 G Bodmin Altarnun A 30 S. Petherwin Launceston A 388 Chillaton N. Bre

0 5 10 km

New Polzeath Port Gaverne St. Teath Moor Lewannick Milton Abbot B 386

Pentire Point Port Isaac Pendoggett Michaelstow 420 Brown S. Petherwin B 3362 Brent

Padstow Bay Trebetherick St. Endellion St. Kew Willy Bolventor Lezant B 3254 B 3257 Lamerton

Trevone St. Minver Rock St. Tudy 301 North Hill Kilmar 35 Stoke Gulworthy Morwellham

St. Merryn Padstow St. Breward 34 Kilmar Tor 390 22 Climsland A 390 Gunnislake 13 Wh

Little Petherick Wadebridge St. Mabyn Helland 21 The Cheesewring Bray Horrabridge

St. Issey St. Breock Pencarrow CORNWALL The Hurlers Shop Kelly Bray Cotehele House Calstock

ance St-Mawgan Bodmin Cardinham Colliford Caradon 369 Callington St. Dominick Bere Alston

13 St. Wenn Lake Hill Pensilva St. Ive 18 St. Mellion Bere Ferrers 32 Buck Abbe

21 Withiel St. Neot St. Cleer A 390 162 Pillaton Tamerton Folio

A 3059 St. Columb Major Lanivet A 389 Lanhydrock A 38 12 19 Dobwalls Liskeard Menheniot Landrake Landulph

13 19 Restormel Castle Liskeard 27 Landrake

8 12 Roche Bugle Lanlivery 18 E Taphouse Widegates 17 13 A 38 Saltash

Fraddon St. Dennis Luxulyan Lostwithiel 29 Duloe St. Germans Antony House

Summercourt Carthew Eden Project St. Blazey Lanreath Morval Hessenford Torpoint

Carlyon St. Austell Tywardreath Golant Pelynt Downderry Crafthole Antony Devonport

Mitchell St. Stephen Par Polkerris Fowey Lansallos W. Looe Cornwall Coast Path Cremyll Mt. Edgcumbe

Ladock Grampound Charlestown Polruan Polperro Talland-by-Looe Whitsand Bay Millbrook Cawsand

Probus Trewithen Sticker St. Austell Bay Gribbin Head Rame Head Wembu Bay

Michael Boswinger Pentewan Black Head

nkevil Tregony Mevagissey Chapel Point

High Lanes Veryan Portloe Gorran Haven Santander Roscoff

Nare Head Dodman Point Veryan Bay

Portscatho in Roseland

wes Point ENGLISH

Eddystone Rocks

Height limit (Feet/Metres)
Hauteur limitée (Pieds/Mètres)
Zulässige Gesamthöhe (Fuß/Meter)
Vrije hoogte (Voet/Meter)
Limite di altezza (piedi/metri)
Altura límite (Pies/Metros)

10' 11' 12' 13' 14' 14'6 15' 16' 16'6
3m 3m5 4m 4m4 4m5 5m

F G H 33 34

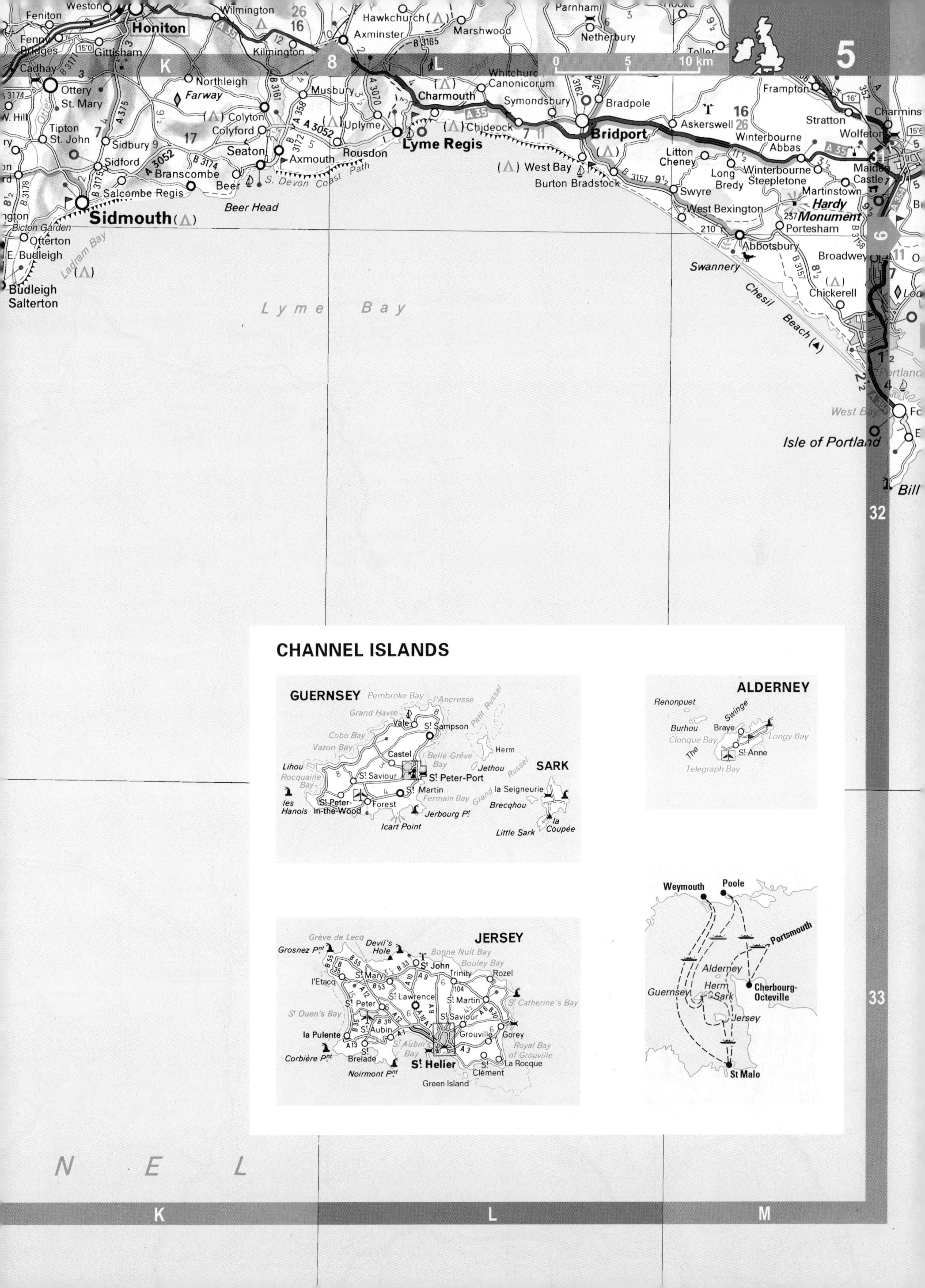

CHANNEL ISLANDS

GUERNSEY

Pembroke Bay
l'Ancresse
Grand Havre
Vale
St Sampson
Cobo Bay
Petit Russel
Vazon Bay
Castel
Herm
Belle Grève Bay
Lihou
Rocquaine Bay
St Saviour
Jethou
St Peter-Port
SARK
les Hanois
St Martin
Fermain Bay
la Seigneurie
St Peter-in-the-Wood
Forest
Jerbourg Pt
Brecqhou
Icart Point
Little Sark
la Coupée

ALDERNEY

Renonpuet
Swinge
Burhou
Braye
Clonque Bay
Longy Bay
The
St Anne
Telegraph Bay

JERSEY

Grève de Lecq
Devil's Hole
Bonne Nuit Bay
Grosnez Pnt
B 55
St John
Bouley Bay
Rozel
l'Etacq
B 35
St Mary's
Trinity
St Lawrence
St Martin
St Catherine's Bay
St Ouen's Bay
St Peter
St Saviour
la Pulente
St Aubin
Gorey
A 13
Grouville
Royal Bay of Grouville
Corbière Pnt
St Brelade
St Helier
La Rocque
Noirmont Pnt
St Clément
Green Island
St Aubin's Bay

Weymouth   Poole
Portsmouth
Alderney
Guernsey   Herm
Sark   Cherbourg-Octeville
Jersey
St Malo

Lyme Bay

0   5   10 km

Honiton
Weston
Wilmington
Hawkchurch
Parnham
Netherbury
Toller
Axminster
Marshwood
Feniton
Fenny Bridges
Gittisham
Kilmington
Whitchurch Canonicorum
Cadhay
Charmouth
Symondsbury
Bradpole
Northleigh
Musbury
Charmouth
Askerswell
Stratton
Ottery St. Mary
Farway
Colyton
Uplyme
Chideock
Bridport
Winterbourne Abbas
Wolfeton
Tipton St. John
Colyford
Lyme Regis
Litton Cheney
Winterbourne Steepletone
Maiden Castle
Sidbury
Seaton
Long Bredy
Martinstown
Sidford
Axmouth
Rousdon
West Bay
Hardy Monument
Branscombe
Beer
Burton Bradstock
Swyre
Portesham
Salcombe Regis
West Bexington
Broadwey
Sidmouth
Beer Head
Abbotsbury
S. Devon Coast Path
Swannery
Chickerell
Bicton Garden
Otterton
E. Budleigh
Ladram Bay
Chesil Beach
Budleigh Salterton
Isle of Portland
West Bay
Bill

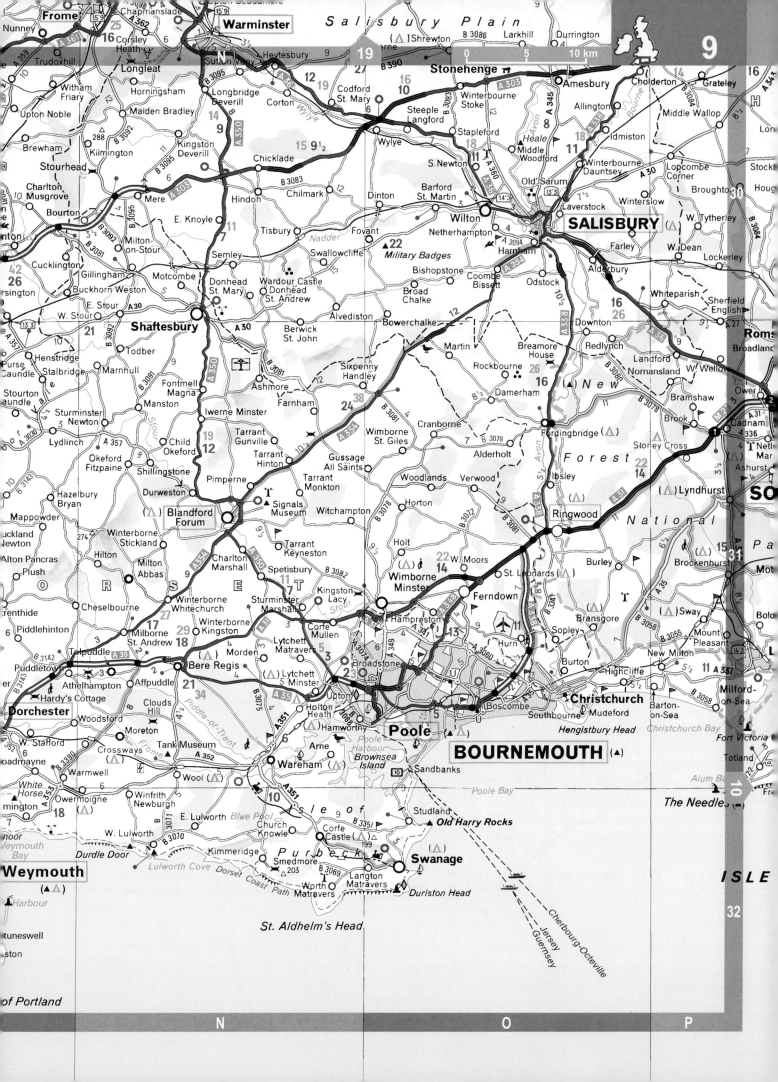

Frome
Nunney
A361
Chapmanslade
Warminster
Salisbury Plain
Shrewton
B 3086
Larkhill
Durrington
25
16
Corsley Heath
A362
Heytesbury
Sutton Veny
19
27
Stonehenge
A303
Amesbury
Cholderton
Grateley
16
H
Longleat
N
Horningsham
12 19
Codford St. Mary
16 10
Steeple Langford
Winterbourne Stoke
12
8
Allington
Middle Wallop
14
Longbridge Deverill
Corton
Wylye
Stapleford
A345
Idmiston
18
11
Maiden Bradley
9
Chicklade
15 9½
S. Newton
18
11
A360
Old Sarum
Winterbourne Dauntsey
11
Kilmington
288
Kingston Deverill
B 3095
Barford St. Martin
Heale
Middle Woodford
A30
Lopcombe Corner
Stockt
Stourhead
Brewham
Charlton Musgrove
Mere
E. Knoyle
Hindon
Chilmark
Dinton
Wilton
SALISBURY
Broughto
30
Houg
Bourton
Milton-on-Stour
7
11
Tisbury
Fovant
Netherhampton
Harnham
Laverstock
Farley
W. Dean
Winterslow
W. Tytherley
B 3084
Cucklington
42 26
Gillingham
Semley
Swallowcliffe
Nadder
Military Badges
22
Bishopstone
Broad Chalke
Coombe Bissett
Odstock
Alderbury
Whiteparish
Lockerley
Sherfield English
Roms
sington
Buckhorn Weston
Motcombe
Donhead St. Mary
Wardour Castle
Donhead St. Andrew
Alvediston
Bowerchalke
12
Martin
Breamore House
Redlynch
16 26
Broadland
26
E. Stour
A30
Berwick St. John
Sixpenny Handley
Rockbourne
26
Landford
Nomansland
W. Wellow
Ower
Shaftesbury
A30
Damerham
16
New
Bramshaw
Brook
M2
Cadnam
A31
A336
Netl
Mar
21
Todber
B 3092
Ashmore
Farnham
24 38
Cranborne
Wimborne St. Giles
Fordingbridge
Forest
1
Ashurst
SO
Purse Caundle
Henstridge
Stalbridge
Marnhull
Fontmell Magna
Iwerne Minster
Gussage All Saints
Alderholt
Ibsley
A338
Stoney Cross
22 14
Lyndhurst
Lydlinch
A357
Child Okeford
19 12
Tarrant Gunville
Tarrant Hinton
Woodlands
Verwood
Ringwood
National
Pa
Okeford Fitzpaine
Shillingstone
Pimperne
Tarrant Monkton
Horton
Holt
Ferndown
Burley
Brockenhurst
31
Hazelbury Bryan
Durweston
Blandford Forum
Signals Museum
Witchampton
A338
Sway
Mappowder
uckland Newton
Winterborne Stickland
Hilton
Tarrant Keyneston
Wimborne Minster
22 14
W. Moors
St. Leonards
Bransgore
Sway
Alton Pancras
Plush
Milton Abbas
R
S
E
Charlton Marshall
Spetisbury
Kingston Lacy
Stour
Hampreston
Hurn
Sopley
Mount Pleasant
Bolo
renthide
Cheselbourne
Winterborne Whitechurch
Sturminster Marshall
Corfe Mullen
13
Burton
New Milton
Highcliffe
Milton St. Andrew
Winterborne Kingston
Lytchett Matravers
Broadstone
Boscombe
Christchurch
Milford-on-Sea
Piddlehinton
17 27
29 18
Morden
23
Upton
Poole
Southbourne
Mudeford
Barton-on-Sea
Dorchester
Telpuddle
A35
Bere Regis
21 34
Lytchett Minster
Holton Heath
Hamworthy
5
BOURNEMOUTH
Hengistbury Head
Christchurch Bay
Fort Victoria
Woodsford
Athelhampton
Hardy's Cottage
Affpuddle
Clouds Hill
Arne
Poole Harbour
Sandbanks
Totland
W. Stafford
Crossways
Moreton
Tank Museum
A352
Wareham
Brownsea Island
Poole Bay
Alum Ba
Fr
Warmwell
White Horse
Owermoigne
Wool
Winfrith Newburgh
10
A351
Isle of
Studland
Old Harry Rocks
The Needle
18
E. Lulworth
Blue Pool
Church Knowle
Corfe Castle
199
Weymouth
W. Lulworth
B 3070
Kimmeridge
Purbeck
Smedmore
203
Langton Matravers
Swanage
Durlston Head
Durdle Door
Lulworth Cove
Dorset Coast Path
Worth Matravers
ISLE
St. Aldhelm's Head
Cherbourg-Octeville
Jersey Guernsey
32
of Portland

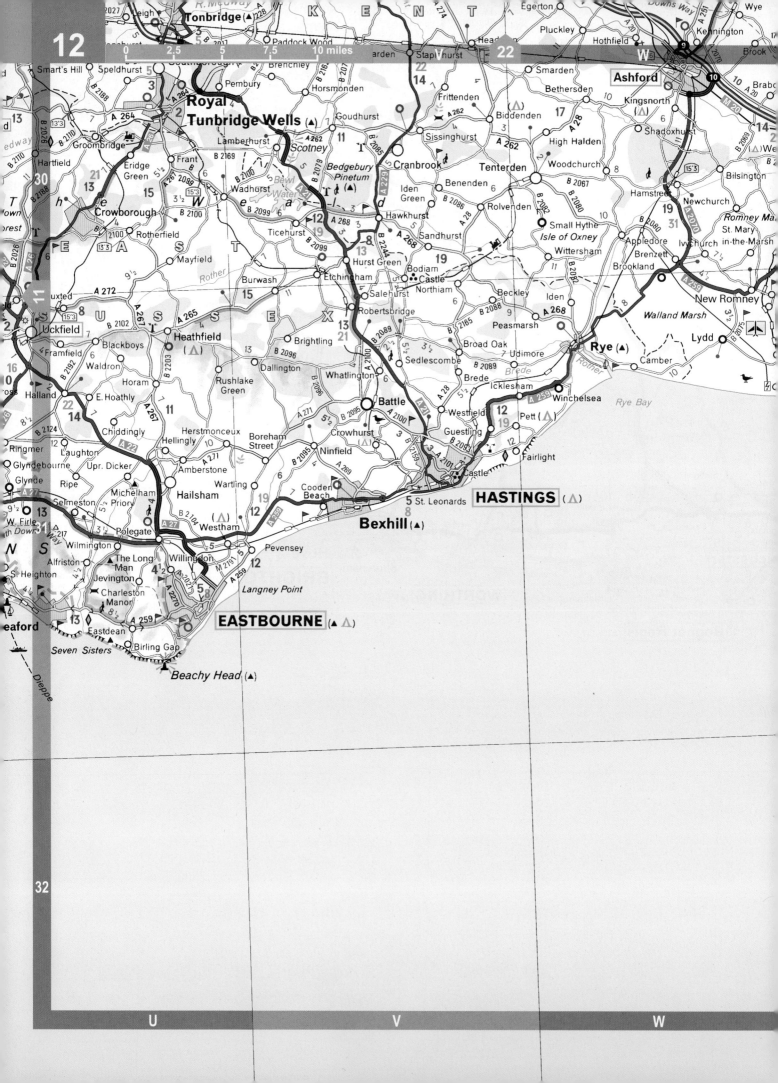

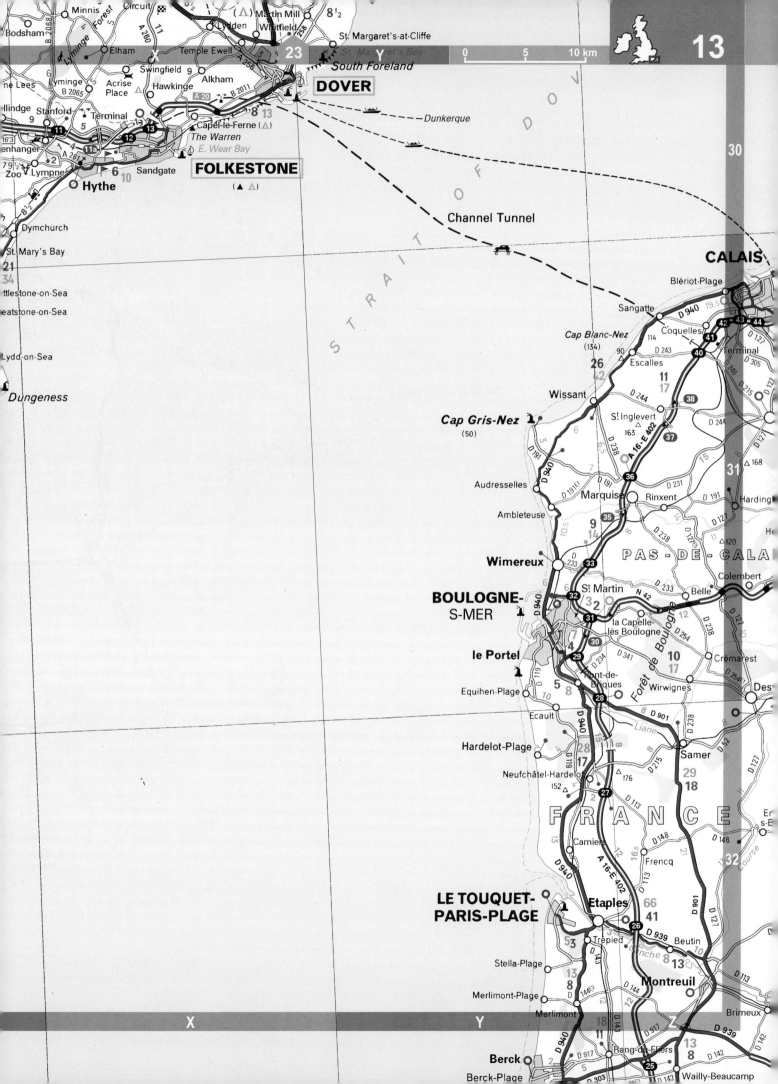

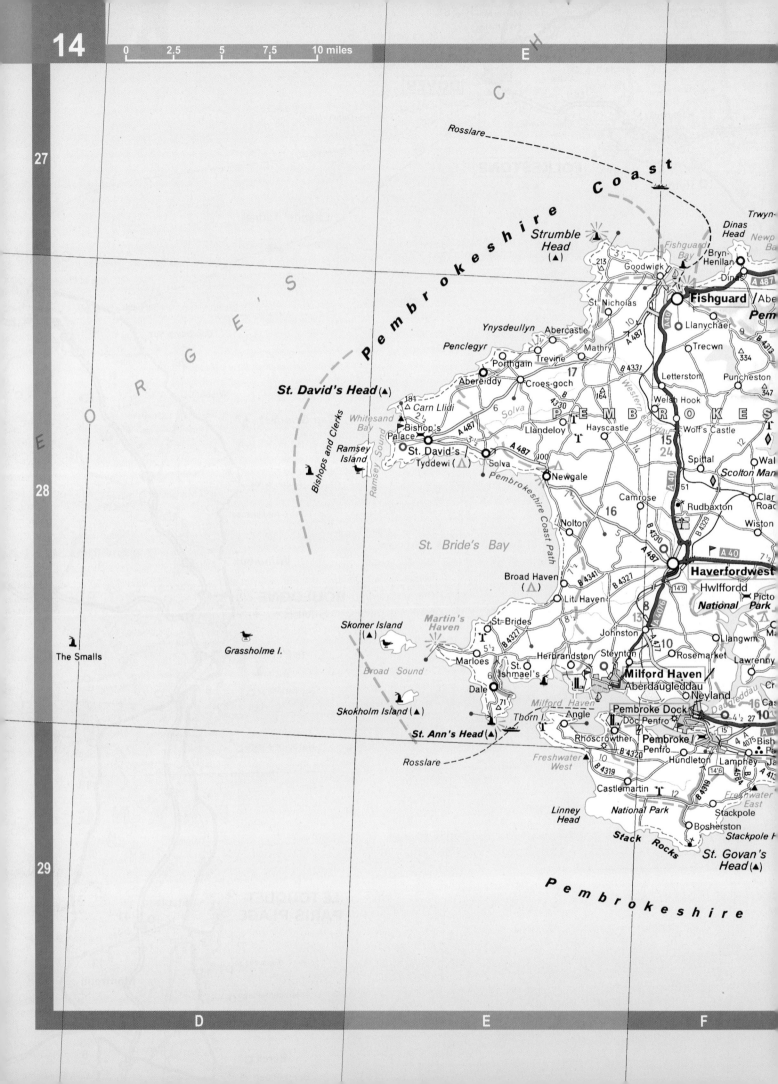

0 2.5 5 7.5 10 miles

Rosslare

Pembrokeshire Coast

TrwynDinas Head

Newp Ba

Strumble
Head
(▲)

Fishguard Bay

Goodwick

Bryn-
Henllan

Dinas

Fishguard | Abe

Pem

St. Nicholas

Llanychaer

Ynysdeullyn

Abercastle

Mathry

Trecwn

334

Penclegyr

Trevine

Letterston

Puncheston

Porthgain

Croes-goch

17

Welsh Hook

347

Abereiddy

181

St. David's Head (▲)

Carn Llidi

Solva

P E M B R O K E S

Wolf's Castle

15
24

Whitesand
Bay

Bishop's
Palace

Llandeloy

Hayscastle

Spittal

Wal

Ramsey
Island

St. David's

Solva

Scolton Man

Tyddewi (△)

100

Newgale

Camrose

Clar
Road

E O R G E'S

Bishops and Clerks

Ramsey Sound

Pembrokeshire Coast Path

16

Nolton

Rudbaxton

Wiston

St. Bride's Bay

Broad Haven
(△)

Haverfordwest
Hwlffordd

National Park

Picto

Lit. Haven

Martin's
Haven

Skomer Island
(▲)

St. Brides

Broad Sound

Herbrandston

Johnston

Llangwm

The Smalls

Grassholme I.

Marloes

Steynton

Rosemarket

Lawrenny

St.
Ishmael's

Milford Haven
Aberdaugleddau

Cr

Dale

Skokholm Island (▲)

Neyland

16

10

Thorn I.

Angle

Pembroke Dock
Doc Penfro

St. Ann's Head (▲)

Rhoscrowther

Pembroke
Penfro

Bish
Pa

Rosslare

Freshwater
West

Hundleton

Lamphey

Ja

Castlemartin

Freshwater
East

Linney
Head

National Park

Stackpole

Bosherston

Stackpole H

Stack Rocks

**St. Govan's
Head** (▲)

P e m b r o k e s h i r e

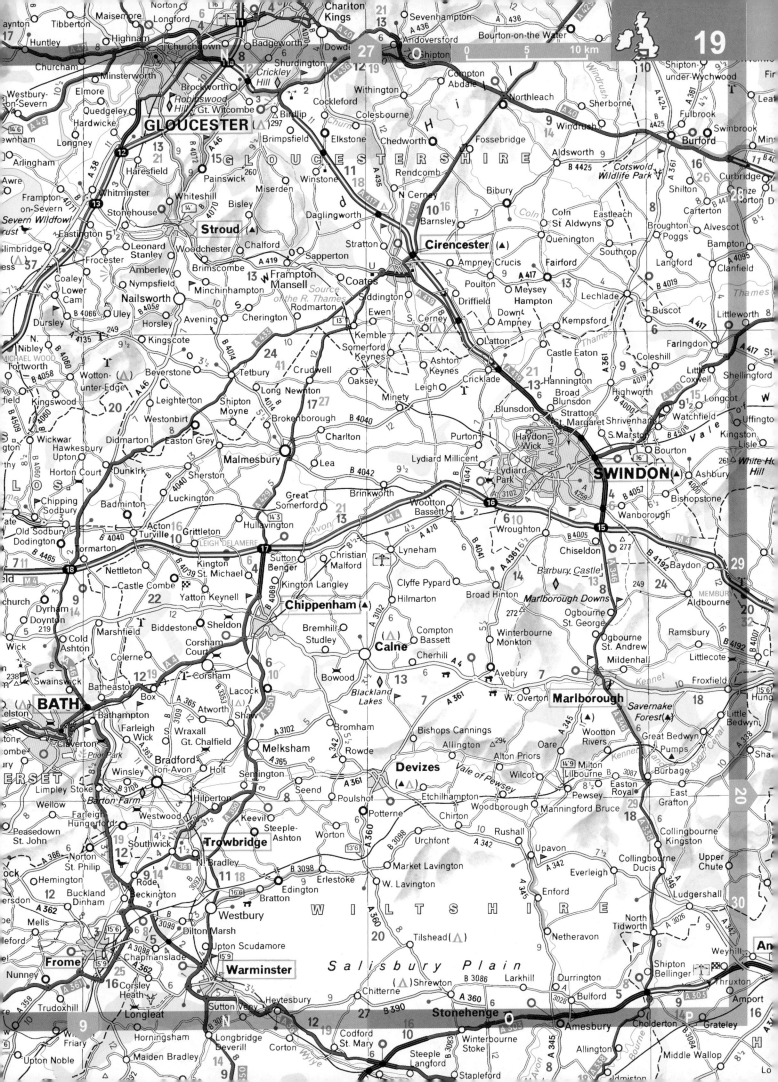

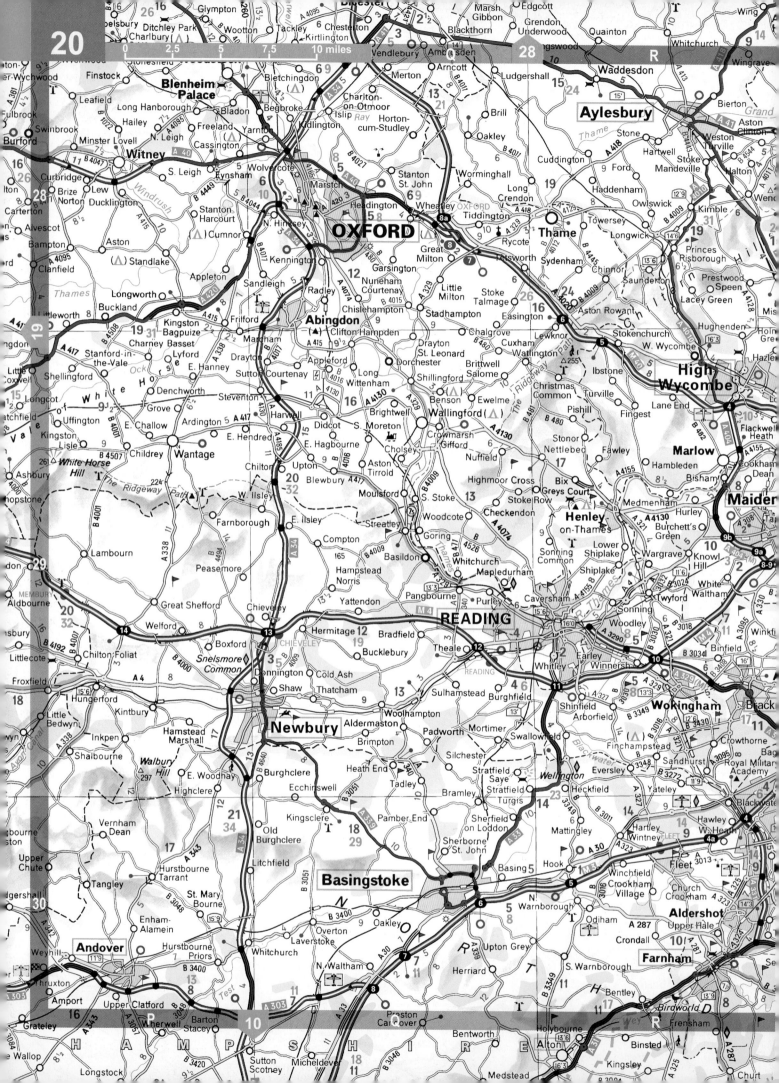

0 5 10 km

Weeley · Thorpe-le-Soken · B 1034
18 · B 1033 · Walton-on-the-Naze
22 · Kirby Cross · Frinton-on-
A 133 · 14 · Little Clacton · 31 · Y

9 · Brightlingsea · B 1027
St. Osyth · **Clacton**-on-Sea (▲)
Grove · Jaywick
Colne Point

(▲) **Margate** · Cliftonville · *Foreness Point*
Westgate-on-Sea · B 2051 · Kingsgate
(△) Birchington · 9 · 6 · B 2052 · *North Foreland*
Herne Bay · Reculver · 6·9 · B 2049 · 13 9 · St. Peter's · 15 3
12 3 · A 299 · A 28 · I. of Thanet · 5 · **Broadstairs** (▲)
B 2205 · 6·9 · St. Nicolas-at-Wade · B 2050 · 3 · 3 3
table · (△) · Sarre · 7 1/2 · A 299 · 4 1/2
15' · A 299 · Hoath · A 253 · Minster · 2 · A 299 · **Ramsgate** (▲ △)
10 · 16 · 5 · Chislet · 11 · Pucks · Abbey · 11 · 7
Yorkletts · A 291 · 18 1 · Gutter · 7 · *Pegwell Bay*
Blean · Sturry · Fordwich · Richborough · *Sandwich Bay*
WAY · 7 · (△) · Preston · A 256
GATE · 7 · **CANTERBURY** · Ash 5 · Sandwich (△)
arbledown · 17 27 · A 257 · Wingham · A 257 · 1
6 · 24 · 39 · 13 · Littlebourne · Woodnesborough · A 258
Chartham · Patrixbourne · 5 1/2 · Eastry · 19
Petham · Bridge · Aylesham · 12 · 6 1/2
Lower Hardres · B 2046 · Barfreston · 13' · **Deal** (▲)
Barham · Ringwould · *The Downs*
Stelling · Lydden · Eythorne · Kingsdown
Minnis · Circuit · 6 1/2 · (△) Martin Mill · 8 1/2
Bodsham · A 260 · 11 · Lydden · Whitfield · A 258 · St. Margaret's-at-Cliffe
Elham · Temple Ewell · A 256 · 4 · *St. Margaret's Bay*
ne Lees · Swingfield · 9 · Alkham · *South Foreland*
Lyminge · Acrise · Hawkinge · B 2011 · Y · 13 · **DOVER**
ellindge · Stanford · B 2065 · Place · A 20 · Z
9 · 11 · 5 · Terminal · 13 · 8 13 · — *Dunkerque*
Capel-le-Ferne (△)

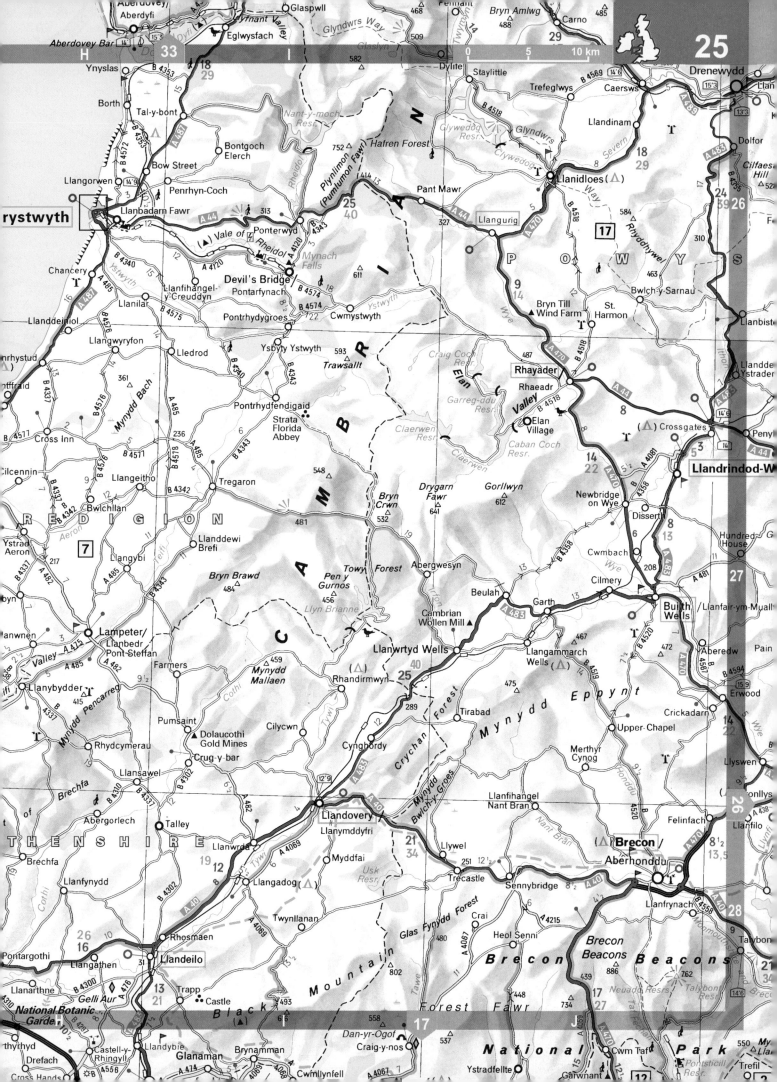

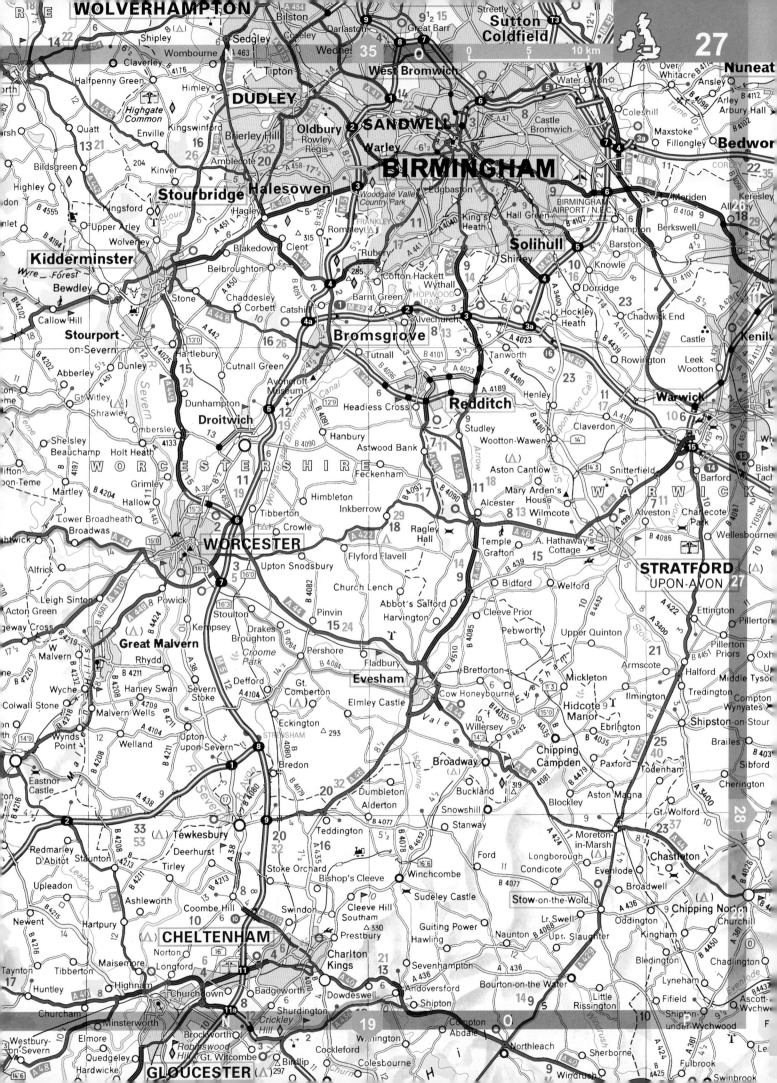

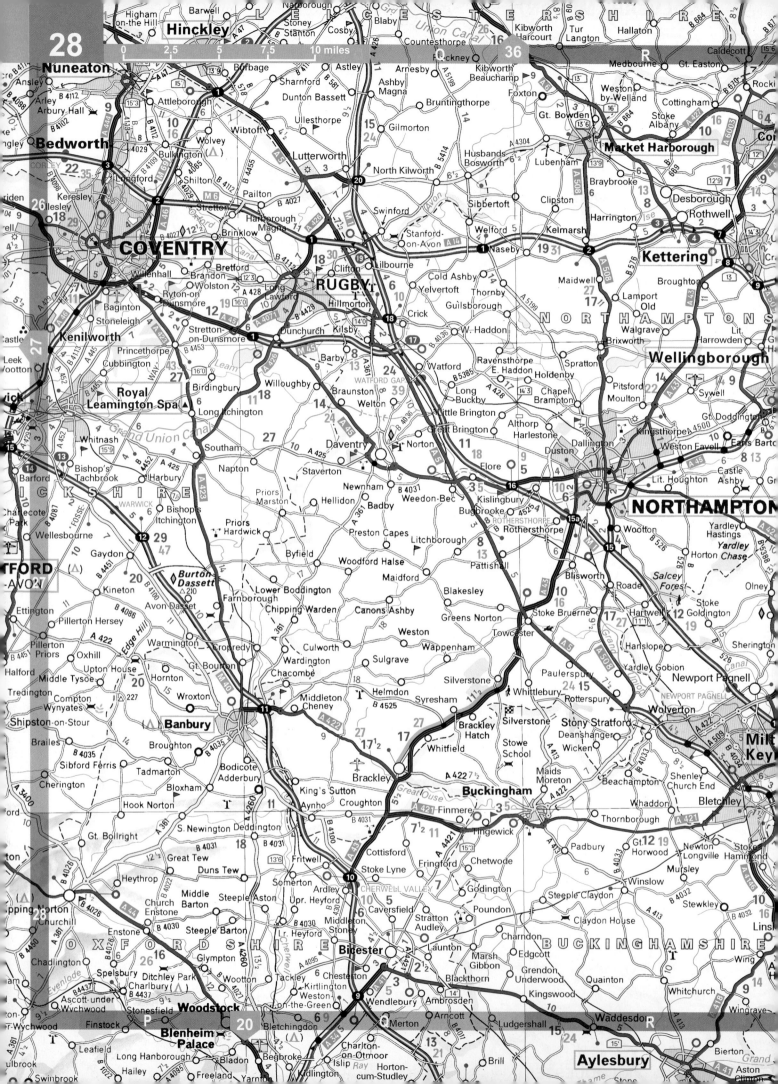

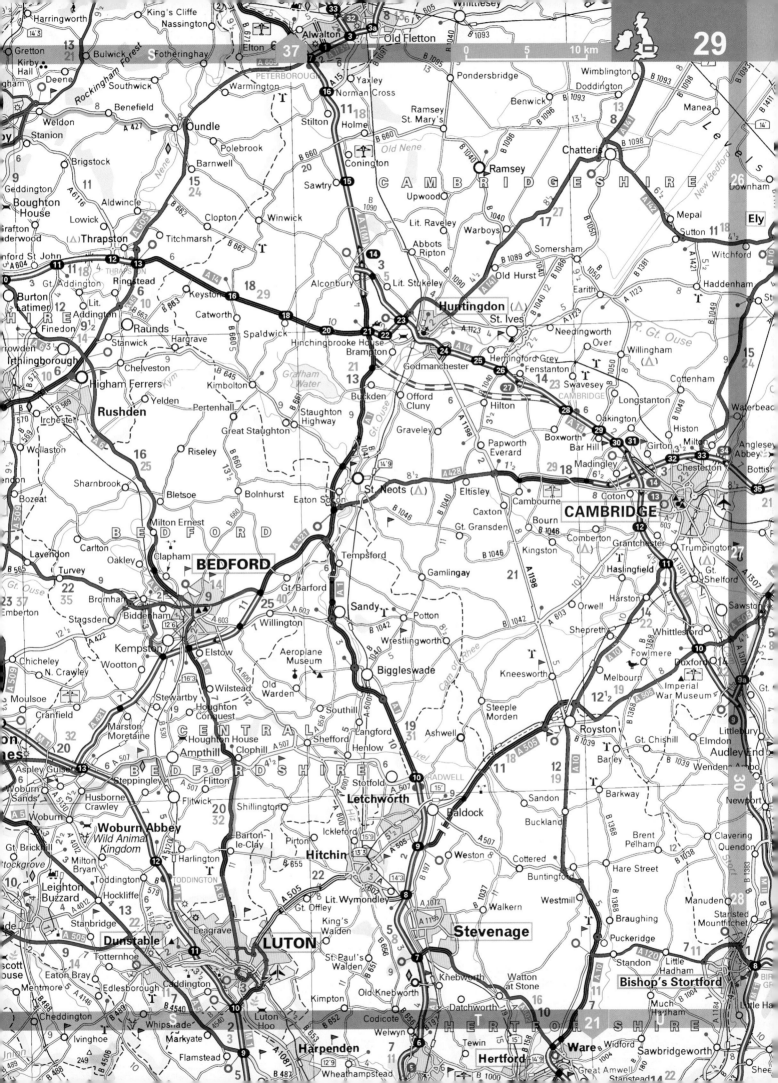

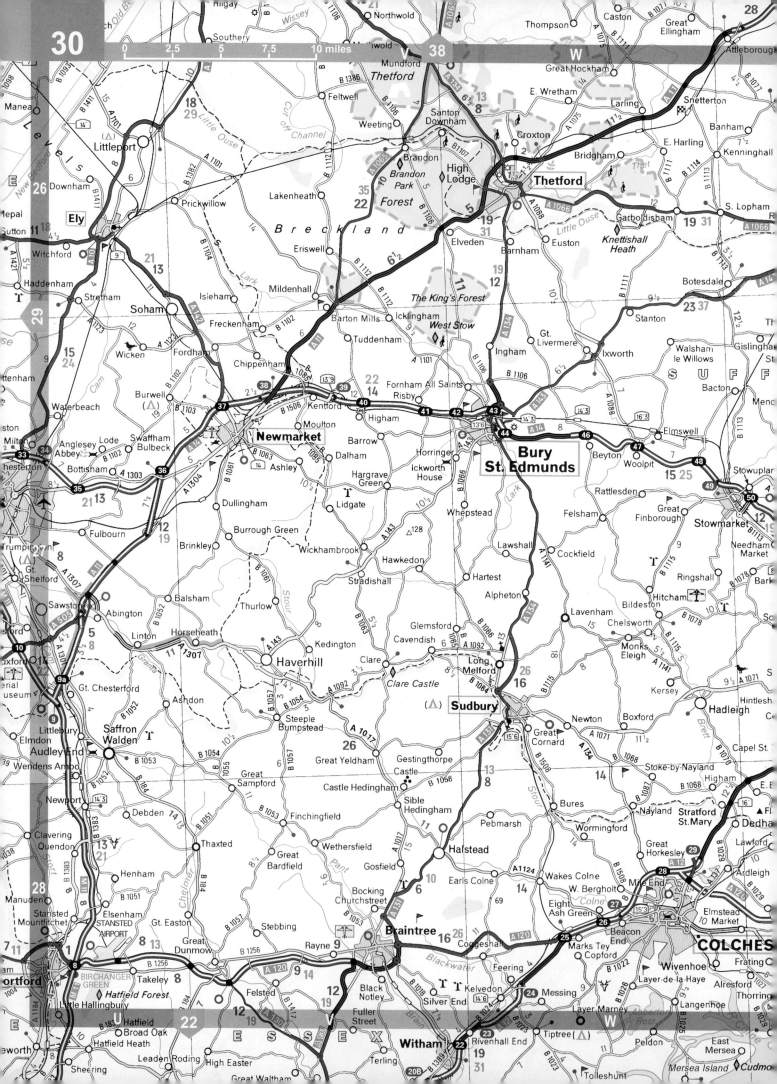

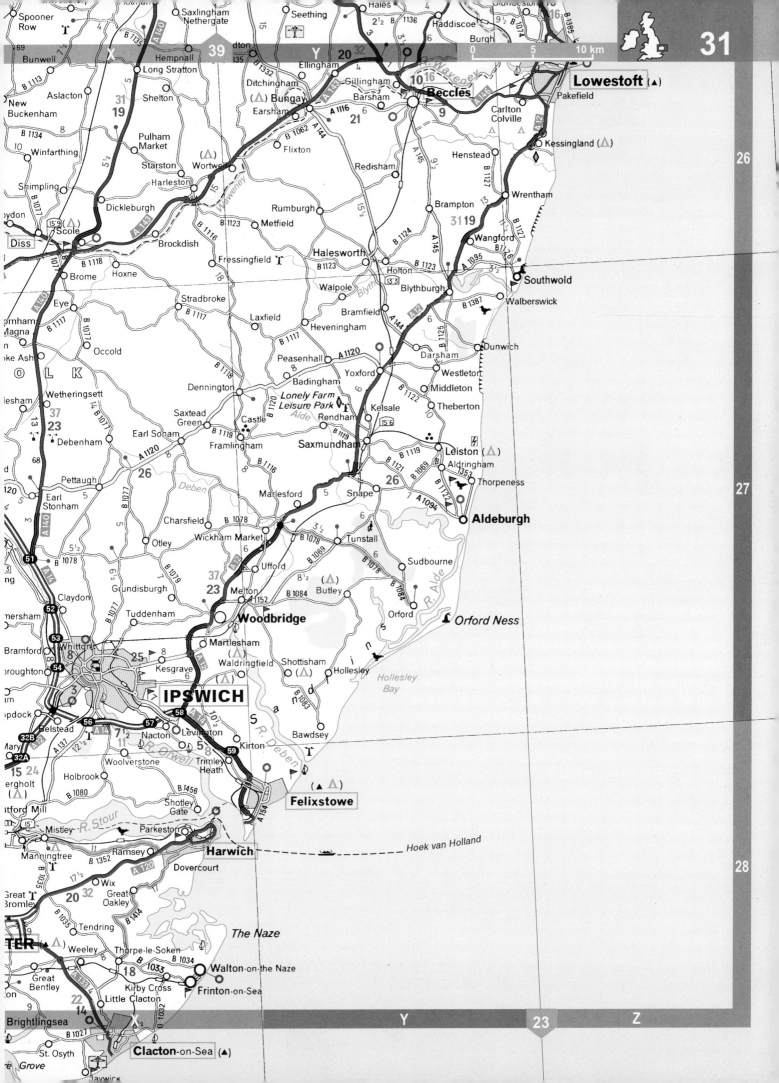

0   2.5   5   7.5   10 miles

F A N L E S E Y 40

Rhosneigr (△)   Llanfaelog   32   5
A 4080   A 4422   B 4422   Pentre Berw   7
Aberffraw   10½   B 4419   Llanfair-Pwl
Bordogan   Brynsiencyn   Bryn-Celli-ddu
A 4080   A 4419   Plas New
Newborough   Mermaid Inn   A 4080
Malltraeth Bay   (△)
Llanddwyn-Island   **Caernarfon**
Bontnewydd

24

C a e r n a r f o n   Bontnewydd
(△)
B a y   Dinas Dinlle   53
Llanwnd
Llandwrog   A 499   14
(△)   Pen-y-gr
Pontlyfni   13½   B 4
(△)   Llanllyfni
Clynnog-Fawr   22
21   35
Trevor   A 499   △   522
Trwyn y Gorlech   Yr Eifl
564   △   Llanaelhaearn
Llithfaen   B 4417   7½   A 4411
Carreg Ddu   6
Morfa Nefyn   **Nefyn**   Y Ffor   (△)   Llanystumdwy
B 4412   B   A 499   (△)   14
Porth Ysgaden   10   A 497   B 4354   7   Chwilog
Tudweiliog   Efailnewydd   A 497   Criccieth
△ 312   B 4415   Pwllheli   9½   (△)
(△)   **Lleyn**
Llangwnnadl   B 4417   Sarn Meyllteyrn   13   T r e m a d o
Penrhyn Mawr   103   A 499   6½   Llanbedrog   B a y
Botwnnog   B 4413   8½
305   A 499
25   4   Llanengan   St. Tudwal's   Abersoch
Aberdaron   Road   Bwlchtocyn
Mynydd Mawr   Y Rhiw   Porth Neigwl   St. Tudwal's Islands
Braich y Pwll   △ 160   or Hell's Mouth
Bardsey Sound   Trwyn Cilan

Bardsey Island (▲)

26

E   F   24   G   **C A R D I G A N   B A Y**

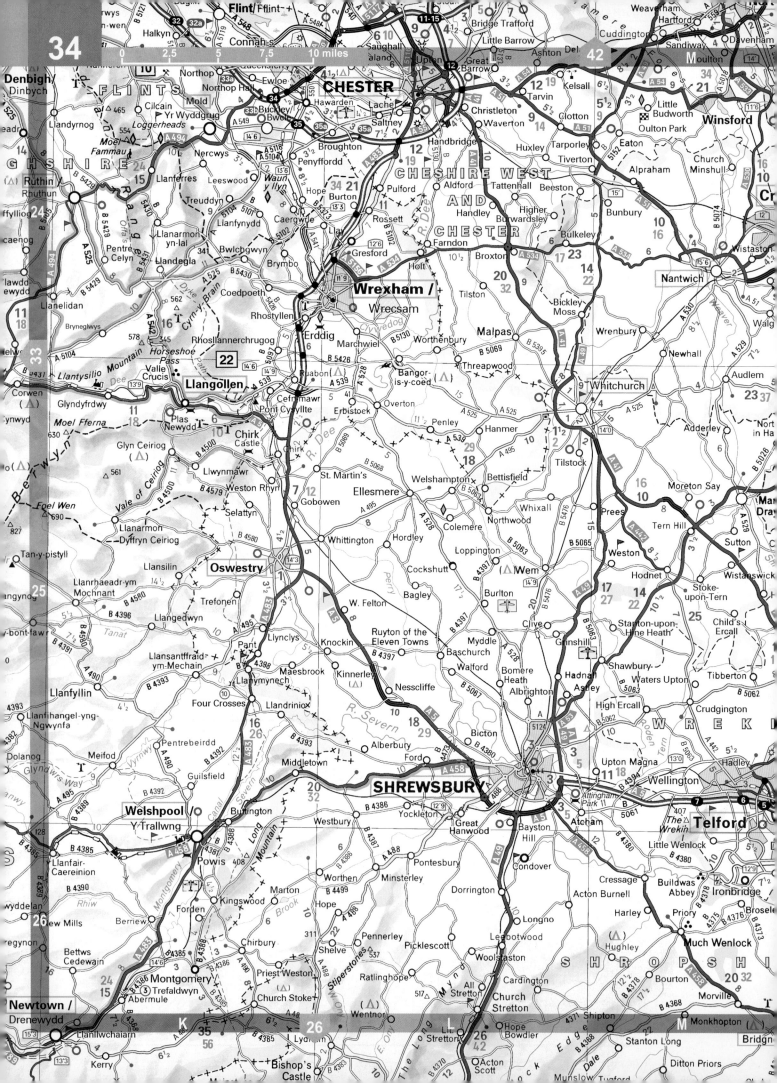

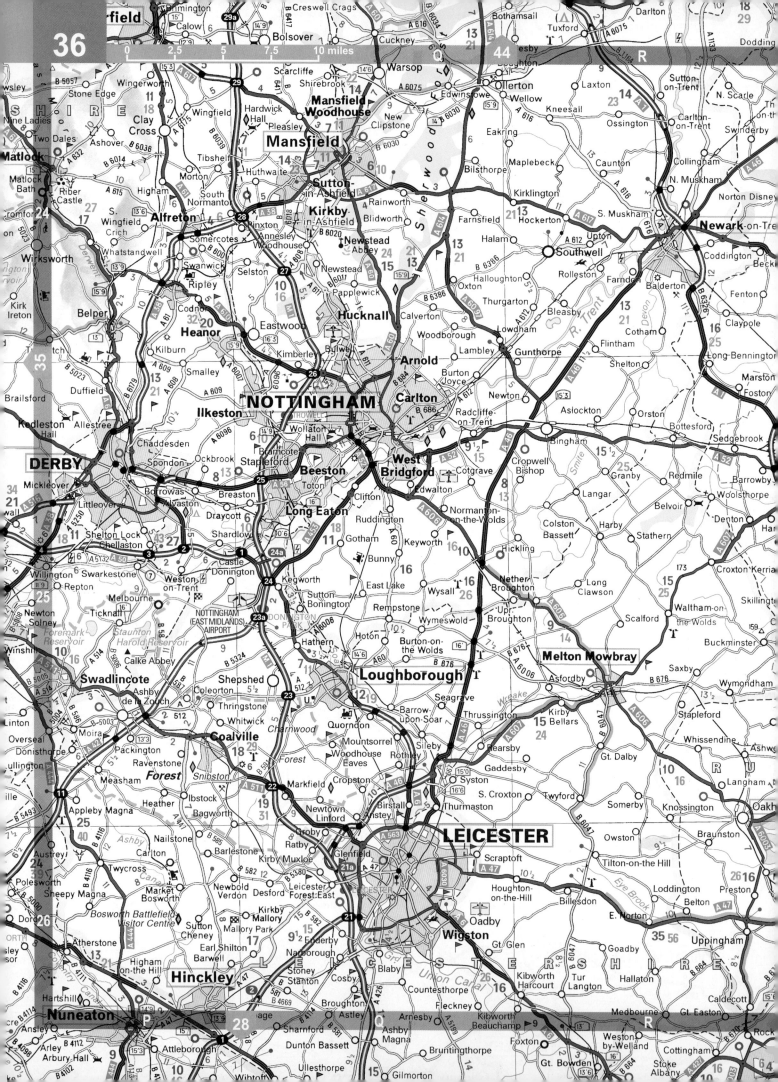

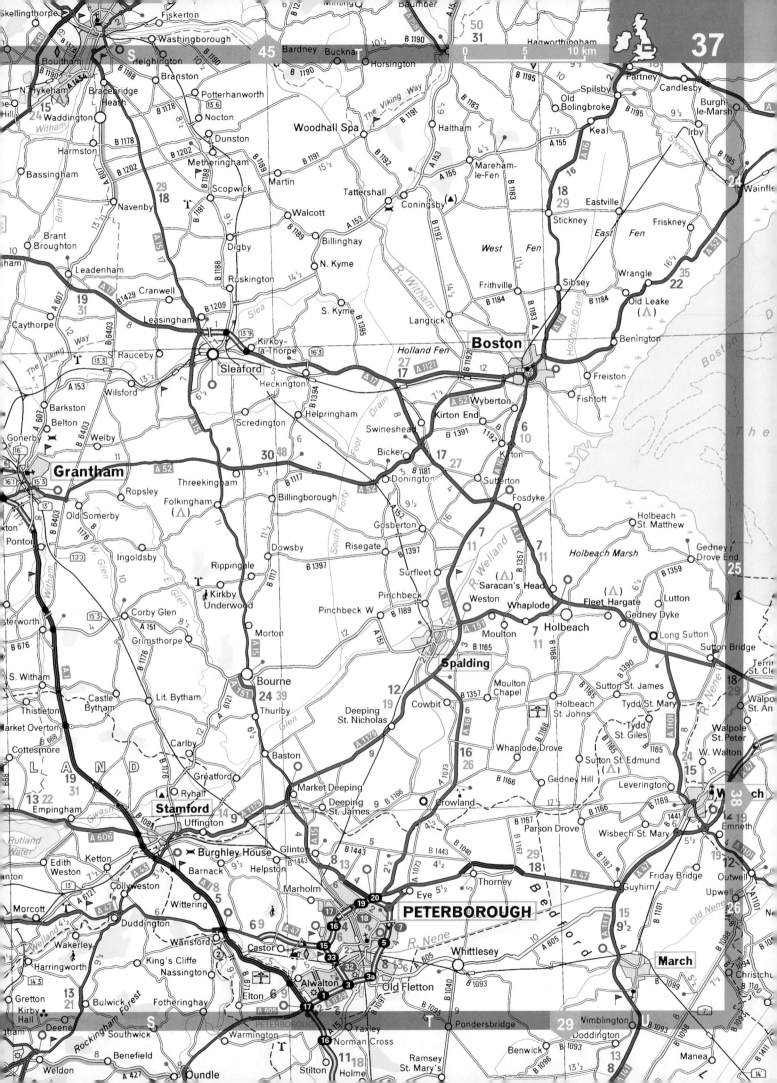

22

The Skerries

Cemlyn Bay

A 5025   Amlwch   Point Lynas

Carmel Head   Cemaes   B 5111

Llanfairynghornwy   Llanfechell   Penysarn

Church Bay   B 5111   128   6

Holyhead Bay   A 5025   Rhosybol   Dulas Bay   Lligwy Bay

Dublin   Llanfaethlu   Llanddeusant   Llyn Alaw   B 5111   Moelfre   12

Llanfwrog   (▲)   Marian–glas

S. Stack   220   Llanfachraeth   112   Llanerchymedd   (▲)   B 5109   Benllech

Holyhead   Caergybi   A N G L E S E Y   Brynteg   Red Wharf Bay   Penmon

Holyhead Mountain   Llanynghenedl   B 5109   Trefor   1   B 5111   Pentraeth   B 5110   Llanddona   Castle   Llangoe

Penrhyn Mawr   2   5   Valley   Bodedern   Bodffordd   B 5109   Talwrn   A 5025   B 5109   Beaum

Trearddur Bay   B 4545   3   A 5025   Bryngwran   B 5112   B 5109   Cefni Resr   Llangefni   A 545   Straits

Holy Island   4   Gwalchmai   20   Llanfair-yn-Neubwll   A 55   A 5   13·3   32   5   A 5114   B 5420   Menai Bridge   Lavan Sar   Bangor

Rhoscolyn   Cymyran Bay   9·6   4080   4   Pentre Berw   6   Porthaethwy   15·6   7a   13·9   Llandygai   12

ISLE OF ANGLESEY   Rhosneigr   (▲)   Llanfaelog   B 4422   Cefni   Llanfair-Pwllgwyngyll   8a   9   10   11   Rac

A 4080   Bryn-Celli-ddu   8   12   B   3   Be

Aberffraw   10·2   Brynsiencyn   Plas Newydd   A 547   A 4244   A 4409

Bordogan   A 4080   B 4419   Felinheli   7·2   Penrhyn Quarries   924   303

Newborough   Bethel   A 487   Llanrug   Penrhyn Quarries   Deiniolen   Llyn Padarn

Malltraeth Bay   Mermaid Inn   (▲)   B 4366   Waunfawr   Castle   Glyder Fawr   Lly

Llanddwyn Island   Caernarfon   (▲)   Llanberis   726   8   Pass of Llanberis   A 4086

Caernarfon   Bontnewydd   A 4086   53   A 4085   Rhyd-Ddu   698   Snowdon / Yr Wyddfa   1085

Caernarfon Bay   (▲)   Dinas Dinlle   Llanwnda   A 499   14   Llyn Cwellyn   747   Nantgwynant

Llandwrog   (▲)   Pen-y-groes   701   Beddgelert Forest   Llyn Di

Pontlyfni   (▲)   13·2   Llanllyfni   B 4418   782   14·9   Beddgelert

24   Trevor   A 499   522   Clynnog-Fawr   22   21   35   11   Moel Hebog   Pass of Aber   14·6

F   32   G   Yr Eifl   Llanaelhaearn   G W Y N E D D

Carreg Ddu   564   Llithfaen   B 4417   6

Morfa Nefyn   Nefyn   eninsula   Y Ffor   Dolbenmaen   (▲)   A 498   Garreg

B   B 4411   (▲)   Llanystumdwy   A 497   15   Tremadog   Vale

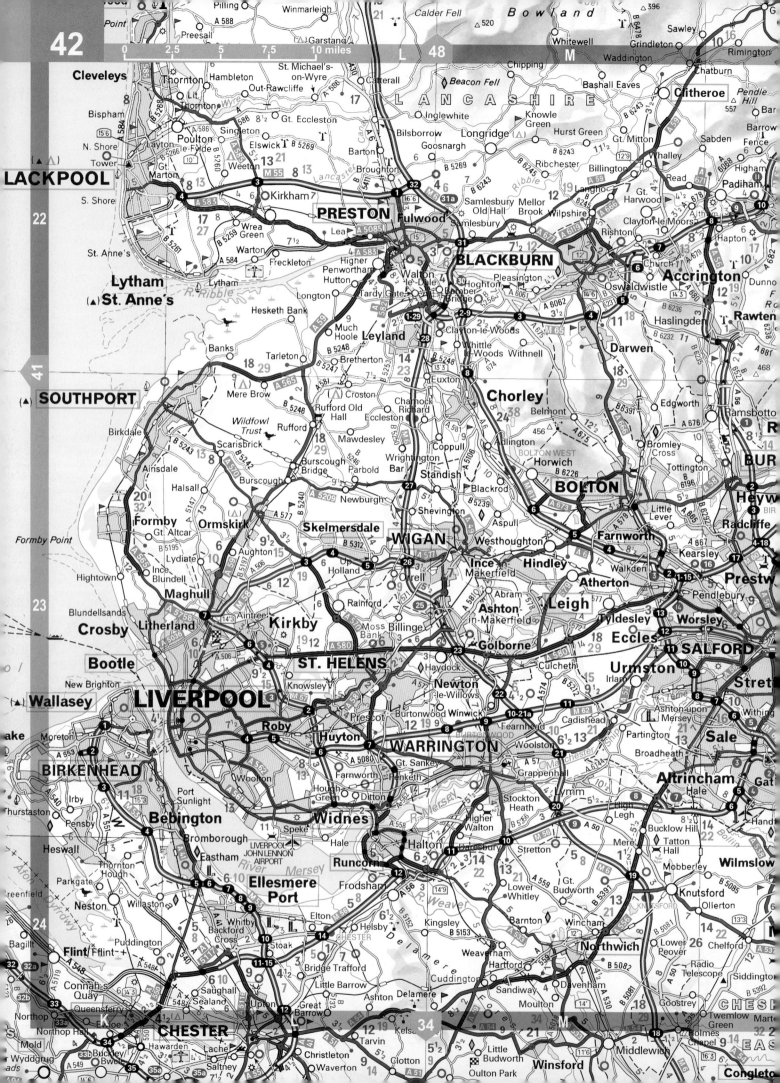

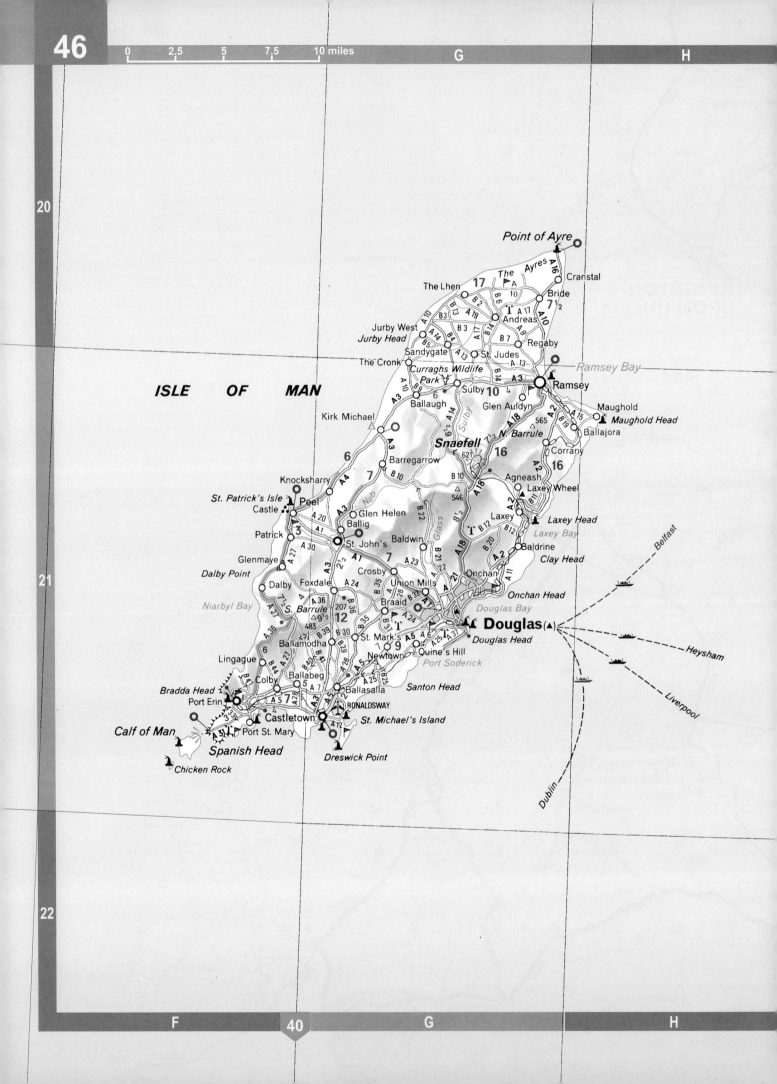

0   2.5   5   7.5   10 miles

G

H

20

Point of Ayre
Cranstal
The Lhen   The Ayres   A16
17   A16
Bride
A   7½
Andreas   A17   A10
Jurby West   B3   A19
Jurby Head   A10   B7   Regaby
B5   B4   A13   A9
Sandygate   St. Judes   A-13
The Cronk   Curraghs Wildlife   B14
Park   A3   Ramsey Bay
A10   B9   Sulby   10   Ramsey
Ballaugh   Glen Auldyn   Maughold
Kirk Michael   A18   Maughold Head
N. Barrule   575   Ballajora
621   16   Corrany
Snaefell   B19   A2   A15
6   Barregarrow   16
7   B10   Agneash
Knocksharry   A4   B10   546   A18   Laxey Wheel
Peel   Nab   Laxey
St. Patrick's Isle   A3   Glen Helen   B22   Laxey Head
Castle   Ballig   Baldwin   Laxey Bay
Patrick   3   A1   A18   Baldrine
A30   St. John's   A23   Clay Head
Glenmaye   A27   2½   B21   A2
Dalby Point   7   Crosby   Onchan
Dalby   Foxdale   A24   Union Mills   Onchan Head
Niarbyl Bay   S. Barrule   207   Braaid   Douglas Bay
12   B30   B31   A24   Douglas
Ballamodha   St. Mark's   A5   A6   Douglas Head
Lingague   6   9   Newtown   Quine's Hill
Colby   Ballabeg   Port Soderick
Bradda Head   5   A7   Ballasalla   Santon Head
Port Erin   A5   A3   RONALDSWAY
Castletown   St. Michael's Island
Calf of Man   Port St. Mary   A12
Spanish Head   Dreswick Point
Chicken Rock

ISLE   OF   MAN

Belfast
Heysham
Liverpool
Dublin

21

22

F

G

40

H

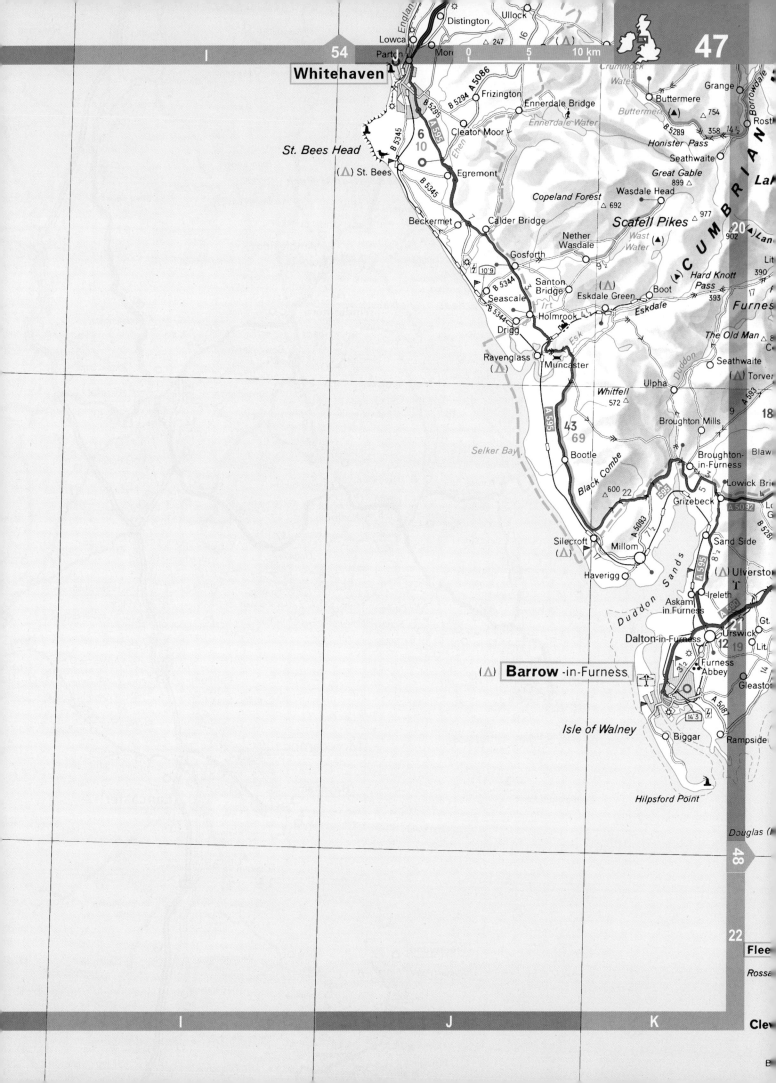

Whitehaven

England

54

Distington
Ullock
Lowca
Parton
Morë
247
16

0   5   10 km

A 5086
B 5294   Frizington
B 5295
Ennerdale Bridge
Crummock Water
Grange
Buttermere
Buttermere (▲)   754
B 5289   358   14½   Rost

Cleator Moor
Ennerdale Water
Honister Pass
Seathwaite

A 595
6
10
Ehen
Egremont
Great Gable
899 △
Wasdale Head
Seathwaite

St. Bees Head

B 5345

(△) St. Bees

B 5345

Copeland Forest
△ 692
Scafell Pikes
977
20
902
CUMBRIAN La

Beckermet
Calder Bridge
7
Nether Wasdale
West Water
Hard Knott Pass
Furnes
390
Lit

Gosforth
10·9
B 5344
Santon Bridge
Eskdale Green
Boot
393
17

Seascale
B 5344
Irt
Holmrook   4½   Eskdale
The Old Man
Seathwaite

Drigg
Esk
Ulpha
(△) Torver

Ravenglass
(△)
Muncaster
Duddon
Whitfell
572 △
18
A 593

Selker Bay
A 595
43
69
Broughton Mills
9

Bootle
Black Combe
600   22
Broughton-in-Furness
Blaw

Silecroft
(△)
Millom
A 5093   7½
Grizebeck
Lowick Bri
A 5092
Lo
B 528

Haverigg
Duddon Sands
Sand Side
A 595   8½
(△) Ulversto

Askam in Furness
Ireleth
A 590
21

Dalton-in-Furness
Urswick
12   19
Gt.
Lit.

(△) **Barrow** -in-Furness
Furness Abbey
14
Gleastot

3½
A 5087
14·3

Isle of Walney
Biggar
Rampside

Hilpsford Point

Douglas (

Flee
Rossa
Cle

I   J   K

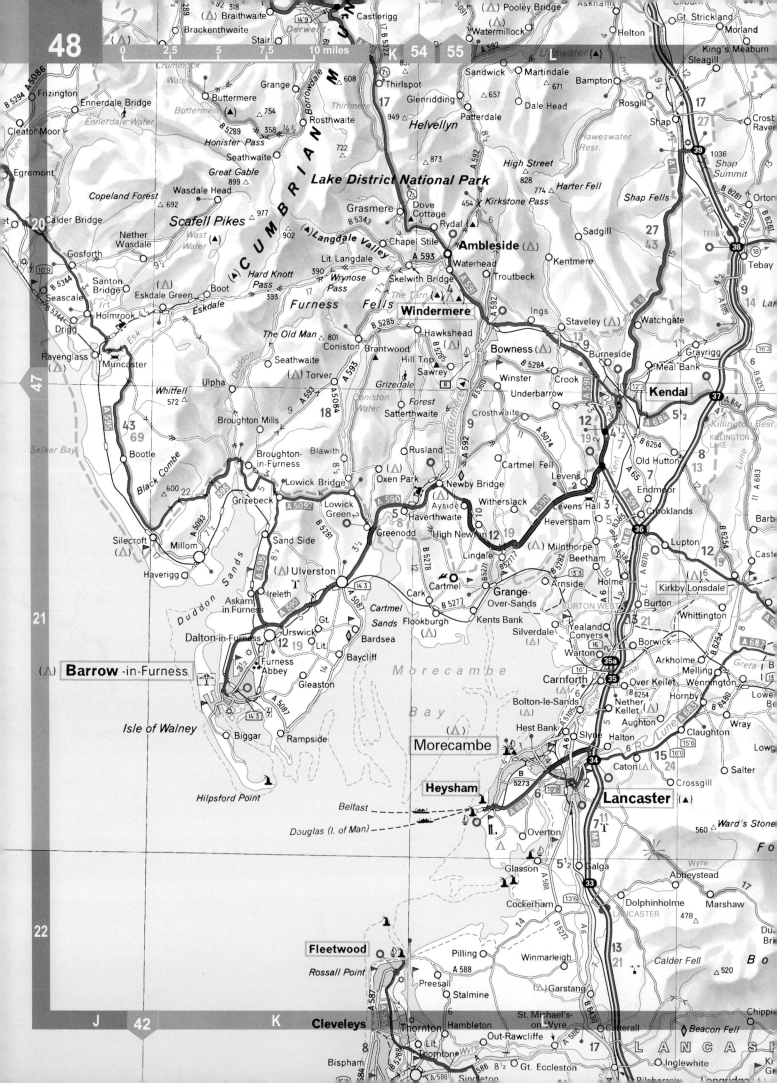

18

SOUTH SHIELDS

Amsterdam

Cleadon

Whitburn

N O R T H   S E A

SUNDERLAND

Ryhope
21

Seaham

19

Hetton

Easington

Horden

Colliery

Peterlee   Blackhall

B 1281   Blackhall Rocks

Hesleden

9

Hart

15'9

B 1280

A 179

HARTLEPOOL

Elwick

Seaton Carew

15
9½

Tees Bay

Greatham

A 1185

Thorpe   Wolviston

hewles

20

Redcar (▲)

Billingham

Marske-by-the-Sea

1275   15'6

Redmarshall

Dormanstown   14 3

Saltburn-by-the-Sea

15

13

15'6

A 1046

Brotton

ckton

Tees

Eston   New Marske

Skelton

Loftus   Staithes

50   S

MIDDLESBROUGH

RE D C A R

Easington   Hinderwell

21 34

Thornaby

Ormesby   5

Boosbeck   Liverton

Runswick Bay

nglewton

on-Tees

A N D

Kettleness

glescliffe

Nunthorpe

Guisborough   Stanghow

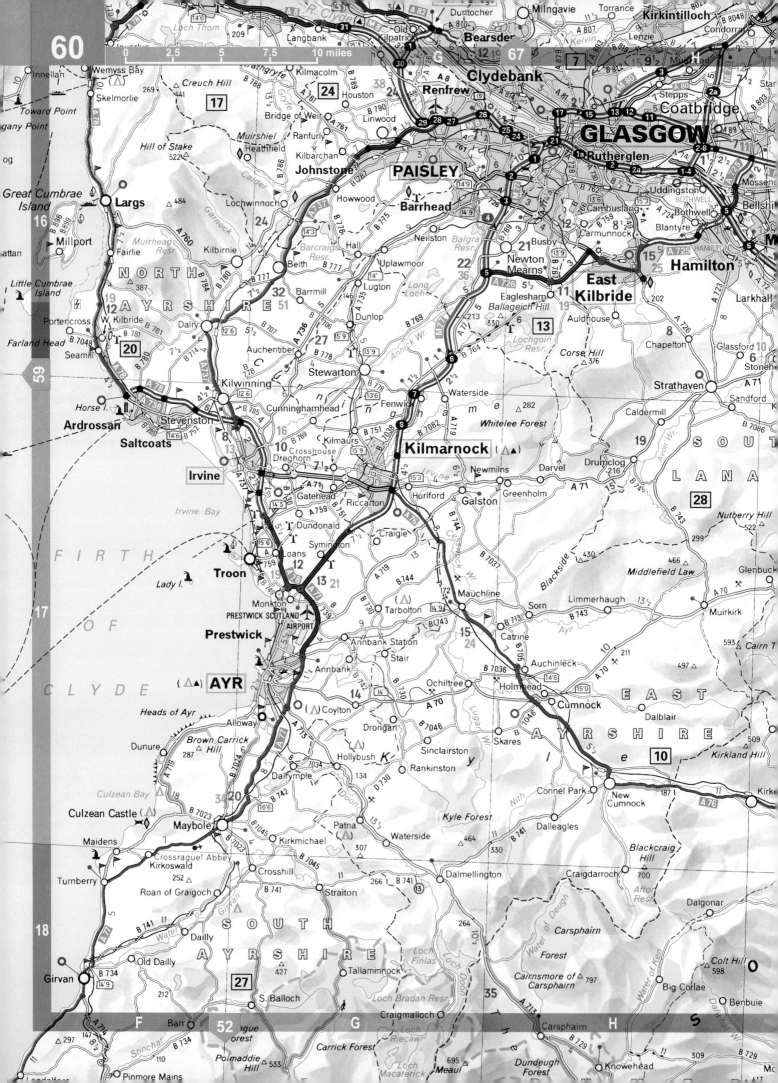

St. Abb's Head
Fast Castle
St. Abbs
A 1107 206
B 6438
11 Coldingham
29 47
15½ A 1
Wr.
encrow
Reston
Ayton
Burnmouth
Eyemouth

Chirnside
B 6355
Foulden
8½
A 6105
Whiteadder Wr.
Paxton
nderston
Allanton
Hutton
B 6461
Tweedmouth
Berwick-upon-Tweed (▲△)
Spittal

Whitsome
B 6460
Horncliffe
11½
A 698
Cheswick

Ladykirk
Castle
Norham
R. Tweed
A 698
15
Ancroft
Goswick
Road submerged at high tide
Chaussée submersible
Holy Island

ean
Cornhill-
on-Tweed
Etal
B 6354
Duddo
Lowick
B 6353
Fenwick
Holy
Island Sands
Holy Island

Wark
Crookham
Ford
143
B 6353
Ross
Farne Islands (▲)

Flodden Field
B 6352
Milfield
126
Doddington
Belford
5½
B 1342
Waren
Mill
Bamburgh Castle
(△)
Seahouses

20
147
Kilham
B 6351
Akeld
B 6525
184
B 6349
Bellshill
Adderstone
B 1341
B 1340
N. Sunderland
Beadnell (△)

Kirk
Yetholm
Hethpool
Kirknewton
A 697
14
Wooler
Chatton
Warenford
Lucker
Newham
Beadnell
Bay

Newton Tors
537
Chillingham
30
48
120
A 1
High
Newton
5½

Middleton
316
15
Embleton
Dunstanburgh
Castle
B 1340

The Cheviot
815
Langleeford
Ilderton
N. Charlton
B 634
B 1339
Craster (△)

Sourhope
605
Wooperton
B 6346
S. Charlton
Eglingham
B 6341
Rennington
Howick

619
44
71
109
11½
B 6346
Longhoughton

Breamish
Ingram
Bolton
Pennington
B 1340
Boulmer

Barrow Burn
Powburn
Glanton
Alnwick
3½
Lesbury
Alnmouth

Prendwick
Aln
Whittingham
B 6341
8
A 1
A 1068

RTHUMBERLAND
Moor
(△)
Alwinton
236
Netherton
Long Crag
Edlingham
135
Shilbottle
Warkworth

Coquet
319
B 6341
Newton-on-
the-Moor
9
4
Coquet Island

Harbottle
Sharperton
Warton
Thropton
278
Cragside
Gardens
6
Swarland (△)
Longframlington
Acklington
Amble
Tooston

s Cairn
412
Watty Bell's Cairn
355
Holystone
Hepple
B 6341
Rothbury (△)
B 6334
6
B 6345
Felton
B 6345
34
21
Druridge
Bay

Rochester
Gt. Tosson
440
Tosson Hill
Brinkburn Priory
17
28
W. Chevington
Widdrington

NATIONAL
Elishaw
B 6341
Otterburn
Elsdon
Forestburn Gate
Longhorsley
A 697
56
Ulgham
Ellington
Lynemouth
Cresswell

adon Hill
378
d's Shaw
356
252
Netherwitton
Longhirst
Ashington
B 1337
A 189
Woodhorn Museum

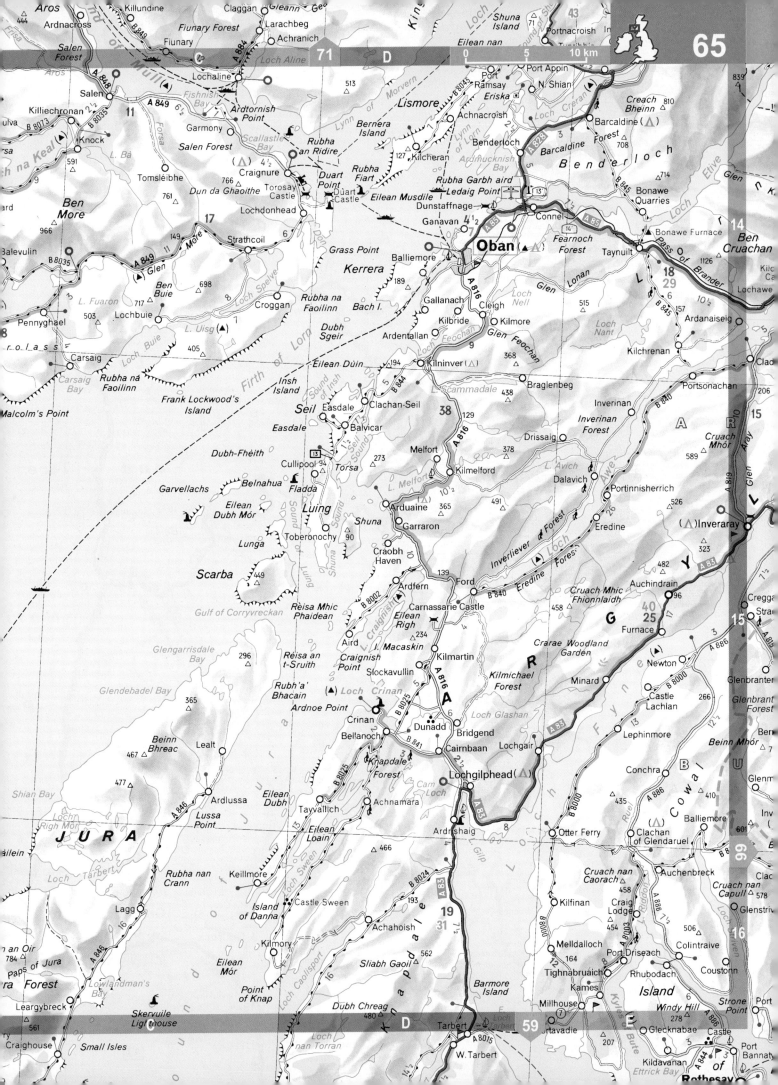

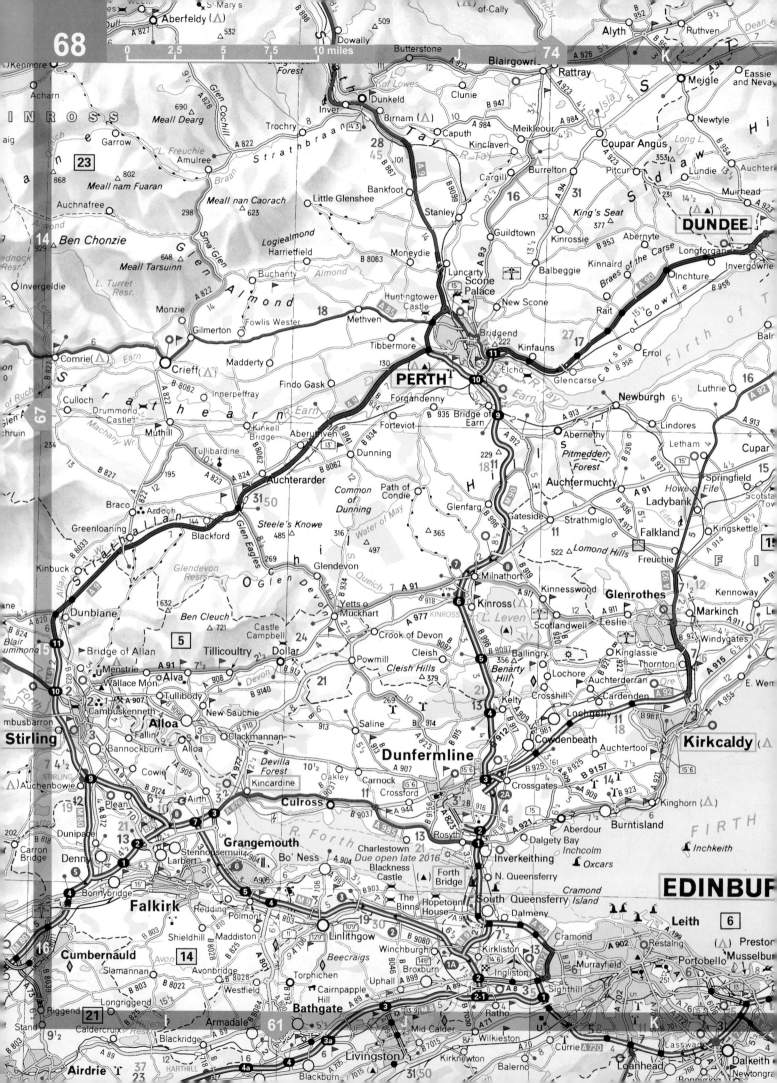

Glamis Castle
Douglastown
Glamis
Kingsmuir
Letham
Lunan Wr
Inverkeilor
Lunan Bay

Balgray
Lumley Den
Inverarity
B 9127
Kirkbuddo
B 9128
Redford
A 933
St. Vigeans
B 961
B 965
A 92
Marywell
Lang Craig

225
A 926
259
Kirkbuddo
Carmyllie
Arbirlot
St. Vigeans
Cliffs
Arbroath

75

M

0   5   10 km

Monikie
Muirdrum
E. Haven
A 930
16
6

Newbigging
Kellas
B 918
B 961
Barry
10
Carnoustie (△)

Kirkton of Strathmartine
MICHELIN
Dighty
A 92
13
Monifieth (△)

9
Broughty Ferry
Buddon Ness

Tay Road Bridge
Newport-on-Tay
B 946
Tayport

14'9
Tentsmuir Forest
Inchcape or Bell Rock

A 914
A 945
A 919
15'3
Leuchars

Kilmany
Balmullo
Guardbridge
Eden Mouth
St. Andrews Bay

Dairsie
A 91
Strathkinness
St. Andrews (△ ▲)
Cath.

B 939
B 940
Craigtoun
A 917
Boarhills
A 915
B 9131
Kingsbarns
Carr Brigs

Hill of Tarvit
Pitscottie
Dunino
B 940
Craighead
Fife Ness

Ceres
Craigrothie
Peat Inn
B 940
17½
9½
113
B 9171
Crail

Backmuir of New Gilston
Largoward
Kellie Castle
4 A 917
B 9171

190
24
Arncroach
B 942
Kilrenny

Kirkton of Largo
A 917
Kilconquhar
Pittenweem
Anstruther

Lundin Links (△)
Lower Largo
Elie
Earlsferry
St. Monans (△)
The East Neuk
Isle of May

Methil
Largo Bay

uckhaven

N O R T H

15

FORTH

Fidra
Craigleith
Bass Rock

North Berwick (△)
Dirleton
187
North Berwick Law
Tantallon Castle
A 198
8

Aberlady Bay
Gullane
Kingston
11
Whitekirk
Tyne Mouth

Aberlady
24
Drem
B 1345
B 1377
Tyninghame
John Muir
Dunbar (△)

GH (△)
A 198
Athelstaneford
Museum of Flight
East Linton
W. Barns
A 1087
Barns Ness

Cockenzie and Port Seton
B 1377
Longniddry
B 1347
B 1343
7
Hailes Castle
10
A 1
Spott
Thorntonloch

21 34
A 1
239
Traprain Law
Stenton
Innerwick
Cockburnspath (△)
Fast Castle

Tranent
A 199
A 6093
Haddington (△)
Garvald
Oldhamstocks
Pease Bay
St. Abb's Head

Ormiston
B 6371
B 6368
B 6369
Dunbar Common
398
Clints Dod
62
245
A 1107
206
St. Abbs

Pencaitland
East Saltoun
Gifford
B 6355
345
391
Heart Law
Grantshouse
Coldingham

12
muir
Hills
29
47

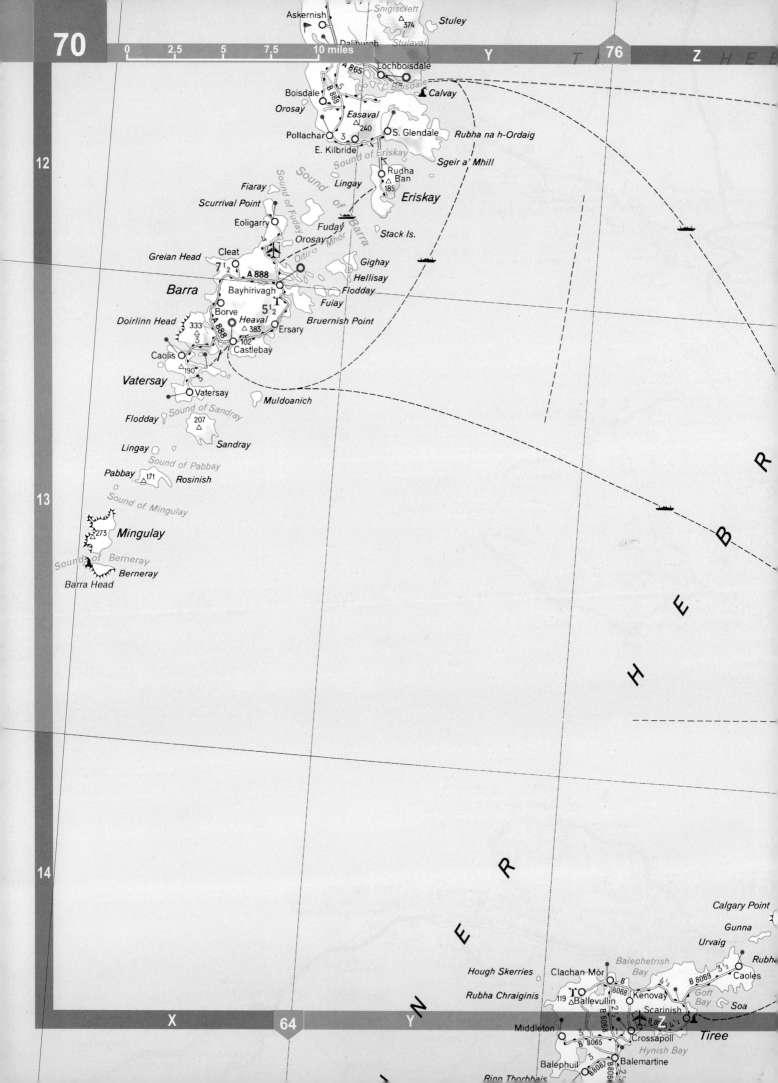

0   2.5   5   7.5   10 miles

Askernish
Snigisclett
374   *Stuley*
Daliburgh
L. Stulaval

12

A 865
Lochboisdale
L. Boisdale
Boisdale
B 888
▲ Calvay
Orosay
Easaval
△ 240
Pollachar   3   S. Glendale   *Rubha na h-Ordaig*
E. Kilbride

Sound of Eriskay
Rudha   *Sgeir a' Mhill*
Ban
△   *Eriskay*
185

Fiaray
Lingay
Sound of Fuday
Sound of Barra
Scurrival Point
Eoligarry
Fuday
Orosay   *Stack Is.*
Greian Head   Cleat   Oitir Mhór
7 1⁄2   *Gighay*
A 888   *Hellisay*
Barra   Bayhirivagh   *Floday*
Borve   5 1⁄2   1 1⁄2   *Fuiay*
Doirlinn Head   *Heaval*   *Bruernish Point*
333   △ 383   Ersary
△   B 888   102
3   Castlebay
Caolis
△ 190
Vatersay
Vatersay

Muldoanich

Sound of Sandray
Flodday   207
Lingay   △   *Sandray*
Sound of Pabbay
Pabbay   171   *Rosinish*
△
Sound of Mingulay

13

273   **Mingulay**
△
Sounds of Berneray
Berneray
Barra Head

14

Calgary Point
Gunna
Urvaig
Hough Skerries   Clachan-Mór   *Balephetrish Bay*   Rubh
B 8069   3 1⁄2
Rubha Chraiginis   B 8068   4 1⁄2   Caoles
119   Kenovay   *Gott*   *Soa*
△ Ballevullin   B 8068   *Bay*
Scarinish
Middleton   5   B 8068   Crossapoll   *Tiree*
B 8065   *Hynish Bay*
Balephuil   3   Balemartine
B 8067
Rinn Thorbhais   Balevullin

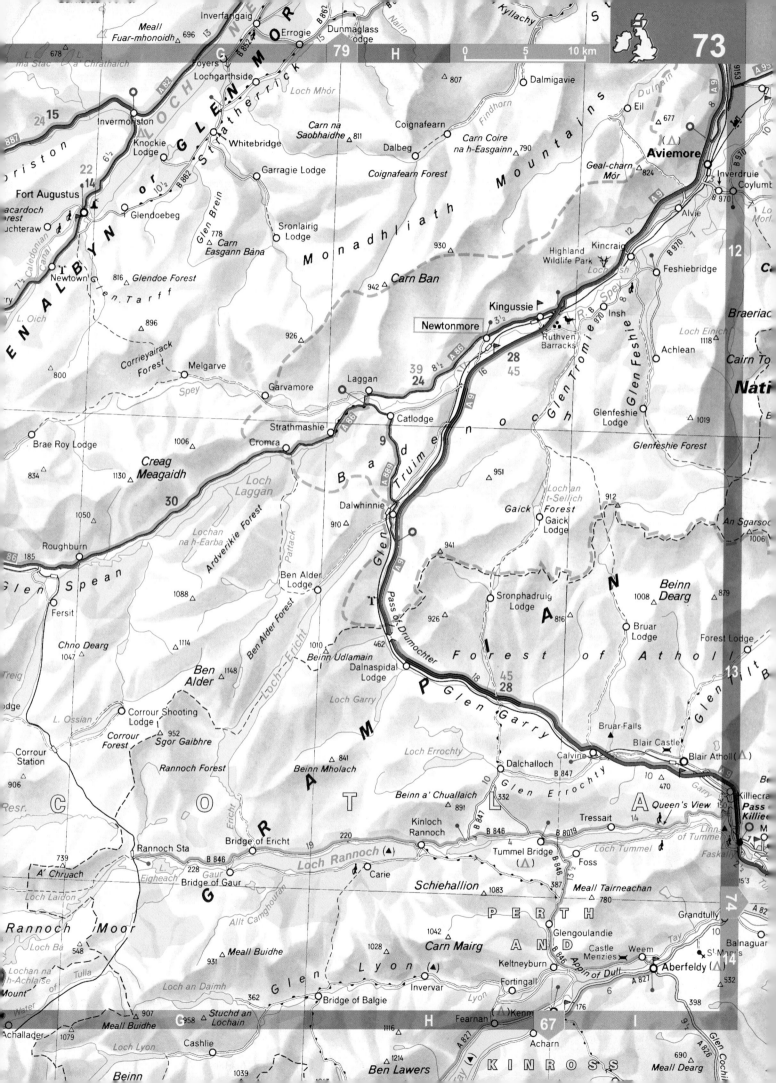

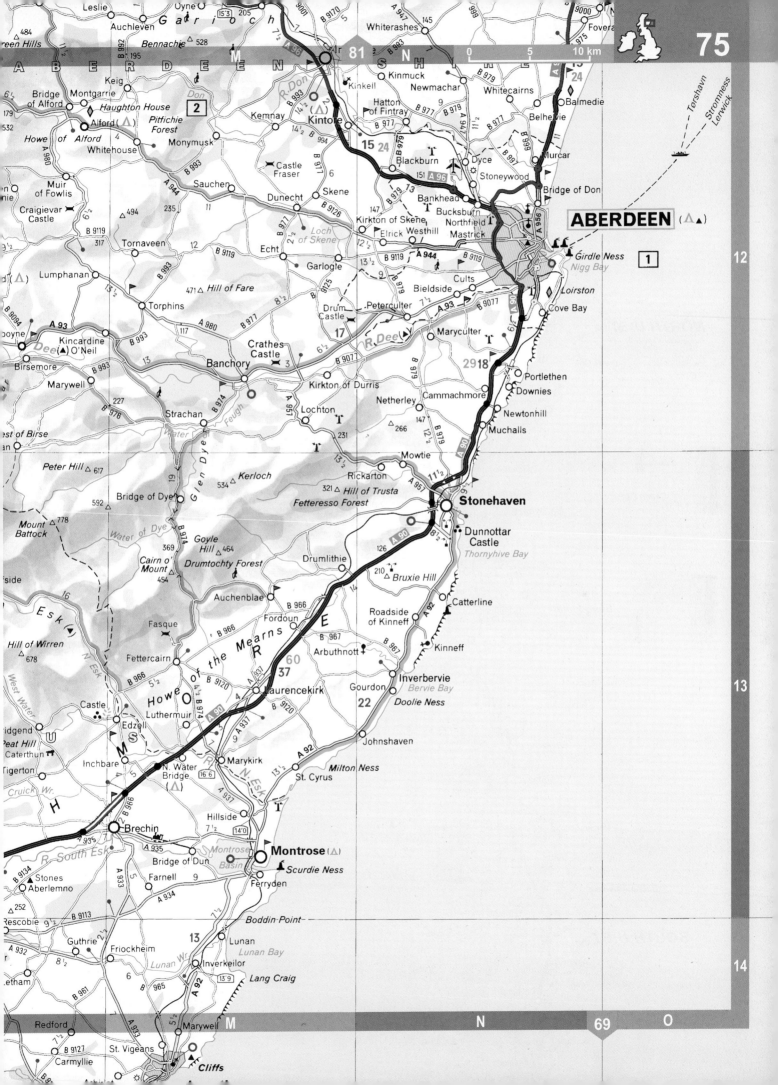

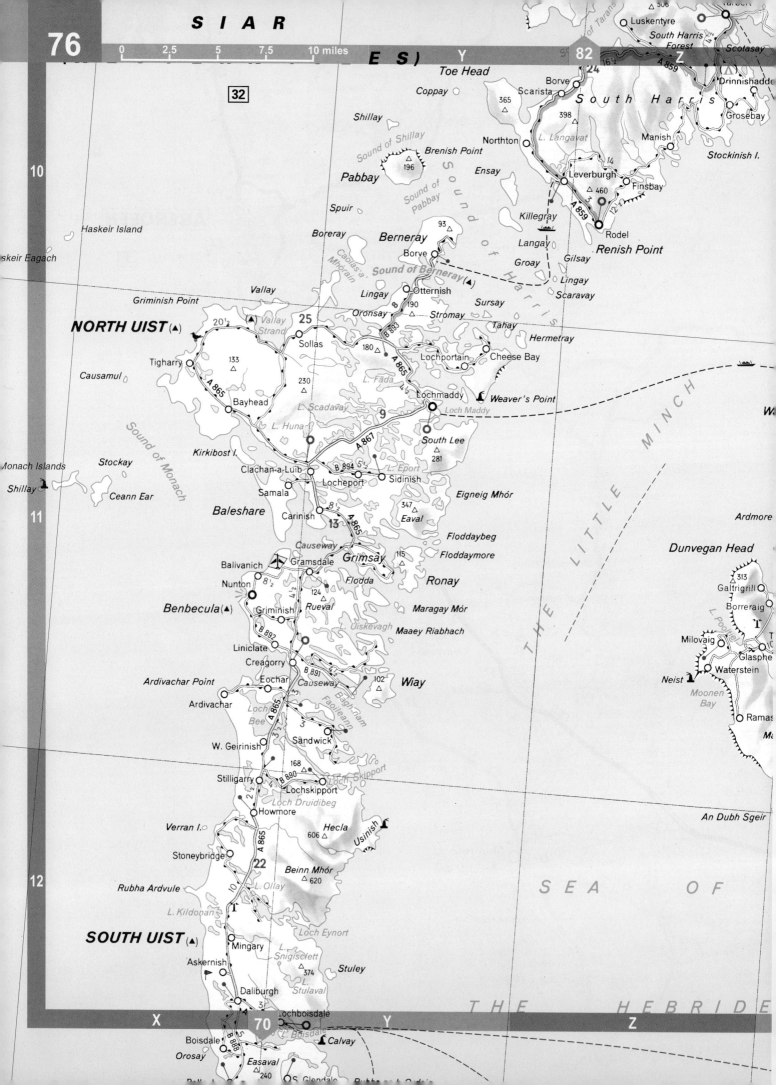

0   2.5   5   7.5   10 miles

32

10

11

12

Toe Head

Coppay ○

Shillay

Sound of Shillay

Brenish Point

Pabbay   196△

Ensay

Spuir

Sound of Pabbay

Boreray

Berneray

Sound of Harris

Haskeir Island

skeir Eagach

Griminish Point

Vallay

NORTH UIST (▲)

Valley Strand   20½

25

Tigharry ○

133△

Causamul ○

230△   L. Scadavay

Bayhead ○

A 865

L. Huna

Sound of Monach

Monach Islands

Stockay

Shillay ◣

Ceann Ear

Kirkibost I.

Clachan-a-Luib ○

B 894

Samala ○

Locheport

Baleshare

Carinish

13

A 865

11

Causeway

Balivanich   Gramsdale

Nunton   8½

Flodda

Benbecula (▲)   Griminish   Rueval   124△

B 892

Liniclate

Creagorry   B 891

Ardivachar Point   Eochar   Causeway

Ardivachar   A 865   3

Loch Bee

W. Geirinish   Sandwick

Stilligarry   B 890

Lochskipport   Loch Skipport

Loch Druidibeg

Howmore

Verran I. ○

A 865

Stoneybridge   22

Rubha Ardvule   L. Ollay

L. Kildonan

SOUTH UIST (▲)

Mingary   L. Snigisclett

Askernish ⚑

Daliburgh   374△   Stuley

L. Stulaval

Lochboisdale

70

Boisdale   L. Boisdale   ◣ Calvay

Orosay   Easaval

B 888   240△   S. Glendale

Borve   Scarista

365△

398△   3   L. Langavat

Northton   14

A 859   Leverburgh   460△   Finsbay

3

Killegray   A 859   12

Langay   Rodel

Groay   Gilsay   **Renish Point**

Lingay

Scaravay

93△

Borve

Otternish

Lingay   190

Oronsay   Stromay   Sursay

B 893   180

A 865   Lochportain   Cheese Bay   Hermetray

Tahay

9   Lochmaddy ◣ Weaver's Point   Loch Maddy

A 867   South Lee   281△

B 894   L. Eport

Sidinish

Eigneig Mhór

347△   Eaval

8½   A 865

Floddaybeg

Floddaymore   115△

Grimsay

Ronay

Maragay Mór

L. Uiskevagh   Maaey Riabhach

102△   **Wiay**

Faoileann   Bagh nam

South Harris Forest   Scotasay   Z

24

S o u t h   H a r r i s

Drinnishadde

Manish   Grosebay

Stockinish I.

T H E   L I T T L E   M I N C H

Ardmore

Dunvegan Head

313△   Galtrigill

Borreraig

L. Pooltiel

Milovaig

Glasphe

Neist ◣   Waterstein

Moonen Bay

Ramas

An Dubh Sgeir

S E A   O F

T H E   H E B R I D E

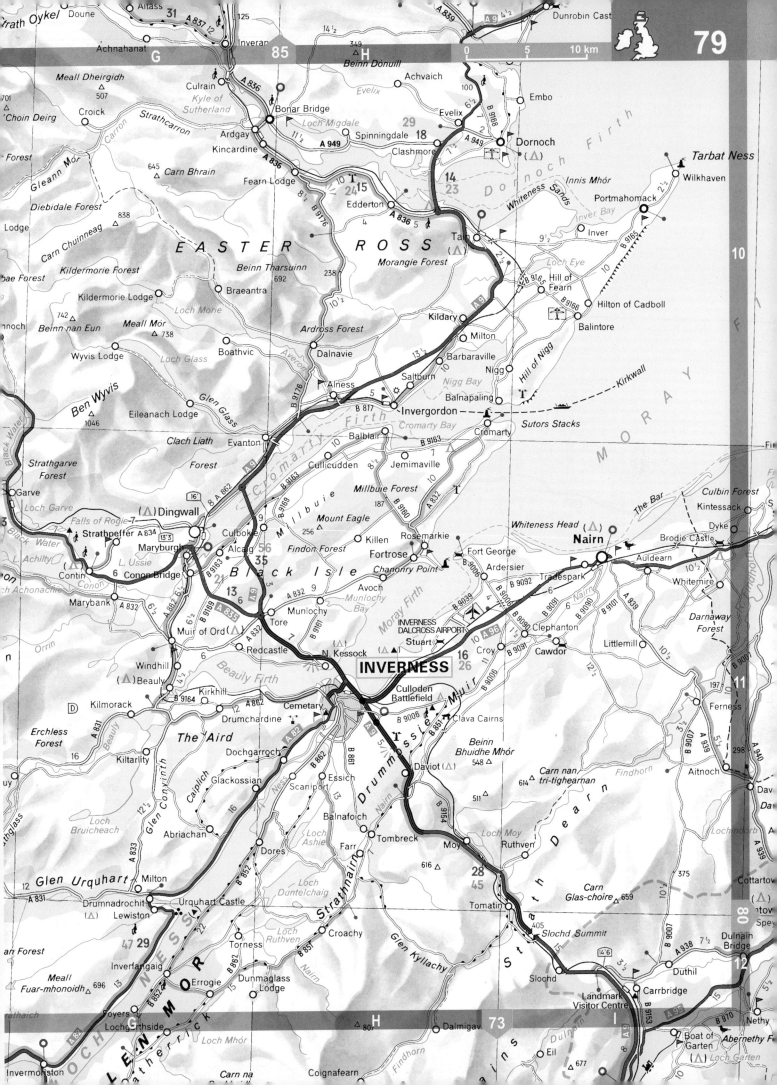

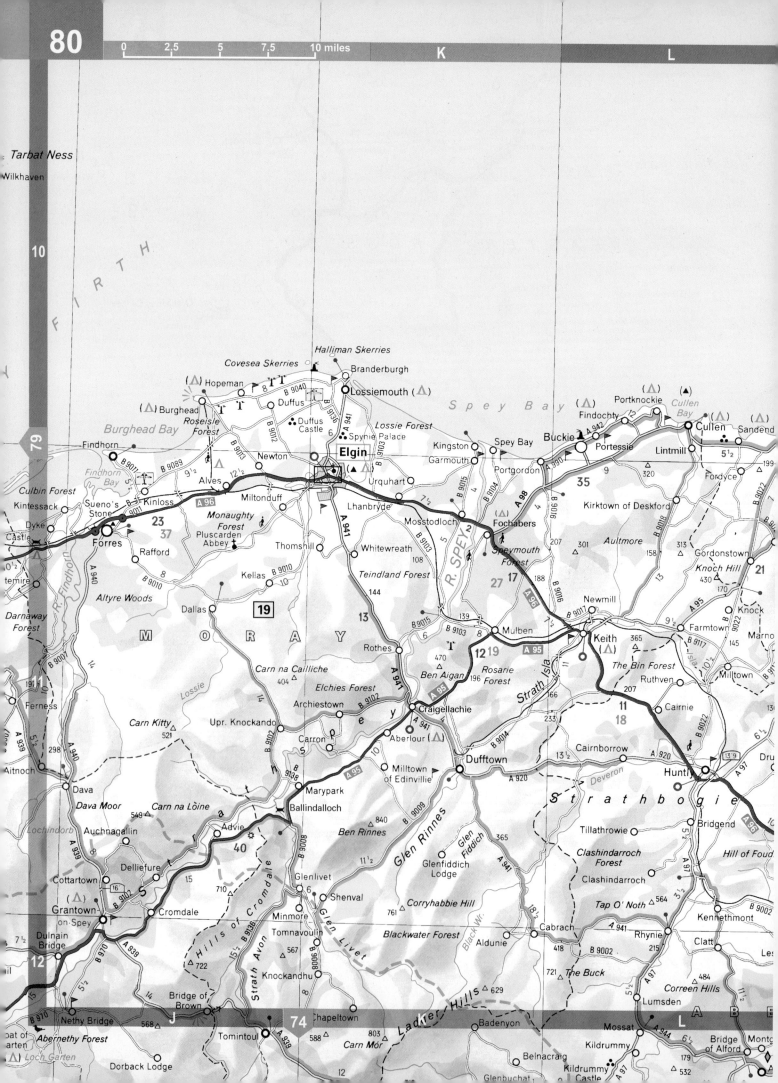

0 2.5 5 7.5 10 miles

Z   A

8

ISLE OF LEWIS
AND HARRIS

Galson

16

Borve

Shader

19

Barvas

Bragar   Arnol

50   12   L. Urrahag   28

Garenin   Shawbost

Carloway   261   Loch Breivat

Little Bernera   Dun Carloway Broch

Gallan Head   Tobson   Tolsta Chaolais   Beinn Mholach   A 857   110

West Loch Roag   292

Aird Uig   Pabay Mór   Breaclete   L. Laxavat Ard   Tong

Valtos   Newmarket

205   Breaclete   Breasclete

Miavaig   Great   Callanish   Stornoway

Timsgarry   Bernera   Eilean

Floday   Vuia Mór   Kearstay   Garynahine   A 858   13 ½   A 859

Camas Uig Uig   Cruilvig   Standing Stones

Mangersta   13   Achmore   112

Islivig   Suainaval   Enaclete   B 8059   B 8011   8   L. Osasay   B 887

574   Leurbost   9

Aird Brenish   20   LEWIS   Crossbost   Ranish

Brenish   L.   Loch Airigh   L. nam   Barkin Isles

Grunavat   na h-Airde   Falcag   Laxay   Keose

L. Trealaval   Eilean Chaluim Chil

Mealasta I.   281   Balallan   Cromore

Kearstay   L. Erisort   Eilean

B 8060   Kershader   Marvig

Scarp   308   Bràigh Mór   Loch Resort   Arivruaich   L. Saibacleit   Glenside

303   Loch Langavat   36   Gravir

Hushinish   492   Seaforth   B 8060

Gasker   Head   Lemreway   Keb

Hushinish Point   B 887   Tirga Mór   Stulaval   401   Park

679   579   17 ½   or   Eishken

Amhuinnsuidhe   Ardvourlie   572   Pairc   Eilean Iubhard

Forest of Harris   Seaforth   Beinn Mhór

Taransay Glorigs   Meavaig   Island   Crionaig   371

Soay Mór   Clisham   467

HARRIS   North Harris   799   Maaruig

Taransay   267   Isay   Rhenigidale   Eilean Mór   Sound of Shiant

506   Ardhasaig   Lo chi   a'Bhàigh

Luskentyre   Tarbert   Trollamarig   Scalpay

South Harris   Kyles   334   Shiant Islands

Forest   Scalpay   104

Scotasay   Scalpay

Toe Head   76   Drinnishadder   Scalpay

Coppay   Scarista   South Harris

365   A 859   A

Shillay   398   Grosebay

B   C   0   5   10 km

8

Butt of Lewis

Eoropie   Port of Ness
Habost   Skigersta
Cross
Dell   B 8015
Ness

Cellar Head

Loch Langavat

248
△
Muirneag   Tolsta
B 895   **Tolsta Head**

Gress

Back

12 ½
△

Tiumpan Head
Portnaguran

Broad Bay
(▲)
Melbost   12   Garrabost   A 866
Knock   Bayble   **Eye Peninsula**

Chicken Head

THE MINCH

Edrachillis Bay

Point of Stoer

Culkein   Eilean Chrona
⌐T   Clashnessie
Stoer
Clachtoll   B 869   L. Cròca

Achmelvich
9
Baddidarach

Soyea Island   Inver

A' Chleit   Kirkaig Point
Inver

Rubha Còigeach   Eilean Mór   11 ½

Rubha Mór   *Enard Bay*   Loch
Reiff   Brae of Achnahaird
6
Eilean   Altandhu   Badnagyle
Mullagrach   ⌐T   Osgaig   Sta
Isle Ristol   Polbain   L. Bad a' Ghaill
Glas-leac Mór   Achiltibuie   Loch
Tanera   Badenscallie
Tanera Beg   Mór
Summer Is.   84
Horse I.   Culnacraig
Eilean Dubh   Achduart   C
Priest Island
Bottle I.
Càrn nan Sgeir   Martin
10

òraidh

ck Head

Mhuire   Greenstone Point   Cailleach Head
Opinan   Rubha Beag   Annat Bay
Mellon Udrigle   Stattic Point   Scoraig
B   C   Gob a' Ghe   77   Gruinard   D   Badluarach   Beinn Ghobhla
Eilean Furadh Mór   Island   Mungasdale   Allt na h-A
Rubha Réidh   Achgarve   Badralloch
Mellon   Laide   A 832   Badcaul
Charles   Gruinard
Cove   Bay   Little Loch Broo

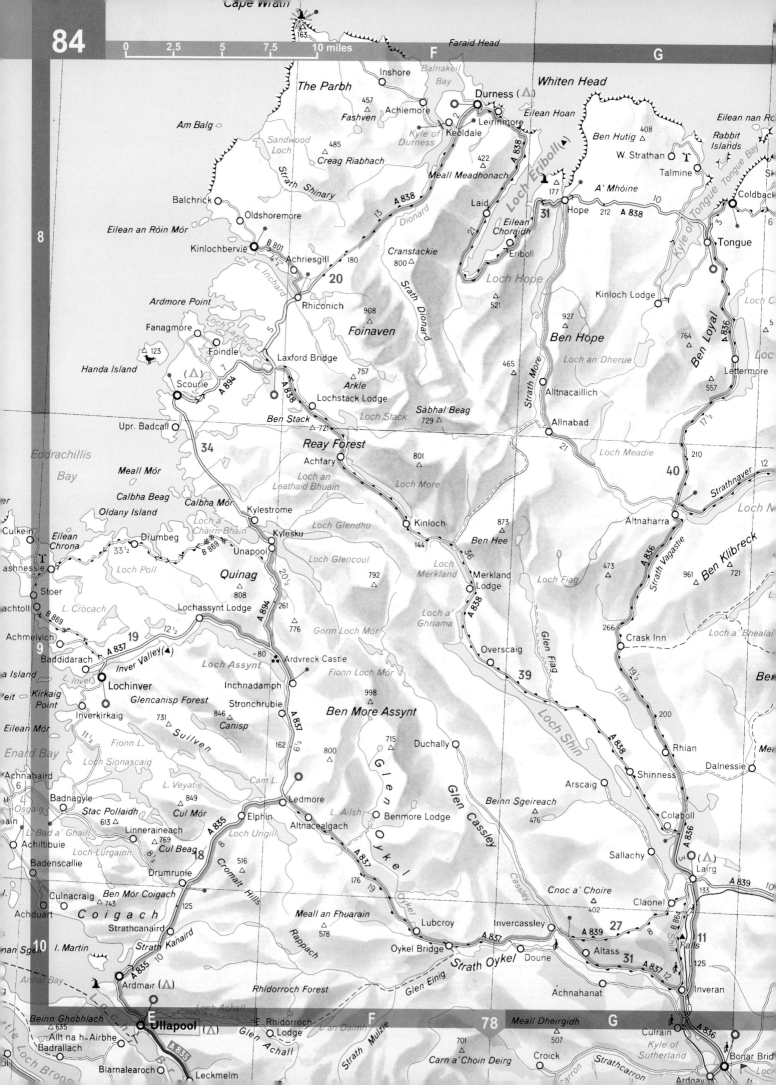

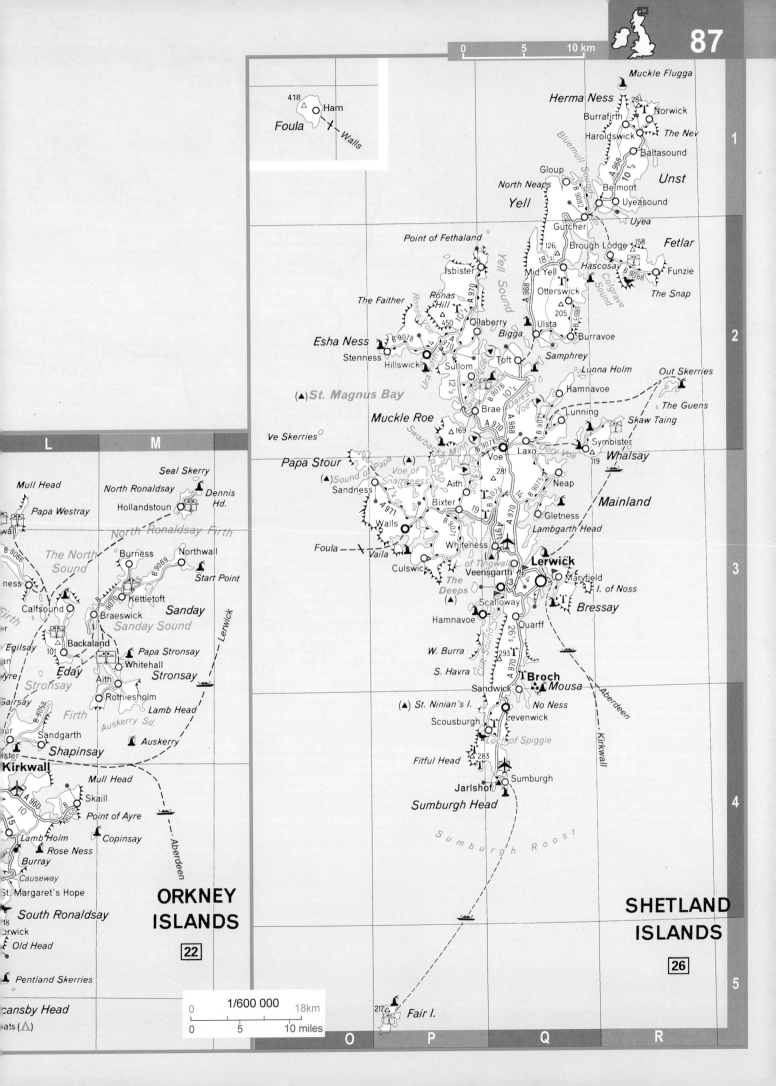

0   5   10 km

Foula
418 △ ⊦ Ham
⊦ Walls

Muckle Flugga ⚑
Herma Ness
Burrafirth   284 △
Haroldswick   Norwick
                   The Nev
Baltasound
Gloup
North Neaps   Belmont   **Unst**
Yell   A 968
               10 ½
Uyeasound
Gutcher   *Uyea*
Point of Fethaland
                   126   Brough Lodge   J 58
Isbister   18 ½   △   **Fetlar**
Ronas   A 970   Mid Yell Hascosay Funzie
Hill   B 9088
The Faither   Otterswick   *The Snap*
450 △   Ollaberry   205 △
Esha Ness   Bigga   Ulsta
B 9078   A   Ulsta   Burravoe
Stenness   A 970
Hillswick   Sullom   Toft   Samphrey
                            Lunna Holm   Out Skerries ⚑
(△)**St. Magnus Bay**   Hamnavoe   *The Guens*
                  B 9076   Lunning   Skaw Taing
Muckle Roe   Brae Dales Voe
169 △   A 970   A 968   Symbister
Ve Skerries ○   119   **Whalsay**
Papa Stour B 9071 Voe Laxo Dury Voe
(△)Sound of Papa   281 △   **Mainland**
Sandness   Aith   Neap
        A 971   Bixter B 9075
Walls   19   Gletness
Foula ─ ─   Vaila   A 970   *Lambgarth Head*
Culswick   Whiteness
                  Lerwick
        Veensgarth   Maryfield
The Deeps 3   *I. of Noss*
        Scalloway   **Bressay**
Hamnavoe   Quarff
W. Burra
S. Havra   293 △
Sandwick   **⊤Broch**
(△) St. Ninian's I.   **Mousa**
Scousburgh   No Ness
        Levenwick
        Loch of Spiggie
Fitful Head 283 △
        Sumburgh
Jarlshof
Sumburgh Head

Aberdeen
Kirkwall
Sumburgh Roost

**SHETLAND
ISLANDS**

26

L   M

Seal Skerry
Mull Head   North Ronaldsay   Dennis
Papa Westray   Hollandstoun   Hd.
North Ronaldsay Firth
The North   Burness   Northwall
Sound   B 9069
                    Start Point
        Kettletoft
Calfsound Braeswick **Sanday**
        Sanday Sound
Egilsay Backaland
101   Papa Stronsay
Eday Whitehall
Aith   **Stronsay**
Stronsay Rothiesholm
Firth   Lamb Head
        Auskerry Sd. Auskerry
Shapinsay
Mull Head
Kirkwall   Skaill
A 960   Point of Ayre
10   B   Copinsay
15
Lamb Holm
Rose Ness
Burray
Causeway
St. Margaret's Hope
South Ronaldsay
Old Head
Pentland Skerries
cansby Head
ats (△)

**ORKNEY
ISLANDS**

22

1/600 000
0   18km
0   5   10 miles

217 △   *Fair I.*

O   P   Q   R

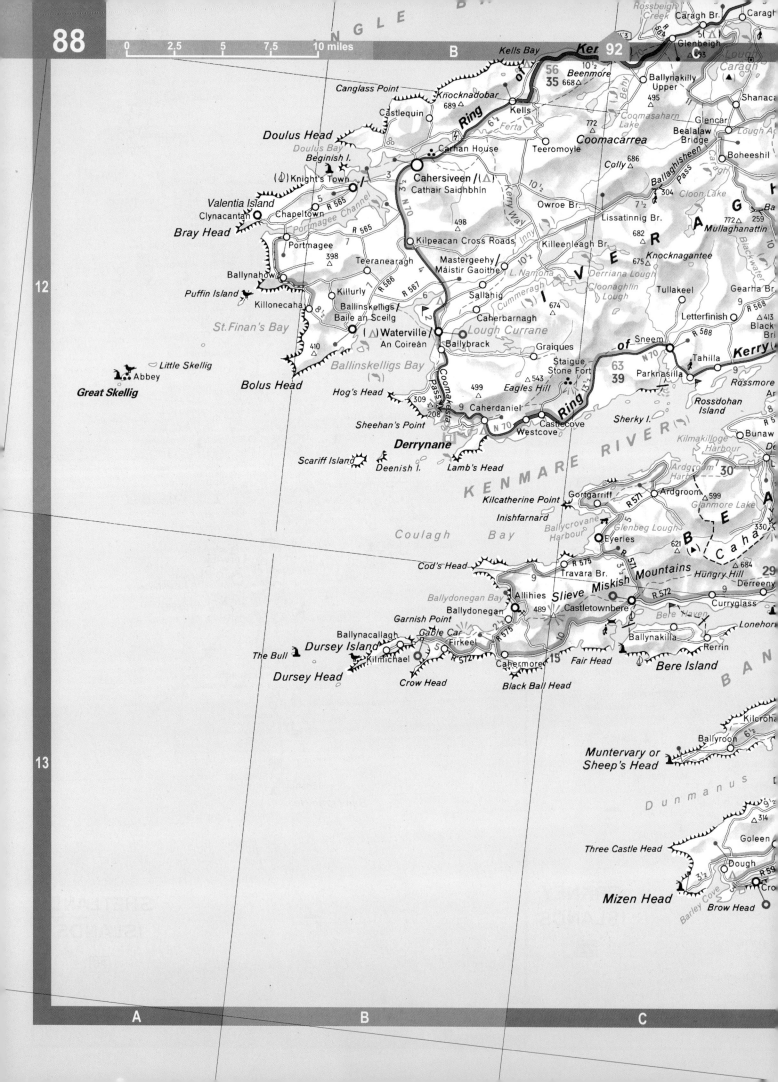

0   2.5   5   7.5   10 miles

B

10

THE

Loop Head

(71)

MOU

Br

Dreenagh

Kerry Head

218

Glenderry

(△) Bally

Ballyheige B

The Seven Hogs or
Magharee Islands

Illauntannig

Fahamore   Rough Point

Brandon Point   Kilshannig

Brandon Head   *Brandon Bay*   *Tralee Bay*

Brandon /   Barr
Cé Bhréanainn   Harbo

Dingle Way   Ballyquin   *Lough Gill*   Castlegregory (△)   Fe

Brandon Creek   **Brandon**   9   **Strand**   Kiltmey   R 560

Tiduff   **Mountain**   Cloghane   Stradbally   Aughacasla   *Derrymore I.*

Ballydavid Head   △ 951   Kilcummin   T 68

Feohanagh   7 1/2   Kilcummin   Camp

Smerwick   *Smerwick*   Ballinloghig   Ballyduff   **Beenoskee**   825

Sybil Head   *Harbour*   Ballydavid   *Feohanagh*   825   L. Slat

Ballyferriter /   Murreagh   Kilmalkedar   **D I N G L E**   (▲) L. Slat   825

Baile an Fheirtéaraigh   Gallarus Oratory   △ 623   594   Lougher   N 86   Caherconree   **Slie**

Clogher Head   Ballynana   (△)   456△ △616   50   Cahersaul   825

Inishtooskert   Ballineanig   5   Connor   31   Anascaul   Aughils   R 561

Dunquin /   Ventry   Milltown   11   Inch   5

Blasket Islands / (▲)   Dún Chaoin   Dingle /   N 86   4 1/2

Na Blascaodaí   516△ Mount Eagle   Daingean Uí Chúis   *Castleman*

Dunmore Head   Beehive   Lispole /   Doonmanagh   *Inch*   *Harbour*

Great Blasket   Huts   *Ventry*   Lios Póil   Castle   *Inch*

Island   *Harbour*   Parkmore Pt.   Cromane   Knockaunnagl

Tearaght I.   **Slea Head**   Bull's Head   Minard Head   Illaunstookagh   Tullig

Inishnabro   L. Yganavan   Caragh

Inishvickillane   **D I N G L E   B A Y** (▲)   Rossbeigh   Caragh Br.   Caragh

Creek   R   564

Kells Bay   **Kerry** (▲)   Glenbeigh   Lough

Canglass Point   Beenmore   Behy   △ 493   **Caragh**

Knocknadobar   668△   Ballynakilly   Shanacas

Castlequin   689 △   10 1/2   Upper

Ring   Kells   495   Glencar

Carhan House   772   Bealalaw   Lough Acc

Doulus Head   Ferta   6 1/2   *Coomasaharn*   Glencar   Bridge

Doulus Bay   Lake   **Coomacarrea**   304   Boheeshil

Beginish I.   Teeromoyle   Colly 686   Cloon Lake

Knight's Town   Cahersiveen /(△)   Owroe Br.   Ballaghisheen

3   Cathair Saidhbhín   7 1/2   **Pass**

Valentia Island   R 565   498   Lissatinnig Br.   772△ 259

Clynacantan   Cha   Kilpeacan Cross Roads   682   Mullaghanattin

Bray Head   88   Killeenleagh Br.   675△ Knocknagantee

Portmagee   7   Mastergeehy /   **V**   Derriana Lough

398   Teeranearagh   Máistir Gaoithe   L. Namona

Ballynahow

A   B   C

11

12

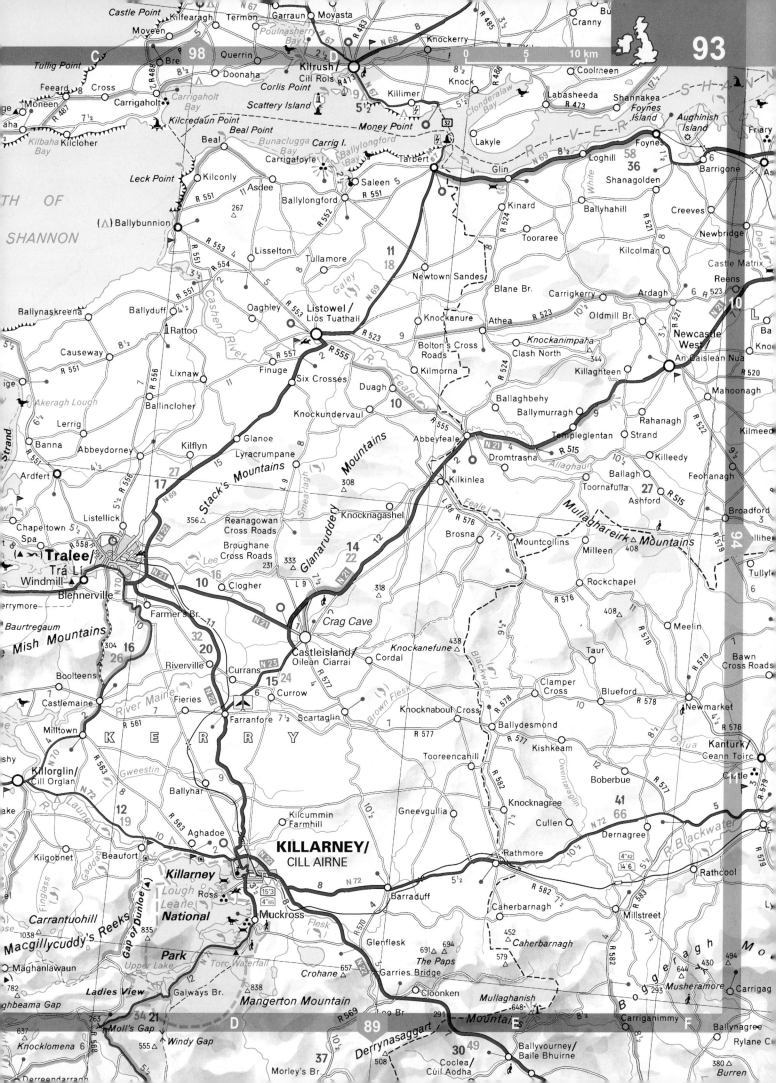

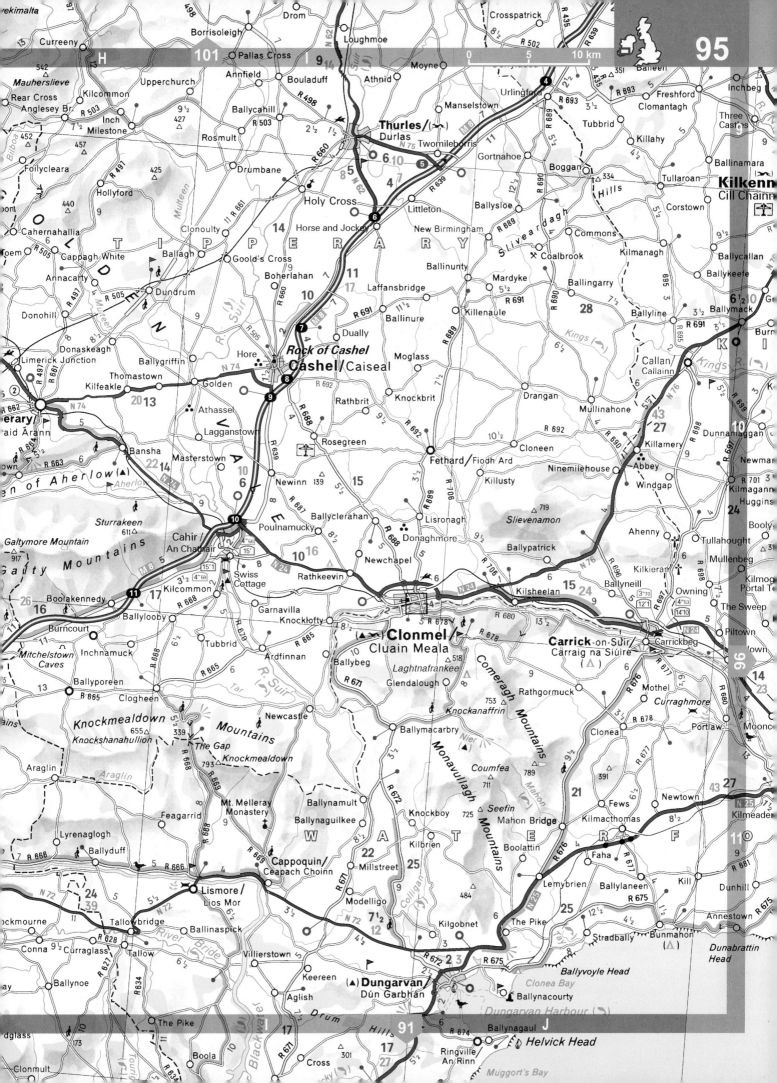

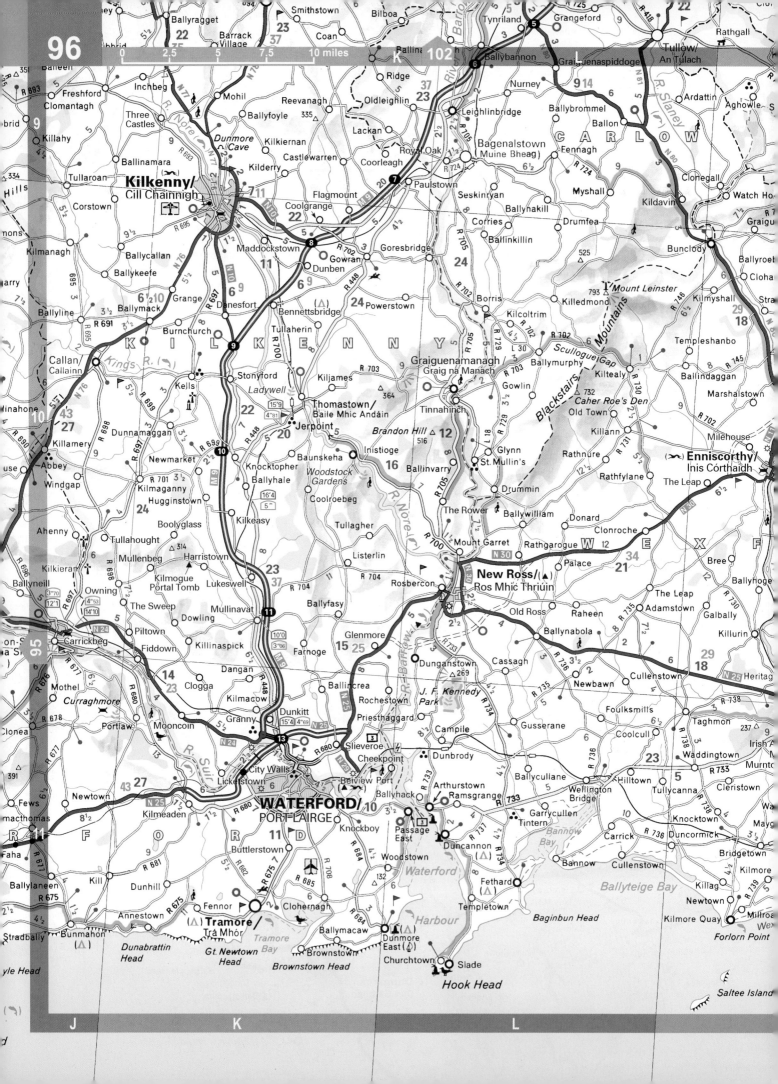

Croaghnakeela Island
L. Skannive
Kylesalia
Mace Head
Carna
Rosmuck
Kinvarra
Ard
St. Macdara's Island
Kilkieran / Cill Chiaráin
Bealadangan
R 340
D

Ardmore
Lettermore Island
Lettercallow
R 374
Lettermore
Costelloe / Casla
Mweenish Island
R 343
R 336
Inishbarra
Téeranea
Rossaveel
Casheen Bay
Carraroe / An Cheathrú Rua
Gorumna
Keeraunnagark
Lettermullan / Leitir Meallain
Island
Ballynahown
Inveran / Indreabhá
Golam Head

North Sound
GALWAY

8

Rock Island
Brannock Islands
Onaght
Kilmurvy
Oghil
Church
Dún Aonghasa
Oatquarter
Castle
Kilronan / Cill Rónáin
Inishmore / Inis Mór
Killeany
Gregory's Sound
(▲)
A R A N   I S L A N D S
Oileáin Árainn
Inishmaan / Inis Meáin
Foul Sound
Inisheer / Inis Oírr
Fardurris Point
(△)
South Sound

N T I C

O'Brien's Tower
206
R 479
R 478
Road
(△) Doolin
R 47

Cliffs of Moher
Cliffs of Moher Visitor Centre
Derreen
R 478
Hags Head
Liscannor
(△) Lahinch
An Leacht

9

Liscannor Bay
Rinneen
N 67
Mal Bay
Milltown Mal
Sráid na Cathra
Spanish Point
R 482
Spanish Point
R 474
Letterkell
R 46
Caherrush Point
Quilty
6
Mutton Island
29
Kilmurry
Mullagh
47
R 483
A N
Carrowmore Point
Cahermurphy
White Strand
Creegh
Leitrim
Killard
Creegh
R 484
Donegal Point
N 67
9
Mountrivers Bridge
Kilmihil
Corbally
Doonbeg
N 68
Bealaha
Doonbeg
Moore Bay
(△)
Kilkee / Cill Chaoi
8½
Moanmore
Cooraclare
13,5
Castle Point
Kilfearagh
Termon
Garraun
Moyasta
Knockerry
R 485
Moveen
Poulnasherry Bay
N 67
R 483
N 68
R 473

10

Tullig Point
R 48
Breaghva
Querrin
Kilrush Cill Ro
Knock
R 486

B
C
Feeard
Cross
Carrigaholt Bay
Corlis Point
Killimer
Bridge
Moneen
Carrigaholt
Scattery Island
Kilbáha
R 487
Kilcredaun Point
Beal Point
Money Point
32

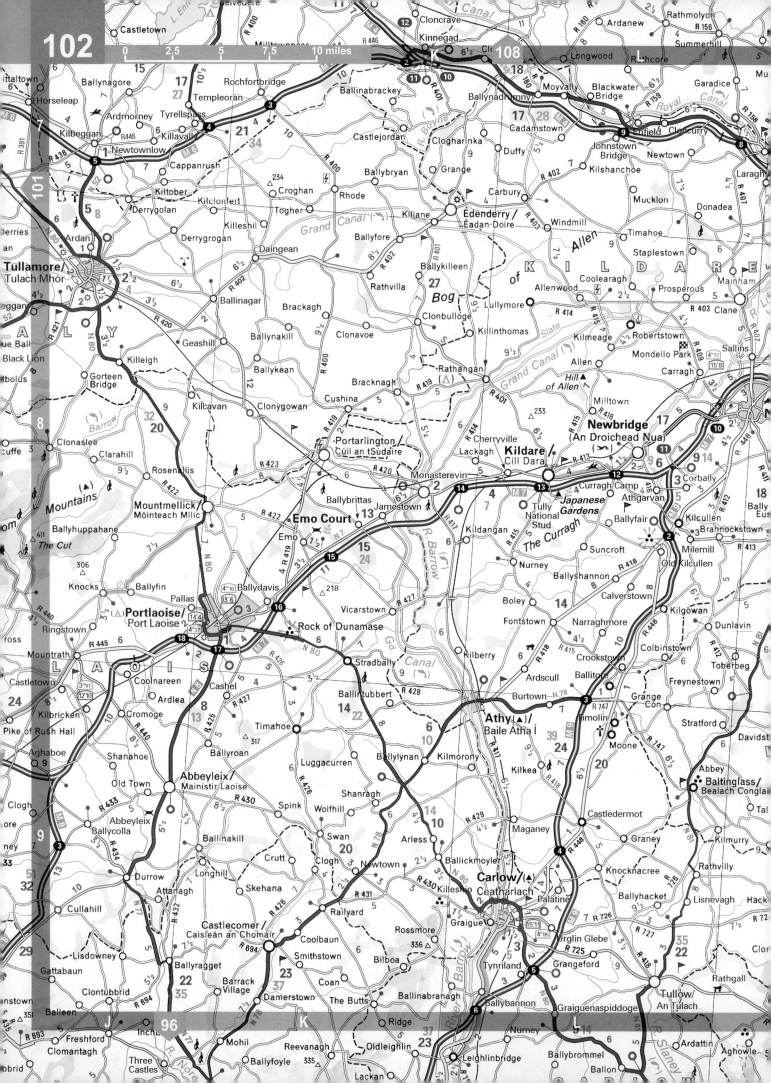

0   2.5   5   7.5   10 miles

A T L A N T

Benwee Hea

Kid Island

Erris Head

Broad Haven

Eagle Island

Rinroe Point

Aghadoon

138

Annagh Head

Corclogh

Knocknalina

Inver

Belmullet /
Béal an Mhuirthead

R 313

Inishglora

An Geata Mór

R 313

Barna
Barr na

R 314

Corraun Point

Drumreagh

Bunnahowen /
Bun na hAbhna

240

Mullet Peninsula

Trawmore
Bay

12

Elly Bay

Doolough Point

Inishkea North

Srahmor

Tristia

Inishkea South

Aghleam

Dooyork

105

Geesala /
Gaoth Saile

Fallmore

Blacksod
Point

Black Rock

Duvillaun More

Duvillaun Beg

Blacksod
Bay

Doohooma

Tullaghan
Bay

Shranama

Saddle Head

Ridge Point

Doona

Fahy Lough

Slievemore

Valley

Ballycroy

Doogort

Achill Head

Croaghaun

Inishbiggle

Castlehill

Bellag

Dooagh

Keel

River

Dooagh

R 319

Bunacurry

Annagh
Island

Moyteoge Head

Keem Strand

Claggan

Cathedral Rocks

Cashel

C

Salia

39

(▲) **ACHILL ISLAND**
Dooega Head

Knockmore

464

340

Achill

Dooega /Dumha Eige

Achill Sound /Gob an Choire

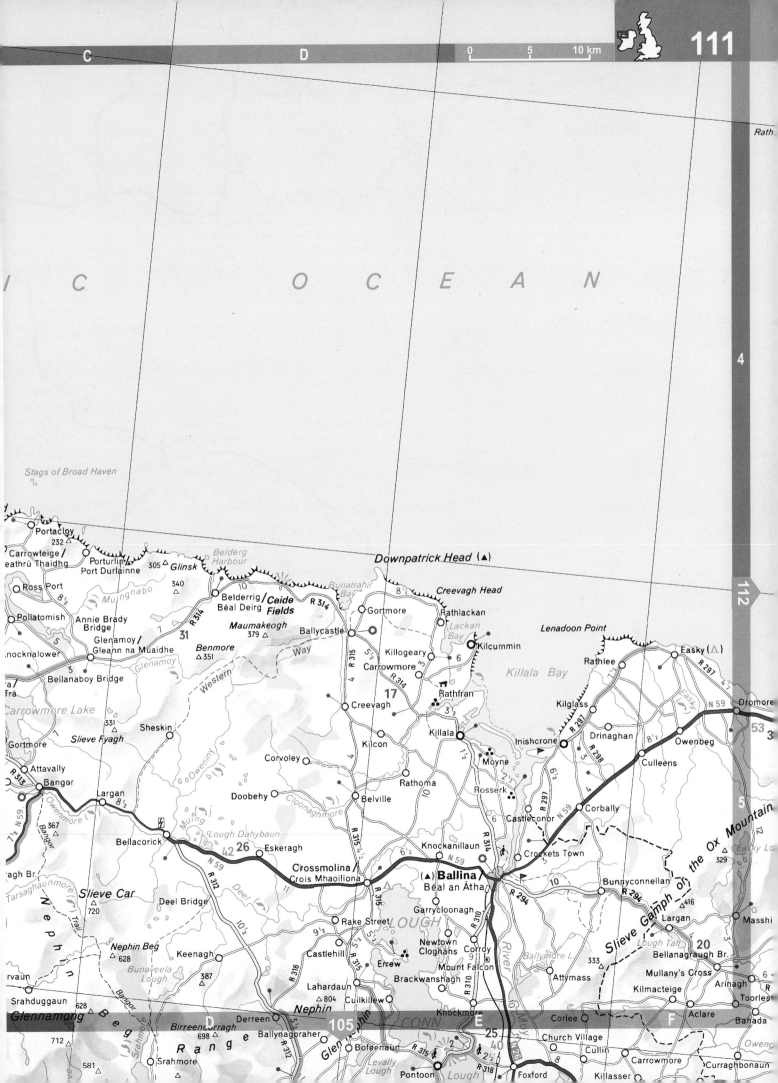

C D

0   5   10 km

4

Rath

112

A T L A N T I C   O C E A N

Stags of Broad Haven

Portacloy
232
Carrowteige /
Ceathrú Thaidhg
Porturlin /
Port Durlainne   305 Glinsk
Belderg Harbour
Ross Port   *Muingnabo*   340
Pollatomish   Annie Brady Bridge   Belderrig / Béal Deirg   **Ceide Fields**
Knocknalower   Glenamoy / Gleann na Muaidhe   *Maumakeogh*   379   Ballycastle
Glenamoy   31   *Benmore*   351   *Way*
Trá /   Bellanaboy Bridge   3   *Western*
Carrowmore Lake   331   Sheskin
Gortmore   *Slieve Fyagh*
Attavally   R 313
Bangor   R 313   *Owenmore*   Largan   8½
N 59   367
Bellacorick   *Muing*   42 26   Eskeragh
Slieve Car   N 59   R 312   *Deel*
agh Br.   *Tarsaghaunmore Trail*   720   Deel Bridge
Nephin   Crossmolina / Crois Mhaoilíona   11
Glennamong Beg   Nephin Beg   628   Keenagh   387
Srahduggaun   628   Rake Street   9½
rvaun   Nephin   Castlehill   Errew
Glennamong   Birreencorragh   Derreen   Lahardaun   Cuilkillew
712   698   Ballynagoraher   Nephin   *Glen Nephin*
581   *Range*   Srahmore   Bofeenaun

Downpatrick Head (▲)
Bunatrahir Bay   8½   *Creevagh Head*
R 314   Gortmore   Rathlackan
10   Killogeary   *Lackan Bay*
R 314   Carrowmore   3   Kilcummin
R 315   5½   4   3   6
17   Rathfran   *Killala Bay*
Creevagh   3   Lenadoon Point
Kilcon   Killala   1½
Corvoley   Moyne
Rathoma   10   Rosserk
Doobehy   *Cloonaghmore*   Belville   6
R 315   8½   Knockanillaun   R 314   Castleconor   R 297
Crossmolina   6½   **Ballina** / Béal an Átha   Crockets Town   Corbally
(▲) **Ballina**   R 294   10
Garrycloonagh   R 310   Bunnyconnellan   R 294
LOUGH   Newtown Cloghans   Corroy   *Ballymore L.*   333
5½   Mount Falcon   Attymass   Mullany's Cross
Brackwanshagh   Corlee
Knockmore   CONN   25   Church Village   Cullin
Levally Lough   2   40   *Lough*   R 318   Carrowmore
Pontoon   R 315   Foxford   Killasser

Rathlee   Easky (△)
R 297   42   N 59   Dromore
7½   *Easky*   53 3
Kilglass   N 59
Inishcrone   Drinaghan   8½   Owenbeg
R 297   R 298   3   Culleens
5
Slieve Gamph or the Ox Mountains   329   *Easky Lo*
416   Largan   Masshi
Bellanagraugh Br.
20   Kilmacteige   Arinagh
Mullany's Cross   Toorles
F   Aclare   Banada
Oweng
Curraghbonaun

D   105   E   F

0   2.5   5   7.5   10 miles

G

West Town
East Town

Tory

Bloody Foreland Head

R 257   M

Brinlack
Bun na Leaca   316   Meenaclady

Gor

Gola Island /
Gabhla   **Gweedore**

Derrybeg   *Tievea*
431

Owey Island /
Llaighe   Bunbeg /
An Bun Beag   Middletown
R 258   Gweedore /
Inishfree   Gaoth Dobh

Cruit   R 257   Dore

Torneady Point   *Island*   **DONEGAL**   Clady
Kincasslagh   **AIRPORT**
Rosses   R 259   Crolly /
Bay   Annagary   Croithlí   L.
Nac

Aran or
Aranmore Island /   228   Leabgarrow   **The**   Loughanure
Árainn Mhór   Burtonport /   *Anure*
Ballintra   Ailt an Chorráin   **Rosses**   519
(▲)   Meencorwic

Rutland   N 56
Island   *Meela*   (▲)   *Owenator*

Inishfree Upper   R 259   *Lough*   396
Croangar   Com

Dungloe /
An Clochán Liath
Crohy Head   Maghery   Meenatotan
Derrydruel   R 252   Doocharry /
Meenacross   *Trawenagh*   An Dúchoraidh
Bay   N 56   *Owen*
Gweebarra   17   384   R 252
Roaninish   *Bay*   Dooey Point   27
Derrylough   Ballynacarrick   Baile

Dunmore Head   Lettermacaward /
(▲)Portnoo   Clooney   Leitir Mhic an Bhaird   *Aghla Mo*
Dawros Head   1½   Narin   5   596
Rossbeg   3   Maas   Gweebarra
Kilclooney   Bridge   335
Loughros More   R 261   D
Bay   N 56   R 250   Graffy
Loughros Point   *Stracashel*
Glendorragha   *L.*   Glenties
Slievetooey   Crannogeboy   *Machugh*   Tanga
443   Maghera   R 253
Port   Laconnell   Kilrean   60
Lough   N 56   6
Glen Head   Olencolmcille   *Nalughraman*   Ardara   Carnaweave
Folk Village   374   50   521
F   Stravally   **G**   502   **Neck of the Ballagh**   **H**
112   31
Rossan Point   Glencolumbkille /   Meenaneary /   Crove   **Glengesh**   Meenybraddan
Malin More   Gleann Cholm Cille   Mín na Aoire   **Pass**
Malin   Meentullynagarn   R 262
Bay   Malin Beg /   R 263   Meenavean   473   Tullynaha
Malinn Bhig   5
Rathlin O'Birne

H   I

0   5   10 km

Malin Head

Inishtrahull Sound

Ballyhillin

Ballygorman

R 242

△ 284

Lag Sand Dunes

Urbalreagh

Lag

Ory Island / Toraigh

Malin

R 243

R 238

Trawbreaga Bay

Dunaff Head

Tullagh Point

Pollan Bay

Doagh Isle

Fanad Head

Rinmore Point

Arryheernabin

Dunaff   8   Kindrohid

Ballyliffin

Carrow

Melmore Head

Doagh Beg / Dumhaigh Bhig

Claggan

Straid

Clonmany

Carndonagh / Carn Domhnach

Tranarossan Bay

Kindrum

△ 505

Raghtin More

Gap of Mamore

262 △

Glasmullan

R 244

7½

Slieve Snaght

Glentoghe

△ 420

R 238

Horn Head

Sheep Haven

Doagh

(▲) *Rosguill*

Downies / Na Dúnaibh

Glinsk

Tawny

Rosnakill

F a n a d

Portsalon

Dunree Head

Magherabane

Drumfree

32

Lough Naminn

Inishbofin / Inis Bó Finne

Dunfanagh

254 △

Rosapenna

Ballyheerin

Ballynashannagh   6

Dunree Head

Magherabane

3½

Ballymagan

Illies

R 240

R 341

Portnablagh

Marble Hill

Carrigart / Carraig Airt

R 245   9

Mulroy Bay

Knockalla Mt.

364 △

Glenvar / Gleann Bhairr

I N I S H O W

(▲)

△ 398

N 56

Ballymore

Ards Forest Park

Cranford

Carrowkeel   6

Lehardan

Buncrana / Bun Cranncha

△ 483

Granias Gap

Ray

Falcarragh / An Fál Carrach

Cashelmore

Doe

R 245

R 246

(▲)

R 247

Lurganboy

Bun Cranncha

Tullydush

Owenkillew

△ 419

Scalp Mountain

58

36

Creeslough

Cashel

Glen

347

Rathmullan

Fahan

R 258

Muff

Crana

Cloghaneely

670 △

Glen Lough

Loughsalt Mt.

470 △

Millford

4

R 245

Ray

1

Inch

R 238

Muff

Q

Errigal Mountain

Glenveagh Mts.

582 △

L. Beagh

L. Keel

Lough Fern

Whale Head

Inch Island

Inch

Scalp Mountain

R 239

752 △

R 251   10½

653 △

Losset

R 255

Barnes Gap

Termon / An Tearmann

Carnaghan

Burnfoot

Culmore

Dunlewy

National

St. Colmcille Oratory

Kilmacrenan

Doon Rock ▲

Treantagh

15

24

Rathmelton

Gortaway

Speenoge

Bridge End

B 194

A 2

Coolkeeragh

Slieve Snaght

683 △

Park

445 △

Gartan Lough

Church Hill

Killyclug

Ellistrin

Fort Stewart

Race End

Newtown Cunningham

22

35

Grianan of Aileach (Stone Fort)

Holywell Hill

261 △

City Walls

LON

538 △

Glendowan Mts.

R 254

Drumbologe

56

Letterkenny / Leitir Ceanainn

N 13

20

R 237

6½

B 193

2½

A 2

Campsey

5½

Glendowan / Gleann Domhain

(Ulster Way)

Breenagh

Rashedoge

Old Town   3½

Pluck

Lismoghry

Gortree

13

Killea

Church Town

New Buildings

Ardmore

118

LONDON DERRY

Drumahoe

B 118

Ervey Cross

Meenanarwa

Commeen / An Coimín

Newmills

Letterleague

N 14

Sheskinapoll

Manorcunningham

256 △

Dooish Mt.

Ardagh

St. Johnstown

Carrigans

Magheramason

Slievekirk

371 △

Killaloo

28

Kingarrow

R 250

Cark Mountain

366 △

12

19

Cornagillagh

Raphoe

R 236

5½

Moyagh

Mountcastle

B 48

Fawney

3

Ballyneaner

△ 568

Cark

Aughkeely

Drumkeen

Aughagault

27

17

Drumbeg

Clonleigh

Ballymagorry

B 49

Dunnamanagh

Fintown / ha Finne

Cloghan / An Clochán

Cloghroe

Convoy

R 264

R 265

Rossgeir

Artigarvan

7½

Ballynamallaght

R 252

R 236

Deele

Ballindrait

Lifford

N 15

Owenreagh Hill

△ 409

Craig

O

N

E

G

A

L

Welchtown

Kilross

Carnowen

Castlefin

Strabane (▲)

Dergalt

Meenglass

△ 547

R 252

Stranorlar

Killygordon

Liscooly

N 15

Sion Mills

Ballybofey / Bealach Féich

Cross Roads

22

14

Clady

Victoria Bridge

Plumbridge

B 47

Blue Stack Mountains

672 △

Croaghnageer

Barnesmore Gap

113

Fearn Hill

230 △

S T R A B A N

B 72

Glenelly

16

26

Lough Mourne

Ardstraw

Douglas Bridge

Craigh

0   2.5   5   7.5   10 miles

L   M

1

Inishtrahull

Inishtrahull Sound

yhillin

Ballygorman

284

rbalreagh

Glengad Head

Lag

Malin R 243   Portaleen

R 242   Culdaff   R 238

Culdaff Bay   Dunmore Head

donagh/   Clonca   Ballymagaraghy   Kinnagoe Bay

Domhnach   Carrowmore   Gleneely   R 238

Glentogher   Leckemy   Crocknasmug   327   Inishowen Head

33   326   Stroove   Dunagree Pt.

S H O W E N   Greencastle   R 241   Magilligan Pt.

Castle Cary   Moville   Bun an Phobail   Magilligan Strand

341   Redcastle   B 202

White Castle   Magilligan   Downhill   Mussenden Temple

Quigley's Point   398   Bellarena   Castlerock

R 238   Binevenagh   Articlave

385   Crindle   B 89   **Coleraine**   Macosquin

Muff   Stradreagh   B 201

Gap   Culmore   Bolea   Springwell Forest   Castleroe

Coolkeeragh   Carrickhugh   A 37   13   Macosquin   Crossgare

Campsey   Greysteel   17   Ballykelly   337   Keady Mountain   B 186   Ballylintagh   Balnamore

Eglinton   27   3   B 66   Ringsend   Mullan   Agivey

LONDONDERRY/ DERRY   Glenhead   B 69   Cam Forest   Boleran   Aghadowey   Ardreagh

Drumahoe   Loug15more   396   Drumsurn   399   Garvagh   Vow

Ervey Cross Roads   B 118   Bovevagh   B 190   B 64   Moneydig

Ness Wood   Burnfoot   **L I M A V A D Y**   B 64

Killaloo   19   31   9   A 6   Dungiven   Kilrea

Claudy   Ballymoney   B 74   Boviel   Swatragh   Lislea

Ballyneaner   Millbrook   Feeny   Banagher   13   Tamlaght

D E R R Y   Park   B 44   Mullaghash   481   Banagher Forest   21   Upperlands   Clady

Carnanreagh   Dreon   Mullaghmore   555   Maghera   Culnady

Craig   **Sperrin Mountains**   678   Lisnamuck   Moneyneany

Mullaghclogha   635   Sawel Mountain   Tobermore   Knockcloghrim

K   **J**   **114**   **M**

Cranagh   Mount Hamilton or Sperrin   562   Draperstown   Curran   Bellaghy

Glenelly Valley   Carnanelly   **M A G H E R A F E L T**   Castledawson

Craignamaddy   Desertmartin

A N T R I M   C O A S T

Benbane Head   Carr Rop

Giant's Causeway   Currysheskin   White Park Bay   Ballinto

The Skerries   Causeway Head   A 2   Castle   Portbradden

Ramore Head   Port Ballintrae   Lisnagunogue   Lagavara   Ba

(△) **Portrush**   Dunluce Castle   Bushmills   Straid

Portstewart   Cloyfin   Ballyloughbeg   Ballinlea   Moyarget

A 2   Ballyrashane   Liscolman   Moss-Side

Derrykeighan   Toberdoney   Dervock

Ballybogy   Stranocum

Damhead   Kirkhills   The Drones

Ballymoney   Milltown   Dunaghy   Kilraghts

Bendoorsgh   43   Killagan Bridge

Garryduff   27   Dunloy   Clogh

B A L L Y M O N

Finvoy

Mac Laughlins Corner   Rasharkin

Kilrea   Glenvale   Glarryford   Mac R

Lisnamuck   Aughnacleagh   Graigs

12

Cullybackey

Portglenone   Galgorm

Ahoghill   Gracehill

B A L L

Gulladuff   A 54

Newferry   Chesney's Corner   Whitesides Corner   Kildr

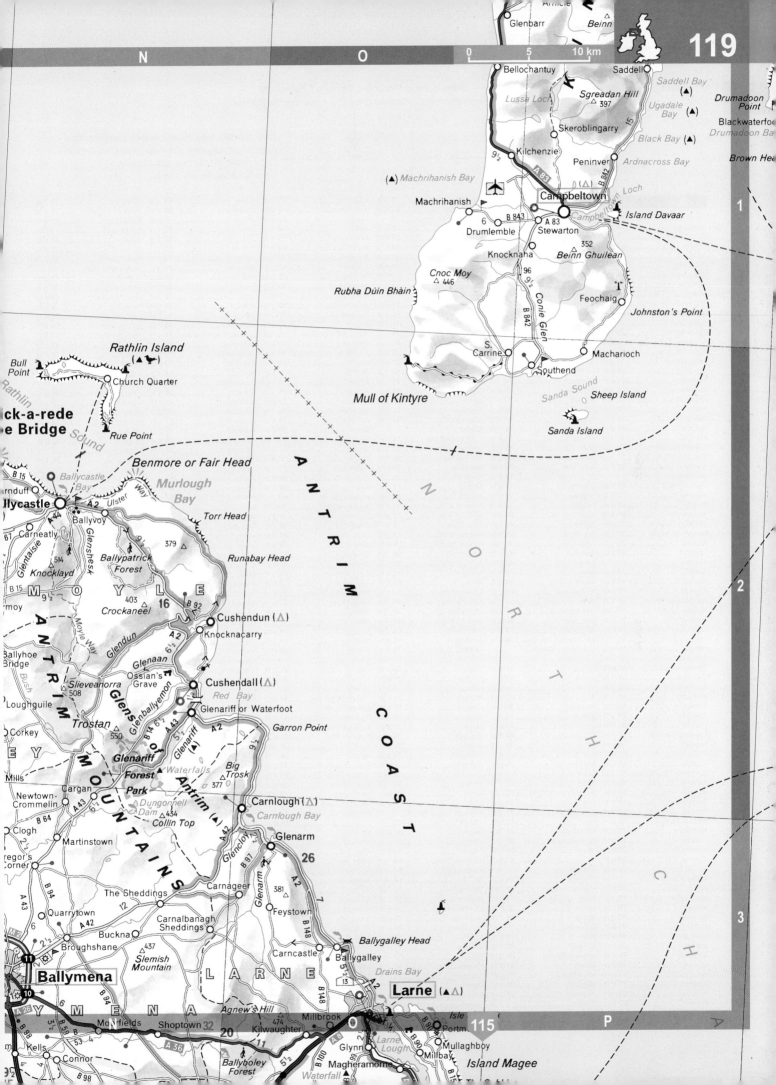

120 Great Britain

A B C D E F G H I J K L M N O P Q R S T U V W X Y Z

Page number / Numéro de page / Seitenzahl
Paginanummer / Numero di pagina / Número de Página

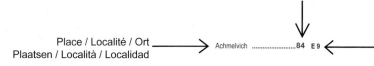

Place / Localité / Ort
Plaatsen / Località / Localidad

Achmelvich ....84 E 9

Grid coordinates / Coordonnées de carroyage
Koordinatenangabe / Verwijstekens ruitsysteem
Coordinate riferite alla quadrettatura
Coordenadas en los mapas

A

A Chill 71 A 12
A La Ronde 4 J 32
Abbas Combe 9 M 30
Abberley 27 M 27
Abbey 23 X 30
Abbey Dore 26 L 28
Abbey Town 54 K 19
Abbeydale 43 P 23
Abbeystead 48 L 22
Abbots Bromley 35 O 25
Abbots Langley 21 S 28
Abbots Leigh 18 M 29
Abbots Ripton 29 T 26
Abbotsbury 5 M 32
Abbotsford House 62 L 17
Abbotskerswell 4 J 32
Aber Banc 15 G 27
Aberaeron 24 H 27
Aberaman 17 J 28
Aberangell 33 I 25
Abercarn 18 K 29
Abercastle 14 E 28
Aberchirder 81 M 11
Abercynon 17 J 29
Aberdâr / Aberdare 17 J 28
Aberdare / Aberdâr 17 J 28
Aberdaron 32 F 25
Aberdaugleddau / Milford Haven 14 E 28
Aberdeen 75 N 12
Aberdour 68 K 15
Aberdour Bay 81 N 10
Aberdovey / Aberdyfi 33 H 26
Aberdyfi / Aberdovey 33 H 26
Aberedw 25 J 27
Abereiddy 14 E 28
Aberfeldy 73 I 14
Aberffraw 32 G 24
Aberford 43 P 22
Aberfoyle 67 G 15
Abergavenny / Y-Fenni 18 K 28
Abergele 41 J 23
Abergolech 15 H 28
Abergwaun / Fishguard 24 F 28
Abergwesyn 25 I 27
Abergwili 15 H 28
Abergwynfi 17 J 29
Abergwyngregyn 41 H 23
Abergynolwyn 33 I 26
Aberhonddu / Brecon 25 J 28
Aberkenfig 17 J 29
Aberlady 69 L 15
Aberlemno 75 L 13
Aberlour 80 K 11
Abermaw / Barmouth 33 H 25
Abermule 34 K 26
Abernethy 68 K 15
Abernyte 68 K 14
Aberpennar / Mountain Ash 17 J 28
Aberporth 15 G 27
Abersoch 32 G 25
Abersychan 18 K 28
Abertawe / Swansea 17 I 29
Aberteifi / Cardigan 15 G 27
Abertillery 18 K 28
Aberuthven 67 J 15
Aberystwyth 25 H 26
Abingdon 20 Q 28
Abinger Common 21 S 30
Abinger Hammer 21 S 30
Abingto *Cambs.* 30 U 27
Abington *South Lanarkshire* 61 I 17
Aboyne 75 L 12
Abriachan 79 G 11
Abridge 21 U 29
Accrington 42 M 22
Achahoish 65 D 16
Achallader 66 F 14
Achanalt 78 F 11
Achaphubuil 72 E 13
Acharacle 71 C 13
Achargary 85 H 8
Acharn 67 H 14
Achduart 83 E 10
Achgarve 78 D 10
Achiemore 84 F 8
Achiltibuie 83 D 9
Achintee 78 D 11
Achintraid 78 D 11
Achlean 73 I 12
Achleck 64 B 14
Achmelvich 84 E 9
Achmore 78 D 11
Achnahanat 84 G 10
Achnamara 65 D 15
Achnanellan 72 E 13
Achnasheen 78 E 11
Achnashellach Forest 78 E 11
Achosnich 71 B 13
Achranich 71 C 14
Achray (Loch) 67 G 15
Achreamie 85 I 8
Achriesgill 84 F 8
Achtalean 77 B 11
Achvaich 79 H 10
Acklington 63 P 18
Ackworth 44 P 23
Acle 39 Y 26
Acomb 55 N 19
Acrise Place 13 X 30
Acton Burnell 34 L 26
Acton Scott 26 L 26
Acton Turville 19 N 29
Adbaston 35 M 25
Adderbury 28 Q 27
Adderley 34 M 25
Adderstone 63 O 17
Addingham 49 O 22
Addlestone 21 S 29
Adfa 33 J 26
Adlington 42 M 23
Adlington Hall 43 N 24
Advie 80 J 11
Adwick-le-Street 44 Q 23
Ae (Forest of) 53 J 18
Ae Village 53 J 18
Afan Argoed 17 J 29
Affric (Glen) 78 F 12
Affric Lodge 78 E 12
Afon Dyfrdwy / Dee (River) 34 K 24
Afon Dyfrdwy (River) / Dee *Wales* 41 K 23
Afon-wen 41 K 23
Agneash 46 G 21
Aikton 54 K 19
Ailort (Loch) 72 C 13
Ailsa Craig 59 E 18
Ainderby Quernhow 50 P 21
Ainort (Loch) 77 B 12
Ainsdale 42 K 23
Air Uig 82 Y 9
Aird 65 D 15
Aird (The) 79 G 11
Aird of Sleat 71 C 12
Airdrie 61 I 16
Airigh na h-Airde (Loch) 82 Z 9
Airor 72 C 12
Airth 67 I 15
Airton 49 N 21
Aith *Orkney Is.* 87 M 6
Aith *Shetland Is.* 87 P 3
Aitnoch 80 I 11
Akeld 63 N 17
Albourne 11 T 31
Albrighton 35 N 26
Albyn or Mor (Glen) 73 F 12
Alcaig 79 G 11
Alcester 27 O 27
Alconbury 29 T 26
Aldborough 39 X 25
Aldbourne 19 P 29
Aldbrough 45 T 22
Aldbrough St. John 49 O 20
Aldbury 21 S 28
Alde (River) 31 Y 27
Aldeburgh 31 Y 27
Aldenham 21 S 28
Alderbury 9 O 30
Alderholt 9 O 31
Alderley Edge 43 N 24
Alderney *Channel I.* 5
Aldershot 20 R 30
Alderton 27 N 28
Aldford 34 L 24
Aldingbourne 11 R 31
Aldridge 35 O 26
Aldringham 31 Y 27
Aldsworth 19 O 28
Aldunie 80 K 12
Aldwick 11 R 31
Alexandria 66 G 16
Alfold Crossways 11 S 30
Alford *Aberdeenshire* 75 L 12
Alford *Lincs.* 45 U 24
Alfreton 36 P 24
Alfrick 27 M 27
Alfriston 12 U 31
Aline (Loch) 65 C 14
Alkborough 44 S 22
Alkham 13 X 30
All Stretton 34 L 26
Allanaquoich 74 J 12
Allanton *North Lanarkshire* 61 I 16
Allanton *Scottish Borders* 63 N 16
Allendale Town 55 N 19
Allenheads 55 N 19
Allensmore 26 L 27
Allerford 17 J 30
Allerston 51 S 21
Allestree 36 P 25
Allhallows 22 V 29
Alligin Shuas 78 D 11
Allington *Kennet* 19 O 29
Allington *Salisbury* 9 O 30
Allnabad 84 G 8
Alloa 67 I 15
Allonby 54 J 19
Alloway 60 G 17
Alltan Fhèarna (Loch an) 85 H 9
Alltnacaillich 84 G 8
Almond (Glen) 67 I 14
Almondbank 68 J 14
Almondsbury 18 M 29
Alness 79 H 10
Alnmouth 63 P 17
Alnwick 63 O 17
Alpheton 30 W 27
Alphington 4 J 31
Alpraham 34 M 24
Alresford 30 X 28
Alrewas 35 O 25
Alsager 35 N 24
Alsh (Loch) 78 D 12
Alston 55 M 19
Alstonefield 35 O 24
Alswear 7 I 31
Altadnduin 85 H 9
Altandhu 83 D 9
Altarnun 3 G 32
Altass 84 G 10
Alternative Technology Centre 33 I 26
Altham 42 M 22
Althorne 22 W 29
Althorpe 44 R 23
Altnabreac Station 85 I 8
Altnacealgach 84 F 9
Altnaharra 84 G 9
Alton *Hants.* 10 R 30
Alton *Staffs.* 35 O 25
Alton Pancras 9 M 31
Alton Priors 19 O 29
Alton Towers 35 O 25
Altrincham 42 M 23
Alum Bay 10 P 31
Alva 67 I 15
Alvaston 36 P 25
Alvechurch 27 O 26
Alvediston 9 N 30
Alves 80 J 11
Alvescot 19 P 28
Alvie 73 I 12
Alvingham 45 U 23
Alwinton 63 N 17
Alyth 74 K 14
Amberley 11 S 31
Amble 63 P 18
Amblecote 27 N 26
Ambleside 48 L 20
Ambrosden 28 Q 28
Amersham 21 S 29
Amesbury 9 O 30
Amhuinnsuidhe 82 Y 10
Amisfield 53 J 18
Amlwch 40 G 22
Ammanford / Rhydaman 15 I 28
Amotherby 50 R 21
Ampleforth 50 Q 21
Amport 20 P 30
Ampthill 29 S 27
Amroth 15 G 28
Amulree 67 I 14
An Riabhachan 78 E 11
An Socach 74 J 13
An Teallach 78 E 10
Anchor 26 K 26
Ancroft 63 O 16
Ancrum 62 M 17
Andover 20 P 30
Andoversford 27 O 28
Andreas 46 G 20
Angle 14 E 28
Anglesey (Isle of) 40
Anglesey Abbey 30 U 27
Angmering 11 S 31
Annan 54 K 19
Annan (River) 61 J 18
Annat 78 D 11
Annat Bay 83 E 10
Annbank 60 G 17
Annbank Station 60 G 17
Anne Hathaway's Cottage 27 O 27
Annesley-Woodhouse 36 Q 24
Annfield Plain 56 O 19
Ansley 28 P 26
Anstey 36 Q 25
Anston 44 Q 23
Anstruther 69 L 15
Anthorn 54 K 19
Antony House 3 H 32
Appin 72 E 14
Appleby *Eden* 55 M 20
Appleby *North Lincolnshire* 44 S 23
Appleby Magna 36 P 25
Applecross 77 C 11
Appledore *Devon* 6 H 30
Appledore *Kent* 12 W 30
Appleford 20 Q 29
Appleton 20 P 28
Appleton Roebuck 44 Q 22
Appleton Wiske 50 P 20
Appletreewick 49 O 21
Aran Fawddwy 33 I 25
Arberth / Narberth 15 F 28
Arbigland 53 J 19
Arbirlot 69 M 14
Arbor Low 35 O 24
Arborfield 20 R 29
Arbroath 69 M 14
Arbury Hall 28 P 26
Arbuthnott 75 N 13
Archiestown 80 K 11
Ard (Loch) 67 G 15
Ardanaiseig 66 E 14
Ardarroch 78 D 11
Ardcharnich 78 E 10
Ardchiavaig 64 B 15
Ardchuilk 78 F 11
Ardchyle 67 G 14
Ardechive 72 E 13
Arden 66 G 15
Ardentallan 65 D 14
Ardeonaig 67 H 14
Ardersier 79 H 11
Ardery 72 C 13
Ardfern 65 D 15
Ardgartan 66 F 15
Ardgay 79 G 10
Ardgour 72 D 13
Ardhasaig 82 Z 10
Ardingly 11 T 30
Ardington 20 P 29
Ardivachar 76 X 11
Ardleigh 30 W 28
Ardley 28 Q 28
Ardlui 66 F 15
Ardlussa 65 C 15
Ardmair 84 E 10
Ardminish 58 C 16
Ardmore Point *Isle of Skye* 77 A 11
Ardnacross 71 C 14
Ardnamurchan 71 B 13
Ardnastang 72 D 13
Ardnave 64 A 16
Ardnave Point 64 B 16
Ardpatrick 59 D 16
Ardrishaig 65 D 15
Ardrossan 59 F 17
Ardshealach 71 C 13
Ardslignish 71 C 13
Ardtalla 58 B 16
Ardtalnaig 67 H 14
Ardtoe 71 C 13
Ardvasar 71 C 12
Ardverikie Forest 73 G 13
Ardvorlich 67 H 14
Ardwell 52 F 19
Argyll 65 D 15
Argyll Forest Park 66 F 15
Arichastlich 66 F 14
Arienas (Loch) 71 C 14
Arileod 71 A 14
Arinacrinachd 77 C 11
Arinagour 71 A 14
Arisaig 71 C 13
Arivruaich 82 Z 9
Arkaig (Loch) 72 E 13
Arkendale 50 P 21
Arkengarthdale 49 O 20
Arkholme 48 M 21
Arklet (Loch) 66 G 15
Arley 27 P 26
Arlingham 19 M 28
Arlington Court 7 I 30
Armadale *Highland* 85 H 8
Armadale *West Lothian* 61 I 16
Armadale Bay 71 C 12
Armitage 35 O 25
Armthorpe 44 Q 23
Arnabost 71 A 14
Arncliffe 49 N 21
Arncott 20 Q 28
Arncroach 69 L 15
Arne 9 N 31
Arnesby 28 Q 26
Arnicle 59 D 17
Arnisdale 72 D 12
Arnish 77 B 11
Arnol 82 A 8
Arnold 36 Q 25
Arnprior 67 H 15
Arnside 48 L 21
Aros 65 B 14
Arram 45 S 22
Arran (Isle of) 59 E 17
Arreton 10 Q 31
Arrochar 66 F 15
Arscaig 84 G 9
Arundel 11 S 31
Ascog 59 E 16
Ascot 21 R 29
Ascott House 29 R 28
Ascott-under-Wychwood 28 P 28
Ascrib Islands 77 A 11
Asfordby 36 R 25
Ash *Kent* 23 X 30
Ash *Surrey* 20 R 30
Ash Mill 7 I 31
Ashbourne 35 O 24
Ashburton 4 I 32
Ashbury 19 P 29
Ashby de la Zouch 36 P 25
Ashby Magna 28 Q 26
Ashcott 8 L 30
Ashdon 30 U 27
Ashford *Kent* 12 W 30
Ashford *Surrey* 21 S 29
Ashford-in-the-Water *Derbs.* 43 O 24
Ashie (Loch) 79 H 11
Ashill *Breckland* 38 W 26
Ashill *South Somerset* 8 L 31
Ashingdon 22 W 29
Ashington *Northumb* 56 P 18
Ashington *West Sussex* 11 S 31
Ashkirk 62 L 17
Ashleworth 27 N 28
Ashley *East Cambridgeshire* 30 V 27
Ashley *Newcastle-under-Lyme* 35 M 25
Ashley *Torridge* 7 I 31
Ashley Green 21 S 28
Ashmore 9 N 31
Ashover 36 P 24
Ashperton 26 M 27
Ashreigney 7 I 31
Ashtead 21 T 30
Ashton 34 L 24
Ashton-in-Makerfield 42 M 23
Ashton Keynes 19 O 29
Ashton-under-Lyne 43 N 23
Ashton-upon-Mersey 42 M 23
Ashurst 10 P 31
Ashwell *North Hertfordshire* 29 T 27
Ashwell *Rutland* 36 R 25
Ashwellthorpe 39 X 26
Askam in Furness 47 K 21
Askern 44 Q 23
Askernish 76 X 12
Askerswell 5 L 31
Askham 55 L 20
Askrigg 49 N 21
Askwith 49 O 22
Aslacton 31 X 26
Aslockton 36 R 25
Aspatria 54 K 19
Aspley Guise 29 S 27
Assynt (Loch) 84 E 9
Astley 34 L 25
Aston *Vale Royal* 44 Q 23
Aston *West Oxfordshire* 20 P 28
Aston Clinton 20 R 28
Aston Magna 27 O 27
Aston Rowant 20 R 28
Aston Tirrold 20 Q 29
Astwood Bank 27 O 27
Atcham 34 L 25
Athelhampton Hall 9 N 31
Athelney 8 L 30
Athelstaneford 69 L 16
Atherington 7 H 31
Athersley 43 P 23
Atherstone 36 P 26
Atherton 42 M 23
Atholl (Forest of) 73 H 13
Attadale 78 D 11
Attleborough *Breckland* 38 X 26
Attleborough *Nuneaton and Bedworth* 28 P 26
Attlebridge 39 X 25
Atwick 51 T 22
Atworth 19 N 29
Aucharnie 81 M 11
Auchavan 74 K 13
Auchenblae 75 M 13
Auchenbowie 67 I 15
Auchenbrack 61 I 18
Auchenbreck 65 E 16
Auchencairn 53 I 19
Auchencrosh 52 F 18
Auchencrow 63 N 16
Auchengray 61 J 16
Auchenmalg 52 F 19
Auchentiber 60 G 16

A

Auchindrean ....78 E 10
Auchinleck ....60 H 17
Auchleven ....81 M 12
Auchlyne ....67 G 14
Auchnafree ....67 I 14
Auchnagallin ....80 J 11
Auchnagatt ....81 N 11
Aucholzie ....74 K 12
Auchronie ....74 L 13
Auchterarder ....67 I 15
Auchteraw ....73 F 12
Auchterderran ....68 K 15
Auchterhouse ....68 K 14
Auchtermuchty ....68 K 15
Auchtertyre ....78 D 12
Auckengill ....86 K 8
Auckley ....44 Q 23
Audenshaw ....43 N 23
Audlem ....34 M 25
Audley ....35 N 24
Audley End ....30 U 27
Aughton *near Lancaster* ....48 L 21
Aughton *near Ormskirk* ....42 L 23
Auldearn ....79 I 11
Auldgirth ....53 I 18
Auldhouse ....60 H 16
Ault a' Chruinn ....72 D 12
Aultbea ....78 D 10
Aust ....18 M 29
Austrey ....35 P 26
Austwick ....49 M 21
Avebury ....19 O 29
Aveley ....22 U 29
Avening ....19 N 28
Aveton Gifford ....4 I 33
Aviemore ....73 I 12
Avoch ....79 H 11
Avon (Glen) ....74 J 12
Avon (River) *R. Severn* ....28 Q 26
Avon (River) *Wilts.* ....9 O 31
Avonbridge ....67 I 16
Avonmouth ....18 L 29
Avonwick ....4 I 32
Awe (Loch) ....65 E 15
Awliscombe ....8 K 31
Awre ....19 M 28
Axbridge ....18 L 30
Axminster ....8 L 31
Axmouth ....5 K 31
Aylburton ....18 M 28
Aylesbury ....20 R 28
Aylesford ....22 V 30
Aylesham ....23 X 30
Aylsham ....39 X 25
Aylton ....26 M 27
Aymestrey ....26 L 27
Aynho ....28 Q 28
Ayr ....60 G 17
Aysgarth ....49 O 21
Ayside ....48 L 21
Ayton *Scarborough* ....51 S 21
Ayton *Scottish Borders* ....63 N 16

B

Bà (Loch) ....65 C 14
Babbacombe Bay ....4 J 32
Babcary ....8 M 30
Babell ....41 K 23
Babworth ....44 R 24
Back ....83 B 9
Backaland ....87 L 6
Backmuir of New Gilston ....69 L 15
Backwater Reservoir ....74 K 13
Backwell West Town ....18 L 29
Baconsthorpe ....39 X 25
Bacton *Mid Suffolk* ....30 X 27
Bacton *North Norfolk* ....39 Y 25
Bacup ....43 N 22
Bad a' Ghaill (Loch) ....84 E 9
Bad an Sgalaig (Loch) ....78 D 10
Badachro ....77 C 10
Badanloch (Loch) ....85 H 9
Badanloch Lodge ....85 H 9
Badcaul ....78 D 10
Baddesley Ensor ....35 P 26
Baddidarach ....84 E 9
Badenoch ....73 H 13
Badenscallie ....83 E 9
Badenyon ....74 K 12
Badlipster ....86 K 8
Badluarach ....78 D 10
Badminton ....19 N 29
Badrallach ....78 E 10
Bae Colwyn / Colwyn Bay ....41 I 23
Bagh nam Faoileann ....76 Y 11
Bagillt ....41 K 23
Bagley ....34 L 25

Bagshot ....21 R 29
Bagworth ....36 P 25
Bagwyllydiart ....26 L 28
Baile Mòr ....64 A 15
Bailiehill ....54 K 18
Bainbridge ....49 N 21
Bainton ....51 S 22
Bakewell ....35 O 24
Bala ....33 J 25
Balallan ....82 A 9
Balbeggie ....68 J 14
Balblair ....79 H 10
Balcary Point ....53 I 19
Balchrick ....84 E 8
Balcombe ....11 T 30
Balderton ....36 R 24
Baldock ....29 T 28
Baldrine ....46 G 21
Baldwin ....46 G 21
Balemartine ....64 Z 14
Balephetrish Bay ....70 Z 14
Balephuil ....64 Z 14
Balephuil Bay ....64 Z 14
Balerno ....61 J 16
Baleshare ....76 X 11
Balevulin ....65 B 14
Balfour ....87 L 6
Balfron ....67 H 15
Balgray ....69 L 14
Balintore *Angus* ....74 K 13
Balintore *Highland* ....79 I 10
Balivanich ....76 X 11
Balk ....50 Q 21
Ballabeg ....46 F 21
Ballachulish ....72 E 13
Balljajora ....46 G 21
Ballamodha ....46 G 21
Ballantrae ....52 E 18
Ballasalla ....46 G 21
Ballater ....74 K 12
Ballaugh ....46 G 21
Ballevullin ....70 Z 14
Balliemore *near Dunoon* ....65 E 15
Balliemore *near Oban* ....65 D 14
Ballig ....46 G 21
Ballingry ....68 K 15
Ballinluig ....74 J 14
Ballochan ....75 L 12
Ballochroy ....59 D 16
Ballyhaugh ....71 A 14
Balmaclellan ....53 H 18
Balmaha ....67 G 15
Balmedie ....75 N 12
Balminnoch ....52 F 19
Balmoral Castle ....74 K 12
Balmullo ....69 L 14
Balnacra ....78 D 11
Balnafoich ....79 H 11
Balnaguard ....74 I 14
Balnahard ....64 B 14
Balnakeil Bay ....84 F 8
Balnaknock ....77 B 11
Balnapaling ....79 H 10
Baltonsborough ....8 M 30
Balvicar ....65 D 15
Balvraid ....72 D 12
Bamburgh Castle ....63 O 17
Bamford ....43 O 23
Bampton *Cumbria* ....48 L 20
Bampton *Devon* ....7 J 31
Bampton *Oxon.* ....20 P 28
Banavie ....72 E 13
Banbury ....28 P 27
Banchory ....75 M 12
Bancyfelin ....15 G 28
Bandenscoth ....81 M 11
Banff ....81 M 10
Bangor ....40 H 23
Bankend ....53 J 18
Bankfoot ....68 J 14
Bankhead ....75 N 12
Banks ....42 L 22
Bankshill ....54 K 18
Banniskirk ....85 J 8
Bannockburn ....67 I 15
Banstead ....21 T 30
Banwell ....18 L 30
Bapchild ....22 W 30
Bar Hill ....29 U 27
Barabaraville ....79 H 10
Barbon ....48 M 21
Barcaldine ....65 E 14
Barcombe Cross ....11 U 31
Bardney ....45 T 24
Bardsea ....48 K 21
Bardsey ....43 P 22
Bardsey Island ....32 F 25

Barford ....39 X 26
Barford-St. Martin ....9 O 30
Barfreston ....23 X 30
Bargoed ....18 K 28
Bargrennan ....52 G 18
Barham ....23 X 30
Barking ....30 X 27
Barking and Dagenham
  London Borough ....21 U 29
Barkston ....37 S 25
Barkway ....29 U 28
Barlaston ....35 N 25
Barlborough ....44 Q 24
Barlestone ....36 P 26
Barley *North Hertfordshire* ....29 U 27
Barley *Pendle* ....42 N 22
Barlow ....43 P 24
Barmby on the Marsh ....44 R 22
Barming ....22 V 30
Barmouth / Abermaw ....33 H 25
Barmouth Bay ....33 H 25
Barmston ....51 T 21
Barnack ....37 S 26
Barnard Castle ....49 O 20
Barnby Dun ....44 Q 23
Barnby Moor
  East Riding of Yorks. ....50 R 22
Barnby Moor *Notts.* ....44 Q 23
Barnet *London Borough* ....21 T 29
Barnetby-le-Wold ....45 S 23
Barney ....38 W 25
Barnham ....30 W 26
Barnham Broom ....38 X 26
Barnhill ....80 J 11
Barnhills ....52 E 18
Barningham ....49 O 20
Barnoldswick ....49 N 22
Barnsley ....43 P 23
Barnstaple ....7 H 30
Barnton ....42 M 24
Barnwell ....29 S 26
Barr ....52 F 18
Barra ....70 X 13
Barra (Sound of) ....70 X 12
Barra Head ....70 X 13
Barregarrow ....46 G 21
Barrhead ....60 G 16
Barrhill ....52 F 18
Barri / Barry ....18 K 29
Barrington ....8 L 31
Barrisdale ....72 D 12
Barrisdale Bay ....72 D 12
Barrmill ....60 G 16
Barrock ....86 K 8
Barrow ....30 V 27
Barrow Burn ....63 N 17
Barrow Gurney ....18 L 29
Barrow-in-Furness ....47 K 21
Barrow-upon-Humber ....45 S 22
Barrow-upon-Soar ....36 Q 25
Barrowby ....36 R 25
Barrowford ....43 N 22
Barry *Angus* ....69 L 14
Barry / Barri
  Vale of Glamorgan ....18 K 29
Barsham ....31 Y 26
Barston ....27 O 26
Bartestree ....26 M 27
Barton Eden ....49 P 20
Barton *Lancs.* ....42 L 22
Barton-le-Clay ....29 S 28
Barton le Willows ....50 R 21
Barton Mills ....30 V 26
Barton-on-Sea ....9 P 31
Barton-under-Needwood ....35 O 25
Barton-upon-Humber ....44 S 22
Barvas ....82 A 8
Barwell ....36 P 26
Barwick-in-Elmet ....43 P 22
Barwick ....8 L 31
Baschurch ....34 L 25
Bashall Eaves ....42 M 22
Basildon *Berks.* ....20 Q 29
Basildon *Essex* ....22 V 29
Basing ....20 Q 30
Basingstoke ....20 Q 30
Baslow ....43 P 24
Bass Rock ....69 M 15
Bassenthwaite ....54 K 19
Bassingham ....37 S 24
Baston ....37 S 25
Bastwick ....39 Y 25
Batcombe ....8 M 31
Bath ....19 M 29
Bathampton ....19 N 29
Batheaston ....19 N 29
Bathgate ....61 J 16
Batley ....43 P 22

Battle ....12 V 31
Baumber ....45 T 24
Bawburgh ....39 X 26
Bawdeswell ....38 X 25
Bawdsey ....31 Y 27
Bawtry ....44 Q 23
Baycliff ....48 K 21
Baydon ....19 P 29
Bayhead ....76 X 11
Bayston Hill ....34 L 25
Beachampton ....28 R 27
Beachy Head ....12 U 31
Beacon (The) ....2 E 33
Beacon End ....30 W 28
Beaconsfield ....21 S 29
Beadlam ....50 R 21
Beadnell Bay ....63 P 17
Beaford ....7 H 31
Beal ....63 O 16
Beaminster ....8 L 31
Beamish Hall ....56 P 19
Beamsley ....49 O 22
Bearsden ....67 G 16
Bearsted ....22 V 30
Beattock ....61 J 18
Beauchief ....43 P 24
Beaufort ....18 K 28
Beaulieu ....10 P 31
Beauly ....79 G 11
Beauly Firth ....79 G 11
Beaumaris ....40 H 23
Beaumont ....54 K 19
Beaupré Castle ....17 J 29
Bebington ....42 L 23
Beccles ....31 Y 26
Beckfoot ....54 J 19
Beckingham ....44 R 23
Beckington ....19 N 30
Beckley ....12 V 31
Beckton ....21 U 29
Bedale ....50 P 21
Beddau ....17 J 29
Beddgelert ....33 H 24
Beddingham ....11 U 31
Bedford ....29 S 27
Bedgebury Pinetum ....12 V 30
Bedlington ....56 P 18
Bedlinog ....17 K 28
Bedrule ....62 M 17
Bedwas ....18 K 29
Bedworth ....28 P 26
Bee (Loch) ....76 X 11
Beer ....5 K 31
Beeston ....36 Q 25
Beeswing ....53 I 18
Begdbroke ....20 Q 28
Beguildy ....26 K 26
Beighton ....44 P 23
Beinn a' Ghlò ....74 I 13
Beinn a' Mheadhoin (Loch) ....78 F 12
Beinn Dearg *Highland* ....78 F 10
Beinn Dearg
  Perthshire and Kinross ....73 I 13
Beinn Heasgarnich ....67 G 14
Beinn Ime ....66 F 15
Beith ....60 G 16
Belbroughton ....27 N 26
Belchford ....45 T 24
Belford ....63 O 17
Belhelvie ....75 N 12
Bellabeg ....74 K 12
Bellanoch ....65 D 15
Bellingham ....55 N 18
Bellshill
  Berwick-upon-Tweed ....63 O 17
Bellshill *North Lanarkshire* ..60 H 16
Belmont ....87 R 1
Belnacraig ....74 K 12
Belnahua ....65 C 15
Belper ....36 P 24
Belsay ....56 O 18
Belstead ....31 X 27
Belstone ....4 I 31
Belton *Lincs.* ....37 S 25
Belton *Norfolk* ....39 Y 26
Belton *North Lincs.* ....44 R 23
Belton *Rutland* ....36 R 26
Belvoir ....36 R 25
Bembridge ....10 Q 31
Bempton ....51 T 21
Ben Alder ....73 G 13
Ben Alder Lodge ....73 G 13
Ben Armine Forest ....85 H 9
Ben Armine Lodge ....85 H 9
Ben Chonzie ....67 I 14
Ben Cruachan ....65 E 14
Ben-damph Forest ....78 D 11

Ben Hope ....84 G 8
Ben Klibreck ....84 G 9
Ben Lawers ....67 H 14
Ben Ledi ....67 H 15
Ben Lomond ....66 G 15
Ben Loyal ....84 G 8
Ben Macdui ....74 I 12
Ben More *Argyll and Bute* ....65 B 14
Ben More *Stirling* ....67 G 14
Ben More Assynt ....84 F 9
Ben Nevis ....72 E 13
Ben Starav ....66 E 14
Ben Vorlich ....67 H 14
Ben Wyvis ....79 G 10
Benbecula ....76 X 11
Benbuie ....60 H 18
Benderloch *Argyll and Bute* ....65 D 14
Benderloch *Mountain* ....65 E 14
Bendronaig Lodge ....78 E 11
Benenden ....12 V 30
Benfleet ....22 V 29
Benigton ....37 U 25
Benllech ....40 H 23
Benmore ....67 G 14
Benmore Lodge ....84 F 9
Benson ....20 Q 29
Bentley *Doncaster* ....44 Q 23
Bentley *East Hampshire* ....20 R 30
Bentpath ....54 K 18
Bentworth ....10 Q 30
Benwick ....29 T 26
Beoraid (Loch) ....72 D 13
Bere Alston ....3 H 32
Bere Ferrers ....3 H 32
Bere Regis ....9 N 31
Berkeley ....18 M 28
Berkhamsted ....21 S 28
Berneray *near Barra* ....70 X 13
Berneray *near North Uist* ....76 Y 10
Bernice ....66 E 15
Bernisdale ....77 B 11
Berriew ....34 K 26
Berrington Hall ....26 L 27
Berrow ....18 K 30
Berry Head ....4 J 32
Berry Hill ....18 M 28
Berry Pomeroy ....4 J 32
Berrynarbor ....17 H 30
Bervie Bay ....75 N 13
Berwick-St. John ....9 N 31
Berwick-upon-Tweed ....63 O 16
Berwyn ....33 J 25
Bessacarr ....44 Q 23
Bethel ....33 H 24
Bethersden ....12 W 30
Bethesda ....33 H 24
Betley ....35 M 24
Bettisfield ....34 L 25
Bettws Cedewain ....34 K 26
Bettws Evan ....15 G 27
Bettws Gwerfil Goch ....33 J 24
Bettws-y-Coed ....33 I 24
Betws yn Rhos ....41 J 23
Beulah *near Cardigan* ....15 G 27
Beulah
  near Llandrindod-Wells ....25 J 27
Beverley ....45 S 22
Beverstone ....19 N 29
Bewaldeth ....54 K 19
Bewcastle ....55 L 18
Bewdley ....27 N 26
Bewholme ....51 T 22
Bexhill ....12 V 31
Bexley *London Borough* ....21 U 29
Beyton ....30 W 27
Bhaid-Luachraich (Loch) ....78 D 10
Bhealaich (Loch') ....84 G 9
Bhraoin (Loch a') ....78 E 10
Bhrollum (Loch) ....82 A 10
Bibury ....19 O 28
Bicester ....28 Q 28
Bicker ....37 T 25
Bickington ....4 I 32
Bickleigh *Mid Devon* ....7 J 31
Bickleigh *South Hams* ....4 H 32
Bicton ....34 L 25
Bicton gardens ....5 K 31
Biddenden ....12 V 30
Biddenham ....29 S 27
Biddestone ....19 N 29
Biddulph ....35 N 24
Bidean nam Bian ....72 E 14
Bideford ....6 H 30
Bidford ....27 O 27
Bieldside ....75 N 12
Bierton ....20 R 28

Big Corlae ....60 H 18
Bigbury ....4 I 33
Bigbury-on-Sea ....4 I 33
Biggar *Barrow-in-Furness* ....47 K 21
Biggar *South Lanarkshire* ....61 J 17
Biggin Hill ....21 U 30
Biggleswade ....29 T 27
Bignor ....11 S 31
Bildeston ....30 W 27
Bildsgreen ....27 M 26
Bill of Portland ....8 M 32
Billericay ....22 V 29
Billesdon ....36 R 26
Billingborough ....37 S 25
Billinge ....42 L 23
Billingford ....57 Q 20
Billinghay ....37 T 24
Billingshurst ....11 S 30
Billingsley ....27 M 26
Billington ....42 M 22
Billockby ....39 Y 26
Billy Row ....56 O 19
Bilsborrow ....42 L 22
Bilsington ....12 W 30
Bilston ....35 N 26
Bilton ....45 T 22
Bimbister ....86 K 6
Binbrook ....45 T 23
Binfield ....20 R 29
Bingham ....36 R 25
Bingley ....43 O 22
Binham ....38 W 25
Binns (The) ....68 J 16
Binsted ....10 R 30
Birchington ....23 X 29
Birdham ....10 R 31
Birdingbury ....28 P 27
Birdwell ....43 P 23
Birdworld ....10 R 30
Birgham ....62 N 17
Birkdale ....42 K 23
Birkenhead ....42 K 23
Birkin ....44 Q 22
Birling Gap ....12 U 31
Birmingham ....27 O 26
Birsay ....86 K 6
Birsemore ....75 L 12
Birstall ....36 Q 25
Birtley *Gateshead* ....56 P 19
Birtley *Tynedale* ....55 N 18
Birtsmorton Court ....27 N 27
Bisham ....20 R 29
Bishop Auckland ....56 P 20
Bishop Burton ....44 S 22
Bishop Monkton ....50 P 21
Bishop Sutton ....18 M 29
Bishop Thornton ....50 P 21
Bishop Wilton ....50 R 22
Bishops Cannings ....19 O 29
Bishop's Castle ....26 L 26
Bishop's Caundle ....9 M 31
Bishop's Cleeve ....27 N 28
Bishop's Itchington ....28 P 27
Bishop's Lydeard ....8 K 30
Bishop's Nympton ....7 I 31
Bishop's Palace
  near St. David's ....14 E 28
Bishop's Palace *near Tenby* ....16 F 28
Bishop's Stortford ....30 U 28
Bishop's Tachbrook ....28 P 27
Bishop's Tawton ....7 H 30
Bishop's Waltham ....10 Q 31
Bishopsteignton ....4 J 32
Bishopstocke ....10 Q 31
Bishopston ....15 H 29
Bishopstone *Salisbury* ....9 O 30
Bishopstone *Swindon* ....19 P 29
Bishopthorpe ....50 Q 22
Bishopton *Darlington* ....56 P 20
Bishopton *Renfrewshire* ....67 G 16
Bishton ....18 L 29
Bisley ....19 N 28
Bispham ....42 K 22
Bix ....20 R 29
Bixter ....87 P 3
Blaby ....36 Q 26
Black Bay ....59 D 17
Black Corries ....72 F 13
Black Down Hills ....8 K 31
Black Isle ....79 G 11
Black Mount ....66 F 14
Black Mountain ....25 I 28
Black Mountains ....26 K 28
Black Notley ....30 V 28
Black Torrington ....6 H 31
Black Water Valley ....78 F 11
Blackawton ....4 I 32

A B C D E F G H I J K L M N O P Q R S T U V W X Y Z

A
B
C
D
E
F
G
H
I
J
K
L
M
N
O
P
Q
R
S
T
U
V
W
X
Y
Z

Blackburn *Aberdeenshire* ...75 N 12
Blackburn *Lancs.* ....42 M 22
Blackburn *West Lothian* .....61 J 16
Blackfield ....10 P 31
Blackford *Cumbria* ....54 L 19
Blackford
   Perthshire and Kinross ..67 I 15
Blackhall ....57 Q 19
Blackhall Rocks ....57 Q 19
Blackhill *Aberdeenshire* ....81 O 11
Blackhill *Highland* ....77 A 11
Blacklunans ....74 J 13
Blackmoor Gate ....17 I 30
Blackmore ....22 U 28
Blackness Castle ....68 J 15
Blacko ....43 N 22
Blackpool ....42 K 22
Blackridge ....61 I 16
Blackthorn ....28 Q 28
Blacktoft ....44 R 22
Blackwater *Hart* ....20 R 30
Blackwater *Isle of Wight* ...10 Q 31
Blackwater (River) ....22 W 28
Blackwater Reservoir ....72 F 13
Blackwaterfoot ....59 D 17
Blackwell ....50 P 20
Blackwood ....18 K 29
Bladnoch ....52 G 19
Bladon ....20 P 28
Blaenannherch ....15 G 27
Blaenau Ffestiniog ....33 I 25
Blaenavon ....17 J 29
Blaengarw ....17 J 29
Blaengrwrach ....17 J 28
Blagdon ....18 L 30
Blaich ....72 E 13
Blaina ....18 K 28
Blair Atholl ....73 I 13
Blair Castle ....73 I 13
Blairgowrie ....68 J 14
Blairmore ....66 F 16
Blakeney *Glos.* ....18 M 28
Blakeney *Norfolk* ....38 X 25
Blakesley ....28 Q 27
Blamerino ....68 K 14
Blandford Forum ....9 N 31
Blanefield ....67 H 16
Blàr a Chaorainn ....72 E 13
Blarmachfoldach ....72 E 13
Blarnalearoch ....78 E 10
Blawith ....48 K 21
Blaxton ....44 R 23
Blaydon ....56 O 19
Bleadon ....18 L 30
Bleaklow Hill ....43 O 23
Blean ....23 X 30
Bleasby ....36 R 24
Blenheim Palace ....20 P 28
Bletchingdon ....20 Q 28
Bletchley ....28 R 27
Bletsoe ....29 S 27
Blewbury ....20 Q 29
Blickling ....39 X 25
Blickling Hall ....39 X 25
Blidworth ....36 Q 24
Blindley Heath ....21 T 30
Blisland ....3 F 32
Blisworth ....28 R 27
Blithe ....35 O 25
Blithfield Hall ....35 O 25
Blithfield Reservoir ....35 O 25
Blockley ....27 O 27
Blofield ....39 Y 26
Bloxham ....28 P 27
Blubberhouses ....49 O 22
Blue John Cavern ....43 O 23
Bluemull Sound ....87 Q 1
Blundeston ....39 Z 26
Blundellsands ....42 K 23
Blyth *Northumb.* ....56 P 18
Blyth *Notts.* ....44 Q 23
Blythburgh ....31 Y 27
Blythe Bridge ....35 N 25
Blyton ....44 R 23
Bo' Ness ....68 J 15
Boarhills ....69 L 15
Boat of Garten ....74 I 12
Boathvic ....79 G 10
Bocking Churchstreet ....30 V 28
Boddam ....81 O 11
Bodedern ....40 G 23
Bodelwyddan ....41 J 23
Bodenham ....26 L 27
Bodfari ....41 J 23
Bodfordd ....40 G 23
Bodham Street ....39 X 25
Bodiam Castle ....12 V 30

Bodicote ....28 Q 27
Bodmin ....3 F 32
Bodmin Moor ....3 G 32
Bodnant Garden ....41 I 23
Bognor Regis ....11 R 31
Bogue ....53 H 18
Boisdale ....70 X 12
Boisdale (Loch) ....70 Y 12
Bolam ....7 J 31
Bollington ....43 N 24
Bolney ....11 T 31
Bolsover ....44 Q 24
Boltby ....50 Q 21
Bolton *Alnwick* ....63 O 17
Bolton *Bolton* ....42 M 23
Bolton Abbey ....49 O 22
Bolton-by-Bowland ....49 N 22
Bolton-le-Sands ....48 L 21
Bolton on Swale ....50 P 20
Bolton-upon-Dearne ....44 Q 23
Bomere Heath ....34 L 25
Bonar Bridge ....79 G 10
Bonawe Quarries ....65 E 14
Bonby ....44 S 23
Boncath ....15 G 27
Bonchester Bridge ....62 M 17
Bonhill ....66 G 16
Bonnybridge ....67 I 16
Bonnyrigg ....61 K 16
Bont-faen / Cowbridge ......17 J 29
Bontgoch Elerch ....25 I 26
Bontnewydd ....32 H 24
Boosbeck ....50 R 20
Boot ....47 K 20
Bootle *Cumbria* ....47 J 21
Bootle *Merseyside* ....42 K 23
Border Forest Park (The) ...55 M 18
Bordogan ....32 G 24
Boreham ....22 V 28
Boreham Street ....12 V 31
Borehamwood ....21 T 29
Boreland ....54 K 18
Borgue
   Dumfries and Galloway ....53 H 19
Borgue *Highland* ....85 J 9
Borness ....53 H 19
Borough Green ....22 U 30
Boroughbridge ....50 P 21
Borreraig ....77 Z 11
Borrobol Forest ....85 H 9
Borrowash ....36 P 25
Borth ....25 H 26
Borve *Barra Isle* ....70 X 13
Borve *Eilean Siar* ....70 X 13
Borve *Isle of Lewis* ....82 A 8
Borve *South Harris* ....76 Y 10
Borwick ....48 L 21
Bosbury ....26 M 27
Boscastle ....6 F 31
Boscombe ....9 O 31
Bosham ....10 R 31
Bosherston ....16 F 29
Bosley ....35 N 24
Boston ....37 T 25
Boston Spa ....50 P 22
Boswinger ....3 F 33
Botesdale ....30 W 26
Bothamsall ....44 R 24
Bothel ....54 K 19
Bothwell ....60 H 16
Botley ....10 Q 31
Bottesfor *Melton* ....36 R 25
Bottesford
   North Lincolnshire ......44 S 23
Bottisham ....30 U 27
Bottwnnog ....32 G 25
Boughton ....36 Q 24
Boughton House ....29 R 26
Boughton Street ....22 W 30
Boulmer ....63 P 17
Boultham ....44 S 24
Bourn ....29 T 27
Bourne ....37 S 25
Bournemouth ....9 O 31
Bourton *North Dorset* ......9 N 30
Bourton
   Vale of White Horse .....19 P 29
Bourton-on-the-Water ....27 O 28
Bovey Tracey ....4 I 32
Bovington ....25 I 28
Bow ....7 I 31
Bow Street ....25 H 26
Bowden ....62 L 17
Bower *Highland* ....85 K 8

Bower *Tynedale* ....55 M 18
Bowerchalke ....9 O 30
Bowes ....49 N 20
Bowhill ....62 L 17
Bowland ....62 L 17
Bowland (Forest of) ....49 M 22
Bowmore ....58 B 16
Bowness ....48 L 20
Bowness-on-Solway ....54 K 19
Bowood House ....19 N 29
Box ....19 N 29
Box Hill ....21 T 30
Boxford *Babergh* ....30 W 27
Boxford *West Berkshire* ...20 P 29
Boxley ....22 V 30
Boxworth ....29 T 27
Boyton ....6 G 31
Bozeat ....29 R 27
Braaid ....46 G 21
Brabourne Lees ....12 W 30
Bracadale (Loch) ....77 A 12
Bracebridge Heath ....37 S 24
Brackley ....28 Q 27
Brackley Hatch ....28 Q 27
Bracknell ....20 R 29
Braco ....67 I 15
Bracora ....72 C 13
Bradan Resr (Loch) ....60 G 18
Bradfield *Sheffield* ....43 P 23
Bradfield *West Berkshire* ..20 Q 29
Bradford *Bradford* ....43 O 22
Bradford *Taunton Deane* ..8 K 31
Bradford Abbas ....8 M 31
Bradford-on-Avon ....19 N 29
Brading ....10 Q 31
Bradninch ....7 J 31
Bradpole ....5 L 31
Bradwell ....43 O 24
Bradwell-on-Sea ....22 W 28
Bradworthy ....6 G 31
Brae ....87 P 2
Brae of Achnahaird ....83 D 9
Brae Roy Lodge ....73 F 13
Braeantra ....79 G 10
Braedownie ....74 K 13
Braehead ....61 J 16
Braemar ....74 J 12
Braemore ....85 J 9
Braeriach ....74 I 12
Braeswick ....87 L 6
Brafferton Helperby ....50 Q 21
Bragar ....82 A 8
Braglenbeg ....65 D 15
Braich y Pwll ....32 F 25
Braidwood ....61 I 16
Bràigh Mór ....82 Y 9
Brailes ....28 P 27
Brailsford ....35 P 25
Braintree ....30 V 28
Braishfield ....10 P 30
Braithwaite ....44 Q 23
Braithwell ....44 Q 23
Bramcote ....36 Q 25
Bramfield ....31 Y 27
Bramford ....31 X 27
Bramhall ....43 N 23
Bramham ....43 P 22
Bramhope ....43 P 22
Bramley
   Basingstoke and Deane ..20 Q 30
Bramley
   South Yorks. ....44 Q 23
Bramley *Surrey* ....21 S 30
Brampton *Cambs.* ....29 T 27
Brampton *Cumbria* ....55 L 19
Brampton *Eden* ....55 M 20
Brampton *Rotherham.* .....43 P 23
Brampton *Suffolk* ....31 Y 26
Brampton Bryan ....26 L 26
Brancaster ....38 V 25
Branderburgh ....80 K 10
Brandesburton ....51 T 22
Brandon *Durham* ....56 P 19
Brandon *Suffolk* ....30 V 26
Brandsby ....50 Q 21
Branscombe ....5 K 31
Bransgore ....9 O 31
Branston ....37 S 25
Brant Broughton ....37 S 24
Brassington ....35 P 24
Bratton ....19 N 30
Bratton Clovelly ....6 H 31
Bratton Fleming ....17 I 30
Braughing ....29 U 28
Braunston *Daventry* ....28 Q 27
Braunston *Rutland* ....36 R 26
Braunton ....6 H 30
Bray-on-Thames ....21 R 29

Bray Shop ....3 G 32
Braybrooke ....28 R 26
Brayford ....7 I 30
Brayton ....44 Q 22
Breaclete ....82 Z 9
Breadalbane ....67 G 14
Breage ....2 D 33
Bream ....18 M 28
Breamore House ....9 O 31
Brean ....18 K 30
Breasclete ....82 Z 9
Breaston ....36 Q 25
Brechin ....75 M 13
Breckland ....30 V 26
Brecon / Aberhonddu ....25 J 28
Brecon Beacons
   National Park ....25 J 28
Bredbury ....43 N 23
Brede ....12 V 31
Bredenbury ....26 M 27
Bredgar ....22 W 30
Bredon ....27 N 27
Bredwardine ....26 L 27
Bremhill ....19 N 29
Brendon ....12 V 30
Brendon Hills ....7 J 30
Brenig Reservoir ....33 J 24
Brenish ....82 Y 9
Brent *London Borough* ....21 T 29
Brent Knoll ....18 L 30
Brent Pelham ....29 U 28
Brentwood ....22 U 29
Brenzett ....12 W 30
Brereton ....35 O 25
Bressay ....87 Q 3
Bretford ....28 P 26
Bretherton ....42 L 22
Brewham ....9 M 30
Brewlands Bridge ....74 K 13
Brewood ....35 N 25
Bride ....46 G 20
Bridestowe ....4 H 31
Bridge ....23 X 30
Bridge of Alford ....75 L 12
Bridge of Allan ....67 I 15
Bridge of Avon ....80 J 11
Bridge of Balgie ....73 H 14
Bridge of Brown ....74 J 12
Bridge of Buchat ....74 L 12
Bridge of Craigisla ....74 K 13
Bridge of Dee ....53 I 19
Bridge of Don ....75 N 12
Bridge of Dun ....75 M 13
Bridge of Dye ....75 M 13
Bridge of Earn ....68 J 14
Bridge of Ericht ....73 G 13
Bridge of Gairn ....74 K 12
Bridge of Gaur ....73 G 13
Bridge of Orchy ....66 F 14
Bridge of Weir ....60 G 16
Bridge Trafford ....42 L 24
Bridgemary ....10 Q 31
Bridgend *Aberdeenshire* ..80 L 11
Bridgend *Angus* ....75 L 13
Bridgend *Argyll and Bute* ..65 D 15
Bridgend *Islay* ....58 B 16
Bridgend
   Perthshire and Kinross ..68 J 14
Bridgend / Pen-y-bont ....17 J 29
Bridgend of Lintrathen ......74 K 13
Bridgerule ....6 G 31
Bridgham ....30 W 26
Bridgnorth ....27 M 26
Bridgwater ....8 L 30
Bridlington ....51 T 21
Bridport ....5 L 31
Brierfield ....43 N 22
Brierley ....43 P 23
Brierley Hill ....27 N 26
Brigg ....44 S 23
Brigham ....54 J 20
Brighouse ....43 O 22
Brighstone ....10 P 32
Brighstone Forest ....10 P 32
Brightling ....12 V 31
Brightlingsea ....22 X 28
Brighton ....11 T 31
Brightwell ....20 Q 29
Brigstock ....29 S 26
Brill ....20 Q 28
Brimfield ....26 L 27
Brimham Rocks ....49 O 21
Brimington ....43 P 24
Brimpsfield ....19 N 28
Brimpton ....20 Q 29
Brinkburn Priory ....63 O 18
Brinkley ....30 V 27

Brinklow ....28 P 26
Brinkworth ....19 O 29
Brinyan ....86 L 6
Brisley ....38 W 25
Brislington ....18 M 29
Bristol ....18 M 29
Briston ....38 X 25
Briton Ferry ....17 I 29
Brittle (Loch) ....71 B 12
Brittwell Salome ....20 Q 29
Brixham ....4 J 32
Brixton ....4 H 32
Brixworth ....28 R 27
Brize Norton ....20 P 28
Broad Bay ....83 B 9
Broad Blunsdon ....19 O 29
Broad Chalke ....9 O 30
Broad Haven ....14 E 28
Broad Hinton ....19 O 29
Broad Law ....61 J 17
Broad Oak ....12 V 31
Broadbridge Heath ....11 S 30
Broadclyst ....7 J 31
Broadford ....77 C 12
Broadlands ....10 P 31
Broadmayne ....9 M 31
Broadstairs ....23 Y 29
Broadstone ....9 O 31
Broadwas ....27 M 27
Broadway ....27 O 27
Broadwell Ho ....55 N 19
Broadwey ....8 M 32
Broadwindsor ....8 L 31
Broadwoodwidger ....6 H 31
Brochel ....77 B 11
Brockdish ....31 X 26
Brockenhurst ....10 P 31
Brockley ....18 L 29
Brockworth ....19 N 28
Brodick ....59 E 17
Brodick Bay ....59 E 17
Brodick Castle ....59 E 17
Brodie Castle ....79 I 11
Brodsworth ....44 Q 23
Brodsworth Hall ....44 Q 23
Brokenborough ....19 N 29
Brolass ....65 B 14
Bromborough ....42 L 24
Brome ....31 X 26
Bromfield ....26 L 26
Bromham *Bedford* ....29 S 27
Bromham *Kennet* ....19 N 29
Bromley *London Borough* ..21 U 29
Brompton *Kent* ....22 V 29
Brompton *near Northallerton* ..50 P 20
Brompton-by-Sawdon ....51 S 21
Brompton on Swale ....49 O 20
Brompton Ralph ....7 K 30
Brompton Regis ....7 J 30
Bromsgrove ....27 N 26
Bromyard ....26 M 27
Bronllys ....26 K 27
Bronwydd ....22 W 30
Brook ....19 Y 26
Brooke ....39 Y 26
Brookmans Park ....21 T 28
Broom (Loch) ....78 E 10
Broomfield *Chelmsford* ....22 V 28
Broomfield *Sedgemoor* ....8 K 30
Broomfleet ....44 S 22
Broomhaugh ....56 O 19
Brora ....85 I 9
Broseley ....34 M 26
Brotherton ....44 Q 22
Brotton ....57 R 20
Brough
   East Riding of Yorkshire ..44 S 22
Brough *Eden* ....49 N 20
Brough *Highland* ....86 J 8
Brough Head ....86 J 6
Brough Lodge ....87 R 2
Broughead ....80 J 10
Broughton *Cumbria* ....54 J 19
Broughton
   Flintshire / Sir y Fflint ..34 L 24
Broughton *Hants.* ....10 P 30
Broughton *Lancs.* ....42 L 22
Broughton *North Lincs.* ...44 S 23
Broughton *Northants.* ......28 R 26
Broughton *Oxon.* ....28 P 27
Broughton *Scottish Borders* ..61 J 17
Broughton-in-Furness ....47 K 21
Broughton Mills ....47 K 21
Broughton Moor ....54 J 19
Broughton Poggs ....19 P 28
Broughty Ferry ....69 L 14
Brownhills ....35 O 26
Brownsea Island ....9 O 31

Broxbourne ....21 T 28
Broxburn ....68 J 16
Bruar Lodge ....73 I 13
Bruichladdich ....58 A 16
Brundall ....39 Y 26
Brushford ....7 J 30
Bruton ....8 M 30
Brydekirk ....54 K 18
Brymbo ....34 K 24
Bryn-Henllan ....24 F 27
Brynamman ....17 I 28
Brynbuga / Usk ....18 L 28
Bryncethin ....17 J 29
Bryneglwys ....34 K 24
Bryngwran ....40 G 23
Bryngwyn ....26 K 27
Brynhoffnant ....15 G 27
Brynmawr ....18 K 28
Brynsiencyn ....32 H 24
Brynteg ....40 H 23
Bualintur ....71 B 12
Bubwith ....44 R 22
Buccleuch ....61 K 17
Buchanty ....67 I 14
Buchlyvie ....67 H 15
Buckden *Cambs.* ....29 T 27
Buckden *North Yorks.* ......49 N 21
Buckfast ....4 I 32
Buckfast Abbey ....4 I 32
Buckfastleigh ....4 I 32
Buckhaven ....68 K 15
Buckhorn Weston ....9 M 30
Buckie ....80 L 10
Buckingham ....28 R 27
Buckland *Herts.* ....29 T 28
Buckland *Oxon.* ....20 P 28
Buckland Abbey ....4 H 32
Buckland Brewer ....6 H 31
Buckland Dinham ....19 M 30
Buckland in-the-Moor ....4 I 32
Buckland Newton ....8 M 31
Buckland St. Mary ....8 K 31
Bucklebury ....20 Q 29
Bucklers Hard ....10 P 31
Buckley / Bwcle ....34 K 24
Buckminster ....36 R 25
Bucknall ....37 T 24
Bucknell ....26 L 26
Bucks green ....11 S 30
Bucksburn ....75 N 12
Bude ....6 G 31
Budleigh Salterton ....5 K 32
Bugbrooke ....28 Q 27
Bugle ....3 F 32
Bugthorpe ....50 R 21
Buildwas Abbey ....34 M 26
Builth Wells /
   Llanfair-ym-Muallt ....25 J 27
Bulford ....19 O 30
Bulkéley ....34 L 24
Bulkington ....28 P 26
Bulwell ....36 Q 24
Bulwick ....37 S 26
Bunarkaig ....72 F 13
Bunessan ....64 B 15
Bungay ....31 Y 26
Bunnahabhainn ....64 B 16
Bunny ....36 Q 25
Buntingford ....29 T 28
Burbage *Leics.* ....28 P 26
Burbage *Wilts.* ....19 O 29
Burchett's Green ....20 R 29
Bures ....30 W 28
Burford ....19 P 28
Burgess Hill ....11 T 31
Burgh-by-Sands ....54 K 19
Burgh Castle ....39 Y 26
Burgh-le-Marsh ....38 U 24
Burgh-St. Peter ....39 Y 26
Burghead ....80 J 10
Burghfield ....20 Q 29
Burghill ....26 L 27
Burghley House ....37 S 26
Burham ....22 V 30
Burley ....9 O 31
Burley-in-Wharfedale ....49 O 22
Burlton ....34 L 25
Burneside ....48 L 20
Burneston ....50 P 21
Burnfoot ....62 L 17
Burnham ....21 S 29
Burnham Market ....38 W 25
Burnham Moor ....22 W 29
Burnham-on-Crouch ....22 W 29
Burnham-on-Sea ....18 L 30
Burnhaven ....81 O 11
Burnhope ....56 O 19
Burniston ....51 S 21

Burnley .... 43 N 22
Burntisland .... 68 K 15
Burrafirth .... 87 R 1
Burravoe .... 87 Q 2
Burray .... 87 L 7
Burrelton .... 68 K 14
Burringham .... 44 R 23
Burrington *North Devon* ...7 I 31
Burrington *North Somerset* . 18 L 30
Burrough Green .... 30 V 27
Burrow Head .... 53 G 19
Burry Port /Porth Tywyn ... 15 H 28
Burscough .... 42 L 23
Burscough Bridge .... 42 L 23
Burshill .... 51 S 22
Bursledon .... 10 Q 31
Burslem .... 35 N 24
Burstwick .... 45 T 22
Burton *Christchurch* ....9 O 31
Burton *Ellesmere*
    Port and Neston .... 48 L 21
Burton *South Lakeland* .. 48 L 21
Burton *Wrecsam / Wrexham* 34 L 24
Burton Agnes .... 51 T 21
Burton Bradstock .... 5 L 31
Burton Constable Hall ... 45 T 22
Burton Fleming .... 51 S 21
Burton in Lonsdale ...... 49 M 21
Burton Joyce .... 36 Q 25
Burton Latimer .... 29 R 26
Burton Leonard .... 50 P 21
Burton Pidsea .... 45 T 22
Burton-upon-Stather .... 44 R 23
Burton-upon-Trent ...... 35 O 25
Burwarton .... 26 M 26
Burwash .... 12 V 31
Burwell *Cambs.* .... 30 U 27
Burwell *Lincs.* .... 45 U 24
Bury *Bury* .... 42 N 23
Bury *Chichester* .... 11 S 31
Bury St. Edmunds ...... 30 W 27
Busby .... 60 H 16
Buscot .... 19 P 28
Bushey .... 21 S 29
Bute (Island of) .... 59 E 16
Bute (Kyles of) .... 59 E 16
Bute (Sound of) .... 59 E 16
Butleigh .... 8 L 30
Butley .... 31 Y 27
Butt of Lewis .... 83 B 8
Buttercrambe .... 50 R 21
Buttermere .... 47 K 20
Butterstone .... 68 J 14
Buttington .... 34 K 25
Buxted .... 12 U 31
Buxton *Derbs.* .... 43 O 24
Buxton *Norfolk* .... 39 X 25
Bwcle / Buckley .... 34 K 24
Bwlch .... 26 K 28
Bwlch Oerddrws .... 33 I 25
Bwlch y Ffridd .... 33 J 26
Bwlch-y-Groes .... 25 I 28
Bwlch-y-Sarnau .... 25 J 26
Bwlchgwyn .... 34 K 24
Bwlchllan .... 25 H 27
Byfield .... 28 Q 27
Byfleet .... 21 S 30
Byland Abbey .... 50 Q 21
Byrness .... 62 M 18

C

Cabrach .... 80 K 12
Cadair Idris .... 33 I 25
Caddington .... 29 S 28
Caddonfoot .... 62 L 17
Cadhay .... 5 K 31
Cadishead .... 42 M 23
Cadnam .... 10 P 31
Cadney .... 44 S 23
Cadwell Park .... 45 T 24
Caerau .... 17 J 29
Caerdydd / Cardiff ...... 18 K 29
Caerffili / Caerphilly ... 18 K 29
Caerfyrddin / Carmarthen ..15 H 28
Caergwrle .... 34 K 24
Caergybi / Holyhead .... 40 G 23
Caerlaverock Castle .... 53 J 19
Caerleon .... 18 L 29
Caernarfon .... 32 H 24
Caernarfon Bay .... 32 G 24
Caerphilly / Caerffili ... 18 K 29
Caersws .... 25 J 26
Caerwent .... 18 L 29
Caerwys .... 41 K 23
Cailliness Point .... 52 F 19
Cairn Edward Forest ... 53 H 18
Cairn Gorm .... 74 J 12

Cairn Table .... 60 H 17
Cairn Toul .... 74 I 12
Cairnborrow .... 80 L 11
Cairndow .... 66 F 15
Cairngaan .... 52 F 20
Cairngarroch .... 52 E 19
Cairnie .... 80 L 11
Cairnpapple Hill .... 67 J 16
Cairnsmore of Carsphairn ..60 H 18
Cairnsmore of Fleet .... 53 G 19
Cairnryan .... 52 E 19
Cairraig Fhada .... 58 B 17
Caister-on-Sea .... 39 Z 26
Caistor .... 45 T 23
Calbourne .... 10 P 31
Caldbeck .... 54 K 19
Caldecott .... 36 R 26
Calder (Loch) .... 85 J 8
Calder Bridge .... 47 J 20
Calder Mains .... 85 J 8
Caldercruix .... 61 I 16
Calderdale .... 43 N 22
Caldermill .... 60 H 17
Caldey Island .... 15 F 28
Caldicot .... 18 L 29
Caldwell .... 49 O 20
Calf of Man .... 46 F 21
Calfsound .... 87 L 6
Calgary .... 71 B 14
Calgary Bay .... 71 B 14
Caliach Point .... 71 B 14
Calke Abbey .... 36 P 25
Callander .... 67 H 15
Callater (Glen) .... 74 J 13
Callington .... 3 H 32
Calne .... 19 N 29
Calow .... 43 P 24
Calstock .... 3 H 32
Calthwaite .... 55 L 19
Calvay .... 70 Y 12
Calver .... 43 P 24
Calverton .... 36 Q 24
Calvine .... 73 I 13
Cam .... 29 U 27
Cam Loch .... 84 E 9
Camas Chil Mhalieu ... 72 D 14
Camas-luinie .... 78 D 12
Camasnacroise .... 72 D 14
Camastianavaig .... 77 B 11
Camber .... 12 W 31
Camberley .... 20 R 30
Camblesforth .... 44 Q 22
Cambo .... 56 O 18
Cambois .... 56 P 18
Camborne .... 2 E 33
Cambrian Mountains ... 25 I 27
Cambridge .... 29 U 27
Cambusbarron .... 67 I 15
Cambuskenneth .... 67 I 15
Camden *London Borough* ...21 T 29
Camelford .... 6 F 32
Cammachmore .... 75 N 12
Campbeltown .... 59 D 17
Campsie Fells .... 67 H 15
Camptown .... 62 M 17
Campville .... 35 P 25
Camrose .... 24 E 28
Camusnagaul .... 78 E 10
Candlesby .... 37 U 24
Canewdon .... 22 W 29
Canisbay .... 86 K 8
Canna .... 71 A 12
Cannich .... 78 F 11
Cannich (Glen) .... 78 F 11
Cannington .... 8 K 30
Cannock .... 35 N 25
Canonbie .... 54 L 18
Canons Ashby .... 28 Q 27
Canterbury .... 23 X 30
Cantley .... 39 Y 26
Canvey Island .... 22 V 29
Caol .... 72 E 13
Caolas a' Mhòrain ...... 76 Y 10
Caoles .... 70 Z 14
Caolis .... 70 X 13
Caolisport (Loch) .... 65 D 16
Cape Cornwall .... 2 C 33
Cape Wrath .... 84 E 8
Capel .... 11 T 30
Capel Curig .... 33 I 24
Capel Garmon .... 33 I 24
Capel Le Ferne .... 13 X 30
Capel St. Mary .... 31 X 27
Capel-y-Ffin .... 26 K 28
Capesthorne Hall .... 43 N 24
Capheaton .... 56 O 18
Cappercleuch .... 61 K 17

Caputh .... 68 J 14
Cara Island .... 58 C 17
Carbis Bay .... 2 D 33
Carbost *Minginish* .... 77 A 12
Carbost *Trotternish* ... 77 B 11
Cardenden .... 68 K 15
Cardiff / Caerdydd ..... 18 K 29
Cardigan / Aberteifi ... 15 G 27
Cardigan Bay .... 24 G 26
Cardington .... 34 L 26
Cardinham .... 3 G 32
Cardrona .... 61 K 17
Cardross .... 66 G 16
Cardurnock .... 54 K 19
Carew .... 15 F 28
Carfraemill .... 62 L 16
Cargill .... 68 J 14
Carhampton .... 7 J 30
Carie .... 73 H 13
Carinish .... 76 Y 11
Carisbrooke .... 10 Q 31
Cark .... 48 L 21
Carlbt .... 37 S 25
Carleen .... 2 D 33
Carleton .... 49 N 22
Carlisle .... 55 L 19
Carlops .... 61 J 16
Carloway .... 82 Z 9
Carlton *Bedford* .... 29 S 27
Carlton *Hambleton* .... 50 Q 20
Carlton
    Hinckley and Bosworth ..36 P 26
Carlton *North Yorks.* .. 44 Q 22
Carlton *Notts.* .... 36 Q 25
Carlton Colville .... 31 Z 26
Carlton in Lindrick ..... 44 Q 23
Carlton-on-Trent .... 36 R 24
Carluke .... 61 I 16
Carmarthen / Caerfyrddin ...15 H 28
Carmel Head .... 40 G 22
Carmunnock .... 60 H 16
Carmyllie .... 69 L 14
Carn Ban .... 73 H 12
Carn Coire na h-Easgainn ..73 H 12
Carn Eige .... 78 E 12
Carn Glas-choire .... 79 I 11
Carn Mairg .... 73 H 14
Carnach .... 78 E 12
Carnaby .... 51 T 21
Carnach .... 78 E 12
Carnassarie Castle ..... 65 D 15
Carnedd Llewelyn ...... 33 I 24
Carnforth .... 48 L 21
Carno .... 33 J 26
Carnock .... 68 J 15
Carnoustie .... 69 L 14
Carnwath .... 61 J 16
Carradale .... 59 D 17
Carradale Bay .... 59 D 17
Carrbridge .... 79 I 12
Carrick .... 66 F 15
Carrick Roads .... 2 E 33
Carron .... 80 K 11
Carron (Loch) .... 77 C 11
Carron Bridge .... 67 H 15
Carrshield .... 55 N 19
Carrutherstown .... 54 J 18
Carsaig .... 65 C 15
Carse of Gowrie .... 68 K 14
Carseriggan .... 52 G 19
Carsethorn .... 53 J 19
Carsluith .... 53 G 19
Carsphairn .... 53 H 18
Carstairs .... 61 I 16
Carterton .... 19 P 28
Carterway Heads .... 56 O 19
Carthew .... 3 F 32
Carthorpe .... 50 P 21
Cartmel .... 48 L 21
Carville .... 56 P 19
Cas-Gwent / Chepstow .. 18 M 29
Cashlie .... 67 G 14
Casnewydd / Newport ... 18 L 29
Cassington .... 20 P 28
Cassley (Glen) .... 84 F 9
Castell-Nedd / Neath ... 17 I 29
Castell Newydd Emlyn /
    Newcastle Emlyn ... 15 G 27
Castell-y-Rhingyll ...... 15 H 28
Castle Acre .... 38 W 25
Castle Ashby .... 28 R 27
Castle Bolton .... 49 O 21
Castle Bytham .... 37 S 25
Castle Campbell .... 67 I 15
Castle Cary .... 8 M 30
Castle Combe .... 19 N 29
Castle Donington .... 36 P 25
Castle Douglas .... 53 I 19

Castle Drogo .... 4 I 31
Castle Eaton .... 19 O 29
Castle Fraser .... 75 M 12
Castle frome .... 26 M 27
Castle Hedingham ...... 30 V 28
Castle Howard .... 50 R 21
Castle Kennedy .... 52 F 19
Castle Lachlan .... 65 E 15
Castle Loch .... 52 F 19
Castle Rising .... 38 V 25
Castlebay .... 70 X 13
Castleford .... 43 P 22
Castlemartin .... 16 E 29
Castlerigg .... 54 K 20
Castleton
    Casnewydd / Newport ...18 K 29
Castleton *Derbs.* ...... 43 O 23
Castleton *North Yorks.* .. 50 R 20
Castletown *Highland* ...85 J 8
Castletown *Isle of Man* . 46 G 21
Caston .... 38 W 26
Catacol .... 59 E 16
Cathcart Bay .... 59 D 16
Caterham .... 21 T 30
Catfield .... 39 Y 25
Catlodge .... 73 H 12
Caton .... 48 L 21
Catrine .... 60 H 17
Catterall .... 42 L 22
Catterick .... 50 P 20
Catterick Garrison ...... 49 O 20
Catterline .... 75 N 13
Cattistock .... 8 M 31
Catton *Broadland* ..... 39 X 26
Catton *Tynedale* ...... 55 N 19
Catworth .... 29 S 26
Cauldcleuch Head ...... 62 L 18
Cauldon .... 35 O 24
Caulkerbush .... 53 I 19
Cautley .... 49 M 20
Cava .... 86 K 7
Cavendish .... 30 V 27
Caversfield .... 28 Q 28
Caversham .... 20 R 29
Cawdor .... 79 I 11
Cawood .... 44 Q 22
Caxton .... 29 T 27
Caynham .... 26 M 26
Caythorpe .... 37 S 24
Cayton .... 51 S 21
Ceall (Loch nan) .... 71 C 13
Cefn Bryn .... 15 H 29
Cefn-Coed-y-cymmer ...17 J 28
Cefn-mawr .... 34 K 25
Cefn-y-Pant .... 15 G 28
Ceinewydd / New Quay ..24 G 27
Ceiriog (Vale of) .... 34 K 25
Cemaes .... 40 G 22
Cemaes Head .... 15 F 27
Cemmaes .... 33 I 26
Cemmaes road .... 33 I 26
Cenarth .... 15 G 27
Ceres .... 69 L 15
Cerne Abbas .... 8 M 31
Cerrigydrudion .... 33 J 24
Chacewater .... 2 E 33
Chacombe .... 28 Q 27
Chadderton .... 43 N 23
Chaddesden .... 36 P 25
Chaddington .... 28 P 28
Chadwell St. Mary ..... 22 V 29
Chagford .... 4 I 31
Chailey .... 11 T 31
Chàirn Bhain (Loch a') ...84 E 9
Chalfont St. Giles ...... 21 S 29
Chalfont St. Peter ...... 21 S 29
Chalford .... 19 N 28
Chalgrove .... 20 Q 29
Challacombe .... 7 I 30
Challoch .... 52 G 19
Challock .... 22 W 30
Chambercombe Manor ... 17 H 30
Chandler's Ford .... 10 P 31
Channel Islands 5
Chapel Brampton ...... 28 R 27
Chapel-en-le-Frith ..... 43 O 24
Chapel Haddlesey ...... 44 Q 22
Chapel le Dale .... 49 M 21
Chapel St. Leonards ... 45 V 24
Chapel Stile .... 48 K 20
Chapelhall .... 61 I 16
Chapelknowe .... 54 K 18
Chapelton .... 60 H 16
Chapeltown *Moray* ... 74 K 12
Chapeltown *Sheffield* . 43 P 23
Chapmanslade .... 19 N 30
Chard .... 8 L 31

Chardstock .... 8 L 31
Charfield .... 19 M 29
Charing .... 22 W 30
Charlbury .... 28 P 28
Charlecote *Park* .... 27 P 27
Charleston *Manor* .... 12 U 31
Charlestown *Highland* ...78 C 10
Charlestown *Restormel* . 3 F 33
Charlton .... 19 N 29
Charlton Horethorne ... 8 M 30
Charlton Kings .... 27 N 28
Charlton Marshall ...... 9 N 31
Charlton Musgrove ..... 9 M 30
Charlton on Otmoor ... 20 Q 28
Charlwood .... 11 T 30
Charminster .... 8 M 31
Charmouth .... 5 L 31
Charney Basset .... 20 P 29
Charsfield .... 31 X 27
Chartham .... 23 X 30
Chartridge .... 21 S 28
Chartwell .... 21 U 30
Chastleton .... 27 P 28
Chatburn .... 42 M 22
Chatham .... 22 V 29
Chatsworth House ...... 43 P 24
Chatteris .... 29 U 26
Chatto .... 62 M 17
Chawleigh .... 7 I 31
Cheadle *Gtr. Mches.* .. 43 N 23
Cheadle *Staffs.* .... 35 O 25
Checkendon .... 20 Q 29
Cheddar .... 18 L 30
Cheddar Gorge .... 18 L 30
Cheddington .... 21 S 28
Cheddleton .... 35 N 24
Chedington .... 8 L 31
Chedworth .... 19 O 28
Cheese Bay .... 76 Y 11
Chelford .... 42 N 24
Chellaston .... 36 P 25
Chelmarsh .... 27 M 26
Chelmsford .... 22 V 28
Cheltenham .... 27 N 28
Chelveston .... 29 S 27
Chelwood Gate .... 11 U 30
Chepstow / Cas-Gwent .. 18 L 29
Cherhill .... 19 O 29
Cherington *Cotswold* .. 19 N 28
Cherington
    Stratford-on-Avon ...27 P 27
Cheriton .... 10 Q 30
Cheriton Bishop .... 4 I 31
Cheriton Fitzpaine ..... 7 J 31
Cherry Burton .... 44 S 22
Chertsey .... 21 S 29
Cherwell (River) .... 28 Q 28
Cheselbourne .... 9 M 31
Chesham .... 21 S 28
Chesham Bois .... 21 S 28
Cheshunt .... 21 T 28
Chesil Beach .... 8 M 32
Chesley Hay .... 35 N 26
Chester .... 34 L 24
Chester-le-Street .... 56 P 19
Chesterfield .... 43 P 24
Chesters .... 62 M 17
Chesters Fort .... 55 N 18
Chesterton *Cambridge* . 29 U 27
Chesterton *Cherwell* .. 28 Q 28
Cheswardine .... 35 M 25
Cheswick .... 63 O 16
Cheviot (The) .... 63 N 17
Cheviot Hills (The) ..... 62 M 17
Chew Magna .... 18 M 29
Chew Stoke .... 18 M 29
Chewton Mendip .... 18 M 30
Chicheley .... 29 R 27
Chichester .... 10 R 31
Chickerell .... 5 M 32
Chicklade .... 9 N 30
Chiddingfold .... 11 S 30
Chiddingly .... 12 U 31
Chiddingstone .... 22 U 30
Chideock .... 5 L 31
Chieveley .... 20 Q 29
Chigwell .... 21 U 29
Chilcompton .... 18 M 30
Child Okeford .... 9 N 31
Childrey .... 20 P 29
Child's Ercall .... 34 M 25
Chilham .... 22 W 30
Chillingham .... 63 O 17
Chilmark .... 9 N 30
Chiltern Hills .... 20 R 29
Chilton *Sedgefield* ... 56 P 20

Chilton
    Vale of White Horse ... 20 Q 29
Chilton Folia .... 20 P 29
Chippenham
    East Cambridgeshire ...30 V 27
Chippenham
    North Wiltshire ...... 19 N 29
Chipping .... 42 M 22
Chipping Campden ..... 27 O 27
Chipping Norton .... 28 P 28
Chipping Ongar .... 22 U 28
Chipping Sodbury ...... 19 M 29
Chipping Warden .... 28 Q 27
Chirbury .... 34 K 26
Chirk .... 34 K 25
Chirk Castle .... 34 K 25
Chirmorie .... 52 F 18
Chirnside .... 63 N 16
Chirton .... 19 O 30
Chiseldon .... 19 O 29
Chislet .... 23 X 30
Chiswell Green .... 21 S 28
Chitterne .... 19 N 30
Chittlehamholt .... 7 I 31
Chittlehampton .... 7 I 30
Chobham .... 21 S 29
Choire (Loch) .... 84 H 9
Cholderton .... 9 O 30
Cholesbury .... 21 S 28
Chollerton .... 55 N 18
Cholsey .... 20 Q 29
Chon (Loch) .... 67 G 15
Chopwell .... 56 O 19
Chorley .... 42 M 23
Chorleywood .... 21 S 29
Christchurch *Christchurch* ..9 O 31
Christchurch *Fenland* .. 38 U 26
Christian Malford ...... 19 N 29
Christleton .... 34 L 24
Christmas Common .... 20 R 29
Christow .... 4 I 32
Chroisg (Loch a') ...... 78 E 11
Chudleigh .... 4 J 32
Chulmleigh .... 7 I 31
Church .... 42 M 22
Church Crookham ..... 20 R 30
Church Eaton .... 35 N 25
Church Enstone .... 28 P 28
Church Fenton .... 44 Q 22
Church Knowle .... 9 N 32
Church Leigh .... 35 O 25
Church Lench .... 27 O 27
Church Minshull .... 34 M 24
Church Stoke .... 34 K 26
Church Stretton .... 34 L 26
Churcham .... 19 M 28
Churchdown .... 27 N 28
Churchill *North Somerset* . 18 L 29
Churchill *Oxon.* .... 27 P 28
Churchingford .... 8 K 31
Churnet .... 35 N 24
Churnsike Lodge .... 55 M 18
Churston Ferrers .... 4 J 32
Churt .... 10 R 30
Chwilog .... 32 H 25
Cifynydd .... 17 K 29
Cilcain .... 34 K 24
Cilcennin .... 25 H 27
Cilgerran .... 15 G 27
Cilmery .... 25 J 27
Cilrhedyn .... 15 G 28
Cilybebyll .... 17 I 28
Cilycwn .... 25 I 27
Cinderford .... 18 M 28
Cirencester .... 19 O 28
City of London
    London Borough .... 21 T 29
Clachaig .... 66 E 16
Clachan *Argyll* .... 66 F 15
Clachan Kintyre .... 59 D 16
Clachan Mór .... 70 Z 14
Clachan of Campsie ... 67 H 16
Clachan of Glendaruel . 65 E 15
Clachtoll .... 83 E 9
Clackavoid .... 74 J 13
Clackmannan .... 67 I 15
Clacton-on-Sea .... 23 X 28
Claggain Bay .... 58 B 16
Claggan .... 71 C 14
Claidh (Loch) .... 82 A 10
Claigan .... 77 A 11
Clandon Park .... 21 S 30
Clanfield .... 10 Q 31
Claonel .... 84 G 9
Clapham *Beds.* .... 29 S 27
Clapham *North Yorks.* . 49 M 21
Clapton-in-Gordano ... 18 L 29

A B C D E F G H I J K L M N O P Q R S T U V W X Y Z

Clàr (Loch nan) .....85 H 9
Clarbeston Road .....24 F 28
Clare .....30 V 27
Clashindarroch .....80 L 11
Clashmore .....79 H 10
Clashnessie .....84 E 9
Clatt .....80 L 12
Clatteringshaws (Loch) .....53 H 18
Clauchlands Point .....59 E 17
Clavering .....29 U 28
Claverley .....27 N 26
Claverton Manor .....19 N 29
Clawdd-newydd .....33 J 24
Clawton .....6 G 31
Claxton Ryedale .....50 R 21
Claxton South Norfolk .....39 Y 26
Clay Cross .....36 P 24
Claydon .....31 X 27
Claydon House .....28 R 28
Claypole .....36 R 24
Clayton .....11 T 31
Clayton-le-Moors .....42 M 22
Clayton West .....43 P 23
Cleadale .....71 B 13
Cleadon .....57 P 19
Cleat .....70 X 12
Cleator Moor .....47 J 20
Cleckheaton .....43 O 22
Cleedownton .....26 M 26
Cleehill .....26 M 26
Cleethorpes .....45 T 23
Cleeve Abbey .....7 J 30
Cleeve Prior .....27 O 27
Clehonger .....26 L 27
Cleigh .....65 D 14
Clenchwarton .....38 V 25
Clent .....27 N 26
Cleobury Mortimer .....26 M 26
Cleobury North .....26 M 26
Clephanton .....79 I 11
Clevedon .....18 L 29
Clevedon-Court .....18 L 29
Cleveland Hills .....50 Q 20
Cleveleys .....42 K 22
Cley Next the Sea .....38 X 25
Cliburn .....55 M 20
Cliffe Edway .....22 V 29
Cliffe Selby .....44 R 22
Clifton
  City of Nottingham .....36 Q 25
Clifton Eden .....55 L 20
Clifton Rugby .....28 Q 26
Clifton Hampden .....20 Q 29
Clifton-upon-Teme .....27 M 27
Clipston .....28 R 26
Clisham .....82 Z 10
Clitheroe .....42 M 22
Clive .....34 L 25
Cliveden House .....21 R 29
Clocaenog .....33 J 24
Clocaenog Forest .....33 J 24
Clola .....81 O 11
Clophill .....29 S 27
Clopton .....29 S 26
Closeburn .....53 I 18
Clotton .....34 L 24
Clouds Hill .....9 N 31
Cloughton .....51 S 20
Clova .....74 K 13
Clova (Glen) .....74 K 13
Clove Lodge .....49 N 20
Clovelly .....6 G 31
Clovenfords .....62 L 17
Clovulin .....72 E 13
Clowne .....44 Q 24
Cluanie Loch .....72 E 12
Cluanie Lodge .....72 E 12
Clumber Park .....44 Q 24
Clun .....26 K 26
Clunbury .....26 L 26
Clunes Forest .....72 F 13
Clungunford .....26 L 26
Clunie .....68 J 14
Clutton .....18 M 30
Clwydian Range .....34 K 24
Clydach .....17 I 28
Clyde (Firth of) .....59 F 17
Clyde (River) .....61 J 17
Clydebank .....60 G 16
Clydesdale .....61 I 16
Clyffe Pypard .....19 O 29
Clynnog-Fawr .....32 G 24
Clyro .....26 K 27
Clyst Honiton .....4 J 31
Clyst Hydon .....7 J 31
Clytha .....18 L 28
Clywedog Resr. .....25 J 26

Coalburn .....61 I 17
Coaley .....19 N 28
Coalville .....36 P 25
Coast .....78 D 10
Coatbridge .....60 H 16
Coates .....19 N 28
Cobham .....21 S 30
Cock Bridge .....74 K 12
Cockayne .....50 Q 20
Cockburnspath .....69 M 16
Cockenzie and Port Seton .....69 L 16
Cockerham .....48 L 22
Cockermouth .....54 J 20
Cockfield Babergh .....30 W 27
Cockfield Teesdale .....56 O 20
Cocking .....10 R 31
Cockleford .....19 N 28
Cockshutt .....34 L 25
Coddington .....36 R 24
Codford St. Mary .....9 N 30
Codicote .....21 T 28
Codnor .....36 P 24
Codsall .....35 N 26
Coe (Glen) .....72 F 14
Coed y Brenin Forest .....33 I 25
Coedpoeth .....34 K 24
Coggeshall .....30 W 28
Coigach .....84 E 10
Coignafearn .....73 H 12
Coignafearn Forest .....73 H 12
Coille Mhorgil .....72 E 12
Colaboll .....84 G 9
Colbost .....77 A 11
Colby Eden .....55 M 20
Colby Isle of Man .....46 F 21
Colchester .....30 W 28
Cold Ash .....20 Q 29
Cold Ashby .....28 Q 26
Cold Ashton .....19 M 29
Cold Fell .....55 M 19
Cold Norton .....22 W 28
Coldbackie .....84 G 8
Colden Common .....10 Q 31
Coldingham .....63 N 16
Coldstream .....63 N 17
Colebrooke .....7 I 31
Coleford Glos. .....18 M 28
Coleford Somerset .....18 M 30
Colemere .....34 L 25
Coleorton .....36 P 25
Coleshill
  North Warwickshire .....27 O 26
Coleshill
  Vale of White Horse .....19 P 29
Colgrave Sound .....87 R 2
Colkirk .....38 W 25
Coll Argyll and Bute .....71 A 14
Coll Eilean Siar .....83 B 9
Colliery Row .....56 P 19
Collieston .....81 O 11
Collin .....53 J 18
Collingbourne Ducis .....19 P 30
Collingbourne Kingston .....19 P 30
Collingham Notts. .....36 R 24
Collingham West Yorks. .....50 P 22
Collington .....26 M 27
Collyweston .....37 S 26
Colmonell .....52 F 18
Coln (River) .....19 O 28
Colnabaichin .....74 K 12
Colne .....43 N 22
Colne (River) .....22 X 28
Colonsay .....64 B 15
Colpy .....81 M 11
Colsterworth .....37 S 25
Coltishall .....39 Y 25
Colwall Stone .....27 M 27
Colwinston .....17 J 29
Colwyn Bay / Bae Colwyn .....41 I 23
Colyton .....5 K 31
Combe Florey .....8 K 30
Combe Martin .....17 H 30
Combe-St. Nicholas .....8 L 31
Combeinteignhead .....4 J 32
Comberton .....29 U 27
Combwich .....8 K 30
Come-to-Good .....2 E 33
Compton Berks. .....20 Q 29
Compton Guildford .....21 S 30
Compton West Sussex .....10 R 31
Compton Abdale .....19 O 28
Compton Basset .....19 O 29
Compton Castle .....4 J 32
Compton Dando .....18 M 29
Compton Wynyates .....28 P 27
Comrie .....67 I 14
Cona Glen .....72 D 13

Conchra .....65 E 15
Condicote .....27 O 28
Condover .....34 L 26
Congleton .....35 N 24
Congresbury .....18 L 29
Coningsby .....37 T 24
Conington .....29 T 26
Conisbrough .....44 Q 23
Coniston .....48 K 20
Connah's Quay .....42 K 24
Connel .....65 D 14
Connel Park .....60 H 17
Conon Bridge .....79 G 11
Consett .....56 O 19
Constantine Bay .....2 E 32
Contin .....79 G 11
Convinth (Glen) .....79 G 11
Conway Falls .....33 I 24
Conwy .....41 I 23
Conwy (River) .....33 I 24
Conwy (Vale of) .....33 I 24
Cooden Beach .....12 V 31
Cookham .....21 R 29
Coolham .....11 S 31
Coombe Bissett .....9 O 30
Copdock .....31 X 27
Copford .....30 W 28
Copley .....56 O 20
Copmanthorpe .....50 Q 22
Copplestone .....7 I 31
Coppull .....42 M 23
Copthorne .....11 T 30
Coquet (River) .....63 N 17
Corbridge .....55 N 19
Corby .....28 R 26
Corby Glen .....37 S 25
Corfe Castle .....9 N 32
Corfe Mullen .....9 N 31
Corgarff Castle .....74 K 12
Corhampton .....10 Q 31
Cornforth .....56 P 19
Cornhill .....81 L 11
Cornhill-on-Tweed .....63 N 17
Cornwood .....4 I 32
Cornworthy .....4 J 32
Corpach .....72 E 13
Corpusty .....39 X 25
Corran .....72 E 13
Corrany .....46 G 21
Corrie .....59 E 17
Corrie Common .....54 K 18
Corrimony .....78 F 11
Corringham Thurrock .....22 V 29
Corringham West Lindsey .....44 R 23
Corris .....33 I 26
Corry .....77 C 12
Corryvreckan (Gulf of) .....65 C 15
Corscombe .....8 L 31
Corsham .....19 N 29
Corsham Court .....19 N 29
Corsley Heath .....19 N 30
Corsock .....53 I 18
Corstopitum .....55 N 19
Corton .....9 N 30
Corwen .....33 J 25
Cosby .....36 Q 26
Cosham .....10 Q 31
Costessey .....39 X 26
Cot-town .....81 N 11
Cotehill .....55 L 19
Cotgrave .....36 Q 25
Cotham .....36 R 24
Cotherstone .....49 O 20
Cothi River .....25 H 28
Coton .....29 U 27
Cotswold Wildlife Park .....19 O 28
Cottenham .....29 U 27
Cottered .....29 T 28
Cottesmore .....37 S 25
Cottingham
  East Riding of Yorks. .....45 S 22
Cottingham Northants. .....28 R 26
Cottisford .....28 Q 28
Cottonshopeburn Foot .....62 M 18
Coulags .....78 D 11
Coulport .....66 F 15
Coulter .....61 J 17
Coundon .....56 P 20
Countesthorpe .....36 Q 26
Coupar Angus .....68 K 14
Coustonn .....66 E 16
Cove Argyll and Bute .....66 F 15
Cove Highland .....78 C 10
Cove Bay .....75 N 12
Coverack .....2 E 33
Cow Honeybourne .....27 O 27

Cowal .....65 E 15
Cowan Bridge .....48 M 21
Cowbit .....37 T 25
Cowbridge / Bont-faen .....17 J 29
Cowdenbeath .....68 J 15
Cowdray House .....10 R 31
Cowes Isle of Wight .....10 Q 31
Cowfold .....11 T 31
Cowie .....67 I 15
Cowling .....43 N 22
Cowplain .....10 Q 31
Coxheath .....22 V 30
Coxhoe .....56 P 19
Coxwold .....50 Q 21
Coylton .....60 G 17
Coylumbridge .....74 I 12
Crackington Haven .....6 G 31
Crafthole .....3 H 32
Craggan .....66 F 15
Cragside Gardens .....63 O 18
Crai .....25 J 28
Craig .....78 E 11
Craig Lodge .....65 E 16
Craig-y-nos .....17 I 28
Craigdarroch .....60 H 18
Craigellachie .....80 K 11
Craigencallie .....53 G 18
Craigendoran .....66 F 16
Craigens .....58 B 16
Craighead .....69 M 15
Craighouse .....58 C 16
Craigie .....60 G 17
Craigievar Castle .....75 L 12
Craigmalloch .....53 G 18
Craignish (Loch) .....65 D 15
Craignure .....65 C 14
Craigrothie .....69 L 15
Craigton .....74 K 14
Craik .....62 K 17
Crail .....69 M 15
Crailing .....62 M 17
Crailinghall .....62 M 17
Crakaig .....85 I 9
Cramlington .....56 P 18
Cramond .....68 K 16
Cranborne .....9 O 31
Cranbrook .....12 V 30
Crane Moor .....43 P 23
Cranford St. John .....29 S 26
Cranleigh .....11 S 30
Cranmore .....18 M 30
Cranshaws .....62 M 16
Cranstal .....46 G 20
Cranwell .....37 S 24
Cranworth .....38 W 26
Crask Inn .....84 G 9
Craster .....63 P 17
Crathes Castle .....75 M 12
Crathie .....74 K 12
Crathorne .....50 Q 20
Craven Arms .....26 L 26
Crawcrook .....56 O 19
Crawford .....61 J 17
Crawfordjohn .....61 I 17
Crawick .....61 I 17
Crawley Hants. .....10 P 30
Crawley West Sussex .....11 T 30
Crawley Down .....11 T 30
Creag Meagaidh .....73 G 13
Creagan .....65 E 14
Creagorry .....76 Y 11
Creake South .....38 W 25
Credenhill .....26 L 27
Crediton .....7 J 31
Creech St. Michael .....8 K 30
Creetown .....53 G 19
Creggans .....66 E 15
Creran (Loch) .....65 D 14
Cressage .....34 M 26
Cresswell Castle Morpeth .....56 P 18
Cresswell Pembrokeshire /
  Sir Benfro .....15 F 28
Creswell .....44 Q 24
Crewe .....35 M 24
Crewkerne .....8 L 31
Crianlarich .....66 G 14
Cribyn .....15 H 27
Criccieth .....33 H 25
Crich .....36 P 24
Crichton .....62 L 16
Crick .....28 Q 26
Crickadarn .....25 K 27
Cricket St. Thomas .....8 L 31
Crickhowell .....26 K 28
Cricklade .....19 O 29
Crickley Hill .....19 N 28
Crieff .....67 I 14

Crimond .....81 O 11
Crimplesham .....38 V 26
Crinan .....65 D 15
Crinan (Loch) .....65 D 15
Cringleford .....39 X 26
Croachy .....79 H 12
Crocketford .....53 I 18
Crockham Hill .....21 U 30
Croes-goch .....14 E 28
Croesyceiliog .....18 L 29
Croft Herefordshire .....26 L 27
Croft Richmondshire .....50 P 20
Croft-on-Tees .....50 P 20
Crofty .....15 H 29
Croggan .....65 C 14
Croglin .....55 M 19
Croick .....79 G 10
Croig .....71 B 14
Cromalt Hills .....84 E 9
Cromar .....74 L 12
Cromarty .....79 H 10
Cromarty Bay .....79 H 10
Cromarty Firth .....79 H 11
Cromdale .....80 J 11
Cromdale (Hills of) .....80 J 12
Cromer .....39 X 25
Cromford .....35 P 24
Cromore .....82 A 9
Cromra .....73 G 13
Crondall .....20 R 30
Cronk (The) .....46 G 21
Crook South Lakeland .....48 L 20
Crook Wear Valley .....56 O 19
Crook of Devon .....68 J 15
Crookham .....63 N 17
Crookham Village .....20 R 30
Crooklands .....48 L 21
Cropredy .....28 Q 27
Cropston .....36 Q 25
Cropwell Bishop .....36 R 25
Crosby Allerdale .....54 J 19
Crosby Isle of Man .....46 G 21
Crosby Sefton .....42 K 23
Crosby Ravensworth .....48 M 20
Croscombe .....18 M 30
Cross .....83 B 8
Cross Fell .....55 M 19
Cross Hands .....15 H 28
Cross Inn .....25 H 27
Crossaig .....59 D 16
Crossapoll .....64 Z 14
Crossbost .....82 A 9
Crossford .....61 I 16
Crossgates .....68 J 15
Crossgill .....48 L 21
Crosshill Fife .....68 K 15
Crosshill South Ayrshire .....60 G 18
Crosshouse .....60 G 17
Crosskeys .....18 K 29
Crosskirk .....85 J 8
Crossmichael .....53 I 19
Crossraguel Abbey .....60 F 18
Crossways .....9 N 31
Croston .....42 L 23
Crouch (River) .....22 W 29
Croughton .....28 Q 28
Crow Hill .....26 M 28
Crowborough .....12 U 30
Crowcombe .....8 K 30
Crowhurst .....12 V 31
Crowland .....37 T 25
Crowle Doncaster .....44 R 23
Crowle Wychavon .....27 N 27
Crowlin Island .....77 C 11
Crowmarsh Gifford .....20 Q 29
Crowthorne .....20 R 29
Croxley Green .....21 S 29
Croxton .....30 W 26
Croxton Kerrial .....36 R 25
Croy .....79 H 11
Croyde .....6 H 30
Croydon London Borough .....21 T 29
Cruden Bay .....81 O 11
Crudgington .....34 M 25
Crudwell .....19 N 29
Crug-y-bar .....25 I 27
Crulivig .....82 Z 9
Crymmych .....15 G 28
Crynant .....17 I 28
Cuaig .....77 C 11
Cubbington .....28 P 27
Cubert .....2 E 32
Cuckfield .....11 T 30
Cucklington .....9 M 30
Cuckney .....44 Q 24
Cuddington Aylesbury .....20 R 28
Cuddington Vale Royal .....42 M 24

Cudworth .....43 P 23
Cuffley .....21 T 28
Cuhxham .....20 Q 29
Cuilicudden .....79 H 11
Cuillin Sound .....71 B 12
Cuillins (The) .....77 B 12
Culbokie .....79 G 11
Culcreuch .....55 M 20
Culkein .....83 D 9
Cullen .....80 L 10
Cullen Bay .....80 L 10
Cullingworth .....43 O 22
Cullipool .....65 D 15
Culloch .....67 I 14
Cullompton .....7 J 31
Culmington .....26 L 26
Culmstock .....8 K 31
Culnacraig .....84 E 10
Culrain .....79 G 10
Culross .....68 J 15
Culshabbin .....52 G 19
Culswic .....87 P 3
Culter Fell .....61 J 17
Cults .....75 N 12
Culzean Castle .....59 F 17
Cumbernauld .....67 I 16
Cumbrian Moutains .....48 K 20
Cuminestown .....81 N 11
Cummersdale .....54 L 19
Cummertrees .....54 J 19
Cumnock .....60 H 17
Cumnor .....20 P 28
Cumwhitton .....55 L 19
Cunninghamhead .....60 G 17
Cupar .....69 K 15
Curbridge .....20 P 28
Curdridge .....10 Q 31
Currie .....61 K 16
Curry Rivel .....8 L 30
Cutcloy .....53 G 19
Cutnall green .....27 N 27
Cuxton .....22 V 29
Cwm .....18 K 28
Cwm Bychan .....33 H 25
Cwm Taf .....17 J 28
Cwmafan .....17 I 29
Cwmaman .....17 J 28
Cwmbach Carmarthenshire /
  Sir Gaerfyrddin .....15 G 28
Cwmbach Powys / Powys .....25 J 27
Cwmbach Rhondda, Cynon, Taf /
  Rhondda, Cynon, Taff .....17 J 28
Cwmbrân .....18 L 29
Cwmcarn .....18 K 29
Cwmcoy .....15 G 27
Cwmllynfell .....17 I 28
Cwmystwyth .....25 I 26
Cwnduad .....15 G 28
Cwnfelin Boeth .....15 G 28
Cwrt-Newydd .....15 H 27
Cydweli / Kidwelly .....15 H 28
Cyffylliog .....33 J 24
Cymmer .....17 J 29
Cymyran Bay .....40 G 23
Cynwyl Elfed .....15 G 28

D

Dacre Eden .....55 L 20
Dacre Harrogate .....49 O 21
Daglingworth .....19 N 28
Dailly .....60 F 18
Daimh (Loch an) .....73 G 14
Dairsie or Osnaburgh .....69 L 14
Dalavich .....65 E 15
Dalbeattie .....53 I 19
Dalbeg .....73 H 12
Dalblair .....60 H 17
Dalby .....46 F 21
Dalchalloch .....73 H 13
Dalchruin .....67 H 15
Dale .....14 E 28
Dale Head .....48 L 20
Dalgonar .....60 H 18
Dalham .....30 V 27
Dalhavaig .....85 I 8
Daliburgh .....76 X 12
Dalkeith .....61 K 16
Dallas .....80 J 11
Dalleagles .....60 H 17
Dallington Northampton .....28 R 27
Dallington Rother .....12 V 31
Dalmally .....66 F 14
Dalmellington .....60 G 18
Dalmeny .....68 J 16
Dalmigavie .....73 H 12
Dalnabreck .....71 C 13

Dalnaspidal Lodge ....73 H 13
Dalnavaid ....74 J 13
Dalnavie ....79 H 10
Dalness ....72 F 14
Dalry
  Dumfries and Galloway ....53 H 18
Dalry North Ayrshire ....60 F 16
Dalrymple ....60 G 17
Dalston ....54 L 19
Dalswinton ....53 I 18
Dalton
  Dumfries and Galloway ....54 J 18
Dalton North Yorks. ....50 P 21
Dalton in Furness ....47 K 21
Damerham ....9 O 31
Damh (Loch) ....78 D 11
Dan-yr-Ogof ....17 I 28
Danbury ....22 V 28
Danby ....50 R 20
Dane ....35 N 24
Danehill ....11 U 30
Darenth ....22 U 29
Darfield ....43 P 23
Darlington ....50 P 20
Darowen ....33 I 26
Darras Hall ....56 O 18
Darrington ....44 Q 22
Darsham ....31 Y 27
Dartford ....22 U 29
Dartford Tunnel ....22 U 29
Dartington ....4 I 32
Dartmeet ....4 I 32
Dartmoor National Park ......4 I 32
Dartmouth ....4 J 32
Darton ....43 P 23
Darvel ....60 H 17
Darwen ....42 M 22
Datchet ....21 S 29
Datchworth ....29 T 28
Dava ....80 J 11
Daventry ....28 Q 27
Davidstow ....6 G 32
Davington ....61 K 18
Daviot ....79 H 11
Dawley ....34 M 26
Dawlish ....4 J 32
Deal ....23 Y 30
Dean ....54 J 20
Dean Forest Park ....18 M 28
Deanich Lodge ....78 F 10
Deanston ....67 H 15
Dearham ....54 J 19
Debden ....30 U 28
Deben (River) ....31 X 27
Debenham ....31 X 27
Deddington ....28 Q 28
Dedham ....30 W 28
Dee / Afon Dyfrdwy (River)
  Wales ....41 K 23
Dee (River) Scotland ....75 N 12
Dee (River) / Afon Dyfrdwy ..34 K 24
Deene ....29 S 26
Deepcut ....21 R 30
Deepdale ....49 M 21
Deeping-St. James ....37 T 25
Deeping St. Nicholas ....37 T 25
Deeps (The) ....87 P 3
Defford ....27 N 27
Deiniolen ....33 H 24
Delabole ....6 F 32
Delamere ....34 M 24
Delamere Forest ....42 L 24
Dell ....83 B 8
Dellifure ....80 J 11
Delnadamph Lodge ....74 K 12
Delph ....43 N 23
Denbigh / Dinbych ....33 J 24
Denby Dale ....43 P 23
Denchworth ....20 P 29
Denham ....21 S 29
Denholm ....62 L 17
Denmead ....10 Q 31
Dennington ....31 Y 27
Denny ....67 I 15
Dent ....49 M 21
Denton South Kesteven ......36 R 25
Denton Stockport ....43 N 23
Denver ....38 V 26
Derby ....36 P 25
Deri ....18 K 28
Dersingham ....38 V 25
Dervaig ....71 B 14
Derwent (River) R. Ouse ....44 R 22
Derwent (River) R. Trent ....36 P 24
Derwent (River) R. Tyne ....56 O 19
Derwent Dale ....43 O 23
Derwent Reservoir Derbs. ..43 O 23

Derwent Reservoir
  Northumb. ....56 N 19
Derwent Water ....54 K 20
Desborough ....28 R 26
Desford ....36 Q 26
Detling ....22 V 30
Devauden ....18 L 28
Deveron (River) ....81 M 11
Devil's Beef Tub ....61 J 17
Devil's Bridge / Pontarfynach 25 I 26
Devil's Elbow ....74 J 13
Devil's Punch Bowl ....10 R 30
Devizes ....19 O 29
Devonport ....3 H 32
Dewsbury ....43 P 22
Dherue (Loch an) ....84 G 8
Dial Post ....11 S 31
Dickleburgh ....31 X 26
Didcot ....20 Q 29
Diddlebury ....26 L 26
Digby ....37 S 24
Dilhorne ....35 N 25
Dilton Marsh ....19 N 30
Dilwyn ....26 L 27
Dinas ....24 F 27
Dinas Dinlle ....32 G 24
Dinas Head ....24 F 27
Dinas-Mawddwy ....33 I 25
Dinas Powys ....18 K 29
Dinbych / Denbigh ....33 J 24
Dinbych-y-pysgod / Tenby ..15 F 28
Dingwall ....79 G 11
Dinnet ....74 L 12
Dinnington
  Newcastle upon Tyne ......56 O 18
Dinnington Rotherham ......44 Q 23
Dinsdale ....50 P 20
Dinton ....9 O 30
Diptford ....4 I 32
Dirleton ....69 L 15
Dishforth ....50 P 21
Diss ....31 X 26
Disserth ....25 J 27
Distington ....53 J 20
Ditcheat ....8 M 30
Ditchingham ....31 Y 26
Ditchling ....11 T 31
Ditton Priors ....26 M 26
Doc Penfro /
  Pembroke Dock ....16 F 28
Docherty (Glen) ....78 E 11
Dochgarroch ....79 H 11
Docking ....38 V 25
Dockray ....54 L 20
Dodburn ....62 L 17
Doddington Cambs. ....29 U 26
Doddington Kent ....22 W 30
Doddington Lincs. ....44 S 24
Doddington Northumb. ......63 O 17
Dodington ....19 M 29
Dodman Point ....3 F 33
Dodworth ....43 P 23
Doirlinn ....71 C 13
Dolanog ....33 J 25
Dolbenmaen ....33 H 25
Dolfor ....26 K 26
Dolgarrog ....33 I 24
Dolgellau ....33 I 25
Dolgoch Falls ....33 I 26
Dollar ....67 I 15
Dolphinholme ....48 L 22
Dolton ....7 H 31
Don (River) R. Ouse ....44 R 22
Don (River) R. Spey ....74 K 12
Doncaster ....44 Q 23
Donhead-St. Andrew ....9 N 30
Donhead-St. Mary ....9 N 30
Donington ....37 T 25
Donington-on-Bain ....45 T 24
Donington Park Circuit ......36 P 25
Donisthorpe ....36 P 25
Donnington Berks. ....20 Q 29
Donnington Salop ....35 M 25
Donyatt ....8 L 31
Doon (Loch) ....60 G 18
Dorback Lodge ....74 J 12
Dorchester Dorset ....8 M 31
Dorchester Oxon. ....20 Q 29
Dordon ....35 P 26
Dore ....43 P 24
Dores ....79 H 11
Dorking ....21 T 30
Dormansland ....11 U 30
Dormanstown ....57 Q 20
Dornie ....78 D 12
Dornoch ....79 H 10

Dornoch Firth ....79 H 10
Dornock ....54 K 19
Dorrington ....34 L 26
Dorstone ....26 K 27
Dorusduain ....78 D 12
Douchary (Glen) ....78 F 10
Dougarie ....59 D 17
Douglas Isle of Man ....46 G 21
Douglas
  South Lanarkshire ....61 I 17
Douglastown ....74 L 14
Doulting ....86 K 6
Doune Highland ....84 G 10
Doune Stirling ....67 H 15
Dove (River) ....35 O 24
Dove Cottage ....48 K 20
Dove Holes ....43 O 24
Dovedale ....35 O 24
Dover ....13 X 30
Dovercourt ....31 X 28
Doveridge ....35 O 25
Dovey / Dyfi (River) ....33 I 26
Dowally ....74 J 14
Dowdeswell ....27 N 28
Dowlish Wake ....8 L 31
Down Ampney ....19 O 28
Downderry ....3 G 32
Downham ....30 U 26
Downham Market ....38 V 26
Downies ....75 N 12
Downton ....9 O 31
Dowsby ....37 S 25
Doynton ....19 M 29
Drakes Broughton ....27 N 27
Draughton ....49 O 22
Drax ....44 R 22
Draycott ....36 P 25
Draycott-in-the-Clay ....35 O 25
Draycott-in-the-Moors ......35 N 25
Drayton Norfolk ....39 X 25
Drayton Oxon. ....20 Q 29
Drayton-St. Leonard ....20 Q 29
Drefach near Carmarthen ..15 H 28
Drefach
  near Newcastle-Emlyn ....15 G 27
Dreghorn ....60 G 17
Drem ....69 L 15
Drenewydd / Newtown ......26 K 26
Dreswick Point ....46 G 21
Driffield ....19 O 28
Drigg ....47 J 20
Drighlington ....43 P 22
Drimnin ....71 C 14
Drinnishadder ....76 Z 10
Drissaig ....65 E 15
Droitwich ....27 N 27
Dronfield ....43 P 24
Drongan ....60 G 17
Droxford ....10 Q 31
Druidibeg (Loch) ....76 Y 12
Druim a' Chliabhain (Loch) .85 H 8
Druimindarroch ....71 C 13
Drum Castle ....75 M 12
Drumbeg ....84 E 9
Drumblade ....81 L 11
Drumburgh ....54 K 19
Drumchardine ....79 G 11
Drumclog ....60 H 17
Drumelzier ....61 J 17
Drumfearn ....71 C 12
Drumlanrig Castle ....61 I 18
Drumlemble ....58 C 17
Drumlithie ....75 M 13
Drummond Castle ....67 I 14
Drummore ....52 F 19
Drummossie Muir ....79 H 11
Drumnadrochit ....79 G 11
Drumrunie ....84 E 9
Drumsallie ....72 D 13
Drumtochty Forest ....75 M 13
Druridge Bay ....63 P 18
Drybrook ....18 M 28
Dryburgh Abbey ....62 M 17
Drygarn Fawr ....25 J 27
Drymen ....67 G 15
Drynoch ....77 B 12
Duchally ....84 F 9
Ducklington ....20 P 28
Duddington ....37 S 26
Duddo ....63 N 16
Dudley Dudley ....27 N 26
Dudley North Tyneside ......56 P 18
Duff House ....81 M 11
Duffield ....36 P 25
Dufftown ....80 K 11
Duffus ....80 J 10
Dufton ....55 M 20

Duggleby ....51 S 21
Duich (Loch) ....78 D 12
Duirinish ....77 C 12
Duke's Pass ....67 G 15
Dukinfield ....43 N 23
Dullingham ....30 V 27
Dulnain Bridge ....80 J 12
Duloe ....3 G 32
Dulverton ....7 J 30
Dumbarton ....67 G 16
Dumbleton ....27 O 27
Dumfries ....53 J 18
Dun Carloway Broch ....82 Z 9
Dunan ....66 F 16
Dunbar ....69 M 15
Dunbeath ....85 J 9
Dunblane ....67 I 15
Duncansby Head ....86 K 8
Dunchurch ....28 Q 26
Duncow ....53 J 18
Duncton ....11 S 31
Dundee ....69 K 14
Dundonald ....60 G 17
Dundrennan ....53 I 19
Dundry ....18 M 29
Dunecht ....75 M 12
Dunfermline ....68 J 15
Dungeness ....13 W 31
Dunholme ....44 S 24
Dunino ....69 L 15
Dunipace ....67 I 15
Dunkeld ....68 J 14
Dunkerque ....13 X 28
Dunkery Beacon ....7 J 30
Dunkeswell ....8 K 31
Dunkirk ....19 N 29
Dunley ....27 N 27
Dunlop ....60 G 16
Dunmaglass Lodge ....79 H 12
Dunnet ....85 J 8
Dunnet Bay ....85 J 8
Dunnet Head ....86 J 7
Dunning ....68 J 15
Dunnington ....50 R 22
Dunnockshaw ....42 N 22
Dunnottar Castle ....75 N 13
Dunoon ....66 F 16
Dunragit ....52 F 19
Dunrobin Castle ....85 I 10
Duns ....62 M 16
Duns Tew ....28 P 28
Dunscore ....53 I 18
Dunsfold ....11 S 30
Dunsford ....4 I 31
Dunsop Bridge ....49 M 22
Dunstable ....29 S 28
Dunstaffnage Castel ....65 D 14
Dunstanburgh Castle ....63 P 17
Dunster ....17 J 30
Dunston ....37 S 24
Dunstone ....4 I 32
Dunsyre ....61 J 16
Duntelchaig (Loch) ....79 H 11
Dunton bassett ....28 Q 26
Dunure ....59 F 17
Dunvegan ....77 A 11
Dunvegan (Loch) ....77 A 11
Dunvegan Castle ....77 A 11
Dunvegan Head ....76 Z 11
Dunwich ....31 Y 27
Durdle Door ....9 N 32
Durham ....56 P 19
Durisdeer ....61 I 18
Durleston Head ....9 O 32
Durness ....84 F 8
Durrington ....19 O 30
Dursley ....19 M 28
Dury Voe ....87 Q 2
Duston ....28 R 27
Duthil ....79 I 12
Duxford ....29 U 27
Dyce ....75 N 12
Dyfi / Dovey (River) ....33 I 26
Dyke ....80 I 11
Dykehead ....74 K 13
Dykends ....74 K 13
Dymchurch ....13 W 30
Dymock ....27 M 28
Dyrham ....19 M 29
Dyserth ....41 J 23

E
Eaglescliffe ....50 P 20
Eaglesfield ....54 K 18
Eaglesham ....60 H 16
Eakring ....36 R 24
Ealing London Borough ....21 T 29
Earba (Lochan na h-) ....73 G 13

Earby ....49 N 22
Eardisley ....26 K 27
Earl Shilton ....36 Q 26
Earl Soham ....31 X 27
Earl Stonham ....31 X 27
Earley Winnersh ....20 R 29
Earlish ....77 A 11
Earls Barton ....28 R 27
Earls Colne ....30 W 28
Earlsferry ....69 L 15
Earlston ....62 L 17
Earn (Loch) ....67 H 14
Earn (River) ....67 J 14
Earsdon ....56 P 18
Earsham ....31 Y 26
Eartham ....11 S 31
Easdale ....65 D 15
Easebourne ....10 R 31
Easington Easington ....57 P 19
Easington
  East Riding of Yorkshire ..45 U 23
Easington
  Redcar and Cleveland ....50 R 20
Easington
  South Oxfordshire ....20 Q 28
Easington Lane ....56 P 19
Easingwold ....50 Q 21
Eassie and Nevay ....68 K 14
East Aberthaw ....17 J 29
East Barkwith ....45 T 24
East Bergholt ....30 X 28
East Brent ....18 L 30
East Budleigh ....5 K 32
East Butterwick ....44 R 23
East-Challow ....20 P 29
East Chinnock ....8 L 31
East Cowes ....10 Q 31
East Cowton ....50 P 20
East Dereham ....38 W 25
East Ferry ....44 R 23
East Glen (River) ....37 S 25
East Grafton ....19 P 29
East Grinstead ....11 T 30
East Hagbourne ....20 Q 29
East-Halton ....45 T 23
East Hanney ....20 P 29
East Hardwick ....44 Q 23
East Harling ....30 W 26
East Haven ....69 L 14
East Hendred ....20 P 29
East Hoathly ....12 U 31
East Horsley ....21 S 30
East Huntspill ....18 L 30
East Ilsley ....20 Q 29
East Keswick ....50 P 22
East Kilbride Eilean Siar ..70 X 12
East Kilbride
  South Lanarkshire ....60 H 16
East-Knoyle ....9 N 30
East-Knoyle ....9 N 30
East Lambrook ....8 L 31
East Leake ....36 Q 25
East Linton ....69 M 16
East Loch Roag ....82 Z 9
East Loch Tarbet ....77 Z 10
East Looe ....3 G 32
East Lulworth ....9 N 32
East-Malling ....22 V 30
East Markham ....44 R 24
East Meon ....10 Q 31
East Mersea ....22 W 28
East Midlands Airport ....36 Q 25
East Moor ....35 P 24
East Norton ....36 R 26
East-Poringland ....39 X 26
East Portlemouth ....4 I 33
East Rhidorroch Lodge ....78 F 10
East-Rudham ....38 W 25
East-Saltoun ....62 L 16
East Tisted ....10 R 30
East Wemyss ....68 K 15
East-Winch ....38 V 25
East Wittering ....10 R 31
East Witton ....49 O 21
East-Woodhay ....20 P 29
East-Wretham ....30 W 26
Eastbourne ....12 U 31
Eastchurch ....22 W 29
Eastdean ....12 U 31
Easter-Compton ....18 M 29
Easter Ross ....79 G 10
Eastergate ....11 S 31
Eastfield ....51 S 21
Eastgate ....55 N 19
Eastham ....42 L 24
Eastington ....19 N 28

Eastleach ....19 O 28
Eastleigh ....10 P 31
Eastoft ....44 R 23
Easton Carlisle ....55 L 18
Easton Dorset ....8 M 32
Easton Norfolk ....39 X 26
Easton-Grey ....19 N 29
Easton-in-Gordano ....18 L 29
Easton-Royal ....19 O 29
Eastriggs ....54 K 19
Eastrington ....44 R 22
Eastry ....23 X 30
Eastville ....37 U 24
Eastwood ....36 Q 24
Eaton ....34 M 24
Eaton Bray ....29 S 28
Eaton Socon ....29 T 27
Ebbw Vale / Glyn Ebwy ....18 K 28
Ebchester ....56 O 19
Ebrington ....27 O 27
Eccels ....62 M 17
Ecchinswell ....20 Q 29
Ecclefechan ....54 K 18
Eccles ....42 M 23
Eccleshall ....35 N 25
Echt ....75 M 12
Eckford ....62 M 17
Eckington Derbs. ....43 P 24
Eckington Worc. ....27 N 27
Edale ....43 O 23
Eday ....87 L 6
Eddelston ....61 K 16
Edderton ....79 H 10
Eddrachillis Bay ....84 E 9
Eden (River) ....55 M 19
Eden Project ....3 F 32
Edenbridge ....21 U 30
Edentaggart ....66 F 15
Edenthorpe ....44 Q 23
Edgefield ....39 X 25
Edgmond ....35 M 25
Edgton ....26 L 26
Edinbane ....77 A 11
Edinburgh ....68 K 16
Edington ....19 N 30
Edith Weston ....37 S 26
Edlesborough ....29 S 28
Edlingham ....63 O 17
Edmondsley ....56 P 19
Edmundbyers ....56 O 19
Ednalton ....36 Q 25
Edwalton ....36 Q 25
Edwinstowe ....36 Q 24
Edzell ....75 M 13
Efailnewydd ....32 G 25
Efenechtyd ....33 K 24
Egerton ....22 W 30
Eggerness Point ....53 G 19
Eggleston ....56 N 20
Egham ....21 S 29
Egilsay ....87 L 6
Eglingham ....63 O 17
Egloskerry ....6 G 32
Eglwys Brewis ....17 J 29
Eglwysfach ....33 I 26
Eglwyswrw ....15 F 27
Egremont ....47 J 20
Egton ....50 R 20
Eigg ....71 B 13
Eigheach (Loch) ....73 G 13
Eight Ash Green ....30 W 28
Eil ....73 I 12
Eil (Loch) ....72 E 13
Eilde Mór (Loch) ....72 F 13
Eilean a' Chalmain ....64 A 15
Eilean Beag ....77 C 11
Eilean Chathastail ....71 B 13
Eilean Donan Castle ....78 D 12
Eilean Flodigarry ....77 B 10
Eilean Mhuire ....82 A 10
Eilean Mòr ....77 C 11
Eilean Mullagrach ....83 D 9
Eilean na Bà ....77 C 11
Eilean nan Each ....71 B 13
Eilean Trodday ....77 A 10
Eileanach Lodge ....79 G 10
Eilt (Loch) ....72 D 13
Eishken ....82 A 9
Eishort (Loch) ....71 C 12
Elan Valley ....25 J 27
Elan Village ....25 J 27
Elcho ....68 J 14
Elgin ....80 K 11
Elgol ....71 B 12
Elham ....23 X 30
Elie ....69 L 15
Eling ....10 P 31
Elkesley ....44 R 24
Elkstone ....19 N 28

A B C D E F G H I J K L M N O P Q R S T U V W X Y Z

Elland .... 43 O 22
Ellastone .... 35 O 25
Ellen's Green .... 11 S 30
Ellerbeck .... 50 P 20
Ellerton .... 44 R 22
Ellesmere .... 34 L 25
Ellesmere Port .... 42 L 24
Ellingham .... 31 Y 26
Ellington .... 56 P 18
Ellon .... 81 N 11
Elloughton .... 44 S 22
Elmdon .... 29 U 27
Elmley Castle .... 27 N 27
Elmore .... 19 N 28
Elmstead Market .... 30 W 28
Elmswell .... 30 W 27
Elphin .... 84 E 9
Elrick .... 75 N 12
Elrig .... 52 G 19
Elsdon .... 55 N 18
Elsenham .... 30 U 28
Elsham .... 45 S 23
Elsrickle .... 61 J 16
Elstead .... 21 R 30
Elstree .... 21 T 29
Elswick .... 42 L 22
Eltisley .... 29 T 27
Elton .... 37 S 26
Elveden .... 30 W 26
Elvington .... 50 R 22
Elwick .... 57 Q 19
Elworth .... 35 M 24
Ely .... 30 U 26
Emberton .... 28 R 27
Embleton *Allerdale* .... 54 K 20
Embleton *Alnwick* .... 63 P 17
Embo .... 79 I 10
Embsay .... 49 O 22
Emneth .... 37 U 26
Empingham .... 37 S 25
Emsworth .... 10 R 31
Enaclete .... 82 Z 9
Enard Bay .... 83 D 9
Enderby .... 36 Q 26
Endmoor .... 48 L 21
Endon .... 35 N 24
Enfield *London Borough* ...... 21 T 29
Enford .... 19 O 30
Englefield Green .... 21 S 29
English Bicknor .... 18 M 28
Englishcombe .... 19 M 29
Enham Alamein .... 20 P 30
Enmore .... 8 K 30
Ensay .... 71 B 14
Enstone .... 28 P 28
Enterkinfoot .... 61 I 18
Enville .... 27 N 26
Eochar .... 76 X 11
Eoligarry .... 70 X 12
Eoropie .... 83 B 8
Eorsa .... 65 B 14
Eport (Loch) .... 76 Y 11
Epping .... 21 U 28
Epping Forest .... 21 U 29
Epsom .... 21 T 30
Epworth .... 44 R 23
Erddig .... 34 K 24
Eredine .... 65 E 15
Eredine Forest .... 65 D 15
Eriboll .... 84 F 8
Eriboll (Loch) .... 84 F 8
Ericht (Loch) .... 73 G 13
Ericstane .... 61 J 17
Eridge Green .... 12 U 30
Eriska .... 65 D 14
Eriskay .... 70 Y 12
Erisort (Loch) .... 82 A 9
Eriswell .... 30 V 26
Erlestoke .... 19 N 30
Ermington .... 4 I 32
Erpingham .... 39 X 25
Erraid .... 64 A 15
Errochty (Loch) .... 73 H 13
Errogie .... 79 G 12
Errol .... 68 K 14
Ersary .... 70 X 13
Erskine Bridge .... 67 G 16
Ervie .... 52 E 19
Erwood .... 25 K 27
Esh Winning .... 56 O 19
Esha Ness .... 87 P 2
Esher .... 21 S 29
Esk (Glen) .... 75 L 13
Esk (River) .... 54 K 19
Eskdale .... 54 K 18
Eskdalemuir .... 61 K 18
Essendon .... 21 T 28

Essich .... 79 H 11
Eston .... 57 Q 20
Etal .... 63 N 17
Etchilhampton .... 19 O 29
Etchingham .... 12 V 30
Etherow (River) .... 43 N 23
Etherow Park .... 43 N 23
Etive (Glen) .... 72 F 14
Etive (Loch) .... 65 E 14
Eton .... 21 S 29
Ettington .... 27 P 27
Ettrick .... 61 K 17
Ettrick Forest .... 62 K 17
Ettrick Pen .... 61 K 17
Etwall .... 35 P 25
Euston .... 30 W 26
Euxton .... 42 L 22
Evanton .... 79 G 11
Evelix .... 79 H 10
Evenlode .... 27 O 28
Evenwood .... 56 O 20
Evercreech .... 8 M 30
Everingham .... 44 R 22
Everleigh .... 19 O 30
Evershot .... 8 M 31
Eversley .... 20 R 29
Everton .... 44 R 23
Evesham .... 27 O 27
Evesham (Vale of) .... 27 O 27
Ewe (Isle of) .... 78 D 10
Ewell .... 21 T 29
Ewelme .... 20 Q 29
Ewenny .... 17 J 29
Ewes .... 54 L 18
Ewhurst .... 11 S 30
Exbourne .... 7 I 31
Exe (River) .... 7 J 31
Exebridge .... 7 J 30
Exeter .... 4 J 31
Exford .... 7 J 30
Exminster .... 4 J 31
Exmoor National Park .... 7 I 30
Exmouth .... 4 J 32
Exton .... 7 J 30
Eyam .... 43 O 24
Eye *Cambs.* .... 37 T 26
Eye *Suffolk* .... 31 X 27
Eye Peninsula .... 83 B 9
Eyemouth .... 63 N 16
Eynort (Loch) .... 77 A 12
Eynort (Loch) *Highland* ...... 77 A 12
Eynort (Loch) *Western Isles* 76 Y 12
Eynsford .... 22 U 29
Eynsham .... 20 P 28
Eyre Point .... 77 B 12
Eythorne .... 23 X 30

F

Fada (Loch) .... 76 Y 11
Failsworth .... 43 N 23
Fair Isle .... 87 P 5
Fair Oak .... 10 Q 31
Fairbourne .... 33 H 25
Fairburn .... 44 Q 22
Fairford .... 19 O 28
Fairlie .... 59 F 16
Fairlight .... 12 V 31
Fakenham .... 38 W 25
Fala .... 62 L 16
Faldingworth .... 45 S 23
Falfield .... 18 M 29
Falkirk .... 67 I 16
Falkland .... 68 K 15
Fallford .... 54 K 18
Fallin .... 67 I 15
Falmer .... 11 T 31
Falmouth .... 2 E 33
Falstone .... 55 M 18
Fanagmore .... 84 E 8
Fangfoss .... 50 R 22
Fannich (Loch) .... 78 E 11
Fannich Lodge .... 78 F 11
Fara .... 86 K 7
Fareham .... 10 Q 31
Faringdon .... 19 P 29
Farlam .... 55 L 19
Farleigh-Hungerford .... 19 N 30
Farley .... 9 O 30
Farley Mount .... 10 P 30
Farlow .... 26 M 26
Farmborough .... 18 M 29
Farmers .... 25 I 27
Farmtown .... 80 L 11
Farnborough *Hants.* .... 20 R 30
Farnborough *Warw.* .... 28 P 27
Farnborough
  West Berkshire .... 20 P 29

Farndon *Chester* .... 34 L 24
Farndon
  Newark and Sherwood .... 36 R 24
Farne Islands .... 63 P 17
Farnell .... 75 M 13
Farnham *Dorset* .... 9 N 31
Farnham *Surrey* .... 20 R 30
Farnham Royal .... 21 S 29
Farningham .... 22 U 29
Farnley .... 49 O 22
Farnsfield .... 36 Q 24
Farnworth .... 42 M 23
Farr .... 85 H 8
Farrington Gurney .... 18 M 30
Farway .... 5 K 31
Fasnakyle .... 78 F 12
Fasnakyle Forest .... 78 F 11
Fasque .... 75 M 13
Fassfern .... 72 E 13
Fauldhouse .... 61 I 16
Faversham .... 22 W 30
Fawley .... 10 P 31
Fazeley .... 35 O 26
Fearby .... 49 O 21
Fearn Lodge .... 79 H 10
Fearnan .... 67 H 14
Fearnmore .... 77 C 11
Featherstone *Staffs.* .... 35 N 26
Featherstone *West Yorks.* ... 43 P 22
Feelindre .... 15 F 27
Feering .... 30 W 28
Feetham .... 49 N 20
Felbridge .... 11 T 30
Felindre *Carmarthenshire /*
  Sir Gaerfyrddin .... 25 I 28
Felindre *Powys* .... 26 K 26
Felinfach .... 25 K 28
Felinheli .... 33 H 24
Felixkirk .... 50 Q 21
Felixstowe .... 31 Y 28
Felling .... 56 P 19
Felmingham .... 39 Y 25
Felpham .... 11 S 31
Felsham .... 30 W 27
Felsted .... 30 V 28
Feltham .... 21 S 29
Felthorpe .... 39 X 25
Felton .... 63 O 18
Feltwell .... 30 V 26
Fence .... 42 N 22
Feniton .... 8 K 31
Fenny Bentley .... 35 O 24
Fenstanton .... 29 T 27
Fenton *Stoke-on-Trent* .... 35 N 25
Fenton *West Lindsey* .... 44 R 24
Fenwick
  Berwick-upon-Tweed ..... 63 O 17
Fenwick *East Ayrshire* .... 60 G 17
Feochaig .... 59 D 17
Feochan (Loch) .... 65 D 14
Feock .... 2 E 33
Feolin Ferry .... 58 B 16
Fern .... 74 L 13
Ferndown .... 9 O 31
Ferness .... 79 I 11
Fernhurst .... 11 R 30
Ferryden .... 75 M 13
Ferryhill .... 56 P 19
Ferryside .... 15 G 28
Fersit .... 73 F 13
Fetterangus .... 81 N 11
Fettercairn .... 75 M 13
Fewston .... 49 O 22
Ffestiniog .... 33 I 25
Ffestiniog (Vale of) .... 33 H 25
Fflint / Flint .... 42 K 24
Fforest Fawr .... 17 J 28
Ffostrasol .... 15 G 27
Fiaray .... 70 X 12
Fiddleton .... 62 L 18
Fifield .... 27 P 28
Filby .... 39 Y 26
Filey .... 51 T 21
Fillongley .... 27 P 26
Filton .... 18 M 29
Finchampstead .... 20 R 29
Finchingfield .... 30 V 28
Findhorn .... 80 J 11
Findhorn (River) .... 73 H 12
Findhorn Bay .... 80 J 11
Findo Gask .... 68 J 14
Findochty .... 80 L 10
Findon .... 11 S 31

Finedon .... 29 S 26
Fingest .... 20 R 29
Fingland .... 60 I 17
Finiskaig .... 72 D 13
Finmere .... 28 Q 28
Finniegill .... 61 K 18
Finningley .... 44 R 23
Finsbay .... 76 Z 10
Finstock .... 20 P 28
Finstown .... 86 K 6
Fintry *Aberdeenshire* .... 81 M 11
Fintry *Stirling* .... 67 H 15
Fionn Loch .... 78 D 10
Fionn Loch Mór .... 84 F 9
Fionnphort .... 64 A 15
Fishbourne *Chichester* .... 10 R 31
Fishbourne *Isle of Wight* .... 10 Q 31
Fishburn .... 56 P 19
Fisherfield Forest .... 78 D 10
Fisherford .... 81 M 11
Fishguard / Abergwaun .... 24 F 28
Fishnish Bay .... 65 B 14
Fishtoft .... 37 U 25
Fiskavaig .... 77 A 12
Fiskerton .... 44 S 24
Fittleworth .... 11 S 31
Fiunary .... 71 C 14
Fivehead .... 8 L 30
Flackwell Heath .... 21 R 29
Fladbury .... 27 N 27
Fladda-Chùain .... 77 A 10
Flagg .... 35 O 24
Flamborough .... 51 T 21
Flamborough Head .... 51 T 21
Flamingo Park .... 50 R 21
Flamstead .... 21 S 28
Flash .... 35 O 24
Flashader .... 77 A 11
Flatford Mill .... 30 X 28
Flax Bourton .... 18 L 29
Flaxton .... 50 R 21
Fleckney .... 36 Q 26
Fleet .... 20 R 30
Fleet (Islands of) .... 53 H 19
Fleet (Loch) .... 79 H 10
Fleet Hargate .... 37 U 25
Fleetwood .... 48 K 22
Flimby .... 53 J 19
Flint / Fflint .... 42 K 24
Flintham .... 36 R 24
Flitton .... 29 S 27
Flitwick .... 29 S 27
Flixton .... 31 Y 26
Flodday *near Hellisay* .... 70 X 13
Flodday *near Sandray* .... 70 X 13
Flodden Field .... 63 N 17
Flodigarry .... 77 B 11
Flookburgh .... 48 L 21
Floors Castle .... 62 M 17
Flotta .... 86 K 7
Flowerdale Forest .... 78 D 11
Flyford Flavell .... 27 N 27
Fochabers .... 80 K 11
Foggathorpe .... 44 R 22
Foinaven .... 84 F 8
Foindle .... 84 E 8
Folkestone .... 13 X 30
Folkingham .... 37 S 25
Folly Gate .... 7 I 31
Fontmell Magna .... 9 N 31
Ford *Argyll and Bute* .... 65 D 15
Ford *Arun* .... 11 S 31
Ford
  Berwick-upon-Tweed ..... 63 N 17
Ford
  Buckinghamshire .... 20 R 28
Ford *Cotswold* .... 27 O 28
Ford
  Shrewsbury and Atcham .. 34 L 25
Forde Abbey .... 8 L 31
Forden .... 34 K 26
Fordham .... 30 V 27
Fordingbridge .... 9 O 31
Fordoun .... 75 M 13
Fordwich .... 23 X 30
Fordyce .... 80 L 11
Foreland .... 10 Q 31
Foreland Point .... 17 I 30
Foremark Reservoir .... 36 P 25
Forest Lodge .... 74 I 13
Forest Row .... 11 U 30
Forestburn Gate .... 63 O 18
Forfar .... 74 L 14
Forganenny .... 68 J 14
Formby .... 42 K 23
Formby Point .... 42 K 23
Fornham All Saints .... 30 W 27

Forres .... 80 J 11
Forrest Lodge .... 53 H 18
Forse .... 85 K 9
Forsinard .... 85 I 8
Fort Augustus .... 73 F 12
Fort George .... 79 H 11
Fort Victoria .... 10 P 31
Fort William .... 72 E 13
Forter .... 74 K 13
Forteviot .... 68 J 14
Forth .... 61 I 16
Forth (Firth of) .... 68 K 15
Forth (River) .... 67 G 15
Forth Bridges .... 68 J 15
Fortingall .... 73 H 14
Forton .... 35 M 25
Fortrose .... 79 H 11
Fortuneswell .... 8 M 32
Fosdyke .... 37 T 25
Foss .... 73 I 13
Foston .... 36 R 25
Foston on the Wolds .... 51 T 22
Fotherby .... 45 T 23
Fotheringhay .... 29 S 26
Foulden .... 63 N 16
Foulness Point .... 22 W 29
Foulridge .... 43 N 22
Foulsham .... 38 X 25
Fountainhall .... 62 L 16
Fountains Abbey .... 50 P 21
Four Crosses .... 34 K 25
Four Elms .... 21 U 30
Four Marks .... 10 Q 30
Fovant .... 9 O 30
Foveran .... 81 N 12
Fowey .... 3 G 32
Fowlmere .... 29 U 27
Fownhope .... 26 M 27
Foxdale .... 46 G 21
Foxholes .... 51 S 21
Foxton .... 28 R 26
Foxup .... 49 N 21
Foyers .... 73 G 12
Fraddon .... 3 F 32
Framfield .... 12 U 31
Framlingham .... 31 Y 27
Frampton-on-Severn .... 19 M 28
Framwellgate Moor .... 56 P 19
Frant .... 12 U 30
Fraserburgh .... 81 O 10
Fraserburgh Bay .... 81 O 10
Freckenham .... 30 V 27
Freckleton .... 42 L 22
Freeland .... 20 P 28
Freethorpe .... 39 Y 26
Freevater Forest .... 79 F 10
Freiston .... 37 U 25
Fremington .... 7 H 30
Frensham .... 10 R 30
Freshwater .... 10 P 31
Freshwater Bay .... 10 P 31
Freshwater East .... 16 F 29
Freshwater West .... 14 E 29
Fressingfield .... 31 X 26
Freswick .... 86 K 8
Freuchie .... 68 K 15
Freuchie (Loch) .... 67 I 14
Friday Bridge .... 37 U 26
Fridaythorpe .... 51 S 21
Frimley .... 21 R 30
Fringford .... 28 Q 28
Frinton-on-Sea .... 31 X 28
Friockheim .... 75 M 14
Frisa (Loch) .... 71 B 14
Friskney .... 37 U 24
Frithville .... 37 T 24
Frittenden .... 12 V 30
Fritwell .... 28 Q 28
Frizington .... 47 J 20
Frocester .... 19 N 28
Frodsham .... 42 L 24
Froggatt .... 43 P 24
Frome .... 19 N 30
Frosterley .... 56 O 19
Froxfield .... 20 P 29
Fuday .... 70 X 12
Fuiay .... 70 X 13
Fulbourn .... 30 U 27
Fulking .... 11 T 31
Fuller Street .... 22 V 28
Fulwood .... 42 M 22
Funtington .... 10 R 31
Funzie .... 87 R 2
Furness Abbey .... 47 K 21
Furness Fells .... 48 K 20
Fyfield .... 22 U 28
Fyvie .... 81 M 11

G

Gaddesby .... 36 R 25
Gaick Lodge .... 73 H 13
Gainford .... 49 O 20
Gainsborough .... 44 R 23
Gairloch .... 78 C 10
Gairlochy .... 72 F 13
Gairsay .... 87 L 6
Gaitsgill .... 54 L 19
Galashiels .... 62 L 17
Galgate .... 48 L 22
Gallan Head .... 82 Y 9
Gallanach .... 65 D 14
Galloway Forest Park .... 52 G 18
Galltair .... 72 D 12
Galmisdale .... 71 B 13
Galmpton .... 4 J 32
Galson .... 82 A 8
Galston .... 60 G 17
Galtrigill .... 76 Z 11
Gamblesby .... 55 M 19
Gamlingay .... 29 T 27
Gamston .... 44 R 24
Ganavan .... 65 D 14
Ganton .... 51 S 21
Garboldisham .... 30 W 26
Gardenstown .... 81 N 10
Garelochhead .... 66 F 15
Garenin .... 82 Z 9
Garforth .... 43 P 22
Gargrave .... 49 N 22
Gargunnock .... 67 H 15
Garioch .... 81 M 12
Garlieston .... 53 G 19
Garlogie .... 75 M 12
Garmony .... 65 C 14
Garmouth .... 80 K 11
Garmston .... 20 Q 28
Garnkirk (Glen) .... 67 G 15
Garrabost .... 83 B 9
Garragie Lodge .... 73 G 12
Garraron .... 65 D 15
Garreg .... 33 H 25
Garrigill .... 55 M 19
Garrisdale Point .... 71 A 12
Garros .... 77 B 11
Garrow .... 67 I 14
Garry (Glen) *Highland* .... 72 E 12
Garry (Glen)
  Perthshire and Kinross ... 73 H 13
Garry (Loch) .... 72 F 12
Garsington .... 20 Q 28
Garten (Loch) .... 74 I 12
Garth .... 25 J 27
Garthorpe .... 44 R 23
Gartmore .... 67 G 15
Gartocharn .... 67 G 15
Garton-on-The-Wolds .... 51 S 21
Garvald .... 69 M 16
Garvamore .... 73 G 12
Garve .... 79 F 11
Garvellachs .... 65 C 15
Garvestone .... 38 W 26
Garvock .... 66 F 16
Garway .... 26 L 28
Garynahine .... 82 Z 9
Gatehouse of Fleet .... 53 H 19
Gateshead .... 56 P 19
Gateside .... 68 K 15
Gatley .... 42 N 23
Gatwick Airport .... 11 T 30
Gaulden Manor .... 8 K 30
Gavard .... 64 B 15
Gaydon .... 28 P 27
Gayton *King's Lynn*
  and West Norfolk .... 38 V 25
Gayton *Stafford* .... 35 N 25
Gaywood .... 38 V 25
Geary .... 77 A 11
Geddington .... 29 R 26
Gedney Drove End .... 37 U 25
Gedney Hill .... 37 T 25
Gelligaer .... 18 K 29
Gelston .... 53 I 19
Georgeham .... 6 H 30
Georth .... 86 K 6
Gerrards Cross .... 21 S 29
Gestingthorpe .... 30 V 27
Gifford .... 62 L 16
Gigha (Sound of) .... 58 C 17
Gigha Island .... 58 C 16
Gighay .... 70 Y 13
Gilberdyke .... 44 R 22
Gilcrux .... 54 J 19
Gildersome .... 43 P 22
Gilfach Goch .... 17 J 29
Gillamour .... 50 Q 21
Gilling East .... 50 Q 21

Gilling West ....49 O 20
Gillingham *Dorset* ....9 N 30
Gillingham *Kent* ....22 V 29
Gillingham *South Norfolk* ....31 Y 26
Gills ....86 K 8
Gilmerton ....67 I 14
Gilmorton ....28 Q 26
Gilston ....62 L 16
Gilwern ....18 K 28
Girthon ....53 H 19
Girton ....29 U 27
Girvan ....59 F 18
Gisburn ....49 N 22
Gisland ....55 M 19
Gittisham ....8 K 31
Gladestry ....26 K 27
Glaisdale ....50 R 20
Glamis ....74 K 14
Glamis Castle ....74 L 14
Glanaman ....17 I 28
Glandwr ....15 G 28
Glanton ....63 O 17
Glas-allt-Shiel ....74 K 13
Glas-leac Mór ....83 D 9
Glas Maol ....74 J 13
Glasbury ....26 K 27
Glascarnoch (Loch) ....78 F 10
Glascwm ....26 K 27
Glasdrum ....72 E 14
Glasgow ....60 H 16
Glasphein ....76 Z 11
Glaspwll ....33 I 26
Glass (Loch) ....79 G 10
Glassburn ....78 F 11
Glasserton ....52 G 19
Glassford ....60 H 16
Glasshouses ....49 O 21
Glasson ....48 L 22
Glassonby ....55 M 19
Glastonbury ....8 L 30
Gleadless ....43 P 23
Gleann Beag ....78 F 10
Gleann Mór ....79 G 10
Gleaston ....48 K 21
Glecknabae ....59 E 16
Glemsford ....30 V 27
Glen auldyn ....46 G 21
Glen Brittle Forest ....77 B 12
Glen Finglas Reservoir ....67 G 15
Glen More Forest Park ....74 I 12
Glen Shee ....74 J 13
Glen Trool Lodge ....52 G 18
Glenbarr ....59 C 17
Glenborrodale ....71 C 13
Glenbranter ....66 E 15
Glenbrittle House ....77 B 12
Glenbuchat Castle ....74 K 12
Glenbuck ....60 I 17
Glencaple ....53 J 18
Glencarse ....68 K 14
Glencoe ....72 E 13
Glencoul (Loch) ....84 F 9
Glendoebeg ....73 G 12
Glendurgan Garden ....2 E 33
Glenegedale ....58 B 16
Glenelg ....72 D 12
Glenelg Bay ....72 D 12
Glenfarg ....68 J 15
Glenfeshie Lodge ....73 I 12
Glenfiddich Lodge ....80 K 11
Glenfield ....36 Q 26
Glenfinnan ....72 D 13
Glenforsa Airport ....65 C 14
Glenfyne Lodge ....66 F 15
Glengorm ....71 B 14
Glengoulandie ....73 H 14
Glengrasco ....77 B 11
Glenkens (The) ....53 H 18
Glenkin die ....74 L 12
Glenkirk ....61 J 17
Glenlivet ....80 J 11
Glenluce ....52 F 19
Glenmassan ....66 E 15
Glenmaye ....46 F 21
Glenmore ....71 C 13
Glenprosen Village ....74 K 13
Glenridding ....48 L 20
Glenrothes ....68 K 15
Glenside ....82 A 9
Glenstriven ....66 E 16
Glentham ....44 S 23
Glentress ....61 K 17
Glentrool Village ....52 G 18
Glentworth ....44 S 23
Glenuachdarach ....77 B 11
Glenuig ....71 C 13
Glespin ....61 I 17

Gletness ....87 Q 3
Glinton ....37 T 26
Glossop ....43 O 23
Gloucester ....27 N 28
Gloup ....87 Q 1
Glusburn ....49 O 22
Glutt Lodge ....85 I 9
Glympton ....28 P 28
Glyn Ceiriog ....34 K 25
Glyn-Ebwy / Ebbw Vale ..18 K 28
Glyn-neath ....17 J 28
Glynde ....11 U 31
Glyndebourne ....11 U 31
Glyndyfrdwy ....34 K 25
Gnosall ....35 N 25
Goadby ....36 R 26
Goat Fell ....59 E 17
Goathland ....50 R 20
Gobowen ....34 K 25
Godalming ....21 S 30
Godmanchester ....29 T 27
Godmanstone ....8 M 31
Godshill ....10 Q 32
Godstone ....21 T 30
Goil (Loch) ....66 F 15
Golborne ....42 M 23
Goldcliff ....18 L 29
Goldhanger ....22 W 28
Goldthorpe ....44 Q 23
Golspie ....85 I 10
Gomersal ....43 O 22
Gometra ....64 B 14
Gomshall ....21 S 30
Gooderstone ....38 V 26
Goodleigh ....7 I 30
Goodrich ....26 M 28
Goodrington ....4 J 32
Goodwick ....24 F 27
Goodwood House ....10 R 31
Goole ....44 R 22
Goonhavern ....2 E 32
Goostrey ....42 M 24
Gordon ....62 M 16
Gordonbush ....85 I 9
Gordonstown ....80 L 11
Gorebridge ....61 K 16
Goring ....20 Q 29
Gorm Loch Mór ....84 F 9
Gorran Haven ....3 F 33
Gorseinon ....15 H 29
Gorsleston-on-Sea ....39 Z 26
Gortantaoid ....64 B 16
Gosberton ....37 T 25
Gosfield ....30 V 28
Gosforth *Cumbria* ....47 J 20
Gosforth
    Newcastle upon Tyne ....56 P 18
Gosport ....10 Q 31
Goswick ....63 O 16
Gotham ....36 Q 25
Gott Bay ....70 Z 14
Goudhurst ....12 V 30
Gourdon ....75 N 13
Gourock ....66 F 16
Gowerton ....15 H 29
Goxhill ....45 T 22
Graemsay ....86 K 7
Grafton Underwood ....29 S 26
Grain ....22 W 29
Grainthorpe ....45 U 23
Granby ....36 R 25
Grandtully ....74 I 14
Grange-over-Sands ....48 L 21
Grangemouth ....67 I 15
Grantchester ....29 U 27
Grantham ....37 S 25
Grantown-on-Spey ....80 J 12
Grantshouse ....62 N 16
Grasby ....45 S 23
Grasmere ....48 K 20
Grassington ....49 O 21
Grateley ....9 P 30
Graveley ....29 T 27
Gravesend ....22 V 29
Gravir ....82 A 9
Grayrigg ....48 M 20
Grays Thurrock ....22 V 29
Grayshott ....10 R 30
Grayswood ....11 R 30
Greasbrough ....43 P 23
Great Addington ....29 S 26
Great Altcar ....42 K 23
Great Amwell ....21 T 28
Great Asby ....49 M 20
Great Ayton ....50 Q 20
Great Baddow ....22 V 28

Great Bardfield ....30 V 28
Great Barford ....29 S 27
Great Barr ....35 O 26
Great Barrow ....34 L 24
Great Barugh ....50 R 21
Great Bedwyn ....19 P 29
Great Bentley ....31 X 28
Great Bernera ....82 Z 9
Great Bircham ....38 V 25
Great-Bollright ....28 P 28
Great Bookham ....21 S 30
Great Bourton ....28 Q 27
Great Bowden ....28 R 26
Great Brickhill ....29 R 28
Great Bridgeford ....35 N 25
Great Bromley ....30 X 28
Great Broughton ....50 Q 20
Great-Budworth ....42 M 24
Great Burdon ....50 P 20
Great Chalfield ....19 N 29
Great Chesterford ....30 U 27
Great Chishill ....29 U 27
Great Clifton ....53 J 20
Great Coates ....45 T 23
Great-Comberton ....27 N 27
Great Cornard ....30 W 27
Great Cubley ....35 O 25
Great Cumbrae Island .....59 F 16
Great-Dalby ....36 R 25
Great Doddington ....28 R 27
Great Driffield ....51 S 21
Great-Dunham ....38 W 25
Great Dunmow ....30 V 28
Great Easton *Essex* ....30 U 28
Great Easton *Leics.* ....28 R 26
Great Eccleston ....42 L 22
Great Ellingham ....38 W 26
Great Finborough ....30 W 27
Great Glen ....36 Q 26
Great Gonerby ....37 S 25
Great Gransden ....29 T 27
Great Harrowden ....28 R 27
Great Harwood ....42 M 22
Great Hockham ....30 W 26
Great Horkesley ....30 W 28
Great Horwood ....28 R 28
Great Houghton ....43 P 23
Great Langton ....50 P 20
Great-Limber ....45 T 23
Great Livermere ....30 W 27
Great Lumley ....56 P 19
Great Malvern ....27 N 27
Great Marton ....42 K 22
Great Massingham ....38 W 25
Great Milton ....20 Q 28
Great Missenden ....21 R 28
Great Mitton ....42 M 22
Great Musgrave ....49 M 20
Great Oakley ....31 X 28
Great Ormes Head ....41 I 22
Great Orton ....54 K 19
Great Ouse (River) ....38 V 25
Great Ouseburn ....50 Q 21
Great Ponton ....37 S 25
Great Ryburgh ....38 W 25
Great Salkeld ....55 L 19
Great Sampford ....30 V 28
Great Shefford ....20 P 29
Great Shelford ....29 U 27
Great Smeaton ....50 P 20
Great Somerford ....19 N 29
Great Stainton ....56 P 20
Great Strickland ....55 L 20
Great Torrington ....6 H 31
Great Tosson ....63 O 18
Great Totham ....22 W 28
Great Urswick ....48 K 21
Great Wakering ....22 W 29
Great Waltham ....22 V 28
Great Whernside ....49 O 21
Great Whittington ....56 O 18
Great Witley ....27 M 27
Great Wolford ....27 P 27
Great Wyrley ....35 N 26
Great Yarmouth ....39 Z 26
Great Yeldham ....30 V 27
Greatford ....37 S 25
Greatham *Cleveland* ....57 Q 20
Greatham *Hants.* ....10 R 30
Greatstone-on-Sea ....12 W 31
Green Hammerton ....50 Q 21
Greenfield
    Flintshire / Sir y Fflint ...41 K 23
Greenfield *Highland* ....72 F 12
Greenhaugh ....55 N 18
Greenhead ....55 M 19
Greenholm ....60 H 17

Greenhow Hill ....49 O 21
Greenlaw ....62 M 16
Greenloaning ....67 I 15
Greenock ....66 F 16
Greenodd ....48 K 21
Greens Norton ....28 Q 27
Greenside ....56 O 19
Greenwich
    London Borough ....21 U 29
Grendon ....28 R 27
Grendon Underwood ....28 Q 28
Gresford ....34 L 24
Greshornish ....77 A 11
Greshornish (Loch) ....77 A 11
Gress ....83 B 9
Gretna ....54 K 19
Gretton ....37 R 26
Greys Court ....20 R 29
Greysouthen ....54 J 20
Greystoke ....55 L 19
Griffithstown ....18 K 28
Griminish ....76 X 11
Grimley ....27 N 27
Grimoldby ....45 U 23
Grimsay ....76 Y 11
Grimston ....38 V 25
Gringley on the Hill ....44 R 23
Grinshill ....34 L 25
Grinton ....49 O 20
Gristhorpe ....51 T 21
Grittleton ....19 N 29
Groby ....36 Q 26
Grogport ....59 D 17
Groombridge ....12 U 30
Grosebay ....76 Z 10
Grosmont *Monmouthshire /*
    Sir Fynwy ....26 L 28
Grosmont *Scarborough* ...50 R 20
Grove ....20 P 29
Gruinard Bay ....78 D 10
Gruinard Island ....78 D 10
Gruinart ....58 B 16
Gruinart (Loch) ....64 B 16
Grunavat (Loch) ....82 Z 9
Grundisburgh ....31 X 27
Gualachulain ....66 E 14
Guardbridge ....69 L 14
Guernsey *Channel I.* 5
Guesting ....12 V 31
Guildford ....21 S 30
Guildtown ....68 J 14
Guilsborough ....28 Q 26
Guisborough ....50 Q 20
Guiseley ....43 O 22
Guist ....38 W 25
Gullane ....69 L 15
Gunna ....70 Z 14
Gunnerside ....49 N 20
Gunnerton ....55 N 18
Gunness ....44 R 23
Gunnislake ....3 H 32
Gunthorpe ....36 R 25
Gurnard ....10 Q 31
Gurness Broch ....86 K 6
Gurnos ....17 I 28
Gussage All Saints ....9 O 31
Gutcher ....87 Q 1
Guthrie ....75 L 14
Guyhirn ....37 U 26
Gwalchmai ....40 G 23
Gwaun-Cae-Gurwen ....17 I 28
Gwbert-on-Sea ....15 F 27
Gweek ....2 E 33
Gwennap ....2 E 33
Gwithian ....2 D 33
Gwyddelwern ....33 J 24
Gwyddgrug ....15 H 28
Gwydir Castle ....33 I 24
Gwytherin ....33 I 24

H

Habost ....83 B 8
Hackney *London Borough* ..21 T 29
Haddenham *Bucks.* ....20 R 28
Haddenham *Cambs.* ....29 U 26
Haddington ....69 L 16
Haddiscoe ....39 Y 26
Haddo House ....81 N 11
Haddon Hall ....35 P 24
Hadfield ....43 O 23
Hadleigh *Essex* ....22 V 29
Hadleigh *Suffolk* ....30 W 27
Hadley ....34 M 25
Hadlow ....22 V 30
Hadnall ....34 L 25
Hadrian's Wall ....55 M 18
Haggbeck ....55 L 18

Hagley ....27 N 26
Hagworthingham ....45 U 24
Hailsham ....12 U 31
Hainford ....39 X 25
Hainton ....45 T 23
Halam ....36 R 24
Halberton ....7 J 31
Hale ....42 M 23
Hales ....39 Y 26
Halesowen ....27 N 26
Halesworth ....31 Y 26
Halford ....27 P 27
Halifax ....43 O 22
Halistra ....77 A 11
Halkirk ....85 J 8
Hall ....60 G 16
Halland ....12 U 31
Hallaton ....36 R 26
Halling ....22 V 29
Hallington ....55 N 18
Halloughton ....36 R 24
Hallow ....27 N 27
Hallsands ....4 J 33
Halsall ....42 L 23
Halse ....8 K 30
Halsetown ....2 D 33
Halstead ....30 V 28
Halstock ....8 M 31
Haltham ....37 T 24
Halton *Aylesbury Vale* ...20 R 28
Halton *Lancaster* ....48 L 21
Halton Gill ....49 N 21
Haltwhistle ....55 M 19
Halwell ....4 I 32
Halwill Junction ....6 H 31
Hamble ....10 Q 31
Hambleden ....20 R 29
Hambledon *Hants.* ....10 Q 31
Hambledon *Surrey* ....11 S 30
Hambleton *Lancs.* ....42 L 22
Hambleton *North Yorks.* ..44 Q 22
Hambleton Hills (The) .....50 Q 21
Hambridge ....8 L 31
Hamilton ....60 H 16
Hammersmith and Fulham
    London Borough ....21 T 29
Hamnavoe *near Brae* ....87 Q 2
Hamnavoe *near Scallway* ..87 P 3
Hampreston ....9 O 31
Hampstead Norris ....20 Q 29
Hampsthwaite ....50 P 21
Hampton Court ....21 S 29
Hampton in Arden ....27 O 26
Hamstead Marshall ....20 P 29
Hamsterley ....56 O 19
Hamstreet ....12 W 30
Hamworthy ....9 N 31
Handa Island ....84 E 8
Handbridge ....34 L 24
Handbury ....27 N 27
Handcross ....11 T 30
Handforth ....43 N 23
Handley ....34 L 24
Handsworth ....43 P 23
Hanham ....18 M 29
Hanley ....35 N 24
Hanley Swan ....27 N 27
Hanningfield ....22 V 28
Hannington ....19 O 29
Hanslope ....28 R 27
Happisburgh ....39 Y 25
Hapton ....42 N 22
Harberton ....4 I 32
Harbertonford ....4 I 32
Harbledown ....23 X 30
Harborough Magna ....28 Q 26
Harbottle ....63 N 17
Harbury ....28 P 27
Harby ....36 R 25
Hardham ....11 S 31
Hardwick ....44 Q 24
Hardwick Hall ....36 Q 24
Hardwicke ....19 N 28
Hardy Monument ....5 M 31
Hardy's Cottage ....9 M 31
Haresfield ....19 N 28
Hare Street ....29 U 28
Harewood House ....50 P 22
Hargrave ....29 S 27
Hargrave Green ....30 V 27
Harlaxton ....36 R 25
Harlech ....33 H 25
Harleston ....31 X 26
Harlestone ....28 R 27
Harley ....34 M 26
Harlington ....29 S 28

Harlosh ....77 A 11
Harlow ....21 U 28
Harlow Hill ....56 O 18
Harmston ....37 S 24
Haroldswick ....87 R 1
Harpenden ....21 S 28
Harpley ....38 V 25
Harport (Loch) ....77 A 12
Harray (Loch of) ....86 K 6
Harrietfield ....67 J 14
Harrington *Allerdale* .....53 J 20
Harrington *Kettering* ....28 R 26
Harringworth ....37 S 26
Harris *Highland* ....71 A 13
Harris *Western Isles* ......82 Y 10
Harris (Sound of) ....76 Y 10
Harrogate ....50 P 22
Harrow *London Borough* ..21 S 29
Harston ....29 U 27
Hartburn ....56 O 18
Hartest ....30 W 27
Harthill *North Lanarkshire* ..61 I 16
Harthill *Rotherham* ....44 Q 24
Harting ....10 R 31
Hartington ....35 O 24
Hartland ....6 G 31
Hartland Quay ....6 G 31
Hartlebury ....27 N 26
Hartlepool ....57 Q 19
Hartley ....22 U 29
Hartley Wintney ....20 R 30
Hartpury ....27 N 28
Hartshill ....36 P 26
Hartshorne ....28 R 28
Hartwell ....28 R 27
Harvington ....27 O 27
Harwich ....31 X 28
Harwood Dale ....51 S 20
Harworth ....44 Q 23
Hascosay ....87 R 2
Haselbury Plucknett ....8 L 31
Hasland ....43 P 24
Haslemere ....11 R 30
Haslingden ....42 N 22
Haslingfield ....29 U 27
Hassocks ....11 T 31
Haster ....86 K 8
Hastings ....12 V 31
Hatch Court ....8 L 31
Hatfield
    County of Herefordshire ..26 M 27
Hatfield *Herts.* ....21 T 28
Hatfield *South Yorks.* .....44 Q 23
Hatfield Broad Oak ....22 U 28
Hatfield Heath ....22 U 28
Hatfield Peverel ....22 V 28
Hatfield Woodhouse ....44 R 23
Hatherleigh ....7 H 31
Hathern ....36 Q 25
Hathersage ....43 P 24
Hatton *Aberdeenshire* ....81 O 11
Hatton *Derbs.* ....35 O 25
Hatton of Fintray ....75 N 12
Haugh of Urr ....53 I 19
Haughton ....35 N 25
Haunn ....71 B 14
Havant ....10 R 31
Haverfordwest / Hwlfford ..16 F 28
Haverhill ....30 V 27
Haverigg ....47 K 21
Havering *London Borough* ..22 U 29
Haverthwaite ....48 K 21
Hawarden ....34 K 24
Hawes ....49 N 21
Hawick ....62 L 17
Hawkchurch ....8 L 31
Hawkedon ....30 V 27
Hawkesbury Upton ....19 M 29
Hawkhurst ....12 V 30
Hawkridge ....7 J 30
Hawkshead ....48 L 20
Hawkwell ....22 V 29
Hawley ....20 R 30
Hawling ....27 O 28
Haworth ....43 O 22
Hawsker ....51 S 20
Haxby ....50 Q 21
Haxey ....44 R 23
Hay-on-Wye ....26 K 27
Haydock ....42 M 23
Haydon Bridge ....55 N 19
Haydon Wick ....19 O 29
Hayfield ....43 O 23

A B C D E F **G** **H** I J K L M N O P Q R S T U V W X Y Z

Hayle ... 2 D 33
Hayling Island ... 10 R 31
Hayscastle ... 14 E 28
Hayton ... 50 R 22
Haywards Heath ... 11 T 31
Hazel Grove ... 43 N 23
Hazelbank ... 61 I 16
Hazelbury Bryan ... 9 M 31
Hazlemere ... 21 R 29
Heacham ... 38 V 25
Headcorn ... 22 V 30
Headington ... 20 Q 28
Headless Cross ... 27 O 27
Headley ... 10 R 30
Heads of Ayr ... 60 F 17
Healey ... 49 O 21
Healing ... 45 T 23
Heanor ... 36 P 24
Heast ... 71 C 12
Heath End ... 20 Q 29
Heath Hayes ... 35 O 25
Heather ... 36 P 25
Heathfield *Renfrewshire* ... 60 F 16
Heathfield *Wealden* ... 12 U 31
Heathrow Airport ... 21 S 29
Hebburn ... 56 P 19
Hebden Bridge ... 43 N 22
Hebrides (Sea of the) ... 76 Z 12
Heckfield ... 20 R 29
Heckington ... 37 T 25
Heddon on the Wall ... 56 O 19
Hedge End ... 10 Q 31
Hednesford ... 35 O 25
Hedon ... 45 T 22
Heighington *Durham* ... 56 P 20
Heighington *Lincs.* ... 44 S 24
Heights of Kinlochewe ... 78 E 11
Helensburgh ... 66 F 15
Helford ... 2 E 33
Hellifield ... 49 N 22
Hellingly ... 12 U 31
Hellisay ... 70 X 12
Hell's Mouth or Porth Neigwl ... 32 G 25
Helmdon ... 28 Q 27
Helmsdale ... 85 J 9
Helmsley ... 50 Q 21
Helpringham ... 37 T 25
Helpston ... 37 S 26
Helsby ... 42 L 24
Helston ... 2 E 33
Helton ... 55 L 20
Helvellyn ... 48 K 20
Hemel Hempstead ... 21 S 28
Hemingbrough ... 44 R 22
Hemingford Grey ... 29 T 27
Hemington ... 19 M 30
Hempnall ... 39 X 26
Hempton ... 38 W 25
Hemsby ... 39 Z 25
Hemswell ... 44 S 23
Hemsworth ... 43 P 23
Hemyock ... 8 K 31
Hendy ... 15 H 28
Henfield ... 11 T 31
Hengoed ... 18 K 29
Henham ... 30 U 28
Henley ... 27 O 27
Henley-on-Thames ... 20 R 29
Henllan ... 33 J 24
Henllys ... 18 K 29
Henlow ... 29 T 27
Hennock ... 4 J 32
Henshaw ... 55 M 19
Henstead ... 31 Y 26
Henstridge ... 9 M 31
Heol Senni ... 25 J 28
Hepple ... 63 N 18
Heptonstall ... 43 N 22
Herbrandston ... 14 E 28
Hereford ... 26 L 27
Heriot ... 62 L 16
Herm *Channel I.* ... 5
Herma Ness ... 87 R 1
Hermitage ... 20 Q 29
Hermitage Castle ... 62 L 18
Herne Bay ... 23 X 29
Herriard ... 20 Q 30
Herrington ... 56 P 19
Herstmonceux ... 12 U 31
Hertford ... 21 T 28
Hesket Newmarket ... 54 K 19
Hesketh Bank ... 42 L 22
Hesleden ... 57 Q 19
Hessenford ... 3 G 32
Hessle ... 45 S 22
Hest Bank ... 48 L 21

Heswall ... 42 K 24
Hethersgill ... 55 L 19
Hethpool ... 63 N 17
Hetton-le-Hole ... 56 P 19
Heveningham ... 31 Y 27
Hever ... 21 U 30
Heversham ... 48 L 21
Hevingham ... 39 X 25
Hewelsfield ... 18 M 28
Hexham ... 55 N 19
Heybridge ... 22 W 28
Heysham ... 48 L 21
Heyshott ... 11 R 31
Heytesbury ... 9 N 30
Heythrop ... 28 P 28
Heywood ... 43 N 23
Hibaldstow ... 44 S 23
Hickling ... 36 R 25
Hickling Green ... 39 Y 25
Hidcote Manor Garden ... 27 O 27
High Bentham ... 49 M 21
High Bickington ... 7 I 31
High Birkwith ... 49 N 21
High Easter ... 22 V 28
High Ercall ... 34 M 25
High Etherley ... 56 O 20
High Force (The) ... 55 N 20
High Halden ... 12 W 30
High Halstow ... 22 V 29
High Ham ... 8 L 30
High Hesket ... 55 L 19
High Newton *Alnwick* ... 63 P 17
High Newton *South Lakeland* ... 48 L 21
High Offley ... 35 N 25
High Ongar ... 22 U 28
High Peak ... 43 O 23
High Willhays ... 4 I 31
High Wycombe ... 20 R 29
Higham *Kent* ... 22 V 29
Higham *Lancs.* ... 42 N 22
Higham *North East Derbyshire* ... 36 P 24
Higham *Suffolk* ... 30 V 27
Higham Ferrers ... 29 S 27
Higham on the Hill ... 36 P 26
Highbridge ... 18 L 30
Highclere ... 20 P 29
Highcliffe ... 9 O 31
Higher Penwortham ... 42 L 22
Highland Wildlife Park ... 73 I 12
Highmoor Cross ... 20 R 29
Highnam ... 27 N 28
Hightae ... 54 J 18
Hightown *Congleton* ... 35 N 24
Hightown *Sefton* ... 42 K 23
Highworth ... 19 O 29
Hilborough ... 38 W 26
Hildenborough ... 22 U 30
Hilderstone ... 35 N 25
Hilgay ... 38 V 26
Hill ... 18 M 29
Hill of Fearn ... 79 I 10
Hill of Tarvit ... 69 L 15
Hillhead ... 52 G 19
Hillingdon *London Borough* ... 21 S 29
Hillington ... 38 V 25
Hillside ... 75 M 13
Hillswick ... 87 P 2
Hilmarton ... 19 O 29
Hilperton ... 19 N 30
Hilpsford Point ... 47 K 21
Hilton *Aberdeenshire* ... 81 N 11
Hilton *Eden* ... 55 M 20
Hilton *Huntingdonshire* ... 29 T 27
Hilton *North Dorset* ... 9 N 31
Hilton *South Derbyshire* ... 35 P 25
Hilton of Cadboll ... 79 I 10
Himbleton ... 27 N 27
Hinchingbrooke House ... 29 T 27
Hinckley ... 36 P 26
Hinderwell ... 50 R 20
Hindhead ... 10 R 30
Hindley ... 42 M 23
Hindolveston ... 38 X 25
Hindon ... 9 N 30
Hingham ... 38 W 26
Hinstock ... 34 M 25
Hintlesham ... 31 X 27
Hinton-Blewett ... 18 M 30
Hirst Courtney ... 44 Q 22
Hirwaun ... 17 J 28
Histon ... 29 U 27
Hitcham ... 30 W 27
Hitchin ... 29 T 28

Hockering ... 38 X 25
Hockerton ... 36 R 24
Hockley ... 22 V 29
Hockley Heath ... 27 O 26
Hockliffe ... 29 S 28
Hoddesdon ... 21 T 28
Hodnet ... 34 M 25
Hodthorpe ... 44 Q 24
Hogsthorpe ... 45 U 24
Holbeach ... 37 U 25
Holbeach-St. Johns ... 37 T 25
Holbeach-St. Matthew ... 37 U 25
Holbeck ... 44 Q 24
Holbrook ... 31 X 28
Holbury ... 10 P 31
Holcombe ... 18 M 30
Holcombe Rogus ... 7 J 31
Holdenby ... 28 R 27
Holford ... 8 K 30
Holkam Hall ... 38 W 25
Hollandstoun ... 87 M 5
Hollesley ... 31 Y 27
Hollesley Bay ... 31 Y 27
Hollingbourne ... 22 V 30
Hollingworth ... 43 O 23
Hollybush ... 60 G 17
Hollym ... 45 U 22
Holmbridge ... 43 O 23
Holme *Huntingdonshire* ... 29 T 26
Holme *South Lakeland* ... 48 L 21
Holme-next-the-Sea ... 38 V 25
Holme upon Spalding-Moor ... 44 R 22
Holmer Green ... 21 R 29
Holmes Chapel ... 35 M 24
Holmesfield ... 43 P 24
Holmfirth ... 43 O 23
Holmhead ... 60 H 17
Holmpton ... 45 U 22
Holnest ... 8 M 31
Holsworthy ... 6 G 31
Holt *Dorset* ... 9 O 31
Holt *Norfolk* ... 38 X 25
Holt *Wilts.* ... 19 N 29
Holt *Wrexham* ... 34 L 24
Holt Heath ... 27 N 27
Holton *Lincs.* ... 45 T 24
Holton *Norfolk* ... 31 Y 26
Holton *South Somerset* ... 8 M 30
Holton Heath ... 9 N 31
Holton-le-Clay ... 45 T 23
Holwick ... 55 N 20
Holy Island *Anglesey* ... 40 F 23
Holy Island *North Ayrshire* ... 59 E 17
Holy Island *Northumb.* ... 63 O 16
Holybourne ... 10 R 30
Holyhead / Caergybi ... 40 G 23
Holystone ... 63 N 18
Holywell ... 2 E 32
Holywell / Treffynnon ... 41 K 23
Holywell Bay ... 2 E 32
Holywood ... 53 J 18
Honing ... 39 Y 25
Honiton ... 8 K 31
Hoo St. Werburgh ... 22 V 29
Hook *Basingstoke and Deane* ... 20 R 30
Hook *East Riding of Yorkshire* ... 44 R 22
Hook Norton ... 28 P 28
Hooke ... 8 M 31
Hope *Derbs.* ... 43 O 23
Hope *Flintshire* ... 34 K 24
Hope *Highland* ... 84 G 8
Hope *South Shropshire* ... 34 L 26
Hope (Loch) ... 84 G 8
Hope Bowdler ... 26 L 26
Hope under Dinmore ... 26 L 27
Hopeman ... 80 J 10
Hopetoun House ... 68 J 16
Hopton ... 39 Z 26
Horam ... 12 U 31
Horbury ... 43 P 23
Horden ... 57 Q 19
Hordley ... 34 L 25
Horeb ... 15 G 27
Horley ... 21 T 30
Hornby ... 48 M 21
Horncastle ... 45 T 24
Hornchurch ... 22 U 29
Horncliffe ... 63 N 16
Horning ... 39 Y 25
Horninglow ... 35 P 25
Horn's Cross ... 6 H 31
Hornsea ... 51 T 22
Hornton ... 28 P 27
Horrabridge ... 4 H 32

Horseheath ... 30 V 27
Horsehouse ... 49 O 21
Horsell ... 21 S 30
Horsford ... 39 X 25
Horsforth ... 43 P 22
Horsham ... 11 T 30
Horsham St. Faith ... 39 X 25
Horsington *East Lindsey* ... 37 T 24
Horsington *South Somerset* ... 9 M 30
Horsley *Stroud* ... 19 N 28
Horsley *Tynedale* ... 56 O 19
Horsmonden ... 12 V 30
Horstead ... 39 Y 25
Horsted Keynes ... 11 T 30
Horton *Abertawe / Swansea* ... 15 H 29
Horton *East Dorset* ... 9 O 31
Horton *South Somerset* ... 8 L 31
Horton Court ... 19 M 29
Horton-in-Ribblesdale ... 49 N 21
Horwich ... 42 M 23
Hoton ... 36 Q 25
Hott ... 55 M 18
Houghton ... 10 P 30
Houghton Hall ... 38 V 25
Houghton House ... 29 S 27
Houghton-le-Spring ... 56 P 19
Houghton-on-the-Hill ... 36 R 26
Hougton ... 55 L 19
Hounslow *London Borough* ... 21 S 29
Hourn (Loch) ... 72 D 12
Housesteads Fort ... 55 N 18
Houston ... 60 G 16
Houstry ... 85 J 9
Hove ... 11 T 31
Hoveton ... 39 Y 25
Hovingham ... 50 R 21
How Caple ... 26 M 28
Howden ... 44 R 22
Howe of the Mearns ... 75 M 13
Howick ... 63 P 17
Howmore ... 76 X 12
Hownam ... 62 M 17
Howwood ... 60 G 16
Hoxa (Sound of) ... 86 K 7
Hoxne ... 31 X 26
Hoy ... 86 J 7
Hoylake ... 41 K 22
Hoyland Nether ... 43 P 23
Huby ... 50 Q 21
Hucknall ... 36 Q 24
Huddersfield ... 43 O 23
Huggate ... 51 S 22
Hugh Town *I. of Scilly* ... 2
Hughenden ... 20 R 29
Hughley ... 34 M 26
Huish Champflower ... 7 J 30
Huish Episcopi ... 8 L 30
Hull (River) ... 45 S 22
Hulland ... 35 P 24
Hullavington ... 19 N 29
Hullbridge ... 22 V 29
Humber (River) ... 45 T 23
Humber Bridge ... 44 S 22
Humberston ... 45 T 23
Humbleton ... 45 T 22
Hume Castle ... 62 M 17
Humshaugh ... 55 N 18
Hundleton ... 16 F 28
Hundred House ... 26 K 27
Hungerford ... 20 P 29
Hunmanby ... 51 T 21
Hunstanton ... 38 V 25
Hunter's Inn ... 17 I 30
Hunter's Quay ... 66 F 16
Huntingdon ... 29 T 26
Huntington ... 50 Q 22
Huntingtower Castle ... 68 J 14
Huntly ... 80 L 11
Hunton ... 49 O 21
Huntspill ... 18 L 30
Hunwick ... 56 O 19
Hurlford ... 60 G 17
Hurn ... 9 O 31
Hursley ... 10 P 30
Hurst Green ... 12 V 30
Hurstbourne Priors ... 20 P 30
Hurstbourne Tarrant ... 20 P 30
Hurstpierpoint ... 11 T 31
Hurworth-on-Tees ... 50 P 20
Hury ... 55 N 20
Husbands Bosworth ... 28 Q 26
Huthwaite ... 36 Q 24
Huttoft ... 45 U 24
Hutton *Scottish Borders* ... 63 N 16

Hutton *South Ribble* ... 42 L 22
Hutton Cranswick ... 51 S 22
Hutton Rudby ... 50 Q 20
Huxley ... 34 L 24
Huyton ... 42 L 23
Hwlffordd / Haverfordwest ... 16 F 28
Hyde ... 43 N 23
Hynish ... 64 Z 14
Hynish Bay ... 64 Z 14
Hythe *Hants.* ... 10 P 31
Hythe *Kent* ... 13 X 30

I

Ibsley ... 9 O 31
Ibstock ... 36 P 25
Ickleford ... 29 T 28
Icklingham ... 30 V 27
Ickworth House ... 30 V 27
Iddesleigh ... 7 H 31
Ideford ... 4 J 32
Iden ... 12 W 31
Iden Green ... 12 V 30
Idmiston ... 9 O 30
Idrigill Point ... 77 A 12
Ightham ... 22 U 30
Ightham Mote ... 22 U 30
Ilchester ... 8 L 30
Ilderton ... 63 O 17
Ilfracombe ... 17 H 30
Ilkeston ... 36 Q 25
Ilkley ... 49 O 22
Illogan ... 2 E 33
Ilmington ... 27 O 27
Ilminster ... 8 L 31
Ilsington ... 4 I 32
Ilton ... 8 L 31
Immingham ... 45 T 23
Immingham Dock ... 45 T 23
Ince Blundell ... 42 K 23
Ince-in-Makerfield ... 42 M 23
Inch Kenneth ... 64 B 14
Inchard (Loch) ... 84 E 8
Inchbare ... 75 M 13
Inchgrundle ... 74 L 13
Inchkeith ... 68 K 15
Inchlaggan ... 72 E 12
Inchmarnock ... 59 E 16
Inchnadamph ... 84 F 9
Inchture ... 68 K 14
Indaal (Loch) ... 58 A 16
Inerval ... 58 B 17
Ingatestone ... 22 V 28
Ingbirchworth ... 43 P 23
Ingham ... 30 W 27
Ingleby Barwick ... 50 Q 20
Ingleton *Durham* ... 56 O 20
Ingleton *North Yorks.* ... 49 M 21
Inglewhite ... 42 L 22
Inglewood Forest ... 55 L 19
Ingliston ... 68 J 16
Ingoldmells ... 38 V 24
Ingoldsby ... 37 S 25
Ingram ... 63 O 17
Ings ... 48 L 20
Inkpen ... 20 P 29
Innellan ... 59 F 16
Inner Hebrides ... 70 Y 14
Inner Sound ... 77 C 11
Innerleithen ... 61 K 17
Innerpeffray ... 67 I 14
Innerwick ... 69 M 16
Insch ... 81 M 11
Insh ... 73 I 12
Inshore ... 84 F 8
Instow ... 6 H 30
Inver *Highland* ... 79 I 10
Inver *Perth and Kinross* ... 68 J 14
Inver (Loch) ... 84 E 9
Inver Bay ... 79 I 10
Inver Mallie ... 72 E 13
Inver Valley ... 84 E 9
Inveralligin ... 78 D 11
Inverallochy ... 81 O 10
Inveran ... 84 G 10
Inveraray ... 66 E 15
Inverarity ... 69 L 14
Inverarnan ... 66 F 15
Inverbeg ... 66 G 15
Inverbervie ... 75 N 13
Invercassley ... 84 G 10
Invercauld House ... 74 J 12
Inverchapel ... 66 F 15
Invercreran ... 72 E 14
Inverdruie ... 73 I 12
Inverewe Gardens ... 78 C 10
Inverey ... 74 J 13
Inverfarigaig ... 79 G 12

Invergarry ... 72 F 12
Invergeldie ... 67 H 14
Invergordon ... 79 H 10
Invergowrie ... 68 K 14
Inverie ... 72 C 12
Inverinan ... 65 E 15
Inverinate ... 78 D 12
Inverkeithing ... 68 J 15
Inverkeithny ... 81 M 11
Inverkip ... 66 F 16
Inverkirkaig ... 84 E 9
Inverliever Forest ... 65 D 15
Inverlochlang ... 67 G 15
Invermoriston ... 73 G 12
Inverness ... 79 H 11
Inversanda ... 72 D 13
Inversnaid Hotel ... 66 F 15
Inveruglas ... 66 F 15
Inverurie ... 81 M 12
Invervar ... 73 H 14
Inwardleigh ... 7 H 31
Iona ... 64 A 15
Ipplepen ... 4 J 32
Ipstones ... 35 O 24
Ipswich ... 31 X 27
Irby *East Lindsey* ... 37 U 24
Irby *Wirral* ... 42 K 23
Irchester ... 29 S 27
Ireby ... 54 K 19
Ireleth ... 47 K 21
Irlam ... 42 M 23
Iron Acton ... 18 M 29
Ironbridge ... 34 M 26
Irthington ... 55 L 19
Irthlingborough ... 29 S 27
Irvine ... 60 F 17
Irwell (River) ... 42 N 23
Isbyty Ystwyth ... 25 I 27
Isla (Glen) ... 74 K 13
Islay (Sound of) ... 64 B 16
Isle of Whithorn ... 53 G 19
Isleham ... 30 V 26
Isleornsay ... 71 C 12
Isleworth ... 21 S 29
Islington *London Borough* ... 21 T 29
Islip ... 20 Q 28
Islivig ... 82 Y 9
Itchingfield ... 11 S 30
Ithon (River) ... 25 K 27
Itteringham ... 39 X 25
Iver ... 21 S 29
Iver Heath ... 21 S 29
Ivinghoe ... 21 S 28
Ivybridge ... 4 I 32
Ivychurch ... 12 W 30
Iwade ... 22 W 29
Iwerne Minster ... 9 N 31
Ixworth ... 30 W 27

J

Jacobstow ... 6 G 31
Jacobstowe ... 7 H 31
Jameston ... 15 F 29
Jamestown *Dumfries and Galloway* ... 61 K 18
Jamestown *West Dunbartonshire* ... 66 G 16
Janetstown ... 85 J 9
Jarrow ... 56 P 19
Jaywick ... 23 X 28
Jedburgh ... 62 M 17
Jedburgh Abbey ... 62 M 17
Jeffreyston ... 15 F 28
Jemimaville ... 79 H 11
Jersey *Channel I.* ... 5
Jevington ... 12 U 31
John Muir ... 69 M 15
John o' Groats ... 86 K 8
Johnshaven ... 75 N 13
Johnston ... 16 F 28
Johnstone ... 60 G 16
Johnstonebridge ... 54 J 18
Jura (Isle of) ... 58 B 16
Jura (Sound of) ... 65 C 16
Jura Forest ... 65 B 16
Jura Ho ... 58 B 16
Jurby West ... 46 G 20

K

Kainakill ... 77 C 12
Kames ... 65 E 16
Katrine (Loch) ... 67 G 15
Kea ... 2 E 33
Keal ... 37 U 24
Keal (Loch na) ... 65 B 14
Kearsley ... 42 M 23
Keasden ... 49 M 21

Kebock Head ....82 A 9
Kedington ....30 V 27
Kedleston Hall ....36 P 25
Keelby ....45 T 23
Keevil ....19 N 30
Kegworth ....36 Q 25
Keig ....75 M 12
Keighley ....43 O 22
Keillmore ....65 C 16
Keinton Mandeville ....8 M 30
Keir Mill ....53 I 18
Keiss ....86 K 8
Keith ....80 L 11
Keld ....49 N 20
Kellas *Angus* ....69 L 14
Kellas *Moray* ....80 J 11
Kelleth ....49 M 20
Kellie Castle ....69 L 15
Kellington ....44 Q 22
Kelloe ....56 P 19
Kelly Bray ....3 H 32
Kelmarsh ....28 R 26
Kelsall ....34 L 24
Kelso ....62 M 17
Kilham
   Berwick-upon-Tweed ......63 N 17
Kelston ....19 M 29
Keltneyburn ....73 H 14
Kelty ....68 J 15
Kelvedon ....30 W 28
Kelvedon Hatch ....22 U 29
Kemble ....19 N 28
Kemnay ....75 M 12
Kempley ....26 M 28
Kempsey ....27 N 27
Kempsford ....19 O 28
Kempston ....29 S 27
Kemsing ....22 U 30
Kendal ....48 L 21
Kenfig ....17 I 29
Kenilworth ....27 P 26
Kenknock ....67 G 14
Kenmore *Highland* ....77 C 11
Kenmore
   Perthshire and Kinross ..67 I 14
Kenn ....18 L 29
Kennet (River) ....19 O 29
Kennethmont ....80 L 11
Kenninghall ....30 X 26
Kennington *Kent* ....22 W 30
Kennington *Oxon.* ....20 Q 28
Kennoway ....68 K 15
Kenovay ....70 Z 14
Kensaleyre ....77 B 11
Kentallen ....72 E 13
Kentford ....30 V 27
Kentisbeare ....7 K 31
Kentmere ....48 L 20
Kenton ....4 J 32
Kents Bank ....48 L 21
Keoldale ....84 F 8
Keresley ....28 P 26
Kerrera ....65 D 14
Kerry ....26 K 26
Kersey ....30 W 27
Kershader ....82 A 9
Kershopefoot ....55 L 18
Kesgrave ....31 X 27
Kessingland ....31 Z 26
Keswick ....54 K 20
Kettering ....28 R 26
Kettleness ....50 R 20
Kettleshulme ....43 N 24
Kettletoft ....87 M 6
Kettlewell ....49 N 21
Ketton ....37 S 26
Kew ....21 T 29
Kewstoke ....18 L 29
Kexbrough ....43 P 23
Kexby ....44 R 23
Keyingham ....45 T 22
Keymer ....11 T 31
Keynsham ....18 M 29
Keyworth ....36 Q 25
Kibworth Harcourt ....36 R 26
Kidderminster ....27 N 26
Kidermorie Lodge ....79 G 10
Kidlington ....20 Q 28
Kidsgrove ....35 N 24
Kidstones ....49 N 21
Kidwelly / Cydweli ....15 H 28
Kielder ....55 M 18
Kielder Forest ....55 M 18
Kielder Reservoir ....55 M 18
Kiiphedir ....85 I 9
Kilamarsh ....44 Q 24
Kilbarchan ....60 G 16
Kilbirnie ....60 F 16
Kilbrannan Sound ....59 D 17

Kilbride ....65 D 14
Kilburn *Amber Valley* ....36 P 24
Kilburn *Hambleton* ....50 Q 21
Kilchattan ....59 E 16
Kilchenzie ....59 C 17
Kilchiaran ....58 A 16
Kilchoan ....71 B 13
Kilchoman ....58 A 16
Kilchrenan ....65 E 14
Kilconquhar ....69 L 15
Kilcreggan ....66 F 16
Kildale ....50 Q 20
Kildary ....79 H 10
Kildavanan ....59 E 16
Kildonan ....59 E 17
Kildonan Lodge ....85 I 9
Kildrummy ....74 L 12
Kildrummy Castle ....74 L 12
Kilfinnan ....72 F 12
Kilgetti ....15 F 28
Kilham
   Berwick-upon-Tweed ......63 N 17
Kilham
   East Riding of Yorkshire ..51 S 21
Kilkhampton ....6 G 31
Killay ....15 H 29
Killean ....59 D 17
Killearn ....67 G 15
Killen ....79 H 11
Killerton ....7 J 31
Killiechronan ....65 C 14
Killilan ....78 D 12
Killin ....67 H 14
Killinghall ....50 P 21
Killundine ....71 C 14
Kilmacolm ....60 G 16
Kilmaluag ....77 B 10
Kilmany ....69 L 14
Kilmarie ....71 B 12
Kilmarnock ....60 G 17
Kilmartin ....65 D 15
Kilmaurs ....60 G 17
Kilmelford ....65 D 15
Kilmersdon ....19 M 30
Kilmington *East Devon* ....8 K 31
Kilmington *Salisbury* ....9 N 30
Kilmorack ....79 G 11
Kilmore ....71 C 12
Kilmory *Ardnamurchan* ....71 B 13
Kilmory *Argyll and Bute* ....65 C 16
Kilmory *I. Rhum* ....71 A 12
Kilmory *North Ayrshire* ....59 E 17
Kilmuir ....77 A 11
Kilmun ....66 F 16
Kilncadzow ....61 I 16
Kilninver ....65 D 14
Kilnsey ....49 N 21
Kiloran ....64 B 15
Kilpeck ....26 L 28
Kilrenny ....69 L 15
Kilsyth ....67 H 16
Kilt Rock ....77 B 11
Kiltarlity ....79 G 11
Kilvaxter ....77 A 11
Kilwinning ....60 F 17
Kimberley *Broxtowe* ....36 Q 25
Kimberley *South Norfolk* ....38 X 26
Kimble ....20 R 28
Kimbolton ....29 S 27
Kimmeridge ....9 N 32
Kimpton ....21 T 28
Kinbrace ....85 I 9
Kinbuck ....67 I 15
Kincardine *Fife* ....67 I 15
Kincardine *Highland* ....79 G 10
Kincardine *O'Neil* ....75 L 12
Kinclaven ....68 J 14
Kincraig ....73 I 12
Kineton ....28 P 27
Kinfauns ....68 J 14
Kingairloch ....72 D 14
Kingarth ....59 E 16
Kinghorn ....68 K 15
Kinglassie ....68 K 15
King's Bromley ....35 O 25
King's Cliffe ....37 S 26
Kings Langley ....21 S 28
King's Lynn ....38 V 25
King's Meaburn ....55 M 20
King's Somborne ....10 P 30
King's Sutton ....28 Q 27
King's Walden ....29 T 28
Kings Worthy ....10 Q 30
Kingsbarns ....69 M 15
Kingsbridge ....4 I 33
Kingsburgh ....77 A 11

Kingsbury Episcopi ....8 L 31
Kingsclere ....20 Q 30
Kingscote ....19 N 29
Kingsdon ....8 L 30
Kingsdown ....23 Y 30
Kingsgate ....23 Y 29
Kingshouse *Highland* ....72 F 14
Kingshouse *Stirling* ....67 H 14
Kingskerswell ....4 J 32
Kingskettle ....68 K 15
Kingsland ....26 L 27
Kingsley *East Hampshire* ....10 R 30
Kingsley
   Staffordshire Moorlands ...35 O 24
Kingsmuir ....74 L 14
Kingsnorth ....12 W 30
Kingsteignton ....4 J 32
Kingsthorpe ....28 R 27
Kingston *Devon* ....4 I 33
Kingston *East Hampshire* ....69 L 15
Kingston *Moray* ....80 K 10
Kingston
   South Cambridgeshire ....29 T 27
Kingston Bagpuize ....20 P 28
Kingston Deverill ....9 N 30
Kingston Lacy ....9 N 31
Kingston Lisle ....20 P 29
Kingston Seymour ....18 L 29
Kingston-St. Mary ....8 K 30
Kingston-upon-Hull ....45 S 22
Kingston-upon-Thames
   London Borough ....21 T 29
Kingstone ....26 L 27
Kingswear ....4 J 32
Kingswinford ....27 N 26
Kingswood ....19 M 29
Kingswood *Powys* ....34 K 26
Kingswood *South Glos.* ....18 M 29
Kington ....26 K 27
Kington Langley ....19 N 29
Kington-St. Michael ....19 N 29
Kingussie ....73 H 12
Kinkell ....75 M 12
Kinkell Bridge ....67 I 15
Kinknockie ....81 O 11
Kinlet ....27 M 26
Kinloch Hourn ....72 D 12
Kinloch Lodge ....84 G 8
Kinloch Rannoch ....73 H 13
Kinlochard ....67 G 15
Kinlochbervie ....84 E 8
Kinlocheil ....72 E 13
Kinlochewe ....78 E 11
Kinlochleven ....72 F 13
Kinlochmoidart ....71 C 13
Kinloss ....80 J 11
Kinmuck ....75 N 12
Kinnaird ....68 K 14
Kinneff ....75 N 13
Kinnelhead ....61 J 18
Kinnerley ....34 L 25
Kinnersley ....26 L 27
Kinnesswood ....68 K 15
Kinninvie ....56 O 20
Kinross ....68 J 15
Kinrossie ....68 K 14
Kintbury ....20 P 29
Kintessack ....80 I 11
Kintore ....75 M 12
Kintra ....58 B 17
Kintyre (Peninsula) ....59 D 17
Kinver ....27 N 26
Kippax ....43 P 22
Kippen ....67 H 15
Kippford ....53 I 19
Kirby Bellars ....36 R 25
Kirby Cross ....31 X 28
Kirhy Hall ....29 S 26
Kirby Misperton ....50 R 21
Kirby Muxloe ....36 Q 26
Kirby Underwood ....37 S 25
Kirdford ....11 S 30
Kirk Ella ....45 S 22
Kirk Ireton ....35 P 24
Kirk Merrington ....56 P 19
Kirk Michael ....46 G 21
Kirk Yetholm ....63 N 17
Kirkbampton ....54 K 19
Kirkbean ....53 J 19
Kirkbride ....54 K 19
Kirkbuddo ....69 L 14
Kirkburn ....51 S 22
Kirkburton ....43 O 23
Kirkby ....42 L 23
Kirkby Fleetham ....50 P 20
Kirkby-in-Ashfield ....36 Q 24

Kirkby-la-Thorpe ....37 S 25
Kirkby Lonsdale ....48 M 21
Kirkby Malham ....49 N 21
Kirkby Mallory ....36 Q 26
Kirkby Malzeard ....49 P 21
Kirkby Overblow ....50 P 22
Kirkby Stephen ....49 M 20
Kirkby Thore ....55 M 20
Kirkbymoorside ....50 R 21
Kirkcaldy ....68 K 15
Kirkcolm ....52 E 19
Kirkconnel ....60 I 17
Kirkcowan ....52 G 19
Kirkcudbright ....53 H 19
Kirkcudbright Bay ....53 H 19
Kirkfieldbank ....61 I 16
Kirkgunzeon ....53 I 19
Kirkham ....42 L 22
Kirkheaton ....56 O 18
Kirkhill ....79 G 11
Kirkhope ....61 J 18
Kirkinner ....52 G 19
Kirkintilloch ....67 H 16
Kirkland
   Dumfries and Galloway ..53 I 18
Kirkland *Eden* ....55 M 19
Kirklees ....43 O 23
Kirklevington ....50 P 20
Kirklington
   North Yorkshire ....50 P 21
Kirklington
   Nottinghamshire ....36 R 24
Kirkliston ....68 J 16
Kirkmaiden ....52 F 19
Kirkmichael
   Perthshire and Kinross ..74 J 13
Kirkmichael
   South Ayrshire ....60 G 17
Kirkmuirhill ....61 I 17
Kirknewton
   Berwick-upon-Tweed ....63 N 17
Kirknewton
   West Lothian ....61 J 16
Kirkoswald ....59 F 18
Kirkpatrick Durham ....53 I 18
Kirkpatrick-Fleming ....54 K 18
Kirkstone Pass ....48 L 20
Kirkton
   Dumfries and Galloway ..53 J 18
Kirkton *Scottish Borders* ..62 L 17
Kirkton Manor ....61 K 17
Kirkton of Culsalmond ....81 M 11
Kirkton of Durris ....75 M 12
Kirkton of Glenisla ....74 K 13
Kirkton of Kingoldrum ....74 K 13
Kirkton of Largo ....69 L 15
Kirkton of Skene ....75 N 12
Kirkton of Strathmartine ..69 K 14
Kirktown of Auchterless ....81 M 11
Kirktown of Deskford ....80 L 11
Kirkwall ....86 L 7
Kirkwhelpington ....56 N 18
Kirmington ....45 T 23
Kirn ....66 F 16
Kirriemuir ....74 K 13
Kirtlebridge ....54 K 18
Kirtlington ....28 Q 28
Kirtomy ....85 H 8
Kirton *Boston* ....37 T 25
Kirton *Suffolk Coastal* ....31 X 27
Kirton End ....37 T 25
Kirton-in-Lindsey ....44 S 23
Kishorn (Loch) ....78 D 11
Kislingbury ....28 R 27
Kitchener Memorial ....86 J 6
Kiveton ....44 Q 23
Knaresborough ....50 P 21
Knarsdale ....55 M 19
Knebworth ....29 T 28
Kneesall ....36 R 24
Kneesworth ....29 T 27
Kneeton ....36 R 25
Knighton / Trefyclawdd ....26 K 26
Knightshayes Court ....7 J 31
Kniveton ....35 O 24
Knock *Argyll and Bute* ..65 C 14
Knock *Moray* ....80 L 11
Knock *Western Isles* ....83 B 9
Knockandhu ....80 K 12
Knockbrex ....53 H 19
Knockie Lodge ....73 G 12
Knockin ....34 L 25
Knocknaha ....59 D 17
Knocksharry ....46 G 21
Knockvennie Smithy ....53 I 18
Knole ....22 U 30
Knossington ....36 R 25
Knottingley ....44 Q 22

Knowe ....52 G 18
Knowehead ....53 H 18
Knowesgate ....55 N 18
Knowle ....27 O 26
Knowsley ....42 L 23
Knoydart ....72 D 12
Knutsford ....42 M 24
Kyle Forest ....60 G 17
Kyle of Durness ....84 F 8
Kyle of Lochalsh ....77 C 12
Kyle of Sutherland ....79 G 10
Kyle of Tongue ....84 G 8
Kyleakin ....77 C 12
Kylerhea ....72 C 12
Kyles Scalpay ....82 Z 10
Kylestrome ....84 E 9
Kynance Cove ....2 E 34
Kyre park ....26 M 27

L

La Rocque *Jersey I.* 5
Laceby ....45 T 23
Lacey Green ....20 R 28
Lache ....34 L 24
Lacock ....19 N 29
Ladder Hills ....74 K 12
Ladock ....3 F 33
Ladybank ....68 K 15
Ladybower Reservoir ....43 O 23
Ladyhill ....55 N 18
Lagg ....65 C 16
Lagg *Argyll and Bute* ....58 B 16
Laggan *near Invergarry* ..72 F 12
Laggan
   near Newtonmore ....73 H 12
Laggan (Loch) ....73 G 13
Laggan Point ....58 B 16
Lagganulva ....64 B 14
Laide ....78 D 10
Lair ....78 E 11
Lairg ....84 G 9
Lake District National Park ..30 V 26
Lakenheath ....30 V 26
Lamanva ....2 E 33
Lamberhurst ....12 V 30
Lambeth *London Borough* ..21 T 29
Lambley *Gedling* ....36 Q 24
Lambley *Tynedale* ....55 M 19
Lambourn ....20 P 29
Lamerton ....3 H 32
Lamington ....61 J 17
Lamlash ....59 E 17
Lamlash Bay ....59 E 17
Lammermuir Hills ....62 L 16
Lampeter /
   Llanbedr Pont Steffan ..15 H 27
Lamplugh ....54 J 20
Lamport ....28 R 26
Lanark ....61 I 16
Lancaster ....48 L 21
Lanchester ....56 O 19
Lancing ....11 T 31
Landmark Visitor Centre ..79 I 12
Landrake ....3 H 32
Land's End ....2 C 33
Landulph ....3 H 32
Lane End ....20 R 29
Laneast ....6 G 32
Lanercost ....55 L 19
Langar ....36 R 25
Langavat (Loch) *Lewis* ..82 Z 9
Langavat (Loch)
   South Harris ....76 Z 10
Langbank ....66 G 16
Langcliffe ....49 N 21
Langdale End ....51 S 21
Langdale Valley ....48 K 20
Langdon Beck ....55 N 19
Langenhoe ....30 W 28
Langford
   Mid Bedfordshire ....29 T 27
Langford
   West Oxfordshire ....19 P 28
Langford Budville ....8 K 31
Langham ....36 R 25
Langholm ....54 L 18
Langleeford ....63 N 17
Langley ....21 S 29
Langley Park ....56 O 19
Langold ....44 Q 23
Langport ....8 L 30
Langrick ....37 T 24
Langsett ....43 O 23
Langshaw ....62 L 17
Langstrothdale
   Chase ....49 N 21

Langthwaite ....49 O 20
Langtoft ....51 S 21
Langton ....50 R 21
Langton Matravers ....9 O 32
Langwathby ....55 L 19
Lanhydrock ....3 F 32
Lanivet ....3 F 32
Lanlivery ....3 F 32
Lanreath ....3 G 32
Lansallos ....3 G 32
Lanton ....62 M 17
Lapford ....7 I 31
Larachbeg ....71 C 14
Larbert ....67 I 15
Largs ....59 F 16
Larkhall ....61 I 16
Larkhill ....19 O 30
Larling ....30 W 26
Lasswade ....61 K 16
Lastingham ....50 R 21
Latchingdon ....22 W 28
Latton ....19 O 29
Lauder ....62 L 16
Lauderdale ....62 L 16
Laugharne ....15 G 28
Laughton *Wealden* ....12 U 31
Laughton *West Lindsey* ....44 R 23
Launcells ....6 G 31
Launceston ....6 G 32
Launton ....28 Q 28
Laurencekirk ....75 M 13
Laurieston ....53 H 19
Lauriston Castle ....68 K 16
Lavendon ....29 S 27
Lavenham ....30 W 27
Laverstock ....9 O 30
Laverstoke ....20 Q 30
Lawford ....30 X 28
Lawrenny ....16 F 28
Lawshall ....30 W 27
Laxay ....82 A 9
Laxey ....46 G 21
Laxey Bay ....46 G 21
Laxfield ....31 Y 27
Laxford (Loch) ....84 E 8
Laxford Bridge ....84 E 8
Laxo ....87 Q 2
Laxton
   East Riding of Yorkshire ..44 R 22
Laxton
   Newark and Sherwood ....36 R 24
Layer-de-la-Haye ....30 W 28
Layer Marney ....22 W 28
Laytham ....44 R 22
Layton ....42 K 22
Lazonby ....55 L 19
Lea *Herefordshire* ....26 M 28
Lea *North Wiltshire* ....19 N 29
Lea *West Lindsey* ....44 R 23
Leaden Roding ....22 U 28
Leadenham ....37 S 24
Leadgate *Derwentside* ....56 O 19
Leadgate *Eden* ....55 M 19
Leadhills ....61 I 17
Leaflied ....20 P 28
Leagrave ....29 S 28
Lealholm ....50 R 20
Lealt ....65 C 15
Leargybreck ....65 C 16
Leasingham ....37 S 24
Leathaid Bhuain (Loch an) ..84 F 9
Leatherhead ....21 T 30
Leathley ....49 P 22
Leavening ....50 R 21
Lebberston ....51 S 21
Lechlade ....19 O 28
Lecht Road ....74 K 12
Leckmelm ....78 E 10
Leconfield ....44 S 22
Ledbury ....27 M 27
Ledmore ....84 F 9
Ledsham ....44 Q 22
Lee ....16 H 30
Lee-on-the-Solent ....10 Q 31
Leebotwood ....34 L 26
Leeds *Kent* ....22 V 30
Leeds *West Yorks.* ....43 P 22
Leedstown ....2 D 33
Leek ....35 N 24
Leek Wootton ....27 P 27
Leeming Bar ....50 P 21
Leeswood ....34 K 24
Legbourne ....45 U 23
Legerwood ....62 M 16
Leicester ....36 Q 26
Leicester Forest East ....36 Q 26
Leigh ....42 M 23

A B C D E F G H I J K L M N O P Q R S T U V W X Y Z

Leigh *Mole Valley* ... 21 T 30
Leigh *North Wiltshire* ... 19 O 29
Leigh *Sevenoaks* ... 22 U 30
Leigh *West Dorset* ... 8 M 31
Leigh-on-Sea ... 22 V 29
Leigh Sinton ... 27 N 27
Leighterton ... 19 N 29
Leighton Buzzard ... 29 S 28
Leim ... 58 C 17
Leintwardine ... 26 L 26
Leirinmore ... 84 F 8
Leiston ... 31 Y 27
Leith ... 68 K 16
Leitholm ... 62 M 16
Lemreway ... 82 A 9
Lendalfoot ... 52 F 18
Lenham ... 22 W 30
Lennoxtown ... 67 H 16
Leominster ... 26 L 27
Leonard Stanley ... 19 N 28
Lepe ... 10 P 31
Lephinmore ... 65 E 15
Lerwick ... 87 Q 3
Lesbury ... 63 P 17
Leslie *Aberdeenshire* ... 81 L 12
Leslie *Fife* ... 68 K 15
Lesmahagow ... 61 I 17
Leswalt ... 52 E 19
Letchworth ... 29 T 28
Letham *Angus* ... 75 L 14
Letham *Fife* ... 68 K 15
Letheringsett ... 38 X 25
Letterewe Forest ... 78 D 10
Letterfearn ... 78 D 12
Lettermore ... 84 G 8
Letters ... 78 E 10
Letterston ... 24 F 28
Leuchars ... 69 L 14
Leurbost ... 82 A 9
Leven
East Riding of Yorks. ... 51 T 22
Leven *Fife* ... 69 K 15
Leven (Loch) ... 72 E 13
Leven (River) ... 72 F 13
Levens ... 48 L 21
Levens Hall ... 48 L 21
Levenwick ... 87 Q 4
Leverington ... 37 U 25
Leverton
with Habblesthorpe ... 44 R 24
Levington ... 31 X 27
Levisham ... 50 R 21
Lewannick ... 3 G 32
Lewdown ... 6 H 32
Lewes ... 11 U 31
Lewis (Isle of) ... 82 Z 9
Lewis and Harris (Isle of) ... 82 Z 8
Lewisham
London Borough ... 21 T 29
Lewknor ... 20 R 28
Leyburn ... 49 O 21
Leyland ... 42 L 22
Leysdown-on-Sea ... 22 W 29
Lezant ... 3 G 32
Lhanbryde ... 80 K 11
Lhen (The) ... 46 G 20
Liathach ... 78 D 11
Libberton ... 61 J 16
Lichfield ... 35 O 25
Liddesdale ... 55 L 18
Lidgate ... 30 V 27
Lifton ... 6 H 32
Ligger or Perran Bay ... 2 E 32
Lilbourne ... 28 Q 26
Lilleshall ... 35 M 25
Lilliesleaf ... 62 L 17
Limmerhaugh ... 60 H 17
Limpsfield ... 21 U 30
Linchmere ... 10 R 30
Lincoln ... 44 S 24
Lincolnshire Wolds ... 45 T 23
Lindfield ... 11 T 30
Lindores ... 68 K 14
Lingague ... 46 F 21
Lingay *near Eriskay* ... 70 X 12
Lingay *near Pabbay* ... 70 X 13
Lingen ... 26 L 27
Lingfield ... 21 T 30
Liniclate ... 76 X 11
Linlithgow ... 67 J 16
Linn of Dee ... 74 J 13
Linn of Tummel ... 74 I 13
Linneraineach ... 84 E 9
Linney Head ... 14 E 29
Linnhe (Loch) ... 72 D 14
Linslade ... 29 R 28
Lintmill ... 80 L 10

Linton *Craven* ... 49 N 21
Linton *Herefordshire* ... 26 M 28
Linton *Scottish Borders* ... 62 M 17
Linton
South Cambridgeshire ... 30 U 27
Linton *South Derbyshire* ... 35 P 25
Linton-on-Ouse ... 50 Q 21
Lintrathen (Loch of) ... 74 K 13
Linwood *Renfrewshire* ... 60 G 16
Linwood *West Lindsey* ... 45 T 23
Liphook ... 10 R 30
Liskeard ... 3 G 32
Lismore ... 65 D 14
Liss ... 10 R 30
Lisset ... 51 T 21
Lisvane ... 18 K 29
Litcham ... 38 W 25
Litchborough ... 28 Q 27
Litchfield ... 20 P 30
Litherland ... 42 L 23
Little-Baddow ... 22 V 28
Little-Barningham ... 39 X 25
Little Berkhamsted ... 21 T 28
Little Brington ... 28 Q 27
Little Budworth ... 34 M 24
Little Bytham ... 37 S 25
Little Chalfont ... 21 S 28
Little Clacton ... 31 X 28
Little Colonsay ... 64 B 14
Little-Coxwell ... 19 P 29
Little Cumbrae Island ... 59 F 16
Little Dewchurch ... 26 L 28
Little Galdenoch ... 52 E 19
Little Glenshee ... 67 J 14
Little Hadham ... 29 U 28
Little Hallingbury ... 22 U 28
Little Harrowden ... 28 R 27
Little Houghton ... 28 R 27
Little Loch Broom ... 78 D 10
Little Loch Roag ... 82 Z 9
Little Mill ... 18 L 28
Little-Milton ... 20 Q 28
Little Minch (The) ... 76 Z 11
Little Moreton Hall ... 35 N 24
Little Ouse (River) ... 30 V 26
Little Ouseburn ... 50 Q 21
Little-Raveley ... 29 T 26
Little Snoring ... 38 W 25
Little-Stretton ... 26 L 26
Little-Stukeley ... 29 T 26
Little Torrington ... 6 H 31
Little Urswick ... 48 K 21
Little Walsingham ... 38 W 25
Little Waltham ... 22 V 28
Little Wenlock ... 34 M 26
Littleborough ... 43 N 23
Littlebourne ... 23 X 30
Littlebury ... 30 U 27
Littlecote House ... 20 P 29
Littleferry ... 79 H 10
Littleham ... 4 J 32
Littlehampton ... 11 S 31
Littlemill ... 79 I 11
Littleport ... 30 U 26
Littlestone-on-Sea ... 12 W 31
Littleton ... 10 P 30
Littleworth ... 20 P 28
Litton Cheney ... 5 M 31
Liverpool ... 42 L 23
Liverton ... 50 R 20
Livet (Glen) ... 80 K 12
Livingston ... 61 J 16
Lizard ... 2 E 34
Lizard Peninsula ... 2 E 33
Llaim ... 35 O 24
Llan ... 33 J 26
Llan-non ... 15 H 28
Llan-y-Bri ... 15 G 28
Llanaelhaearn ... 32 G 25
Llanaethney ... 15 H 28
Llanasa ... 41 J 23
Llanbadarn Fawr ... 25 H 26
Llanbedr ... 33 H 25
Llanbedr Pont Steffan /
Lampeter ... 15 H 27
Llanbedrog ... 32 G 25
Llanberis ... 33 H 24
Llanberis (Pass of) ... 33 H 24
Llanbister ... 26 K 26
Llanboidy ... 15 G 28
Llanbradach ... 18 K 29
Llanbrynmair ... 33 J 26
Llanddarog ... 15 H 28
Llanddeiniol ... 25 H 27
Llanddderfel ... 33 J 25
Llanddeusant ... 40 G 22

Llanddewi Brefi ... 25 I 27
Llanddewi Ystradenni ... 26 K 27
Llanddona ... 40 H 23
Llanddowror ... 15 G 28
Llanddulas ... 41 J 23
Llandegla ... 34 K 24
Llandeilo ... 15 I 28
Llandenny ... 18 L 28
Llandinam ... 25 J 26
Llandissilio ... 15 F 28
Llandogo ... 18 L 28
Llandovery / Llanymddyfri ... 25 I 28
Llandrindod Wells ... 25 J 27
Llandrinio ... 34 K 25
Llandudno ... 41 I 23
Llandudno Junction ... 41 I 23
Llandwrog ... 32 H 24
Llandybie ... 15 H 28
Llandyfaelog ... 15 H 28
Llandygai ... 40 H 23
Llandysul ... 15 H 27
Llanegryn ... 33 H 26
Llanelidan ... 34 K 24
Llanellen ... 18 K 28
Llanelli ... 15 H 28
Llanelltyd ... 33 I 25
Llanengan ... 32 G 25
Llanerchymedd ... 40 G 23
Llanerfyl ... 33 J 25
Llanfachraeth ... 40 G 23
Llanfaethlu ... 40 G 22
Llanfair ... 33 H 25
Llanfair-Caereinion ... 34 K 26
Llanfair-Pwllgwyngyll ... 40 H 23
Llanfair-ym-Muallt /
Builth Wells ... 25 J 27
Llanfair-yn-Neubwll ... 40 G 23
Llanfairfechan ... 41 I 23
Llanfairynghornwy ... 40 G 22
Llanfechell ... 40 G 22
Llanferres ... 34 K 24
Llanfihangel-ar-arth ... 15 H 28
Llanfihangel Glyn Myfyr ... 33 J 24
Llanfihangel Nant Bran ... 25 J 28
Llanfihangel Rhyditon ... 26 K 27
Llanfihangel-y-Creuddyn ... 25 I 26
Llanfilo ... 26 K 28
Llanfoist ... 18 K 28
Llanfrynach ... 25 J 28
Llanfwrog ... 40 G 23
Llanfyllin ... 34 K 25
Llanfynydd *Carmarthenshire /*
Sir Gaerfyrddin ... 15 H 28
Llanfynydd *Flintshire /*
Sir y Fflint ... 34 K 24
Llanfyrnach ... 15 G 28
Llangadfan ... 33 J 25
Llangadog ... 15 I 28
Llangain ... 15 G 28
Llangammarch Wells ... 25 J 27
Llangarron ... 26 L 28
Llangathen ... 15 H 28
Llangedwyn ... 34 K 25
Llangefni ... 40 H 23
Llangeinor ... 17 J 29
Llangeitho ... 25 H 27
Llangeler ... 15 G 27
Llangenith ... 15 H 29
Llangennech ... 15 H 28
Llangernyw ... 33 I 24
Llangoed ... 40 H 23
Llangollen ... 34 K 25
Llangorse ... 26 K 28
Llangorwen ... 25 H 26
Llangrannog ... 15 G 27
Llangunllo ... 26 K 27
Llangunnor ... 15 H 28
Llangurig ... 25 J 26
Llangwm *Monmouthshire /*
Sir Fynwy ... 18 L 28
Llangwm *Pembrokeshire /*
Sir Benfro ... 16 F 28
Llangwnnadl ... 32 F 25
Llangwyryfon ... 25 H 27
Llangybi ... 15 H 27
Llangyndeyrn ... 15 H 28
Llangynidr ... 26 K 28
Llangynog *Carmarthenshire /*
Sir Gaerfyrddin ... 15 G 28
Llangynog *Powys* ... 33 J 25
Llangynwyd ... 17 J 29
Llangywer ... 33 J 25
Llanharan ... 17 J 29
Llanharry ... 17 J 29
Llanhilleth ... 18 K 28
Llanidloes ... 25 J 26

Llanilar ... 25 H 26
Llanishen ... 18 L 28
Llanllwchaiarn ... 26 K 26
Llanllyfni ... 32 H 24
Llanmadoc ... 15 H 29
Llannefydd ... 41 J 23
Llanon ... 25 H 27
Llanpumsaint ... 15 H 28
Llanrhaeadr ... 33 J 24
Llanrhaeadr-ym-
Mochnant ... 34 K 25
Llanrhidian ... 15 H 29
Llanrhystud ... 25 H 27
Llanrug ... 33 H 24
Llanrwst ... 33 I 24
Llansanffraid Glan Conwy ... 41 I 23
Llansannan ... 33 J 24
Llansantffraid ... 25 H 27
Llansantffraid-ym-Mechain ... 34 K 25
Llansawel ... 15 H 27
Llansilin ... 34 K 25
Llansoy ... 18 L 28
Llanstephan ... 15 G 28
Llanthony ... 26 K 28
Llanthony Priory ... 26 K 28
Llantilio Crossenny ... 18 L 28
Llantrisant ... 17 J 29
Llantwit Major ... 17 J 29
Llanuwchllyn ... 33 I 25
Llanvetherine ... 18 L 28
Llanwddyn ... 33 J 25
Llanwenog ... 15 H 27
Llanwnda ... 32 H 24
Llanwnen ... 15 H 27
Llanwnog ... 25 J 26
Llanwrda ... 25 I 28
Llanwrin ... 33 I 26
Llanwrtyd Wells ... 25 J 27
Llanwyddelan ... 33 J 26
Llanybydder ... 15 H 27
Llanychaer ... 24 F 28
Llanymawddwy ... 33 J 25
Llanymddyfri / Llandovery ... 25 I 28
Llanymynech ... 34 K 25
Llanynghenedl ... 40 G 23
Llanystumdwy ... 32 H 25
Llawhaden ... 15 F 28
Llechryd ... 15 G 27
Lledrod ... 25 I 27
Lleyn Peninsula ... 32 G 25
Llithfaen ... 32 G 25
Llowes ... 26 K 27
Llston ... 15 H 29
Llwydafydd ... 24 G 27
Llwyngwril ... 33 H 25
Llwynmawr ... 34 K 25
Llyfnant Valley ... 33 I 26
Llyn Brianne ... 25 I 27
Llyn Celyn ... 33 I 25
Llyn Tegid or Bala Lake ... 33 J 25
Llyswen ... 26 K 27
Llysworney ... 17 J 29
Llywel ... 25 J 28
Loanhead ... 61 K 16
Lochailort ... 72 D 13
Lochaline ... 65 C 14
Lochans ... 52 E 19
Locharbriggs ... 53 J 18
Lochassynt Lodge ... 84 E 9
Lochawe ... 66 E 14
Lochay (Glen) ... 67 G 14
Lochboisdale ... 70 Y 12
Lochbuie ... 65 C 14
Lochcarron ... 78 D 11
Lochdonhead ... 65 C 14
Lochdrum ... 78 F 10
Lochearnhead ... 67 H 14
Locheport ... 76 Y 11
Locherben ... 61 J 18
Lochfoot ... 53 I 18
Lochgair ... 65 D 15
Lochgarthside ... 73 G 12
Lochgelly ... 68 K 15
Lochgilphead ... 65 D 15
Lochgoilhead ... 66 F 15
Lochinver ... 84 E 9
Lochluichart ... 78 F 11
Lochmaben ... 54 J 18
Lochmaddy ... 76 Y 11
Lochore ... 68 K 15
Lochportain ... 76 Y 11
Lochranza ... 59 E 16
Lochsie (Glen) ... 74 J 13
Lochstack ... 84 F 8
Lochton *Aberdeenshire* ... 75 M 12
Lochton *South Ayrshire* ... 52 F 18
Lochtyn / Ynys ... 15 G 27

Lochuisge ... 72 D 14
Lochwinnoch ... 60 G 16
Lochy (Loch) ... 72 F 13
Lockerbie ... 54 J 18
Lockerley ... 9 P 30
Locking ... 18 L 30
Loddington ... 28 R 26
Loddon ... 39 Y 26
Lode ... 30 U 27
Lodsworth ... 11 R 31
Lofthouse ... 49 O 21
Loftus ... 50 R 20
Logan Gardens ... 52 F 19
Loggerheads ... 35 M 25
Logie Coldstone ... 74 L 12
Logiealmond ... 67 I 14
Login ... 15 F 28
Lomond (Loch) ... 66 G 15
Londesborough ... 51 R 22
London ... 21 T 29
London Colney ... 21 T 28
Long (Loch) *Angus* ... 68 K 14
Long (Loch)
Argyll and Bute ... 66 F 15
Long Ashton ... 18 M 29
Long Bennington ... 36 R 25
Long Bredy ... 5 M 31
Long Buckby ... 28 Q 27
Long Clawson ... 36 R 25
Long Crendon ... 20 R 28
Long Eaton ... 36 Q 25
Long Hanborough ... 20 P 28
Long Itchington ... 28 P 27
Long Lawford ... 28 Q 26
Long Man (The) ... 12 U 31
Long Marston ... 50 Q 22
Long Marton ... 55 M 20
Long Melford ... 30 W 27
Long Mountain ... 34 K 26
Long Mynd (The) ... 26 L 26
Long Preston ... 49 N 21
Long Stratton ... 31 X 26
Long Sutton *Lincs.* ... 37 U 25
Long Sutton *Somerset* ... 8 L 30
Long Wittenham ... 20 Q 29
Longay ... 77 C 12
Longbenton ... 56 P 18
Longborough ... 27 O 28
Longbridge Deverill ... 9 N 30
Longburton ... 8 M 31
Longcot ... 19 P 29
Longdon ... 35 O 25
Longfield ... 22 U 29
Longford
Derbyshire Dales ... 35 O 25
Longford *Tewkesbury* ... 27 N 28
Longforgan ... 68 K 14
Longformacus ... 62 M 16
Longham ... 38 W 25
Longhirst ... 56 P 18
Longhorsley ... 56 O 18
Longhoughton ... 63 P 17
Longleat House ... 19 N 30
Longmanhill ... 81 M 11
Longnewton ... 50 P 20
Longney ... 19 M 28
Longniddry ... 69 L 16
Longnor ... 35 O 24
Longridge *Ribble Valley* ... 42 M 22
Longridge
South Staffordshire ... 35 N 25
Longridge *West Lothian* ... 61 I 16
Longside ... 81 O 11
Longstanton ... 29 U 27
Longton *South Ribble* ... 42 L 22
Longton *Stoke-on-Trent* ... 35 N 25
Longtown *Carlisle* ... 54 L 18
Longtown *Herefordshire* ... 26 L 28
Longwick ... 20 R 28
Longworth ... 20 P 28
Lonmore ... 77 A 11
Looe ... 3 G 32
Loose ... 22 V 30
Loppington ... 34 L 25
Lorn ... 65 E 14
Lorn (Firth of) ... 65 D 14
Lossiemouth ... 80 K 10
Lostwithiel ... 3 G 32
Lothbeg ... 85 I 9
Lothersdale ... 49 N 22
Lothmore ... 85 I 9
Loudwater ... 21 R 29
Loughborough ... 36 Q 25
Loughor (River) ... 17 H 29
Loughton ... 21 U 29
Louth ... 45 U 23
Lovington ... 8 M 30

Low Bradley ... 49 O 22
Low Crosby ... 55 L 19
Low Row *Carlisle* ... 55 M 19
Low Row *Richmondshire* ... 49 N 20
Low Street ... 39 Y 25
Lowca ... 53 J 20
Lowdham ... 36 Q 24
Lower Beeding ... 11 T 30
Lower Bentham ... 49 M 21
Lower Boddington ... 28 Q 27
Lower Broadheath ... 27 N 27
Lower Cam ... 19 M 28
Lower Diabaig ... 78 C 11
Lower Dounreay ... 85 I 8
Lower Dunsforth ... 50 Q 21
Lower Halstow ... 22 W 29
Lower Hardres ... 23 X 30
Lower Heyford ... 28 Q 28
Lower Killeyan ... 58 B 17
Lower Largo ... 69 L 15
Lower Mayland ... 22 W 28
Lower Peover ... 42 M 24
Lower Upham ... 10 Q 31
Lower-Whitley ... 42 M 24
Lowestoft ... 31 Z 26
Lowgill ... 49 M 21
Lowick
Berwick-upon-Tweed ... 63 O 17
Lowick
East Northamptonshire ... 29 S 26
Lowick Bridge ... 48 K 21
Lowther ... 55 L 20
Lowther Hills ... 61 J 18
Loxwood ... 11 S 30
Loyal (Loch) ... 84 G 8
Loyne (Loch) ... 72 E 12
Lùb Score ... 77 A 10
Lubcroy ... 84 F 10
Lubenham ... 28 R 26
Lubnaig (Loch) ... 67 H 15
Luccombe ... 17 J 30
Luce Bay ... 52 F 19
Lucker ... 63 O 17
Luddesdown ... 22 V 29
Ludford *East Lindsey* ... 45 T 23
Ludford *South Shropshire* ... 26 L 26
Ludgershall *Bucks.* ... 20 Q 28
Ludgershall *Wilts.* ... 19 P 30
Ludgvan ... 2 D 33
Ludham ... 39 Y 25
Ludlow ... 26 L 26
Lugton ... 60 G 16
Luib *Highland* ... 77 B 12
Luib *Stirling* ... 67 G 14
Luichart (Loch) ... 78 F 11
Luing ... 65 D 15
Lullington ... 35 P 25
Lulsgate Bottom ... 18 L 29
Lulworth Cove ... 9 N 32
Lumphanan ... 75 L 12
Lumsden ... 80 L 12
Lunan ... 75 M 14
Lunanhead ... 74 L 14
Luncarty ... 68 J 14
Lund ... 51 S 22
Lundie ... 68 K 14
Lundie (Loch) ... 78 C 11
Lundin Links ... 69 L 15
Lundy ... 16 G 30
Lunning ... 87 Q 2
Lurgainn (Loch) ... 84 E 9
Lurgashall ... 11 S 30
Luskentyre ... 82 Z 10
Luss ... 66 G 15
Lusta ... 77 A 11
Lustleigh ... 4 I 32
Luston ... 26 L 27
Luthermuir ... 75 M 13
Luthrie ... 68 K 14
Luton ... 29 S 28
Luton Hoo ... 21 S 28
Lutterworth ... 28 Q 26
Lutton ... 37 U 25
Luxborough ... 7 J 30
Lybster ... 86 K 9
Lydbury North ... 26 L 26
Lydd ... 12 W 31
Lydd-on-Sea ... 12 W 31
Lydden ... 23 X 30
Lydeard-St. Lawrence ... 8 K 30
Lydford *Mendip* ... 8 M 30
Lydford *West Devon* ... 4 H 32
Lydiard Millicent ... 19 O 29
Lydiard Park ... 19 O 29
Lydiate ... 42 L 23
Lydlinch ... 9 M 31

Lydney ... 18 M 28
Lydstep ... 15 F 29
Lyme Bay ... 5 L 32
Lyme Park ... 43 N 23
Lyme Regis ... 5 L 31
Lyminge ... 13 X 30
Lymington ... 10 P 31
Lymm ... 42 M 23
Lympne ... 13 X 30
Lympstone ... 4 J 32
Lyndhurst ... 10 P 31
Lyne ... 61 K 17
Lyneham *North Wiltshire* ... 19 O 29
Lyneham *West Oxfordshire* ... 27 P 28
Lynemouth ... 56 P 18
Lyness ... 86 K 7
Lynmouth ... 17 I 30
Lynton ... 17 I 30
Lyon (Glen) ... 73 H 14
Lyonshall ... 26 L 27
Lytchett Matravers ... 9 N 31
Lytchett Minster ... 9 N 31
Lytes Cary ... 8 L 30
Lyth ... 86 K 8
Lytham ... 42 L 22
Lytham St. Anne's ... 42 K 22
Lythe ... 51 R 20

M

Maaruig ... 82 Z 10
Mabie ... 53 J 18
Mablethorpe ... 45 U 23
Macaskin (Island) ... 65 D 15
Macclesfield ... 43 N 24
Macduff ... 81 M 10
Machars (The) ... 52 G 19
Machen ... 18 K 29
Machir Bay ... 58 A 16
Machrihanish ... 58 C 17
Machrihanish Bay ... 58 C 17
Machynlleth ... 33 I 26
Madderty ... 67 I 14
Maddiston ... 67 I 16
Maddy (Loch) ... 76 Y 11
Madeley *Staffs* ... 35 M 24
Madeley *Telford and Wrekin* ... 35 M 26
Madingley ... 29 U 27
Madron ... 2 D 33
Maenclochog ... 15 F 28
Maentwrog ... 33 I 25
Maerdy *Conwy* ... 33 J 25
Maerdy *Rhondda, Cynon, Taf* ... 17 J 28
Maes Howe ... 86 K 7
Maesbrook ... 34 K 25
Maesteg ... 17 J 29
Maghull ... 42 L 23
Magor ... 18 L 29
Maiden Bradley ... 9 N 30
Maiden Castle ... 8 M 31
Maiden Newton ... 8 M 31
Maidenhead ... 20 R 29
Maidens ... 59 F 17
Maidford ... 28 Q 27
Maids Morelon ... 28 R 27
Maidstone ... 22 V 30
Maidwell ... 28 R 26
Mainland *Orkney Islands* ... 86 J 6
Mainland *Shetland Islands* ... 87 R 3
Mainstone ... 26 K 26
Maisemore ... 27 N 28
Malborough ... 4 I 33
Maldon ... 22 W 28
Malham ... 49 N 21
Mallaig ... 71 C 12
Mallory Park Circuit ... 36 P 26
Mallwyd ... 33 I 25
Malmesbury ... 19 N 29
Malpas ... 34 L 24
Maltby ... 44 Q 23
Maltby-le-Marsh ... 45 U 24
Malton ... 50 R 21
Malvern Wells ... 27 N 27
Mamble ... 26 M 26
Mamore Forest ... 72 F 13
Man (Isle of) ... 46 G 21
Manaccan ... 2 E 33
Manaton ... 4 I 32
Manchester ... 43 N 23
Manderston ... 62 N 16
Manea ... 29 U 26
Mangersta ... 82 Y 9
Manish ... 76 Z 10
Manningford Bruce ... 19 O 30

Mannings Heath ... 11 T 30
Manningtree ... 31 X 28
Manorbier ... 15 F 29
Mansfield ... 36 Q 24
Mansfield Woodhouse ... 36 Q 24
Manstone ... 9 N 31
Manton ... 36 R 26
Manuden ... 30 U 28
Maplebeck ... 36 R 24
Mapledurham ... 20 Q 29
Mappleton ... 45 T 22
Mappowder ... 9 M 31
Mar (Forest of) ... 74 J 12
Marazion ... 2 D 33
March ... 37 U 26
Marcham ... 20 P 29
Marchington ... 35 O 25
Marchwood ... 10 P 31
Marden ... 22 V 30
Maree (Loch) ... 78 D 10
Mareham-le-Fen ... 37 T 24
Maresfield ... 11 U 31
Margam ... 17 I 29
Margaretting ... 22 V 28
Margate ... 23 Y 29
Margnaheglish ... 59 E 17
Marham ... 38 V 26
Marholm ... 37 T 26
Marian-Glas ... 40 H 22
Marishader ... 77 B 11
Mark *Sedgemoor* ... 18 L 30
Mark *South Ayrshire* ... 52 E 18
Market Bosworth ... 36 P 26
Market Deeping ... 37 T 25
Market Drayton ... 34 M 25
Market Harborough ... 28 R 26
Market Lavington ... 19 O 30
Market Overton ... 36 R 25
Market Rasen ... 45 T 23
Market Weighton ... 44 S 22
Markfield ... 36 Q 25
Markinch ... 68 K 15
Marks Tey ... 30 W 28
Marksbury ... 18 M 29
Markyate ... 21 S 28
Marlborough ... 19 O 29
Marldon ... 4 J 32
Marlesford ... 31 Y 27
Marloes ... 14 E 28
Marlow ... 20 R 29
Marnhull ... 9 N 31
Marple ... 43 N 23
Marros ... 15 G 28
Marsden ... 43 O 23
Marsett ... 49 N 21
Marsh Gibbon ... 28 Q 28
Marsham ... 39 X 25
Marshaw ... 48 M 22
Marshchapel ... 45 U 23
Marshfield *Casnewydd / Newport* ... 18 K 29
Marshfield *South Gloucestershire* ... 19 N 29
Marshwood ... 8 L 31
Marske ... 49 O 20
Marske-by-the-Sea ... 57 Q 20
Marstch ... 20 Q 28
Marston ... 37 R 25
Marston Magna ... 8 M 31
Marston Moretaine ... 29 S 27
Martham ... 39 Y 25
Martin *New Forest* ... 9 O 31
Martin *North Kesteven* ... 37 T 24
Martin (Isle) ... 84 E 10
Martin Mill ... 23 Y 30
Martindale ... 48 L 20
Martinstown ... 5 M 31
Martlesham ... 31 X 27
Martletwy ... 15 F 28
Martley ... 27 M 27
Martock ... 8 L 31
Marton *Harrogate* ... 50 P 21
Marton *Macclesfield* ... 35 N 24
Marvig ... 82 A 9
Marwell Zoological Park ... 10 Q 31
Mary Arden's House ... 27 O 27
Mary Tavy ... 4 H 32
Marybank ... 79 G 11
Maryburgh ... 79 G 11
Maryculter ... 75 N 12
Maryfield ... 87 Q 3
Marykirk ... 75 M 13
Marypark ... 80 J 11
Maryport *Allerdale* ... 53 J 19
Maryport *Dumfries and Galloway* ... 52 F 19

Marywell *Aberdeenshire* ... 75 L 12
Marywell *Angus* ... 69 M 14
Masham ... 49 P 21
Matching Green ... 22 U 28
Mathry ... 14 E 28
Matlock ... 36 P 24
Matlock Bath ... 35 P 24
Mattersey ... 44 R 23
Mattingley ... 20 R 30
Mattishall ... 38 X 26
Mauchline ... 60 G 17
Maud ... 81 N 11
Maughold ... 46 H 21
Maughold Head ... 46 H 21
Mawbray ... 54 J 19
Mawnan ... 2 E 33
Maxstoke ... 27 P 26
Maxton ... 62 M 17
Maybole ... 60 F 17
Mayfield *East Sussex* ... 12 U 30
Mayfield *Staffs* ... 35 O 24
Mc Arthur's Head ... 58 B 16
Meadie (Loch) ... 84 G 9
Meal Bank ... 48 L 20
Mealsgate ... 54 K 19
Meare ... 8 L 30
Measach (Falls of) ... 78 E 10
Measham ... 36 P 25
Meavaig ... 82 Z 10
Meavy ... 4 H 32
Medbourne ... 28 R 26
Medmenham ... 20 R 29
Medstead ... 10 Q 30
Medway (River) ... 22 W 29
Meidrim ... 15 G 28
Meifod ... 34 K 25
Meigle ... 68 K 14
Meikleour ... 68 J 14
Melbost ... 83 B 9
Melbourn ... 29 U 27
Melbourne *East Riding of Yorkshire* ... 44 R 22
Melbourne *South Derbyshire* ... 36 P 25
Melbury Osmond ... 8 M 31
Meldon ... 56 O 18
Melfort ... 65 D 15
Melgarve ... 73 G 12
Melksham ... 19 N 29
Melldalloch ... 65 E 16
Mellerstain ... 62 M 17
Melling ... 48 M 21
Mellon Charles ... 78 D 10
Mellon Udrigle ... 78 D 10
Mells ... 19 M 30
Melmerby *Eden* ... 55 M 19
Melmerby *Harrogate* ... 50 P 21
Melrose ... 62 L 17
Meltham ... 43 O 23
Melton ... 31 X 27
Melton Mowbray ... 36 R 25
Melvaig ... 77 C 10
Melvich ... 85 I 8
Memsie ... 81 N 11
Menai Bridge / Porthaethwy ... 40 H 23
Menai Strait ... 33 H 24
Mendip Hills ... 18 L 30
Mendlesham ... 31 X 27
Menheniot ... 3 G 32
Mennock ... 61 I 17
Menston ... 43 O 22
Menstrie ... 67 I 15
Menteith Hills ... 67 H 15
Mentmore ... 29 R 28
Meonstoke ... 10 Q 31
Meopham ... 22 V 29
Mepal ... 29 U 26
Mere *Cheshire* ... 42 M 24
Mere *Wilts* ... 9 N 30
Mereworth ... 22 V 30
Meriden ... 27 P 26
Merkland Lodge ... 84 F 9
Mermaid Inn ... 32 H 24
Merrick ... 52 G 18
Merriott ... 8 L 31
Merrylaw ... 62 K 18
Mersey (River) ... 42 M 23
Merthyr Cynog ... 25 J 27
Merthyr Tydfil ... 17 J 28
Merton *Cherwell* ... 20 Q 28
Merton *Devon* ... 7 H 31
Merton *London Borough* ... 21 T 29
Meshaw ... 7 I 31
Messing ... 30 W 28
Messingham ... 44 S 23
Metfield ... 31 Y 26

Metheringham ... 37 S 24
Methil ... 69 K 15
Methlick ... 81 N 11
Methven ... 68 J 14
Methwold ... 38 V 26
Mevagissey ... 3 F 33
Mexborough ... 44 Q 23
Mhòr (Loch) ... 73 G 12
Miavaig ... 82 Z 9
Michaelchurch Escley ... 26 L 27
Michaelstow ... 3 F 32
Micheldever ... 10 Q 30
Michelham Priory ... 12 U 31
Micklefield ... 44 Q 22
Mickleover ... 36 P 25
Mickleton *Cotswold* ... 27 O 27
Mickleton *Teesdale* ... 55 N 20
Mid Ardlaw ... 81 N 10
Mid Calder ... 61 J 16
Mid Lavant ... 10 R 31
Mid Sannox ... 59 E 17
Mid Yell ... 87 Q 2
Midbea ... 86 L 6
Middle Barton ... 28 P 28
Middle Rasen ... 45 S 23
Middle Tysoe ... 28 P 27
Middle Wallop ... 9 P 30
Middle Woodford ... 9 O 30
Middlebie ... 54 K 18
Middleham ... 49 O 21
Middlesbrough ... 57 Q 20
Middlestown ... 43 P 23
Middleton *Argyll and Bute* ... 64 Z 14
Middleton *Berwick-upon-Tweed* ... 63 O 17
Middleton *Bradford* ... 49 O 22
Middleton *Gtr. Mches* ... 43 N 23
Middleton Cheney ... 28 Q 27
Middleton-in-Teesdale ... 55 N 20
Middleton-on-Sea ... 11 S 31
Middleton on the Wolds ... 51 S 22
Middleton St. George ... 50 P 20
Middleton Tyas ... 49 P 20
Middletown *Powys* ... 34 K 25
Middlewich ... 35 M 24
Midgeholme ... 55 M 19
Midhurst ... 10 R 31
Midlem ... 62 L 17
Midsomer Norton ... 18 M 30
Midtown ... 78 C 10
Miefield ... 53 H 19
Migdale (Loch) ... 79 H 10
Milborne Port ... 8 M 31
Milborne St. Andrew ... 9 N 31
Milbourne ... 56 O 18
Milburn ... 55 M 20
Mildenhall *Forest Heath* ... 30 V 26
Mildenhall *Kennet* ... 19 O 29
Mile End ... 30 W 28
Milfield ... 63 N 17
Milford ... 11 S 30
Milford Haven / Aberdaugleddau ... 14 E 28
Milford-on-Sea ... 9 P 31
Milland ... 10 R 30
Millbrook ... 3 H 32
Millhouse ... 59 E 16
Millmeece ... 35 N 25
Millom ... 47 K 21
Millport ... 59 F 16
Milltown *Dumfries and Galloway* ... 54 K 18
Milltown *Highland* ... 78 F 11
Milltown *Moray* ... 80 L 11
Milnathort ... 68 J 15
Milnavgie ... 67 H 16
Milnrow ... 43 N 23
Milnthorpe ... 48 L 21
Milovaig ... 76 Z 11
Milton ... 79 H 10
Milton *Cambs* ... 29 U 27
Milton *Carlisle* ... 55 L 19
Milton *Dumfries* ... 53 I 18
Milton *Highland* ... 79 G 11
Milton *Stranraer* ... 52 F 19
Milton Abbas ... 9 N 31
Milton Abbot ... 3 H 32
Milton Bryan ... 29 S 28
Milton Ernest ... 29 S 27
Milton Keynes ... 28 R 27
Milton Libourne ... 19 O 29
Milton of Campsie ... 67 H 16
Milton of Cushnie ... 75 L 12
Milton-on-Stour ... 9 N 30
Miltonduff ... 80 J 11
Miltown of Edinvillie ... 80 K 11
Milverton ... 8 K 30

Milwich ... 35 N 25
Minard ... 65 E 15
Minch (The) ... 83 C 9
Minehead ... 17 J 30
Minety ... 19 O 29
Mingary ... 76 X 12
Minginish ... 77 B 12
Mingulay ... 70 X 13
Minnigaff ... 52 G 19
Minster *near Sheerness* ... 22 W 29
Minster *near Ramsgate* ... 23 X 29
Minsterley ... 34 L 26
Minsterworth ... 19 N 28
Minterne Magna ... 8 M 31
Minting ... 45 T 24
Mintlaw ... 81 O 11
Minto ... 62 L 17
Mirfield ... 43 O 22
Miserden ... 19 N 28
Misson ... 44 R 23
Misterton *Notts* ... 44 R 23
Misterton *Somerset* ... 8 L 31
Mistley ... 31 X 28
Mitcheldean ... 26 M 28
Mitchell ... 2 E 32
Mitford ... 56 O 18
Mithcham ... 21 T 29
Mithian ... 2 E 33
Moaness ... 86 K 7
Mochdre ... 41 I 23
Mochrum ... 52 G 19
Modbury ... 4 I 32
Moelfre ... 40 H 22
Moffat ... 61 J 17
Moidart ... 72 C 13
Moira ... 36 P 25
Mol-Chlach ... 71 B 12
Mold / Yr Wyddgrug ... 34 K 24
Molland ... 7 I 30
Monach Islands ... 76 W 11
Monadhliath Mountains ... 73 H 12
Monar (Loch) ... 78 E 11
Monar Lodge ... 78 F 11
Monaughty Forest ... 80 J 11
Moneydie ... 68 J 14
Moniaive ... 53 I 18
Monifieth ... 69 L 14
Monikie ... 69 L 14
Monk Fryston ... 44 Q 22
Monkland ... 26 L 27
Monkokehampton ... 7 H 31
Monks Eleigh ... 30 W 27
Monksilver ... 7 K 30
Monkton ... 60 G 17
Monmouth / Trefynwy ... 18 L 28
Monreith ... 52 G 19
Montacute ... 8 L 31
Montgarrie ... 75 L 12
Montgomery / Trefaldwyn ... 34 K 26
Montrose ... 75 M 13
Monyash ... 35 O 24
Monymusk ... 75 M 12
Monzie ... 67 I 14
Moonen Bay ... 76 Z 11
Moor Monkton ... 50 Q 21
Moorends ... 44 R 23
Moorfoot Hills ... 61 K 16
Moors (The) ... 52 F 19
Moortown ... 45 S 23
Morar ... 71 C 13
Moray Firth ... 79 H 11
Morchard Bishop ... 7 I 31
Morcott ... 37 S 26
Morden ... 9 N 31
Mordiford ... 26 M 27
More (Glen) ... 67 H 16
More (Loch) *near Kinloch* ... 84 F 9
More (Loch) *near Westerdale* ... 85 J 8
Morebath ... 7 J 30
Morebattle ... 62 M 17
Morecambe ... 48 L 21
Morecambe Bay ... 48 L 21
Moresby ... 53 J 20
Moreton *Epping Forest* ... 22 U 28
Moreton *Purbeck* ... 9 N 31
Moreton-in-Marsh ... 27 O 28
Moreton-on-lugg ... 26 L 27
Moreton Say ... 34 M 25
Moretonhampstead ... 4 I 32
Morfa Nefyn ... 32 G 25
Morie (Loch) ... 79 G 10
Moriston (Glen) ... 72 F 12
Morland ... 55 M 20
Morley ... 43 P 22
Morlich (Loch) ... 74 I 12

Morpeth ... 56 O 18
Morriston ... 17 I 29
Morte Bay ... 6 H 30
Mortehoe ... 16 H 30
Mortimer ... 20 Q 29
Morton *near Bourne* ... 37 S 25
Morton *near Gainsborough* ... 44 R 23
Morton *North East Derbyshire* ... 36 P 24
Morton on Swale ... 50 P 21
Morval ... 3 G 32
Morven ... 85 I 9
Morvern ... 71 C 14
Morvich ... 72 D 12
Morville ... 34 M 26
Morwelham ... 3 H 32
Morwenstow ... 6 G 31
Mosborough ... 43 P 24
Moss Bank ... 42 L 23
Mossdale ... 53 H 18
Mossend ... 60 H 16
Mossley ... 43 N 23
Mosstodloch ... 80 K 11
Mostyn ... 41 K 23
Motherwell ... 61 I 16
Moulin ... 74 I 13
Moulton *Forest Heath* ... 30 V 27
Moulton *Lincs* ... 37 T 25
Moulton *Northants* ... 28 R 27
Moulton Chapel ... 37 T 25
Mount Pleasant ... 9 P 31
Mountain Ash / Aberpennar ... 17 J 28
Mount's Bay ... 2 D 33
Mountsorrel ... 36 Q 25
Mousa ... 87 Q 4
Mousehole ... 2 D 33
Mouswald ... 54 J 18
Mow Cop ... 35 N 24
Mowtie ... 75 N 13
Moy ... 79 H 11
Muasdale ... 59 C 17
Much Dewchurch ... 26 L 28
Much Hadham ... 29 U 28
Much Hoole ... 42 L 22
Much Marcle ... 26 M 28
Much Wenlock ... 34 M 26
Muchalls ... 75 N 12
Muchelney ... 8 L 30
Muchrachd ... 78 F 11
Muck ... 71 B 13
Muckle Roe ... 87 P 2
Mucklestone ... 35 M 25
Muddiford ... 7 H 30
Mudford ... 8 M 31
Mugeary ... 77 B 11
Muick (Loch) ... 74 K 13
Muie ... 85 H 9
Muir of Fowlis ... 75 L 12
Muir of Ord ... 79 G 11
Muirdrum ... 69 L 14
Muirhead ... 60 H 16
Muirkirk ... 60 H 17
Muirshearlich ... 72 E 13
Muker ... 49 N 20
Mulbarton ... 39 X 26
Mulben ... 80 K 11
Muldoanich ... 70 X 13
Mull (Isle of) ... 64 B 14
Mull (Sound of) ... 71 C 14
Mull of Galloway ... 52 F 20
Mull of Oa ... 58 A 17
Mullardoch (Loch) ... 78 E 11
Mullardoch House ... 78 F 11
Mullion ... 2 E 33
Mumbles (The) ... 15 H 29
Mumby ... 45 U 24
Mundesley ... 39 Y 25
Mundford ... 30 V 26
Mundham ... 10 R 31
Munlochy ... 79 H 11
Munlochy Bay ... 79 H 11
Munslow ... 26 L 26
Murlaggan ... 72 E 13
Murrayfield ... 68 K 16
Mursley ... 28 R 28
Murton *Easington* ... 57 P 19
Murton *Eden* ... 55 M 20
Musbury ... 5 K 31
Musselburgh ... 68 K 16
Muston ... 51 T 21
Muthill ... 67 I 15
Mybster ... 85 J 8
Myddfai ... 25 I 28
Myddle ... 34 L 25

Mydroilyn .....15 H 27
Mynach Falls .....25 I 26
Mynachlog-ddu .....15 F 28
Mynydd Eppynt .....25 J 27
Mynydd Mawr .....32 F 25
Mynydd Preseli .....15 F 28
Myrelandhorn .....86 K 8
Mytchett .....21 R 30
Mytholmroyd .....43 O 22

N

Na Cùiltean .....58 C 16
Naburn .....50 Q 22
Nacton .....31 X 27
Nafferton .....51 S 21
Nailsea .....18 L 29
Nailstone .....36 P 26
Nailsworth .....19 N 28
Nairn .....79 I 11
Nant (Loch) .....65 E 14
Nant-y-Moch Reservoir ..25 I 26
Nant-y-moel .....17 J 29
Nantgwynant Valley .....33 H 24
Nantwich .....34 M 24
Nantyglo .....18 K 28
Napton .....28 Q 27
Narberth / Arberth .....15 F 28
Narborough Blaby .....36 Q 26
Narborough Breckland .....38 V 25
Naseby .....28 R 26
Nash Point .....17 J 29
Nassington .....37 S 26
Nateby .....49 M 20
National Exhibition Centre ..27 O 26
National Motor Museum .....10 P 31
Naunton .....27 O 28
Navenby .....37 S 24
Naver (Loch) .....84 G 9
Nayland .....30 W 28
Naze (The) .....31 X 28
Neap .....87 Q 3
Neath / Castell-nedd .....17 I 29
Neath (River) .....17 I 28
Nebo .....33 I 24
Necton .....38 W 26
Needham Market .....31 X 27
Needingworth .....29 T 27
Needles (The) .....10 P 32
Nefyn .....32 G 25
Neidpath Castle .....61 K 17
Neilston .....60 G 16
Neist Point .....76 Z 11
Nelson
  Caerffili / Caerphilly .....18 K 29
Nelson Pendle .....43 N 22
Nene (River) .....37 T 26
Nenthead .....55 M 19
Nercwys .....34 K 24
Nereabolls .....58 A 16
Ness .....83 B 8
Ness (Loch) .....73 G 12
Nesscliffe .....34 L 25
Nestley Marsh .....10 P 31
Neston .....42 K 24
Nether Broughton .....36 R 25
Nether Kellet .....48 L 21
Nether Langwith .....44 Q 24
Nether Stowey .....8 K 30
Nether Wasdale .....47 J 20
Nether Whitecleuch .....61 I 17
Netheravon .....19 O 30
Netherbrae .....81 M 11
Netherbury .....8 L 31
Netherend .....18 M 28
Netherhampton .....9 O 30
Nethermill .....54 J 18
Netherthong .....43 O 23
Netherton .....63 N 17
Nethertown .....86 K 7
Netherwitton .....56 O 18
Nethy Bridge .....74 J 12
Netley .....10 P 31
Nettlebed .....20 R 29
Nettleham .....44 S 24
Nettleton .....45 T 23
Nevern .....15 F 27
Nevis (Glen) .....72 E 13
Nevis (Loch) .....72 C 12
New Abbey .....53 J 19
New Aberdour .....81 N 11
New Alresford .....10 Q 30
New Buckenham .....31 X 26
New Byth .....81 N 11
New Clipstone .....36 Q 24
New Cumnock .....60 H 17
New Deer .....81 N 11
New Edlington .....44 Q 23

New Forest National Park .....9 P 31
New Galloway .....53 H 18
New Holland .....45 S 22
New Hythe .....22 V 30
New Leeds .....81 N 11
New Luce .....52 F 19
New Marske .....57 Q 20
New Mills .....43 O 23
New Mills Powys .....33 K 26
New Milton .....9 P 31
New Pitsligo .....81 N 11
New Quay / Ceinewydd .....24 G 27
New Rackheath .....39 Y 26
New Radnor .....26 K 27
New Romney .....12 W 31
New Rossington .....44 Q 23
New Sauchie .....67 I 15
New Scone .....68 J 14
New Silksworth .....57 P 19
New Tredegar .....18 K 28
New Waltham .....45 T 23
Newark-on-Trent .....36 R 24
Newbiggin Eden .....55 L 19
Newbiggin Teesdale .....55 N 20
Newbiggin-by-the-Sea .....56 P 18
Newbigging Angus .....69 L 14
Newbigging
  South Lanarkshire .....61 J 16
Newbold Verdon .....36 P 26
Newborough
  Isle of Anglesey .....32 G 24
Newborough
  East Staffordshire .....35 O 25
Newbridge Caerffili /
  Caerphilly .....18 K 29
Newbridge Isle of Wight .....10 P 31
Newbridge-on-Wye .....25 J 27
Newbrough .....55 N 18
Newburgh Aberdeenshire .....81 N 12
Newburgh Fife .....68 K 14
Newburgh Lancashire .....42 L 23
Newburn .....56 O 19
Newbury .....20 Q 29
Newby Bridge .....48 L 21
Newby Hall .....50 P 21
Newcastle Monmouthshire /
  Sir Fynwy .....18 L 28
Newcastle
  South Shropshire .....26 K 26
Newcastle Emlyn /
  Castell Newydd Emlyn .....15 G 27
Newcastle-under-Lyme .....35 N 24
Newcastle-upon-Tyne .....56 P 19
Newcastle-upon-Tyne
  Airport .....56 O 18
Newcastleton .....55 L 18
Newchapel .....15 G 27
Newchurch Carmarthenshire /
  Sir Gaerfyrddin .....15 G 28
Newchurch Isle of Wight .....10 Q 32
Newchurch Powys .....26 K 27
Newchurch Shepway .....12 W 30
Newdigate .....11 T 30
Newent .....27 M 28
Newgale .....14 E 28
Newhall .....34 M 24
Newham Isle of Wight .....63 O 17
Newham London Borough ..21 U 29
Newhaven .....11 U 31
Newick .....11 U 31
Newington .....22 V 29
Newland .....18 M 28
Newlyn .....2 D 33
Newmachar .....75 N 12
Newmains .....61 I 16
Newmarket Isle of Lewis .....82 A 9
Newmarket Suffolk .....30 V 27
Newmill Moray .....80 L 11
Newmill Scottish Borders .....62 L 17
Newmilns .....60 G 17
Newnham Daventry .....28 Q 27
Newnham Glos......18 M 28
Newnham Kent .....22 W 30
Newnham Bridge .....26 M 27
Newport Essex .....30 U 28
Newport I.O.W. .....10 Q 31
Newport Pembrokes .....15 F 27
Newport Stroud .....19 M 28
Newport
  Telford and Wrekin .....35 M 25
Newport /
  Casnewydd Newport .....18 L 29
Newport-on-Tay .....69 L 14
Newport Pagnell .....28 R 27
Newquay .....2 E 32
Newsham .....49 O 20
Newstead .....36 Q 24

Newstead Abbey .....36 Q 24
Newton Aberdeenshire .....81 O 11
Newton Argyll and Bute .....65 E 15
Newton Babergh .....30 W 27
Newton Moray .....80 J 11
Newton Ribble Valley .....49 M 22
Newton Rushcliffe .....36 R 25
Newton Abbot .....4 J 32
Newton Arlosh .....54 K 19
Newton-Aycliffe .....56 P 20
Newton Ferrers .....4 H 33
Newton Flotman .....39 X 26
Newton-le-Willows .....42 M 23
Newton Longville .....28 R 28
Newton Mearns .....60 H 16
Newton-on-Rawcliffe .....50 R 21
Newton-on-Trent .....44 R 24
Newton Poppleford .....5 K 31
Newton Reigny .....55 L 19
Newton St. Cyres .....7 J 31
Newton Stewart .....52 G 19
Newton Tracey .....7 H 30
Newton Wamphray .....54 J 18
Newtongrange .....61 K 16
Newtonhill .....75 N 12
Newtonmore .....73 H 12
Newtown Cheshire .....43 N 23
Newtown Heref......26 M 27
Newtown Highland .....73 F 12
Newtown Isle of Man .....46 G 21
Newtown /
  Drenewydd Powys .....26 K 26
Newtown Linford .....36 Q 25
Newtown St. Boswells .....62 L 17
Newtyle .....68 K 14
Neyland .....16 F 28
Nicholaston .....15 H 29
Nigg .....79 H 10
Nigg Bay .....79 H 10
Nine Ladies .....35 P 24
Ninebanks .....55 M 19
Ninfield .....12 V 31
Nisbet .....62 M 17
Nith (River) .....53 J 19
Niths .....61 I 18
Niton .....10 Q 32
Nocton .....37 S 24
Nolton .....14 E 28
Nordelph .....38 U 26
Norfolk Broads .....39 Y 25
Norham .....63 N 16
Normanby .....50 R 21
Normandy .....21 S 30
Normanton .....43 P 22
Normanton-on-the-Wolds ..36 Q 25
North Baddesley .....10 P 31
North Ballachulish .....72 E 13
North Berwick .....69 L 15
North Bovey .....4 I 32
North Bradley .....19 N 30
North Brentor .....4 H 32
North Cadbury .....8 M 30
North Cave .....44 S 22
North-Cerney .....19 O 28
North-Charlton .....63 O 17
North Cliffe .....44 R 22
North Cowton .....50 P 20
North Crawley .....29 S 27
North Creake .....38 W 25
North Curry .....8 L 30
North Dalton .....51 S 22
North Deighton .....50 P 22
North Erradale .....77 C 10
North Esk (Riv.) .....75 L 13
North Fearns .....77 B 11
North Foreland .....23 Y 29
North Frodingham .....51 T 22
North Grimston .....51 R 21
North Harris .....82 Z 10
North Hill .....3 G 32
North Hinksey .....20 Q 28
North Holmwood .....21 T 30
North Hykeham .....37 S 24
North Kelsey .....45 S 23
North Kessock .....79 H 11
North Kyme .....37 T 24
North Leigh .....20 P 28
North-Molton .....7 I 30
North Morar .....72 C 13
North Newbald .....44 S 22
North Nibley .....19 M 29
North Otterington .....50 P 21
North Petherton .....8 K 30
North Petherwin .....6 G 31
North Rigton .....50 P 22
North Ronaldsay .....87 M 5
North-Scarle .....36 R 24

North-Shian .....65 D 14
North Shields .....56 P 18
North Shore .....42 K 22
North Somercotes .....45 U 23
North Sound (The) .....87 L 6
North Stainley .....50 P 21
North Stainmore .....49 N 20
North Sunderland .....63 P 17
North Tamerton .....6 G 31
North-Tawton .....7 I 31
North Thoresby .....45 T 23
North Tidworth .....19 P 30
North Uist .....76 X 11
North Walsham .....39 Y 25
North Warnborough .....20 R 30
North Water Bridge .....75 M 13
North Weald Bassett .....22 U 28
North Wootton .....38 V 25
North York Moors
  National Park .....50 R 20
Northallerton .....50 P 20
Northam .....6 H 30
Northampton .....28 R 27
Northaw .....21 T 28
Northchapel .....11 S 30
Northchurch .....21 S 28
Northfleet .....22 V 29
Northiam .....12 V 31
Northleach .....19 O 28
Northleigh .....5 K 31
Northlew .....7 H 31
Northop .....34 K 24
Northrepps .....39 Y 25
Northton .....76 Y 10
Northumberland
  National Park .....63 N 18
Northwich .....42 M 24
Northwold .....38 V 26
Northwood .....34 L 25
Norton Daventry .....28 Q 27
Norton Doncaster .....44 Q 23
Norton Ryedale .....50 R 21
Norton Tewkesbury .....27 N 28
Norton Disney .....36 R 24
Norton Fitzwarren .....8 K 30
Norton in Hales .....35 M 25
Norton St. Philip .....19 N 30
Norwich .....39 X 26
Norwick .....87 R 1
Noss (Isle of) .....87 Q 3
Noss Head .....86 K 8
Nottingham .....36 Q 25
Nuffield .....20 Q 29
Nunburnholme .....51 R 22
Nuneaton .....28 P 26
Nuneham Courtenay .....20 Q 28
Nunney .....19 M 30
Nunthorpe .....50 Q 20
Nunton .....76 X 11
Nutley .....11 U 30
Nympsfield .....19 N 28

O

Oa (The) .....58 B 17
Oadby .....36 Q 26
Oakamoor .....35 O 24
Oakdale .....18 K 28
Oakengates .....35 M 25
Oakford .....7 J 31
Oakham .....36 R 25
Oakhill .....18 M 30
Oakington .....29 U 27
Oakley Aylesbury Vale .....20 Q 28
Oakley Bedfordshire .....29 S 27
Oakley Fife .....68 J 15
Oaksey .....19 N 29
Oakworth .....43 O 22
Oare Kennet .....19 O 29
Oare Swale .....22 W 30
Oare West Somerset .....17 I 30
Oathlaw .....74 L 13
Oban .....65 D 14
Occold .....31 X 27
Ochil Hills .....68 I 15
Ochiltree .....60 G 17
Ockbrook .....36 P 25
Ockle .....71 C 13
Ockley .....11 S 30
Odiham .....20 R 30
Odland .....18 M 29
Odstock .....9 O 30
Offa's Dyke Path .....26 K 26
Offord Cluny .....29 T 27
Ogbourne St. Andrew .....19 O 29
Ogbourne St. George .....19 O 29
Ogil .....74 L 13
Ogle .....56 O 18

Ogmore-by-Sea .....17 J 29
Ogmore Vale .....17 J 29
Oich (Loch) .....73 F 12
Oidhche (Loch na h-) .....78 D 11
Oigh-Sgeir .....71 Z 13
Okeford Fitzpaine .....9 N 31
Okehampton .....4 H 31
Old Alresford .....10 Q 30
Old Bolingbroke .....37 U 24
Old Burghclere .....20 Q 30
Old Castleton .....55 L 18
Old Colwyn .....41 I 23
Old Dailly .....59 F 18
Old Deer .....81 N 11
Old Fletton .....37 T 26
Old Harry Rocks .....9 O 32
Old Head .....87 L 7
Old Hurst .....29 T 26
Old Hutton .....48 L 21
Old Kilpatrick .....67 G 16
Old Knebworth .....29 T 28
Old Leake .....37 U 24
Old Man of Hoy .....86 J 7
Old Man of Storr .....77 B 11
Old Radnor .....26 K 27
Old Rayne .....81 M 11
Old' Sarum .....9 O 30
Old Sodbury .....19 M 29
Old Somerby .....37 S 25
Old Warden .....29 S 27
Old Windsor .....21 S 29
Oldany Island .....84 E 9
Oldbury .....27 N 26
Oldbury on Severn .....18 M 29
Oldcotes .....44 Q 23
Oldham .....43 N 23
Oldhamstocks .....69 M 16
Oldmeldrum .....81 N 11
Oldshoremore .....84 E 8
Olgrinmore .....85 J 8
Ollaberry .....87 P 2
Ollach .....77 B 11
Ollay (Loch) .....76 X 12
Ollerton Macclesfield .....42 M 24
Ollerton
  Newark and Sherwood .....36 Q 24
Olney .....28 R 27
Olveston .....18 M 29
Ombersley .....27 N 27
Once Brewed .....55 M 19
Onchan .....46 G 21
Onecote .....35 O 24
Onich .....72 E 13
Onllwyn .....17 I 28
Opinan .....83 D 10
Orchy (Glen) .....66 F 14
Ord .....71 C 12
Ordie .....74 L 12
Orford .....31 Y 27
Orford Ness .....31 Y 27
Orkney Islands 87
Orleton .....26 L 27
Ormesby .....50 Q 20
Ormesby St. Margaret .....39 Z 26
Ormiston .....62 L 16
Ormskirk .....42 L 23
Oronsay .....64 B 15
Orosay near Fuday .....70 X 12
Orosay near Lochboisdale ..70 X 12
Orphir .....86 K 7
Orrin (Glen) .....78 F 11
Orrin Reservoir .....78 F 11
Orsay .....58 A 16
Orsett .....22 V 29
Orston .....36 R 25
Orton .....48 M 20
Orwell .....29 T 27
Orwell (River) .....31 X 28
Osborne House .....10 Q 31
Osdale .....77 A 11
Osgaig (Loch) .....83 E 9
Osgodby .....45 S 23
Oskaig .....77 B 11
Osmington .....9 M 32
Ossett .....43 P 22
Ossington .....36 R 24
Oswaldtwistle .....42 M 22
Oswestry .....34 K 25
Otford .....22 U 30
Othery .....8 L 30
Otley Suffolk .....31 X 27
Otley West Yorks......49 O 22
Otterbourne .....10 P 30
Otterburn .....55 N 18
Otternish .....76 Y 10
Otterswick .....87 Q 2
Otterton .....5 K 32

Ottery St. Mary .....5 K 31
Ottringham .....45 T 22
Oulton Broad .....39 Z 26
Oulton Park Circuit .....34 M 24
Oundle .....29 S 26
Ouse (River)
  English Channel .....11 T 30
Ouse (River) North Sea .....50 Q 21
Out-Rawcliffe .....42 L 22
Out Skerries .....87 R 2
Outer Hebrides .....82 Y 9
Outhgill .....49 M 20
Outwell .....38 U 26
Over .....29 U 27
Over Compton .....8 M 31
Overseal .....35 P 25
Overstrand .....39 Y 25
Overton Hants. .....20 Q 30
Overton Lancs. .....48 L 21
Overton Wrexham .....34 L 25
Overtown .....61 I 16
Ower .....10 P 31
Owermoigne .....9 N 32
Owlswick .....20 R 28
Owlsbury .....10 Q 30
Owston .....36 R 26
Owston Ferry .....44 R 23
Oxburgh Hall .....38 V 26
Oxen Park .....48 K 21
Oxenhope .....43 O 22
Oxford .....20 Q 28
Oxnam .....62 M 17
Oxted .....21 T 30
Oxton
  Newark and Sherwood .....36 Q 24
Oxton Scottish Borders .....62 L 16
Oxwich .....15 H 29
Oxwich Bay .....15 H 29
Oykel (Glen) .....84 F 9
Oykel Bridge .....84 F 10
Oyne .....81 M 12

P

Pabay .....77 C 12
Pabbay near Harris .....76 Y 10
Pabbay near Mingulay .....70 X 13
Pabbay (Sound of) .....76 Y 10
Packington .....36 P 25
Padbury .....28 R 28
Paddock Wood .....22 V 30
Paddockhole .....54 K 18
Padiham .....42 N 22
Padstow .....3 F 32
Pagham .....10 R 31
Paignton .....4 J 32
Pailton .....28 Q 26
Painscastle .....26 K 27
Painswick .....19 N 28
Paisley .....60 G 16
Pakefield .....31 Z 26
Palnackie .....53 I 19
Pamber End .....20 Q 30
Pandy
  Monmouthshire / Sir Fynwy .26 L 28
Pandy Powys .....33 J 26
Pangbourne .....20 Q 29
Pant .....34 K 25
Pantymenyn .....15 F 28
Papa Stour .....87 O 3
Papa Westray .....87 L 5
Papplewick .....36 Q 24
Paps of Jura .....65 B 16
Papworth Everard .....29 T 27
Parbh (The) .....84 F 8
Parbold .....42 L 23
Parc Cefn Onn .....18 K 29
Parham House .....11 S 31
Park Gate .....10 Q 31
Park of Pairc .....82 A 9
Parkeston .....31 X 28
Parkgate .....53 J 18
Parkhurst .....10 Q 31
Parnham House .....8 L 31
Parracombe .....17 I 30
Parrett (River) .....8 K 30
Parson Drove .....37 U 26
Partney .....37 U 24
Parton Copeland .....54 J 20
Parton
  Dumfries and Galloway .....53 H 18
Partridge Green .....11 T 31
Parwich .....35 O 24
Patchway .....18 M 29
Pateley Bridge .....49 O 21
Path of Condie .....68 J 15
Pathhead .....62 L 16
Patna .....60 G 17

A B C D E F G H I J K L M N O P Q R S T U V W X Y Z

Patrick ....46 F 21
Patrington ....45 T 22
Patrixbourne ....23 X 30
Patterdale ....48 L 20
Pattingham ....35 N 26
Pattishall ....28 Q 27
Paulerspury ....28 R 27
Paull ....45 T 22
Paulton ....18 M 30
Paxton ....63 N 16
Peacehaven ....11 T 31
Peak District
  National Park ....43 O 23
Pearsie ....74 K 13
Peasedown St. John ..19 M 30
Peasemore ....20 P 29
Peasenhall ....31 Y 27
Peaslake ....21 S 30
Peasmarsh ....12 W 31
Peat Inn ....69 L 15
Peatknowe ....81 M 11
Pebmarsh ....30 W 28
Pebworth ....27 O 27
Peebles ....61 K 17
Peel ....46 F 21
Peel Fell ....62 M 18
Pegswood ....56 P 18
Pegwell Bay ....23 Y 30
Peinchorran ....77 B 12
Peldon ....22 W 28
Pelton ....56 P 19
Pelynt ....3 G 32
Pembrey ....15 H 28
Pembridge ....26 L 27
Pembroke / Penfro ..16 F 28
Pembroke Dock /
  Doc Penfro ....16 F 28
Pembrokeshire Coast
  National Park ....15 F 29
Pembury ....12 V 30
Pen-y-bont / Bridgend ..17 J 29
Pen-y-groes ....32 H 24
Penalun ....15 F 29
Penarth ....18 K 29
Pencader ....15 H 27
Pencaitland ....62 L 16
Pencarrow ....3 F 32
Penclawdd ....15 H 29
Pencombe ....26 M 27
Penderyn ....17 J 28
Pendine ....15 G 28
Pendine Sands ......15 G 28
Pendlebury ....42 N 23
Pendoylan ....17 J 29
Penelewey ....2 E 33
Penfro / Pembroke ..16 F 28
Pengethley ....26 M 28
Penhow ....18 L 29
Penicuik ....61 K 16
Penifiler ....77 B 11
Peninver ....59 D 17
Penistone ....43 P 23
Penketh ....42 L 23
Penkridge ....35 N 25
Penley ....34 L 25
Penmaen ....15 H 29
Penmaenmawr ....41 I 23
Penmaenpool ....33 I 25
Penmark ....17 J 29
Penmon ....40 H 23
Pennal ....33 I 26
Pennant ....33 J 26
Pennerley ....34 L 26
Pennines (The) ......49 N 20
Pennyghael ....65 B 14
Penpont ....53 I 18
Penrhiwpal ....15 G 27
Penrhyn ....40 H 23
Penrhyn Bay ....41 I 23
Penrhyndeudraeth ..33 H 25
Penrith ....55 L 19
Penruddock ....55 L 20
Penryn ....2 E 33
Pensarn ....41 J 23
Penshaw ....56 P 19
Penshurst ....22 U 30
Pensilva ....3 G 32
Pentewan ....3 F 33
Pentire Point ....3 F 32
Pentland Firth ....86 K 7
Pentland Hills ....61 J 16
Pentland Skerries ..87 L 7
Pentraeth ....40 H 23
Pentre-Berw ....40 H 23
Pentre-Celyn ....34 K 24
Pentrebeirdd ....34 K 25
Penwith ....2 D 33

Penybont ....26 K 27
Penysarn ....40 H 22
Penzance ....2 D 33
Pernrhyn-Coch ....25 I 26
Perranaworthal ....2 E 33
Perranporth ....2 E 32
Perranzabuloe ....2 E 33
Pershore ....27 N 27
Pertenhall ....29 S 27
Perth ....68 J 14
Peterborough ....37 T 26
Peterculter ....75 N 12
Peterhead ....81 O 11
Peterlee ....57 P 19
Petersfield ....10 R 30
Peterstone Wentlooge ..18 K 29
Peterstow ....26 M 28
Petham ....23 X 30
Petrockstowe ....7 H 31
Pett ....12 V 31
Pettaugh ....31 X 27
Petworth ....11 S 31
Pevensey Bay ....12 V 31
Pewsey ....19 O 29
Pickering ....50 R 21
Picklescott ....34 L 26
Picton Castle ....16 F 28
Piddlehinton ....9 M 31
Piddletrenthide ....9 M 31
Piercebridge ....49 O 20
Pierowall ....86 L 6
Pilgrims Hatch ....22 U 29
Pillerton Hersey .....28 P 27
Pillerton Priors ......27 P 27
Pilley ....43 P 23
Pilling ....48 L 22
Pilning ....18 M 29
Pilton ....8 M 30
Pinchbeck ....37 T 25
Pinchbeck-West .....37 T 25
Pinhoe ....4 J 31
Pinmore Mains ......52 F 18
Pinner ....21 S 29
Pinvin ....27 N 27
Pinwherry ....52 F 18
Pinxton ....36 Q 24
Pirbright ....21 S 30
Pirnmill ....59 D 17
Pirton ....29 T 28
Pishill ....20 R 29
Pitcaple ....81 M 12
Pitcombe ....8 M 30
Pitcur ....68 K 14
Pitlochry ....74 I 13
Pitmedden ....81 N 11
Pitminster ....8 K 31
Pitscottie ....69 L 15
Pitsford ....28 R 27
Pittentrail ....85 H 10
Pittenweem ....69 L 15
Pladda ....59 E 17
Plaistow ....11 S 30
Plas Newydd Anglesey ..33 H 24
Plas Newydd
  Denbighshire ....34 K 25
Plean ....67 I 15
Pleasington ....42 M 22
Pleasley ....36 Q 24
Plenmeller ....55 M 19
Plockton ....78 D 11
Pluckley ....22 W 30
Plumbland ....54 K 19
Plumpton ....11 T 31
Plymouth ....4 H 32
Plympton ....4 H 32
Plymstock ....4 H 32
Plymtree ....7 J 31
Plynlimon
  (Pumlumon Fawr) ..25 I 26
Pocklington ....50 R 22
Point Lynas ....40 H 22
Point of Ayr Flintshire ..41 K 22
Point of Ayre Isle of Man ..46 G 20
Polbain ....83 D 9
Pole of Itlaw (The) ..81 M 11
Polebrook ....29 S 26
Polegate ....12 U 31
Polesden Lacey .....21 S 30
Polesworth ....35 P 26
Polkerris ....3 F 32
Polloch ....72 D 13
Pollock House ......60 H 16
Polmont ....67 I 16
Polperro ....3 G 33
Polruan ....3 G 33
Polwarth ....62 M 16
Pondersbridge ....29 T 26

Pont-ar-Gothi ....15 H 28
Pontardawe ....17 I 28
Pontarddulais ....15 H 28
Pontarfynach /
  Devil's Bridge ......25 I 26
Pontargothi ....15 H 28
Pontarsais ....15 H 28
Pontefract ....44 Q 22
Ponteland ....56 O 18
Ponterwyd ....25 I 26
Pontesbury ....34 L 26
Pontlottyn ....18 K 28
Pontllyfni ....32 G 24
Pontneddfechan ....17 J 28
Pontrhydfendigaid ..25 I 27
Pontrhydygroes .....25 I 26
Pontrilas ....26 L 28
Pontyates ....15 H 28
Pontyberem ....15 H 28
Pontyclun ....17 J 29
Pontycymer ....17 J 29
Pontypool / Pontypwl ..18 K 28
Pontypridd ....17 J 29
Pontypwl / Pontypool ..18 K 28
Poole ....9 O 31
Poole Bay ....9 O 31
Poolewe ....78 D 10
Pooley Bridge ....55 L 20
Pooltiel (Loch) ....76 Z 11
Porlock ....17 J 30
Port Appin ....65 D 14
Port Askaig ....58 B 16
Port Bannatyne .....59 E 16
Port Carlisle ....54 K 19
Port Charlotte ....58 A 16
Port Driseach ....65 E 16
Port Ellen ....58 B 17
Port Erin ....46 F 21
Port-Eynon ....15 H 29
Port-Eynon Point ...15 H 29
Port Gaverne ....3 F 32
Port Glasgow ....66 F 16
Port Henderson .....77 C 10
Port Isaac ....3 F 32
Port Lamont ....59 E 16
Port Logan ....52 F 19
Port Mór ....71 B 13
Port of Menteith ....67 H 15
Port of Ness ....83 B 8
Port Ramsay ....65 D 14
Port St. Mary ....46 F 21
Port Talbot ....17 I 29
Port William ....52 G 19
Portavadie ....59 E 16
Portchester ....10 Q 31
Portencross ....59 F 16
Portesham ....5 M 31
Portgordon ....80 K 11
Portgower ....85 I 9
Porth ....17 J 29
Porth Neigwl
  or Hell's Mouth ....32 G 25
Porth Tywyn /Burry Port ..15 H 28
Porthaethwy /
  Menai Bridge ....40 H 23
Porthcawl ....17 I 29
Porthcothan ....2 E 32
Porthcurno ....2 D 33
Porthgwarra ....2 D 33
Porthkerry ....17 K 29
Porthleven ....2 E 33
Porthmadog ....33 H 25
Porthtowan ....2 E 33
Porthyrhyd ....15 H 28
Portinnisherrich .....65 E 15
Portishead ....18 L 29
Portknockie ....80 L 10
Portland (Isle of) ....8 M 32
Portlethen ....75 N 12
Portmahomack ....79 I 10
Portmeirion ....33 H 25
Portnacroish ....72 D 14
Portnaguran ....83 B 9
Portnahaven ....58 A 16
Portnalong ....77 A 12
Portobello ....68 K 16
Portreath ....2 E 33
Portree ....77 B 11
Portscatho ....3 F 33
Portskerra ....85 I 8
Portskewett ....18 L 29
Portslade ....11 T 31
Portslogan ....52 E 19
Portsmouth ....10 Q 31
Portsoy ....81 L 10
Portuairk ....71 B 13

Postbridge ....4 I 32
Potten End ....21 S 28
Potter Heigham ......39 Y 25
Potter Street ....21 U 28
Potterhanworth ......37 S 24
Potterne ....19 N 30
Potters Bar ....21 T 28
Potton ....29 T 27
Poughill ....6 G 31
Poulshot ....19 N 29
Poulton ....19 O 28
Poulton-le-Fylde ....42 L 22
Poundstock ....6 G 31
Powburn ....63 O 17
Powerstock ....8 L 31
Powick ....27 N 27
Powis ....34 K 26
Powmill ....68 J 15
Poynings ....11 T 31
Poynton ....43 N 23
Praa Sands ....2 D 33
Prawle Point ....4 I 33
Praze-an-Beeble ......2 E 33
Prees ....34 M 25
Preesall ....48 L 22
Prendwick ....63 O 17
Prescot ....42 L 23
Prestatyn ....41 J 22
Prestbury Cheltenham ..27 N 28
Prestbury Macclesfield ..43 N 24
Presteigne ....26 K 27
Preston
  East Riding of Yorks. ..45 T 22
Preston Kent ....23 X 30
Preston Lancs. ....42 L 22
Preston Rutland .....36 R 26
Preston West Sussex ..11 S 31
Preston Candover ..10 Q 30
Preston Capes ....28 Q 27
Prestonpans ....69 L 16
Prestwich ....42 N 23
Prestwick ....60 G 17
Prestwood ....20 R 28
Prickwillow ....30 V 26
Priest Island ....83 D 10
Priest Weston ....34 K 26
Princes Risborough ..20 R 28
Princethorpe ....28 P 26
Princetown ....4 I 32
Priors Marston ....28 Q 27
Probus ....3 F 33
Prosen (Glen) ....74 K 13
Prudhoe ....56 O 19
Puckeridge ....29 U 28
Pucklechurch ....19 M 29
Pucks Gutter ....23 X 30
Puddletown ....9 M 31
Pudsey ....43 P 22
Pulborough ....11 S 31
Pulford ....34 L 24
Pulham ....9 M 31
Pulham Market ......31 X 26
Puncheston ....24 F 28
Purbeck (Isle of) .....9 N 32
Purbrook ....10 Q 31
Puriton ....8 L 30
Purleigh ....22 V 28
Purley ....20 Q 29
Purse Caundle Manor ..9 M 31
Purston Jaglin ....43 P 22
Purton ....19 O 29
Putsborough ....6 H 30
Pwllheli ....32 G 25
Pyecombe ....11 T 31
Pyle ....17 I 29
Pylle ....8 M 30

Q

Quainton ....28 R 28
Quantock Hills ....8 K 30
Quarff ....87 Q 3
Quarr ....10 Q 31
Quatt ....27 M 26
Quedgeley ....19 N 28
Queen Camel ....8 M 30
Queen Elizabeth
  Forest Park ....67 G 15
Queenborough ....22 W 29
Queensbury ....43 O 22
Queensferry ....34 K 24
Quendon ....30 U 28
Quenington ....19 O 28
Quinag ....84 E 9
Quines's Hill ....46 G 21
Quinish Point ....71 B 14
Quiraing ....77 B 11

Quoich (Loch) ....72 E 12
Quorndon ....36 Q 25
Quothquan ....61 J 17

R

Raasay (Island of) ..77 B 11
Raasay (Sound of) ..77 B 11
Raasay Ho ....77 B 11
Rachub ....33 H 24
Rackenford ....7 J 31
Rackwick ....86 J 7
Radcliffe ....42 N 23
Radcliffe-on-Trent ..36 Q 25
Radlett ....21 T 28
Radley ....20 Q 28
Radnor Forest ....26 K 27
Radstock ....18 M 30
Radyr ....18 K 29
Rafford ....80 J 11
Raglan ....18 L 28
Ragley Hall ....27 O 27
Rainford ....42 L 23
Rainham ....22 V 29
Rainworth ....36 Q 24
Rait ....68 K 14
Ramasaig ....76 Z 11
Rampisham ....8 M 31
Rampside ....47 K 21
Rampton ....44 R 24
Ramsbottom ....42 N 23
Ramsbury ....19 P 29
Ramsey Cambs. .....29 T 26
Ramsey Isle of Man ..46 G 21
Ramsey Bay ....46 G 21
Ramsey Island ....14 D 28
Ramsey St. Mary's ..29 T 26
Ramsgate ....23 Y 29
Ramsgill-in-Nidderdale ..49 O 21
Ranby ....44 Q 24
Ranfurly ....60 G 16
Rangeworthy ....18 M 29
Ranish ....82 A 9
Rankinston ....60 G 17
Rannoch (Loch) .....73 H 13
Rannoch Moor ....73 F 14
Rannoch Sta ....73 G 13
Ranskill ....44 Q 23
Ranton ....35 N 25
Ranworth ....39 Y 25
Rapness ....87 L 6
Rappach ....84 F 10
Ratby ....36 Q 26
Rathen ....81 O 11
Rathmell ....49 N 21
Ratho ....68 J 16
Ratlinghope ....34 L 26
Rattlesden ....30 W 27
Rattray ....68 K 14
Rattray Head ....81 O 11
Raunds ....29 S 26
Ravenglass ....47 J 20
Ravenscar ....51 S 20
Ravensthorpe ....28 Q 27
Ravenstone ....36 P 25
Ravenstonedale .....49 M 20
Ravensworth ....49 O 20
Rawcliffe ....44 R 22
Rawmarsh ....44 P 23
Rawtenstall ....42 N 22
Rayleigh ....22 V 29
Rayne ....30 V 28
Read ....42 M 22
Reading ....20 R 29
Rearsby ....36 Q 25
Reay ....85 I 8
Reay Forest ....84 F 9
Reculver ....23 X 29
Red Wharf Bay ......40 H 23
Redbourn ....21 S 28
Redbourne ....44 S 23
Redbridge
  London Borough ..21 U 29
Redcar ....57 Q 20
Redcliff Bay ....18 L 29
Reddding ....67 I 16
Redditch ....27 O 27
Redesmouth ....55 N 18
Redford ....69 L 14
Redhill North Somerset ..18 L 29
Redhill
  Reigate and Banstead ..21 T 30
Redisham ....31 Y 26
Redmarley d'Abitot ..27 M 28
Redmarshall ....57 P 20
Redmire ....49 O 21
Redpoint ....77 C 11
Redruth ....2 E 33

Redwick ....18 L 29
Reedham ....39 Y 26
Reekie Linn ....74 K 13
Reepham ....45 S 24
Reeth ....49 O 20
Regarby ....46 G 20
Reiff ....83 D 9
Reigate ....21 T 30
Reighton ....51 T 21
Reiss ....86 K 8
Relubbus ....2 D 33
Rempstone ....36 Q 25
Rendcomb ....19 O 28
Rendham ....31 Y 27
Renfrew ....60 G 16
Renish Point ....76 Z 10
Renishaw ....44 P 24
Rennington ....63 O 17
Renton ....66 G 16
Renwick ....55 M 19
Repton ....36 P 25
Rescobie ....75 L 14
Resipole ....72 C 13
Resolven ....17 I 28
Resort (Loch) ....82 Z 9
Restalrig ....68 K 16
Reston ....63 N 16
Restormel Castle .....3 G 32
Retford ....44 R 24
Rettendon ....22 V 29
Reynoldston ....15 H 29
Rhaeadr / Rhayader ..25 J 27
Rhaeadr Ddu ....33 I 25
Rhandirmwyn ....25 I 27
Rhayader / Rhaeadr ..25 J 27
Rheidol (Vale of) ...25 I 26
Rhenigidale ....82 Z 10
Rhian ....84 G 9
Rhiconich ....84 F 8
Rhigos ....17 J 28
Rhilochan ....85 H 9
Rhinns of Galloway (The) ..52 E 19
Rhinns of Kells ......53 G 18
Rhondda ....17 J 29
Rhoose ....17 J 29
Rhos ....17 I 28
Rhoscolyn ....40 G 23
Rhoscrowther ....14 E 28
Rhoslanerchrugog ..34 K 24
Rhosmaen ....25 I 28
Rhosneigr ....40 G 23
Rhossili ....15 H 29
Rhostyllen ....34 K 24
Rhosybol ....40 G 22
Rhu ....66 F 15
Rhuddlan ....41 J 23
Rhum ....71 A 13
Rhuthun / Ruthin ...34 K 24
Rhyd-Ddu ....33 H 24
Rhydaman / Ammanford ..15 I 28
Rhydcymerau ....15 H 27
Rhydd ....27 N 27
Rhyddhywel ....25 J 26
Rhydowen ....15 H 27
Rhyl ....41 J 23
Rhymmi / Rhymney ..18 K 28
Rhymney / Rhymmi ..18 K 28
Rhynie ....80 L 12
Ribble (River) ....49 N 22
Ribblesdale ....49 N 21
Ribchester ....42 M 22
Riber Castle ....36 P 24
Riccall ....44 Q 22
Riccarton ....60 G 17
Richards Castle .....26 L 27
Richborough ....23 X 30
Richmond ....49 O 20
Richmond-upon-Thames
  London Borough ..21 T 29
Rickarton ....75 N 13
Rickmansworth ......21 S 29
Ridgeway Cross .....27 M 27
Ridgeway Path (The) ..20 P 29
Ridsdale ....55 N 18
Rievaulx Abbey .....50 Q 21
Rigg ....77 B 11
Rigside ....61 I 17
Rillington ....51 R 21
Rimington ....49 N 22
Rimsdale (Loch) ....85 H 9
Ringford ....53 H 19
Ringmer ....11 U 31
Ringshall ....30 W 27
Ringstead
  East Northamptonshire ..29 S 26
Ringstead King's Lynn
  and West Norfolk ..38 V 25

A B C D E F G H I J K L M N O P Q R S T U V W X Y Z

A B C D E F G H I J K L M N O P Q R S T U V W X Y Z

Ringwood ....9 O 31
Ringwould ....23 Y 30
Rinnes (Glen) ....80 K 11
Rinns of Islay ....58 A 16
Rinns Point ....58 A 16
Ripe ....12 U 31
Ripley *Derbs.* ....36 P 24
Ripley *North Yorks.* ....50 P 21
Ripley *Surrey* ....21 S 30
Riplingham ....44 S 22
Ripon ....50 P 21
Rippingale ....37 S 25
Rippondcn ....43 O 22
Risabus ....58 B 17
Risby ....30 V 27
Risca ....18 K 29
Risegate ....37 T 25
Riseley ....29 S 27
Rishton ....42 M 22
Risplith ....50 P 21
Ristol (Isle) ....83 D 9
Roadside of Kinneff ....75 N 13
Roag ....77 A 11
Roag (Loch) ....82 Z 9
Roan of Graigoch ....60 F 18
Roberton
  Dumfries and Galloway ....61 I 17
Roberton
  Scottish Borders ....62 L 17
Robertsbridge ....12 V 31
Robin Hood's Bay ....51 S 20
Roby ....42 L 23
Rocester ....35 O 25
Rochdale ....43 N 23
Roche ....3 F 32
Rochester ....22 V 29
Rochester
  Northumberland ....63 N 18
Rochford ....22 W 29
Rock ....3 F 32
Rockcliffe *Cumbria* ....54 K 19
Rockcliffe
  Dumfries and Galloway ....53 I 19
Rockfield ....18 L 28
Rockingham ....28 R 26
Rode ....19 N 30
Rode Heath ....35 N 24
Rodel ....76 Z 10
Rodmel ....11 U 31
Rodney Stoke ....18 L 30
Rogart ....85 H 9
Rogerstone ....18 K 29
Rogiet ....18 L 29
Rokeby Hall ....49 O 20
Rolleston *Notts.* ....36 R 24
Rolleston-on-Dove *Staffs.* ....35 P 25
Rolvenden ....12 V 30
Romannobridge ....61 J 16
Romiley ....43 N 23
Romney Marsh ....12 W 30
Romsey ....10 P 31
Romsley ....27 N 26
Rona (Island of) ....77 C 11
Ronaldsway ....46 G 21
Ronas Voe ....87 P 2
Ronay ....76 Y 11
Rookhope ....55 N 19
Roos ....45 T 22
Rootpark ....61 I 16
Ropley ....10 Q 30
Ropsley ....37 S 25
Rora ....81 O 11
Rora Head ....86 J 7
Rosedale Abbey ....50 R 20
Rosehearty ....81 N 10
Rosemarket ....16 F 28
Rosemarkie ....79 H 11
Rosewell ....61 K 16
Rosgill ....48 L 20
Roshven ....71 C 13
Rosley ....54 K 19
Roslin ....61 K 16
Rosliston ....35 P 25
Rosneath ....66 F 15
Ross
  Berwick-upon-Tweed ....63 O 17
Ross
  Dumfries and Galloway ....53 H 19
Ross of Mull ....64 B 15
Ross-on-Wye ....26 M 28
Rossall Point ....48 K 22
Rossett ....34 L 24
Rosudgeon ....2 D 33
Rosyth ....68 J 15
Rothbury ....63 O 18
Rothbury Forest ....63 O 18
Rotherfield ....12 U 30

Rotherham ....43 P 23
Rothersthorpe ....28 R 27
Rothes ....80 K 11
Rothesay ....59 E 16
Rothienorman ....81 M 11
Rothiesholm ....87 M 6
Rothwell *Leeds.* ....43 P 22
Rothwell *Northamp.* ....28 R 26
Rotterspury ....28 R 27
Rottingdean ....11 T 31
Roughburn ....73 F 13
Roughsike ....55 L 18
Roughton ....39 X 25
Rounton ....50 P 20
Rousay ....86 K 6
Rousdon ....5 L 31
Routh ....45 S 22
Rowardennan Lodge ....66 G 15
Rowington ....27 O 27
Rowland's Castle ....10 R 31
Rowland's Gill ....56 O 19
Rownhams ....10 P 31
Rowsley ....35 P 24
Roxburgh ....62 M 17
Roxwell ....22 V 28
Roy (Glen) ....72 F 13
Royal Leamington Spa ....28 P 27
Royal Military Academy ....20 R 29
Royal Tunbridge Wells ....12 U 30
Roybridge ....72 F 13
Roydon *Essex* ....21 U 28
Roydon *Norfolk* ....31 X 26
Royston *Herts.* ....29 T 27
Royston *South Yorks.* ....43 P 23
Royton ....43 N 23
Ruabon ....34 K 25
Ruan High Lanes ....3 F 33
Ruan Minor ....2 E 34
Ruardean ....18 M 28
Rubbha na Faing ....58 A 16
Rubha a' Mhail ....64 B 16
Rubha Còigeach ....83 D 9
Rubha Dubh ....70 Z 14
Rubha Hunish ....77 A 10
Rubha na h-Easgainne ....71 B 12
Rubha Réidh ....77 C 10
Rubha Suisnish ....71 B 12
Rubh'an Dùnain ....71 A 12
Rudbaxton ....24 F 28
Ruddington ....36 Q 25
Rudgeway ....18 M 29
Rudgwick ....11 S 30
Rudha Ban ....70 Y 12
Rudston ....51 T 21
Rufford Old Hall ....42 L 23
Rufforth ....50 Q 22
Rugby ....28 Q 26
Rugeley ....35 O 25
Rumburgh ....31 Y 26
Rumney ....18 K 29
Runcorn ....42 L 23
Runswick Bay ....50 R 20
Runtaleave ....74 K 13
Runwell ....22 V 29
Rushall ....19 O 30
Rushden ....29 S 27
Ruskington ....37 S 24
Rusland ....48 K 21
Rusper ....11 T 30
Ruspidge ....18 M 28
Rustington ....11 S 31
Ruswarp ....51 S 20
Rutherglen ....60 H 16
Ruthin / Rhuthun ....34 K 24
Ruthven *Aberdeenshire* ....80 L 11
Ruthven *Angus* ....74 K 14
Ruthven *Highland* ....79 I 11
Ruthven (Loch) ....79 H 12
Ruthven Barracks ....73 H 12
Ruthwell ....54 J 19
Rutland Water ....37 S 26
Ruyton
  of the Eleven Towns ....34 L 25
Ryal ....56 O 18
Ryan (Loch) ....52 E 19
Rycote ....20 Q 28
Rydal ....48 L 20
Ryde ....10 Q 31
Rye ....12 W 31
Ryhall ....37 S 25
Ryhill ....43 P 23
Ryhope ....57 P 19
Ryton ....56 O 19

S
Sabden ....42 M 22
Sacriston ....56 P 19

Sadberge ....50 P 20
Saddell ....59 D 17
Saddell Bay ....59 D 17
Sadgill ....48 L 20
Saffron Walden ....30 U 27
Saham Toney ....38 W 26
St. Abbs ....63 N 16
St. Abb's Head ....63 N 16
St. Agnes ....2 E 33
St. Albans ....21 T 28
St. Aldhelm's Head ....9 N 32
St. Andrews ....69 L 14
St. Ann's ....54 J 18
St. Ann's Head ....14 E 28
St. Arvans ....18 L 29
St. Asaph ....41 J 23
St. Athan ....17 J 29
St. Austell ....3 F 32
St. Bees ....47 J 20
St. Bees Head ....47 J 20
St. Blazey ....3 F 32
St. Boswells ....62 M 17
St. Breock ....3 F 32
St. Breward ....3 F 32
St. Briavels ....18 M 28
St. Brides ....14 E 28
St. Bride's Bay ....14 E 28
St. Brides Major ....17 J 29
St. Brides-Super-Ely ....17 J 29
St. Bride-Wentlooge ....18 K 29
St. Buryan ....2 D 33
St. Catherine's Point ....10 Q 32
St. Clears / Sanclêr ....15 G 28
St. Cleer ....3 G 32
St. Columb Major ....3 F 32
St. Combs ....81 O 11
St. Cyrus ....75 M 13
St. David's / Tyddewi ....14 E 28
St. David's Head ....14 D 28
St. Day ....2 E 33
St. Dennis ....3 F 32
St. Dogmaels ....15 F 27
St. Dominick ....3 H 32
St. Donats ....17 J 29
St. Endellion ....3 F 32
St. Erth ....2 D 33
St. Ewe ....3 F 33
St. Fagans ....18 K 29
St. Fergus ....81 O 11
St. Fillans ....67 H 14
St. Florence ....15 F 28
St. Gennys ....6 G 31
St. Germans ....3 H 32
St. Giles ....51 N 19
St. Giles-on-the-Heath ....6 H 31
St. Govan's Head ....16 F 29
St. Harmon ....25 J 26
St. Helen Auckland ....56 O 20
St. Helens *I.O.W.* ....10 Q 31
St. Helens *Merseyside* ....42 L 23
St. Helier *Jersey* 5
St. Ishmael's ....14 E 28
St. Issey ....3 F 32
St. Ive ....3 G 32
St. Ives *Cambs.* ....29 T 27
St. Ives *Cornwall* ....2 D 33
St. John's ....46 G 21
St. John's Chapel ....55 N 19
St. John's Loch ....86 J 8
St. Jude ....46 G 20
St. Just ....2 C 33
St. Just in Roseland ....2 F 33
St. Keverne ....2 E 33
St. Kew ....3 F 32
St. Leonards *Dorset* ....9 O 31
St. Leonards *East Sussex* ....12 V 31
St. Mabyn ....3 F 32
St. Magnus Bay ....87 P 2
St. Margaret's at Cliffe ....23 Y 30
St. Margaret's Bay ....23 Y 30
St. Margaret's Hope ....87 L 7
St. Mark's ....46 G 21
St. Martin's ....34 K 25
St. Mary in the Marsh ....12 W 30
St. Mary's *Orkney Islands* ....86 L 7
St. Mary's
  Perth and Kinross ....73 I 14
St. Mary's-Bay ....13 W 30
St. Mary's-Hoo ....22 V 29
St. Mary's Loch ....61 K 17
St. Mawes ....2 E 33
St. Mawgan ....3 F 32
St. Mellion ....3 H 32
St. Mellons ....18 K 29
St. Merryn ....3 F 32
St. Michael Penkevil ....2 E 33
St. Michael's Mount ....2 D 33

St. Michaels-on-Wyre ....42 L 22
St. Minver ....3 F 32
St. Monans ....69 L 15
St. Neot ....3 G 32
St. Neots ....29 T 27
St. Nicholas *Pembrokes* ....14 E 28
St. Nicholas
  Vale of Glamorgan ....17 K 29
St. Nicholas-at-Wade ....23 X 29
St. Ninian's Isle ....87 P 4
St. Osyth ....23 X 28
St. Patrick's Isle ....46 F 21
St. Paul's Walden ....29 T 28
St. Peter Port *Guernsey* 5
St. Peter's ....23 Y 29
St. Pool ....4 I 33
St. Stephen ....3 F 32
St. Teath ....3 F 32
St. Tudwal's Islands ....32 G 25
St. Tudy ....3 F 32
St. Vigeans ....69 M 14
St. Wenn ....3 F 32
St. Weonards ....26 L 28
Saxby ....36 R 25
Salcombe ....4 I 33
Salcombe Regis ....5 K 31
Sale ....42 N 23
Salehurst ....12 V 31
Salen *Argyll and Bute* ....65 C 14
Salen *Highland* ....71 C 13
Salford ....42 N 23
Salfords ....21 T 30
Salhouse ....39 Y 25
Saline ....68 J 15
Salisbury ....9 O 30
Salisbury Plain ....19 O 30
Sallachy
  Ben More Assybt ....84 G 9
Sallachy
  near Kyle of Lochalsh ....78 D 12
Saltash ....3 H 32
Saltburn ....79 H 10
Saltburn-by-the-Sea ....57 R 20
Saltcoats ....59 F 17
Salter ....48 M 21
Saltfleet ....45 U 23
Saltford ....18 M 29
Salthouse ....38 X 25
Saltney ....34 L 24
Salton ....50 R 21
Samala ....76 X 11
Samlesbury Old Hall ....42 M 22
Sampford Courtenay ....7 I 31
Sampford Peverell ....7 J 31
Sanaigmore ....58 A 16
Sanclêr / St. Clears ....15 G 28
Sancreed ....2 D 33
Sancton ....44 S 22
Sand Side ....47 K 21
Sanda Island ....59 D 18
Sanday *Highland* ....71 A 12
Sanday *Orkney Islands* ....87 M 6
Sandbach ....35 M 24
Sandbank ....66 F 16
Sandbanks ....9 O 31
Sandend ....80 L 10
Sandford *Eden* ....49 M 20
Sandford *Mid Devon* ....7 I 31
Sandford *North Somerset* ....18 L 30
Sandford
  South Lanarkshire ....60 H 17
Sandford Orcas ....8 M 31
Sandgate ....13 X 30
Sandgreen ....53 H 19
Sandhaven ....81 N 10
Sandhead ....52 F 19
Sandhurst *Berks.* ....20 R 29
Sandhurst *Kent* ....12 V 30
Sandleigh ....20 Q 28
Sandlins ....31 Y 27
Sandness ....87 P 3
Sandon
  North Hertfordshire ....29 T 28
Sandon *Stafford* ....35 N 25
Sandown ....10 Q 32
Sandray ....70 X 13
Sandridge ....21 T 28
Sandringham House ....38 V 25
Sandsend ....51 R 20
Sandwell ....27 O 26
Sandwich ....23 Y 30
Sandwick *Eden* ....48 L 20
Sandwick *Eilean Siar* ....76 Y 11
Sandwick *Shetland Islands* ....87 Q 4
Sandwood Loch ....84 E 8
Sandy ....29 T 27
Sandygate ....46 G 20
Sandyhills ....53 I 19

Sanna ....71 B 13
Sanquhar ....61 I 17
Santon Downham ....30 W 26
Santon Head ....46 G 21
Sapperton ....19 N 28
Saracen's Head ....37 T 25
Sarclet ....86 K 8
Sarisbury ....10 Q 31
Sark *Channel I.* 5
Sarn Meyllteyrn ....32 G 25
Sarre ....23 X 29
Satley ....56 O 19
Satterthwaite ....48 K 21
Sauchen ....75 M 12
Saughall ....42 L 24
Saughtree ....62 L 18
Saundersfoot ....15 F 28
Saunderton ....20 R 28
Sawbridgeworth ....21 U 28
Sawrey ....48 L 20
Sawston ....29 U 27
Sawtry ....29 T 26
Saxby ....36 R 25
Saxilby ....44 S 24
Saxlingham Nethergate ....39 X 26
Saxmundham ....31 Y 27
Saxtead Green ....31 X 27
Scadavay (Loch) ....76 Y 11
Scaddle (Glen) ....72 D 13
Scafell Pikes ....47 K 20
Scagglethorpe ....50 R 21
Scalasaig ....64 B 15
Scalby ....51 S 21
Scaleby ....55 L 19
Scalford ....36 R 25
Scalloway ....87 Q 3
Scalpay *Highland* ....77 C 12
Scalpay *Western Isles* ....77 A 10
Scamblesby ....45 T 24
Scampton ....44 S 24
Scaniport ....79 H 11
Scapa Flow ....86 K 7
Scarba ....65 C 15
Scarborough ....51 S 21
Scarcliffe ....44 Q 24
Scardroy ....78 F 11
Scarfskerry ....86 K 8
Scarisbrick ....42 L 23
Scarista ....76 Y 10
Scarp ....82 Y 9
Scavaig (Loch) ....71 B 12
Scawby ....44 S 23
Schiehallion ....73 H 13
Scilly (Isles of) ....2 B 34
Scone Palace ....68 J 14
Scopwick ....37 S 24
Scoraig ....83 D 10
Scorton ....50 P 20
Scotby ....55 L 19
Scotch-Corner ....49 P 20
Scothern ....45 S 24
Scotlandwell ....68 K 15
Scotney ....12 V 30
Scotstown ....72 D 13
Scotter ....44 S 23
Scotton *Harrogate* ....50 P 21
Scotton *Richmondshire* ....49 O 20
Scottow ....39 Y 25
Scourie ....84 E 8
Scousburgh ....87 Q 4
Scrabster ....85 J 8
Scraptoft ....36 Q 26
Scredington ....37 S 25
Scridain (Loch) ....64 B 14
Scruton ....50 P 21
Sculthorpe ....38 W 25
Scunthorpe ....44 S 23
Sea Palling ....39 Y 25
Seaford ....12 U 31
Seaforth (Loch) ....82 Z 10
Seaforth Head ....82 A 9
Seagrave ....36 Q 25
Seaham ....57 P 19
Seale ....21 R 30
Sealga (Loch na) ....78 D 10
Seamer *Hambleton* ....50 Q 20
Seamer *Scarborough* ....51 S 21
Seamill ....59 F 16
Seasalter ....23 X 29
Seascale ....47 J 20
Seaton *Allerdale* ....53 J 20
Seaton *East Devon* ....5 K 31
Seaton Carew ....57 Q 20
Seaton Delaval ....56 P 18
Seaton Delaval Hall ....56 P 18
Seaton Ross ....44 R 22
Seaton Sluice ....56 P 18

Seave Green ....50 Q 20
Seaview ....10 Q 31
Sebergham ....54 L 19
Sedbergh ....49 M 21
Sedgebrook ....36 R 25
Sedgley ....27 N 26
Sedlescombe ....12 V 31
Seend ....19 N 29
Seething ....39 Y 26
Seighford ....35 N 25
Seil (Isle of) ....65 D 15
Seilich (Loch an t-) ....73 H 13
Selattyn ....34 K 25
Selborne ....10 R 30
Selby ....44 Q 22
Selker Bay ....47 J 21
Selkirk ....62 L 17
Sellindge ....13 W 30
Selmeston ....12 U 31
Selsey ....10 R 31
Selston ....36 Q 24
Selworthy ....17 J 30
Semley ....9 N 30
Senghenydd ....18 K 29
Sennen ....2 C 33
Sennybridge ....25 J 28
Sessay ....50 Q 21
Settle ....49 N 21
Seven Sisters
  East Sussex ....12 U 31
Seven Sisters
  Neath and Port Talbot ....17 I 28
Sevenhampton ....27 O 28
Sevenoaks ....22 U 30
Severn (River) ....27 M 28
Severn Bridge ....18 M 29
Severn Stoke ....27 N 27
Sgibacleit (Loch) ....82 A 9
Sgiwen ....17 I 29
Sgurr Mòr ....78 E 10
Shader ....82 A 8
Shaftesbury ....9 N 30
Shalbourne ....20 P 29
Shaldon ....4 J 32
Shalfleet ....10 P 31
Shalford ....21 S 30
Shandon ....66 F 15
Shanklin ....10 Q 32
Shap ....48 L 20
Shapinsay ....87 L 6
Shapwick ....8 L 30
Shardlow ....36 P 25
Sharlston ....43 P 23
Sharnbrook ....29 S 27
Sharnford ....28 Q 26
Sharperton ....63 N 18
Sharpness ....18 M 28
Shavington ....34 M 24
Shaw *Gtr. Mches.* ....43 N 23
Shaw *West Berkshire* ....20 Q 29
Shaw *Wilts.* ....19 N 29
Shawbost ....82 Z 9
Shawbury ....34 M 25
Shawford ....10 Q 30
Shawhead ....53 I 18
Shebbear ....6 H 31
Shebster ....85 I 8
Sheepwash ....6 H 31
Sheepy Magna ....36 P 26
Sheering ....22 U 28
Sheerness ....22 W 29
Sheffield ....43 P 23
Sheffield Park ....11 T 31
Shefford ....29 S 27
Sheldon ....19 N 29
Sheldon Manor ....19 N 29
Sheldwich ....22 W 30
Shell or Sealg (Loch) ....82 A 9
Shelley ....43 O 23
Shellingford ....20 P 29
Shelsley Beauchamp ....27 M 27
Shelton *Rushcliffe* ....36 R 25
Shelton *South Norfolk* ....31 X 26
Shelton Lock ....36 P 25
Shelve ....34 L 26
Shenley Church End ....28 R 27
Shenstone ....27 O 26
Shenval ....80 K 11
Shepley ....43 O 23
Sheppey (Isle of) ....22 W 29
Shepreth ....29 U 27
Shepshed ....36 Q 25
Shepton Mallet ....18 M 30
Sherborne *Cotswold* ....19 O 28
Sherborne *West Dorset* ....8 M 31
Sherborne St. John ....20 Q 30
Sherburn *Durham* ....56 P 19

Sherburn *Ryedale* .....51 S 21
Sherburn-in-Elmet .....44 Q 22
Shere .....21 S 30
Sherfield English .....9 P 31
Sheriff Hutton .....50 Q 21
Sheriffhales .....35 M 25
Sheringham .....39 X 25
Sherington .....28 R 27
Shernborne .....38 V 25
Sherston .....19 N 29
Sherwood Forest .....36 Q 24
Shetland Islands 87
Shevington .....42 L 23
Shiant (Sound of) .....82 A 10
Shiant Island .....82 A 10
Shiel (Glen) .....72 D 12
Shiel (Loch) .....72 D 13
Shieldaig *Loch Gairloch* .....78 C 10
Shieldaig *Loch Torridon* .....78 D 11
Shieldaig (Loch) .....78 C 11
Shieldhill .....67 I 16
Shifnal .....35 M 25
Shilbottle .....63 O 17
Shildon .....56 P 20
Shillay .....76 W 11
Shillingford .....7 J 30
Shillingstone .....9 N 31
Shillington .....29 S 28
Shilton *Rugby* .....28 P 26
Shilton *West Oxfordshire* .....19 P 28
Shimpling .....31 X 26
Shin (Loch) .....84 G 9
Shiney Row .....56 P 19
Shinfield .....20 R 29
Shipdham .....38 W 26
Shiplake .....20 R 29
Shipley *Salop* .....35 N 26
Shipley *West Yorks.* .....43 O 22
Shipston-on-Stour .....27 P 27
Shipton *Bridgnorth* .....26 M 26
Shipton *Cotswold* .....27 O 28
Shipton *Hambleton* .....50 Q 21
Shipton Moyne .....19 N 29
Shipton-under-Wychwood .....19 P 28
Shiptonthorpe .....44 R 22
Shira (Lochan) .....66 F 14
Shirebrook .....36 Q 24
Shiremoor .....56 P 18
Shirenewton .....18 L 29
Shirley *Derbyshire* .....35 O 25
Shirley *Solihull* .....27 O 26
Shoadoxhurst .....12 W 30
Shobdon .....26 L 27
Shoeburyness .....22 W 29
Shoreham .....11 T 31
Shorne .....22 V 29
Shotesham .....39 X 26
Shotley Bridge .....56 O 19
Shotley Gate .....31 X 28
Shottenden .....22 W 30
Shottermill .....10 R 30
Shotton Colliery .....57 P 19
Shotts .....61 I 16
Shouldham .....38 V 26
Shrewsbury .....34 L 25
Shrewton .....19 O 30
Shrivenham .....19 P 29
Shuna Sound .....65 D 15
Shurdington .....27 N 28
Shurrery .....85 J 8
Sibbertoft .....28 Q 26
Sibford Ferris .....28 P 27
Sible Hedingham .....30 V 28
Sibsey .....37 U 24
Sidbury .....5 K 31
Siddington .....19 O 28
Siddlington .....43 N 24
Sidford .....5 K 31
Sidinish .....76 Y 11
Sidlaw Hills .....68 K 14
Sidlesham .....10 R 31
Sidmouth .....5 K 31
Sighthill .....68 K 16
Sileby .....36 Q 25
Silecroft .....47 K 21
Silkstone .....43 P 23
Silloth .....54 J 19
Silsden .....49 O 22
Silver End .....30 V 28
Silverdale *Lancaster* .....48 L 21
Silverdale
  Newcastle-under-Lyme .....35 N 24
Silverstone .....28 Q 27
Silverstone Circuit .....28 Q 27
Silverton .....7 J 31
Simonburn .....55 N 18
Simonsbath .....7 I 30

Sinclair's Bay .....86 K 8
Sinclairston .....60 G 17
Singleton *Chichester* .....10 R 31
Singleton *Fylde* .....42 L 22
Sionascaig (Loch) .....84 E 9
Sissinghurst .....12 V 30
Sithney .....2 E 33
Sittingbourne .....22 W 29
Sixpenny Handley .....9 N 31
Skara Brae .....86 J 6
Skares .....60 H 17
Skeabost .....77 B 11
Skegness .....38 V 24
Skellingthorpe .....44 S 24
Skelmanthorpe .....43 P 23
Skelmersdale .....42 L 23
Skelmorlie .....59 F 16
Skelpick .....85 H 8
Skelton *Cleveland* .....50 R 20
Skelton *Cumbria* .....55 L 19
Skelwith Bridge .....48 K 20
Skene .....75 M 12
Skene (Loch of) .....75 M 12
Skenfrith .....26 L 28
Skeroblingarry .....59 D 17
Skerray .....85 H 8
Skervuile Lighthouse .....65 C 16
Skidby .....44 S 22
Skiddaw .....54 K 20
Skigersta .....83 B 8
Skilgate .....7 J 30
Skillington .....37 S 25
Skinburness .....54 J 19
Skipness .....59 D 16
Skipport (Loch) .....76 Y 12
Skipsea .....51 T 22
Skipton .....49 N 22
Skipton-on-Swale .....50 P 21
Skipwith .....44 R 22
Skirlaugh .....45 T 22
Skirling .....61 J 17
Skirwith .....55 M 19
Skirza .....86 K 8
Skokholm Island .....14 E 28
Skomer Island .....14 E 28
Skye (Isle of) .....77 B 12
Slaggyford .....55 M 19
Slaidburn .....49 M 22
Slaithwaite .....43 O 23
Slamannan .....67 I 16
Slapin (Loch) .....71 B 12
Slapton .....4 J 33
Sleaford .....37 S 25
Sleagill .....48 M 20
Sleat (Sound of) .....71 C 12
Sledmere .....51 S 21
Sleekburn .....56 P 18
Sleights .....51 S 20
Slickly .....86 K 8
Sligachan .....77 B 12
Sligachan (Loch) .....77 B 12
Slimbridge .....19 M 28
Slindon .....11 S 31
Slingsby .....50 R 21
Slochd .....79 I 12
Slockavullin .....65 D 15
Slough .....21 S 29
Sloy (Loch) .....66 F 15
Slumbay .....78 D 11
Slyne .....48 L 21
Smailholm .....62 M 17
Smailholm Tower .....62 M 17
Small Dole .....11 T 31
Small Hythe .....12 W 30
Smallfield .....11 T 30
Smarden .....12 W 30
Smart'Hill .....12 U 30
Smedmore .....9 N 32
Smithfield .....55 L 19
Snaefell .....46 G 21
Snainton .....51 S 21
Snaith .....44 Q 22
Snape .....31 Y 27
Snetterton Circuit .....30 W 26
Snettisham .....38 V 25
Snitterfield .....27 O 27
Snizort (Loch) .....77 A 11
Snodland .....22 V 30
Snowdon / Yr Wyddfa .....33 H 24
Snowdonia National Park .....33 I 24
Snowshill .....27 O 27
Soa .....70 Z 14
Soa Island .....64 A 15
Soar (River) .....36 Q 25
Soay .....71 B 12
Soay Sound .....71 B 12
Soham .....30 V 26

Solent (The) .....10 Q 31
Solihull .....27 O 26
Sollas .....76 X 11
Solva .....14 E 28
Solway Firth .....53 J 19
Somerby .....36 R 25
Somercotes .....36 P 24
Somerford Keynes .....19 O 29
Somersham
  Huntingdonshire .....29 U 26
Somersham *Mid Suffolk* .....31 X 27
Somerton *Norfolk* .....39 Y 25
Somerton *Oxon.* .....28 Q 28
Somerton *Somerset* .....8 L 30
Sompting .....11 S 31
Sonning Common .....20 R 29
Sopley .....9 O 31
Sorbie .....52 G 19
Sorisdale .....71 A 13
Sorn .....60 H 17
Sortat .....86 K 8
Soulby .....49 M 20
Sound (The) .....4 H 32
Sourhope .....63 N 17
South-Alloa .....67 I 15
South Balloch .....60 G 18
South Brent .....4 I 32
South Cairn .....52 E 19
South Carrine .....59 C 18
South Cave .....44 S 22
South Cerney .....19 O 28
South Charlton .....63 O 17
South Croxton .....36 R 25
South Downs .....11 R 31
South Elmsall .....44 Q 23
South Esk (River) .....75 L 13
South Ferriby .....44 S 22
South Foreland .....23 Y 30
South Glendale .....70 Y 12
South Hanningfield .....22 V 29
South Harris .....76 Z 10
South Harris Forest .....82 Z 10
South Hayling .....10 R 31
South-Heighton .....11 U 31
South Hetton .....56 P 19
South Kelsey .....45 S 23
South Killingholme .....45 T 23
South Kirkby .....44 Q 23
South Kyme .....37 T 24
South Lancing .....11 T 31
South Leverton .....44 R 24
South Lopham .....30 X 26
South-Marston .....19 O 29
South Mary Bourne .....20 P 30
South Mimms .....21 T 28
South Molton .....7 I 30
South Morar .....72 C 13
South Moreton .....20 Q 29
South Newington .....28 P 28
South-Newton .....9 O 30
South Normanton .....36 P 24
South Ockendon .....22 U 29
South Otterington .....50 P 21
South Oxhey .....21 S 29
South Petherton .....8 L 31
South Petherwin .....3 G 32
South Queensferry .....68 J 16
South Rauceby .....37 S 25
South Raynham .....38 W 25
South Ronaldsay .....87 L 7
South Shields .....56 P 19
South Shore .....42 K 22
South Stack .....40 F 23
South Stainley .....50 P 21
South Tawton .....4 I 31
South Thoresby .....45 U 24
South Uist .....70 X 12
South Walls .....86 K 7
South Warnborough .....20 R 30
South Witham .....37 S 25
South Woodham Ferrers .....22 V 29
South Wootton .....38 V 25
South Wraxall .....19 N 29
South Zeal .....4 I 31
Southam
  Stratford-on-Avon .....28 P 27
Southam *Tewkesbury* .....27 N 28
Southampton .....10 P 31
Southborough .....12 U 30
Southbourne *Dorset* .....9 O 31
Southbourne *West Sussex* .....10 R 31
Southend .....59 D 18
Southend-on-Sea .....22 W 29
Southerness .....53 J 19
Southery .....38 V 26
Southill .....29 T 27
Southminster .....22 W 29

Southport .....42 K 23
Southrop .....19 O 28
Southsea .....10 Q 31
Southwaite .....55 L 19
Southwater .....11 S 30
Southwell .....36 R 24
Southwick
  East Northamptonshire .....29 S 26
Southwick *Sunderland* .....56 P 19
Southwick *West Sussex* .....11 T 31
Southwick *Wilts.* .....19 N 30
Southwick *Widley* .....10 Q 31
Southwold .....31 Z 27
Sowerby Bridge .....43 O 22
Spalding .....37 T 25
Spaldwick .....29 S 26
Spanish Head .....46 F 21
Sparkford .....8 M 30
Spaxton .....8 K 30
Spean (Glen) .....73 F 13
Spean Bridge .....72 F 13
Speeton .....51 T 21
Speldhurst .....12 U 30
Spelsbury .....28 P 28
Spelve (Loch) .....65 C 14
Spennymoor .....56 P 19
Spey (River) .....73 G 12
Spey Bay .....80 K 10
Speymouth Forest .....80 K 11
Spilsby .....37 U 24
Spinningdale .....79 H 10
Spital *Dumfries*
  and Galloway .....52 G 19
Spital *Highland* .....85 J 8
Spital *Northumb.* .....63 O 16
Spittal *Pembrokeshire /*
  Sir Benfro .....24 F 28
Spittal of Glenshee .....74 J 13
Spixworth .....39 X 25
Spofforth .....50 P 22
Spondon .....36 P 25
Spooner Row .....39 X 26
Spott .....69 M 16
Spreyton .....7 I 31
Spridlington .....44 S 23
Springfield .....68 K 15
Springholm .....53 I 18
Sproatley .....45 T 22
Sprotbrough .....44 Q 23
Sproughton .....31 X 27
Sprouston .....62 M 17
Sprowston .....39 X 26
Spurn Head .....45 U 23
Sronlairig Lodge .....73 G 12
Sronphadruig Lodge .....73 H 13
Stack (Loch) .....84 F 8
Stack Island .....70 Y 12
Stack Rocks .....16 E 29
Staffa .....64 A 14
Staffin Bay .....77 B 11
Stafford .....35 N 25
Stagsden .....29 S 27
Staincross .....43 P 23
Staindrop .....56 O 20
Staines .....21 S 29
Stainforth *North Yorks.* .....49 N 21
Stainforth *South Yorks.* .....44 Q 23
Stainton .....55 L 20
Stainton-le-Vale .....45 T 23
Staintondale .....51 S 20
Stair *Allerdale* .....54 K 20
Stair *South Ayrshire* .....60 G 17
Staithes .....50 R 20
Stakeford .....56 P 18
Stalbridge .....9 M 31
Stalham .....39 Y 25
Stalisfield .....22 W 30
Stalling Busk .....49 N 21
Stallingborough .....45 T 23
Stalmine .....48 L 22
Stalybridge .....43 N 23
Stamford .....37 S 26
Stamford Bridge .....50 R 22
Stamfordham .....56 O 18
Stanbridge .....29 S 28
Standford-in-the-Vale .....20 P 29
Standing Stones .....82 Z 9
Standish .....42 M 23
Standlake .....20 P 28
Standon .....29 U 28
Stane .....61 I 16
Stanford .....13 X 30
Stanford-le-Hope .....22 V 29
Stanford-on-Avon .....28 Q 26
Stanghow .....50 R 20
Stanhoe .....38 W 25

Stanhope .....55 N 19
Stanion .....29 S 26
Stanley *Durham* .....56 O 19
Stanley
  Perthshire and Kinross .....68 J 14
Stanley *Wakefield.* .....43 P 22
Stanmer Park .....11 T 31
Stannington .....43 P 23
Stansted Abbotts .....21 U 28
Stansted Mountfitchet .....30 U 28
Stanton .....30 W 27
Stanton Harcourt .....20 P 28
Stanton Long .....26 M 26
Stanton-upon-Hine-Heath .....34 M 25
Stanway .....27 O 28
Stanwell .....21 S 29
Stanwick .....29 S 27
Staple Fitzpaine .....8 K 31
Stapleford *Melton* .....36 R 25
Stapleford *Notts.* .....36 Q 25
Stapleford *Wilts.* .....9 O 30
Staplehurst .....22 V 30
Starcross .....4 J 32
Start Point .....4 J 33
Startforth .....49 O 20
Stathern .....36 R 25
Staughton Highway .....29 S 27
Staunton *Forest of Dean* .....27 N 28
Staunton *Monmouthshire /*
  Sir Fynwy .....18 M 28
Staveley *Cumbria* .....48 L 20
Staveley *Derbs.* .....43 P 24
Staxigoe .....86 K 8
Staxton .....51 S 21
Staylittle .....25 J 26
Steart .....18 K 30
Stebbing .....30 V 28
Stedham .....10 R 31
Steep .....10 R 30
Steeple .....22 W 28
Steeple Ashton .....19 N 30
Steeple Aston .....28 Q 28
Steeple Barton .....28 P 28
Steeple Bumpstead .....30 V 27
Steeple Claydon .....28 R 28
Steeple Langford .....9 O 30
Steeple Morden .....29 T 27
Steeton .....49 O 22
Stelling Minnis .....23 X 30
Stenhousemuir .....67 I 15
Stenness *Orkney Islands* .....86 K 7
Stenness *Shetland Islands* .....87 P 2
Stenton .....69 M 16
Steppingley .....29 S 27
Stevenage .....29 T 28
Stevenston .....60 F 17
Stewartby .....29 S 27
Stewarton .....60 G 16
Stewkley .....28 R 28
Steyning .....11 T 31
Steynton .....16 E 28
Stichill .....62 M 17
Sticker .....3 F 33
Sticklepath .....4 I 31
Stickney .....37 U 24
Stiffkey .....38 W 25
Stillgarry .....76 X 12
Stillingfleet .....44 Q 22
Stillington *Hambleton* .....50 Q 21
Stillington
  Stockton-on-Tees .....56 P 20
Stilton .....29 T 26
Stirling .....67 I 15
Stithians .....2 E 33
Stob Choire Claurigh .....72 F 13
Stobo .....61 K 17
Stobs Castle .....62 L 17
Stock .....22 V 29
Stockbridge .....10 P 30
Stocke Talmage .....20 Q 28
Stockland .....8 K 31
Stockland Bristol .....18 K 30
Stockport .....43 N 23
Stocksbridge .....43 P 23
Stocksfield .....56 O 19
Stockton Heath .....42 M 23
Stockton-on-Tees .....50 P 20
Stockton-on-Teme .....27 M 27
Stockton on the Forest .....50 R 22
Stoer .....83 D 9
Stogumber .....7 K 30
Stogursey .....18 K 30
Stoke .....22 V 29
Stoke Albany .....28 R 26
Stoke Ash .....31 X 27
Stoke-by-Nayland .....30 W 28

Stoke Climsland .....3 H 32
Stoke Fleming .....4 J 33
Stoke Gabriel .....4 J 32
Stoke Goldington .....28 R 27
Stoke Hammond .....28 R 28
Stoke Lacy .....26 M 27
Stoke Lyne .....28 Q 28
Stoke Mandeville .....20 R 28
Stoke-on-Trent .....35 N 24
Stoke Orchard .....27 N 28
Stoke Poges .....21 S 29
Stoke-St. Mary .....8 K 31
Stoke-St. Michael .....18 M 30
Stoke St. Milborough .....26 M 26
Stokeham .....44 R 24
Stokenchurch .....20 R 29
Stokenham .....4 I 33
Stokesay .....26 L 26
Stokesley .....50 Q 20
Stone *Bucks.* .....20 R 28
Stone *Staffs.* .....35 N 25
Stone Edge .....36 P 24
Stonehaugh .....55 N 18
Stonehaven .....75 N 13
Stonehenge .....9 O 30
Stonehouse *Glos.* .....19 N 28
Stonehouse
  South Lanarkshire .....61 I 16
Stoneleigh .....28 P 26
Stonesfield .....20 P 28
Stoney Cross .....9 P 31
Stoney Stanton .....36 Q 26
Stoneybridge .....76 X 12
Stoneykirk .....52 F 19
Stoneywood .....75 N 12
Stony Stratford .....28 R 27
Stornoway .....82 A 9
Storr (The) .....77 B 11
Storrington .....11 S 31
Stort (River) .....29 U 28
Stotfold .....29 T 27
Stottesdon .....26 M 26
Stoughton .....10 R 31
Stoul .....72 C 13
Stoulton .....27 N 27
Stour (River)
  English Channel .....9 N 31
Stour (River) *North Sea* .....30 V 27
Stour (River) *R. Severn* .....27 N 26
Stourbridge .....27 N 26
Stourhead House .....9 N 30
Stourport-on-Severn .....27 N 26
Stourton Caundle .....9 M 31
Stow .....62 L 16
Stow-on-the-Wold .....27 O 28
Stowbridge .....38 V 26
Stowe-by-Chartley .....35 O 25
Stowe School .....28 Q 27
Stowmarket .....30 W 27
Stowupland .....30 X 27
Straad .....59 E 16
Strachan .....75 M 12
Strachur .....66 E 15
Stradbroke .....31 X 27
Stradishall .....30 V 27
Stradsett .....38 V 26
Straiton .....60 G 18
Straloch .....74 J 13
Stranraer .....52 E 19
Strata Florida Abbey .....25 I 27
Stratfield Saye .....20 Q 29
Stratford St. Mary .....30 W 28
Stratford-upon-Avon .....27 O 27
Strath Brora .....85 H 9
Strath Dearn .....79 I 11
Strath Halladale .....85 I 8
Strath Isla .....80 K 11
Strath Morc .....78 E 10
Strath Mulzie .....78 F 10
Strath of Kildonan .....85 I 9
Strath Oykel .....84 F 10
Strath Skinsdale .....85 H 9
Strath Tay .....68 J 14
Strathallan .....67 I 15
Strathan .....72 E 13
Strathardle .....74 J 13
Strathaven .....60 H 16
Strathblane .....67 H 16
Strathbogie .....80 L 11
Strathbraan .....67 I 14
Strathcanaird .....84 E 10
Strathcarron .....78 D 11
Strathcoil .....65 C 14
Strathconon .....78 F 11
Strathconon Forest .....78 F 11

A B C D E F G H I J K L M N O P Q R S T U V W X Y Z

Strathearn 67 I 14
Stratherrick 73 G 12
Strathkinness 69 L 14
Strathmashie 73 H 13
Strathmiglo 68 K 15
Strathmore 75 M 13
Strathnairn 79 H 11
Strathnaver 85 H 8
Strathpeffer 79 G 11
Strathrannoch 79 F 10
Strathspey 80 J 11
Strathvaich Lodge 78 F 10
Strathy 85 I 8
Strathy Point 85 H 8
Strathyre 67 H 15
Stratton *Cornwall* 6 G 31
Stratton *Glos.* 19 O 28
Stratton *West Dorset* 5 M 31
Stratton Audley 28 Q 28
Stratton-on-the-Fosse 18 M 30
Stratton-St. Margaret 19 O 29
Streatley 20 Q 29
Street 8 L 30
Strensall 50 Q 21
Stretford 42 N 23
Stretham 30 U 26
Stretton *Cheshire* 42 M 23
Stretton *Staffs.* 35 N 25
Stretton-on-Dunsmore 28 P 26
Strichen 81 N 11
Striven (Loch) 66 E 16
Stroma (Island of) 86 K 7
Stromeferry 78 D 11
Stromemore 78 D 11
Stromness 86 K 7
Stronachlachar 66 G 15
Stroncheggan 72 E 13
Stronchrubie 84 F 9
Strone 66 F 16
Stronmilchan 66 F 14
Stronsay 87 M 6
Stronsay Firth 87 L 6
Strontian 72 D 13
Stroud 19 N 28
Strumble Head 14 E 27
Stuart Castel 79 H 11
Stuartfield 81 N 11
Stubbington 10 Q 31
Studland 9 O 32
Studley *Warw.* 27 O 27
Studley *Wilts.* 19 N 29
Studley Royal Gardens 50 P 21
Stuley 76 Y 12
Sturminster Marshall 9 N 31
Sturminster Newton 9 N 31
Sturry 23 X 30
Sturton-le-Steeple 44 R 23
Suainaval (Loch) 82 Z 9
Sudbourne 31 Y 27
Sudbury *Derbs.* 35 O 25
Sudbury *Suffolk* 30 W 27
Sudbury Hall 35 O 25
Sudeley Castle 27 O 28
Sùil Ghorm 71 A 13
Sulby 46 G 21
Sulgrave 28 Q 27
Sulhamstead 20 Q 29
Sullom 87 P 2
Sullom Voe 87 P 2
Sully 18 K 29
Sumburgh 87 Q 4
Sumburgh Roost 87 P 4
Summer Island 83 D 9
Summerbridge 49 O 21
Summercourt 3 F 32
Sunart 72 D 13
Sunart (Loch) 71 C 13
Sunbury 21 S 29
Sunderland 57 P 19
Sunderland Bridge 56 P 19
Sunk Island 45 T 23
Sunningdale 21 S 29
Sunninghill 21 S 29
Surfleet 37 T 25
Surlingham 39 Y 26
Sutterton 37 T 25
Sutton *Bassetlaw* 44 R 23
Sutton *Cambs.* 29 U 26
Sutton *Guildford* 21 S 30
Sutton *London Borough* 21 T 29
Sutton *Shrops.* 34 M 25
Sutton Bank 50 Q 21
Sutton Benger 19 N 29
Sutton Bonington 36 Q 25
Sutton Bridge 37 U 25
Sutton Cheney 36 P 26
Sutton Coldfield 35 O 26
Sutton Courtenay 20 Q 29
Sutton-in-Ashfield 36 Q 24
Sutton-on-Hull 45 T 22
Sutton-on-Sea 45 U 24
Sutton-on-the-Forest 50 Q 21
Sutton-on-the-Hill 35 P 25
Sutton-on-Trent 36 R 24
Sutton Scotney 10 P 30
Sutton St. Edmund 37 U 25
Sutton St. James 37 U 25
Sutton-St. Nicholas 26 L 27
Sutton
under Whitestonecliffe 50 Q 21
Sutton Valence 22 V 30
Sutton Veny 9 N 30
Swadlincote 36 P 25
Swaffham 38 W 26
Swaffham Bulbeck 30 U 27
Swainby 50 Q 20
Swainswick 19 M 29
Swale (River) 50 P 21
Swale (The) 22 W 29
Swale Dale 49 O 20
Swallow 45 T 23
Swallow Falls 33 I 24
Swallowcliffe 9 N 30
Swallowfield 20 R 29
Swanage 9 O 32
Swanbridge 18 K 29
Swanland 44 S 22
Swanley 22 U 29
Swannery 5 M 32
Swanscombe 22 U 29
Swansea / Abertawe 17 I 29
Swanton Abbot 39 Y 25
Swanton Morley 38 W 25
Swanwick 36 P 24
Swarbacks Minn 87 P 2
Swavesey 29 T 27
Sway 9 P 31
Swaythling 10 P 31
Swimbridge 7 I 30
Swinbrook 19 P 28
Swinderby 36 R 24
Swindon *Cheltenham* 27 N 28
Swindon *Swindon* 19 O 29
Swinefleet 44 R 22
Swineshead 37 T 25
Swinford 28 Q 26
Swingfield 23 X 30
Swinton *Rotherham.* 44 Q 23
Swinton *Scottish Borders* 63 N 16
Swynnerton 35 N 25
Swyre 5 M 31
Sydenham 20 R 28
Syderstone 38 W 25
Sydling St. Nicholas 8 M 31
Sykehouse 44 Q 23
Symbister 87 Q 2
Symington *South Ayrshire* 60 G 17
Symington
South Lanarkshire 61 J 17
Symonds Yat 18 M 28
Symonds Yat Rock 18 M 28
Symondsbury 5 L 31
Syresham 28 Q 27
Syston 36 Q 25
Sywell 28 R 27

T

Tackley 28 Q 28
Tadcaster 44 Q 22
Taddington 43 O 24
Tadley 20 Q 29
Tadmarton 28 P 27
Tadworth 21 T 30
Taff (River) 18 K 29
Taibach 17 I 29
Tain 79 H 10
Takeley 30 U 28
Tal-y-bont *Dyfed* 25 I 26
Tal-y-Bont *Gwynedd* 33 H 25
Tal-y-Cafn 41 I 23
Tal-y-Llyn Lake 33 I 25
Talacre 41 K 22
Talaton 7 K 31
Talgarreg 15 H 27
Talgarth 26 K 28
Talke 35 N 24
Tall-y-llyn 33 I 26
Talladale 78 D 10
Tallaminnock 60 G 18
Talley 25 I 28
Talsarnau 33 H 25
Talwrn 40 H 23
Talybont-on-Usk *Powys* 26 K 28
Talywern 33 I 26
Tamanavay (Loch) 82 Y 9
Tamar (River) 6 G 31
Tamerton Foliot 4 H 32
Tamworth 35 O 26
Tan Hill 49 N 20
Tan-y-pistill 33 J 25
Tanera Beg 83 D 9
Tanera Mòr 83 D 9
Tangley 20 P 30
Tangmere 11 R 31
Tannach 86 K 8
Tannadice 74 L 13
Tantallon Castle 69 M 15
Taransay 82 Y 10
Taransay (Sound of) 82 Z 10
Tarbat Ness 79 I 10
Tarbert *Argyll and Bute* 59 D 16
Tarbert *Gigha Island* 65 C 16
Tarbert *Western Isles* 82 Z 10
Tarbert (Loch) 65 C 16
Tarbet *Argyll and Bute* 66 F 15
Tarbet *Highland* 72 D 13
Tarbolton 60 G 17
Tardy Gate 42 L 22
Tarfside 74 L 13
Tarland 74 L 12
Tarleton 42 L 22
Tarn (The) 48 L 20
Tarporley 34 M 24
Tarrant Gunville 9 N 31
Tarrant Hinton 9 N 31
Tarrant Keyneston 9 N 31
Tarrington 26 M 27
Tarskavaig 71 C 12
Tarskavaig Point 71 B 12
Tarves 81 N 11
Tarvin 34 L 24
Tathwell 45 T 24
Tattersett 38 W 25
Tattershall 37 T 24
Tatton Hall 42 M 24
Taunton 8 K 30
Taunton Deane 7 K 30
Taverham 39 X 25
Tavernspite 15 G 28
Tavistock 4 H 32
Taw (River) 7 I 31
Tay (Firth of) 68 K 14
Tay (Loch) 67 H 14
Tay Road Bridge 69 L 14
Taynton 27 M 28
Taynuilt 65 E 14
Tayport 69 L 14
Tayvallich 65 D 15
Teacuis (Loch) 71 C 14
Tealby 45 T 23
Teangue 71 C 12
Tebay 48 M 20
Tedburn St. Mary 4 I 31
Teddington 27 N 28
Tees (River) 50 P 20
Teesdale 55 N 20
Teifi (River) 15 G 27
Teignmouth 4 J 32
Telford 34 M 25
Teme (River) 27 M 27
Templand 54 J 18
Temple 61 K 16
Temple Ewell 23 X 30
Temple Grafton 27 O 27
Temple Sowerby 55 M 20
Templeton 15 F 28
Tempsford 29 T 27
Tenbury Wells 26 M 27
Tenby / Dinbych-y-pysgod 15 F 28
Tendring 31 X 28
Tenterden 12 W 30
Terling 22 V 28
Tern Hill 34 M 25
Terrington St. Clement 38 U 25
Test (River) 20 P 30
Tetbury 19 N 29
Tetford 45 T 24
Tetney 45 T 23
Tetsworth 20 Q 28
Tettenhall 35 N 26
Tewin 21 T 28
Tewkesbury 27 N 28
Texa 58 B 17
Teynham 22 W 30
Thakeham 11 S 31
Thame 20 R 28
Thame (River) 20 R 28
Thames (River) 20 Q 29
Thanet (Isle of) 23 Y 29
Thankerton 61 J 17
Thatcham 20 Q 29
Thaxted 30 V 28
Theale *Berks.* 20 Q 29
Theale *Somerset* 18 L 30
Theddlethorpe St. Helen 45 U 23
Thetford 30 W 26
Theviothead 62 L 17
Theydon Bois 21 U 28
Thirlestane 62 L 16
Thirlspot 48 K 20
Thirsk 50 P 21
Thistleton 37 S 25
Thixendale 51 R 21
Thompson 38 W 26
Thomshill 80 K 11
Thoralby 49 N 21
Thoresway 45 T 23
Thorganby 44 R 22
Thornaby-on-Tees 50 Q 20
Thornborough 28 R 28
Thornbury *Heref.* 26 M 27
Thornbury *South Glos.* 18 M 29
Thornbury *Torridge* 6 H 31
Thornby 28 Q 26
Thorncombe 8 L 31
Thorne 44 R 23
Thorner 43 P 22
Thorney 37 T 26
Thornford 8 M 31
Thornham 38 V 25
Thornhill
Dumfries and Galloway 61 I 18
Thornhill *Stirling* 67 H 15
Thornton *Fife* 68 K 15
Thornton *Lancs.* 42 K 22
Thornton Curtis 45 S 23
Thornton-in-Craven 49 N 22
Thornton-le-Dale 51 R 21
Thorntonloch 69 M 16
Thornyhive Bay 75 N 13
Thorpe *Derbs.* 35 O 24
Thorpe *Essex* 22 W 29
Thorpe-le-Soken 31 X 28
Thorpe-on-the-Hill 37 S 24
Thorpe Thewles 57 P 20
Thorpeness 31 Y 27
Thorrington 31 X 28
Thorverton 7 J 31
Thrapston 29 S 26
Threapwood 34 L 24
Three Cocks 26 K 27
Three Crosses 15 H 29
Threekingham 37 S 25
Threlkeld 54 K 20
Thringstone 36 P 25
Throckley 56 O 19
Thropton 63 O 18
Throwleigh 4 I 31
Thrumster 86 K 8
Thruxton Circuit 20 P 30
Thrybergh 44 Q 23
Thundersley 22 V 29
Thurcroft 44 Q 23
Thurgarton 36 R 24
Thurgoland 43 P 23
Thurlby 37 S 25
Thurlestone 4 I 33
Thurlow 30 V 27
Thurlton 39 Y 26
Thurmaston 36 Q 25
Thurne 39 Y 25
Thurnham 22 V 30
Thurnscoe 44 Q 23
Thursby 54 K 19
Thurso 85 J 8
Thurstaston 42 K 23
Thurstonfield 54 K 19
Thurton 39 Y 26
Thwaite 49 N 20
Tibbermore 68 J 14
Tibberton *Glos.* 27 M 28
Tibberton *Salop* 34 M 25
Tibberton *Wychavon* 27 N 27
Tibshelf 36 P 24
Ticehurst 12 V 30
Tickhill 44 Q 23
Ticknall 36 P 25
Tiddington 20 Q 28
Tidenham 18 M 29
Tideswell 43 O 24
Tigerton 75 L 13
Tigharry 76 X 11
Tighnabruaich 65 E 16
Tilbury 22 V 29
Tillathrowie 80 L 11
Tillicoultry 67 I 15
Tillington 11 S 31
Tilney St. Lawrence 38 U 25
Tilshead 19 O 30
Tilstock 34 L 25
Tilt (Glen) 73 I 13
Tilton-on-the-Hill 36 R 26
Timberscombe 7 J 30
Timsbury 18 M 30
Timsgarry 82 Y 9
Tingewick 28 Q 28
Tingwall (Loch) 87 P 3
Tintagel 6 F 32
Tintern Abbey 18 L 28
Tintinhull 8 L 31
Tintwistle 43 O 23
Tinwald 53 J 18
Tipton 27 N 26
Tipton-St. john 5 K 31
Tiptree 22 W 28
Tirabad 25 J 27
Tiree 64 Z 14
Tirga Mòr 82 Z 10
Tirley 27 N 28
Tiroran 65 B 14
Tisbury 9 N 30
Titchfield 10 Q 31
Titchmarsh 29 S 26
Tiumpan Head 83 B 9
Tiverton *Chester* 34 L 24
Tiverton *Mid Devon* 7 J 31
Tobermory 71 B 14
Toberonochy 65 D 15
Tobson 82 Z 9
Tockwith 50 Q 22
Todber 9 N 31
Toddington 29 S 28
Todenham 27 P 27
Todmorden 43 N 22
Toe Head 76 Y 10
Togston 63 P 18
Tokavaig 71 C 12
Toll of Birness 81 O 11
Toller Porcorum 8 M 31
Tollerton 50 Q 21
Tollesbury 22 W 28
Tolleshunt d'Arcy 22 W 28
Tolpuddle 9 N 31
Tolquhon Castle 81 N 11
Tolsta 83 B 8
Tolsta Chaolais 82 Z 9
Tolsta Head 83 B 8
Tomatin 79 I 11
Tombreck 79 H 11
Tomcrasky 72 F 12
Tomdoun 72 E 12
Tomich 78 F 12
Tomintoul 74 J 12
Tomnavoulin 80 K 12
Tomsléibhe 65 C 14
Tonbridge 22 U 30
Tondu 17 J 29
Tong 82 A 9
Tongham 20 R 30
Tongland 53 H 19
Tongue 84 G 8
Tongwynlais 18 K 29
Tonna 17 I 28
Tonypandy 17 J 29
Tonyrefail 17 J 29
Topcliffe 50 P 21
Topsham 4 J 31
Tor Ness 86 K 7
Torbay 4 J 32
Torcross 4 J 33
Torksey 44 R 24
Torlundy 72 E 13
Tormarton 19 N 29
Tornapress 78 D 11
Tornaveen 75 M 12
Torness 79 G 12
Torphichen 67 J 16
Torphins 75 M 12
Torpoint 3 H 32
Torquay 4 J 32
Torquhan 62 L 16
Torridon (Loch) 77 C 11
Torrin 71 B 12
Torrisdale Bay 85 H 8
Torthorwald 53 J 18
Tortworth 19 M 29
Torver 48 K 20
Toscaig 77 C 11
Totaig *Loch Alsh* 78 D 12
Totaig *Loch Dunvegan* 77 A 11
Totland 10 P 31
Totley 43 P 24
Totnes 4 I 32
Toton 36 Q 25
Totscore 77 A 11
Totternhoe 29 S 28
Totton 10 P 31
Tournaig 78 D 10
Tow Law 56 O 19
Towcester 28 R 27
Tower Hamlets
London Borough 21 T 29
Towie 74 L 12
Town Yetholm 62 N 17
Towneley Hall 43 N 22
Townhead 53 H 19
Townhead of Greenlaw 53 I 19
Tradespark 79 I 11
Trallwng / Welshpool 34 K 26
Tranent 69 L 16
Trapp 25 I 28
Traquair House 61 K 17
Trawden 43 N 22
Trawsfynydd 33 I 25
Trealaval (Loch) 82 A 9
Trearddur Bay 40 G 23
Trecastle 25 J 28
Trecwn 24 F 28
Tredington 27 P 27
Treen 2 D 33
Trefaldwyn / Montgomery 34 K 26
Trefeglwys 25 J 26
Treffynnon / Holywell 41 K 23
Trefil 18 K 28
Trefnant 41 J 23
Trefonen 34 K 25
Trefor 40 G 23
Trefyclawdd / Knighton 26 K 26
Trefynwy / Monmouth 18 L 28
Tregaron 25 I 27
Tregony 3 F 33
Tregurrian 2 E 32
Tregynon 33 J 26
Treharris 18 K 29
Treherbert 17 J 28
Treig (Loch) 73 F 13
Trelawnyd 41 J 23
Trelech 15 G 28
Trelech a'r Betws 15 G 28
Trelissick Gardens 2 E 33
Trelleck 18 L 28
Tremadog 33 H 25
Tremadog Bay 32 H 25
Trenance 2 E 32
Trengwainton Garden 2 D 33
Trent 8 M 31
Trent (River) 36 R 24
Trentham 35 N 25
Treorchy 17 J 29
Trerice 2 E 32
Treshnish Isles 64 A 14
Treshnish Point 71 A 14
Tressait 73 I 13
Tretower 26 K 28
Treuddyn 34 K 24
Trevine 14 E 28
Trevone 3 F 32
Trevor 32 G 25
Trevose Head 2 E 32
Trewithen 3 F 33
Trimdon 56 P 19
Trimley Heath 31 X 28
Trimsaran 15 H 28
Tring 21 R 28
Trispen 2 E 33
Trochry 67 J 14
Troedyrhiw 17 J 28
Trollamarig (Loch) 82 Z 10
Tromie (Glen) 73 H 12
Troon 60 G 17
Trossachs (The) 67 G 15
Trotternish 77 B 11
Troutbeck *Eden* 54 L 20
Troutbeck *South Lakeland* 48 L 20
Trowbridge 19 N 30
Trudoxhill 19 M 30
Truim (Glen) 73 H 13
Trull 8 K 31
Trumpington 29 U 27
Trunch 39 Y 25
Truro 2 E 33
Trusthorpe 45 U 24
Trwyn Cilan 32 G 25
Tuath (Loch) 64 B 14
Tuddenham *Forest Heath* 30 V 27
Tuddenham
Suffolk Coastal 31 X 27
Tudhoe 56 P 19
Tudweiliog 32 G 25
Tugford 26 M 26
Tulla (Loch) 66 F 14
Tullibardine 67 I 15

Tullibody ....67 I 15
Tullymurdoch ....74 K 14
Tumble ....15 H 28
Tummel (Loch) ....73 I 13
Tunstall
  East Riding of Yorkshire ...45 T 22
Tunstall Staffs. ....35 N 24
Tunstall Suffolk ....31 Y 27
Tur Langton ....36 R 26
Turnberry ....59 F 18
Turnditch ....35 P 24
Turret
  (Loch and Reservoir) ......67 I 14
Turriff ....81 M 11
Turvey ....29 S 27
Tusker Rock ....17 I 29
Tutbury ....35 O 25
Tuxford ....44 R 24
Twatt ....86 K 6
Tweed (River) ....61 J 17
Tweeddale ....61 J 17
Tweedmouth ....63 N 16
Tweedsmuir Hills ....61 J 17
Twemlow Green ....35 N 24
Twickenham ....21 S 29
Two Dales ....35 P 24
Twyford Berks. ....20 R 29
Twyford Hants. ....10 Q 30
Twyford Leics. ....36 R 25
Twynholm ....53 H 19
Twynllanan ....25 I 28
Tydd-St. Giles ....37 U 25
Tydd St. Mary ....37 U 25
Tyddewi / St. David's ....14 E 28
Tyldesley ....42 M 23
Tylorstown ....17 J 29
Tyne (River) ....56 P 19
Tynehead ....62 L 16
Tynemouth ....56 P 18
Tynewydd ....17 J 29
Tynron ....53 I 18
Tythegston ....17 J 29
Tytherington ....18 M 29
Tywardreath ....3 F 32
Tywi (River) ....25 I 27
Tywyn ....33 H 26

U

Ubiey ....18 L 30
Uckfield ....11 U 31
Uddingston ....60 H 16
Udimore ....12 V 31
Uffculme ....7 K 31
Uffington ....37 S 26
Ufford ....31 Y 27
Ugadale Bay ....59 D 17
Ugborough ....4 I 32
Ugbrooke House ....4 J 32
Ugthorpe ....50 R 20
Uig Highland ....77 A 11
Uig Western Isles ....82 Y 9
Uisg (Loch) ....65 C 14
Uiskevagh (Loch) ....76 Y 11
Ulbster ....86 K 8
Ulceby East Lindsey ....45 U 24
Ulceby North Lincolnshire ...45 T 23
Ulcombe ....22 V 30
Uldale ....54 K 19
Uley ....19 N 28
Ulgham ....56 P 18
Ullapool ....78 E 10
Ulleskelf ....44 Q 22
Ullesthorpe ....28 Q 26
Ullinish ....77 A 11
Ullock ....54 J 20
Ullswater ....48 L 20
Ulpha ....47 K 21
Ulsta ....87 Q 2
Ulva ....64 B 14
Ulverston ....48 K 21
Unapool ....84 E 9
Union Mills ....46 G 21
Unst ....87 R 1
Upavon ....19 O 30
Upchurch ....22 V 29
Uphall ....68 J 16
Uphill ....18 L 30
Upleadon ....27 M 28
Uplyme ....5 L 31
Upottery ....8 K 31
Upper Arley ....27 M 26
Upper Badcall ....84 E 9
Upper Beeding ....11 T 31
Upper Bighouse ....85 I 8
Upper Broughton ....36 R 25
Upper Chapel ....25 J 27
Upper Chute ....20 P 30

Upper Dicker ....12 U 31
Upper Hale ....20 R 30
Upper Heyford ....28 Q 28
Upper Hindhope ....62 M 17
Upper Knockando ....80 J 11
Upper Loch Torridon ....78 D 11
Upper Poppleton ....50 Q 22
Upper Sandaig ....72 D 12
Upper Tean ....35 O 25
Uppertown ....86 K 7
Uppingham ....36 R 26
Upton Dorset ....9 N 31
Upton Notts. ....36 R 24
Upton Vale of White Horse ...20 Q 29
Upton Wakefield ....44 Q 23
Upton West Somerset ....7 J 30
Upton Grey ....20 Q 30
Upton House ....28 P 27
Upton Magna ....34 M 25
Upton Noble ....9 M 30
Upton Scudamore ....19 N 30
Upton-upon-Severn ....27 N 27
Upwell ....38 U 26
Upwood ....29 T 26
Ure (River) ....50 Q 21
Urigill (Loch) ....84 F 9
Urmston ....42 M 23
Urquhart ....80 K 11
Urquhart (Glen) ....79 G 11
Urquhart Castle ....79 G 12
Urrahag (Loch) ....82 A 8
Ushaw Moor ....56 P 19
Usk / Brynbuga ....18 L 28
Usk (River) ....18 K 28
Uttoxeter ....35 O 25
Uyea ....87 R 2
Uyeasound ....87 R 1

V

Vallay Strand ....76 X 11
Valle Crucis ....34 K 25
Valley ....40 G 23
Valtos ....82 Z 9
Vatersay ....70 X 13
Vatten ....77 A 11
Ve Skerries ....87 O 2
Venachar (Loch) ....67 H 15
Ventnor ....10 Q 32
Verham Dean ....20 P 30
Verulamium ....21 S 28
Verwood ....9 O 31
Veryan ....3 F 33
Veyatie (Loch) ....84 E 9
Vindolanda ....55 M 19
Voe ....87 Q 2
Voil (Loch) ....67 G 14
Vowchurch ....26 L 27
Vyrnwy (Lake) ....33 J 25

W

Waddesdon ....20 R 28
Waddingham ....44 S 23
Waddington Lancs. ....42 M 22
Waddington Lincs. ....37 S 24
Wadebridge ....3 F 32
Wadhurst ....12 U 30
Wag ....85 I 9
Wainfleet All Saints ....38 U 24
Wainstalls ....43 O 22
Wakefield ....43 P 22
Wakerley ....37 S 26
Wakes Colne ....30 W 28
Walberswick ....31 Y 27
Walcott ....37 T 24
Walden Head ....49 N 21
Walderslade ....22 V 29
Waldringfield ....31 X 27
Waldron ....12 U 31
Walesby ....44 R 24
Walford ....34 L 25
Walgherton ....34 M 24
Walgrave ....28 R 26
Walkden ....42 M 23
Walkeringham ....44 R 23
Walkern ....29 T 28
Wall ....35 O 26
Wallace Monument ....67 I 15
Wallasey ....42 K 23
Wallend ....22 W 29
Wallingford ....20 Q 29
Wallington House ....56 O 18
Walls ....87 P 3
Wallsend ....56 P 18
Wallyford ....69 K 16
Walney (Isle of) ....47 K 21
Walpole ....31 Y 27

Walpole St. Andrew ....38 U 25
Walpole St. Peter ....38 U 25
Walsall ....35 O 26
Walsden ....43 N 22
Walsham le Willows ....30 W 27
Walshford ....50 P 22
Walston ....61 J 16
Waltham Kent ....23 X 30
Waltham North East Lincs. ...45 T 23
Waltham Abbey ....21 U 28
Waltham Forest
  London Borough ....21 T 29
Waltham-on-the-Wolds ......36 R 25
Walton Carlisle ....55 L 19
Walton Leeds ....50 Q 22
Walton Powys ....26 K 27
Walton-East ....24 F 28
Walton-in-Gordano ....18 L 29
Walton-le-Dale ....42 M 22
Walton-on-Thames ....21 S 29
Walton-on-the-Naze ....31 X 28
Walton-Upon-Trent ....35 O 25
Walworth ....49 P 20
Wanborough ....19 O 29
Wandsworth
  London Borough ....21 T 29
Wangford ....31 Y 26
Wanlockhead ....61 I 17
Wansford
  East Riding of Yorkshire ...51 S 22
Wansford Peterborough .....37 S 26
Wanstrow ....9 M 30
Wantage ....20 P 29
Wappenham ....28 Q 27
Warboys ....29 T 26
Warbstow ....6 G 31
Warcop ....49 M 20
Wardington ....28 Q 27
Wardour Castle ....9 N 30
Ware ....21 T 28
Wareham ....9 N 31
Wargrave ....20 R 29
Wark near Coldstream ....63 N 17
Wark near Hexham ....55 N 18
Wark Forest ....55 M 18
Warkworth ....63 P 17
Warley ....27 O 26
Warlingham ....21 T 30
Warmington
  East Northamptonshire ....29 S 26
Warmington
  Stratford-on-Avon ....28 P 27
Warminster ....19 N 30
Warmsworth ....44 Q 23
Warmwell ....9 M 31
Warnborough ....20 R 30
Warnford ....10 Q 30
Warnham ....11 S 30
Warren ....43 N 24
Warren (The) ....13 X 30
Warrington ....42 M 23
Warsash ....10 Q 31
Warslow ....35 O 24
Warsop ....36 Q 24
Warter ....51 R 22
Warton Alnwick ....63 O 18
Warton near Morecambe .....48 L 21
Warton near Preston ....42 L 22
Warwick ....27 P 27
Warwick Bridge ....55 L 19
Wasbister ....86 K 6
Wasdale Head ....47 K 20
Wash (The) ....38 U 25
Washington
  Tyne and Wear ....56 P 19
Washington West Sussex ...11 S 31
West Water ....47 K 20
Watchet ....17 K 30
Watchfield ....19 P 29
Watchgate ....48 L 20
Water Orton ....27 O 26
Waterbeach ....30 U 27
Waterbeck ....54 K 18
Watergate Bay ....2 E 32
Waterhead ....74 L 13
Waterhouses ....35 O 24
Wateringbury ....22 V 30
Waterlooville ....10 Q 31
Waternish Point ....77 A 11
Waters Upton ....34 M 25
Waterside ....60 G 17
Waterstein ....76 Z 11
Watford Watford ....21 S 29
Watford Daventry ....28 Q 27
Wath ....50 P 21
Wath-upon-Dearne ....44 P 23
Watlington ....20 Q 29

Watten ....85 K 8
Watton Breckland ....38 W 26
Watton
  East Riding of Yorkshire ...51 S 22
Watton at Stone ....29 T 28
Waunfawr ....33 H 24
Waveney (River) ....31 Y 26
Waverton Allerdale ....54 K 19
Waverton Chester ....34 L 24
Wawne ....45 S 22
Wear (River) ....56 O 20
Weardale ....55 N 19
Weasenham St. Peter ....38 W 25
Weaver (River) ....34 M 24
Weaverthorpe ....51 S 21
Wedmore ....18 L 30
Wednesbury ....35 N 26
Wednesfield ....35 N 26
Weedon-Bec ....28 Q 27
Week St. Mary ....6 G 31
Weeley ....31 X 28
Weem ....73 I 14
Weeting ....30 V 26
Weeton ....42 L 22
Welburn ....50 R 21
Welby ....37 S 25
Welcombe ....6 G 31
Welford Daventry ....28 Q 26
Welford Stratford-on-Avon ...27 O 27
Welford West Berkshire ......20 P 29
Welham Green ....21 T 28
Welland ....27 N 27
Welland (River) ....37 T 25
Wellesbourne ....27 P 27
Wellingborough ....29 R 27
Wellington
  Herefordshire ....26 L 27
Wellington Salop ....34 M 25
Wellington Somerset ....8 K 31
Wellow
  Bath and North East ....19 M 30
Wellow
  Newark and Sherwood .....36 R 24
Wells ....18 M 30
Wells-next-the-Sea ....38 W 25
Wells of Ythan ....81 M 11
Welney ....38 U 26
Welsh Newton ....26 L 28
Welshampton ....34 L 25
Welshpool / Trallwng ....34 K 26
Welton Allerdale ....54 K 19
Welton Daventry ....28 Q 27
Welton West Lindsey ....44 S 24
Welton-le-Wold ....45 T 23
Welwyn ....21 T 28
Welwyn Garden City ....21 T 28
Wem ....34 L 25
Wembdon ....8 K 30
Wembley ....21 T 29
Wembury ....4 H 33
Wembworthy ....7 I 31
Wemyss Bay ....59 F 16
Wendens Ambo ....30 U 27
Wendlebury ....28 Q 28
Wendover ....20 R 28
Wendron ....2 E 33
Wenlock Edge ....26 L 26
Wennington ....48 M 21
Wensley ....49 O 21
Wensleydale ....49 O 21
Wentbridge ....44 Q 23
Wentnor ....26 L 26
Wentworth ....43 P 23
Wenvoe ....18 K 29
Weobley
  Hereford and Worcester ...26 L 27
Wereham ....38 V 26
Werrington ....6 G 32
West Alvington ....4 I 33
West Auckland ....56 O 20
West-Barns ....69 M 16
West Bergholt ....30 W 28
West-Bradenham ....38 W 26
West Bridgford ....36 Q 25
West Bromwich ....27 O 26
West-Buckland
  North Devon ....7 I 30
West-Buckland
  Taunton Deane ....8 K 31
West Butterwick ....44 R 23
West Calder ....61 J 16
West Camel ....8 M 30
West Charleton ....4 I 33
West Chevington ....63 P 18
West Chiltington ....11 S 31

Watten ....85 K 8
West-Chinnock ....8 L 31
West Coker ....8 L 31
West Dean ....9 P 30
West-Dereham ....38 V 26
West Down ....7 H 30
West End ....10 Q 31
West Farleigh ....22 V 30
West-Felton ....34 L 25
West-Firle ....11 U 31
West Geirinish ....76 X 11
West-Grinstead ....11 T 31
West Hanningfield ....22 V 28
West Harptree ....18 M 30
West Heath ....20 R 30
West Heslerton ....51 S 21
West-Hill ....5 K 31
West Hoathly ....11 T 30
West-Huntspill ....18 L 30
West Kilbride ....59 F 16
West Kingsdown ....22 U 29
West Kirby ....41 K 22
West Langwell ....85 H 9
West Lavington ....19 O 30
West Linton ....61 J 16
West Loch Roag ....82 Z 9
West Loch Tarbert
  Argyll and Bute ....59 D 16
West Loch Tarbert
  Western Isles ....82 Z 10
West Looe ....3 G 32
West Lulworth ....9 N 32
West Lutton ....51 S 21
West Malling ....22 V 30
West Malvern ....27 M 27
West Meon ....10 Q 30
West Mersea ....22 W 28
West Moors ....9 O 31
West-Overton ....19 O 29
West Putford ....6 G 31
West-Quantoxhead ....8 K 30
West Rainton ....56 P 19
West Runton ....39 X 25
West-Stafford ....9 M 31
West Strathan ....84 G 8
West Tanfield ....50 P 21
West-Tarbert ....59 D 16
West Thorney ....10 R 31
West Town ....18 L 29
West-Tytherley ....9 P 30
West Walton ....37 U 25
West Wellow ....9 P 31
West Wickam ....21 T 29
West Winch ....38 V 25
West Wittering ....10 R 31
West Witton ....49 O 21
West Woodburn ....55 N 18
West Wycombe ....20 R 29
Westbourne ....10 R 31
Westbury Cheshire ....34 L 25
Westbury Wilts. ....19 N 30
Westbury-on-Severn ....19 M 28
Westcliff ....22 W 29
Westcott ....21 S 30
Westenhanger ....13 X 30
Wester Ross ....78 D 11
Westerdale Highland ....85 J 8
Westerdale Scarborough .....50 R 20
Westerham ....21 U 30
Westerleigh ....19 M 29
Western Cleddau ....24 E 28
Westfield Highland ....85 J 8
Westfield Rother ....12 V 31
Westfield West Lothian ....67 I 16
Westgate-on-Sea ....23 Y 29
Westham ....12 U 31
Westhoughton ....42 M 23
Westleton ....31 Y 27
Westmeston ....11 T 31
Westmill ....29 T 28
Westnewton ....54 J 19
Weston Devon ....8 K 31
Weston
  North Hertfordshire ....29 T 28
Weston South Holland ....37 T 25
Weston
  South Northamptonshire ...28 Q 27
Weston Staffs. ....35 N 25
Weston-by-Welland ....28 R 26
Weston Favell ....28 R 27
Weston-on-the-Green ....28 Q 28
Weston-on-Trent ....36 P 25
Weston Rhyn ....34 K 25
Weston-super-Mare ....18 L 29
Weston Turville ....20 R 28
Weston-under-Lizard ....35 N 25
Weston-under-Penyard ......26 M 28

Westonzoyland ....8 L 30
Westray ....86 K 6
Westruther ....62 M 16
Westward ....54 K 19
Westward Ho ....6 H 30
Westwood ....19 N 30
Wetheral ....55 L 19
Wetherby ....50 P 22
Wetheringsett ....31 X 27
Wethersfield ....30 V 28
Wetwang ....51 S 21
Wey (River) ....10 R 30
Weybourne ....39 X 25
Weybridge ....21 S 29
Weyhill ....20 P 30
Weymouth ....8 M 32
Whaddon ....28 R 28
Whaley Bridge ....43 O 24
Whalley ....42 M 22
Whalsay ....87 R 2
Whalton ....56 O 18
Whaplode ....37 T 25
Whaplode Drove ....37 T 25
Wharfe (River) ....44 Q 22
Wharfedale ....49 O 22
Whatlington ....12 V 31
Whatsandwell ....36 P 24
Whauphill ....52 G 19
Whaw ....49 N 20
Wheathampstead ....21 T 28
Wheatley Notts. ....44 R 23
Wheatley Oxon. ....20 Q 28
Wheatley Hill ....56 P 19
Wheaton Aston ....35 N 25
Wheldrake ....50 R 22
Whepstead ....30 W 27
Whernside ....49 M 21
Wherwell ....10 P 30
Whickham ....56 O 19
Whimple ....7 J 31
Whipsnade ....21 S 28
Whissendine ....36 R 25
Whissonsett ....38 W 25
Whitburn South Tyneside ...57 P 19
Whitburn West Lothian ....61 I 16
Whitby ....51 S 20
Whitchurch
  Basingstoke and Deane ...20 P 30
Whitchurch
  Bath and N.E. Somerset ...18 M 29
Whitchurch Bucks. ....28 R 28
Whitchurch
  Caerdydd / Cardiff ....18 K 29
Whitchurch Devon ....4 H 32
Whitchurch Oxon. ....20 Q 29
Whitchurch Salop ....34 L 25
Whitchurch
  Heref. and Worc. ....18 M 28
White Coomb ....61 K 17
White Horse Hill ....20 P 29
White Scarcaves ....49 M 21
White Waltham ....20 R 29
Whitebridge ....73 G 12
Whitecairns ....75 N 12
Whitechurch Canonicorum ...5 L 31
Whitefield ....42 N 23
Whitehall ....87 M 6
Whitehaven ....47 J 20
Whitehill ....10 R 30
Whitehills ....81 M 10
Whitehouse
  Aberdeenshire ....75 M 12
Whitehouse
  Argyll and Bute ....59 D 16
Whitekirk ....69 M 15
Whiten Head ....84 G 8
Whiteness Sands ....79 I 10
Whiteparish ....9 P 30
Whitcrashes ....81 N 12
Whitemire ....79 I 11
Whitesand Bay Cornwall .....2 C 33
Whitesand Bay
  Pembrokes ....14 E 28
Whiteshill ....19 N 28
Whiteside ....55 M 18
Whitewall ....49 M 22
Whitewreath ....80 K 11
Whitfield Dover ....23 X 30
Whitfield
  South Northamptonshire ...28 Q 27
Whitfield Tynedale ....55 M 19
Whitgift ....44 R 22
Whithorn ....52 G 19
Whiting Bay ....59 E 17
Whitland ....15 G 28
Whitley ....28 R 28
Whitley Bay ....56 P 19

A B C D E F G H I J K L M N O P Q R S T U V W X Y Z

A B C D E F G H I J K L M N O P Q R S T U V W X Y Z

Whitley Bridge ....44 Q 22
Whitley Chapel ....55 N 19
Whitminster ....19 N 28
Whitmore ....35 N 25
Whitnash ....28 P 27
Whitsand Bay ....3 H 32
Whitstable ....23 X 29
Whitstone ....6 G 31
Whittingham ....63 O 17
Whittington *Derbs.* ....43 P 24
Whittington *King's Lynn
   and West Norfolk* ....38 V 26
Whittington *Lancaster* ......48 M 21
Whittington *Shrops.* ....34 L 25
Whittle le Woods ....42 M 22
Whittlebury ....28 R 27
Whittlesey ....37 T 26
Whittlesford ....29 U 27
Whitton *North Lincolnshire* ..44 S 22
Whitton *Powys* ....26 K 27
Whitton *Suffolk* ....31 X 27
Whittonstall ....56 O 19
Whitwell *Derbs.* ....44 Q 24
Whitwell *I.O.W.* ....10 Q 32
Whitwell-on-the-Hill ....50 R 21
Whitwick ....36 P 25
Whitworth ....43 N 23
Whixall ....34 L 25
Whygate ....55 M 18
Wiay *Highland* ....77 A 11
Wiay *Western Isles* ....76 Y 11
Wibtoft ....28 Q 26
Wick *Bro Morgannwg /
   The Vale of Glamorgan* ....17 J 29
Wick *Highland* ....86 K 8
Wick *South Glos.* ....19 M 29
Wicken *Cambs.* ....28 R 27
Wicken *Northants.* ....30 U 27
Wickenby ....45 S 24
Wickersley ....44 Q 23
Wickford ....22 V 29
Wickham ....10 Q 31
Wickham Market ....31 Y 27
Wickhambrook ....30 V 27
Wickwar ....19 M 29
Widdrington ....63 P 18
Wide Open ....56 P 18
Widecombe-in-the-Moor ......4 I 32
Wideford Hill Cairn ....86 K 7
Widemouth Bay ....6 G 31
Widford ....21 U 28
Widnes ....42 L 23
Wigan ....42 M 23
Wiggenhall
   St. Mary Magdalen ....38 V 25
Wigglesworth ....49 N 21
Wight (Isle of) ....10 P 32
Wighton ....38 W 25
Wigmore *Herefordshire* ....26 L 27
Wigmore *Medway* ....22 V 29
Wigston ....36 Q 26
Wigton ....54 K 19
Wigtown ....52 G 19

Wigtown Bay ....53 H 19
Wilberfoss ....50 R 22
Wilcot ....19 O 29
Wild Animal Kingdom ....29 S 28
Wilkhaven ....79 I 10
Wilkieston ....61 J 16
Willand ....7 J 31
Willenhall *Coventry* ....28 P 26
Willenhall *Walsall* ....35 N 26
Willerby ....45 S 22
Willersey ....27 O 27
Willingdon ....12 U 31
Willingham ....29 U 27
Willingham Forest ....45 T 23
Willington *Beds.* ....29 S 27
Willington *Derbs.* ....35 P 25
Willington *Durham* ....56 O 19
Williton ....7 K 30
Willoughby ....28 Q 27
Wilmcote ....27 O 27
Wilmington *East Essex* ....12 U 31
Wilmington *Kent* ....22 U 29
Wilmslow ....43 N 24
Wiloughby ....45 U 24
Wilpshire ....42 M 22
Wilsford ....37 S 25
Wilstead ....29 S 27
Wilton ....9 O 30
Wimbledon ....21 T 29
Wimblington ....29 U 26
Wimborne Minster ....9 O 31
Wimborne St. Giles ....9 O 31
Wincanton ....9 M 30
Wincham ....42 M 24
Winchburgh ....68 J 16
Winchcombe ....27 O 28
Winchelsea ....12 W 31
Winchester ....10 Q 30
Winchfield ....20 R 30
Wincle ....35 N 24
Windermere ....48 L 20
Windhill ....79 G 11
Windlesham ....21 S 29
Windrush ....19 O 28
Windrush (River) ....19 O 28
Windsor ....21 S 29
Windsor Great Park ....21 S 29
Windygates ....68 K 15
Winestead ....45 T 22
Winfarthing ....31 X 26
Winford ....18 M 29
Winforton ....26 K 27
Winfrith Newburgh ....9 N 32
Wing ....28 R 28
Wingate ....57 P 19
Wingerworth ....36 P 24
Wingfield *near Alfreton* ....36 P 24
Wingfield
   near Chesterfield ....36 P 24
Wingham ....23 X 30
Wingrave ....28 R 28
Winkfield ....21 R 29
Winkleigh ....7 I 31

Winksley ....50 P 21
Winmarleigh ....48 L 22
Winnersh ....20 R 29
Winscombe ....18 L 30
Winsford *Cheshire* ....34 M 24
Winsford *Somerset* ....7 J 30
Winsham ....8 L 31
Winshill ....35 P 25
Winslow ....28 R 28
Winster *Derbyshire Dales* ....35 P 24
Winster *South Lakeland* .....48 L 20
Winston ....49 O 20
Winstone ....19 N 28
Winterborne Kingston ....9 N 31
Winterborne Stickland ....9 N 31
Winterborne Whitechurch ......9 N 31
Winterbourne ....18 M 29
Winterbourne Abbas ....5 M 31
Winterbourne Dauntsey ....9 O 30
Winterbourne Monkton ....19 O 29
Winterbourne Stoke ....9 O 30
Winteringham ....44 S 22
Winterton ....44 S 23
Winterton-on-Sea ....39 Z 25
Winton ....49 N 20
Wintringham ....51 S 21
Winwick ....29 S 26
Wirksworth ....35 P 24
Wirral ....42 K 24
Wisbech ....37 U 25
Wisbech-St. Mary ....37 U 26
Wisborough Green ....11 S 30
Wishaw ....61 I 16
Wisley ....21 S 30
Wissey (River) ....38 V 26
Wistanstow ....26 L 26
Wistanswick ....34 M 25
Wistaston ....34 M 24
Wiston
   Dumfries and Galloway ....61 J 17
Wiston *Pembrokeshire /
   Sir Benfro* ....16 F 28
Wistow ....44 Q 22
Witchampton ....9 N 31
Witchford ....30 U 26
Witham ....22 V 28
Witham (River) ....37 T 24
Witham Friary ....9 M 30
Witheridge ....7 I 31
Withern ....45 U 24
Withernsea ....45 U 22
Withernwick ....45 T 22
Withington *Cotswold* ....19 O 28
Withington *Herefordshire* ...26 M 27
Withnell ....42 M 22
Withycombe ....4 J 32
Withypool ....7 J 30
Witley ....11 S 30
Witney ....20 P 28
Witsome ....63 N 16
Wittering ....37 S 26
Wittersham ....12 W 30
Witton le Wear ....56 O 19

Wiveliscombe ....7 K 30
Wivelsfield ....11 T 31
Wivenhoe ....30 W 28
Woburn ....29 S 28
Woburn Abbey ....29 S 28
Woburn Sands ....29 S 27
Woking ....21 S 30
Wokingham ....20 R 29
Wold Newton ....45 T 23
Woldingham ....21 T 30
Wollaston ....29 S 27
Wollaton Hall ....36 Q 25
Wolsingham ....56 O 19
Wolston ....28 P 26
Wolvercote ....20 Q 28
Wolverhampton ....35 N 26
Wolverton ....28 R 27
Wolvey ....28 P 26
Wolviston ....57 Q 20
Wombleton ....50 R 21
Wombourne ....27 N 26
Wombwell ....43 P 23
Womersley ....44 Q 22
Wonersh ....21 S 30
Wood Dalling ....39 X 25
Woodborough ....36 Q 24
Woodbridge ....31 X 27
Woodbury ....4 J 31
Woodchurch ....12 W 30
Woodcote ....20 Q 29
Woodford Halse ....28 Q 27
Woodhall Spa ....37 T 24
Woodham Ferrers ....22 V 29
Woodhouse ....43 P 23
Woodhouse Eaves ....36 Q 25
Woodingdean ....11 T 31
Woodland ....56 O 20
Woodlands ....9 O 31
Woodley ....20 R 29
Woodnesborough ....23 X 30
Woodseaves ....35 N 25
Woodsetts ....44 Q 23
Woodsford ....9 M 31
Woodstock ....20 P 28
Woodton ....39 Y 26
Woody Bay ....17 I 30
Wookey ....18 L 30
Wookey Hole ....18 L 30
Wool ....9 N 31
Woolacombe ....16 H 30
Wooler ....63 N 17
Woolfardisworthy ....6 G 31
Woolhampton ....20 Q 29
Woolpit ....30 W 27
Woolsthorpe ....36 R 25
Wooperton ....63 O 17
Woore ....35 M 25
Wootton *Bedford* ....29 S 27
Wootton *Northampton* ......28 R 27
Wootton Bassett ....19 O 29
Wootton Brige ....10 Q 31
Wootton Courtenay ....17 J 30
Wootton Rivers ....19 O 29

Wootton-Wawen ....27 O 27
Worcester ....27 N 27
Workington ....53 J 20
Worksop ....44 Q 24
Worle ....18 L 29
Wormbridge ....26 L 28
Wormingford ....30 W 28
Worminghall ....20 Q 28
Wormit ....69 L 14
Worms Head ....15 H 29
Wormsley ....26 L 27
Worplesdon ....21 S 30
Worsbrough ....43 P 23
Worsley ....42 M 23
Worsthorne ....43 N 22
Worth Matravers ....9 N 32
Worthen ....34 L 26
Worthenbury ....34 L 24
Worthing ....11 S 31
Wortley ....43 P 23
Worton ....19 N 30
Wortwell ....31 Y 26
Wotton-under-Edge ....19 M 29
Wrafton ....6 H 30
Wragby *East Lindsey* ....45 T 24
Wragby *Wakefield* ....43 P 23
Wrangle ....37 U 24
Wrawby ....44 S 23
Wray ....48 M 21
Wrea Green ....42 L 22
Wreay ....55 L 19
Wrecsam / Wrexham ....34 L 24
Wrekenton ....56 P 19
Wremtham ....31 Z 26
Wrenbury ....34 M 24
Wrestlingworth ....29 T 27
Wrexham / Wrecsam ....34 L 24
Wrington ....18 L 29
Writtle ....22 V 28
Wroot ....44 R 23
Wrotham ....22 U 30
Wroughton ....19 O 29
Wroxall ....10 Q 32
Wroxham ....39 Y 25
Wroxton ....28 P 27
Wyberton ....37 T 25
Wyche ....27 M 27
Wye ....22 W 30
Wye (River) ....26 M 28
Wykeham ....51 S 21
Wylam ....56 O 19
Wylye .... 9 O 30
Wymeswold ....36 Q 25
Wymondham *Leics.* ....36 R 25
Wymondham *Norfolk* ....39 X 26
Wyre ....87 L 6
Wysall ....36 Q 25
Wyvis Lodge ....79 G 10

Y

Y-Fenni / Abergavenny ....18 L 28
Y Ffor ....32 G 25
Y Llethr ....33 I 25

Y Rhiw ....32 G 25
Yafforth ....50 P 20
Yalding ....22 V 30
Yapton ....11 S 31
Yardley Gobion ....28 R 27
Yardley Hastings ....28 R 27
Yare (River) ....38 W 26
Yarm ....50 P 20
Yarmouth ....10 P 31
Yarnton ....20 Q 28
Yarrow ....62 K 17
Yate ....19 M 29
Yateley ....20 R 29
Yatton ....18 L 29
Yatton Keynell ....19 N 29
Yaxham ....38 W 26
Yaxley ....29 T 26
Yeadon ....43 O 22
Yealand Conyers ....48 L 21
Yealmpton ....4 I 32
Yedingham ....51 S 21
Yelden ....29 S 27
Yell ....87 Q 1
Yelvertoft ....28 Q 26
Yelverton ....4 H 32
Yeolmbridge ....6 G 32
Yeovil ....8 M 31
Yeovilton ....8 M 30
Yesnaby ....86 J 6
Yetminster ....8 M 31
Yetts o' Muckhart ....68 J 15
Yielden ....29 S 27
Ynys / Lochtyn ....15 G 27
Ynysddu ....18 K 29
Ynyslas ....25 H 26
Ynysybwl ....17 J 29
Yockenthwaite ....49 N 21
Yockleton ....34 L 25
York ....50 Q 22
Yorkletts ....23 X 30
Yorkley ....18 M 28
Yorkshire Dales
   National Park ....49 N 21
Yorkshire Wolds ....51 S 21
Youlgreave ....35 O 24
Yoxall ....35 O 25
Yoxford ....31 Y 27
Yr Wyddfa / Snowdon ....33 H 24
Yr Wyddgrug / Mold ....34 K 24
Ysbyty Ifan ....33 I 24
Ystalyfera ....17 I 28
Ystrad-Aeron ....25 H 27
Ystrad Mynach ....18 K 29
Ystradfellte ....17 I 28
Ystradgynlais ....17 I 28
Ystradowen ....17 J 29
Ystwyth (River) ....25 H 26

Z

Zennor ....2 D 33

A
B
C
D
E
F
G
H
I
J
K
L
M
N
O
P
Q
R
S
T
U
V
W
X
Y
Z

A

Aasleagh	105	D 7
Abbert	106	F 7
Abbey	100	G 8
Abbeydorney	93	C 10
Abbeyfeale	93	E 10
Abbeylara	107	J 6
Abbeyleix /		
Mainistir Laoise	101	J 9
Abbeyshrule	107	J 7
Abington	94	G 10
Achill	104	C 6
Achill Head	110	B 6
Achill Island	104	B 6
Achill Sound	104	C 6
Achillbeg Island	104	C 6
Achonry	112	G 5
Aclare	112	F 5
Acoose (Lough)	89	C 11
Adamstown	96	L 10
Adare	94	F 10
Adrigole	89	C 12
Aghaboe	101	J 9
Aghabullogue	90	F 12
Aghada	90	H 12
Aghadiffin	106	F 6
Aghadoe	89	D 11
Aghadoon	110	B 5
Aghadowey	118	M 2
Aghagallon	114	N 4
Aghagower	105	D 6
Aghalane	113	J 5
Aghalee	114	N 4
Aghamore Leitrim	107	I 6
Aghamore Mayo	105	F 6
Aghamuck	106	H 6
Aghavannagh	103	M 9
Aghavas	107	I 6
Aghaville	89	D 13
Aghinlig	114	M 4
Aghla Mountain	116	H 3
Aghleam	110	B 5
Aghnablaney	113	I 4
Aghnacliff	107	J 6
Aghnamullen	108	L 5
Aghowle	96	M 9
Agivey	118	M 2
Aglish Tipperary	100	H 8
Aglish Waterford	91	I 11
Agnew's Hill	115	O 3
Ahakista	89	D 13
Ahalia (Loughs)	105	D 7
Ahascragh	106	G 7
Ahenny	95	J 10
Aherla	90	F 12
Aherlow	94	H 10
Aherlow (Glen of)	95	H 10
Ahoghill	118	M 3
Aillwee Cave	99	E 8
Ailt an Chorráin /		
Burtonport	116	G 3
Aird Mhór / Ardmore	91	I 12
Akeragh Lough	93	C 10
Aldergrove	115	N 4
Allaghaun	93	E 10
Allen	102	L 8
Allen (Bog of)	102	K 8
Allen (Lough)	112	H 5
Allenwood	102	L 8
Allihies	88	B 13
Allistragh	114	L 4
Alloon Lower	106	G 7
Allow	94	F 11
Allua (Lough)	89	E 12
Altagowlan	112	H 5
Altan Lough	117	H 2
Altnamackan	114	M 5
Altnapaste	117	I 3
An Blascaod Mór /		
Blasket Islands	92	A 11
An Bun Beag / Bunbeg	116	H 2
An Caisleán Nua /		
Newcastle West	93	E 10
An Caisleán Riabhach /		
Castlerea	106	G 6
An Chathair / Caher	95	I 10
An Cheathrú Rua /		
Carraroe	98	D 8
An Chloich Mhóir /		
Cloghmore	104	C 6
An Clochán / Clifden	104	B 7
An Clochán / Cloghan		
Donegal	117	I 3
An Clochán Liath /		
Dungloe	116	G 3
An Cloigeann / Cleegan	104	B 7

An Cóbh / Cobh	90	H 12
An Coimín / Commeen	117	I 3
An Coireán / Waterville	88	B 12
An Corrán / Currane	104	C 6
An Creagán /		
Mount Bellew	106	G 7
An Daingean / Dingle	92	B 11
An Dúchoraidh /		
Doocharry	116	H 3
An Fál Carrach /		
Falcarragh	117	H 2
An Fhairche / Clonbur	105	D 7
An Geata Mór	110	B 5
An Gleann Garbh /		
Glengarriff	89	D 12
An Gort / Gort	99	F 8
An Gort Mór / Gortmore	105	D 7
An Leacht / Lahinch	98	D 9
An Longfort / Longford	107	I 6
An Mám / Maam Cross	105	D 7
An Mhala Raithní /		
Mulrany	104	C 6
An Móta / Moate	101	I 7
An Muileann gCearr /		
Mullingar	107	J 7
An Nás / Naas	102	M 8
An Ráth / Charleville	94	F 10
An Ros / Rush	109	N 7
An Sciobairín / Skibbereen	89	E 13
An Seanchaisleán /		
Oldcastle	108	K 6
An Spidéal / Spiddal	99	E 8
An tAonach / Nenagh	100	H 9
An Teampall Mór /		
Templemore	101	I 9
An Tearmann / Termon	117	I 2
An tInbhear Mór / Arklow	97	N 9
An Tulach / Tullow	102	L 9
An Uaimh / Navan	108	L 7
Anascaul	92	B 11
Anayalla	114	L 5
Anglesborough	94	H 10
Anglesey Bridge	95	H 9
Annacarriga	99	G 9
Annacarty	95	H 10
Annaclone	115	N 5
Annacloy	115	O 4
Annacotty	94	G 9
Annadorn	115	O 5
Annagary	116	H 2
Annagassan	109	M 6
Annageeragh (River)	98	D 9
Annagh Head	110	B 5
Annagh Island	110	C 6
Annaghdown	105	E 7
Annaghmore Lough	106	H 6
Annahilt	115	N 4
Annalee	107	J 5
Annalong	109	O 5
Annamoe	103	N 8
Annes Grove Gardens	94	G 11
Annestown	91	K 11
Annfield	95	I 9
Annie Brady Bridge	111	C 5
Annsborough	115	O 5
Antrim	115	N 3
Antrim (Glens of)	119	N 2
Antrim Coast	119	O 2
Antrim Mountains	119	N 2
Anure (Lough)	116	H 3
Araglin	95	H 11
Árainn Mhór /		
Aran or Aranmore Island	116	G 2
Aran Islands /		
Oileáin Árainn	98	C 8
Archdale (Castle)	113	I 4
Archerstown	108	K 7
Ard	104	C 8
Ardagh Donegal	117	J 3
Ardagh Limerick	93	E 10
Ardan	101	I 9
Ardanairy	103	N 9
Ardanew	108	L 7
Ardara	116	G 3
Ardattin	96	L 9
Ardboe	114	M 4
Ardcath	109	M 7
Ardcloon	105	F 7
Ardcrony	100	H 9
Ardea	89	C 12
Arderin	101	J 8
Ardfert	93	C 11
Ardfinnan	89	F 13
Ardgehane	90	F 13
Ardglass	115	P 5
Ardglass	90	H 11

Ardgroom	88	C 12
Ardgroom Harbour	88	C 12
Ardkeen	115	P 4
Ardlea	101	J 9
Ardlougher	107	J 5
Ardmillan	115	O 4
Ardmoney	113	J 5
Ardmore Derry	117	K 3
Ardmore Galway	104	C 8
Ardmore Point Antrim	114	N 4
Ardmore Point Craigavon	114	M 4
Ardmore Point		
Dunganstown East	103	N 9
Ardmorney	101	J 7
Ardmoy	106	G 6
Ardnagreevagh	104	B 7
Ardnasodan	105	F 7
Ardpatrick	94	G 10
Ardrahan	99	F 8
Ardreagh	118	M 2
Ardress House	114	M 4
Ards Forest Park	117	I 2
Ards Peninsula	115	P 4
Ardscull	102	L 8
Ardshankill	113	I 4
Ardstraw	113	J 3
Argideen	89	F 13
Argory (The)	114	M 4
Arigna	112	H 5
Arinagh	112	F 5
Arless	102	K 9
Armagh	114	M 4
Armaghbrague	114	M 5
Armoy	118	N 2
Arney	113	I 5
Arra Mountains	100	G 9
Arrow (Lough)	106	H 5
Arryheernabin	117	J 2
Artane	103	N 7
Arthurstown	96	L 11
Articlave	118	L 2
Artigarvan	117	J 3
Arvagh	107	J 6
Asdee	93	D 10
Ashbourne	109	M 7
Ashford Glenealy	103	N 8
Ashford Limerick	93	E 10
Ashford Castle	105	E 7
Ashleam Bay	104	B 6
Ashton	90	F 12
Askamore	97	M 9
Askanagap	103	M 9
Askeaton	94	F 10
Askill	112	H 4
Áth Cinn / Headford	105	E 7
Athassel Abbey	95	I 10
Athboy	108	L 7
Athea	93	E 10
Athgarvan	102	L 8
Athlacca	94	G 10
Athleague	106	H 7
Athnid	95	I 9
Athy / Baile Átha Í	102	L 9
Atlantic Drive (The)	104	C 6
Atorick (Lough)	99	G 8
Attanagh	101	J 9
Attavally	111	C 5
Attical	109	N 5
Attymass	111	E 5
Attymon	99	G 8
Aucloggen	105	F 7
Audley's Castle	115	P 4
Aughacasla	92	C 11
Aughagault	117	I 3
Aughamullan	114	M 4
Augher	114	K 4
Aughils	92	C 11
Aughinish	99	E 8
Aughinish Island	93	E 10
Aughkeely	117	I 3
Aughnacleagh	118	M 3
Aughnacloy	114	L 4
Aughnanure Castle	105	E 7
Aughnasheelan	107	I 5
Aughrim Galway	100	H 8
Aughrim Wicklow	103	N 9
Aughris	112	F 5
Aughris Head	112	F 5
Aughrus More	104	B 7
Avoca	103	N 9
Avoca (River)	103	N 9
Avoca (Vale of)	103	N 9
Avonbeg	103	M 9
Avondale Forest Park	103	N 9
Avonmore (River)	103	N 9
Awbeg	94	G 11

B

Baginbun Head	96	L 11
Baile an Fheirtéaraigh /		
Ballyferriter	92	A 11
Baile an Mhóta /		
Ballymote	112	G 5
Baile an Róba /		
Ballinrobe	105	E 7
Baile an Sceilg /		
Ballinskelligs	88	B 12
Baile Átha an Rí / Athenry	99	F 8
Baile Átha Cliath / Dublin	103	N 8
Baile Átha Fhirdhia / Ardee	108	M 6
Baile Átha Luain / Athlone	107	I 7
Baile Átha Troim / Trim	108	L 7
Baile Brigín / Balbriggan	109	N 7
Baile Chláir / Claregalway	99	F 7
Baile Locha Riach /		
Loughrea	99	G 8
Baile Mhic Andáin /		
Thomastown	96	K 10
Baile Mhistéala /		
Mitchelstown	94	H 11
Baile na Finne / Fintown	117	H 3
Baile na Lorgan /		
Castleblayney	108	L 5
Baile Uí Fhiacháin /		
Newport	105	D 6
Baile Uí Mhatháin /		
Ballymahon	107	I 7
Baileysmill	115	O 4
Baldoyle	103	N 7
Balla	105	E 6
Ballaba	99	F 8
Ballagan Point	109	N 5
Ballagh Fermanagh	113	J 5
Ballagh Galway	106	F 7
Ballagh Limerick	93	E 10
Ballagh near Curraghroe	107	H 6
Ballagh near Nahara	106	H 7
Ballagh Tipperary	95	I 10
Ballagh (Neck of the)	112	G 3
Ballaghaderreen /		
Bealach an Doirín	106	G 6
Ballaghbeama Gap	89	C 12
Ballaghbehy	93	E 10
Ballaghisheen Pass	88	C 12
Ballaghkeen	97	M 10
Ballaghmore	101	I 9
Ballaghnatrillick	112	G 4
Ballard	97	M 9
Ballardiggan	99	F 8
Balleen	101	J 9
Ballickmoyler	102	K 9
Balliggan	115	P 4
Ballina	99	G 9
Ballina / Béal an Átha	111	E 5
Ballinaboy	104	B 7
Ballinabrackey	102	K 7
Ballinaclash	103	N 9
Ballinacor	103	N 9
Ballinadee	90	G 12
Ballinafad Aghanagh	106	G 5
Ballinafad Galway	104	C 7
Ballinagleragh	113	H 5
Ballinakill	101	K 9
Ballinalack	107	J 7
Ballinalea	103	N 8
Ballinalee	107	J 6
Ballinamallard	113	J 4
Ballinamara	95	J 9
Ballinameen	106	H 6
Ballinamore Bridge	106	G 7
Ballinamuck	107	I 6
Ballinascarty	90	F 12
Ballinaspick	91	I 11
Ballinclashet	90	G 12
Ballinclea	103	M 9
Ballincloher	93	C 10
Ballincollig	90	G 12
Ballincrea	96	K 11
Ballincurrig	90	H 12
Ballindaggan	96	L 10
Ballinderreen	99	F 8
Ballinderry Cookstown	114	M 4
Ballinderry Terryglass	100	H 8
Ballinderry Wicklow	103	N 9
Ballinderry Bridge	114	M 4
Ballindine	105	F 6
Ballindrait	117	J 3
Ballineanig	92	A 11
Ballineen	89	F 12
Ballingarrane	94	F 10

Ballingarry Galway	100	H 8
Ballingarry Limerick	94	F 10
Ballingarry Tipperary	95	J 10
Ballingeary / Béal Átha		
an Ghaorthaidh	89	E 12
Ballingurteen	89	E 12
Ballinhassig	90	G 12
Ballinkillin	96	L 10
Ballinlea	118	M 2
Ballinleeny	94	F 10
Ballinloghig	92	B 11
Ballinlough Meath	108	K 6
Ballinlough Roscommon	106	G 6
Ballinluska	90	H 12
Ballinruan	99	F 9
Ballinskelligs Bay	88	B 12
Ballinspittle	90	G 12
Ballintober	106	G 6
Ballintogher	112	G 5
Ballintotty	100	H 9
Ballintra Donegal	112	H 4
Ballintra near Leabgarrow	116	G 3
Ballintubber	105	E 6
Ballinunty	95	I 10
Ballinure	95	I 10
Ballinure (River)	100	H 8
Ballinvarry	96	L 10
Ballitore	102	L 8
Ballivor	108	L 7
Ballon	96	L 9
Balloo Cross Roads	115	O 4
Balloor	112	G 4
Balloughter	97	M 10
Ballure	112	H 4
Ballyagran	94	F 10
Ballyallinan	94	F 10
Ballyalton	115	P 5
Ballyard	113	J 4
Ballybannon	102	L 9
Ballybay		
near Carrickmacross	108	L 5
Ballybay		
near Castleblayney	108	L 5
Ballybeg	95	I 11
Ballyboghil	109	N 7
Ballybofey	118	M 2
Ballyboy	101	I 8
Ballybrack Dublin	103	N 8
Ballybrack Kerry	88	B 12
Ballybrittas	101	K 8
Ballybrommel	96	L 9
Ballybrood	94	G 10
Ballybrophy	101	J 9
Ballybryan	101	K 7
Ballybunnion	93	D 10
Ballycahill	95	I 9
Ballycallan	95	J 10
Ballycanew	97	M 10
Ballycarney	97	M 10
Ballycarry	115	O 3
Ballycastle Mayo	111	D 5
Ballycastle Moyle	119	N 2
Ballycastle Bay	119	N 2
Ballyclare Newtonabbey	115	N 3
Ballyclare Roscommon	107	I 6
Ballyclerahan	95	I 10
Ballyclery	99	F 8
Ballyclogh	94	F 11
Ballycolla	101	J 9
Ballycommon	100	H 9
Ballyconneely	104	B 7
Ballyconneely Bay	104	B 7
Ballyconnell Cavan	113	J 5
Ballyconnell Sligo	112	G 4
Ballycorick	99	E 9
Ballycotton	91	I 12
Ballycotton Bay	91	H 12
Ballycrossaun	100	H 8
Ballycrovane Harbour	88	C 12
Ballycuirke Lough	99	E 8
Ballycullane	96	L 11
Ballycullen	103	N 8
Ballycumber	101	I 8
Ballydangan	100	H 7
Ballydavid Galway	100	G 8
Ballydavid Kilmalkedar	92	A 11
Ballydavid Head	92	A 11
Ballydavis	101	K 8
Ballydehob	89	D 13
Ballydesmond	93	E 11
Ballydonegan	88	B 13
Ballydonegan Bay	88	B 13
Ballyduff Dingle	92	B 11

Ballyduff Kerry	93	D 10
Ballyduff Waterford	91	H 11
Ballyduff Wexford	97	M 10
Ballyeaston	115	O 3
Ballyeighter Loughs	99	F 9
Ballyfad	97	N 9
Ballyfair	102	L 8
Ballyfarnagh	105	F 6
Ballyfarnan	106	H 5
Ballyfasy	96	K 10
Ballyfeard	90	G 12
Ballyferis Point	115	P 4
Ballyfin	101	J 8
Ballyfinboy	100	H 8
Ballyforan	106	H 7
Ballyfore	102	K 8
Ballyfoyle	96	K 9
Ballygalley	119	O 3
Ballygalley Head	119	O 3
Ballygar	106	H 7
Ballygarrett	97	N 10
Ballygarries	105	E 6
Ballygarvan	90	G 12
Ballygawley Dungannon	114	K 4
Ballygawley Sligo	112	G 5
Ballyglass		
near Cornanagh	105	E 6
Ballyglass near		
Kilmovee	106	G 6
Ballygorman	117	K 1
Ballygowan Ards	115	O 4
Ballygowan		
Newry-Mourne	109	N 5
Ballygriffin	95	I 10
Ballyhack	96	L 11
Ballyhacket	102	L 9
Ballyhaght	94	G 10
Ballyhahill	93	E 10
Ballyhaise	107	K 5
Ballyhalbert	115	P 4
Ballyhale Galway	105	E 7
Ballyhale Kilkenny	96	K 10
Ballyhar	93	D 11
Ballyhaunis /		
Béal Átha hAmhnais	106	F 6
Ballyhean	105	E 6
Ballyhear	105	E 7
Ballyheelan	107	J 6
Ballyheerin	117	I 2
Ballyheige	93	C 10
Ballyheige Bay	93	C 10
Ballyhillin	117	J 1
Ballyhoe Bridge	118	N 2
Ballyhoe Lough	108	L 6
Ballyhoge	96	M 10
Ballyhooly	94	G 11
Ballyhornan	115	P 5
Ballyhoura Mountains	94	G 11
Ballyhuppahane	101	J 8
Ballyjamesduff	107	K 6
Ballykean	101	K 8
Ballykeefe	95	J 10
Ballykeel	115	N 4
Ballykeeran	107	I 7
Ballykelly	118	K 2
Ballykilleen	102	K 8
Ballykinler	115	O 5
Ballyknockan	103	M 8
Ballylacy	97	N 9
Ballylaghnan	99	G 9
Ballylanders	94	G 10
Ballylaneen	91	J 11
Ballylesson	115	O 4
Ballylickey	89	D 12
Ballyliffin	117	J 2
Ballyline	95	J 10
Ballylintagh	118	L 2
Ballylongford	93	D 10
Ballylongford Bay	93	D 10
Ballyloughbeg	118	M 2
Ballylynan	102	K 9
Ballymacarbry	95	I 11
Ballymacaw	96	K 11
Ballymachugh	107	K 6
Ballymack	96	K 10
Ballymackey	100	H 9
Ballymackilroy	114	K 4
Ballymacoda	91	I 12
Ballymacrevan	115	O 4
Ballymacurly	106	H 6
Ballymacward	106	G 7
Ballymadog	91	I 12
Ballymagan	117	J 2
Ballymagaraghy	118	K 2
Ballymagorry	117	J 3
Ballymakeagh	91	I 12

Ballymakeery / Baile Mhic Íre ...89 E 12
Ballymakenny ...109 M 6
Ballymartin ...109 O 5
Ballymartle ...90 G 12
Ballymena ...119 N 3
Ballymoe ...106 G 6
Ballymoney Ballymoney ...118 M 2
Ballymoney Limavady ...118 K 3
Ballymore Donegal ...117 I 2
Ballymore Westmeath ...107 I 7
Ballymore Eustace ...103 M 8
Ballymore Lough ...111 E 5
Ballymurphy ...96 L 10
Ballymurragh ...93 E 10
Ballymurray ...106 H 7
Ballynabola ...96 L 10
Ballynacallagh ...88 B 13
Ballynacally ...99 E 9
Ballynacarrick ...116 H 3
Ballynacarriga ...89 E 12
Ballynacarrigy ...107 J 7
Ballynacarrow ...112 G 5
Ballynaclogh ...100 H 9
Ballynacorra ...90 H 12
Ballynacourty ...91 J 11
Ballynadrumny ...102 L 7
Ballynafid ...107 J 7
Ballynagaul ...91 J 11
Ballynagoraher ...105 D 6
Ballynagore ...101 J 7
Ballynagree ...90 F 12
Ballynaguilkee ...95 I 11
Ballynahinch ...115 O 4
Ballynahinch Lake ...104 C 7
Ballynahow ...88 A 12
Ballynahown Kilcummin ...98 D 8
Ballynahown Westmeath ...101 I 7
Ballynakill Carlow ...96 L 9
Ballynakill Offaly ...101 K 8
Ballynakill Westmeath ...107 I 7
Ballynakill Harbour ...104 B 7
Ballynakilla ...88 C 13
Ballynakilly Upper ...88 C 11
Ballynamallaght ...117 K 3
Ballynamona ...90 G 11
Ballynamult ...95 I 11
Ballynana ...92 A 11
Ballynare ...103 M 7
Ballynashannagh ...117 J 2
Ballynaskeagh ...114 N 5
Ballynaskreena ...93 C 10
Ballynastangford ...105 E 6
Ballynastraw ...97 M 10
Ballynchatty ...113 K 4
Ballyneaner ...118 K 3
Ballyneety ...94 G 10
Ballyneill ...95 J 10
Ballynoe Cork ...90 H 11
Ballynoe Down ...115 O 5
Ballynure ...115 O 3
Ballyorgan ...94 G 11
Ballypatrick ...95 J 10
Ballypatrick Forest ...119 N 2
Ballyporeen ...95 H 11
Ballyquin ...92 B 11
Ballyquintin Point ...115 P 5
Ballyragget ...101 J 9
Ballyrashane ...118 M 2
Ballyreagh Dungannon ...114 L 4
Ballyreagh Fermanagh ...113 J 4
Ballyroan ...101 K 9
Ballyroddy ...106 H 6
Ballyroebuck ...97 M 10
Ballyronan ...114 M 3
Ballyroney ...115 N 5
Ballyroon ...88 C 13
Ballysadare ...112 G 5
Ballysadare Bay ...112 G 5
Ballyshannon Donegal ...112 H 4
Ballyshannon Kildare ...102 L 8
Ballysloe ...95 J 10
Ballysteen ...94 F 10
Ballyteige Bay ...96 L 11
Ballytoohy ...104 C 6
Ballyvaughan ...99 E 8
Ballyvaughan Bay ...99 E 8
Ballyvester ...115 P 4
Ballyvoge / Baile Uí Bhuaigh ...89 E 12
Ballyvoneen ...106 G 7
Ballyvourney / Baile Bhuirne ...89 E 12
Ballyvoy ...119 N 2
Ballyvoyle Head ...91 J 11
Ballywalter ...115 P 4
Ballyward ...115 N 5

Ballywilliam ...96 L 10
Balnamore ...118 M 2
Balrath ...108 M 7
Balrothery ...109 N 7
Balscaddan ...109 N 7
Baltimore ...89 D 13
Baltray ...109 N 6
Banada ...106 F 5
Banagher ...101 I 8
Banagher Forest ...118 L 3
Banbridge ...114 N 4
Bandon River ...89 F 12
Bangor Mayo ...111 C 5
Bangor North-Down ...115 O 4
Bangor Trail ...111 C 5
Bann (River) / Lough Neagh ...115 N 5
Bann (River) River Slaney ...97 M 10
Banna ...93 C 10
Banna Strand ...93 C 11
Bannow ...96 L 11
Bannow Bay ...96 L 11
Bansha ...95 H 10
Banteer ...94 F 11
Bantry / Beanntrai ...89 D 12
Bantry Bay ...89 C 13
Barefield ...99 F 9
Barley Cove ...88 C 13
Barna Limerick ...94 H 10
Barna Offaly ...101 I 9
Barnacahoge ...105 F 6
Barnaderg ...106 F 7
Barnesmore ...113 H 3
Barnesmore Gap ...113 I 3
Barmeen ...115 N 5
Barnycarroll ...105 F 6
Baronscourt Forest ...113 J 3
Barr na Trá / Barnatra ...110 C 5
Barra (Lough) ...117 H 3
Barrack Village ...101 K 9
Barraduff ...89 D 11
Barrigone ...93 E 10
Barringtonsbridge ...94 G 10
Barrow (River) ...102 K 8
Barrow Harbour ...93 C 11
Barry ...107 I 7
Barry's Point ...90 F 13
Batterstown ...108 M 7
Baunskeha ...96 K 10
Bauntlieve ...99 E 9
Baurtregaum ...93 C 11
Bawn Cross Roads ...94 F 11
Bawnboy ...113 I 5
Beagh Galway ...105 F 7
Beagh Roscommon ...112 H 5
Beagh (Lough) ...117 I 2
Beagh (Slieve) ...113 K 4
Beal ...93 D 10
Béal an Átha / Ballina ...111 E 5
Béal an Átha Mhóir / Ballinamore ...107 I 5
Béal an Mhuirthead / Belmullet ...110 C 5
Béal Átha an Ghaorthaidh / Ballingeary ...89 E 12
Béal Átha na Muice / Swinford ...106 F 6
Béal Átha na Sluaighe / Ballinasloe ...100 H 8
Béal Átha Seanaidh / Ballyshannon ...112 H 4
Béal Deirg / Belderrig ...111 D 5
Beal Point ...93 D 10
Béal Tairbirt / Belturbet ...107 J 5
Bealach Conglais / Baltinglass ...102 L 9
Bealach Féich / Ballybofey ...117 I 3
Bealaclugga / New Quay ...99 E 8
Bealad Cross Roads ...89 F 13
Bealadangan ...105 D 8
Bealaha ...98 D 9
Bealalaw Bridge ...88 C 12
Bealanabrack ...104 C 7
Bealin ...107 I 7
Bealnablath ...90 F 12
Beara ...89 C 12
Bearna / Barna ...99 E 8
Beaufort ...89 D 11
Bective ...108 L 7
Beehive Huts ...92 A 11
Beenmore ...88 B 11
Beennaskehy ...90 G 11
Beenoskee ...92 B 11
Beg (Lough) Antrim ...114 N 4
Beg (Lough) River Bann ...114 M 3
Beginish Island ...88 B 12

Behy ...88 C 11
Bekan ...105 F 6
Belcarra ...105 E 6
Belclare ...105 F 7
Belcoo ...113 I 5
Belderg Harbour ...111 D 5
Belfarsad ...104 C 6
Belfast ...115 O 4
Belfast Lough ...115 O 3
Belgooly ...90 G 12
Belhavel Lough ...112 H 5
Bellacorick ...111 D 5
Belladrihid ...112 G 5
Bellagarvaun ...110 C 6
Bellaghy ...114 M 3
Bellahy ...106 F 6
Bellameeny ...106 H 7
Bellamont Forest ...108 K 5
Bellanaboy Bridge ...111 C 5
Bellanacargy ...107 K 5
Bellanagare ...106 G 6
Bellanagraugh Bridge ...112 F 5
Bellanaleck ...113 J 5
Bellanamore ...117 H 3
Bellanamullia ...107 H 7
Bellananagh ...107 J 6
Bellanode ...114 K 5
Bellarena ...118 L 2
Bellavary ...105 E 6
Belleek ...114 M 5
Belleek ...113 H 4
Bellewstown ...109 M 7
Belmont ...101 I 8
Belmore Mountain ...113 I 5
Beltra Croaghmoyle ...105 D 6
Beltra Sligo ...112 G 5
Beltra Lough ...105 D 6
Belvelly ...90 H 12
Belview Port ...96 K 11
Belville ...111 D 5
Ben Gorm ...104 C 7
Benbane Head ...118 M 2
Benbaun ...104 C 7
Benbo ...112 H 5
Benbrack ...113 I 5
Benbreen ...104 C 7
Benbulben ...112 G 4
Benburb ...114 L 4
Bere Haven ...88 C 13
Bere Island ...88 C 13
Bernish Rock ...114 M 5
Berrings ...90 F 12
Bertraghboy Bay ...104 C 7
Bessbrook ...114 M 5
Bettystown ...109 N 6
Big Dog Forest ...113 I 4
Big Island ...100 H 8
Big Trosk ...119 N 2
Bilboa ...102 K 9
Bilboa (River) ...95 H 10
Billis Bridge ...108 K 6
Bills Rocks ...104 B 6
Binevenagh ...118 L 2
Binn Éadair / Howth ...103 N 7
Biorra / Birr ...101 I 8
Birdhill ...99 G 9
Birreencorragh ...105 D 6
Bishops Court ...115 P 5
Black Galway ...105 E 7
Black (River) Longford ...107 I 6
Black Ball Head ...88 B 13
Black Bull ...103 M 7
Black Gap (The) ...113 I 4
Black Head Clare ...99 E 8
Black Head Larne ...115 O 3
Black Lion ...101 J 8
Black Rock ...110 B 5
Blacklion ...113 I 5
Blackpool ...94 G 10
Blackrock Cork ...90 G 12
Blackrock Louth ...109 M 6
Blackrock Rathdown ...103 N 8
Blackskull ...114 N 4
Blacksod Bay ...110 B 5
Blacksod Point ...110 B 5
Blackstairs Mountains ...96 L 10
Blackwater ...97 M 10
Blackwater (River) Cork ...89 F 11

Blackwater (River) / Lough Neagh ...114 L 4
Blackwater (River) / River Boyne ...108 L 6
Blackwater Bridge Innfield ...102 L 7
Blackwater Bridge Tahilla ...88 C 12
Blackwater Harbour ...97 N 10
Blackwatertown ...114 L 4
Blanchardstown ...103 M 7
Blane Bridge ...93 E 10
Blaney ...113 I 4
Blarney ...90 G 12
Blasket Sound ...92 A 11
Bleach ...99 G 8
Bleach Lake ...94 F 10
Blennerville ...93 C 11
Blessington ...103 M 8
Bloody Foreland ...116 H 2
Blue Ball ...101 J 8
Blue Stack Mountains ...113 H 3
Blueford ...93 E 11
Boa Island ...113 I 4
Boardmills ...115 O 4
Boderg (Lough) ...107 I 6
Bodyke ...99 G 9
Bofeenaun ...105 E 6
Bofin (Lough) Galway ...105 D 7
Bofin (Lough) Roscommon ...107 I 6
Bogay ...117 J 2
Boggan Meath ...108 L 6
Boggan Tipperary ...95 J 9
Boggaun ...101 I 9
Boggeragh Mountains ...89 F 11
Bohateh ...99 G 9
Bohaun ...105 D 6
Boheeshil ...88 C 12
Boher ...94 G 10
Boheraphuca ...101 I 8
Boherbue ...93 E 11
Bohereen ...94 G 10
Boherlahan ...95 I 10
Bohermeen ...108 L 7
Boherquill ...107 J 6
Boho ...113 I 4
Bola ...105 E 6
Bola (Lough) ...104 C 7
Bolea ...118 L 2
Boleran ...118 L 2
Boley ...102 L 8
Bolinglanna ...104 C 6
Boliska Lough ...99 E 8
Bolton's Cross Roads ...93 D 10
Bolus Head ...88 A 12
Bonet ...112 H 5
Boola ...91 I 11
Boolakennedy ...95 H 10
Boolattin ...95 J 11
Boolyduff ...99 E 9
Boolyglass ...96 K 10
Borris ...96 L 10
Borris in Ossory ...101 J 9
Borrisoleigh ...100 I 9
Boston ...99 F 8
Bottlehill ...90 G 11
Bouladuff ...95 I 9
Boviel ...118 L 3
Bow ...99 G 9
Boyerstown ...108 L 7
Boyle (River) ...106 H 6
Boyne (River) ...102 K 7
Brackagh ...101 K 8
Brackley Lough ...113 I 5
Bracklin ...108 K 7
Brackloon Mayo ...106 F 6
Brackloon Roscommon ...106 G 6
Bracknagh Offaly ...102 K 8
Bracknagh Roscommon ...107 H 7
Brackwanshagh ...111 E 5
Brandon Bay ...92 B 11
Brandon Head ...92 B 11
Brandon Hill ...96 L 10
Brannock Islands ...98 C 8
Brannockstown ...102 L 8
Bray Head Kerry ...88 A 12
Bray Head Wicklow ...103 N 8
Bré / Bray ...103 N 8
Breaghva ...98 C 10
Breaghwy ...105 E 6
Bree ...96 M 10
Breenagh ...117 I 3
Brickeens ...105 F 6
Bricklieve Mountains ...106 G 5
Bride Cork ...89 F 12

Bride River Blackwater ...91 I 11
Bridebridge ...90 H 11
Brideswell Ballyellis ...97 M 9
Brideswell Ballynamona ...106 H 7
Bridge End ...117 J 2
Bridgeland ...103 M 9
Bridget Lough ...99 G 9
Bridgetown Cannock Chase ...96 M 11
Bridgetown Clare ...99 G 9
Bridgetown Donegal ...112 H 4
Briensbridge ...99 G 9
Brittas Limerick ...94 G 10
Brittas Saggart ...103 M 8
Brittas Bay ...103 N 9
Britway ...90 H 11
Broad Haven ...110 C 5
Broad Meadow ...109 N 7
Broadford Clare ...99 G 9
Broadford Limerick ...94 F 10
Broadway ...97 M 11
Brookeborough ...113 J 5
Broomfield ...108 L 5
Brosna ...93 E 11
Brosna (River) ...101 I 8
Broughal ...101 I 8
Broughane Cross Roads ...93 D 11
Brougher Mount ...113 J 4
Broughshane ...119 N 3
Brow Head ...88 C 13
Brown Flesk ...93 D 11
Brownstown ...96 K 11
Brownstown Head ...96 K 11
Bruckless ...112 G 4
Bruff ...94 G 10
Bruree ...94 G 10
Bryansford ...115 O 5
Buckna ...119 N 3
Buckode ...112 H 4
Buiríos Uí Chéin / Borrisokane ...100 H 9
Bulgaden ...94 G 10
Bull (The) ...88 B 13
Bull Point ...119 N 2
Bullaba ...117 I 3
Bullaun ...99 G 8
Bull's Head ...92 B 11
Bun Cranncha / Buncrana ...117 J 2
Bun Dobhráin / Bundoran ...112 H 4
Bun na hAbhna / Bunnahowen ...110 C 5
Bun na Leaca / Brinlack ...116 H 2
Bunaclugga Bay ...93 D 10
Bunacurry ...110 C 6
Bunatrahir Bay ...111 D 5
Bunaveela Lough ...111 D 5
Bunaw ...88 C 12
Bunbrosna ...107 J 7
Bunclody ...96 M 10
Bunlahy ...107 J 6
Bunmahon ...91 J 11
Bunnafollistran ...105 E 7
Bunnaglass ...99 F 8
Bunnahown ...104 C 7
Bunnanaddan ...112 G 5
Bunny (Lough) ...99 F 8
Bunnyconnellan ...111 E 5
Bunowen ...105 D 6
Bunratty ...99 F 9
Burncourt ...95 H 11
Burnchurch ...96 K 10
Burnfoot Birdstown ...117 J 2
Burnfoot Limavady ...118 L 3
Burnfort ...90 G 11
Burr Point ...115 P 4
Burren Clare ...99 E 8
Burren Cork ...90 F 12
Burren Mayo ...105 E 6
Burren (The) ...99 E 8
Burren Centre Kifenora ...99 E 9
Burrenfadda ...99 E 9
Burrishoole Abbey ...105 D 6
Burrow ...97 M 11
Burtown ...102 L 9
Bush ...118 M 2
Bush (The) Dungannon ...114 L 4
Bush (The) Rathcor ...109 N 6
Bushfield ...100 G 9
Bushmills ...118 M 2
Butler's Bridge ...107 J 5
Butlerstown ...90 F 13
Buttevant ...94 F 11
Butts (The) ...101 K 9
Bweeng ...90 G 11

C

Cabragh ...114 L 4

Cadamstown Kildare ...102 L 7
Cadamstown Offaly ...101 J 8
Caddy ...114 N 3
Caggan ...105 D 7
Caha Mountains ...89 C 12
Caha pass ...89 D 12
Caher Clare ...99 G 9
Caher Mayo ...105 E 7
Caher Island ...104 B 6
Caher Roe's Den ...96 L 10
Caheradrine ...99 F 8
Caheragh ...89 E 13
Caherbarnagh Corcaigh / Cork ...89 E 11
Caherbarnagh Kerry ...88 B 12
Caherconlish ...94 G 10
Caherconnel ...99 E 8
Caherconree ...92 C 11
Caherdaniel ...88 B 12
Caherea ...99 E 9
Caherlistrane ...105 E 7
Cahermore Cork ...88 B 13
Cahermore Galway ...99 F 8
Cahermurphy ...98 D 9
Cahernahallia ...95 H 10
Cahore Point ...97 N 10
Caiseal / Cashel ...95 I 10
Caisleán an Bharraigh / Castlebar ...105 E 6
Caisleán an Chomair / Castlecomer ...101 K 9
Calafort Ros Láir / Rosslare Harbour ...97 M 11
Caledon ...114 L 4
Calf Islands ...89 D 13
Callaghansmills ...99 F 9
Callainn / Callan ...95 J 10
Callow Galway ...104 B 7
Callow Mayo ...105 E 6
Callow Roscommon ...106 G 6
Caltra ...106 G 7
Caltraghlea ...100 H 7
Calverstown ...102 L 8
Cam Forest ...118 L 2
Camlin (River) ...107 I 6
Camlough ...114 M 5
Camoge ...94 G 10
Camolin ...97 M 10
Camowen ...113 K 4
Camp ...92 C 11
Campile ...96 L 11
Campsey ...118 K 2
Camross ...101 J 8
Camus Bay ...105 D 8
Canglass Point ...88 B 12
Canningstown ...108 K 6
Canon Island ...99 E 9
Cappagh Dungannon ...114 L 4
Cappagh Limerick ...94 F 10
Cappagh River ...100 G 8
Cappagh White ...95 H 10
Cappaghmore ...99 F 8
Cappalinnan ...101 J 9
Cappamore ...94 G 10
Cappanacreha ...105 D 7
Cappanrush ...101 J 7
Cappataggle ...100 G 8
Cappeen ...89 F 12
Car (Slieve) ...111 D 5
Caragh (Lough) ...88 C 11
Caragh (River) ...89 C 12
Caragh Bridge ...92 C 11
Caragh Lake ...92 C 11
Carbery's Hundred Isles ...89 D 13
Carbury ...102 L 7
Cardy ...115 P 4
Cargan ...119 N 3
Carhan House ...88 B 12
Cark Mountain ...117 I 3
Carland ...114 L 4
Carlanstown ...108 L 6
Carlingford ...109 N 6
Carlingford Lough ...109 N 5
Carn ...113 I 4
Carna ...104 C 8
Carnageer ...119 O 3
Carnaghan ...117 J 2
Carnalbanagh Sheddings ...119 N 3
Carnanelly ...114 L 3
Carnanreagh ...118 K 3
Carnaross ...108 L 6
Carnaween ...112 H 3
Carncastle ...119 O 3
Carndonagh / Carn Domhnach ...118 K 2
Carnduff ...119 N 2

Carne .....97 M 11
Carneatly .....119 N 2
Carnew .....97 M 9
Carney *Sligo* .....112 G 4
Carney *Tipperary* .....100 H 9
Carnlough .....119 O 3
Carnlough Bay .....119 O 3
Carnmore .....99 F 8
Carnoneen .....105 F 7
Carnowen .....117 J 3
Carnsore Point .....97 M 11
Carnteel .....114 L 4
Carntogher .....118 L 3
Carra (Lough) .....105 E 6
Carracastle .....106 F 6
Carragh .....102 L 8
Carraholly .....105 D 6
Carraig Airt / Carrigart .....117 I 2
Carraig Mhachaire Rois /
  Carrickmacross .....108 L 6
Carraig na Siúire /
  Carrick-on-Suir .....95 J 10
Carran .....99 E 8
Carrantuohill .....89 C 11
Carrick *Wexford* .....96 L 11
Carrick / An Charraig
  Donegal .....112 G 4
Carrick-a-Rede
  Rope Bridge .....118 M 2
Carrick-on-Shannon /
  Cora Droma Rúisc .....107 H 6
Carrickaboy .....107 K 6
Carrickashedoge .....108 L 6
Carrickboy .....107 I 7
Carrickfergus .....115 O 3
Carrickhugh .....118 K 2
Carrickmore .....114 K 4
Carrickroe .....114 K 4
Carrig .....94 G 11
Carrig Island .....93 D 10
Carrigadrohid .....90 F 12
Carrigafoyle Castle .....93 D 10
Carrigagulla .....90 F 11
Carrigaholt .....93 C 10
Carrigaholt Bay .....93 C 10
Carrigahorig .....100 H 8
Carrigaline .....90 G 12
Carrigallen .....107 J 6
Carrigan .....107 J 6
Carrigan Head .....112 F 4
Carriganimmy .....89 E 12
Carrigans .....117 J 3
Carrigatogher .....100 H 9
Carrigfadda .....89 E 13
Carrigglass Manor .....107 I 6
Carriggower .....103 N 8
Carrigkerry .....93 E 10
Carrignavar .....90 G 12
Carrigrohane .....90 G 12
Carrigtohill .....90 H 12
Carrowbehy .....106 G 6
Carrowdore .....115 P 4
Carrowkeel *Donegal* .....117 J 2
Carrowkeel *Galway* .....99 G 8
Carrowkennedy .....105 D 6
Carrowmore *Galway* .....99 F 8
Carrowmore *Kilmacowen* .....112 G 5
Carrowmore
  near *Cloonacool* .....112 F 5
Carrowmore
  near *Crossboyne* .....105 E 6
Carrowmore
  near *Killasser* .....105 F 6
Carrowmore
  near *Killogeary* .....111 E 5
Carrowmore Lake .....110 C 5
Carrowmore Point .....98 D 9
Carrowmoreknock .....105 E 7
Carrownacon .....105 E 6
Carrowneden .....112 F 5
Carrownisky .....104 C 6
Carrowntanlis .....105 F 7
Carrowreagh
  Roscommon .....100 H 7
Carrowreagh *Sligo* .....112 F 5
Carrowrory .....107 I 7
Carry Bridge .....113 J 5
Carrybeg .....95 J 10
Carryduff .....115 O 4
Casheen bay .....98 C 8
Cashel *Donegal* .....117 I 2
Cashel *Mayo* .....104 C 6
Cashel
  near *Glennamaddy* .....106 G 7
Cashel / An Caiseal
  Galway .....104 C 7
Cashel (Rock of) .....95 I 10

Cashelgarran .....112 G 4
Cashelmore .....117 I 2
Cashen River .....93 D 10
Cashla .....99 F 8
Cashla Bay .....98 D 8
Cashleen .....104 B 7
Casla / Costelloe .....98 D 8
Casltepollard .....107 K 6
Cassagh .....96 L 10
Castle Carry .....118 K 2
Castle Coole .....113 J 4
Castle Gardens .....90 F 13
Castle Haven .....89 E 13
Castle Island .....89 D 13
Castle Point .....98 C 10
Castlebaldwin .....112 G 5
Castlebar (River) .....105 E 6
Castlebellingham .....109 M 6
Castleblakeney .....106 G 7
Castlebridge .....97 M 10
Castlecaulfield .....114 L 4
Castleconnell .....99 G 9
Castleconor .....111 E 5
Castlecor .....94 F 11
Castlecove .....88 B 12
Castlecuffe .....101 J 8
Castledawson .....114 M 3
Castlederg .....113 J 3
Castledermot .....102 L 9
Castlefinn .....117 J 3
Castlefreke .....89 F 13
Castlegal .....112 G 4
Castlegar .....99 E 8
Castlegregory .....92 B 11
Castlehill *Ballycroy South* ..110 C 6
Castlehill
  near *Rake Street* .....111 D 5
Castlejordan .....102 K 7
Castleknock .....103 M 7
Castlellis .....97 M 10
Castlelyons .....90 H 11
Castlemaine .....93 C 11
Castlemaine Harbour .....92 C 11
Castlemartyr .....90 H 12
Castleplunket .....106 G 6
Castlequin .....88 B 12
Castlerahan .....108 K 6
Castlerock .....118 L 2
Castleroe .....118 M 2
Castleshane .....114 L 5
Castletown *Clare* .....99 E 8
Castletown *Cork* .....89 F 12
Castletown *Laois* .....101 J 9
Castletown *Limerick* .....94 F 10
Castletown *Meath* .....108 L 6
Castletown near *Finnea* .....107 K 6
Castletown *Westmeath* .....107 J 7
Castletown *Wexford* .....97 N 9
Castletown House .....103 M 7
Castletownbere .....88 C 13
Castletownroche .....94 G 11
Castletownshend .....89 E 13
Castleville .....105 E 7
Castleward House .....115 P 4
Castlewarren .....96 K 9
Castlewellan .....115 O 5
Castlewellan Forest Park .....115 O 5
Cathair na Mart /
  Westport .....105 D 6
Cathair Saidhbhín /
  Cahersiveen .....88 B 12
Cathedral Rocks .....104 B 6
Causeway .....93 C 10
Causeway Head .....118 M 2
Cavan / An Cabhán .....107 J 6
Cavanagarvan .....114 L 5
Cavangarden .....112 H 4
Cé Bhréanainn / Brandon ..92 B 11
Ceanannas / Ceanannus Mór
  (Kells) .....108 L 6
Ceann Toirc / Kanturk .....94 F 11
Ceapach Choinn /
  Cappoquin .....91 I 11
Ceathlarlach / Carlow .....102 L 9
Ceathrú Thaidhg /
  Carrowteige .....111 C 5
Cecilstown .....94 F 11
Celbridge .....103 M 7
Chanonrock .....108 M 6
Chapelfinn *Down* .....115 P 5
Chapeltown
  near *Portmagee* .....88 A 12
Chapeltown near *Tralee* ..93 C 11
Charlemont .....114 L 4
Charlestown *Craigavon* .....114 M 4
Charlestown *Mayo* .....106 F 6
Cheekpoint .....96 K 11

Cherryville .....102 L 8
Chesney's Corner .....114 M 3
Church Ballee .....115 P 5
Church Cross .....89 D 13
Church Hill *Donegal* .....117 I 3
Church Hill *Fermanagh* .....113 I 4
Church Quarter .....119 N 2
Church Town .....117 J 3
Church Village .....105 E 6
Churchstreet .....106 G 6
Churchtown *Cookstown* .....114 L 3
Churchtown *Cork* .....90 H 12
Churchtown *Down* .....115 P 4
Churchtown *Wexford* .....96 L 11
Churchtown Point .....114 M 3
Cill Airne / Killarney .....89 D 11
Cill Chainnigh / Kilkenny ..96 K 10
Cill Chaoi / Kilkee .....98 D 9
Cill Dalua / Killaloe .....99 G 9
Cill Dara / Kildare .....102 L 8
Cill Mhantáin / Wicklow ....103 N 9
Cill Mocheallóg /
  Kilmallock .....94 G 10
Cill Orglan / Killorglin .....93 C 11
Cill Rois / Kilrush .....93 D 10
Cill Rónáin / Kilronan .....98 C 8
Cionn tSáile / Kinsale .....90 G 12
City Walls .....96 K 11
Clabby .....113 J 4
Cladagh .....113 I 5
Claddagh .....106 F 7
Claddaghduff .....104 B 7
Clady *Antrim* .....115 N 4
Clady *Magherafelt* .....118 M 3
Clady *Strabane* .....117 J 3
Clady (River) .....116 H 2
Clady Milltown .....114 M 5
Claggan *Donegal* .....117 J 2
Claggan *Mayo* .....104 C 6
Clamper Cross .....93 E 11
Clanabogan .....113 J 4
Clane .....102 L 8
Clár Chlainne Mhuiris /
  Claremorris .....105 F 6
Clara .....103 N 9
Clara (Valle of) .....103 N 9
Clarahill .....101 J 8
Clare *Armagh* .....114 M 5
Clare *Craigavon* .....114 N 4
Clare (River) .....105 F 7
Clare Island .....104 B 6
Clarecastle .....99 F 9
Clareen .....101 I 8
Clarina .....94 F 10
Clarinbridge .....99 F 8
Clark's Cross Roads .....107 J 7
Clash .....100 H 9
Clash North .....93 E 10
Clashmore .....91 I 11
Claudy .....118 K 3
Clear (Cape) .....89 D 13
Cleggan / An Cloigeann ....104 B 7
Cleggan Bay .....104 B 7
Cléire (Oilean) /
  Clear Island .....89 D 13
Cleristown .....96 M 11
Clew Bay .....104 C 6
Clifden Bay .....104 B 7
Cliff .....112 H 4
Clifferna .....108 K 6
Cliffony .....112 G 4
Clogga *Kilkenny* .....96 K 11
Clogga *Wicklow* .....97 N 9
Clogh *Ballymena* .....119 N 3
Clogh *Kilkenny* .....101 K 9
Clogh *Laois* .....101 J 9
Clogh *Wexford* .....97 M 10
Clogh Mills .....118 N 3
Cloghan *Offaly* .....101 I 8
Cloghan *Westmeath* .....107 K 7
Cloghane .....92 B 11
Cloghaneely .....117 H 2
Clogharinka .....102 K 7
Cloghaun .....105 F 7
Cloghboley .....112 G 4
Cloghbrack *Cloonbur* .....105 D 7
Cloghbrack *Meath* .....108 K 7
Clogheen .....95 I 11
Clogher *Dungannon* .....113 K 4
Clogher *Kerry* .....93 D 11
Clogher
  near *Carrownacon* .....105 E 6
Clogher near *Westport* .....105 D 6
Clogher *Roscommon* .....107 H 6
Clogher Head *Kerry* .....92 A 11
Clogher Head *Louth / Lú* ..109 N 6
Cloghera .....99 G 9

Clogherhead .....109 N 6
Cloghjordan .....100 H 9
Cloghmacoo .....108 L 6
Cloghoge .....109 M 5
Cloghroe *Cork* .....90 G 12
Cloghroe *Donegal* .....117 I 3
Cloghy .....115 P 4
Cloghy Bay .....115 P 4
Clohamon .....96 M 10
Clohernagh .....96 K 11
Cloich na Coillte /
  Clonakilty .....89 F 13
Clóirtheach / Clara .....101 J 7
Clomantagh .....95 J 9
Clonakenny .....101 I 9
Clonakilty Bay .....90 F 13
Clonalis House .....106 G 6
Clonalvy .....109 M 7
Clonard .....108 K 7
Clonaslee .....101 J 8
Clonavoe .....101 K 8
Clonbern .....106 G 7
Clonbulloge .....102 K 8
Cloncagh .....94 F 10
Clonco Bridge .....100 G 8
Cloncrave .....108 K 7
Cloncullen .....107 I 7
Cloncurry .....102 L 7
Clondalkin .....103 M 8
Clondaw .....97 M 10
Clonderalaw Bay .....93 E 10
Clondulane .....90 H 11
Clonea .....95 J 11
Clonea Bay .....91 J 11
Clonee .....103 M 7
Cloneen .....95 J 10
Clonelly .....113 I 4
Clonevin .....97 N 10
Clonfert .....100 H 8
Clonfert Cross Roads .....100 H 8
Clonkeevy .....112 G 5
Clonleigh .....117 J 3
Clonlost .....107 K 7
Clonmacnoise .....101 I 8
Clonmany .....117 J 2
Clonmellon .....108 K 7
Clonmore *Carlow* .....103 M 9
Clonmore *Tipperary* .....101 I 9
Clonmult .....90 H 12
Clonony .....101 I 8
Clonoulty .....95 I 10
Clonroche .....96 L 10
Clonsilla .....103 M 7
Clontarf .....103 N 7
Clontibret .....114 L 5
Clontubbrid .....101 J 9
Clonycavan .....108 L 7
Clonygowan .....101 K 8
Cloon Lake .....88 C 12
Cloonacleigha Lake .....112 G 5
Cloonacool .....112 F 5
Cloonagh Lough .....106 F 6
Cloonaghlin Lough .....88 C 12
Cloonaghmore .....111 D 5
Cloonboo .....105 E 7
Cloondaff .....105 D 6
Cloondara .....107 I 6
Cloone .....107 I 6
Cloone Grange .....107 I 6
Cloonee Loughs .....89 C 12
Clooneen .....107 J 6
Clooney .....116 G 3
Cloonfad *Kiltullagh* .....106 F 6
Cloonfad near *Old Town* ....100 H 8
Cloonfallagh .....105 F 6
Cloonfinish .....105 F 6
Cloonfower .....106 G 6
Cloonfree Lough .....106 H 6
Cloonkeen *Kerry* .....89 E 12
Cloonkeen *Mayo* .....105 D 6
Cloonkeen *Roscommon* .....106 G 6
Cloonlara .....99 G 9
Cloonloogh .....106 G 6
Cloonlusk .....94 H 10
Cloonmore .....106 G 6
Cloonoon .....100 H 8
Cloonteen .....94 H 10
Cloonta .....106 G 6
Cloonusker .....99 G 9
Cloonymorris .....100 G 8
Cloonyquin .....106 H 6
Cloran .....108 L 7
Clough .....115 O 5
Cloverhill *Cavan* .....107 J 5
Cloverhill *Galway* .....105 E 7
Cloyfin .....118 M 2

Cloyne .....90 H 12
Cluain Eois / Clones .....113 K 5
Cluain Meala / Clonmel .....95 I 10
Cluainín / Manorhamilton ..112 H 5
Clydagh .....105 E 6
Clynacantan .....88 A 12
Coachford .....90 F 12
Coagh .....114 M 4
Coalbrook .....95 J 10
Coalisland .....114 L 4
Coan .....101 K 9
Cod's Head .....88 B 13
Coill an Chollaigh /
  Bailieborough .....108 L 6
Colbinstown .....102 L 8
Coldwood .....99 F 8
Colebrooke .....113 J 5
Coleraine .....118 L 2
Colgagh .....112 G 5
Colgagh Lough .....112 G 5
Colligan (River) .....95 I 11
Collin Top .....119 N 3
Collinstown .....107 K 7
Collon .....109 M 6
Collooney .....112 G 5
Colly .....88 C 12
Colmanstown .....106 G 7
Comber .....115 O 4
Comeragh Mountains .....95 J 11
Commeen .....117 H 3
Commons .....95 J 10
Conay Island .....112 G 5
Cong / Conga .....105 E 7
Conlig .....115 O 4
Conn (Lough) .....111 E 5
Conna .....90 H 11
Connagh .....100 G 9
Connemara .....104 C 7
Connemara
  National Park .....104 C 7
Connolly .....99 E 9
Connonagh .....89 E 13
Connor .....115 N 3
Connor Pass .....92 B 11
Convoy .....117 I 3
Coogue .....105 F 6
Coolagarry .....106 H 7
Coolaney .....112 G 5
Coolattin .....97 M 9
Coolbaun .....101 K 9
Coolbawn .....100 H 9
Coolboy .....97 M 9
Coolcull .....96 L 11
Coolderry .....101 I 8
Coole (Castle) .....113 J 4
Coole Abbey .....90 H 11
Coolea / Cúil Aodha .....89 E 12
Coolearagh .....102 L 8
Cooley Point .....109 N 6
Coolgrange .....96 K 10
Coolgreany .....97 N 9
Coolkeeragh .....117 K 2
Coolkellure .....89 E 12
Coolmeen .....93 E 10
Coolmore .....112 H 4
Coolnareen .....101 J 9
Coolrain .....101 J 9
Coolroebeg .....96 K 10
Coolshaghtena .....107 H 6
Coolteige .....106 H 6
Coomacarrea .....88 B 12
Coomakesta Pass .....88 B 12
Coomasaharn Lake .....88 C 12
Coomhola .....89 D 12
Coomhola Bridge .....89 D 12
Coonagh .....94 F 10
Cooraclare .....98 D 9
Coorleagh .....96 K 10
Coornagillagh .....89 C 12
Cootehall .....106 H 6
Copany .....113 H 4
Copeland Island .....115 P 3
Coppanagh .....108 L 6
Cora Droma Rúisc /
  Carrick-on-Shannon .....107 H 6
Corbally
  Castleconor West .....111 E 5
Corbally *Clare* .....98 D 9
Corbally *Kildare* .....102 L 8
Corbay Upper .....107 I 6
Corbet Milltown .....115 N 4
Corcaigh / Cork .....90 G 12
Corclogh .....110 B 5
Corcomroe Abbey .....99 E 8

Cordal .....93 D 11
Cordarragh .....105 D 6
Corduff .....109 N 7
Cork Harbour .....90 H 12
Corkey .....119 N 2
Corkscrew Hill .....99 E 8
Corlea .....107 I 7
Corlee .....105 E 5
Corlis Point .....93 D 10
Corn Hill .....107 I 6
Cornafulla .....101 H 7
Cornagillagh .....117 I 3
Cornamona .....105 D 7
Cornanagh .....105 E 6
Corracloona .....113 H 4
Corrakyle .....99 G 9
Corraleehan .....113 I 5
Corran Cross Roads .....114 M 5
Corrandulla .....105 F 7
Corraree .....106 H 7
Corrib (Lough) .....105 E 7
Corries .....96 L 10
Corrigeenroe .....106 H 5
Corrofin .....99 E 9
Corronoher .....94 F 10
Corroy .....111 E 5
Corry .....112 H 5
Corstown .....95 J 10
Cortowm .....108 L 6
Corvally .....106 L 6
Corvoley .....111 D 5
Cottoners .....89 C 11
Coulagh Bay .....88 B 12
Coumfea .....95 J 11
Courtmacsherry .....90 F 13
Courtmacsherry Bay .....90 G 13
Courtown .....97 N 10
Cousane Gap .....89 E 12
Craanford .....97 M 9
Craffield .....103 M 9
Crag Cave .....93 D 11
Craggaunowen
  Megalithic Centre .....99 F 9
Craig .....118 K 3
Craigantlet .....115 O 4
Craigavad .....115 O 4
Craigavon .....114 M 4
Craignamaddy .....114 K 3
Craigs .....118 M 3
Crana .....117 J 2
Cranagh .....114 K 3
Cranfield Point .....109 N 5
Cranford .....117 I 2
Crannogeboy .....116 G 3
Cranny .....99 E 9
Cratloe .....99 F 9
Craughwell .....99 F 8
Crawfordsburn .....115 O 4
Crazy Corner .....107 K 7
Creagh .....113 J 4
Creagh (The) .....114 M 3
Creaghanroe .....114 L 5
Crean's Cross Roads .....90 F 12
Crecora .....94 F 10
Creegh .....98 D 9
Creeslough .....117 I 2
Creevagh .....111 D 5
Creevagh Head .....111 E 5
Creeves .....93 E 10
Creevykeel .....112 G 4
Cregg *Clare* .....99 E 8
Cregg *Cork* .....89 E 13
Cregg *Galway* .....105 E 7
Cregg *Sligo* .....112 G 5
Creggan *Armagh* .....108 M 5
Creggan *Dungannon* .....114 K 4
Cregganbaun .....104 C 6
Creggaun .....94 F 10
Creggs .....106 G 7
Crilly .....114 L 4
Crindle .....118 L 2
Crinkill .....101 I 8
Croagh *Donegal* .....112 G 3
Croagh *Limerick* .....94 F 10
Croagh Patrick .....105 C 6
Croaghmoyle .....105 D 6
Croaghnageer .....113 I 3
Croaghnakeela Island .....104 C 8
Croaghrimbeg .....105 D 6

A
B
C
D
E
F
G
H
I
J
K
L
M
N
O
P
Q
R
S
T
U
V
W
X
Y
Z

A
B
C
D
E
F
G
H
I
J
K
L
M
N
O
P
Q
R
S
T
U
V
W
X
Y
Z

Croan (Lough) .... 106 H 7
Croangar (Lough) ....116 H 3
Crockaneel ....119 N 2
Crockets Town ....111 E 5
Crockmore ....113 I 4
Crocknasmug ....118 L 2
Croghan *Offaly* ....101 K 7
Croghan *Roscommon* .....106 H 6
Croghan Mountain ....103 N 9
Crohane ....89 D 12
Crohy Head ....116 G 3
Crois Mhaoilíona /
    Crossmolina ....111 E 5
Croithlí / Crolly ....116 H 2
Cromane ....92 C 11
Cromoge ....101 J 9
Croob (Slieve) ....115 N 4
Crookedwood ....107 K 7
Crookhaven ....88 C 13
Crookstown *Kildare* ....102 L 8
Crookstown *Moviddy* ......90 F 12
Croom ....94 F 10
Croos ....106 H 7
Cross *Cong* ....105 E 7
Cross *Waterford* ....91 I 11
Cross (River) ....105 D 7
Cross Barry ....90 G 12
Cross Keys *Cavan* ....107 K 6
Cross Keys *Meath* ....108 K 6
Cross Keys *Meath* ....108 M 7
Cross Roads ....117 I 3
Crossabeg ....97 M 10
Crossakeel ....108 K 6
Crossboyne ....105 E 6
Crossconnell ....100 H 8
Crossdoney ....107 J 6
Crossea ....107 J 7
Crosserlough ....107 K 6
Crossgar ....115 O 4
Crossgare ....118 L 2
Crosshaven ....90 H 12
Crossmaglen ....108 M 5
Crossna ....106 H 5
Crossooha ....99 F 8
Crosspatrick *Kilkenny* .....101 J 9
Crosspatrick *Wicklow* .....97 M 9
Crosswell ....106 G 7
Crove ....112 G 3
Crow Head ....88 B 13
Crownarad ....112 G 4
Cruit Island ....116 G 2
Crumlin *Antrim* ....115 N 4
Crumlin *Cong* ....105 D 7
Crusheen ....99 F 9
Crutt ....101 K 9
Cúil an tSúdaire /
    Portarlington ....101 K 8
Cuilcagh ....113 I 5
Cuilkillew ....111 E 5
Cuilmore ....105 F 6
Culdaff ....118 K 2
Culdaff Bay ....118 K 2
Culfadda ....106 G 5
Culfin ....104 C 7
Culky ....113 J 5
Cullahill ....101 J 9
Cullane ....94 G 10
Cullaun ....94 H 10
Cullaville ....108 M 5
Culleens ....111 F 5
Cullen *Cork* ....94 H 10
Cullen *Tipperary* ....93 E 11
Cullenagh (River) ....99 E 9
Cullenstown
    near Duncormick ......96 L 11
Cullenstown
    near Newbawn ....96 L 10
Cullin ....105 E 6
Cullin (Lough) ....105 E 6
Cullybackey ....118 M 3
Cullyhanna ....108 M 5
Culmore ....117 K 2
Culnady ....118 M 3
Cummeragh ....88 B 12
Cunningburn ....115 P 4
Curlew Mountains ....106 G 6
Curracloe ....97 M 10
Curragh ....91 I 12
Curragh (The) ....102 L 8
Curragh Camp ....102 L 8
Curragh West ....106 G 7
Curragha ....109 M 7
Curraghbonaun ....106 F 6
Curraghboy ....106 H 7
Curraghmore Gardens .....95 J 11
Curraghroe ....107 H 6
Curraglass ....91 H 11

D

Currahchase Forest Park ...94 F 10
Curran ....114 M 3
Currane (Lough) ....88 B 12
Currans ....93 D 11
Curraun ....105 D 7
Curreel (Lough) ....104 C 7
Curreeny ....100 H 9
Currow ....93 D 11
Curry ....105 E 6
Curryglass ....88 C 12
Curryskeskin ....118 M 2
Cushendall ....119 N 2
Cushendun ....119 N 2
Cusher ....114 M 5
Cushina ....101 K 8
Cut (The) ....101 J 8
Cutra (Lough) ....99 F 8

Dahybaun (Lough) ....111 D 5
Daingean ....101 K 8
Dalgar ....105 F 7
Dalkey ....103 N 8
Damastown ....109 N 7
Damerstown ....101 K 9
Damhead ....118 M 2
Dan (Lough) ....103 N 8
Danesfort *Kilkenny* ....96 K 10
Danesfort *Longford* ....107 I 6
Dangan *Cork* ....91 H 12
Dangan *Waterford* ....96 K 11
Darby's Gap ....97 M 10
Darkley ....114 L 5
Darragh ....99 E 9
Dartry Mountains ....112 G 4
Davagh Forest Park ....114 L 3
Davidstown ....103 M 9
Dawros ....104 C 7
Dawros Head ....116 G 3
Dead ....94 H 10
Dealagh ....98 D 9
Dee ....108 L 6
Deel *Limerick* ....94 F 10
Deel *Mayo* ....111 D 5
Deel *Westmeath* ....108 K 7
Deel Bridge ....111 D 5
Deele (River) ....117 I 3
Deelish ....89 E 12
Deenish Island ....88 B 12
Delamont ....115 O 4
Delgany ....103 N 8
Delphi ....104 C 7
Delvin ....108 K 7
Delvin (River) ....109 N 7
Dennet (Burn) ....117 J 3
Derg ....113 J 3
Derg (Lough)
    near Donegal ....113 I 4
Derg (Lough)
    near Nenagh ....100 H 9
Dergalt ....117 J 3
Dernagree ....93 E 11
Derravaragh (Lough) ....107 J 7
Derreen
    near Ballynagoraher ....105 D 6
Derreen near Cloghmore ...104 C 6
Derreen near Formoyle ......99 E 8
Derreen near Lahinch ....98 D 9
Derreen Gardens ....89 C 12
Derreendarragh ....89 C 12
Derreeny ....88 C 12
Derreeny Bridge ....89 E 13
Derriana Lough ....88 C 12
Derries ....101 J 8
Derry ....112 G 5
Derryadd ....114 M 4
Derryanvil ....114 M 4
Derrybeg ....116 H 2
Derryboye ....115 O 4
Derrybrien ....99 G 8
Derryclare Lough ....104 C 7
Derrycooly ....101 I 8
Derrycraff ....105 D 6
Derrydruel ....116 G 3
Derryerglinna ....105 D 7
Derryfadda ....101 J 9
Derrygolan ....101 J 8
Derrygonnelly ....113 I 4
Derrygoolin ....100 G 9
Derrygrogan ....101 J 8
Derrykeevan ....114 M 4
Derrykeighan ....118 M 2
Derrylea ....104 C 7
Derrylin ....113 J 5
Derrylough ....116 G 3
Derrymore ....93 C 11

Derrymore Island ....93 C 11
Derrynane ....88 B 12
Derrynane House ....88 B 12
Derrynasaggart Mountains ..89 E 11
Derrynawilt ....113 K 5
Derryneen ....104 C 7
Derrynoose ....114 L 5
Derryrush ....104 C 7
Derrytrasna ....114 M 4
Derryveagh Mountains .....117 H 3
Derryvohy ....105 E 6
Derrywode ....106 G 6
Dervock ....118 M 2
Desertmartin ....114 L 3
Devenish Island ....113 J 4
Devilsbit ....101 I 9
Devilsmother ....105 D 7
Diamond (The) *Antrim* ....114 N 4
Diamond (The)
    Cookstown ....114 M 4
Diamond (The) *Omagh* ...113 J 4
Dingle /
    Daingean Uí Chúis ......92 B 11
Dingle Bay ....92 B 11
Dingle Harbour ....92 B 11
Divis ....115 N 4
Doagh *Newtownabbey* ...115 N 3
Doagh *Rosguill* ....117 I 2
Doagh Beg /
    Dumhaigh Bhig ....117 J 2
Doagh Isle ....117 J 2
Dodder ....103 M 8
Doe Castle ....117 I 2
Dolla ....100 H 9
Dollingstown ....114 N 4
Domhnach Phádraig /
    Donaghpatrick ....108 L 6
Donabate ....109 N 7
Donacarney ....109 N 6
Donadea ....102 L 7
Donagh ....113 J 5
Donaghadee ....115 P 4
Donaghaguy ....109 N 5
Donaghcloney ....114 N 4
Donaghey ....114 L 4
Donaghmore ....114 L 4
Donaghmore *Meath* ......109 M 7
Donard *Wexford* ....96 L 10
Donard *Wicklow* ....103 M 8
Donard (Slieve) ....115 O 5
Donaskeagh ....95 H 10
Donegal / Dún na nGall ...113 H 4
Donegal Airport ....116 G 2
Donegal Bay ....112 G 5
Donegal Point ....98 D 9
Doneraile ....94 G 11
Donohill ....95 H 10
Donore ....109 M 6
Donoughmore ....90 F 12
Doo (Lough) ....99 E 9
Doo Lough ....104 C 7
Doo Lough Pass ....104 C 7
Dooagh ....110 B 6
Doobehy ....111 D 5
Doocastle ....106 G 5
Dooega Head ....104 B 6
Dooey Point ....116 G 3
Doogary ....107 J 5
Dooghbeg ....104 C 6
Doogort ....110 B 5
Doohooma ....110 C 5
Dooish Mount ....117 J 3
Doolough Point ....110 C 5
Doon *Galway* ....100 G 7
Doon *Limerick* ....94 H 10
Doon Lough ....99 F 9
Doona ....110 C 5
Doonaha ....93 D 10
Doonbeg ....98 D 9
Doonloughan ....104 B 7
Doonmanagh ....92 B 11
Doorin Point ....112 H 4
Dooyork ....110 C 5
Dore ....116 H 2
Dorrusawillin ....107 H 5
Dough ....88 C 13
Douglas ....90 G 12
Douglas Bridge ....113 J 3
Doulus Bay ....88 A 12
Doulus Head ....88 A 12
Dowdallshill ....109 M 5
Dowling ....96 K 10
Downhill ....118 L 2
Downpatrick ....115 O 5
Downpatrick Head ....111 D 5
Downs (The) ....107 K 7
Dowra ....113 H 5

Dowth ....109 M 6
Drains Bay ....119 O 3
Drangan ....95 J 10
Draperstown ....114 L 3
Dreen ....118 K 3
Dreenagh ....92 C 10
Drimnagh *Cork* ....89 E 13
Drinagh *Wexford* ....97 M 11
Drinaghan ....111 E 5
Dring ....107 J 6
Dripsey ....90 F 12
Dripsey (River) ....90 F 11
Drishaghaun ....105 D 7
Drishane Bridge ....89 D 13
Droichead Átha /
    Drogheda ....109 M 6
Droichead na Bandan /
    Bandon ....90 F 12
Drom ....101 I 9
Dromahair ....112 H 5
Dromara ....115 N 4
Dromcolliher ....94 F 10
Dromin *Limerick* ....94 G 10
Dromin *Louth* ....109 M 6
Dromina ....94 F 11
Dromineer ....100 H 9
Dromiskin ....109 M 6
Dromkeen ....94 G 10
Drommahane ....90 F 11
Dromod ....107 I 6
Dromoland Castle ....99 F 9
Dromore *Banbridge* ....115 N 4
Dromore *Omagh* ....113 J 4
Dromore Lake ....94 F 10
Dromore West ....112 F 5
Dromtrasna ....93 E 10
Drones (The) ....118 M 2
Drowes ....112 H 4
Drum *Monaghan* ....108 K 5
Drum *Roscommon* ....101 H 7
Drum *Sligo* ....112 G 5
Drum Hills ....91 I 11
Drum Manor
    Forest Park ....114 L 4
Drumahoe ....117 K 3
Drumandoora ....99 F 8
Drumaness ....115 O 4
Drumanoo Head ....112 G 4
Drumatober ....100 G 8
Drumbane ....95 I 10
Drumbeg *Feddyglass* .....117 J 3
Drumbeg *Lisburn* ....115 O 4
Drumbo ....115 O 4
Drumbologe ....117 I 3
Drumcar ....109 M 6
Drumcard ....113 I 5
Drumcliff ....112 G 5
Drumcliff Bay ....112 G 5
Drumcondra ....108 M 6
Drumcong ....107 I 5
Drumcree ....108 K 7
Drumcullen ....114 M 3
Drumduff ....113 J 4
Drumena Cashel ....115 O 5
Drumfea ....96 L 10
Drumfin ....112 G 5
Drumfree ....117 J 2
Drumgoft ....103 M 9
Drumintee ....109 M 5
Drumkeary ....100 G 8
Drumkeen ....117 I 3
Drumkeeran ....112 H 5
Drumlaheen Lough ....107 I 5
Drumlea ....107 I 5
Drumlegagh ....113 J 4
Drumlish ....107 I 6
Drumlosh ....101 I 7
Drummannon ....114 M 4
Drummin ....96 L 10
Drummullin ....106 H 6
Drumnakilly ....114 K 4
Drumone ....108 K 6
Drumquin ....113 J 4
Drumraney ....107 I 7
Drumreagh ....110 B 5
Drumshanbo ....107 H 5
Drumsna ....107 H 6
Drumsurn ....118 L 3
Duagh ....93 D 10
Dually ....95 I 10
Dublin Bay ....103 N 7
Duff ....112 H 4
Duffy ....102 L 7
Duleek ....109 M 7
Dumha Éige / Dooega ....104 B 6
Dún Aengus ....98 C 8

Dún A'Rí Forest Park ....108 L 6
Dún Chaoin / Dunquin ......92 A 11
Dún Dealgan / Dundalk ...109 M 5
Dún Garbhán /Dungarvan ..91 J 11
Dun Laoghaire ....103 N 8
Dún Mánmhaí /
    Dunmanway ....89 E 12
Dún Mór / Dunmore ....106 F 7
Dún na nGall / Donegal ...113 H 4
Dunabrattin Head ....91 K 11
Dunadry ....115 N 3
Dunaff ....117 J 2
Dunaff Head ....117 J 2
Dunaghy ....118 M 2
Dunagree Point ....118 L 2
Dunamase (Rock of) ....101 K 8
Dunamon ....106 H 7
Dunany ....109 N 6
Dunany Point ....109 N 6
Dunbel ....96 K 10
Dunboyne ....103 M 7
Dunbrody Abbey ....96 L 11
Dunbulcaun Bay ....99 F 8
Duncannon ....96 L 11
Duncormick ....96 M 11
Dundalk Bay ....109 N 6
Dunderrow ....90 G 12
Dunderry ....108 L 7
Dundonald ....115 O 4
Dundrod ....115 N 4
Dundrum *Down* ....115 O 5
Dundrum *Dublin* ....103 N 8
Dundrum *Tipperary* ....95 H 10
Dundrum Bay ....115 O 5
Dunfanaghy ....117 I 2
Dungannon ....114 L 4
Dunganstown ....96 L 10
Dungarvan Harbour ....91 J 11
Dungiven ....118 L 3
Dungloe /
    An Clochán Liath ....116 G 3
Dungonnell Dam ....119 N 3
Dungourney ....90 H 12
Dunguaire Castle ....99 F 8
Dunhill ....91 K 11
Duniry ....100 G 8
Dunkellin ....99 F 8
Dunkerrin ....101 I 9
Dunkineely ....112 G 4
Dunkitt ....96 K 11
Dunlavin ....102 L 8
Dunleer ....109 M 6
Dunlewy ....117 H 2
Dunloe (Gap of) ....89 D 11
Dunloy ....118 M 2
Dunluce Castle ....118 M 2
Dunmanus ....89 D 13
Dunmanus Bay ....88 C 13
Dunmore ....109 O 5
Dunmore Cave ....96 K 9
Dunmore East ....96 L 11
Dunmore Head *Dunquin* ..92 A 11
Dunmore Head
    near Culdaff ....118 K 2
Dunmore Head
    near Portnoo ....116 G 3
Dunmurry ....115 N 4
Dunnamaggan ....96 K 10
Dunnamanagh ....117 K 3
Dunnamore ....114 L 3
Dunnycove Bay ....89 F 13
Dunowen Head ....89 F 13
Dunree Head ....117 J 2
Dunsany ....108 M 7
Dunshaughlin ....108 M 7
Dunworly Bay ....90 F 13
Durlas / Thurles ....95 I 9
Durrow ....101 J 9
Durrus ....89 D 13
Dursey Head ....88 B 13
Dursey Island ....88 B 13
Duvillaun Beg ....110 B 5
Duvillaun More ....110 B 5
Dyan ....114 L 4
Dysart ....107 J 7
Dysert O'Dea ....99 E 9

E

Éadan Doire / Edenderry .102 K 7
Eagle (Mount) ....92 A 11
Eagle Island ....110 B 5
Eagles Hill ....88 B 12
Eany ....112 H 3
Easky ....111 F 5
Easky Lough ....112 F 5
East Ferry ....90 H 12

East Town ....116 H 2
Eddy Island ....99 F 8
Eden ....115 O 3
Ederny ....113 J 4
Edgeworthstown ....107 J 6
Edgeworthstown /
    Meathas Troim ....107 J 6
Egish (Lough) ....108 L 5
Eglinton ....118 K 2
Eglish ....114 L 4
Eighter ....108 K 6
Eleven Lane Ends ....114 M 5
Ellistrin ....117 I 3
Elly Bay ....110 B 5
Elphin ....106 H 6
Elton ....94 G 10
Elva (Slieve) ....99 E 8
Emlagh Point ....104 C 6
Emly ....94 G 10
Emmoo ....106 H 7
Emo ....101 K 8
Emo Court ....101 K 8
Emyvale ....114 L 4
Ennel (Lough) ....107 J 7
Ennis / Inis ....99 F 9
Enniscorthy /
    Inis Córthaidh ....97 M 10
Enniskean ....89 F 12
Enniskerry ....103 N 8
Enniskillen ....113 J 4
Ennistimon / Inis Diomáin ...99 E 9
Eochaill / Youghal ....91 I 12
Erne (Lower Lough) ....113 I 4
Erne (River) ....107 J 6
Erne (Upper Lough) ....113 J 5
Erra ....107 I 6
Errew Abbey ....111 E 5
Erriff (River) ....105 D 7
Errigal Mountain ....117 H 2
Erril ....101 I 9
Erris Head ....110 B 5
Errisbeg ....104 C 7
Errislannan ....104 B 7
Errit Lough ....106 F 6
Ervey Cross Roads ....118 K 3
Eshnadarragh ....113 K 5
Eshnadeelada ....113 K 5
Eske ....113 H 3
Eske (Lough) ....113 H 3
Esker ....99 F 8
Esker South ....107 I 6
Eskeragh ....111 D 5
Eskragh ....113 K 4
Eyeries ....88 C 12
Eyrecourt ....100 H 8

F

Faha ....91 J 11
Fahamore ....92 B 11
Fahan ....117 J 2
Fahy ....100 H 8
Fahy Lough ....110 C 5
Fair Green ....99 F 9
Fair Head ....88 C 13
Fairyhouse ....108 M 7
Fairymount ....106 G 6
Fallmore ....110 B 5
Fanad ....117 I 2
Fanad Head ....117 J 2
Fane River ....108 M 5
Fanore ....99 E 8
Farahy ....94 G 11
Fardrum ....101 I 7
Fardurris Point ....98 D 8
Farmer's Bridge ....93 D 11
Farnagh ....101 I 7
Farnaght ....107 I 6
Farnanes Cross Roads .....90 F 12
Farnoge ....96 K 10
Farran ....90 F 12
Farran Forest Park ....90 F 12
Farrancassidy
    Cross Roads ....112 H 4
Farranfore ....93 D 11
Fastnet Rock ....89 D 13
Faughan ....118 K 3
Fawney ....117 K 3
Fea (Lough) ....114 L 3
Feagarrid ....95 I 11
Feakle ....99 G 9
Feale (River) ....93 D 10
Fearn Hill ....113 J 3
Fedamore ....94 G 10
Fee (Lough) ....104 C 7
Feeagh (Lough) ....105 D 6
Feeard ....93 C 10
Feenagh ....94 F 10

Feeny … 118 K 3
Feevagh … 106 H 7
Fenagh … 107 I 5
Fenit … 92 C 11
Fennagh … 96 L 9
Fennor … 91 K 11
Feohanagh *Kerry* … 92 A 11
Feohanagh *Limerick* … 94 F 10
Feohanagh (River) … 92 B 11
Ferbane … 101 I 8
Fergus (River) … 99 E 9
Fern (Lough) … 117 I 2
Ferns … 97 M 10
Ferry Bridge … 94 F 10
Ferrybank … 97 N 9
Ferrycarrig … 97 M 10
Ferta … 88 B 12
Fethard … 96 L 11
Fews … 95 J 11
Feystown … 119 O 3
Fiddown … 96 K 10
Fieries … 93 D 11
Finavarra … 99 E 8
Finglas … 103 N 7
Finglass … 89 C 11
Finn (Lough) … 117 H 3
Finn (River) … 117 J 3
Finnea … 107 J 6
Finnisglin … 104 C 7
Fintona … 113 K 4
Fintragh Bay … 112 G 4
Finuge … 93 D 10
Finvoy … 118 M 2
Fiodh Ard / Fethard … 95 I 10
Fionnaithe / Finny … 105 D 7
Firkeel … 88 B 13
Fisherhill … 105 E 6
Five Corners … 115 N 3
Fivealley … 101 I 8
Fivemilebridge … 90 G 12
Fivemiletown … 113 K 4
Flagmount *Corlea* … 99 G 9
Flagmount *Kilkenny* … 96 K 10
Flat Head … 90 G 12
Flesk … 89 D 11
Florence Court … 113 I 5
Florence Court
  Forest Park … 113 I 5
Foaty Island/Fota Island … 90 H 12
Foilycleara … 95 H 10
Folk Park … 99 F 9
Fontstown … 102 L 8
Forbes (Lough) … 107 I 6
Fordstown … 108 L 6
Fore … 107 K 6
Forkill … 109 M 5
Forlorn Point … 96 M 11
Formoyle *Lonford* … 107 I 7
Formoyle *Mayo* … 104 C 6
Formoyle
  near Ballivaghan … 99 E 8
Formoyle *near Inagh* … 99 E 9
Formoyle (Lough) … 105 D 7
Fort Stewart … 117 J 2
Forthill … 107 I 7
Fota Island … 90 H 12
Foul Sound … 98 D 8
Foulksmills … 96 L 11
Fountain Cross … 99 E 9
Four Mile House … 106 H 6
Four Roads … 106 H 7
Fourknocks … 109 N 7
Foxford … 105 E 6
Foxhall … 105 E 7
Foyle (Lough) … 118 K 2
Foynes … 93 E 10
Foynes Island … 93 E 10
Francis' Gap … 99 G 8
Freemount … 94 F 11
Frenchpark … 106 G 6
Freshford … 95 J 9
Freynestown … 102 L 8
Frosses … 112 H 3
Frower Point … 90 G 12
Fuerty … 106 H 7
Funshin More … 99 F 8
Funshinagh (Lough) … 106 H 7
Funshion … 94 G 11
Furbogh … 99 E 8
Furnace … 105 D 7
Furnace Lough … 105 D 6
Furness … 103 M 8
Fyagh (Slieve) … 111 D 5

G

Gabriel (Mount) … 89 D 13
Gaddagh … 89 C 11

Gaillimh / Galway … 99 E 8
Gainestown … 107 K 7
Galbally *Dungannon* … 114 L 4
Galbally *Limerick* … 94 H 10
Galbally *Wexford* … 96 M 10
Galbolie … 108 K 6
Galey … 93 D 10
Galgorm … 118 N 3
Gallarus Oratory … 92 A 11
Galley Head … 89 F 13
Gallion (Slieve) … 114 L 3
Galmoy … 101 J 9
Galty Mountains … 95 H 10
Galtymore Mountain … 95 H 10
Galway Bay … 98 D 8
Galways Bridge … 89 D 12
Gaoth Dobhair /
  Gweedore … 116 H 2
Gaoth Sáile / Geesala … 110 C 5
Gap (The) … 95 I 11
Gara (Lough) … 106 G 6
Garadice … 102 L 7
Garadice Lough … 107 I 5
Garbally … 100 H 8
Garinish Island … 88 C 12
Garnavilla … 95 I 10
Garnish Point … 88 B 13
Garrane … 89 E 12
Garranlahan … 106 G 6
Garraun *Clare* … 98 D 9
Garraun *Galway* … 100 G 8
Garraun (Mount) … 104 C 7
Garries Bridge … 89 D 12
Garrison … 112 H 4
Garristown … 109 M 7
Garron Point … 119 O 2
Garrycloonagh … 111 E 5
Garrycullen … 96 L 11
Garryduff … 118 M 2
Garryfine … 94 F 10
Garrykennedy … 100 G 9
Garryspillane … 94 G 10
Garryvoe … 91 H 12
Gartan Lough … 117 I 3
Gartree Point … 114 N 4
Garty Lough … 107 J 6
Garvagh *Coleraine* … 118 L 3
Garvagh *Rowan* … 107 I 6
Garvaghy … 114 K 4
Garvary … 113 J 4
Gattabaun … 101 J 9
Gearagh (The) … 90 F 12
Gearha Bridge … 88 C 12
Geashill … 101 K 8
Geevagh … 112 H 5
George (Lough) … 99 F 9
Gerahies … 89 D 13
Giant's Causeway … 118 M 2
Giles Quay … 109 N 6
Gilford … 114 M 4
Gill (Lough) *near Sligo* … 112 G 5
Gill (Lough) *nearTralee* … 92 B 11
Glandore … 89 E 13
Glandore Harbour … 89 E 13
Glangevlin … 113 I 5
Glanmire … 90 G 12
Glanmore Lake … 89 C 12
Glanoe … 93 D 10
Glantane … 90 F 11
Glanworth … 94 G 11
Glarryford … 118 M 3
Glasdrumman … 109 O 5
Glaslough … 114 L 5
Glasmullan … 117 J 2
Glassan … 107 I 7
Glasshouse Lake … 107 J 5
Glassillaun … 104 C 6
Glastry … 115 P 4
Gleann Cholm Cille /
  Glencolumbkille … 112 F 3
Gleann Domhain /
  Glendowan … 117 I 3
Gleann na Muaidhe /
  Glenamoy … 111 C 5
Glenamoy (River) … 111 D 5
Glenaan … 119 N 2
Glenade … 112 H 4
Glenade Lough … 112 H 4

Glenariff Forest Park … 119 N 2
Glenariff or Waterfoot … 119 N 2
Glenarm … 119 O 3
Glenavy … 115 N 4
Glenballyemon … 119 N 2
Glenbeg Lough … 88 C 12
Glenbeigh … 92 C 11
Glenboy … 112 H 5
Glenbridge Lodge … 103 M 8
Glenbrohane … 94 G 10
Glenbrook … 90 G 12
Glencar … 88 C 12
Glencar Lough … 112 G 4
Glencloy … 119 O 3
Glencolmcille Folk Village … 112 F 3
Glencree … 103 N 8
Glencullen … 103 N 8
Glendalough *Brockagh* … 103 M 8
Glendalough *Waterford* … 95 J 11
Glenderry … 92 C 10
Glendorragha … 116 G 3
Glendree … 99 F 9
Glendum … 119 N 2
Glenealy … 103 N 9
Gleneely *near Ballybofey* … 113 I 3
Gleneely *near Cardonagh* … 118 K 2
Glenelly … 114 K 3
Glenelly Valley … 114 K 3
Glenfarne … 113 I 5
Glenflesk … 89 D 11
Glengad Head … 118 K 1
Glengarriff (River) … 89 D 12
Glengarriff Harbour … 89 D 12
Glengesh Pass … 112 G 3
Glengormley … 115 O 3
Glenhead … 118 K 2
Glenhull … 114 K 3
Glenicmurrin Lough … 98 D 8
Glenmacnass … 103 M 8
Glenmalur … 103 M 9
Glenmore *Clare* … 99 E 9
Glenmore *Kilkenny* … 96 K 10
Glennagevlagh … 105 D 7
Glennamaddy … 106 G 7
Glennascaul … 99 F 8
Glenoe … 115 O 3
Glenshane Pass … 118 L 3
Glenshesk … 119 N 2
Glentaisie … 119 N 2
Glentane … 106 G 7
Glenties … 116 H 3
Glentogher … 118 K 2
Glentrasna … 105 D 7
Glenvale … 118 M 3
Glenvar / Gleann Bhairr … 117 J 2
Glenveagh National Park … 117 I 2
Glenville … 90 G 11
Glin … 93 E 10
Glin Castle … 93 E 10
Glinsce / Glinsk … 104 C 7
Glinsk *Donegal* … 117 I 2
Glinsk *Mayo* … 111 D 5
Glounthaune … 90 G 12
Glowra … 109 N 5
Glyde (River) … 108 M 6
Glynn *Carlow* … 96 L 10
Glynn *Larne* … 115 O 3
Gneevgullia … 93 E 11
Gob an Choire /
  Achill Sound … 104 C 6
Gobbins (The) … 115 O 3
Gokane Point … 89 E 13
Gola Island / Gabhla … 116 G 2
Golagh Lough … 113 H 4
Golam Head … 98 C 8
Golden … 95 I 10
Golden Vale … 95 H 10
Goleen … 88 C 13
Goold's Cross … 95 I 10
Goresbridge … 96 K 10
Gorey / Guaire … 97 N 9
Gormanston … 109 N 7
Gort an Choirce /
  Gortahork … 117 H 2
Gortaclare … 113 K 4
Gortahill … 113 I 5
Gortaleam … 106 F 7
Gortarevan … 100 H 8
Gortaroo … 91 I 12
Gortaway … 117 J 2
Gorteen … 106 G 6
Gorteen Bridge … 101 J 8
Gorteeny … 100 G 8
Gortgarriff … 88 C 12
Gortgarrigan … 112 H 5
Gortin … 113 K 3
Gortin Glen Forest Park … 113 K 3

Gortletteragh … 107 I 6
Gortmore *near Ballycastle* … 111 D 5
Gortmore *near Bangor* … 111 C 5
Gortmullan … 113 J 5
Gortnadeeve … 106 G 7
Gortnahoo … 95 J 9
Gortnasillagh … 106 G 6
Gortree … 117 J 3
Gortymadden … 100 G 8
Gorumna Island … 98 C 8
Gosford Forest Park … 114 M 5
Gougane Barra
  Forest Park … 89 D 12
Gougane Barra Lake … 89 E 12
Gouladoo … 89 C 13
Gowla … 104 C 7
Gowlaun … 104 C 7
Gowlin … 96 L 10
Gowna (Lough) … 107 J 6
Gowran … 96 K 10
Gracehill … 118 N 3
Graffy … 116 H 3
Gráig na Manach /
  Graiguenamanagh … 96 L 10
Graigue … 102 L 9
Graigue Hill … 96 L 9
Graigue More … 96 M 10
Graigues … 88 B 12
Grand Canal … 101 I 8
Graney … 102 L 9
Graney (Lough) … 99 G 9
Graney (River) … 99 G 9
Grange *Kildare* … 102 K 7
Grange *Kilkenny* … 96 K 10
Grange *Louth* … 109 N 5
Grange *Sligo* … 112 G 4
Grange *Waterford* … 91 I 12
Grange (River) … 106 F 7
Grange Con … 102 L 9
Grangebellew … 109 M 6
Grangeford … 102 L 9
Grangegeeth … 108 M 6
Granias Gap … 117 K 2
Grannagh … 99 F 8
Gransha … 115 O 3
Granville … 114 L 4
Greagh … 107 I 6
Great Blasket Island … 92 A 11
Great Island … 90 H 12
Great Newtown Head … 96 K 11
Great Skellig … 88 A 12
Great Sugar Loaf … 103 N 8
Greatman's Bay … 98 D 8
Greenan … 103 N 9
Greenanstown … 109 N 7
Greencastle *Donegal* … 118 L 2
Greencastle
  Newry-Mourne … 109 N 5
Greencastle *Omagh* … 114 K 3
Greenfield … 105 E 7
Greenisland … 115 O 3
Greenore … 109 N 5
Greenore Point … 97 N 11
Gregans Castle … 99 E 8
Gregory's Sound … 98 D 8
Grenagh … 90 G 11
Grey Abbey … 115 P 4
Grey Point … 115 O 3
Greysteel … 118 K 2
Greystone … 114 L 4
Greystones … 103 N 8
Grianan of Aileach … 117 J 2
Grogan … 101 I 8
Groomsport … 115 P 3
Gubaveeny … 113 I 5
Gubbaroe Point … 113 I 4
Gulladoo Lough … 107 J 6
Gulladuff … 118 M 3
Gullion (Slieve) … 109 M 5
Gur (Lough) … 94 G 10
Gurteen *Cappalusk* … 99 G 7
Gurteen *Leitrim* … 112 H 5
Gusserane … 96 L 11
Gweebarra Bridge … 116 H 3
Gweebarra … 116 H 3
Gweebarra Bay … 116 G 3
Gweestin … 93 D 11
Gweestion … 105 E 6
Gyleen … 90 H 12

H

Hacketstown … 103 M 9
Hags Head … 98 D 9
Hamiltonsbawn … 114 M 4
Hand Cross Roads (The) … 99 E 9
Hannahstown … 115 N 4

Hare Island … 89 D 13
Harristown … 96 K 10
Harrow (The) … 97 M 10
Healy Pass … 89 C 12
Helen's Bay … 115 O 3
Helvick Head … 91 J 11
Herbertstown … 94 G 10
High Island … 104 B 7
Highwood … 112 H 5
Hill Street … 107 H 6
Hillsborough … 115 N 4
Hilltown *Harristown* … 96 L 11
Hilltown
  Newry and Mourne … 115 N 5
Hind … 106 H 7
Hog's Head … 88 B 12
Holeopen Bay West … 90 G 13
Hollyford … 95 H 10
Hollyfort … 97 M 9
Hollymount … 105 E 7
Hollywood … 103 M 8
Holy Cross … 95 I 10
Holy Island … 99 G 9
Holycross … 94 G 10
Holywell … 113 I 5
Holywell Hill … 117 J 2
Holywood … 115 O 4
Hook Head … 96 L 11
Hore Abbey … 95 I 10
Horn Head … 117 I 2
Horse and Jockey … 95 I 10
Horse Island … 89 D 13
Horseleap … 101 J 7
Hospital … 94 G 10
Hugginstown … 96 K 10
Hurlers Cross … 99 F 9
Hurley … 109 M 7
Hyne (Lough) … 89 E 13

I

Ilen … 89 E 13
Illaunstookagh … 92 C 11
Illauntannig … 92 B 11
Illies … 117 J 2
Illnacullin … 89 D 12
Inagh … 99 E 9
Inagh (Lough) … 104 C 7
Inch … 92 C 11
Inch *Donegal* … 117 J 2
Inch *near Whitegate* … 90 H 12
Inch *near Youghal* … 91 I 12
Inch *Tipperary* … 95 H 9
Inch *Wexford* … 97 N 9
Inch Abbey … 115 O 4
Inch Island … 117 J 2
Inchagoill … 105 E 7
Inchamore Bridge … 108 L 7
Inchbeg … 96 J 9
Inchcleraun … 107 H 7
Inchee Bridge … 89 D 12
Inchicronan Lough … 99 F 9
Inchigeelagh … 89 E 12
Inchiquin … 105 E 7
Inchiquin Lough *Clare* … 99 E 9
Inchiquin Lough *Kerry* … 89 D 12
Inchmore … 107 I 7
Inchnamuck … 95 H 11
Inchydoney Island … 90 F 13
Indreabhán / Inveran … 98 D 8
Inis / Ennis … 99 F 9
Inis Bó Finne / Inishbofin … 117 H 2
Inis Meáin / Inishmaan … 98 D 8
Inis Mór / Inishmore … 98 C 8
Inis Oírr / Inisheer … 98 D 8
Inishannon … 90 G 12
Inishbarra … 98 C 8
Inishbiggle … 110 C 5
Inishbofin … 104 B 7
Inishcarra … 90 G 12
Inishcarra Reservoir … 90 F 12
Inishcrone … 111 E 5
Inishdoorus … 105 D 7
Inishfarnard … 88 B 12
Inishfree Bay … 116 G 2
Inishfree Upper … 116 G 3
Inishglora … 110 B 5
Inishkea North … 110 B 5
Inishkea South … 110 B 5
Inishmaine Island … 105 E 7
Inishmicatreer … 105 E 7
Inishmurray … 112 G 4
Inishnabro … 92 A 11
Inishnee … 104 C 7
Inishowen … 117 J 2
Inishowen Head … 118 L 2
Inishshark … 104 B 7

Inishtooskert … 92 A 11
Inishtrahull … 118 K 1
Inishtrahull Sound … 118 K 1
Inishturk … 104 B 6
Inishvickillane … 92 A 11
Inistioge … 96 K 10
Innfield … 102 L 7
Innisfree … 112 G 5
Inniskeen … 108 M 5
Inny (River) … 107 J 6
Inver *Donegal* … 112 H 4
Inver *Mayo* … 110 C 5
Inver Bay … 112 H 4
Ireland's Eye … 103 N 7
Irish Agricultural
  Museum … 97 M 11
Irishtown … 105 F 7
Iron (Lough) … 107 J 7
Iron Mountains … 113 I 5
Irvinestown … 113 J 4
Island Lake … 106 F 6
Island Reavy (Lough) … 115 N 5
Islandmore … 115 P 4
Iveragh … 88 B 12

J

J. F. Kennedy Park … 96 L 11
Jamestown *Cloonteem* … 107 H 6
Jamestown *Laois* … 101 K 8
Japanese Gardens … 102 L 8
Jerpoint Abbey … 96 K 10
Jerrettspass … 114 M 5
Johnstown *Kildare* … 103 M 8
Johnstown *Kilkenny* … 101 J 9
Johnstown *Meath* … 108 M 7
Johnstown *near Arklow* … 103 N 9
Johnstown
  near Coolgreany … 97 N 9
Johnstown Bridge … 107 I 6
Johnstownbridge … 102 L 7
Jonesborough … 109 M 5
Joyce … 105 D 7
Julianstown … 109 N 6

K

Kanturk Castle … 94 F 11
Katesbridge … 115 N 5
Keadew … 107 H 5
Keady … 114 L 5
Keady Mountain … 118 L 2
Kealduff … 89 C 12
Kealkill … 89 D 12
Kearney … 115 P 4
Kearney Point … 115 P 4
Keeagh … 99 E 8
Keel … 110 B 6
Keel (Lough) … 117 I 2
Keel Lough … 110 B 6
Keeloges … 106 G 7
Keem Strand … 110 B 6
Keenagh *Longford* … 107 I 7
Keenagh *Mayo* … 111 D 5
Keeraunagark … 98 D 8
Keereen … 91 I 11
Keimaneigh (The pass of) … 89 E 12
Kells *Ballymena* … 115 N 3
Kells *Kerry* … 88 B 12
Kells *Kilkenny* … 96 K 10
Kells (Ceanannus Mor) /
  Ceanannas *Meath* … 108 L 6
Kells Bay … 88 B 11
Kells Priory … 96 K 10
Kellysgrove … 100 H 8
Kenmare River … 88 B 12
Kentstown … 108 M 7
Kerry (Ring of) … 88 B 12
Kerry Head … 92 C 10
Kesh *Fermanagh* … 113 I 4
Kesh *Toomour* … 106 G 5
Keshcarrigan … 107 I 5
Key (Lough) … 106 H 5
Kid Island … 110 C 5
Kilbaha … 93 C 10
Kilbaha Bay … 93 C 10
Kilbane … 99 G 9
Kilbarry … 89 E 12
Kilbeacanty … 99 F 8
Kilbeggan … 101 J 7
Kilbeheny … 94 H 11
Kilbennan … 105 F 7
Kilberry *Bert* … 108 L 6
Kilberry *Kildare* … 102 K 8
Kilbreedy … 94 F 10
Kilbrickan … 105 D 7
Kilbricken … 101 J 9
Kilbride *near Blessington* … 103 M 8
Kilbride *near Ratoah* … 103 M 7

A B C D E F G H I J K L M N O P Q R S T U V W X Y Z

Kilbride *near Trim* 108 L7
Kilbride *near Wicklow* 103 N9
Kilbrien 95 J11
Kilbrin 94 F11
Kilbrittain 90 F12
Kilcaimin 99 F8
Kilcar 112 G4
Kilcarn 108 L7
Kilcatherine Point 88 B12
Kilcavan 101 J8
Kilchreest 99 G8
Kilclaran 99 G9
Kilclief 115 P5
Kilcloher 93 C10
Kilclonfert 101 J8
Kilclooney 116 G3
Kilcock 102 L7
Kilcogy 107 J6
Kilcolgan 99 F8
Kilcolman *Cashel* 90 F12
Kilcolman
 Dunmoylan East 93 E10
Kilcoltrim 96 L10
Kilcomin 101 I9
Kilcommon *near Caher* 95 I10
Kilcommon *near Milestone* ..95 H9
Kilcon 111 E5
Kilconly *Galway* 105 F7
Kilconly *Kerry* 93 D10
Kilcoo 115 N5
Kilcoole 103 N8
Kilcormac 101 I8
Kilcornan 94 F10
Kilcotty 97 M10
Kilcredan 91 I12
Kilcredaun Point 93 C10
Kilcrohane 89 C13
Kilcrow 100 H8
Kilcullen 102 L8
Kilcummin *Kerry* 92 B11
Kilcummin *Mayo* 111 E5
Kilcummin Farmhill 93 D11
Kilcurly 109 M5
Kilcurry 109 M5
Kildalkey 108 L7
Kildangan 102 K8
Kildavin 96 L9
Kilderry 96 K9
Kildoney Point 112 H4
Kildorrery 94 G11
Kildress 114 L4
Kildrum 115 N3
Kilfeakle 95 H10
Kilfearagh 98 D10
Kilfenora 99 E9
Kilfinnane 94 G10
Kilfinny 94 F10
Kilflyn 93 D10
Kilgarvan 89 D12
Kilglass *Galway* 106 G7
Kilglass *Sligo* 111 E5
Kilglass Lough 107 H6
Kilgobnet *Kerry* 89 C11
Kilgobnet *Waterford* 91 J11
Kilgory Lough 99 F9
Kilgowan 102 L8
Kiljames 96 K10
Kilkea 102 L9
Kilkeary 100 H9
Kilkeasy 96 K10
Kilkeel 109 N5
Kilkeeran High Crosses 95 J10
Kilkerrin 106 G7
Kilkieran / Cill Chiaráin 104 C8
Kilkieran Bay 104 C7
Kilkiernan 96 K9
Kilkinamurry 115 N5
Kilkinlea 93 E10
Kilkishen 99 F9
Kill *Cavan* 108 K5
Kill *Waterford* 91 J11
Killabunane 89 D12
Killaclug 94 H11
Killacolla 94 F10
Killadangan 105 D6
Killadeas 113 I4
Killadoon 104 C6
Killadysert 99 E9
Killafeen 99 E9
Killag 96 M11
Killagan Bridge 118 M2
Killaghteen 93 E10
Killahy 95 J9
Killakee 103 N8
Killala 111 E5
Killala Bay 111 E5

Killallon 108 K6
Killaloo 118 K3
Killamery 95 J10
Killane 102 K8
Killanena 99 F9
Killann 96 L10
Killard 98 D9
Killard Point 115 P5
Killarga 112 H5
Killarney National Park 89 D11
Killarone 105 E7
Killary Harbour 104 C7
Killashandra 107 J5
Killashee 107 I6
Killasser 105 F6
Killavally *Mayo* 105 D6
Killavally *Westmeath* 101 J7
Killavil 106 G5
Killavullen 94 G11
Killea *Donegal* 117 J3
Killea *Tipperary* 101 I9
Killeagh 91 H12
Killealy 115 N3
Killeany 98 D8
Killedmond 96 L10
Killeedy 93 E10
Killeen *Ardamullivan* 99 F9
Killeen *Armagh* 114 M5
Killeen *Dungannon* 114 M4
Killeenaran 99 F8
Killeenleagh Bridge 88 B12
Killeevan 113 K5
Killeglan 106 H7
Killeigh 101 J8
Killen 113 J3
Killenagh 97 N10
Killenaule 95 I10
Killeshil 101 K8
Killeshin 102 K9
Killeter 113 I3
Killeter Forest 113 I3
Killevy 109 M5
Killevy Churches 109 M5
Killilan Bridge 99 G8
Killimer 93 D10
Killimor 100 H8
Killinaboy 99 E9
Killinaspick 96 K10
Killinchy 115 O4
Killincooly 97 N10
Killiney *Dublin* 103 N8
Killiney *Kerry* 92 B11
Killiney Bay 103 N8
Killinick 97 M11
Killinierin 97 N9
Killinkere 108 K6
Killinny 99 F8
Killinthomas 102 K8
Killinure Lough 107 I7
Killiskey 103 N8
Killkelly 105 F6
Killmuckbridge 97 N10
Killogeary 111 E5
Killogeenaghan 101 I7
Killonecaha 88 B12
Killoran 100 G8
Killoscobe 106 G7
Killough 115 P5
Killough 103 N8
Killowen 109 N5
Killucan 108 K7
Killukin 107 H6
Killurin 96 M10
Killurly 88 B12
Killusty 95 J10
Killwaughter 115 O3
Killyclogher 113 K4
Killyclug 117 I3
Killycolpy 114 M4
Killygar 107 J5
Killygordon 117 I3
Killykeen Forest Park 107 J5
Killylea 114 L4
Killyleagh 115 P4
Killyon 101 I8
Kilmacanoge 103 N8
Kilmacduagh Monastery 99 F8
Kilmacoo 103 N9
Kilmacow 96 K11
Kilmacrenan 117 I2
Kilmacteige 111 F5
Kilmacthomas 95 J11
Kilmactranny 106 H5
Kilmacurragh 103 N9
Kilmaganny 96 K10
Kilmaine 105 E7

Kilmainham Wood 108 L6
Kilmakilloge Harbour 88 C12
Kilmaley 99 E9
Kilmalkedar 92 B11
Kilmanagh 95 J10
Kilmeadan 96 K11
Kilmeage 102 L8
Kilmeedy 94 F10
Kilmeelickin 105 D7
Kilmeena 105 D6
Kilmessan 108 M7
Kilmichael
 near Castletownbere 88 B13
Kilmichael *near Macroom* ..89 E12
Kilmichael Point 97 N9
Kilmihil 98 E9
Kilmona 90 G12
Kilmoon 89 D13
Kilmore *Armagh* 114 M4
Kilmore *Clare* 99 G9
Kilmore *Down* 115 O4
Kilmore *Mayo* 105 E6
Kilmore *Roscommon* 107 H6
Kilmore *Wexford* 96 M11
Kilmore Quay 96 M11
Kilmorna 93 D10
Kilmorony 102 L9
Kilmovee 106 F6
Kilmurry *Cork* 90 F12
Kilmurry *Limerick* 94 G10
Kilmurry *near Kilkishen* 99 F9
Kilmurry *near Milltown* 98 D9
Kilmurry *Wicklow* 102 L9
Kilmurry Mac Mahon 93 E10
Kilmyshall 96 M10
Kilnagross 107 I6
Kilnalag 106 G6
Kilnaleck 107 K6
Kilnamanagh 97 M10
Kilnamona 99 E9
Kilntown 115 N4
Kilpatrick 90 F12
Kilpeacan Cross Roads 88 B12
Kilpedder 103 N8
Kilquiggin 97 M9
Kilraghts 118 M2
Kilrane 97 M11
Kilrea 118 M3
Kilrean 116 H3
Kilreekill 100 G8
Kilroghter 99 E8
Kilross *Donegal* 117 I3
Kilross *Tipperary* 94 H10
Kilruddery 103 N8
Kilsallagh *Galway* 106 G7
Kilsallagh *Mayo* 104 C6
Kilsallaghan 103 N7
Kilsally 114 M4
Kilsaran 109 M6
Kilshanchoe 102 L7
Kilshannig 92 B11
Kilshanny 99 E9
Kilsheelan 95 J10
Kilskeer 108 L6
Kilskeery 113 J4
Kiltealy 96 L10
Kilteel 103 M8
Kilteely 94 G10
Kiltegan 103 M9
Kilternan 103 N8
Kiltimagh 105 E6
Kiltober 101 J7
Kiltoom 107 H7
Kiltormer 100 H8
Kiltullagh 99 G8
Kiltyclogher 113 H4
Kilvine 105 F7
Kilworth 94 H11
Kilworth Mountains 94 H11
Kinale (Lough) 107 J6
Kinard 93 E10
Kinawley 113 J5
Kincasslagh 116 G2
Kindrohid 117 J2
Kindrum 117 I2
Kingarrow 117 H3
Kings River 95 J10
Kingscourt 108 L6
Kingsland 106 G6
Kingsmill 114 M4
Kingstown 104 B7
Kinlough 112 H4
Kinnadoohy 104 C6
Kinnagoe Bay 118 K2
Kinnegad 108 K7
Kinnitty 101 I8

Kinsale (Old Head of) 90 G13
Kinsale Harbour 90 G12
Kinsalebeg 91 I12
Kinvarra
 near Camus Bay 105 D7
Kinvarra
 near Kinvarra Bay 99 F8
Kinvarra Bay 99 F8
Kippure 103 N8
Kircubbin 115 P4
Kirkhills 118 M2
Kirkistown 115 P4
Kishkeam 93 E11
Kitconnell 100 G8
Knappagh 105 D6
Knappogue Castle 99 F9
Knight's Town 88 B12
Knock *Clare* 93 E10
Knock *Mayo* 105 F6
Knock *Tipperary* 101 I9
Knockaderry 94 F10
Knockadoon Head 91 I12
Knockainy 94 G10
Knockalla Mount 117 J2
Knockalongy 112 F5
Knockalough 99 E9
Knockanaffrin 95 J11
Knockananna 103 M9
Knockanefune 93 E11
Knockanevin 94 G11
Knockanillaun 111 E5
Knockanimpaha 93 E10
Knockanure 93 D10
Knockaunalour 90 G11
Knockaunavoher 94 G10
Knockaunnaglashy 92 C11
Knockboy *near Dungarvan* ..95 I11
Knockboy *near Waterford* 96 K11
Knockboy (Mount) 89 D12
Knockbrack 117 I3
Knockbrandon 97 M9
Knockbride 108 L6
Knockbridge 109 M6
Knockbrit 95 I10
Knockcloghrim 114 M3
Knockcroghery 106 H7
Knockdrin 107 K7
Knockerry 98 D10
Knockferry 105 E7
Knocklayd 119 N2
Knocklofty 95 I10
Knocklomena 89 C12
Knocklong 94 G10
Knockmealdown 95 I11
Knockmealdown
 Mountains 95 H11
Knockmore 104 B6
Knockmore (Mount) 104 C6
Knockmourne 90 H11
Knockmoy Abbey 106 F7
Knocknaboul Cross 93 E11
Knocknacarry 119 N2
Knocknacree 102 L9
Knocknadobar 88 B12
Knocknagantee 88 C12
Knocknagashel 93 D11
Knocknagree 93 E11
Knocknahilan 90 F12
Knocknalina 110 C5
Knocknalower 110 C5
Knockowen 89 C12
Knockraha 90 G12
Knocks *Cork* 89 F12
Knocks *Fermanagh* 113 J5
Knocks *Laois* 101 J8
Knockshanahullion 95 H11
Knockskagh 89 F12
Knocktopher 96 K10
Knocktown 96 M11
Knockundervaul 93 D10
Knockvicar 106 H5
Knowth 108 M6
Kylemore 100 H8
Kylemore Abbey 104 C7
Kylemore Lough 104 C7

L

Laban 99 F8
Labasheeda 93 E10
Lack 113 J4
Lackagh 102 K8
Lackan *Carlow* 96 K9
Lackan *Wicklow* 103 M8
Lackan bay 111 E5
Lackareagh 89 F12
Laconnell 116 G3

Ladies View 89 D12
Lady's Island Lake 97 M11
Ladysbridge 90 H12
Ladywell 96 K10
Laffansbridge 95 I10
Lag 117 K2
Lagan (River) 115 N4
Lagan Valley 115 O4
Lagavara 118 M2
Lagganstown 95 I10
Laghey Corner 114 L4
Laghtnafrankee 95 J11
Laghy 113 H4
Lahardaun 111 E5
Lakyle 93 E10
Lambay Island 109 N7
Lambeg 115 N4
Lamb's Head 88 B12
Lanesborough 107 I6
Laney (River) 89 F12
Laracor 108 L7
Laragh *Kildare* 102 L7
Laragh *Monaghan* 108 L5
Laragh *Wicklow* 103 N8
Largan *Mayo* 111 D5
Largan *Sligo* 111 F5
Largy 112 G4
Largydonnell 112 H4
Larne 115 O3
Larne Lough 115 O3
Lattin 94 H10
Laune (River) 93 C11
Lauragh 88 C12
Laurelvale 114 M4
Laurencetown 100 H8
Lavagh 112 F5
Lavagh More 117 H3
Lawrencetown 114 N4
Leabgarrow 116 G3
League (Slieve) 112 F4
League Point 89 D13
Leamaneh Castle 99 E9
Leamlara 90 H12
Leamore Strand 103 N8
Leane (Lough) 89 D11
Leannan (River) 117 I2
Leap 89 E13
Leap (The)
 near Enniscorthy 96 M10
Leap (The) *near New Ross* .96 L10
Lecale Peninsula 115 O5
Lecarrow *Leitrim* 112 H5
Lecarrow *Roscommon* 107 H7
Leckanarainey 112 H4
Leckanvy 105 C6
Leckaun 112 H5
Leckavrea Mountain 105 D7
Leckemy 118 K2
Lee 93 C11
Lee (River) 90 G12
Lee Reservoir 90 F12
Leek Point 93 C10
Leenane 104 C7
Legan or Lenamore 107 J7
Leganany Dolmen 115 N5
Leggah 107 J6
Legoniel 115 O4
Lehardan 117 J2
Leighlinbridge 96 L9
Leinster (Mount) 96 L10
Leitir Meallàin /
 Lettermullan 98 C8
Leitir Mhic an Bhaird /
 Lettermacaward 116 H3
Leitrim *Banbridge* 115 O5
Leitrim *Creegh* 98 D9
Leitrim *Leitrim* 107 H6
Leixlip 103 M7
Lemanaghan 101 I8
Lemybrien 91 J11
Lenadoon Point 111 E5
Lenan Head 117 J2
Lene (Lough) 107 K7
Lerrig 93 C10
Leslie Hill 114 L5
Letterbarra 112 H3
Letterbreen 113 I5
Lettercallow 98 C8
Lettercraffroe Lough 105 D7
Letterfinish 88 C12
Letterfrack 104 C7
Letterkelly 99 E9
Letterkenny /
 Leitir Ceanainn 117 I3
Letterleague 117 I3
Lettermore 98 D8
Lettermore Island 98 C8

Levally 106 F7
Levally Lough 105 E6
Licketstown 96 K11
Liffey (River) 102 M8
Lifford 117 J3
Light House Island 115 P3
Limavady 118 L2
Limerick / Luimneach 94 G10
Limerick Junction 95 H10
Lios Dúin Bhearna /
 Lisdoonvarna 99 E8
Lios Mór / Lismore 91 I11
Lios Póil / Lispole 92 B11
Lios Tuathail / Listowel 93 D10
Lisacul 106 G6
Lisbane 115 O4
Lisbellaw 113 J5
Lisburn 115 N4
Liscannor 98 D9
Liscannor Bay 98 D9
Liscarney 105 D6
Liscarroll 94 F11
Liscolman 118 M2
Liscooly 117 J3
Lisdoart 114 K4
Lisdowney 101 J9
Lisduff *Cavan* 108 K6
Lisduff *Leitrim* 107 I6
Lisduff *Offaly* 101 I8
Lisgarode 100 H9
Lisgoold 90 H12
Lislea *Magherafelt* 118 M3
Lislea *Newry-Mourne* 114 M5
Lismacaffry 107 J6
Lismoghry 117 J3
Lismoyle 106 H7
Lisnacree 109 N5
Lisnageer 108 K5
Lisnagleer 114 L4
Lisnagry 94 G9
Lisnagunogue 118 M2
Lisnamuck 118 L3
Lisnarrick 113 I4
Lisnaskea 113 J5
Lisnavagh 102 L9
Lispatrick 90 G13
Lisroe 99 E9
Lisronagh 95 I10
Lisryan 107 J6
Lissadell House 112 G4
Lissalway 106 G6
Lissamona 89 D13
Lissatinnig Bridge 88 C12
Lissavaird 89 F13
Lisselton 93 D10
Lissinagroagh 112 H5
Lissiniska 112 H4
Lissycasey 99 E9
Listellick 93 C11
Listerlin 96 K10
Listooder 115 O4
Lisvarrinane 94 H10
Little Bray 103 N8
Little Island 90 G12
Little Skellig 88 A12
Littleton 95 I10
Lixnaw 93 D10
Loanends 115 N4
Lobinstown 108 M6
Loch Garman / Wexford 97 M10
Loghill 93 E10
Lombardstown 94 F11
Londonderry 117 K3
Lonehort Point 88 C13
Long Island 89 D13
Longford 101 I8
Longhill 101 K9
Longwood 108 L7
Loo Bridge 89 D12
Loobagh 94 G10
Loop Head 92 C10
Lorrha 100 H8
Loskeran 91 J11
Losset *Cavan* 107 J6
Losset *Donegal* 117 I2
Lough Bradan Forest 113 J4
Lough Gowna 107 J6
Lough Key Forest Park 106 H6
Lough Navar Forest 113 I4
Loughanavally 107 J7
Loughanillaunmore 98 D8
Loughanure 116 H2
Loughbrickland 114 N5
Lougher 92 C11
Loughermore 118 K3
Loughfad Hill 113 I4
Loughgall 114 M4

Loughglinn .... 106 G 6
Loughguile .... 119 N 2
Loughinisland .... 115 O 4
Loughlinstown .... 103 N 8
Loughmoe .... 101 I 9
Loughmorne .... 108 L 5
Loughros More Bay ....116 G 3
Loughros Point ....116 G 3
Loughsalt Mount ....117 I 2
Loughshinny .... 109 N 7
Louisburgh .... 104 C 6
Loup (The) .... 114 M 3
Louth .... 108 M 6
Lower Ballinderry .... 114 N 4
Lower Lake .... 103 N 8
Lowertown ....89 D 13
Lowerymore .... 113 I 3
Lowtown .... 115 N 5
Lucan .... 103 M 7
Luggacurren .... 101 K 9
Lugnaquillia Mountain .... 103 M 9
Luimneach / Limerick ....94 G 10
Lukeswell ....96 K 10
Lullymore .... 102 L 8
Lurgan Craigavon .... 114 N 4
Lurgan Frenchpark .... 106 G 6
Lurganboy Donegal ....117 J 2
Lurganboy Leitrim ....112 H 5
Lusk .... 109 N 7
Lyle .... 115 N 3
Lyracrumpane ....93 D 10
Lyre ....90 F 11
Lyrenagloagh ....95 H 11

M

Maas ....116 G 3
Mac Gregor's Corner ....119 N 3
Mac Laughlins Corner ....118 M 3
Mac Mahon's Town ....114 K 4
Mac Swyne's Bay ....112 G 4
Mace .... 105 D 6
Mace Head .... 104 C 8
Macgillycuddy's Reeks .....89 C 12
Machugh (Lough) ....116 G 3
Mackan .... 113 J 5
Macnean Lower (Lough) ...113 I 5
Macnean Upper (Lough) ...113 I 5
Macosquin ....118 L 2
Macroom/
Maigh Chromtha ....89 F 12
Maddan .... 114 L 5
Maddockstown ....96 K 10
Maganey .... 102 L 9
Magee (Island) ....115 O 3
Maghaberry .... 115 N 4
Maghanlawaun ....89 C 12
Maghera Clare ....99 F 9
Maghera Donegal ....116 G 3
Maghera Down .... 115 O 5
Maghera Magherafelt ....118 L 3
Magherabane ....117 J 2
Magherafelt .... 114 M 3
Magheragall .... 115 N 4
Magheralin .... 114 N 4
Magheramason ....117 J 3
Magheramorne .... 115 O 3
Magheraveely .... 113 K 5
Maghery near Dungannon .114 M 4
Maghery near Dunglow ....116 G 3
Magilligan .... 118 L 2
Magilligan Point .... 118 L 2
Magilligan Strand .... 118 L 2
Maguiresbridge ....113 J 5
Mahee Island ....115 P 4
Mahon ....95 J 11
Mahon (Lough) ....90 G 12
Mahoonagh ....93 E 10
Maigh Chromtha /
Macroom ....89 F 12
Maigh Cuilinn /
Moycullen .... 105 E 7
Maigh Nuad / Maynooth ..103 M 7
Maigue (River) ....94 F 10
Main ....118 N 3
Maine (River) ....93 C 11
Mainham .... 102 L 8
Mainistir Fhear Maí /
Fermoy ....90 H 11
Mainistir na Búille /
Boyle .... 106 H 6
Mainistir na Corann /
Midleton ....90 H 12
Máistir Gaoithe /
Mastergeehy ....88 B 12
Mal Bay ....98 D 9
Mala / Mallow ....94 G 11
Málainn Bhig / Malin Beg ..112 F 3

Malin ....118 K 2
Malin Bay ....112 F 3
Malin Head ....117 J 1
Malin More ....112 F 3
Mallusk ....115 N 3
Mamore (Gap of) ....117 J 2
Manger ....112 H 4
Mangerton Mountain ....89 D 12
Mannin Bay .... 104 B 7
Mannin Lake .... 105 F 6
Manorcunningham ....117 J 3
Manselstown ....95 I 9
Mansfieldstown .... 109 M 6
Mantua .... 106 H 6
Manulla .... 105 E 6
Manulla (River) .... 105 E 6
Maothail / Mohill .... 107 I 6
Marble Arch Caves ....113 I 5
Marble Hill ....117 I 2
Mardyke ....95 J 10
Markethill .... 114 M 5
Marshalstown ....96 M 10
Martin .... 90 G 12
Martinstown Emlygrennan ..94 G 10
Martinstown
Grennanstown ....108 L 7
Martinstown
South Somerset ....119 N 3
Mask (Lough) .... 105 D 7
Massford .... 115 N 4
Masshill ....112 F 5
Masterstown ....95 I 10
Matehy ....90 G 12
Matrix (Castle) ....94 F 10
Mattock (River) ....108 M 6
Mauherslieve ....95 H 9
Maum .... 105 D 7
Maumakeogh ....111 D 5
Maumeen Lough .... 104 B 7
Maumtrasna .... 105 D 7
Maumturk Mountains ...... 104 C 7
Mauricesmills ....99 E 9
Mayo .... 105 E 6
Mayo (Plains of) .... 105 E 6
Mayobridge .... 114 N 5
Mazetown .... 115 N 4
Mealagh ....89 D 12
Meanus ....94 G 10
Meathas Troim /
Edgeworthstown .... 107 J 6
Meela (Lough) ....116 G 3
Meelick .... 100 H 8
Meelin ....93 E 11
Meenaclady ....116 H 2
Meenacross ....116 G 3
Meenanarwa ....117 H 3
Meenaneary /
Min na Aoire .... 112 G 3
Meenatotan ....116 H 3
Meenavean ....112 F 3
Meencorwick ....116 H 3
Meenglass ....113 I 3
Meenlaragh ....117 H 2
Meenreagh ....113 I 3
Meentullynagarn ....112 G 3
Meenybraddan ....112 H 3
Meeting of the Waters ..... 103 N 9
Mellifont Abbey .... 109 M 6
Melmore Head ....117 I 2
Melvin (Lough) ....112 H 4
Menlough .... 106 G 7
Mew Island ....115 P 4
Michelstown Caves ....95 H 11
Middletown ....116 H 2
Middletown Armagh .... 114 L 5
Midfield .... 105 F 6
Mile ....117 J 2
Milebush ....115 O 3
Milehouse ....96 M 10
Milemill .... 102 L 8
Milestone ....95 H 9
Milford Armagh .... 114 L 5
Milford Cork ....94 F 10
Mill Town .... 114 L 5
Millbay ....115 O 3
Millbrook Derry ....118 K 3
Millbrook Larne .... 115 O 3
Millbrook Oldcastle .... 108 K 6
Milleen ....93 E 11
Millford ....117 I 2
Millisle ....115 P 4
Millroad ....96 M 11
Millstreet Cork ....89 E 11
Millstreet Waterford ....91 I 11
Milltown Armagh .... 114 L 5
Milltown Ballymoney ....118 M 2
Milltown Banbridge .... 114 N 5

Milltown Cavan .... 107 J 5
Milltown Craigavon .... 114 M 4
Milltown Dublin .... 103 M 8
Milltown Kildare .... 102 L 8
Milltown near Dingle ....92 B 11
Milltown
near Mount Bellew ..... 106 G 7
Milltown near Tralee ....93 C 11
Milltown near Tuam .... 105 F 7
Milltown Omagh ....114 K 4
Milltown Wexford ....97 M 10
Miltownpass .... 107 K 7
Minane Bridge ....90 G 12
Minard Head ....92 B 11
Mine Head ....91 J 12
Minerstown ....115 O 5
Minterburn .... 114 L 4
Mizen Head ....88 C 13
Moanmore ....98 D 9
Modelligo ....91 I 11
Modreeny .... 100 H 9
Mogeely ....90 H 12
Moglass ....95 I 10
Moher (Cliffs of) ....98 D 9
Moher Lough .... 105 D 6
Mohil ....96 K 9
Móinteach Milic /
Mountmellick .... 101 K 8
Moira .... 115 N 4
Moll's Gap ....89 D 12
Monard ....95 H 10
Monaseed ....97 M 9
Monàster ....94 G 10
Monasteraden .... 106 G 6
Monasteranenagh Abbey ..94 G 10
Monasterboice .... 109 M 6
Monasterevin .... 102 K 8
Monavullagh Mountains ...95 J 11
Mondello Park .... 102 L 8
Monea ....113 I 4
Moneen Clare ....93 C 10
Moneen Galway .... 105 F 7
Money Point ....93 D 10
Moneydig ....118 M 3
Moneygall .... 101 I 9
Moneyglass .... 114 M 3
Moneygold ....112 G 4
Moneylahan ....112 G 4
Moneymore .... 114 L 3
Moneyneany ....118 L 3
Moneyreagh ....115 O 4
Monilea .... 107 K 7
Monivea .... 106 F 7
Monkstown Cork ....90 G 12
Monkstown
Newtownabbey ....115 O 3
Monroe .... 107 J 7
Montpelier ....99 G 9
Mooncoin ....96 K 11
Moone .... 102 L 9
Moord ....91 I 12
Moore Bay ....98 C 9
Moorfields ....115 N 3
More (Island) .... 105 D 6
Morenane ....94 F 10
Morley's Bridge ....89 D 12
Morningstar ....94 G 10
Mornington .... 109 N 6
Mosney .... 109 N 7
Moss-Side ....118 M 2
Mossley ....115 O 3
Mothel ....95 J 11
Motte Stone .... 103 N 9
Mount Falcon .... 111 E 5
Mount Garret ....96 L 10
Mount Hamilton or Sperrin 114 K 3
Mount Melleray Monastery .95 I 11
Mount Norris .... 114 M 5
Mount Nugent .... 107 K 6
Mount Stewart Gardens ...115 P 4
Mount Talbot .... 106 H 7
Mount Temple .... 107 I 7
Mount Uniacke ....91 H 12
Mount Usher Gardens ..... 103 N 8
Mountbolus .... 101 J 8
Mountcastle ....117 J 3
Mountcharles ....112 H 4
Mountcollins ....93 E 11
Mountfield .... 114 K 4
Mountfinn .... 114 K 4
Mounthenry .... 105 E 7
Mountjoy Dungannon ....114 M 4
Mountjoy Omagh .... 113 J 4
Mountrath .... 101 J 8
Mountrivers Bridge ....98 D 9
Mountshannon .... 100 G 9
Mourne (Lough)
near Ballybofey ....113 I 3

Mourne (Lough)
near Carrickfergus ....115 O 3
Mourne Beg .... 113 I 3
Mourne Mountains .... 109 N 5
Mourne River .... 113 J 3
Moveen .... 98 C 10
Moville / Bun an Phobail ..118 K 2
Mowhan .... 114 M 5
Moy .... 114 L 4
Moy (River) .... 111 E 5
Moyagh ....117 J 3
Moyallan .... 114 M 4
Moyard .... 104 B 7
Moyarget .... 118 N 2
Moyasta ....98 D 9
Moydow .... 107 I 7
Moygashel .... 114 L 4
Moyglass ....99 G 8
Moylough Galway .... 106 G 7
Moylough Sligo .... 106 F 5
Moynalty .... 108 L 6
Moynalvy .... 108 L 7
Moyne Roscommon .... 106 G 6
Moyne Tipperary .... 107 J 6
Moyne Wicklow .... 103 M 9
Moyne Abbey .... 111 E 5
Moyrus .... 104 C 7
Moyteoge Head .... 110 B 6
Moyvally .... 102 L 7
Moyvore .... 107 J 7
Moyvoughly .... 107 I 7
Muck (Isle of) .... 115 O 3
Muckamore .... 115 N 3
Muckanagh Lough ....99 F 9
Muckish Mountain ....117 H 2
Mucklon .... 102 L 7
Muckno Lake .... 108 L 5
Muckros Head ....112 G 4
Muckross ....89 D 11
Muff .... 117 K 2
Muggort's Bay ....91 J 11
Muinchille / Cootehill ..... 108 K 5
Muine Bheag /
Bagenalstown ....96 L 9
Muineachán / Monaghan ..114 L 5
Muing .... 111 D 5
Muingnabo .... 111 C 5
Mulhuddart .... 103 M 7
Mulkear ....94 G 10
Mullach Íde / Malahide ... 103 N 7
Mullagh Cavan .... 108 L 6
Mullagh Galway .... 100 G 8
Mullagh Mayo .... 104 C 6
Mullagh Meath .... 103 M 7
Mullaghanattin ....88 C 12
Mullaghanish ....89 E 12
Mullaghareirk Mountains ..93 E 10
Mullaghash .... 118 K 3
Mullaghbane .... 109 M 5
Mullaghboy ....115 O 3
Mullaghcarn .... 113 K 3
Mullaghcleevaun .... 103 M 8
Mullaghclogha .... 114 K 3
Mullaghmore
Cliffony North .... 112 G 4
Mullaghmore Magherafelt .118 L 3
Mullaghmore Head .... 112 G 4
Mullaghroe .... 106 G 6
Mullan Coleraine ....118 L 2
Mullan Figullar ....114 L 4
Mullany'sCross .... 111 F 5
Mullartown .... 109 O 5
Mullen .... 106 G 6
Mullenbeg ....96 K 10
Mullet Peninsula .... 110 B 5
Mullinahone ....95 J 10
Mullinasole .... 112 H 4
Mullinavat ....96 K 10
Mulroy Bay ....117 I 2
Multyfarnham .... 107 J 7
Mungret ....94 F 10
Muntervary
or Sheep's Head ....88 C 13
Murley .... 113 K 4
Murlough Bay .... 119 N 2
Murntown ....97 M 11
Murreagh ....92 A 11
Murrisk .... 105 D 6
Murroogh ....99 E 8
Murroe ....94 G 10
Musheramore ....89 F 11
Mussenden Temple ....118 L 2
Mutton Island ....98 D 9
Mweelrea Mountains .... 104 C 7
Mweenish Island .... 104 C 8
Myshall ....96 L 9

N

Na Cealla Beaga /
Killybegs ....112 G 4
Na Clocha Liatha /
Greystones .... 103 N 8
Na Dúnaibh / Downies ......117 I 2
Na Sceirí / Skerries .... 109 N 7
Nacorra (Lough) .... 105 D 6
Nacung (Lough) ....117 H 2
Nad ....90 F 11
Nafooey (Lough) .... 105 D 7
Nagles Mountains ....90 G 11
Nalughraman (Lough) ......116 G 3
Naminn (Lough) ....117 J 2
Namona (Lough) ....88 B 12
Nanny .... 108 M 7
Narin ....116 G 3
Narraghmore .... 102 L 8
Narrow Water Castle .... 109 N 5
Naul .... 109 N 7
Neagh (Lough) .... 114 M 4
Neale .... 105 E 7
Nealstown .... 101 I 9
Neidín / Kenmare ....89 D 12
Nephin .... 111 D 5
Nephin (Glen) .... 105 D 6
Nephin Beg .... 111 D 5
Nephin Beg Range .... 111 C 5
New Birmingham ....95 J 10
New Buildings ....117 J 3
New Inn Cavan .... 108 K 6
New Inn Galway .... 100 G 8
New Kildimo ....94 F 10
New Quay / Bealaclugga ...99 E 8
New Twopothouse Village ..94 G 11
Newbawn ....96 L 10
Newbliss .... 113 K 5
New Inn Cavan .... 108 K 6
Newbridge
near Tuomard .... 106 G 7
Newbridge /
An Droichead Nua ...... 102 L 8
Newcastle Down .... 115 O 5
Newcastle Dublin .... 103 M 8
Newcastle Tipperary ....95 I 11
Newcastle Wicklow .... 103 N 8
Newcestown ....90 F 12
Newchapel ....95 I 10
Newferry .... 114 M 3
Newgrange .... 109 M 6
Newmarket Cork ....93 E 11
Newmarket Kilkenny ....96 K 10
Newmarket on Fergus ....99 F 9
Newmills Donegal ....117 I 3
Newmills Dungannon .... 114 L 4
Newport Tipperary .... 100 G 9
Newport Bay .... 105 C 6
Newport Trench .... 114 M 4
Newry .... 114 M 5
Newtown Cork ....94 G 11
Newtown Galway ....99 F 8
Newtown Kildare .... 102 L 7
Newtown Laois .... 101 K 9
Newtown Limerick ....94 G 10
Newtown near Knock ...... 101 I 9
Newtown near Nenagh .... 100 H 9
Newtown Offaly .... 100 H 8
Newtown Roscommon ..... 100 H 7
Newtown Tipperary ....95 H 10
Newtown Waterford ....95 J 11
Newtown Wexford ....96 M 11
Newtown Cashel .... 107 I 7
Newtown Cloghans .... 111 E 5
Newtown-Crommelin .... 119 N 3
Newtown Cunningham ..... 117 J 3
Newtown Forbes .... 107 I 6
Newtown Gore .... 107 I 5
Newtown
Mount Kennedy .... 103 N 8
Newtown Sandes ....93 D 10
Newtownabbey ....115 O 4
Newtownards .... 115 O 4
Newtownbreda .... 115 O 4
Newtownbutler .... 113 K 5
Newtownhamilton .... 114 M 5
Newtownlow .... 101 J 7
Newtownlynch ....99 E 8
Newtownshandrum ....94 F 10
Newtownstewart .... 113 J 3
Nier ....95 J 11
Ninemilehouse ....95 J 10
Nobber .... 108 L 6

Nohaval ....90 G 12
Nore .... 101 J 9
Nore (River) ....96 K 10
North Channel .... 119 O 2
North Ring ....90 F 13
North Sound ....98 C 8
Nose of Howth .... 103 N 7
Noughaval Doora ....99 F 9
Noughaval Noughaval ....99 E 8
Nowen Hill ....89 E 12
Nuns Quarter ....115 O 4
Nurney Carlow ....96 L 9
Nurney Kildare .... 102 L 8
Nutt's Corner ....115 N 4

O

Oaghley ....93 D 10
Oatfield ....99 F 9
Oatquarter ....98 C 8
O'Brien's Tower ....98 D 9
O'Flynn (Lough) .... 106 G 6
Oghil Clare .... 100 H 8
Oghil Galway ....98 C 8
Ogonnelloe ....99 G 9
O'Grady (Lough) ....99 G 9
Oileán Ciarraí /
Castleisland ....93 D 11
Oilgate ....97 M 10
Oily ....112 G 4
Old Court ....89 E 13
Old Head Ballymackean ....90 G 13
Old Head Louisburgh ...... 104 C 6
Old Kilcullen .... 102 L 8
Old Kildimo ....94 F 10
Old Ross ....96 L 10
Old Town Donegal ....117 I 3
Old Town Laois .... 101 J 9
Old Town Roscommon ..... 100 H 8
Old Town Wexford ....96 L 10
Old Twopothouse ....94 G 11
Oldleighlin ....96 K 9
Oldmill Bridge ....93 E 10
Oldtown Dublin .... 109 N 7
Oldtown Roscommon ...... 101 I 7
Omagh .... 113 K 4
Omeath .... 109 N 5
Omey Island .... 104 B 7
Onaght ....98 C 8
Oola ....94 H 10
Oorid Lough .... 105 D 7
Oranmore ....99 F 8
Oriel (Mount) .... 108 M 6
Oristown .... 108 L 6
Oritor .... 114 L 4
Ossian's Grave .... 119 N 2
Oughter (Lough) .... 107 J 6
Oulart ....97 M 10
Ovens ....90 G 12
Owel (Lough) .... 107 J 7
Owenascaul ....92 B 11
Owenator ....116 H 3
Owenavorragh ....97 M 10
Owenbeagh ....117 H 3
Owenbeg .... 111 F 5
Owenbeg (River) ....112 G 5
Owenboliska ....99 E 8
Owenboy ....90 G 12
Owenbristy ....99 F 8
Owencarrow ....117 I 2
Owendalulleegh ....99 G 8
Owenea ....116 G 3
Owengarve Clew Bay ...... 105 D 6
Owengarve River Moy ..... 106 F 5
Owenglin .... 104 C 7
Oweniny .... 111 D 5
Owenkillew Glenelly .... 114 K 3
Owenkillew Lough Swilly ..117 J 2
Owenmore Bridge .... 105 D 6
Owenmacurra ....90 H 12
Owenreagh Hill ....117 J 3
Owenriff .... 105 D 7
Owentaraglin ....93 E 11
Owentocker .... 116 H 3
Owenur (River) .... 106 H 6
Ower .... 105 E 7
Owning ....95 J 10
Owroe Bridge ....88 B 12
Owvane ....89 D 12
Oysterhaven ....90 G 12

P

Palace ....96 L 10
Palatine .... 102 L 9
Pallas .... 101 J 8
Pallas Cross .... 100 I 9
Pallas Green ....94 G 10
Pallaskenry ....94 F 10

A B C D E F G H I J K L M N O P Q R S T U V W X Y Z

A B C D E F G H I J K L M N O P Q R S T U V W X Y Z

Paps (The) ... 89 E 11
Park Bellavary ... 105 E 6
Park Derry ... 118 K 3
Parke's Castle ... 112 H 5
Parkgate ... 115 N 3
Parkmore ... 99 F 8
Parkmore Point ... 92 A 11
Parknasilla ... 88 C 12
Parteen ... 99 G 9
Partry ... 105 E 6
Partry Mountains ... 105 D 7
Passage ... 106 H 7
Passage East ... 96 L 11
Passage West ... 90 G 12
Patrickswell ... 94 F 10
Patterson's Spade Mill ... 115 N 3
Paulstown ... 96 K 9
Peake ... 90 F 12
Peatlands ... 114 M 4
Peterswell ... 99 F 8
Pettigoe ... 113 I 4
Phoenix Park ... 103 M 7
Piercetown ... 97 M 11
Pigeons (The) ... 107 I 7
Pike ... 100 H 8
Pike (The) near Boola ... 91 I 11
Pike (The) near Lamybrien ... 91 J 11
Pike (The) Tipperary ... 100 H 8
Pike Corner ... 108 L 7
Pike of Rush Hall ... 101 J 9
Piltown ... 95 K 10
Pluck ... 117 J 3
Plumbridge ... 113 K 3
Pollagh ... 101 I 8
Pollan Bay ... 117 J 2
Pollatomish ... 111 C 5
Pollnalaght ... 113 J 4
Pollshask ... 106 G 7
Pomeroy ... 114 L 4
Pontoon ... 105 E 6
Port ... 116 F 3
Port Ballintrae ... 118 M 2
Port Durlainne / Porturlin ... 111 C 5
Port Láirge / Waterford ... 96 K 11
Port Laoise / Portlaoise ... 101 K 8
Port Omna / Portumna ... 100 H 8
Portacloy ... 111 C 5
Portadown ... 114 M 4
Portaferry ... 115 P 4
Portaleen ... 118 K 2
Portavogie ... 115 P 4
Portbradden ... 118 M 2
Portglenone ... 118 M 3
Portland ... 100 H 8
Portlaw ... 96 K 11
Portmagee ... 88 A 12
Portmagee Channel ... 88 A 12
Portmarnock ... 103 N 7
Portmuck ... 115 O 3
Portnablagh ... 117 I 2
Portnoo ... 116 G 3
Portrane ... 109 N 7
Portroe ... 100 G 9
Portrush ... 118 M 2
Portsalon ... 117 J 2
Portstewart ... 118 L 2
Poulaphouca Reservoir ... 103 M 8
Poulnamucky ... 95 I 10
Poulnasherry Bay ... 98 D 10
Power Head ... 90 H 12
Power's Cross ... 100 H 8
Powerscourt Demesne ... 103 N 8
Powerstown ... 96 K 10
Poyntz Pass ... 114 M 5
Priesthaggard ... 96 L 11
Prosperous ... 102 L 8
Puckaun ... 100 H 9
Puffin Island ... 88 A 12
Punchestown ... 103 M 8

Q
Quarrytown ... 119 N 3
Querrin ... 93 D 10
Quigley's Point ... 118 K 2
Quilty ... 98 D 9
Quin ... 99 F 9
Quoile ... 115 O 4

R
Rabbit Islands ... 89 E 13
Race End ... 117 I 2
Raffrey ... 115 O 4
Raghly ... 112 G 5
Raghtin More ... 117 J 2
Rahan ... 101 J 8
Rahanagh ... 93 E 10
Rahara ... 106 H 7

Raharney ... 108 K 7
Raheen ... 96 L 10
Raigh ... 105 D 7
Railyard ... 101 K 9
Rake Street ... 111 D 5
Ram Head ... 91 I 12
Ramor (Lough) ... 108 K 6
Ramore Head ... 118 M 2
Rams Island ... 114 N 4
Ramsgrange ... 96 L 11
Randalstown ... 114 N 3
Rapemills ... 101 I 8
Raphoe ... 117 J 3
Rasharkin ... 118 M 3
Rashedoge ... 117 I 3
Rath ... 101 I 8
Ráth Caola / Rathkeale ... 94 F 10
Ráth Droma / Rathdrum ... 103 N 9
Rathangan ... 102 L 8
Rathaspick ... 107 J 7
Rathbrit ... 95 I 10
Rathcabban ... 100 H 8
Rathconrath ... 107 J 7
Rathcool ... 89 F 11
Rathcoole ... 103 M 8
Rathcor ... 109 N 6
Rathcore ... 102 L 7
Rathcormack near Fermoy ... 90 H 11
Rathcormack near Sligo ... 112 G 5
Rathcroghan ... 106 H 6
Rathdangan ... 103 M 9
Rathdowney ... 101 J 9
Rathduff ... 90 G 11
Rathedan ... 96 L 9
Rathfeigh ... 108 M 7
Rathfriland ... 115 N 5
Rathfylane ... 96 L 10
Rathgarogue ... 96 L 10
Rathgormuck ... 95 J 11
Rathkeevin ... 95 I 10
Rathkenny ... 108 M 6
Rathlackan ... 111 E 5
Rathlee ... 111 E 5
Rathlin Island ... 119 N 2
Rathlin O'Birne Island ... 112 F 4
Rathlin Sound ... 119 N 2
Rathmelton ... 117 J 2
Rathmines ... 103 N 8
Rathmolyon ... 108 L 7
Rathmore ... 89 E 11
Rathmullan ... 117 J 2
Rathnew ... 103 N 9
Rathnure ... 96 L 10
Rathoma ... 111 E 5
Rathowen ... 107 J 7
Rathvilla ... 101 K 8
Rathvilly ... 102 L 9
Ratoath ... 108 M 7
Raven Point (The) ... 97 M 10
Ravensdale ... 109 M 5
Ray near Dunfanaghy ... 117 H 2
Ray near Rathmullan ... 117 J 2
Ray (River) ... 117 H 2
Rea (Lough) ... 99 G 8
Reaghstown ... 108 M 6
Reananeree / Rae na nDoirí ... 89 E 12
Reanascreena ... 89 E 13
Rear Cross ... 95 H 9
Red Bay ... 119 N 2
Redcastle ... 118 K 2
Redcross ... 103 N 9
Redgate ... 97 M 10
Redhills ... 107 K 5
Ree (Lough) ... 107 I 7
Reelan ... 117 H 3
Reen ... 89 D 12
Reens ... 94 F 10
Reevanagh ... 96 K 9
Relaghbeg ... 108 L 6
Rerrin ... 88 C 13
Rhode ... 101 K 7
Richhill ... 114 M 4
Ridge ... 96 K 9
Ridge Point ... 110 C 5
Rine (River) ... 99 F 9
Rineanna Point ... 99 F 9
Ringabella Bay ... 90 H 12
Ringarogy Island ... 89 D 13
Ringaskiddy ... 90 H 12
Ringboy ... 115 P 4
Ringfad Point ... 115 P 5
Ringsend ... 118 L 2
Ringstown ... 101 J 8
Ringville / An Rinn ... 91 J 11
Rinmore Point ... 117 I 2

Rinn (River) ... 107 I 6
Rinn Lough ... 107 I 6
Rinneen Clare ... 98 D 9
Rinneen Cork ... 89 E 13
Rinroe Point ... 110 C 5
Rinville ... 99 F 8
Rinvyle ... 104 C 7
Rinvyle Castle ... 104 B 7
Rinvyle Point ... 104 B 7
River ... 110 B 6
Riverchapel ... 97 N 10
Riverstick ... 90 G 12
Riverstown Cork ... 90 G 12
Riverstown Sligo ... 112 G 5
Riverstown Tipperary ... 101 I 8
Riverville ... 93 D 11
Roadford ... 98 D 8
Roaninish ... 116 G 3
Roaringwater Bay ... 89 D 13
Robe ... 105 E 6
Robert's Head ... 90 H 12
Robertstown ... 102 L 8
Robinstown ... 108 L 7
Roche's Point ... 90 H 12
Rochestown ... 96 K 11
Rochfortbridge ... 101 K 7
Rock (The) ... 114 L 4
Rock Island ... 98 C 8
Rockabill ... 109 N 7
Rockchapel ... 93 E 11
Rockcorry ... 108 K 5
Rockhill ... 94 F 10
Rockmills ... 94 G 11
Rodeen ... 107 H 6
Roe ... 118 L 3
Roe Valley ... 118 L 2
Roney Point ... 97 N 10
Rooaun ... 100 H 8
Roonagh Quay ... 104 C 6
Roonah Lough ... 104 C 6
Roosky Leitrim ... 112 H 4
Roosky Mayo ... 106 F 6
Roosky Roscommon ... 107 I 6
Ropefield ... 112 G 5
Ros an Mhil / Rossaveel ... 98 D 8
Ros Comáin / Roscommon ... 106 H 7
Ros Cré / Roscrea ... 101 I 9
Ros Láir / Rosslare ... 97 M 11
Ros Mhic Thriúin / New Ross ... 96 L 10
Rosapenna ... 117 I 2
Rosbercon ... 96 L 10
Rosegreen ... 95 I 10
Rosenallis ... 101 J 8
Rosguill ... 117 I 2
Roskeeragh Point ... 112 F 4
Rosmuck ... 105 D 7
Rosmult ... 95 I 9
Rosnakill ... 117 I 2
Ross near Dunfanaghy ... 89 D 11
Ross Lough Leane ... 89 D 11
Ross Lough Sheelin ... 107 K 6
Ross Abbey ... 105 E 7
Ross Lake ... 105 E 7
Ross Port ... 111 C 5
Ross West ... 105 E 6
Rossan Point ... 112 F 3
Rossbeg ... 116 G 3
Rossbeigh Creek ... 92 C 11
Rossbrin ... 89 D 13
Rosscahill ... 105 E 7
Rosscarbery ... 89 E 13
Rosscarbery Bay ... 89 E 13
Rosscor ... 113 H 4
Rossdohan Island ... 88 C 12
Rosserk Abbey ... 111 E 5
Rosses (The) ... 116 G 2
Rosses Bay ... 116 G 2
Rosses Point ... 112 G 5
Rossgeir ... 117 J 3
Rossglass ... 115 O 5
Rossinver ... 112 H 4
Rosslare Bay ... 97 M 11
Rosslare Point ... 97 M 11
Rosslea ... 113 K 5
Rossmore Cork ... 89 F 12
Rossmore Laois ... 102 K 9
Rossmore Forest Park ... 114 L 5
Rossmore Island ... 88 C 12
Rossnowlagh ... 112 H 4
Rostellan ... 90 H 12
Rostrevor ... 109 N 5
Rosturk ... 105 C 6
Rough Point ... 92 B 11
Roughty ... 89 D 12
Roundfort ... 105 E 7
Roundstone ... 104 C 7

Roundwood ... 103 N 8
Roury ... 89 E 13
Rousky ... 114 K 3
Rowallane Gardens ... 115 O 4
Rower (The) ... 96 L 10
Royal Canal ... 107 I 7
Royaloak ... 96 L 9
Ruan ... 99 F 9
Rubane ... 115 P 4
Rue Point ... 119 N 2
Runabay Head ... 119 N 2
Runnabackan ... 106 H 6
Rushen (Slieve) ... 113 J 5
Russborough House ... 103 M 8
Rutland Island ... 116 G 3
Ryefield ... 108 K 6
Ryehill ... 106 F 7
Rylane Cross ... 90 F 12

S
Saddle Head ... 110 B 5
Saggart ... 103 M 8
St. Finan's Bay ... 88 A 12
St. John's Lough ... 107 I 5
St. John's Point ... 115 P 5
St. John's Point ... 112 G 4
St. Johnstown ... 117 J 3
St. Macdara's Island ... 104 C 8
St. Margaret's ... 103 N 7
St. Mochta's House ... 108 M 6
St. Mullin's ... 96 L 10
Saintfield ... 115 O 4
Saleen Cork ... 90 H 12
Saleen Kerry ... 93 D 10
Salia ... 104 C 6
Sallahig ... 88 B 12
Sallins ... 102 M 8
Sally Gap ... 103 N 8
Sallybrook ... 90 G 12
Sallypark ... 100 H 9
Salrock ... 104 C 7
Saltee Islands ... 96 M 11
Salthill ... 99 E 8
Sandholes ... 114 L 4
Sandyford ... 103 N 8
Santry ... 103 N 7
Saul ... 115 O 4
Sawel Mountain ... 118 K 3
Scalp Mountain ... 117 J 2
Scardaun Mayo ... 105 E 7
Scardaun Roscommon ... 106 H 7
Scarnagh ... 97 N 9
Scarriff / An Scairbh ... 99 G 9
Scarriff Island ... 88 B 12
Scartaglin ... 93 D 11
Scarva ... 114 M 5
Scattery Island ... 93 D 10
Schull / Skull ... 89 D 13
Scolban (Lough) ... 113 H 4
Scotch Town ... 114 K 3
Scotshouse ... 113 K 5
Scotstown ... 114 K 5
Scrabo Hill ... 115 O 4
Scramoge ... 107 H 6
Screeb Cross ... 105 D 7
Screen ... 97 M 10
Screggan ... 101 J 8
Scribbagh ... 113 H 4
Scullogue Gap ... 96 L 10
Scur (Lough) ... 107 I 5
Seaforde ... 115 O 5
Seapatrick ... 114 N 4
Seefin ... 95 J 11
Seskinore ... 113 K 4
Seskinryan ... 96 L 9
Seven Heads ... 90 F 13
Seven Hogs or Magharee Islands (The) ... 92 B 11
Shalwy ... 112 G 4
Shanacashel ... 88 C 11
Shanagarry ... 90 H 12
Shanaglish ... 99 F 8
Shanagolden ... 93 E 10
Shanahoe ... 101 J 9
Shanballard ... 99 G 7
Shanbally Cork ... 90 G 12
Shanbally Galway ... 106 G 7
Shanballymore ... 94 G 11
Shanco ... 114 L 4
Shanes Castle ... 114 N 3
Shankill ... 103 N 8
Shanlaragh ... 89 E 12
Shanlis ... 108 M 6
Shannagh (Lough) ... 115 N 5
Shannakea ... 93 E 10
Shannawona ... 105 D 7
Shannon ... 99 F 9

Shannon (River) ... 100 H 8
Shannon Airport ... 99 F 9
Shannon Harbour ... 101 I 8
Shannonbridge ... 100 H 8
Shanragh ... 101 K 9
Shantonagh ... 108 L 5
Sharavogue ... 101 I 8
Sheddings (The) ... 119 N 3
Sheeanamore ... 103 M 9
Sheeaun ... 99 G 9
Sheeffry Hills ... 105 C 6
Sheehan's Point ... 88 B 12
Sheelin (Lough) ... 107 K 6
Sheep Haven ... 117 I 2
Sheever (Lough) ... 107 K 7
Shehy Mountains ... 89 D 12
Shercock ... 108 L 6
Sherkin Island ... 89 D 13
Sherky Island ... 88 C 12
Sheskin ... 111 D 5
Sheskinapoll ... 117 J 3
Shillelagh ... 97 M 9
Shinrone ... 101 I 9
Shiven ... 106 G 7
Shoptown ... 115 N 3
Shot Head ... 89 C 13
Shranamanragh Bridge ... 110 C 5
Shrule ... 105 E 7
Silent Valley ... 109 O 5
Sillan (Lough) ... 108 L 5
Silver Bridge ... 108 M 5
Silver Strand ... 104 C 6
Silvermine Mountains ... 100 H 9
Silvermines ... 100 H 9
Sinking ... 106 F 7
Sion Mills ... 113 J 3
Six Crosses ... 93 D 10
Six Road Ends ... 115 P 4
Six Towns (The) ... 114 L 3
Sixmilebridge ... 99 F 9
Sixmilecross ... 114 K 4
Skannive (Lough) ... 104 C 8
Skeagh ... 107 J 7
Skehana ... 101 K 9
Skehanagh ... 106 G 7
Skerries (The) ... 118 M 2
Skreen Meath ... 108 M 7
Skreen Sligo ... 112 F 5
Sky Road ... 104 B 7
Slade ... 96 L 11
Slane ... 108 M 6
Slane (Hill of) ... 108 M 6
Slaney (River) ... 97 M 10
Slat (Lough) ... 92 B 11
Slate (River) ... 102 L 8
Slea Head ... 92 A 11
Slemish Mountain ... 119 N 3
Sliabh na Caillighe ... 108 K 6
Slieve Anierin ... 113 I 5
Slieve Aught Mountains ... 99 G 8
Slieve Bernagh ... 99 G 9
Slieve Bloom Mountains ... 101 J 8
Slieve Gamph or the Ox Mountains ... 111 F 5
Slieve Mish Mountains ... 93 C 11
Slieve Miskish Mountains ... 88 C 13
Slieveanorra ... 119 N 2
Slievecallan ... 99 E 9
Slievefelim Mountains ... 94 H 9
Slievekimalta ... 100 H 9
Slievekirk ... 117 K 3
Slievemore Dungannon ... 114 K 4
Slievemore Mayo ... 110 B 5
Slievemurry ... 106 G 7
Slievenamon ... 95 J 10
Slieveroe ... 96 K 11
Slievetooey ... 116 G 3
Sligeach / Sligo ... 112 G 5
Sligo Bay ... 112 F 5
Sliveardagh Hills ... 95 J 10
Slyne Head ... 104 B 7
Smerwick ... 92 A 11
Smerwick Harbour ... 92 A 11
Smithborough ... 114 K 5
Smithstown ... 101 K 9
Snagh (Slieve) Derryveagh Mts. ... 117 H 3
Snaght (Slieve) Inishowen ... 117 J 2
Snave ... 89 D 12
Sneem ... 88 C 12
Soldierstown ... 115 N 4
Sord / Swords ... 103 N 7
South Sound ... 98 D 8
Spa ... 93 C 11
Spa (The) ... 115 O 4
Spanish Point Locality ... 98 D 9
Spanish Point Mal Bay ... 98 D 9

Speenoge ... 117 J 2
Spelga Dam ... 115 N 5
Sperrin Mountains ... 118 K 3
Spink ... 101 K 9
Spittaltown ... 101 J 7
Springfield ... 113 I 4
Springhill ... 114 M 3
Springwell Forest ... 118 L 2
Squires Hill ... 115 O 4
Sraghmore ... 103 N 8
Srah / An tSraith ... 105 E 6
Srahduggaun ... 111 C 6
Srahmore near Bangor ... 111 C 5
Srahmore near Newport ... 105 D 6
Srahmore River ... 105 D 6
Sráid na Cathrach / Milltown Malbay ... 98 D 9
Stabannan ... 109 M 6
Stackallan ... 108 M 6
Stack's Mountains ... 93 D 11
Staffordstown ... 114 M 3
Stags (The) ... 89 E 13
Stags of Broad Haven ... 111 C 4
Staigue Stone Fort ... 88 B 12
Stamullin ... 109 N 7
Staplestown ... 102 L 8
Stepaside ... 103 N 8
Stewartstown ... 114 L 4
Stickstown ... 90 F 12
Stillorgan ... 103 N 8
Stone Bridge ... 113 K 5
Stonyford Kilkenny ... 96 K 10
Stonyford Lisburn ... 115 N 4
Stormont ... 115 O 4
Strabane ... 117 J 3
Stracashel ... 117 H 3
Stradbally Kerry ... 92 B 11
Stradbally Laois ... 101 K 8
Stradbally Waterford ... 91 J 11
Strade ... 105 E 6
Stradone ... 107 K 6
Stradreagh ... 118 L 2
Straffan ... 103 M 8
Stragar ... 112 G 3
Strahart ... 96 M 10
Straid Donegal ... 117 J 2
Straid Larne ... 115 O 3
Straid Moyle ... 118 M 2
Straith Salach / Recess ... 104 C 7
Strand ... 93 E 10
Strandhill ... 112 G 5
Strangford ... 115 P 4
Strangford Lough ... 115 P 4
Stranocum ... 118 M 2
Stranorlar ... 117 I 3
Stratford ... 102 L 9
Stravally ... 112 G 3
Streamstown ... 104 B 7
Streedagh Point ... 112 G 4
Streek Head ... 89 C 13
Street ... 107 J 6
Strokestown ... 106 H 6
Stroove ... 118 L 2
Struell Wells ... 115 O 5
Strule ... 113 J 3
Sturrakeen ... 95 H 10
Suck (River) ... 106 G 6
Suir (River) ... 101 I 9
Summercove ... 90 G 12
Summerhill ... 108 L 7
Suncroft ... 102 L 8
Sunderlin (Lough) ... 107 I 7
Swan ... 101 K 9
Swanlinbar ... 113 I 5
Swan's Cross Roads ... 114 K 5
Swatragh ... 118 L 3
Sweep (The) ... 95 J 10
Swilly (Lough) ... 117 J 2
Swilly (River) ... 117 J 2
Sybil Head ... 92 A 11

T
Table Mountain ... 103 M 8
Tacumshane ... 97 M 11
Tacumshin Lake ... 97 M 11
Taghmon ... 96 M 11
Taghshinny ... 107 I 7
Tagoat ... 97 M 11
Tahilla ... 88 C 12
Talbot Island ... 104 B 7
Talbotstown ... 102 M 9
Tallaght ... 103 M 8
Tallanstown ... 108 M 6
Tallow ... 91 H 11
Tallowbridge ... 91 H 11
Talt (Lough) ... 111 F 5
Tamlaght Fermanagh ... 113 J 5

Tamlaght *Magherafelt* ....118 M 3
Tamnamore ....114 M 4
Tandragee ....114 M 4
Tang ....107 I 7
Tangaveane ....116 H 3
Tappaghan Mount ....113 J 4
Tara (Hill of) ....108 M 7
Tarbert ....93 D 10
Tardree Forest ....115 N 3
Tarker (Lough) ....108 L 5
Tarmon ....112 H 5
Tarsaghaunmore ....111 C 5
Tassagh ....114 L 5
Taughblane ....115 N 4
Taur ....93 E 11
Tawin ....99 E 8
Tawin Island ....99 E 8
Tawny ....117 I 2
Tawnyinah ....106 F 6
Tawnylea ....112 H 5
Tay ....95 J 11
Tay (Lough) ....103 N 8
Taylor's Cross ....101 I 8
Tearaght Island ....92 A 11
Tedavnet ....114 K 5
Teelin ....112 G 4
Teemore ....113 J 5
Teeranea ....98 D 8
Teeranearagh ....88 B 12
Teerelton ....89 F 12
Teermaclane ....99 E 9
Teernakill ....105 D 7
Teeromoyle ....88 B 12
Teevurcher ....108 L 6
Temple (The) ....115 O 4
Temple of the Winds .....115 P 4
Templeboy ....112 F 5
Templederry ....100 H 9
Templeglentan ....93 E 10
Templehouse Lake ....112 G 5
Templemartin ....90 F 12
Templenoe ....89 C 12
Templeoran ....101 J 7
Templepatrick ....115 N 3
Templeshanbo ....96 L 10
Templetouhy ....101 I 9
Templetown ....96 L 11
Tempo ....113 J 4
Terenure ....103 N 8
Termon ....98 D 10
Termonbarry ....107 I 6
Termonfeckin ....109 N 6

Terryglass ....100 H 8
Tevrin ....107 K 7
Thomas Street ....106 H 7
Thomastown *Meath* ....108 L 6
Thomastown *Tipperrary* ....95 H 10
Thoor Ballylee ....99 F 8
Three Castle Head ....88 C 13
Three Castles ....96 J 9
Three Rock ....103 N 8
Tiduff ....92 B 11
Tievealehid ....116 H 2
Tievemore ....113 I 4
Tillyvoos ....112 H 4
Tiltinbane ....113 I 5
Timahoe ....102 L 8
Timoleague ....90 F 13
Timolin ....102 L 9
Tinahely ....103 M 9
Tinnahinch ....96 L 10
Tinriland ....102 L 9
Tiobraid Árann /
   Tipperary ....95 H 10
Tirnaneill ....114 L 5
Tirneevin ....99 F 8
Toames ....89 F 12
Tobar an Choire /
   Tubbercurry ....112 F 5
Tober ....101 J 7
Toberbeg ....102 M 8
Toberdoney ....118 M 2
Tobermore ....114 L 3
Tobernadarry ....105 E 7
Toberscanavan ....112 G 5
Toe Head ....89 E 13
Toem ....95 H 10
Togher *Cork* ....89 E 12
Togher *Louth* ....109 N 6
Togher *Offaly* ....101 K 8
Tolka ....103 M 7
Tollymore Forest Park ....115 O 5
Tombrack ....97 M 10
Tomdarragh ....103 N 8
Tomhaggard ....97 M 11
Tonabrocky ....99 E 8
Tonakeera Point ....104 C 7
Tonyduff ....108 K 6
Toomaghera ....99 E 8
Toomard ....106 G 7
Toombeola ....104 C 7
Toome ....114 M 3
Toomyvara ....100 H 9
Toor ....100 H 9

Tooraree ....93 E 10
Tooreencahill ....93 E 11
Toorlestraun ....112 F 5
Toormore ....89 D 13
Toormore Bay ....89 D 13
Toornafulla ....93 E 10
Toraigh /
   Tory Island ....116 H 2
Torc Waterfall ....89 D 11
Torneady Point ....116 G 2
Torr Head ....119 N 2
Tory Sound ....117 H 2
Tourig (River) ....91 I 11
Tower ....90 G 12
Trá Lí / Tralee ....93 C 11
Trá Mhór /
   Tramore ....96 K 11
Trabane Strand ....112 F 4
Tracton ....90 G 12
Trafrask ....89 D 12
Tragumna ....89 E 13
Tralee Bay ....92 C 11
Tramore Bay ....96 K 11
Tranarossan Bay ....117 I 2
Travara Bridge ....88 C 12
Trawbreaga Bay ....117 K 2
Trawenagh Bay ....116 G 3
Trawmore Bay ....110 C 5
Trean ....105 D 7
Treantagh ....117 I 2
Treehoo ....107 K 5
Trien ....106 G 6
Trillick ....113 J 4
Tristia ....110 C 5
Trory ....113 J 4
Trostan ....119 N 2
Truskmore ....112 G 4
Trust ....100 G 7
Tuaim / Tuam ....105 F 7
Tuamgraney ....99 G 9
Tuar Mhic Éadaigh /
   Tourmakeady ....105 D 7
Tubber ....99 F 8
Tubbrid *Kilkenny* ....95 J 9
Tubbrid *Tipperary* ....95 I 11
Tulach Mhór /
   Tullamore ....101 J 8
Tulla *near Ennis* ....99 F 9
Tulla *near Gort* ....99 F 8
Tullagh Point ....117 J 2
Tullaghan ....112 G 4
Tullaghan Bay ....110 C 5

Tullaghanstown ....108 L 7
Tullagher ....96 K 10
Tullaghobegly ....117 H 2
Tullaherin ....96 K 10
Tullahought ....95 J 10
Tullakeel ....88 C 12
Tullamore ....93 D 10
Tullaroan ....95 J 10
Tullig ....92 C 11
Tullig Point ....93 C 10
Tullokyne ....105 E 7
Tully
   Lower Lough Erne ......113 I 4
Tully *near Ballyshannon* ....113 H 4
Tully *Upper Lough Erne* ....113 J 5
Tully Cross ....104 C 7
Tully National Stud ....102 L 8
Tullyallen ....109 M 6
Tullyamalra ....108 L 5
Tullycanna ....96 L 11
Tullydush ....117 J 2
Tullyhogue ....114 L 4
Tullylease ....94 F 11
Tullymacreeve ....109 M 5
Tullynaha ....112 H 3
Tullynally Castle ....107 J 6
Tullyroan ....114 M 4
Tullyvin ....108 K 5
Tulrohaun ....105 F 6
Tulsk ....106 H 6
Turlough ....105 E 6
Turloughmore ....105 F 7
Turner's Rock Tunnel .....89 D 12
Turreen ....107 I 7
Tuskar Rock ....97 N 11
Twelve Pins (The) ....104 C 7
Twomileborris ....95 I 9
Tylas ....108 M 7
Tynagh ....100 G 8
Tynan ....114 L 5
Tyrella ....115 O 5
Tyrellspass ....101 J 7

Union Hall ....89 E 13
Unshin ....112 G 5
Upper Ballinderry ....115 N 4
Upper Lake ....103 M 8
Upperchurch ....95 H 9
Upperlands ....118 M 3
Urbalreagh ....117 K 1
Urglin Glebe ....102 L 9
Urlaur ....106 F 6
Urlaur Lough ....106 F 6
Urlingford ....95 J 9

V

Valencia Island ....88 A 12
Valley ....110 C 5
Valleymount ....103 M 8
Vartry Reservoir ....103 N 8
Ventry ....92 A 11
Ventry Harbour ....92 A 11
Vicarstown ....102 K 8
Victoria Bridge ....113 J 3
Villierstown ....91 I 11
Virginia ....108 K 6
Virginia Road ....108 K 6
Vow ....118 M 3

W

Waddingtown ....96 M 11
Walshestown ....97 M 11
Walshtown ....90 H 12
Ward (River) ....103 N 7
Ward ....103 N 7
Waringsford ....115 N 4
Waringstown ....114 N 4
Warrenpoint ....109 N 5
Washing Bay ....114 M 4
Watch Ho.-Village ....96 M 9
Waterfall ....90 G 12
Waterfoot or Glenariff ....119 N 2
Waterford Harbour ....96 L 11
Watergrasshill ....90 G 11
Waterworks ....114 L 3
Wattle Bridge ....113 J 5
Welchtown ....117 I 3
Wellington Bridge ....96 L 11
Wells Cross ....114 M 4
Wesport Bay ....105 C 6
West Town ....116 H 2
Westcove ....88 B 12
Westport House ....105 D 6
Westport Quay ....105 D 6
Wexford Bay ....97 N 10

Wexford Harbour ....97 M 10
Whale Head ....117 J 2
Wheathill ....113 I 5
Whiddy Island ....89 D 12
White *Limerick* ....93 E 10
White *Louth* ....109 M 6
White Castle ....118 K 2
White Hall ....89 D 13
White Island ....113 I 4
White Park Bay ....118 M 2
White Strand ....98 D 9
Whiteabbey ....115 O 3
Whitechurch *Cork* ....90 G 12
Whitechurch *Waterford* ....91 I 11
Whitecross ....114 M 5
Whitegate ....90 H 12
Whitehall *Roscommon* ....107 I 6
Whitehall *Westmeath* .....107 K 7
Whitehead ....115 O 3
Whites Town ....109 N 6
White'sCross ....90 G 12
Whitesides Corner ....114 M 3
Wicklow Gap ....103 M 8
Wicklow Mountains ......103 N 8
Wicklow Way ....103 N 8
Wildfowl
   and Wetlands Trust ....115 O 4
Wilkinstown ....108 L 6
Willbrook ....99 E 9
Williamstown *Galway* ....106 G 6
Williamstown
   Westmeath ....107 I 7
Windgap ....95 J 10
Windmill ....102 L 7
Windy Gap *Kerry* ....89 D 12
Windy Gap *Louth* ....109 N 5
Windy Gap *Mayo* ....105 E 6
Wolfhill ....101 K 9
Womanagh ....91 I 12
Woodburn ....115 O 3
Woodcock Hill ....99 F 9
Woodenbridge ....103 N 9
Woodford (River) ....99 G 8
Woodstown ....96 L 11

Y

Yellow Furze ....108 M 6
Yganavan (Lough) ....92 C 11
Youghal ....100 H 9
Youghal Bay ....91 I 12

U

Uachtar Ard /
   Oughterard ....105 E 7
Uaigh / Owey Island ....116 G 2
Ugga Beg (Lough) ....98 D 8
Ulster American
   Folk Park ....113 J 4
Ulster Folk
   Museum (The) ....115 O 4

A
B
C
D
E
F
G
H
I
J
K
L
M
N
O
P
Q
R
S
T
U
V
W
X
Y
Z

Town plans

Sights
Place of interest
Interesting place of worship:
Church - Protestant church

Roads
Motorway - Dual carriageway
Numbered junctions: complete, limited
Major thoroughfare
Unsuitable for traffic or street subject to restrictions
Pedestrian street - Tramway
Car park - Park and Ride
Tunnel
Station and railway
Funicular
Cable-car

Various signs
Tourist Information Centre
Mosque - Synagogue
Tower - Ruins
Windmill
Garden, park, wood
Cemetery

Stadium - Golf course - Racecourse
Outdoor or indoor swimming pool
View - Panorama
Monument - Fountain
Pleasure boat harbour
Lighthouse
Airport - Underground station
Coach station
Ferry services:
passengers and cars - passengers only

Main post office with poste restante - Hospital
Covered market
Gendarmerie - Police
Town Hall
University, College
Public buildings located by letter:
Museum
Theatre

Plans

Curiosités
Bâtiment intéressant
Édifice religieux intéressant : catholique - protestant

Voirie
Autoroute - Double chaussée de type autoroutier
Échangeurs numérotés : complet - partiels
Grande voie de circulation
Rue réglementée ou impraticable
Rue piétonne - Tramway
Parking - Parking Relais
Tunnel
Gare et voie ferrée
Funiculaire, voie à crémaillère
Téléphérique, télécabine

Signes divers
Information touristique
Mosquée - Synagogue
Tour - Ruines
Moulin à vent
Jardin, parc, bois
Cimetière

Stade - Golf - Hippodrome
Piscine de plein air, couverte
Vue - Panorama
Monument - Fontaine
Port de plaisance
Phare
Aéroport - Station de métro
Gare routière
Transport par bateau :
passagers et voitures, passagers seulement

Bureau principal de poste restante - Hôpital
Marché couvert
Gendarmerie - Police
Hôtel de ville
Université, grande école
Bâtiment public repéré par une lettre :
Musée
Théâtre

Stadtpläne

Sehenswürdigkeiten
Sehenswertes Gebäude
Sehenswerter Sakralbau:Katholische - Evangelische Kirche

Straßen
Autobahn - Schnellstraße
Nummerierte Voll - bzw. Teilanschlussstellen
Hauptverkehrsstraße
Gesperrte Straße oder mit Verkehrsbeschränkungen
Fußgängerzone - Straßenbahn
Parkplatz - Park-and-Ride-Plätze
Tunnel
Bahnhof und Bahnlinie
Standseilbahn
Seilschwebebahn

Sonstige Zeichen
Informationsstelle
Moschee - Synagoge
Turm - Ruine
Windmühle
Garten, Park, Wäldchen
Friedhof

Stadion - Golfplatz - Pferderennbahn
Freibad - Hallenbad
Aussicht - Rundblick
Denkmal - Brunnen
Yachthafen
Leuchtturm
Flughafen - U-Bahnstation
Autobusbahnhof
Schiffsverbindungen:
Autofähre, Personenfähre
Hauptpostamt (postlagernde Sendungen) - Krankenhaus
Markthalle
Gendarmerie - Polizei
Rathaus
Universität, Hochschule
Öffentliches Gebäude, durch einen Buchstaben gekennzeichnet:
Museum
Theater

Plattegronden

Bezienswaardigheden
Interessant gebouw
Interessant kerkelijk gebouw: Kerk - Protestantse kerk

Wegen
Autosnelweg - Weg met gescheiden rijbanen
Knooppunt / aansluiting: volledig, gedeeltelijk
Hoofdverkeersweg
Onbegaanbare straat, beperkt toegankelijk
Voetgangersgebied - Tramlijn
Parkeerplaats - P & R
Tunnel
Station, spoorweg
Kabelspoor
Tandradbaan

Overige tekens
Informatie voor toeristen
Moskee - Synagoge
Toren - Ruïne
Windmolen
Tuin, park, bos
Begraafplaats

Stadion - Golfterrein - Renbaan
Zwembad: openlucht, overdekt
Uitzicht - Panorama
Gedenkteken, standbeeld - Fontein
Jachthaven
Vuurtoren
Luchthaven - Metrostation
Busstation
Vervoer per boot:
Passagiers en auto's - uitsluitend passagiers

Hoofdkantoor voor poste-restante - Ziekenhuis
Overdekte markt
Marechaussee / rijkswacht - Politie
Stadhuis
Universiteit, hogeschool
Openbaar gebouw, aangegeven met een letter::
Museum
Schouwburg

Piante

Curiosità
Edificio interessante
Costruzione religiosa interessante: Chiesa - Tempio

Viabilità
Autostrada - Doppia carreggiata tipo autostrada
Svincoli numerati: completo, parziale
Grande via di circolazione
Via regolamentata o impraticabile
Via pedonale - Tranvia
Parcheggio - Parcheggio Ristoro
Galleria
Stazione e ferrovia
Funicolare
Funivia, cabinovia

Simboli vari
Ufficio informazioni turistiche
Moschea - Sinagoga
Torre - Ruderi
Mulino a vento
Giardino, parco, bosco
Cimitero

Stadio - Golf - Ippodromo
Piscina: all'aperto, coperta
Vista - Panorama
Monumento - Fontana
Porto turistico
Faro
Aeroporto - Stazione della metropolitana
Autostazione
Trasporto con traghetto:
passeggeri ed autovetture - solo passeggeri

Ufficio centrale di fermo posta - Ospedale
Mercato coperto
Carabinieri - Polizia
Municipio
Università, scuola superiore
Edificio pubblico indicato con lettera:
Museo
Teatro

Planos

Curiosidades
Edificio interessante
Edificio religioso interessante: católica - protestante

Vías de circulación
Autopista - Autovía
Enlaces numerados: completo, parciales
Via importante de circulacion
Calle reglamentada o impracticable
Calle peatonal - Tranvia
Aparcamiento - Aparcamientos «P+R»
Túnel
Estación y línea férrea
Funicular, línea de cremallera
Teleférico, telecabina

Signos diversos
Oficina de Información de Turismo
Mezquita - Sinagoga
Torre - Ruinas
Molino de viento
Jardín, parque, madera
Cementerio

Estadio - Golf - Hipódromo
Piscina al aire libre, cubierta
Vista parcial - Vista panorámica
Monumento - Fuente
Puerto deportivo
Faro
Aeropuerto - Estación de metro
Estación de autobuses
Transporte por barco:
pasajeros y vehículos, pasajeros solamente

Oficina de correos - Hospital
Mercado cubierto
Policía National - Policía
Ayuntamiento
Universidad, escuela superior
Edificio público localizado con letra :
Museo
Teatro

Plans de ville
Town plans / Stadtpläne / Stadsplattegronden
Piante di città / Planos de ciudades

GREAT BRITAIN

- Aberdeen 150
- Bath 150
- Birmingham............ 151
- Bournemouth 152
- Brighton and Hove 153
- Bristol 154
- Cambridge............. 155
- Canterbury............. 156
- Cardiff 157
- Chester 158
- Coventry............... 159
- Dundee................ 159
- Durham................ 160
- Edinburgh 161
- Exeter................. 162
- Glasgow 163
- Leeds 164
- Leicester 165
- Lincoln................ 165
- Liverpool 166-167
- Greater London 168-169
- London 170-171
- Manchester 172
- Newcastle-upon-Tyne ... 173
- Norwich 174
- Nottingham............ 174
- Oxford 175
- Perth 176
- Plymouth 177
- Portsmouth
  and Southsea 178
- Southampton 179
- Stirling................ 180
- Stratford-upon-Avon 181
- Winchester............. 182
- Windsor................ 183
- York 184

IRELAND

- Belfast 185
- Cork 186
- Galway................. 187
- Dublin 188-189
- Killarney 190
- Limerick 191

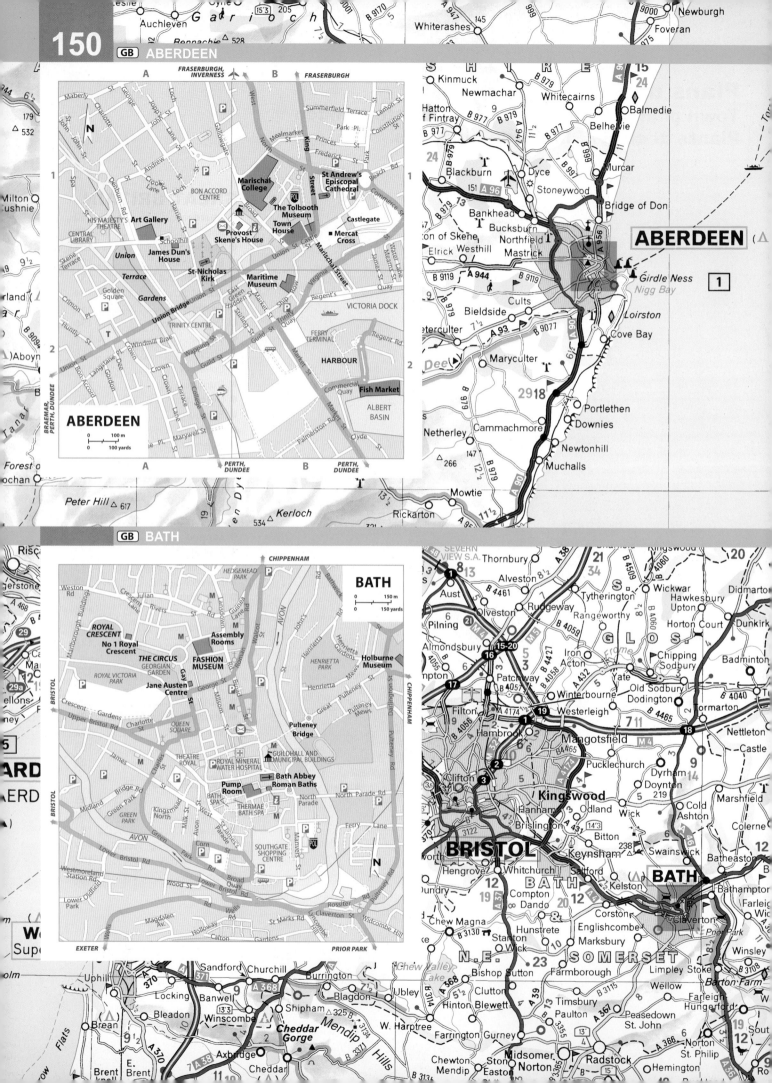

A27
PORTSMOUTH   CRAWLEY   LEWES

WORTHING

**BRIGHTON
AND HOVE**

0   300 m
0   300 yards

N

HOVE

St. Ann's
Well Gardens

St.
Bartholomews

BRIGHTON

Brighton Museum
and Art Gallery

ROYAL
PAVILION

THE LANES

Queen's Park

NEWHAVEN

Bucks
Green
Loxwood

A 281
Broadbridge
Heath

Horsham

St. Leonard's
Forest

Wakehurst
Place

Wych Cross

Ashdown
Forest

Crowbo

Plaistow
chapel

Kirdford

Mannings
Heath

Balcombe

Chelwood Gate

Handcross

Ardingly

Horsted Keynes

Nutley

Itchingfield

Ouse
Nymans

Danehill

Fletching

Wisborough
Green

Billingshurst

Southwater

Lr. Beeding

Cuckfield

Haywards
Heath

Maresfield
Sheffield Park

Buxted

A 272

Petworth

Coolham

Cowfold

Bolney

Burgess Hill

Newick

Uckfield

Framfield

Blackb

Pulborough

W. Chiltington

Dial Post

W. Grinstead

Partridge Green

Hickstead

Hurstpierpoint

Keymer

Wivelsfield

Chailey

Ditchling Common

Barcombe Cross

Halland

E. Hoath

Hardham

Thakeham

Albourne

Hassocks

Ditchling

Westmeston

Plumpton

Waldron

Parham
House

Storrington

Henfield

Clayton

Pyecombe

Ditchling
Beacon
248

Lewes

Ringmer

Laughton

Bury

Amberley

Washington

Small Dole

Stanmer Park

Castle

Glyndebourne

Upr. Dicke

South Downs Way

Steyning

Fulking

Poynings

Falmer

Glynde

Ripe

n
S

Arundel

Upr. Beeding

Findon

Southwick

Beddingham

W. Firle

Mich
Prior

Angmering

Sompting

Lancing

Portslade

Hove

Woodingdean

Rodmell

S. Heighton

Alfriston

Ford

Preston

Rustington

Shoreham

BRIGHTON

Rottingdean

Wilmington

Jevingto

Climping

Littlehampton

WORTHING

Peacehaven

Newhaven

Charles
Mano

Middleton-on-Sea

or Regis

Seaford

Eastdean

Seven Sisters

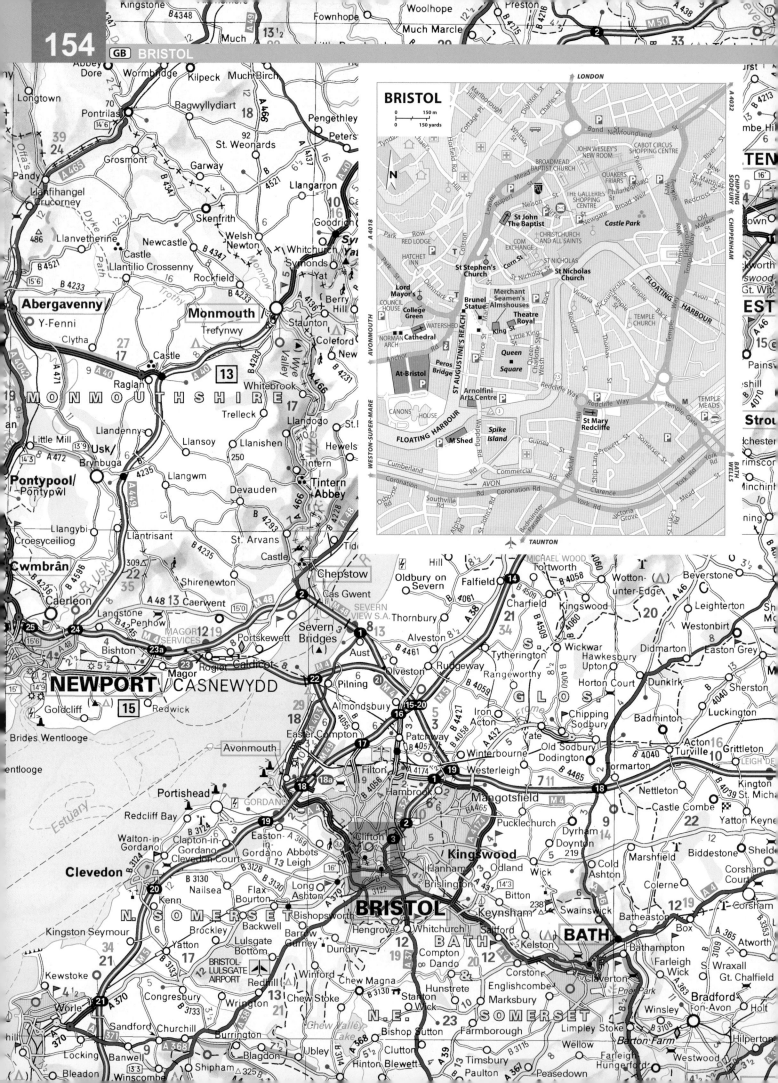

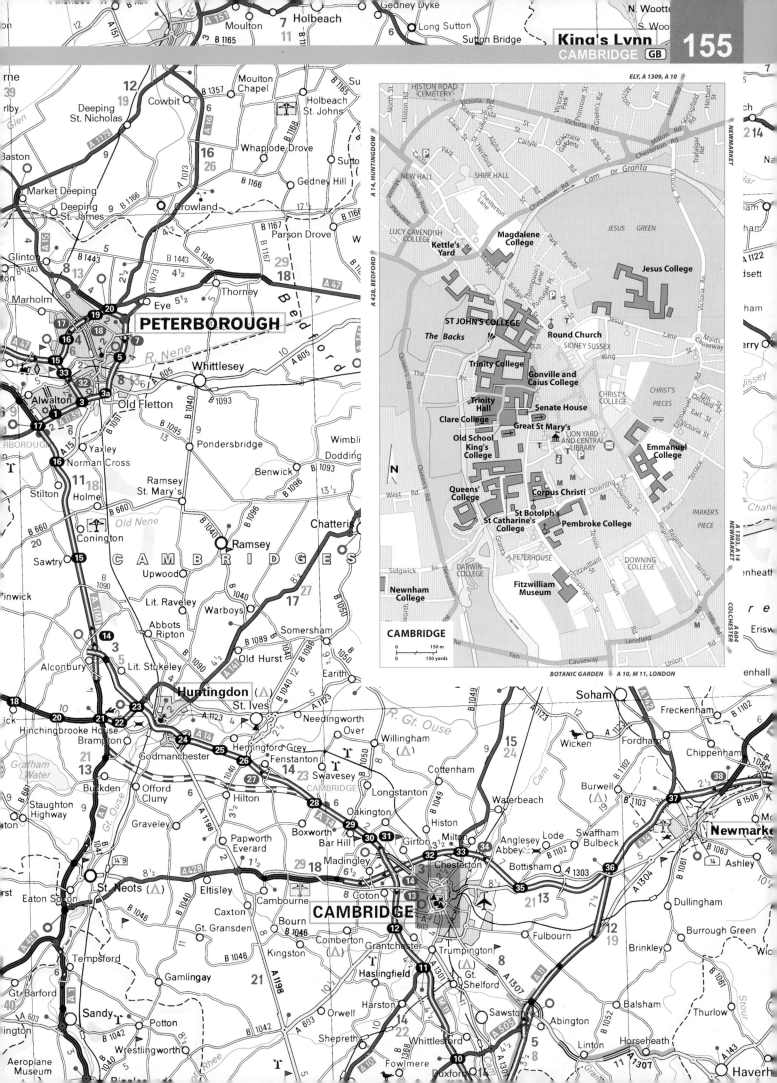

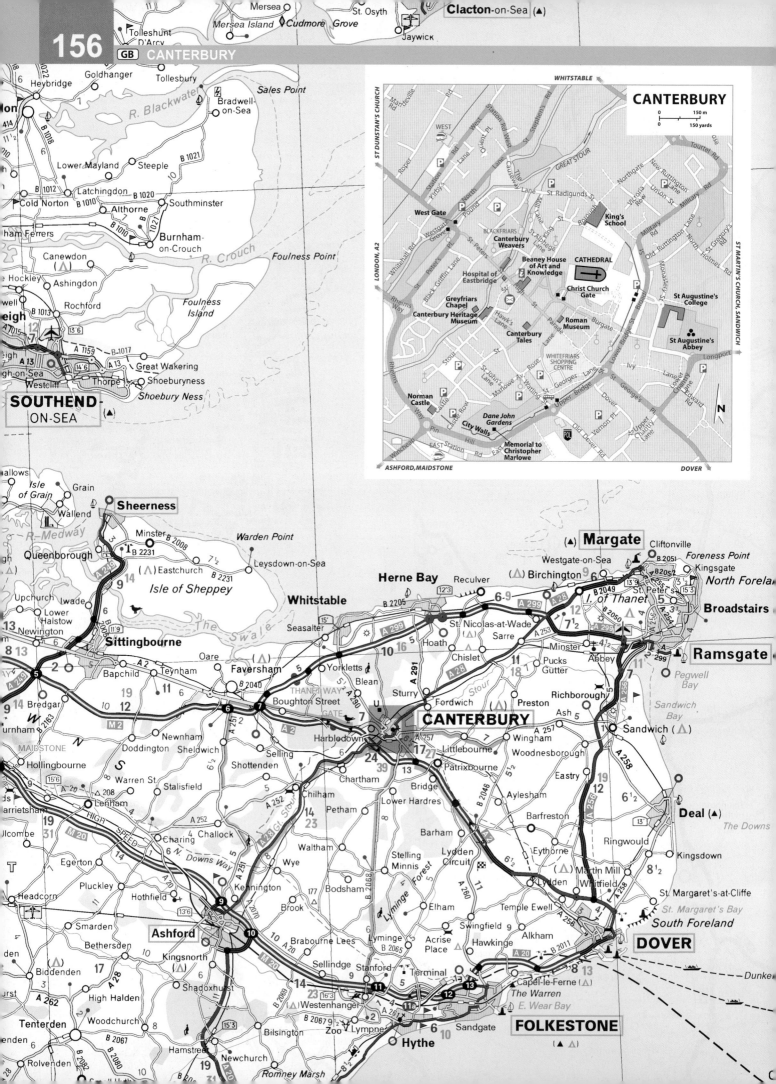

CARDIFF

SWANSEA · MERTHYR TYDFIL · CAERPHILLY · A 48 Bristol

NATIONAL MUSEUM OF WALES

WELSH OFFICE · UNIVERSITY COLLEGE · TEMPLE OF PEACE · ALEXANDRA GARDENS · OLD COUNTY HALL · City Hall · Gorsedd Gardens · CARDIFF NEW SYNAGOGUE

Bute Park · Law Courts · Cardiff Castle · Military Museums · High St. Arcade · St John's Church · St David's Shopping Centre · CAPITOL CENTRE · QUEEN ST

Castle Arcade · Cardiff Arms Park · Central Market · Millennium Stadium · Morgan Arcade · Royal Arcade · TABERNACLE

CARDIFF CENTRAL · SWAMINARAYANA TEMPLE · CALLAGHAN SQUARE

THOMPSON'S PARK · Bute East Dock

SEVENOAKS PARK · GRANGETOWN MUSLIM CULTURAL CENTRE · CARDIFF BAY · THE RED DRAGON CENTRE

BUTETOWN · Coal Exchange · THE SALVATION ARMY · ST CUTHBERT'S

Wales Millennium Centre · Pierhead Building · Y Senedd · Techniquest · MERMAID QUAY · Norwegian Church · CARDIFF BAY

HAMADRYAD PARK · CARDIFF BAY WETLANDS RESERVE · CARDIFF YACHT CLUB · QUEEN ALEXANDRA DOCK

N
LECKWITH WOODS

CARDIFF
0   200 m
0   200 yards

PENARTH · BRIGEND

CAERPHILLY · Cymmer · Senghenydd · Llanbradach · Machen · Risca · Caerleon · Langstone · Penhow · MAGOR SERVICES · SEVERN VIEW S.A.

Tonyrefail · Pontypridd · Beddau · Bedwas · Rogerstone · Bishton · Severn Bridges · Aust

Talbot Green · Caerphilly / Caerffili · Parc Cefn Onn · Thornhill · NEWPORT CASNEWYDD · Magor · Rogiet · Caldicot · Pilning

Pontyclun · Llanharry · Miskin · Pentyrch · Tongwynlais · Lisvane · Castleton · Marshfield · Goldcliff · Redwick · Almondsbury · Easter Compton · Filton

Hensol · St-Brides Super-Ely · Whitchurch · Radyr · Llanishen · St. Mellons · St. Brides Wentlooge · Peterstone Wentlooge · Avonmouth · Portishead

VALE OF · Beaupre Castle · Eglwys Brewis · St-Fagans · Ely · Rumney · Portishead · Redcliff Bay · GORDANO · Clifton

Bonvilston · St Nicholas · Pendoylan · Wenvoe · Dinas Powys · **CARDIFF / CAERDYDD** · Walton-in-Gordano · Clapton-in-Gordano · Clevedon Court · Abbots Leigh

GLAMORGAN · Penmark · Penarth · Clevedon · Nailsea · Flax Bourton · Long Ashton · BRIST

Penkerry · Sully · Swanbridge · Kenn · N. SOMERSET · Backwell · Barrow Gurney · Dundry

East Aberthaw · Rhoose · CARDIFF AIRPORT · **Barry / Barri** · Flat Holm · Kingston Seymour · Brockley · Lulsgate Bottom · BRISTOL-LULSGATE AIRPORT · Winford · Chew Magna

Weston-Super-Mare · Worle · Congresbury · Wrington · Chew Stoke

Chester (inset map)

HOYLAKE — A 41, ELLESMERE PORT — M 56, MANCHESTER / M 53, LIVERPOOL

NORTHGATE ARENA

Garden Lane · Bouverie St · Walpole St · Victoria Rd · Liverpool Rd · Walter St · Cornwall St · Trafford St · Talbot St · Anne St · Brook St · Francis St · Egerton St · Crewe St

Louise St · Raymond St · Chichester St · St Oswalds Way · George St · Gloucester St · Hoole Way · Milton St · Leadworks Lane · City Rd

St Oswalds Way

NORTHGATE · King Charles' Tower

The Walls · Kaleyards Gate

South View Rd · Raymond St · Tower Rd · King St · Martin's · St Werburgh St · York St · Canal Side · Steam Mill St · Russell St

Chester Cathedral

Town Hall · Bedward Row · FORUM SHOPPING CENTRE · EASTGATE · The Bars

Walls Ave · New Crane St · Nicholas St · Watergate · Bridge St · Eastgate · Love St · Union St · Bath Lane · Dee Lane

QUEENSFERRY · WATERGATE · Stanley Palace · Dewa Roman Experience · Grey Friars · White Friars · Black Friars · NEWGATE · Roman Amphitheatre · Grosvenor Park · St John's · The Groves

THE ROWS

Grosvenor Museum · Duke St · Lower Park Rd · Upper Park Rd

N · Roodee · The Walls · CASTLE · BRIDGEGATE · The DEE · Old Dee Bridge · QUEEN'S PARK · Victoria Crescent · Queen's Park Rd · St George's Crescent · Crescent

CHESTER
0 — 150 m
0 — 150 yards

WREXHAM — A 55, CONWY

MANCHESTER, NANTWICH · A 5115, A 41 · A 5115, A 41, WHITCHURCH

Main map

Hesketh Bank · Much Hoole · Ley

A 59 · A 565 · B 5247 · Croston · A 581 · Rufford Old Hall · Mere Brow · Eccl

SOUTHPORT

Birkdale · Ainsdale · Wildfowl Trust · Rufford · Scarisbrick · Burscough Bridge · Parbold · Newburgh

Halsall · Burscough · A 5209

B 5243 · B 5242 · B 5240

Formby · Gt. Altcar · **Ormskirk** · **Skelmersdale** · Up Holland

Lydiate · Aughton · B 5195 · A 570 · A 59 · B 5197 · A 506 · B 5312

Hightown · Ince Blundell · **Maghull** · A 5147 · Rainford

Blundellsands · **Crosby** · **Litherland** · Aintree · **Kirkby** · Mossley · Bank

Bootle · Knowsley · **ST. HELENS**

New Brighton · **LIVERPOOL** · Roby · Huyton · Presco

Wallasey · Woolton · Farnworth · Hough Green · Ditto

BIRKENHEAD · A 553 · A 540 · Irby · Port Sunlight · **Widnes** · Hale · **Runcorn** · Frodsha

West Kirby · Thurstaston · Pensby · **Bebington** · Bromborough · Speke · **LIVERPOOL JOHN LENNON AIRPORT** · River Mersey

Heswall · Eastham · Thornton Hough · Parkgate · Neston · Willaston · **Ellesmere Port** · Elton · Helsb

Welsh Channel · River Dee / Afon Dyfrdwy · Greenfield · Whitby · Backford Cross · Stoak · **CHESTER**

Point of Ayr · Talacre · Puddington · Saughall · Sealand · Bridge Trafford · Little Barrow

(△) **Rhyl** · Prestatyn · A 548 · Llanasa · Mostyn · Holywell / Treffynnon · Flint / Fflint · Connah's Quay · Upton · Great Barrow

Kinmel Bay · Trelawnyd · Dyserth · Bagillt · Queensferry · Lache · Christleton

A 525 · A 547 · Rhuddlan · Castle · Rhualt · Babell · Halkyn · Northop · Ewloe · Saltney · Waverton · Huxley

Pensarn · Bodelwyddan · St Asaph · Caerwys · Afon-wen · Northop Hall · Hawarden · Buckley · Broughton · Handbridge

Abergele · Tremeirchion · Bodfari · Nannerch · Mold · Bwlch · **CHESHIRE WEST AND CHESTER**

Llannefydd · Trefnant · **Denbigh / Dinbych** · **FLINTS** · Yr Wyddgrug / Loggerheads · Hawarden · Pulford · Aldford · Tattenhall

Henllan · Llandyrnog · Cilcain · Moel Fammau · Nercwys · Penyffordd · Higher Burwardsley

Bylchau · Llanrhaeadr · Llanferres · Leeswood · Waun y llyn · Hope · Burton · Rossett · Handley

A 544 · **DENBIGHSHIRE** · **Ruthin / Rhuthun** · Offa's Dyke Path · Treuddyn · Caergwrle · Farndon · Broxton

Cyffylliog · Llandegla · Llanfynydd · Llanarmon-yn-Ial · Bwlchgwyn · Gresford · Holt · Tilston

Clocaenog Forest · Clawdd newydd · Llanelidan · Pentre Celyn · Brymbo · Coedpoeth · **Wrexham / Wrecsam** · Erddig · Marchwiel · Worthenbury · Malpas

Llanfihangel Glyn Myfyr · Bettws Gwerfil Goch · Gwyddelwern · Bryneglwys · Rhosllannerchrugog · Rhostyllen · Clywedog

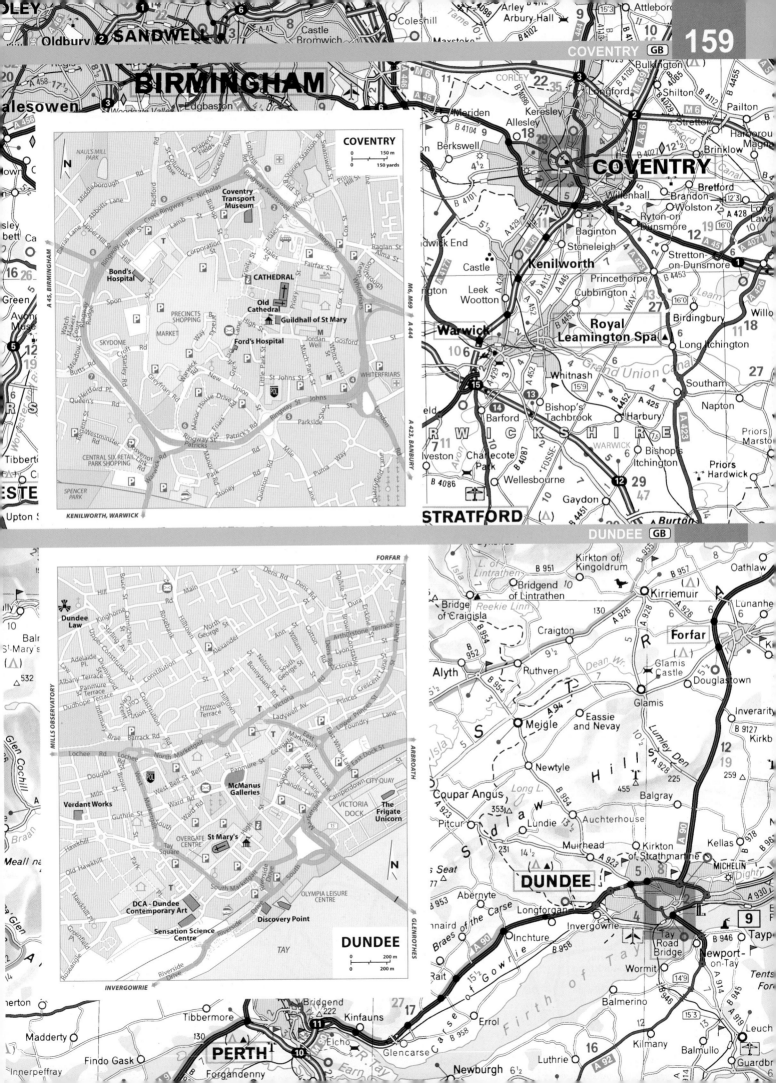

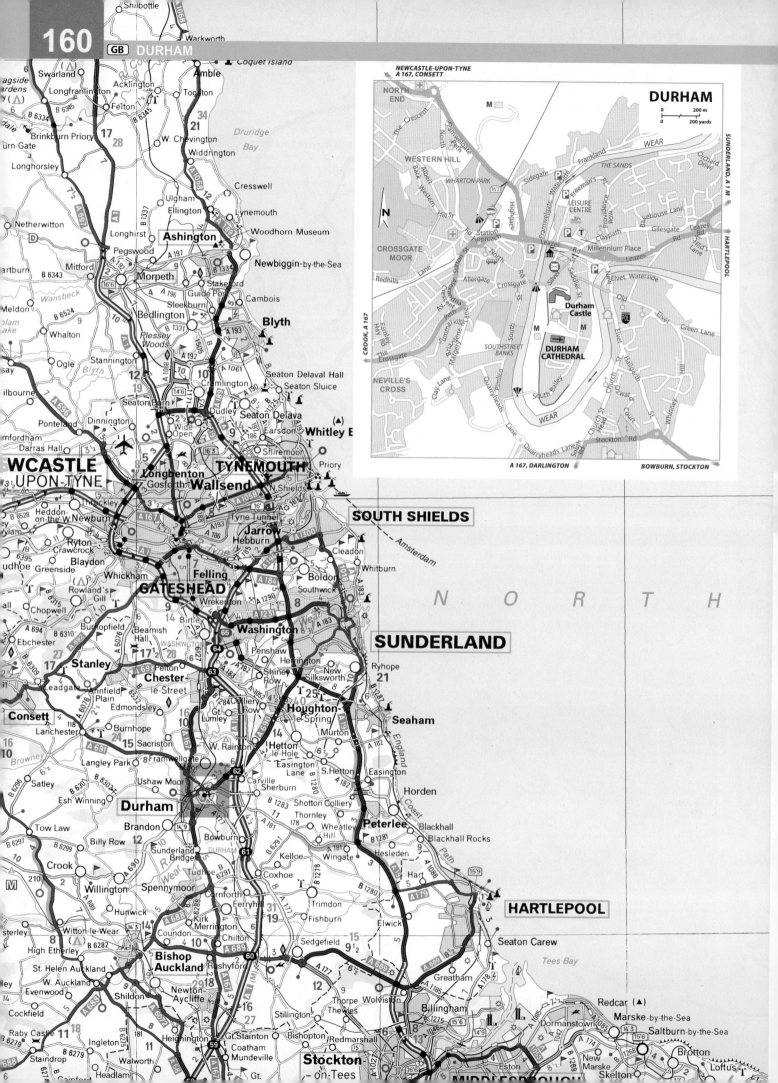

DURHAM (inset map)

NEWCASTLE-UPON-TYNE
A 167, CONSETT

Scale: 0 — 200 m / 0 — 200 yards

NORTH END

WESTERN HILL

WHARTON PARK

THE SANDS

WEAR

LEISURE CENTRE

CROSSGATE MOOR

Millennium Place

Durham Castle

SOUTHSTREET BANKS

DURHAM CATHEDRAL

NEVILLE'S CROSS

WEAR

A 167, DARLINGTON

BOWBURN, STOCKTON

SUNDERLAND, A 1 M

HARTLEPOOL

CROOK, A 167

Main map place names

Shilbottle, Warkworth, Amble, Coquet Island, Swarland, Longframlington, Acklington, Togston, Felton, Brinkburn Priory, W. Chevington, Widdrington, Cresswell, Druridge Bay, Longhorsley, Netherwitton, Ulgham, Ellington, Lynemouth, Woodhorn Museum, Longhirst, Pegswood, Ashington, Newbiggin-by-the-Sea, Mitford, Morpeth, Stakeford, Cambois, Guide Post, Sleekburn, Bedlington, Blyth, Whalton, Meldon, Plessey Woods, Seaton Delaval Hall, Stannington, Cramlington, Seaton Sluice, Ogle, Ponteland, Seaton Burn, Dudley, Seaton Delaval, Dinnington, Wide Open, Earsdon, Shiremoor, Whitley Bay, Darras Hall, Priory

WCASTLE UPON-TYNE, TYNEMOUTH, Wallsend, Longbenton, Gosforth, N. Shields, Throckley, Heddon-on-the-W, Newburn, Jarrow, Hebburn, SOUTH SHIELDS, Amsterdam, Cleadon, Whitburn, Ryton, Crawcrook, Blaydon, Greenside, Whickham, Felling, Boldon, Southwick, Chopwell, Rowland's Gill, GATESHEAD, Wrekenton, Burnopfield, Beamish Hall, Birtley, WASHINGTON, Penshaw, Herrington, Ebchester, Stanley, Pelton, Chester-le-Street, Shiney Row, New Silksworth, SUNDERLAND, Ryhope, Consett, Annfield Plain, Edmondsley, Gt. Lumley, Colliery Row, Houghton-le-Spring, Seaham, Lanchester, Burnhope, Sacriston, W. Rainton, Hetton le-Hole, Murton, Langley Park, Framwellgate Moor, Easington Lane, S. Hetton, Easington, Satley, Esh Winning, Ushaw Moor, Carville, Sherburn, Horden, DURHAM, Brandon, Shotton Colliery, Thornley, Peterlee, Blackhall, Blackhall Rocks, Tow Law, Billy Row, Bowburn, Wheatley Hill, Hesleden, Wingate, Hart, Crook, Willington, Spennymoor, Kelloe, Coxhoe, Trimdon, Elwick, HARTLEPOOL, Hunwick, Kirk Merrington, Ferryhill, Fishburn, Seaton Carew, Witton-le-Wear, Coundon, Chilton, Sedgefield, Tees Bay, High Etherley, Bishop Auckland, Rushyford, Greatham, St. Helen Auckland, W. Auckland, Newton Aycliffe, Shildon, Thorpe Thewles, Wolviston, Billingham, Redcar, Marske-by-the-Sea, Cockfield, Evenwood, Heighington, Stillington, Saltburn-by-the-Sea, Raby Castle, Ingleton, Gt. Stainton, Coatham Mundeville, Bishopton, Redmarshall, Eston, New Marske, Skelton, Brotton, Staindrop, Gainford, Headlam, Walworth, Stockton-on-Tees, MIDDLESBROUGH, Dormanstown, Loftus

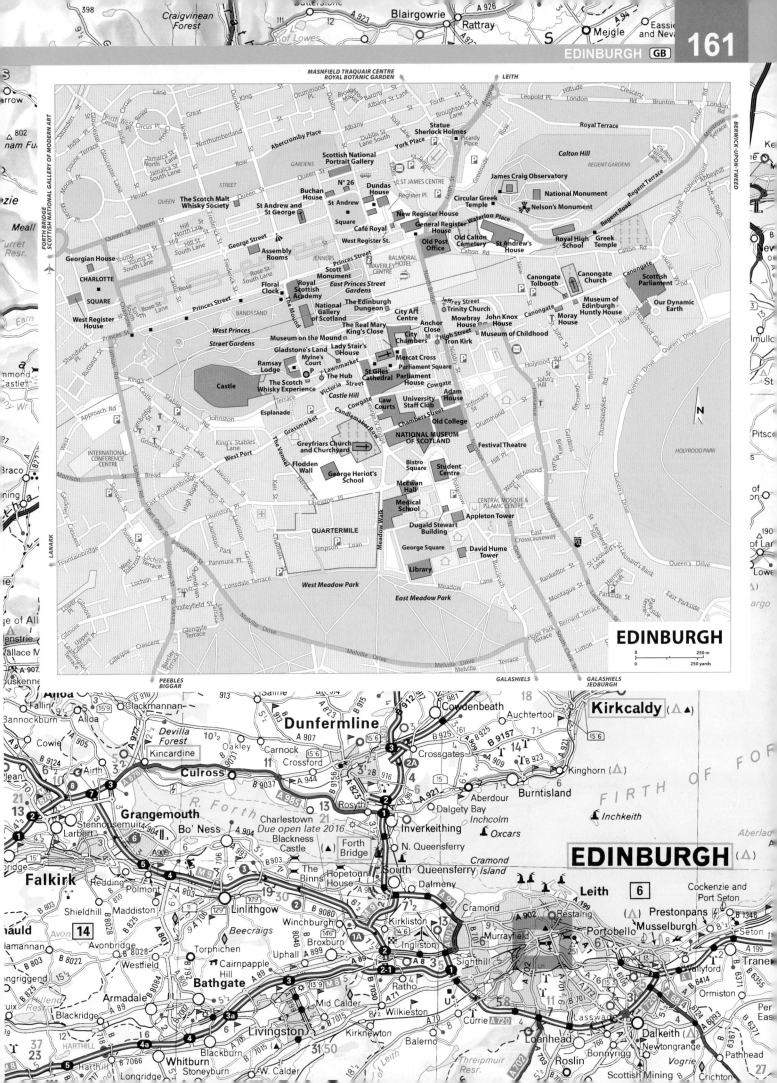

EDINBURGH

0 — 250 m
0 — 250 yards

EXETER (inset map)

St Martin's Church
Mol's Coffee House
Royal Albert Memorial Museum
Guildhall
St Nicholas Priory
Cathedral
Cathedral Close
City
TUCKER'S HALL
WHITE HART
ST MARY STEPS
Quay House Visitor Centre
CUSTOM HOUSE
HISTORIC QUAYSIDE
ST THOMAS
HARLEQUINS SHOPPING CENTRE
PRINCESSHAY SHOPPING CENTRE
GUILDHALL CENTRE
ROUGEMONT HOUSE
CASTLE
CENTRAL
WYNARD'S HOSPITAL
SHIP INN
Bridge Court
Dinham Mount
Dinham Crescent

0   150 m
0   150 yards

A 30, OKEHAMPTON
A 38, PLYMOUTH

Main map place names:

Bishop's Tawton, W. Buckland, Swimbridge, N. Molton, Hawkridge, Upton, Huish Cham, Regis

DEVON

Brushford, Exebridge, Morebath, Shillingford, Bampton, Oakford, Holcombe Rogus, Knightshayes Court, Sampford Peverel, Rackenford, Witheridge, Bolham, Tiverton, Halberton, Willand, Cullompton, Bickleigh, Cheriton Fitzpaine, Bradninch, Silverton, Plymtree, Killerton, Clyst Hydon, Stoke Canon, Talaton, Whimple, Broadclyst, Sandford, Thorverton, Newton St. Cyres, Crediton, Pinhoe, Clyst Honiton, EXETER AIRPORT, Venn Ottery, Newton Poppleford, Clyst St Mary, Woodbury, Yetti

Okehampton, Sticklepath, S. Tawton, S. Zeal, Belstone, Whiddon Down, Spreyton, Tedburn St. Mary, Cheriton Bishop, Ide, Alphington, EXETER, Topsham, Exminster, Exton, Lympstone, A La Ronde, Withycombe, Littleham, Exmouth

Sourton, Throwleigh, Sandy Park, Easton, Castle Drogo, Fingle Bridge, Drewsteignton, Spinster's Rock, Chagford, Scorhill, High Willhays, Dunsford, Doddiscombsleigh, Kennford, Trusham, Kenton, Starcross, Dawlish

Dartmoor Forest, Shovel Down, Moretonhampstead, N. Bovey, Christow, Manaton, Lustleigh, Hennock, Chudleigh, Ideford, Bishopsteignton

N. Brenton, Brent Tor, Mary Tavy, Dartmoor, Wistman's Wood, Postbridge, Cut Hill, Grey Wethers, Great Mis Tor, Becky Falls, Haytor Rocks, Bovey Tracey, Widecombe-in-the-Moor, Ilsington, Kingsteignton, Newton Abbot, Teignmouth, Shaldon, Combeinteignhead, Maidencombe, Babbacombe Bay

Two Bridges, Dartmoor Prison, Princetown, Dartmeet, Buckland-in-the-Moor, Bickington, Abbotskerswell, Kingskerswell, Compton, Cockington, Babbacombe, TORQUAY, TORBAY

Tavistock, Whitchurch, National Park, Ryder's Hill, Holne, Ashburton, Buckfast, Buckfastleigh, Staverton, Dartington, Ipplepen, Marldon, Berry Pomeroy, Paignton, Tor Bay, Goodrington, Churston Ferrers

Yelverton, Meavy, Buckland Abbey, Bickleigh, Cornwood, S. Brent, Avonwick, Diptford, Harberton, Ashprington, Stoke Gabriel, Galmpton, Berry Head, Brixham

PLYMOUTH, Plympton, Ivybridge, Ugborough, Ermington, Harbertonford, Cornworthy, Dittisham, Totnes

GLASGOW

Scale: 0 — 450 m / 0 — 450 yards

City Centre Map Labels

DUMBARTON · STIRLING · KIRKINTILLOCH · LIVINGSTON · HAMILTON MOTHERWELL · PAISLEY · KILMARNOCK · MOTHERWELL HAMILTON · EAST KILBRIDE

Botanic Gardens · Hunterian Art Gallery · MACKINTOSH HOUSE · University Gilmorehill Building · Hunterian Museum · WESTERN INFIRMARY · Park Circus · Kelvingrove Park · KELVINGROVE ART GALLERY AND MUSEUM · Kelvin Hall · Queen's Cross Church · Tenement House · The National Piping Centre · Beresford · Glasgow School of Art · CCA · The Mitchell Library · Willow Tearoom · Sauciehall Street · BUCHANAN STREET BUS STATION · BUCHANAN GALLERIES · Martyr's School · Royal Infirmary · CATHEDRAL · Necropolis · St Mungo Museum of Religious Life and Art · Provand's Lordship · Scottish Exhibition and Conference Center · EXHIBITION CENTRE STATION · Merchants' House · Daily Record Building · Willow Tea Rooms · The Lighthouse · Gallery of Modern Art · Princes Square · City Chambers · George Street · Trades Hall · Merchant Square · Clyde Auditorium The "Armadillo" · La grue Finnieston · Glasgow Tower · Science Centre · CENTRAL STATION · ST ENOCH SHOPPING CENTRE · Glasgow Cross · Tolbooth Steeple · The Barras · Bridgegate Steeple · Scotland Street School Museum · Glasgow Green · People's Palace · Doulton Fountain · Templeton Business Centre

Regional Map Labels

Greenock · Port Glasgow · Dumbarton · Erskine Bridge · Duntocher · Bearsden · Milngavie · Torrance · Kirkintilloch · Lenzie · Cumbernauld · Condorrat · Slamannan · Longriggend · Riggend · Caldercruix · Langbank · Bishopton · Old Kilpatrick · Clydebank · Renfrew · Stepps · Coatbridge · Airdrie · Chapelhall · Bridge of Weir · Linwood · GLASGOW · Rutherglen · Mossend · Holytown · Salsburg · Johnstone · Kilbarchan · PAISLEY · Uddingston · Bothwell · Bellshill · Newarthill · Garfin · Cleland · Muirshiel · Ranfurly · Heathfield · Barrhead · Cambuslang · Blantyre · Carmunnock · HAMILTON · Motherwell · Wishaw · Kilmacolm · Houston · Kilmalcolm · Lochwinnoch · Howwood · Neilston · Busby · Newton Mearns · Uddingston · East Kilbride · Eaglesham · Ballageich Hill · Auldhouse · Larkhall · Overtown · Beith · Barrmill · Uplawmoor · Kilbirnie · Dunlop · Dalry · Dalserf · Law

Rivers/features: R. Clyde · Kelvin · Loch Thom · Creuch Hill · Strathgryfe · Gryfe · Stake · Garnock · Barcraigs Resr. · Long Loch · Balgray Resr.

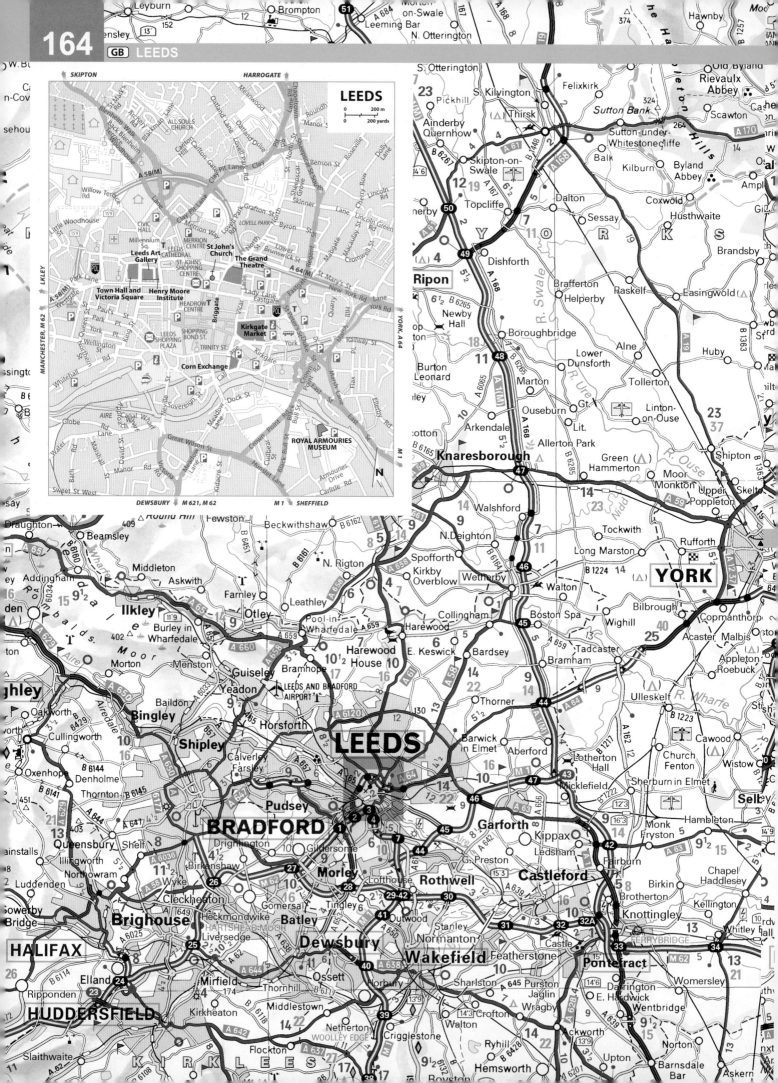

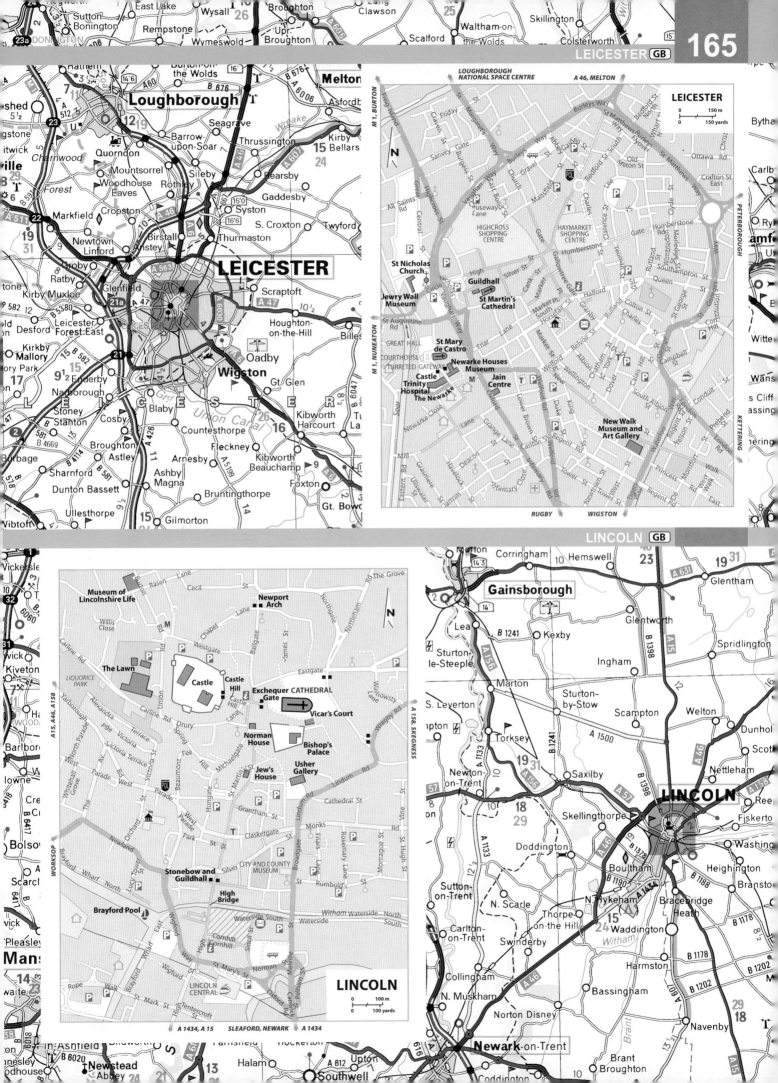

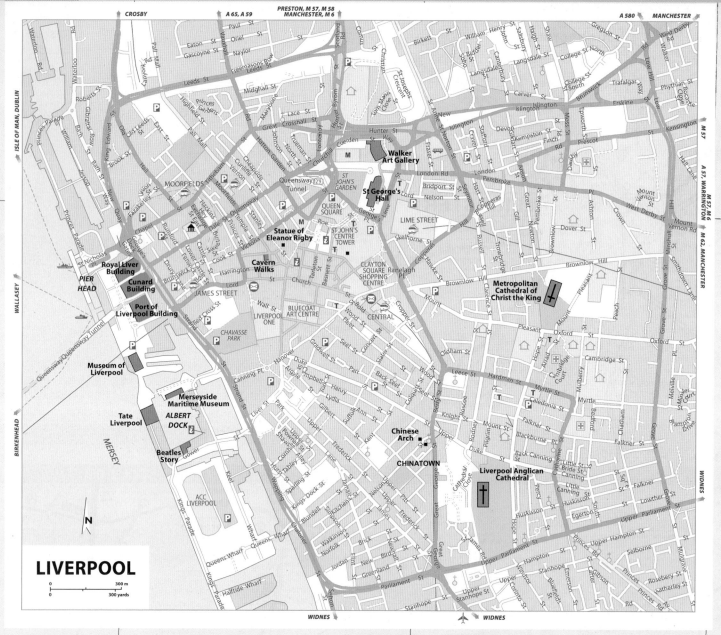

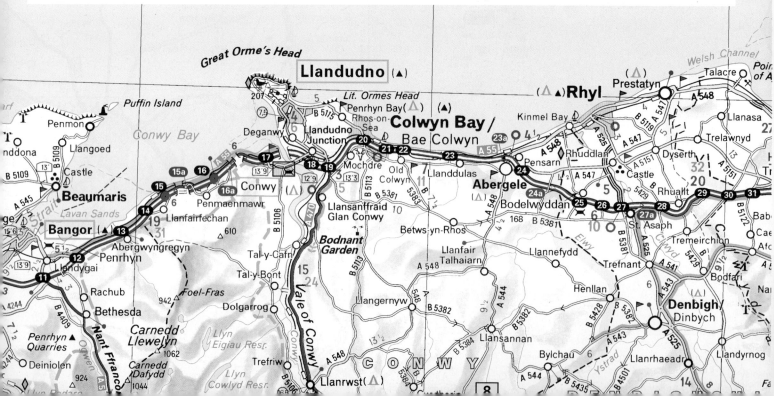

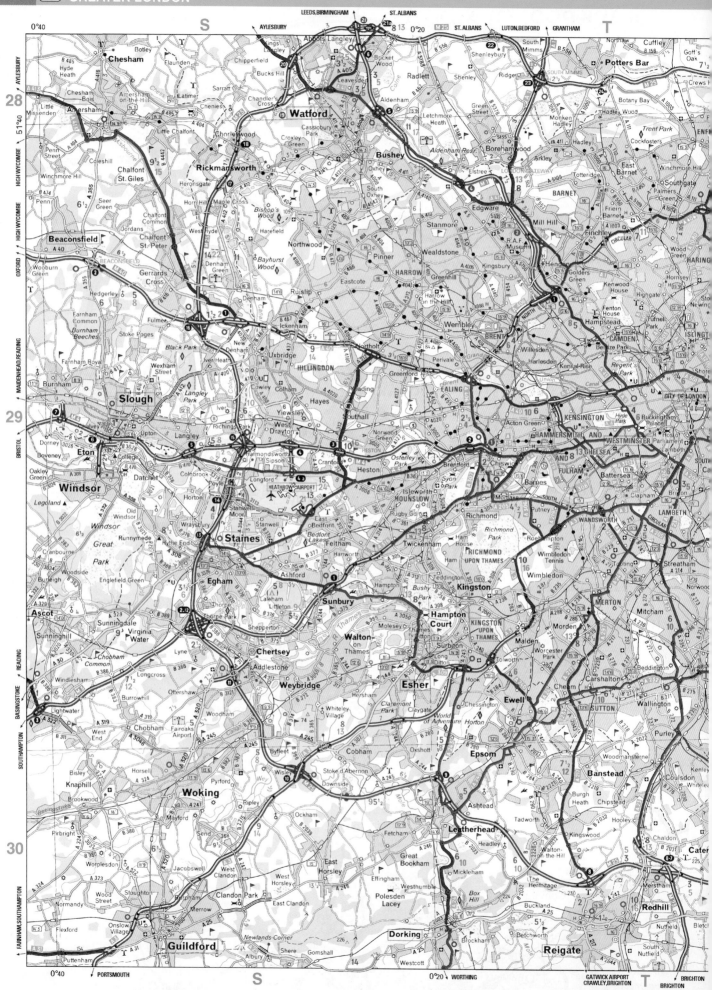

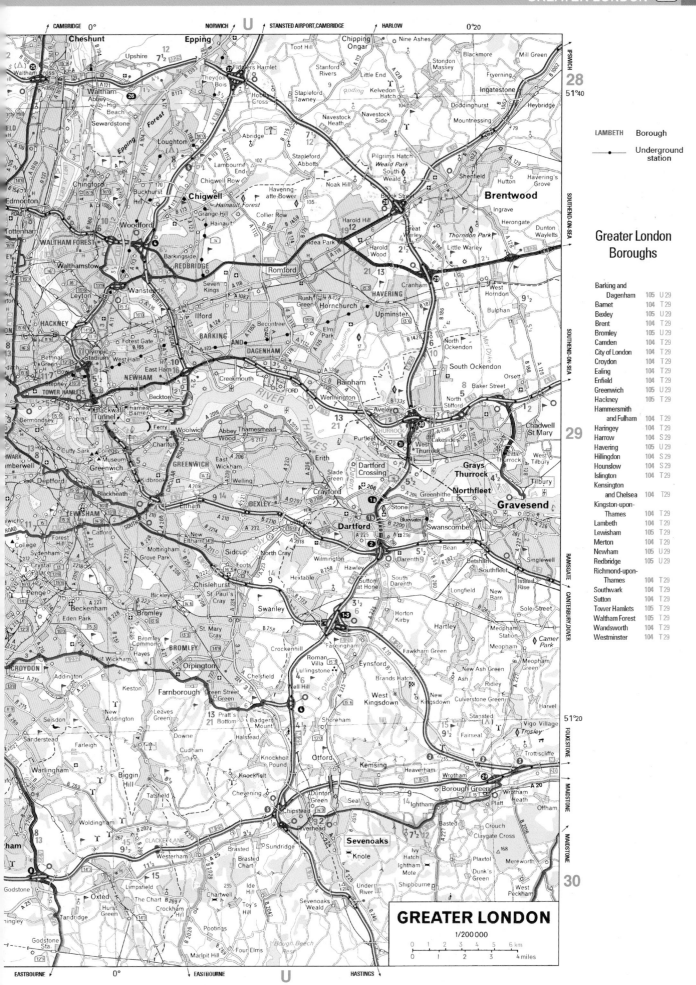

LAMBETH Borough
Underground station

Greater London Boroughs

Barking and Dagenham	105	U 29
Barnet	104	T 29
Bexley	105	U 29
Brent	104	T 29
Bromley	105	U 29
Camden	104	T 29
City of London	104	T 29
Croydon	104	T 29
Ealing	104	T 29
Enfield	104	T 29
Greenwich	105	U 29
Hackney	105	T 29
Hammersmith and Fulham	104	T 29
Haringey	104	T 29
Harrow	104	S 29
Havering	105	U 29
Hillingdon	104	S 29
Hounslow	104	S 29
Islington	104	T 29
Kensington and Chelsea	104	T 29
Kingston-upon-Thames	104	T 29
Lambeth	104	T 29
Lewisham	105	T 29
Merton	104	T 29
Newham	105	U 29
Redbridge	105	U 29
Richmond-upon-Thames	104	T 29
Southwark	104	T 29
Sutton	104	T 29
Tower Hamlets	105	T 29
Waltham Forest	105	T 29
Wandsworth	104	T 29
Westminster	104	T 29

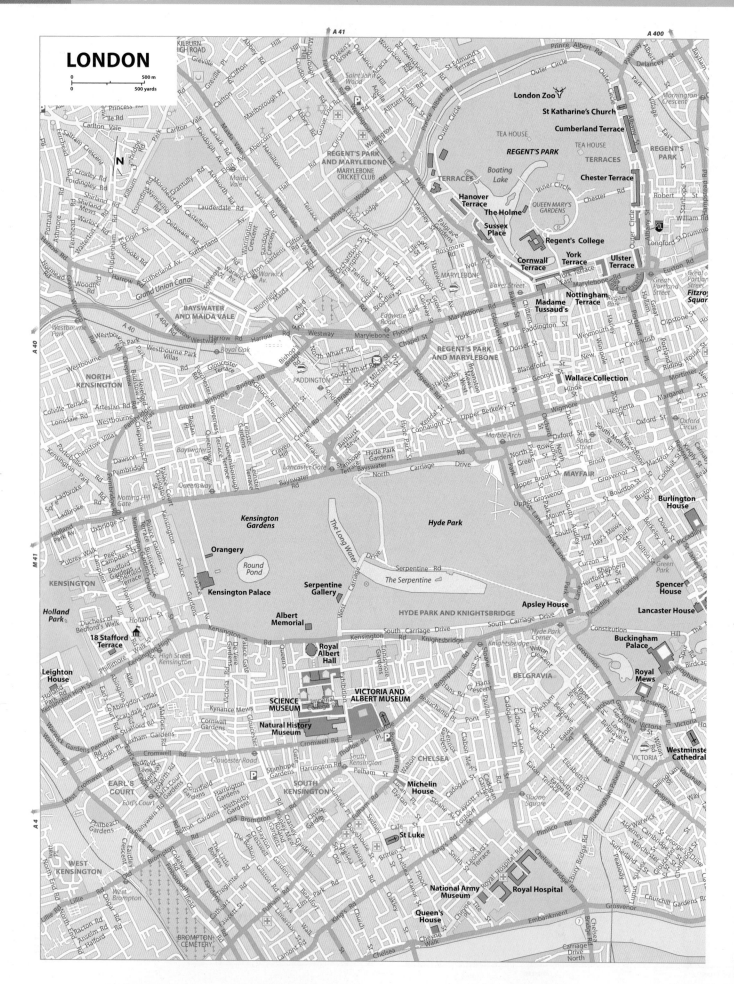

LONDON

0 — 500 m
0 — 500 yards

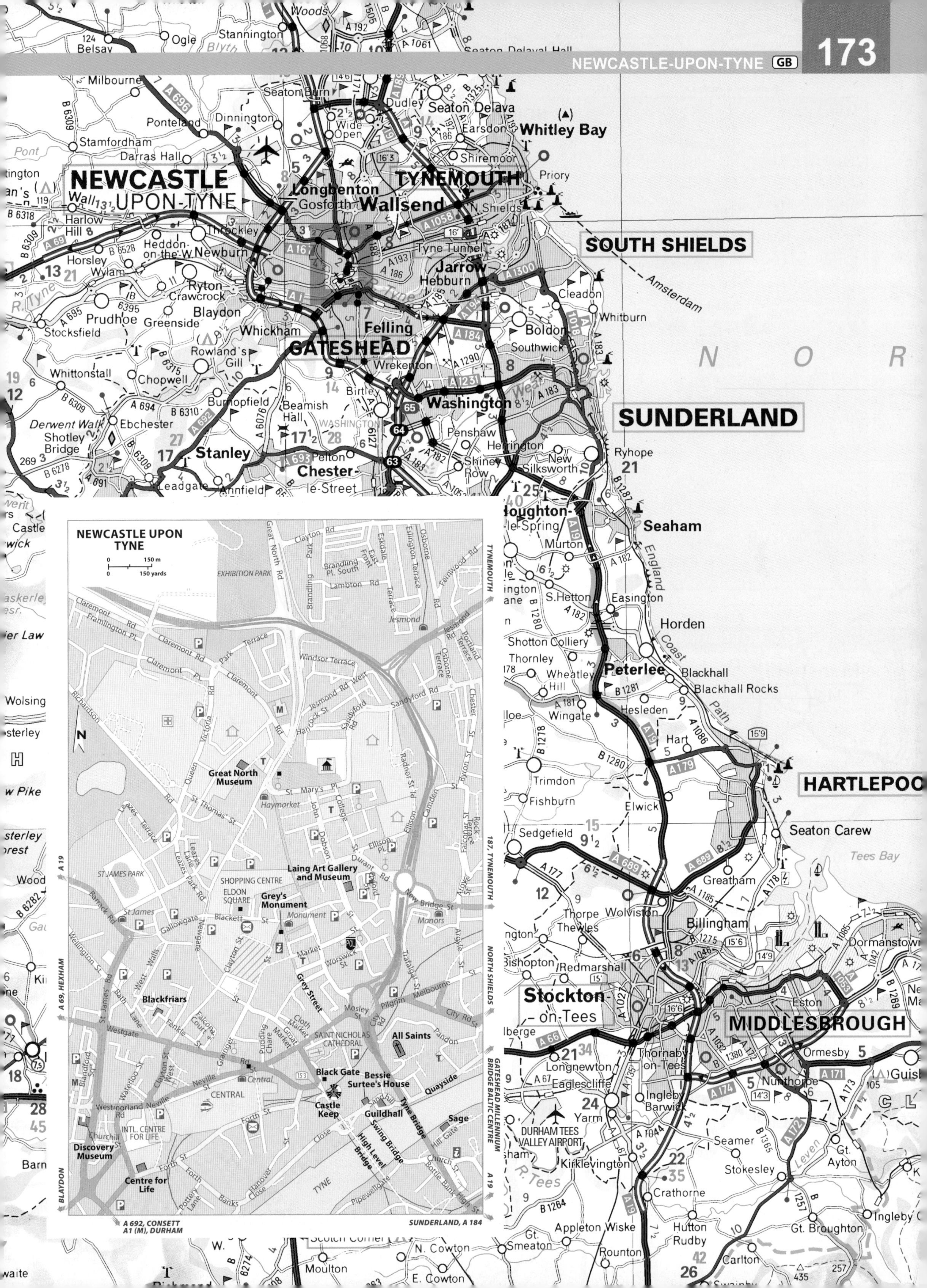

Woods
A 192
Stannington
124 Belsay
Ogle
A 1061
Seaton Delaval Hall
A 1605
Blyth
Milbourne
Dudley
Seaton Delava
Whitley Bay
Seaton Burn
Wide Open
Earsdon
Shiremoor
Ponteland
Dinnington
Priory
Stamfordham
Darras Hall
TYNEMOUTH
N. Shields
NEWCASTLE
UPON-TYNE
Longbenton
Gosforth
Wallsend
SOUTH SHIELDS
Wall 13½
Harlow Hill
Throckley
Tyne Tunnel
Heddon-on-the-W Newburn
A 167
A 193
Jarrow
Amsterdam
Horsley
Wylam
Hebburn
A 1300
Cleadon
Ryton Crawcrock
Blaydon
Greenside
Whickham
Felling
Boldon
Whitburn
Stocksfield
A 695
GATESHEAD
Southwick
N O R
Prudhoe
Rowland's Gill
Wrekenton
A 1290
SUNDERLAND
Whittonstall
Chopwell
Birtley
Washington
Beamish Hall
WASHINGTON
Penshaw
Herrington
Ebchester
Burnopfield
65
Shiney Row
New Silksworth
Ryhope
Shotley Bridge
Stanley
64
63
Pelton
Houghton-le-Spring
Seaham
Leadgate
Chester-le-Street
Murton
Arnfield
S. Hetton
Easington
Horden
Shotton Colliery
Thornley
Peterlee
Blackhall
Wheatley Hill
Blackhall Rocks
Wingate
Hesleden
Hart
HARTLEPOO
Trimdon
A 179
Fishburn
Elwick
Seaton Carew
Sedgefield
Tees Bay
Greatham
Thorpe Wolviston
Thewles
Billingham
Bishopton
Redmarshall
Dormanstow
Stockton-on-Tees
Eston
MIDDLESBROUGH
Longnewton
Thornaby-on-Tees
Ormesby
Eaglescliffe
Ingleby Barwick
Nunthorpe
Guis
Yarm
DURHAM TEES VALLEY AIRPORT
Seamer
Gt. Ayton
Kirklevington
Stokesley
Crathorne
Appleton Wiske
Hutton Rudby
Gt. Broughton
Ingleby
Moulton
N. Cowton
Carlton
E. Cowton
Rounton
Swinby

Inset map:

NEWCASTLE UPON TYNE
0   150 m
0   150 yards
N

EXHIBITION PARK
Great North Museum
Laing Art Gallery and Museum
SHOPPING CENTRE
ELDON SQUARE
Grey's Monument
Monument
ST JAMES PARK
Blackfriars
All Saints
SAINT NICHOLAS CATHEDRAL
Black Gate
Bessie Surtee's House
Quayside
Castle Keep
Guildhall
Sage
CENTRAL
INTL. CENTRE FOR LIFE
Discovery Museum
Centre for Life
High Level Bridge
Swing Bridge
Tyne Bridge
TYNE
GATESHEAD MILLENNIUM BRIDGE BALTIC CENTRE

A 692, CONSETT
A1 (M), DURHAM
SUNDERLAND, A 184
A 69, HEXHAM
BLAYDON
TYNEMOUTH
NORTH SHIELDS
187. TYNEMOUTH
A 19

NORWICH

Holkham · Wells-next-the-Sea · Salthouse · Cley-next-the-Sea · Sheringham · W. Runton · **Cromer** · Brancaster · Blakeney

CROMER · WROXHAM · A 1151

NORWICH
0 — 200 m
0 — 200 yards

St Crispin's Rd · Cowgate · Barrack · COW TOWER · Cotman Fields · St Andrew's and Blackfriars Hall · Elm Hill · St Simion and St Jude · Norwich Cathedral · St Peter Hungate · Erpingham Gate · Pull's Ferry · St Michael at Plea · St Ethelbert's Gate · St Benedicts St · Pottergate · Guildhall · City Hall · Market Place · Castle · Castle Museum · Royal Arcade · MILLENNIUM BUILDING · St Peter Mancroft · CHAPEL FIELD GARDENS · CASTLE MALL SHOPPING CENTRE · SAINSBURY CENTER FOR VISUAL ARTS · CHAPELFIELD SHOPPING CENTRE · Walls · St Stephens · Queens Rd · Victoria · Queens Rd · Rouen · Thorn Lane · Ber St · Horns Lane · King St · RIVERSIDE · Carrow Bridge · Walls · Carrow Hill · Trafalgar St · Southwell · Ipswich Grove · Newmarket Rd · Brunswick Rd

THETFORD · IPSWICH · LOWESTOFT · GREAT YARMOUTH · N

A 47, SWAFFHAM · A 149

Bodham Street · A 148 · Holt · Aylmerton · Baconsthorpe · Roughton · Northrepps · Mundesley · Edgefield · Aldborough · Thorpe Market · Trunch · Bacton · Little Barningham · Itteringham · Erpingham · Knapton · Corpusty · Blickling Hall · Felmingham · North Walsham · Honing · Blickling · Swanton Abbott · Worstead · Stalham · Reepham · Marsham · Scottow · Low Street · Cawston · Buxton · Neatishead · Catfield · Hevingham · Norfolk Wildlife Park · Coltishall · Norfolk Broads · Lenwade · Felthorpe · Horstead · Hoveton · Ludham · Attlebridge · Hainford · Wroxham · Horning · Ranworth · Taverham · Drayton · Horsford · Horsham St. Faith · Spixworth · Salhouse · S. Walsham · Hockering · Sprowston · New Rackheath · Coltessey · Catton · **NORWICH** · Easton · Thorpe St. Andrew · Acle · Barford · Bawburgh · Blofield · Hethersett · Cringleford · Surlingham · Brundall · Caistor St. Edmund · R. Yare · Mulbarton · Stoke Holy Cross · East Poringland · Claxton · Cantley · Thurton · Newton · Brooke · Shotesham · Loddon · Ashwellthorpe

---

NOTTINGHAM

Pleasley · Clipstone · Eakring · **Mansfield** · Maplebe · Huthwaite · Bilsthorpe · **Sutton-in-Ashfield** · Rainworth · Kirkling · **Kirkby-in-Ashfield** · Blidworth · Farnsfield · Hocke · Pinxton · Annesley Woodhouse · **Newstead** · Newstead Abbey · Halam · Selston · Newstead · Halloughton · Oxton · Thurgarton · Papplewick · Eastwood · **Hucknall** · Calverton · Lowdham · Kimberley · Bulwell · Woodborough · Lambley · Gunth · **NOTTINGHAM** · **Arnold** · Burton Joyce · Newton · Wollaton Hall · **Carlton** · Radcliffe-on-Trent · Aslockton · Orston · Bottesford · Barkston · Belton · Bramcote · Stapleford · **West Bridgford** · Cotgrave · Cropwell Bishop · Bingham · Sedgebrook · Gt. Gonerby · Welby · **Beeston** · Toton · Edwalton · Granby · Redmile · Barrowby · **Grantham** · **Long Eaton** · Clifton · Normanton-on-the-Wolds · Langar · Belvoir · Woolsthorpe · Denton · Ruddington · Colston Bassett · Harby · Stathern · Harlaxton · Gotham · Keyworth · Hickling · Gt. Ponton · Bunny · Nether Broughton · Croxton Kerrial · Kegworth · East Lake · Wysall · Long Clawson · Skillington · Sutton Bonington · Rempstone · Upr. · Waltham-on- · Ingolds

MANSFIELD · M 1 MANCHESTER

NOTTINGHAM
0 — 200 m
0 — 200 yards

Raleigh Rd · Hampden · Shelton · Portland · Cromwell · Shakespeare · Bluecoat St · Talbot St · Chaucer St · Goldsmith · Derby Rd · Wollaton St · VICTORIA CENTRE · Newcastle Drive · Upper Parliament · Lincoln St · Tennis Drive · Park Valley · Pelham · Woolpack Lane · Barker Gate · Huntingdon Drive · Lenton · St Mary's · Weekday Cross · Fisher Gate · Clumber Rd · **Castle** · Peveril Drive · Collin · London Rd · Lenton Rd · Fishpond Drive · Nottingham Canal · Station St · MIDLAND · Queen's Rd

DERBY · BEESTON · BIRMINGHAM · LEICESTER · GRANTHAM · N

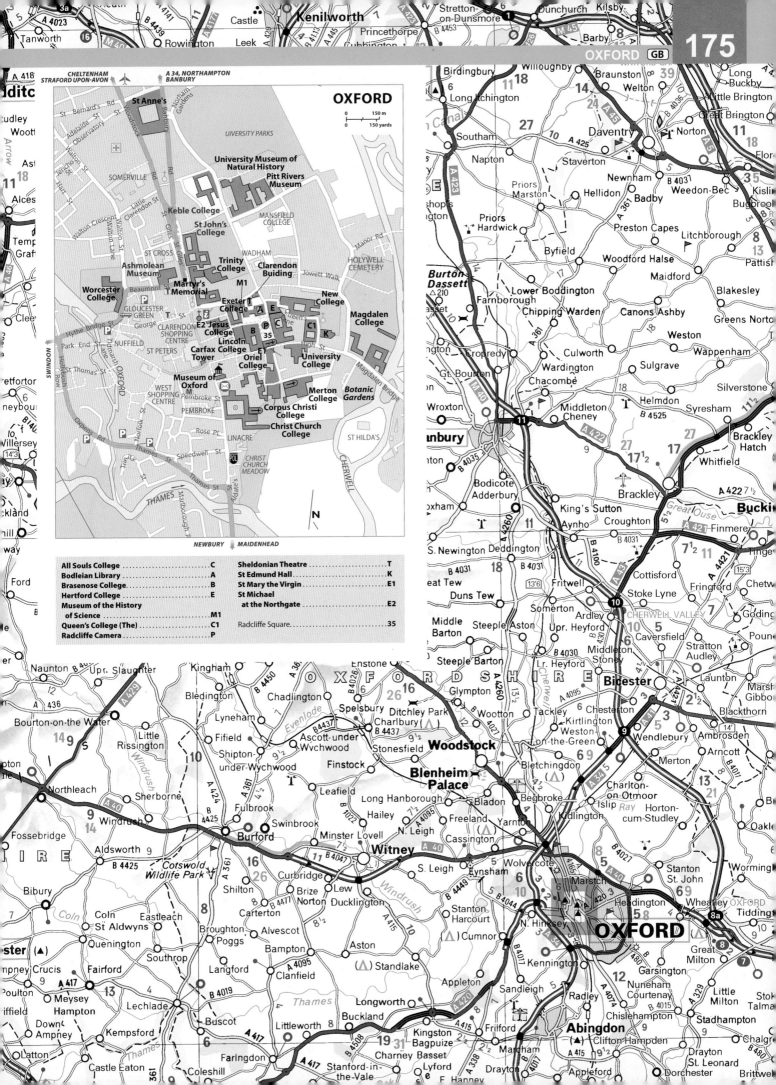

PERTH (city inset)

Black Watch Regimental Museum

North

Bell's Sports Centre

Inch

Barossa Place

N°10

Rose Terrace

Georgian Terraces

Old Perth Academy

Atholl Crescent

Charlotte St

Fair Maids House

Perth Bridge

Black Watch Gardens

Foundry Lane

Lower City Mills

Charlotte Square

Museum and Art Gallery

St CATHERINE'S RETAIL PARK SHOPPING CENTRE

High St

ST JOHN'S CENTRE

St John's

City Hall

Maison des Evêques de Dunkeld

King James VI Hospital

Salutation Hotel

Sheriff Court

Water Works et Fergusson Gallery

South Inch

MONCREIFFE ISLAND

M 90, FORTH ROAD BRIDGE

BRAEMAR SCONE PALACE   COUPAR ANGUS

A9 INVERNESS CAITHNESS GLASS

CRIANLARICH CRIEFF

A9 STIRLING CHERRYBANK

KINNOULL HILL

BRANKLYN GARDEN FRIARTON BRIDGE

Main map

Glas-allt

Loch Muick

Loch Lee

Inchgrundle

Glen

Braedownie

Glen Clova

West Knock

Ben Tirran

White Hill

Clova

Waterhead

Runtaleave

Glen Prosen

Glenprosen Village

N

Isla Forest

Cat Law 678

Dykehead

Ogil

Fern

Backwater Resr.

3

Balintore

Pearsie

Tannadice

Dykends

Kirkton of Kingoldrum

Oathlaw

Bridgend of Lintrathen

Kirriemuir

Lunanhead

Kingsmuir

Craigisla

Reekie Linn

Craigton

Forfar

Ruthven

Glamis Castle

Douglastown

Inverarity

Meigle

Eassie and Nevay

Glamis

Kirkbuddo

Newtyle

Lumley Den

Balgray

Coupar Angus

Siddlaw Hills

Lundie

Auchterhouse

Kellas

Newbigging

Pitcur

Kof Lowes

Clunie

Muirhead

Kirkton of Strathmartine

Dunkeld

Birnam

Meikleour

Strathbraan

Tay

Caputh

King's Seat 377

Dundee

Michelin

Dighty

Inver

Trochry

Kinclaven

R. Isla

Strathbraan

Cargill

Burrelton

Abernyte

Longforgan

Invergowrie

Tay Road Bridge

Broughty Ferry

Little Glenshee

Bankfoot

Stanley

Guildtown

Kinrossie

Braes of the Carse

Inchture

9

Tayport

Caorach

Logiealmond

Harrietfield

Moneydie

Balbeggie

Kinnaird

Longforgan

Newport-on-Tay

Wormit

Buchanty

Almond

Luncarty

Scone Palace

New Scone

Rait

Firth of Tay

Balmerino

Tentsmuir Forest

Huntingtower Castle

Carse of Gowrie

Methven

Tibbermore

Bridgend

Kinfauns

Errol

Balmullo

Leuchars

Findo Gask

PERTH

Elcho

Glencarse

Newburgh

Luthrie

Kilmany

Guardbridge

R. Earn

Forgandenny

Bridge of Earn

Abernethy

Lindores

Dairsie

Strathkinness

Aberuthven

Forteviot

Pitmedden Forest

Letham

Cupar

Craigtoun

Pitscottie

Dunning

Auchtermuchty

Howe of Fife

Springfield

Hill of Tarvit

Ceres

Peat Inn

Auchterarder

Common of Dunning

Path of Condie

Glenfarg

Gateside

Strathmiglo

Ladybank

Scotstarvit Tower

Craigrothie

Steele's Knowe

Water of May

Lomond Hills

Freuchie

Falkland

Kingskettle

Backmuir of New Gilston

Largoward

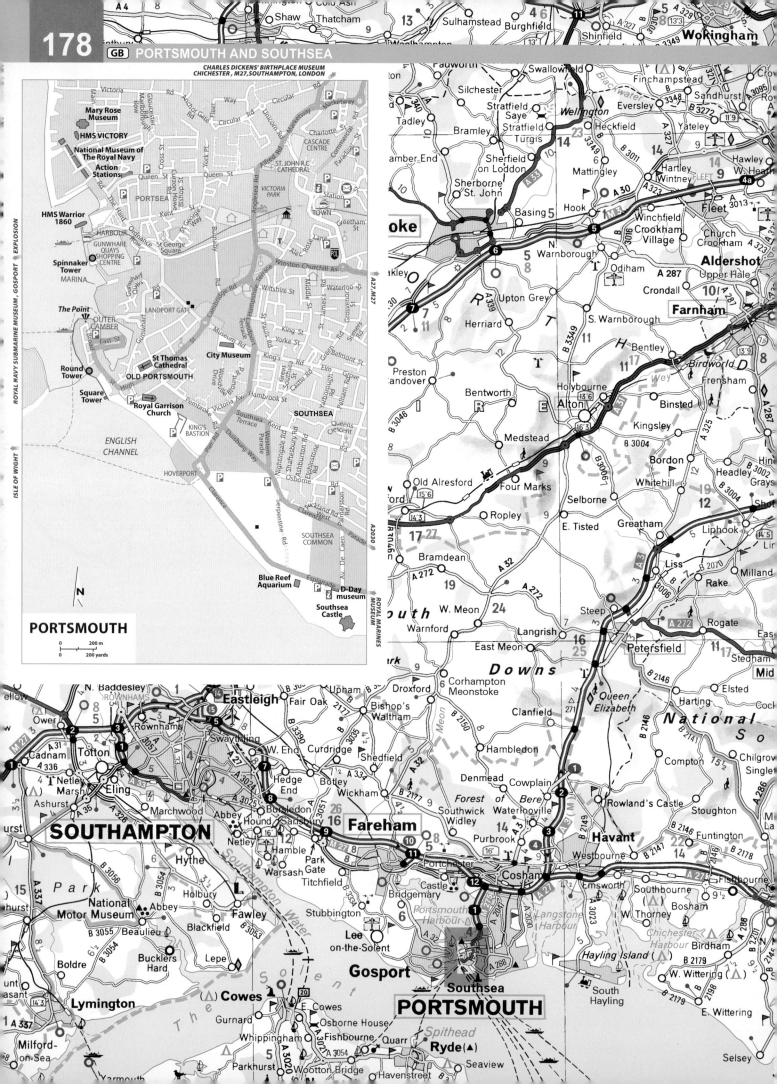

PORTSMOUTH

Inset map labels:
CHARLES DICKENS' BIRTHPLACE MUSEUM
CHICHESTER , M27, SOUTHAMPTON, LONDON

Mary Rose Museum
HMS VICTORY
National Museum of The Royal Navy
Action Stations
HMS Warrior 1860
GUNWHARF QUAYS SHOPPING CENTRE
Spinnaker Tower
MARINA
The Point
OUTER CAMBER
East St
Round Tower
Square Tower
Royal Garrison Church
OLD PORTSMOUTH
St Thomas Cathedral
City Museum
KING'S BASTION
SOUTHSEA
ENGLISH CHANNEL
HOVERPORT
SOUTHSEA COMMON
Blue Reef Aquarium
D-Day museum
Southsea Castle
ROYAL NAVY SUBMARINE MUSEUM, GOSPORT, EXPLOSION
ISLE OF WIGHT
ROYAL MARINES MUSEUM
PORTSEA
LANDPORT
VICTORIA PARK
ST. JOHN R.C. CATHEDRAL
CASCADE CENTRE
LANDPORT GATE
TOWN

Scale: 0 – 200 m / 0 – 200 yards

Main map place names

A4, Shaw, Thatcham, Sulhamstead, Burghfield, Woolhampton, Shinfield, **Wokingham**

Padworth, Swallowfield, Finchampstead, Sandhurst, Crowthorne
Silchester, Stratfield Saye, Stratfield Turgis, Wellington, Eversley, Yateley
Tadley, Bramley, Sherfield on Loddon, Mattingley, Heckfield, Hartley Wintney, Hawley, Hawley Heath
Sherborne St. John, Basing, Hook, Winchfield, Crookham Village, Church Crookham, **Fleet**, **Aldershot**
N. Warnborough, Odiham, Upper Hale
-oke, **Farnham**, Crondall
Upton Grey, S. Warnborough, Bentley, Birdworld
Herriard, Frensham
Preston Candover, Bentworth, Holybourne, Alton, Binsted, Kingsley, Bordon, Headley
Medstead, Whitehill, Grayshott
Old Alresford, Four Marks, Selborne, Greatham, Liphook, Milland
Ropley, E. Tisted, Liss, Rake
Bramdean, Steep, Rogate, Stedham, Midhurst
W. Meon, Warnford, Langrish, East Meon, Petersfield, Harting
Corhampton, Meonstoke, Droxford, Clanfield, Queen Elizabeth, Elsted
Downs, Hambledon, Denmead, Cowplain, Compton, Chilgrove, Singleton
SOUTHAMPTON, N. Baddesley, ROWNHAMS, **Eastleigh**, Fair Oak, Upham, Bishop's Waltham, Shedfield, Southwick, Widley, Waterlooville, Rowland's Castle, Stoughton, Funtington
Ower, Cadnam, Totton, Rownhams, Swaythling, W. End, Curdridge, **Fareham**, Purbrook, **Havant**, Westbourne, Emsworth, Southbourne, Bosham
Netley Marsh, Eling, Ashurst, Marchwood, Abbey, Hound, Netley, Hamble, Botley, Wickham, Forest of Bere, Portchester, **Cosham**, W. Thorney, Fishbourne, Birdham
Hythe, Hedge End, Bursledon, Sarisbury, Park Gate, Titchfield, Castle, Bridgemary, Langstone Harbour, Hayling Island, W. Wittering
Holbury, Warsash, Stubbington, **Portsmouth Harbour**
National Motor Museum, Fawley, Blackfield, Lee on-the-Solent, **Gosport**, **Southsea**, South Hayling, E. Wittering, Selsey
Beaulieu, Bucklers Hard, Lepe, **PORTSMOUTH**
Boldre, Lymington, **Cowes**, E. Cowes, Gurnard, Osborne House, Whippingham, Fishbourne, Quarr, **Ryde**, Seaview
Milford-on-Sea, Yarmouth, Parkhurst, Wootton Bridge, Havenstreet, Haven
The Solent, Spithead

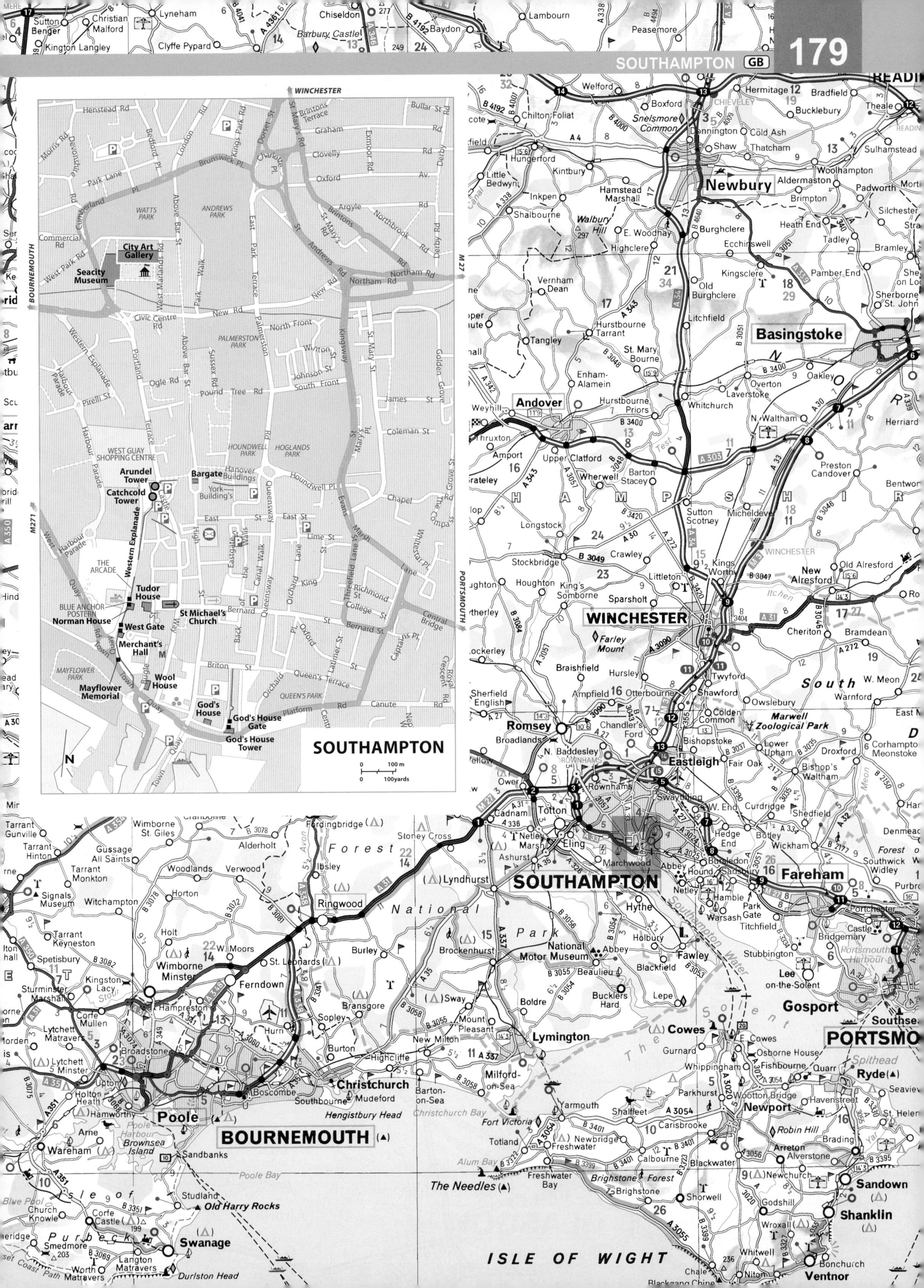

SOUTHAMPTON (city inset)

City Art Gallery
Seacity Museum
Civic Centre
WEST QUAY SHOPPING CENTRE
Arundel Tower
Catchcold Tower
Bargate
Hanover Buildings
York Building's
THE ARCADE
Tudor House
BLUE ANCHOR POSTERN
Norman House
West Gate
Merchant's Hall
Wool House
Mayflower Memorial
God's House
God's House Gate
God's House Tower
St Michael's Church
WATTS PARK
ANDREWS PARK
PALMERSTON PARK
HOUNDWELL PARK
HOGLANDS PARK
QUEEN'S PARK
MAYFLOWER PARK

WINCHESTER
BOURNEMOUTH
PORTSMOUTH

0 100 m
0 100 yards

Main regional map:

READING
Newbury
Basingstoke
Andover
WINCHESTER
Romsey
Eastleigh
SOUTHAMPTON
Fareham
PORTSMO(UTH)
Gosport
Southse(a)
Ryde
Newport
Sandown
Shanklin
Ventnor
ISLE OF WIGHT
Lymington
Cowes
Yarmouth
The Needles
Freshwater Bay
BOURNEMOUTH
Christchurch
Poole
Swanage
Wareham
Corfe Castle
Old Harry Rocks
Wimborne Minster
Ferndown
Ringwood
Lyndhurst
Brockenhurst
National Motor Museum
Beaulieu
Fawley
Totton
New Forest National Park

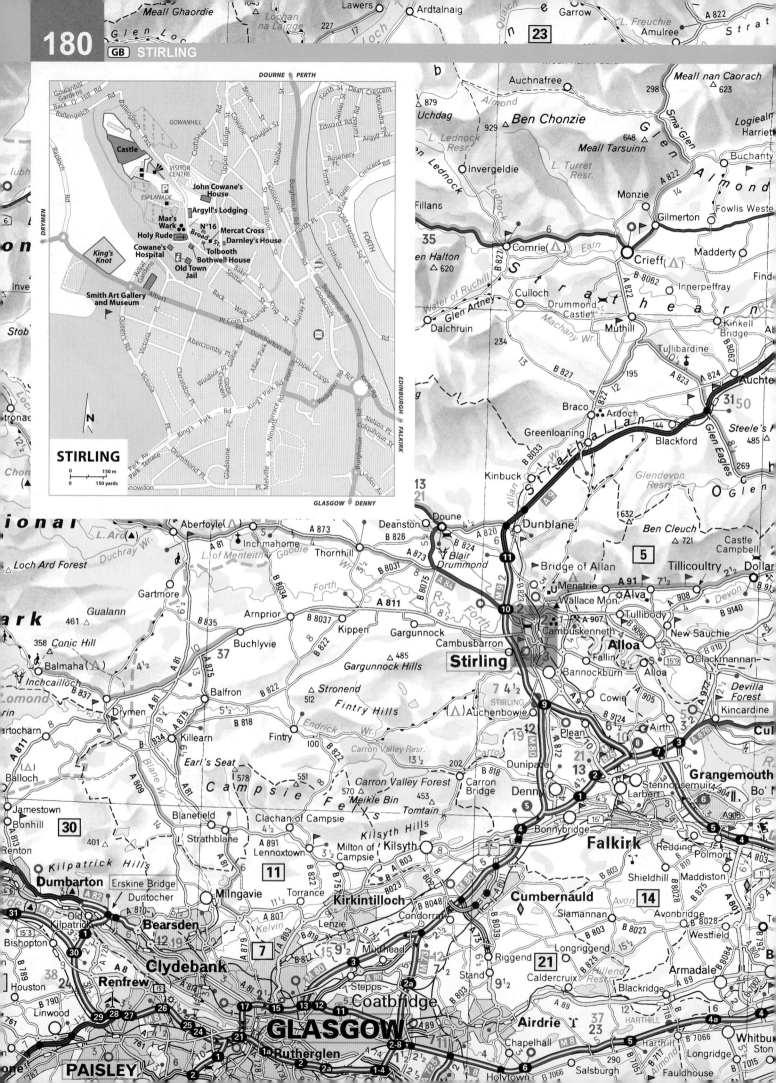

WINCHESTER (inset map)

0   200 m
0   200 yards

N

NEWBURY   LONDON

Bereweeke Rd
Andover Rd
Brassey Rd
Owen's Rd
Hatherley
Fairfield Rd
Clifton
St Pauls Hill
Clifton Terrace
Upper High St
Romsey
St James Terrace
St James' Lane
Compton Rd
Beaufort Rd
Christchurch Rd
Ranelagh
Edgar Rd
St Cross Rd
Kingsgate Rd
Romans Rd
St Michael's Rd
St Swithun St
Canon St
Dome Alley
Kingsgate St
Thomas St
Southgate St
Archery Lane
Symonds St
Culver Rd
KINGSGATE PARK
Wharf Hill
College Walk
College St
Winchester College
The Close
CATHEDRAL
Market Lane
God Begot House
Castle Great Hall
WINCHESTER
RECREATION CENTRE
King Alfred Pl
Hyde Close
Nuns Rd
Arthur Rd
Saxon Rd
Egb...
Worthy Lane
Station Rd
Sussex St
City Rd
Swan Lane
Gordon Rd
North Walls
Hyde St
POL
Middle Brook St
Upper Brook St
Lower Brook St
Friarsgate
Eastgate St
Water Lane
Chesil St
Magdalen Hill
Blue Ball Hill
Alresford Rd
Wales St
St Martin's Close
Beggar's Lane
Moss Rd
Firmstone Rd
Northbrook Av.
Stratton Rd
Baring Rd
Quarry Rd
Petersfield Rd
St John's St
St Catherine's Rd
Bar End
Portal Rd
Milland Rd
Barfield Close
Domum Rd
ITCHEN
SOUTHAMPTON   SOUTHAMPTON
SALISBURY
ROMSEY
GUILDFORD

Main map

Wootton Rivers
Oare
Milton
Great Bedwyn
Pumps
Shalbourne
Inkpen
Walbury
Hamstead Marshall
Brimpton
Padworth
Silch...
Newbu...
Kennet and Avon Canal
A 338

Highclere
Ecchinswell
B 3051
Tadley
Bram...
Kingsclere
21 34
18 29
Pamber End
Sher... St.
Old Burghclere
A 34
A 339
17
A 343
Litchfield
B 3051
Basingstoke
Hurstbourne Tarrant
St. Mary Bourne
B 3048
15·9
Oakley
B 3400
Overton
Laverstoke
9
A 30
7 11 5
Enham-Alamein
Hurstbourne Priors
Whitchurch
N. Waltham
2 11
He...
B 3400
13 8
A 303
A 33
8
Clatford
B 3048
Test
11 7
A 303
Preston Candover
Be...
Wherwell
Barton Stacey
M   P   S   H   I   R...
B 3420
Sutton Scotney
Micheldever
18 11
B 3046
24
A 30
A 34
A 272
9½
Crawley
Kings Worth
15·6
New Alresford
Old Alresford
B 3049
23
Littleton
A 30
9
WINCHESTER
B 3047
14·3
...orne
...g's
Sparsholt
A 3420
9
WINCHESTER
B 3404
A 31
Cheriton
B 3046
17 27
Bramdean
A 272
Farley Mount
A 3090
10
11
11
Twyford
South
W. Meon
Warnford
Lockerley
Alderbury
Braishfield
Hursley
Ampfield 16
Otterbourne
Shawford
Owslebury
Marwell Zoological Park
Coombe Bissett
A 354
Odstock
16 26
Whiteparish
Sherfield English
A 27
A 3090
7½
12
Colden Common
Lower Upham
Droxford
Corhar Meons
Downton
A 36
14·3
A 27
10·6
Chandler's Ford
12
Bishopstoke
B 3037
Fair Oak
Bishop's Waltham
Martin
Breamore House
26 16
Redlynch
Landford Nomansland
W. Wellow
Romsey
Broadlands
N. Baddesley
ROWNHAMS
13
Eastleigh
B 3390
B 2150
Rockbourne
Damerham
8½ 11
New Forest
Bramshaw
Ower
8 5
Rownhams
15
Swaythling
W. End
Curdridge
Shedfield
A 32
Fordingbridge (Δ)
B 3078
Brook
Cadnam 4 336
Totton
A 3057
A 31
Stoney Cross
Netley Marsh
Eling
Ashurst
A 35
A 33
A 326
Marchwood
Hedge End
Botley
Wickham
B 2177
Forest Southwic...
Widley
Alderholt
Ibsley
Forest
22 14
Lyndhurst
SOUTHAMPTON
A 3024
W. End
A 3025
Burseldon
Sarisbury
16
Fareham
Verwood
B 3072
National
Hythe
Abbey
Hound
Netley
Hamble
Warsash
Park Gate
Titchfield
M 27
Portchester
Castle
Ringwood
A 338
B 3054
Holbury
Bridgemary
Portsmouth Harbour
W. Moors
St. Leonards (Δ)
Burley
A 337
National Motor Museum
Abbey
Blackfield
Fawley
Stubbington
Lee on-the-Solent
Gosport
PORTSM...
Ferndown
Bransgore
Sopley
Brockenhurst
B 3055
Beaulieu
Bucklers Hard
Lepe
The Solent
20
Cowes
E. Cowes
South
A 338
Sway
Boldre
Mount Pleasant
New Milton
Lymington
11 A 337
Milford-on-Sea
Barton-on-Sea
Yarmouth
Gurnard
Whippingham
Fishbourne
Quarr
Spithead
Ryde (Δ)
BOURNEMOUTH (Δ)
Boscombe
Southbourne
Christchurch
Mudeford
Hengistbury Head
Christchurch Bay
Fort Victoria
Totland
Freshwater
Shalfleet
A 3054
Newbridge
Carisbrooke
Newport
Wootton Bridge
Havenstreet
Parkhurst
Robin Hill
Brading
Arreton
Alverstone

WINDSOR

0 — 250 m
0 — 250 yards

Eton College
Home Park

WINDSOR AND ETON RIVERSIDE

CLEWER PARK
CLEWER
LEISURE CENTRE

THAMES
ALEXANDRA GARDENS
WINDSOR ROYAL STATION
CENTRAL

WINDSOR CASTLE
ST GEORGE'S CHAPEL

KING EDWARD COURT CENTRE

CLEWER WITHIN

Home Park

FROGMORE

A322 STAINES-UPON-THAMES

N

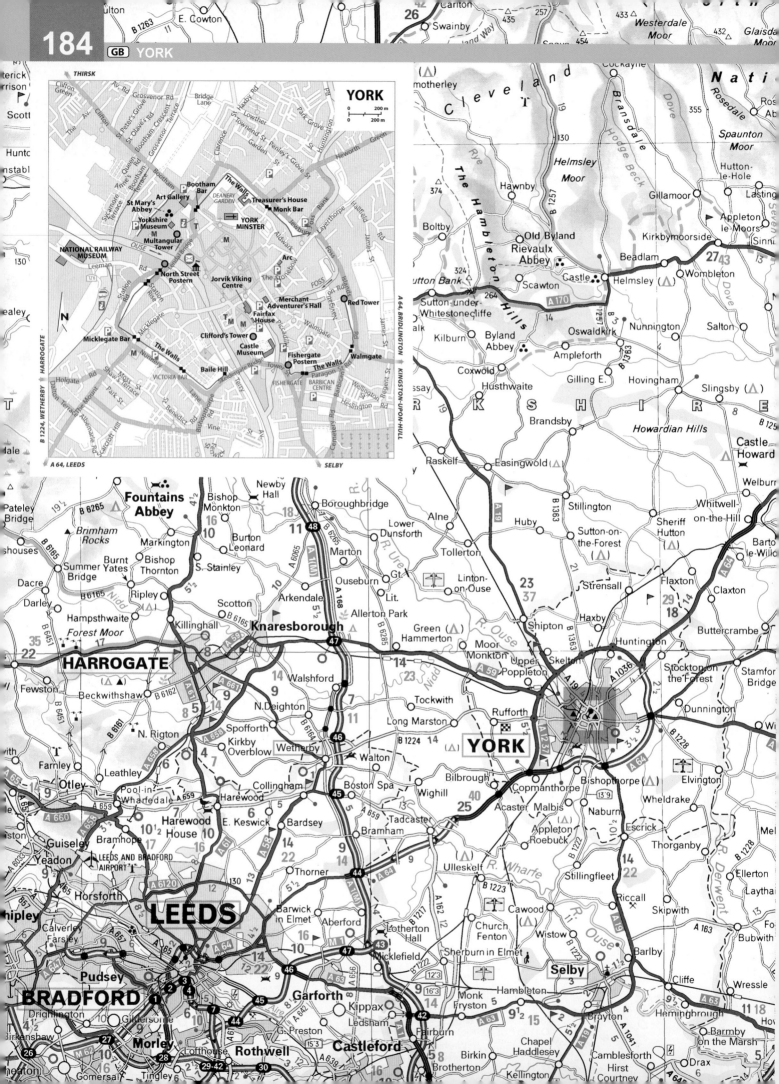

YORK

THIRSK

Clifton
Green
Av. Rd Grosvenor Rd
St Peter's Grove Rd
Bridge
Lane
Haxby Rd
Lowther
Townend St Penley's Gr Garden St
Clarence
St
Park Grove
Huntington
Heworth
Green
Bootham Bar
The Walls
St Mary's Abbey
Art Gallery
Yorkshire Museum
Multangular Tower
Treasurer's House
Monk Bar
DEANERY GARDEN
YORK MINSTER
North Street Postern
Jorvik Viking Centre
Arc
Micklegate Bar
The Walls
Merchant Adventurer's Hall
Fairfax House
Red Tower
Clifford's Tower
Castle Museum
Baile Hill
Fishergate Postern
Walmgate
The Walls
VICTORIA BAR
Paragon St
BARBICAN CENTRE
FISHERGATE

NATIONAL RAILWAY MUSEUM

N

B 1224, WETHERBY, HARROGATE

A 64, LEEDS

A 64, BRIDLINGTON
KINGSTON-UPON-HULL

SELBY

0   200 m
0   200 m

Cleveland

Nati

Helmsley Moor

Spaunton Moor

The Hambleton Hills

Bransdale

Hodge Beck

Dove

Rosedale

Ros Ab

Hawnby

Gillamoor

Hutton-le-Hole

Lasting

374

Appleton le Moors

Boltby

Old Byland

Rievaulx Abbey

Kirkbymoorside

Sinni

Beadlam

27 43

Sutton Bank

264

Scawton

Castle

Helmsley (Λ)

Wombleton

13

Sutton-under-Whitestonecliffe

A 170

14

B 3

Kilburn

Byland Abbey

Oswaldkirk

Nunnington

Salton

Coxwold

Ampleforth

B 1363

Husthwaite

Gilling E.

Hovingham

Slingsby (Λ)

B 125

Brandsby

Howardian Hills

Castle Howard

Raskelf

Easingwold (Λ)

Whitwell-on-the-Hill

Welburr

Stillington

Sheriff Hutton

Barto le-Will

Alne

Huby

Sutton-on-the-Forest (Λ)

Flaxton

Claxton

23 37

Strensall

29 14

18

Lower Dunsforth

Tollerton

Linton-on-Ouse

Lit.

Buttercrambe

Boroughbridge

Marton

Ouseburn

Green (Λ) Hammerton

Shipton

Haxby

Huntington

Stockton-on-the-Forest

Stamfor Bridge

Fountains Abbey

Bishop Monkton

Newby Hall

18

11 48

Moor Monkton

Upper Poppleton

Skelton

A 19

A 1036

Markington

Burton Leonard

S. Stainley

Arkendale

Allerton Park

YORK

Dunnington

Brimham Rocks

Pateley Bridge

shouses

B 6265

16
10

Ripley

Scotton

B 6165

Knaresborough

47

14

A 59

Rufforth

Copmanthorpe

13·9

Bishopthorpe (Λ)

Elvington

Summer Bridge

Bishop Thornton

Killinghall

Walshford

Tockwith

HARROGATE

14
9

N.Deighton

7

Long Marston

B 1224 14

Bilbrough

Wheldrake

Dacre

Darley

Hampsthwaite

Forest Moor

Beckwithshaw

B 6162

Spofforth

11

46

Walton

Acaster Malbis (Λ)

Thorganby

35

22

Fewston

N. Rigton

Kirkby Overblow

Wetherby

Boston Spa

Wighill

Appleton Roebuck

B 1222

Escrick

Farnley

Leathley

Collingham

45

Bardsey

Tadcaster

Bramham

40

25

Naburn

Stillingfleet

14

22

Otley

Pool-in-Wharfedale

Harewood

E. Keswick

A 659

Ulleskelf

Riccall

Skipwith

Guiseley

Yeadon

Bramhope

Harewood House

Thorner

Barwick in Elmet

A 64

Church Fenton

Cawood

Wistow

Barlby

Horsforth

LEEDS AND BRADFORD AIRPORT

Aberford

Lotherton Hall

Sherburn in Elmet

Selby

Ellerton

Bubwith

Calverley Farsley

LEEDS

Micklefield

Monk Fryston

Cliffe

Wressle

Pudsey

Garforth

Kippax

Fairburn

Brayton

Barmby on the Marsh

BRADFORD

Morley

Rothwell

Castleford

Ledsham

G. Preston

Birkin

Brotherton

Chapel Haddlesey

Drax

Morley

Tingley

Lofthouse

Hemingbrough

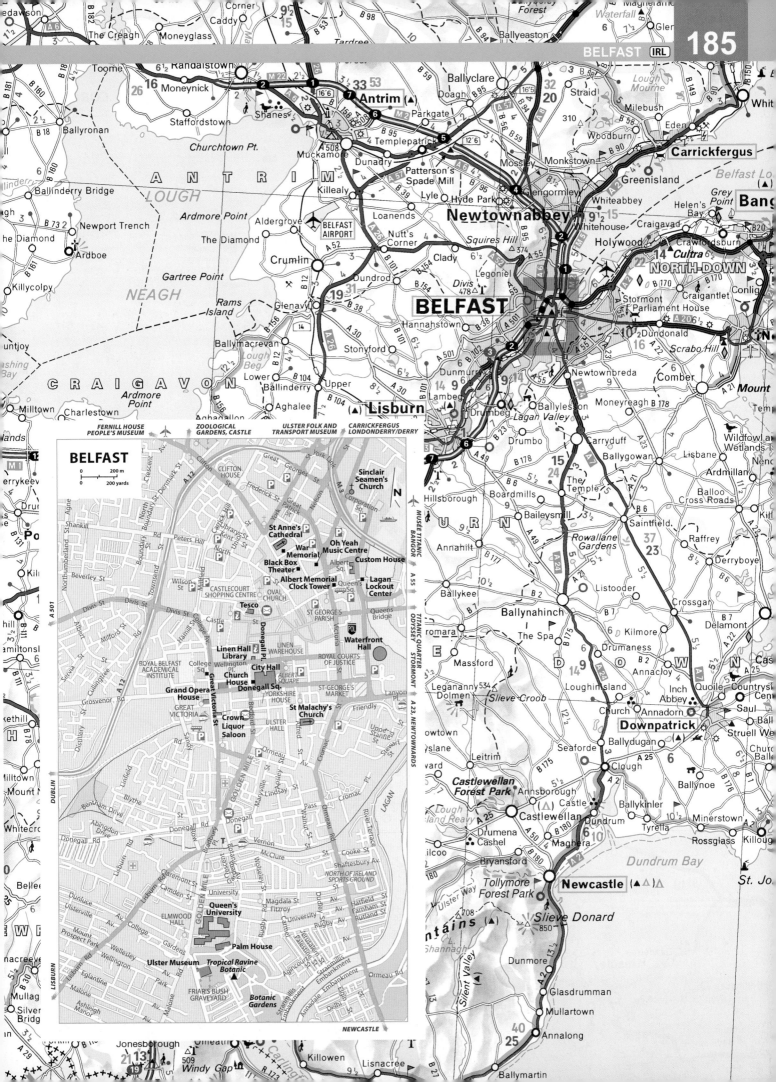

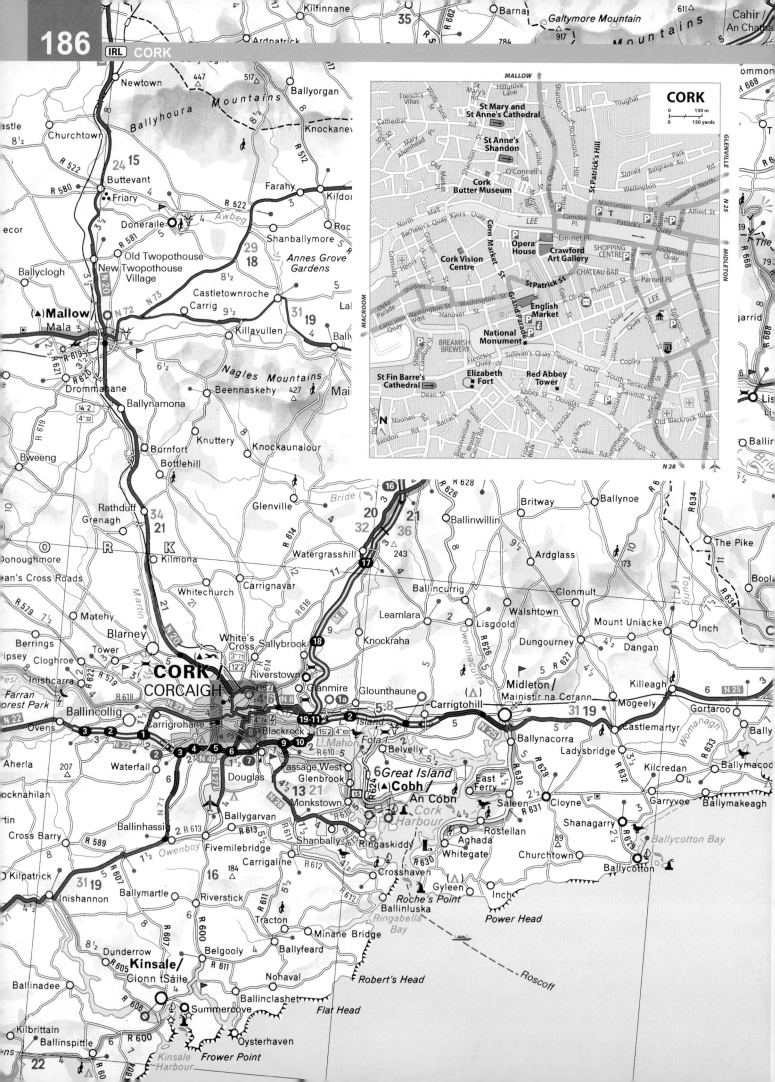

CORK

0   150 m
0   150 yards

St Mary and
St Anne's Cathedral

St Anne's
Shandon

Cork
Butter Museum

Opera
House

Crawford
Art Gallery

Cork Vision
Centre

SHOPPING
CENTRE

St Patrick St

CHATEAU BAR

English
Market

National
Monument

BREAMISH
BREWERY

St Fin Barre's
Cathedral

Elizabeth
Fort

Red Abbey
Tower

GALWAY
0 — 100 m
0 — 100 yards

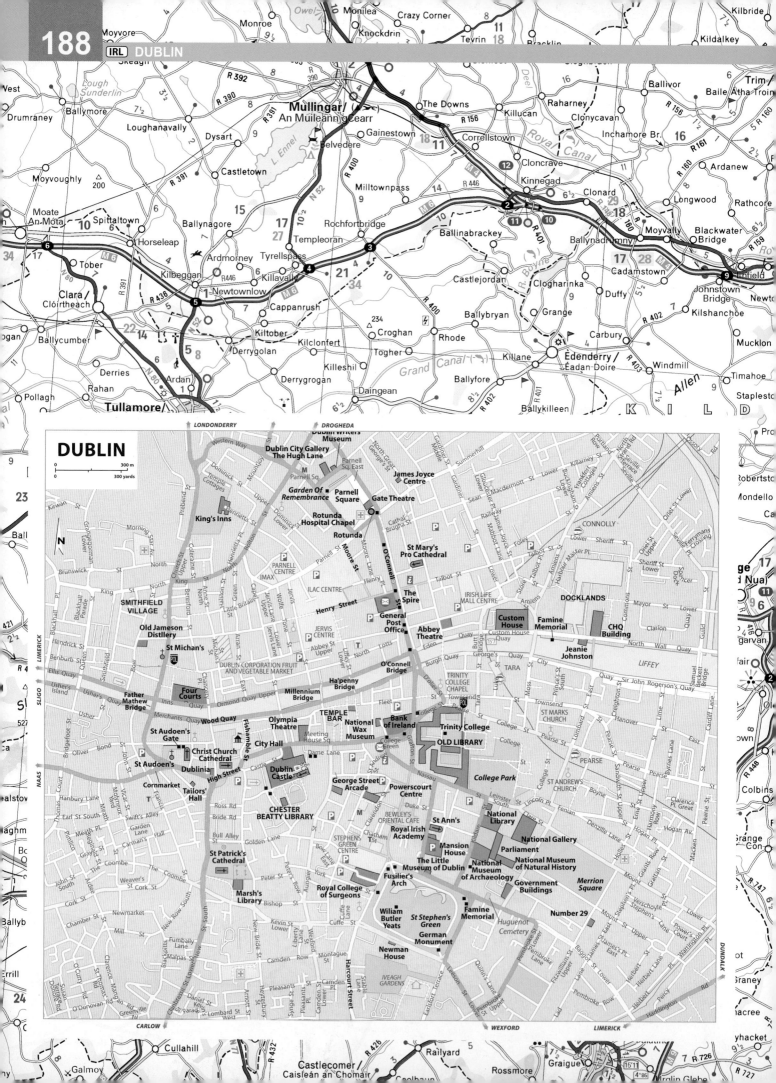

DUBLIN / BAILE ÁTHA CLIATH

Dún Laoghaire

Howth / Binn Éadair

Bray / Bré

Naas / An Nás

Russborough House

Glendalough

Wicklow / Cill Mhantáin

Greystones / Na Clocha Liatha

Powerscourt Demesne

Baltinglass / Bealach Conglais

Skerries / Na Sceirí
Rush / An Ros
Malahide / Mullach Íde
Lambay Island
Ireland's Eye
Nose of Howth
Dublin Bay
Killiney Bay
Leamore Strand
Wicklow Head
Ardmore Point
Brittas Bay

WICKLOW MOUNTAINS NATIONAL PARK

FINGAL

Kippure
Lugnaquilla Mountain
Mullaghcleevaun
Table Mountain
Three Rock Mt.
Great Sugar Loaf
Bray Head

Poulaphouca Reservoir
Vartry Reservoir
Lough Tay
Lough Dan
Upper Lake
Lower Lake

Sally Gap
Wicklow Gap
Meeting of the Waters
Vale of Clara
Avondale Forest Park
Mount Usher
The Devil's Glen

Douglas (I. of M)
Holyhead
Liverpool

Selected towns and villages:
Tara, Skreen, Ardcath, Fourknocks, Clonalvy, Balbriggan / Baile Brigín, Balrothery, Loughshinny, Robinstown, Kilmessan, Pike Corner, Dunsany, Tylas, Curragha, Garristown, Damastown, Oldtown, Ballyboghil, Corduff, Lusk, Portrane, Donabate, Newbridge, Laracor, Cross Keys, Moynalvy, Ratoath, Ashbourne, Donaghmore, Kilsallaghan, Swords / Sord, St. Margaret's, Kinsaley, Portmarnock, Baldoyle, Clontarf, Summerhill, Garadice, Mullagh, Batterstown, Fairyhouse, Kilbride, Ward, Santry, Artane, Maynooth / Maigh Nuad, Dunboyne, Clonee, Mulhuddart, Blanchardstown, Finglas, Kilcock, Leixlip, Clonsilla, Lucan, Phoenix Park, Rathmines, Castletown House, Celbridge, Milltown, Clondalkin, Rathgar, Blackrock, Dalkey, Killiney, Newcastle, Rathcoole, Saggart, Tallaght, Dundrum, Stillorgan, Sandyford, Ballybrack, Loughlinstown, Shankill, Naas / An Nás, Kill, Johnstown, Furness, Kilteel, Brittas, Kilbride, Killakee, Glencullen, Kilternan, Enniskerry, Killiney, Little Bray, Sallins, Punchestown, Blessington, Corbally, Ballymore Eustace, Valleymount, Ballyknockan, Hollywood, Glencree, Powerscourt, Killough, Kilmacanoge, Greystones, Delgany, Kilcullen, Brannockstown, Milemill, Dunlavin, Granabeg, Glenbridge Lodge, Sraghmore, Newtown Mt. Kennedy, Carriggower, Kilpedder, Kilcoole, Stratford, Davidstown, Donard, Ballinclea, Roundwood, Annamoe, Laragh, Tomdarragh, Killiskey, Ashford, Ballinalea, Rathnew, Abbey, Talbotstown, Drumgoff, Ballinderry, Clara, Glenealy, Kilmacurragh, Kilbride, Kilpoole, Kilmurry, Kiltegan, Rathdangan, Aghavannagh, Greenan, Rath Droma / Rathdrum, Kilmacoo, Redcross, Ballinacor, Lisnevagh, Hacketstown, Knockananna, Moyne, Craffield, Aughrim, Sheeanamore, Ballinaclash, Motte Stone, Ardanairy

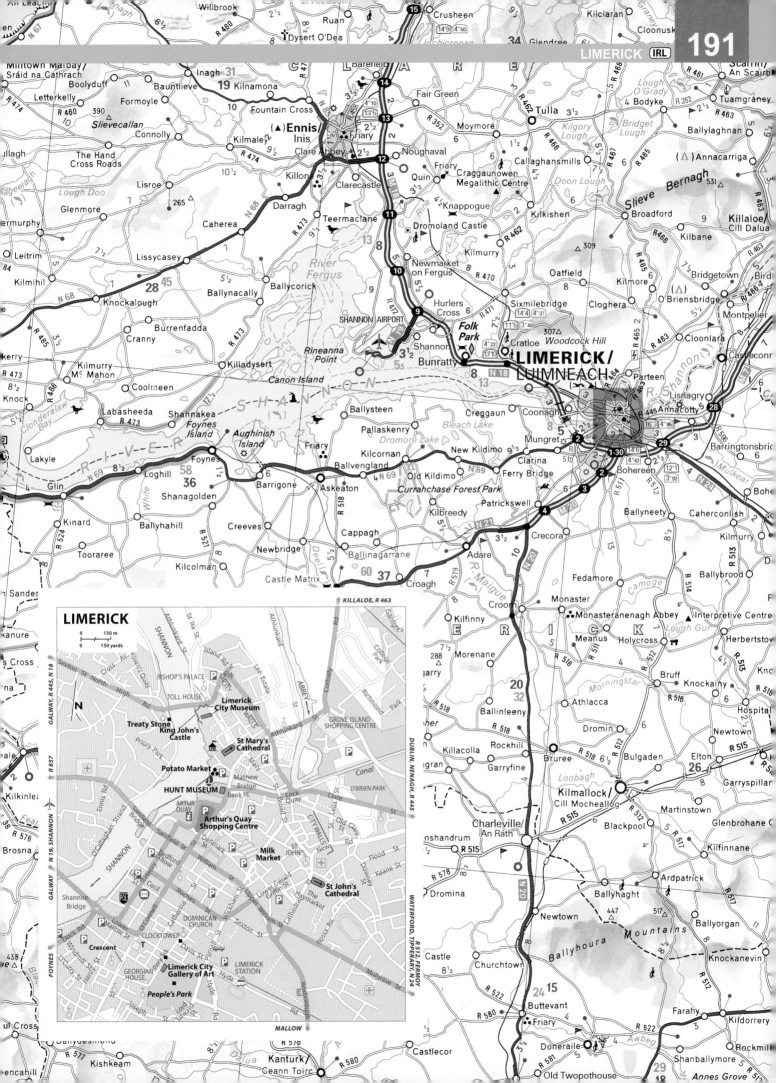

Eochair

Bóithre
Mótarbhealach - Limistéar seirbhíse
Carrbhealach dúbailte le saintréithe mótarbhealaigh
Acomhail mótarbhealaigh: iomlán - teoranta
Vimhreacha ceangail
Líonra idirmáisiúnta agus náisiúnta bóithre
Bóthar idir-réigiúnach nach bhfuil chomh plódaithe
Bóthar nuadheisithe - gan réitiú
Cosán - Conair mharcáilte / Cosán marcaíochta
Mótarbhealach, bóthar á dhéanamh
(an dáta oscailte sceidealta, mas eol)

Leithead bóithre
Carrshlí dhéach
4 lána - 2 leathanlána
2 lána - 2 chunglána

Fad bóthar (iomlán agus meánfhad)
Bhóithre dola ar an mótarbhealach
Saor ó dhola ar an mótarbhealach
i míle - i gciliméadair
ar an mbóthar

Aicmiú oifigiúil bóthair
Mótarshl - GB: Priomhbhealach

IRL: Bóithre eile ,

Príomhbóithre agus fobhóithre náisiúnta
Ceann scribe ar ghréasán bóithre príomha

Constaicí
Timpeall - Bearnas agus a airde os cionn leibhéal na mara (i méadair)
Fána ghéar (suas treo an gha)
IRL: Bealach deacair nó baolach
Bóthar cúng le hionaid phasála (in Albain)
Crosaire comhréidh: iamród ag dul, faoi bhóthar, os cionn bóthair
Bóthar toirmeasctha - Bóthar faoi theorannú
Bacainn dola - Bóthar aonslí
(Ar phríomhbóithre agus ar bhóithre réigiúnacha)
Teorainneacha airde (faoi 15'6" IRL, faoi 16'6" GB)
Teorann Mheáchain (faoi 16t)

Iompar
Leithead caighdeánach - Staisiún paisinéiri
Aerfort - Aerpháirc
Longsheirbhísí : (Seirbhísí séasúracha: dearg)
Árthach foluaineach - Bád
Fartha (uas - ulach : tonnaí méadracha)
Coisithe agus lucht rothar

Lóistín - Riarachán
Teorainneacha riaracháin
Teorainn na hAlban agus teorainn na Breataine Bige

Teorainn idirnáisiúnta - Custam

Áiseanna Spóirt agus Súgartha
Machaire Gailf - Ráschúrsa
Timpeall rásaíochta - Cuan bád aeraíochta
Láthair champa , láthair charbhán
Conair mharcáilte - Páirc thuaithe
Zú - Tearmannéan mara
IRL: Lascaireacht - Ráschúrsa con Lamród thraein gaille
Traein cábla
Carr cábla , cathaoir cábla

Amhairc
Príomhradharcanna:
féach AN EOLAÍ UAINE
Bailte nó áiteanna inspéise, baill lóistín
Foirgneamh Eaglasta - Caisleán
Fothrach - Leacht meigiliteach - Pluais
Páirc, Gáirdíní - Ionad eile spéisiúla
IRL: Dunfort - Cros Cheilteach - Cloigtheach
Lánléargas - Cothrom Radhairc - Bealach Aoibhinn

Comharthaí Eile
Cáblashlí thionsclaíoch
Crann teileachumarsáide - Teach solais
Stáisiún Giniúna - Cairéal
Mianach - Tionsclaíocht
Scaglann - Aill
Páirc Fhoraoise Naisiúnta - Páirc Naisiúnta

Allwedd

Ffyrdd
Traffordd - Mannau gwasanaeth
Ffordd ddeuol â nodweddion traffordd
Cyfnewidfeyd: wedi'i chwblhau - cyfyngedig
Rhifau'r cyffyrdd
Ffordd ar rwydwaith rhyngwladol a chenedlaethol
Ffordd rhyngranbarthol a llai prysur
Ffordd ac wyneb iddi - heb wyneb
Llwybr troed - Llwybr troed ag arwyddion / Llwybr ceffyl
Traffordd - ffordd yn cael ei hadeiladu
(Os cyfodi yr achos: dyddiad agor disgwyliedig)

Ffyrdd
ffordd ddeuol
4 lôn - 2 lôn lydan
2 lôn - 2 lôn gul

Pellter (cyfanswm a'r rhyng-bellter)
Tollffyrdd ar y drafford
Rhan di-doll ar y drafford
mewn miltiroedd - mewn kilometrau
ar y ffordd

Dosbarthiad ffyrdd swyddogol
Traffordd - GB : Prif ffordd

IRL: Prif ffordd genedlaethol a ffordd eilradd

Ffyrdd eraill
Cylchfan ar rwydwaith y prif ffyrdd

Rhwystrau
Cylchfan - Bwlch a'i uchder uwchlaw lefel y môr (mewn metrau)
Rhiw serth (esgyn gyda'r saeth)
IRL: Darn anodd neu beryglus o ffordd
Yn yr Alban : ffordd gul â mannau pasio
Croesfan rheilffordd: croesfan rheilffordd, o dan y ffordd, dros y ffordd
Ffordd waharddedig - Ffordd a chyfyngiadau arni
Rhwystr Toll - Unffordd
(Ar brif ffyrdd a ffyrdd rhanbarthol)
Terfyn uchder (llai na 15'6" IRL, 16'6" GB)
Terfyn pwysau (llai na 16t)

Cludiant
Lled safonol - Gorsaf deithwyr
Maes awyr - Maes glanio
Llongau ceir: (Gwasanaethau tymhorol: mewn coch)
llong hofran - llong
Fferi (llwyth uchaf: mewn tunelli metrig)
Teithwyr ar droed neu feic yn unig

Llety - Gweinyddiaeth
Ffiniau gweinyddol
Ffin Cymru, ffin yr Alban

Ffin ryngwladol - Tollau

Cyfleusterau Chwaraeon a Hamdden
Cwrs golf - Rasio Ceffylau
Rasio Cerbydau - Harbwr cychod pleser
Leoedd i wersylla
Llwybr troed ag arwyddion - Parc gwlad
Parc saffari, sw - Gwarchodfa natur
IRL: Pysgota - Maes rasio milgwn
Trên twristiaid
Rhaffordd, car cêbl, cadair esgyn

Golygfeydd
Gweler Llyfr Michelin

Trefi new fannau o ddiddordeb, mannau i aros
Adeilag eglwysig - Castell
Adfeilion - Heneb fegalithig - Ogof
Gerddi, parc - Mannau eraill o ddiddordeb
IRL: Caer - Croes Geltaidd - twr crwn
Panorama - Golygfan - Ffordd dygfeydd

Symbolau eraill
Lein gêbl ddiwydiannol
Mast telathrebu - Goleudy
Gorsaf bwer - Chwarel
Mwyngloddio - Gweithgarwch diwydiannol
Purfa - Clogwyn
Parc Coedwig Cenedlaethol - Parc Cenedlaethol

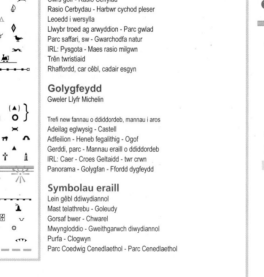

Comnarthaí ar phleanna bailte

Ionaid inspéise
Ionad inspéise agus
Ionad inspéise adhartha

Bóithre
Mótarbhealach, carrbhealach dúbailte le saintréithe mótarbhea
Acomhail mótarbhealaigh : iomlán - teoranta
Priomh-thrébhealach
Sráid: neamhoiriúnach do thrácht, ach í stáit speisialta
Sráid: coisithe
Carrchlós

Comharthaí Éagsúla
Aerfort
Leithead caighdeánach - Staisiún paisinéiri
Ionad eolais turasóireachta - Ospidéal
Gairdín, páirc, coill - Reilig
Staidiam
Galfchúrsa
Stáisiún traenach faoi thalamh
Príomhoifi g phoist le poste restante
Foirgneamh poiblí curtha in iúl le litir thagartha:
Músaem
Amharclann
Póitíní (ceanncheathrú)

Symbolau ar gynlluniau'r trefi

Golygfeydd
Man diddorol
Lle diddorol o addoliad

Ffyrdd
Traffordd, ffordd ddeuol
Cyfnewidfeyd : wedi'i chwblhau - cyfyngedig
Prif ffordd drwodd
Stryd : Anaddas i draffi g, cyfyngedig
Stryd: Cerddwr
Parc ceir

Arwyddion amrywiol
Maes awyr
Lled safonol - Gorsaf deithwyr
Canolfan croeso - Ysbyty
Gardd, parc, coedwig - Mynwent
Stadiwm
Cwrs golff
Gorsaf danddaearol
Prif swyddfa bost gyda poste restante
Adeilad cyhoeddus a ddynodir gan lythyren:
Amgueddfa
Theatr
Yr Heddlu (pencadlys)

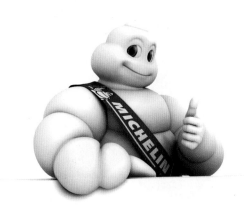

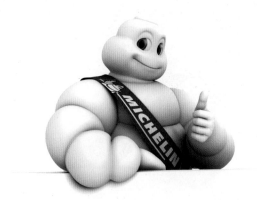